THE MORAL OF THE STORY

An Introduction to Questions of Ethics and Human Nature

Nina Rosenstand
San Diego State University

Mayfield Publishing Company
Mountain View, California
London • Toronto

THE MORAL OF THE STORY

LIBRARY OF CONGRESS CATALOGING-IN-PUBLICATION DATA
Rosenstand, Nina.
    The moral of the story : an introduction to questions of ethics and human nature /
Nina Rosenstand.
        p.   cm.
    Includes bibliographical references and index.
        ISBN 1-55934-027-4
        1. Ethics.   2. Man.   I. Title.
BJ1012.R59   1993
171—dc20   93-25790
                                                                                     CIP

Manufactured in the United States of America
10   9   8   7   6   5   4

Mayfield Publishing Company
1280 Villa Street
Mountain View, California 94041

Sponsoring editor, James Bull; production editor, April Wells-Hayes; manuscript editor,
Jane Townsend; text and cover designer, David Bullen; art editor, Susan Breitbard; art
director, Jeanne M. Schreiber; manufacturing manager, Martha Branch. The text was set in
10-1/2/12-1/2 Bembo and printed on 50# Butte des Morts by The Banta Company.

Photo and illustration credits appear at the back of the book on page 516, which constitutes
an extension of the copyright page.

Cover image and "Blacky" story, Karen Barbour, from *Speak! Children's Book Illustrators Brag
About Their Dogs,* © 1993 Harcourt Brace & Company.

 This book is printed on recycled paper.

For Craig and my parents

Immorality may be fun, but it isn't fun enough to take the place of 100 percent virtue and three square meals a day.

—Noel Coward, *Design for Living*

PREFACE

The Moral of the Story is an introduction to ethical theory written primarily for college courses such as Introduction to Ethics, Moral Problems, and Introduction to Philosophy: Values. Although many textbooks in value theory or ethics present problems of social importance for students to discuss, such as abortion, euthanasia, and capital punishment, in my experience it is better for students to be introduced to basic ethical theory before they are plunged into discussions involving moral judgments. The main focus of this book is thus an overview of some classical and modern approaches to ethical theory—such as ethical relativism, egoism, utilitarianism, deontology, virtue theory—and, in addition, a selection of influential theories about human nature. However, because I believe that a full understanding of any ethical theory is possible only through the application of that theory to specific cases, I have chosen to use examples primarily from the world of fiction.

There is a growing interest in narrative theory among American as well as European philosophers; ethicists and other thinkers are beginning to include stories in their courses as well as in their professional papers, not only as examples of problem solving but also as illustrations of an epistemological phenomenon. Humans are, in Alasdair MacIntyre's words, story-telling animals, and humans seem to choose the narrative form as their favorite way to structure meaning as they attempt to make sense of their reality. Recognizing this trend, and taking advantage of most students' natural interest in films and stories in general, I have selected a number of narrative illustrations of moral problems rather than relying solely on real-life case stories.

Organization

The Moral of the Story is divided into four major sections. Part I introduces the topic of ethics and places the phenomenon of story-telling within the context of cross-cultural moral education and discussion. Part 2 examines the *conduct theories* of ethical relativism, psychological and ethical egoism, utilitarianism, and Kantian deontology. Part 3 explores the topic of *virtue theory* and contains chapters on Plato, Aristotle, theories of virtues and values of non–Western/non-contemporary traditions, and contemporary virtue theories in the American tradition as well as in Continental philosophy. Part 4 focuses on the question of ethics in relation to theories of *human nature*; topics discussed are theories of personhood, determinism and freedom of the will, gender theories, theories of good and evil human nature, and theories of humans as social, psychological, and story-telling beings.

The Moral of the Story contains three chapters with summaries of narratives and accompanying study questions. Chapter 7 concludes the section on theory of conduct, Chapter 13 concludes the section on virtue theory, and Chapter 20 concludes the section on human nature.

All four parts are intended to be used in introductory ethics courses, but Part 4 may also serve as an independent text for courses at colleges and universities in Philosophy of Human Nature/Philosophy of Man. Additionally, with its emphasis on stories and their moral relevance I hope that this book may prove useful in Philosophy of Literature courses as well. However, since no one-semester syllabus will allow for a detailed study of all the topics in this book, various teaching approaches are possible. The accompanying Instructor's Manual lists some suggestions for alternative organizations of the material.

Using the Narrative Summaries and Boxes

The narratives have been chosen from a wide variety of sources ranging from epic prose, poems, and novels to films. I wish to emphasize that from a literary and artistic point of view these outlines of course do not do the originals justice; a story worth experiencing, be it a novel, short story, or film, can't be reduced to a mere plot outline and still retain all of its essence. As Martha Nussbaum says, the form is an inherent part of the story content. There also usually is more to the story than the bare bones of a moral problem, and in writing these summaries I have had to disregard much of the richness of story and character development. Nevertheless, I have chosen the outline format in order to discuss a number of different stories and genres as they relate to specific issues in ethics. Because I believe it is important to show that there is a cross-cultural, historic tradition of exploring moral problems through telling a story, I have opted for a broad selection of narrative outlines. There are, of course, other ways in which stories and ethical theory can be brought together; one might, for instance, select one or two short stories or films in their original format for class discussion. I hope that instructors will indeed select a few stories—novels, short stories, or videos—for their classes to experience firsthand. However, the outlines are written so that firsthand experience should not be necessary to a discussion of the problem presented by the story. The outlines give readers just enough information to enable them to discuss the moral problem presented. I hope that some readers will become inspired to seek out the originals on their own.

Because space is limited, I have not been able to include more than a sampling of stories, and I readily admit that my choices are subjective ones; I personally find them interesting as illustrations and effective in a classroom context where students come from many different cultural backgrounds. Because I am a native of Denmark, I have chosen to include a few stories from the Scandinavian literary tradition. I am fully aware that others might choose other stories or even choose completely different ethical problems to illustrate, and I would be delighted to hear from instructors and students how this selection of stories might be expanded and improved. However, should the instructor prefer to use this book strictly to emphasize ethical theory, without using stories as examples, the three chapters containing narrative summaries can be bypassed without loss of theoretical content.

The Moral of the Story contains a number of boxes that serve an important function: to provide a closeup of one aspect of the material being discussed or a narrow-focus discussion of some specific issue presented in the general text.

I would like to express my gratitude to the many people who in some way have contributed to the completion of this book. I would like to thank Jim Bull of Mayfield Publishing Company for his encouragement and suggestions, and not least for his patience and faith during the time between our first conversation about *The Moral of the Story* and the day he received a prospectus from me. I would like also to express my gratitude to Gina Kinsella, Melissa Kreischer, Julianne Rovesti, Julianna Scott, and Pam Trainer of Mayfield Publishing Company. In particular I am grateful to April Wells-Hayes for being not only an effective and helpful production editor but also an understanding one; and to Jane Townsend for her skillful and knowledgeable editing. I also thank Lynn Rabin-Bauer and Margaret Moore for their work on the Instructor's Manual.

For professional support and helpful discussions about ethics I thank my colleagues from California State University, Long Beach: Cheryl Clark, Paul Tang, Shane Andre, William Johnson, Daniel Guerriere, Steven Davis, Betsy Decyk, and G. A. Spangler. I would like to thank Lawrence Hinman of the University of San Diego for sharing his thoughts on narratives and philosophy with me; Michael Kuttnauer of Mesa College for reminding me of Kafka's version of the Abraham legend and for sharing his views on the history of liberalism; Flemming Lundgreen-Nielsen of the University of Copenhagen for providing philological research data; Per Kølle of Sesam Publishing Company, Copenhagen, Denmark, for his helpful information; and Niels Oxenvad of the H. C. Andersen Museum, Odense, Denmark, for gracious and expeditious assistance. Furthermore, I would like to thank these reviewers for their support and their excellent and enlightening suggestions: L. E. Andrade, Illinois State University, Normal; Linda Bomstad, California Polytechnic State University, San Luis Obispo;

Karen Hanson, Indiana University; Sterling Harwood, San Jose State University; Anita Silvers, San Francisco State University; and Becky White, California State University, Chico.

In addition, I am grateful to the following colleagues and friends for their support and assistance: T. Peter Kemp, University of Copenhagen; Kaare Schmidt, University of Copenhagen; Kirsten Jensen, San Diego State University; Deborah Chaffin, San Diego State University; Mary McGregor, San Diego State University; Andrew Feenberg, San Diego State University; Stanley Weismann, San Diego State University; Thomas Weston, San Diego State University; Jack Zupko, San Diego State University; Beth Snyder, San Diego State University; Randi McKenzie, San Diego State University; Bill Puett, San Diego Miramar College; Cheryl Harris, California State University, San Bernardino; Susan Jahoda, Amherst University; Patrick Pidgeon, San Diego Mesa College; Søren Peter and Jytte Hansen, Copenhagen; Palle and Elsebeth Hansen, Copenhagen; Charles Bub, Toby Kovalivker, Tiffany O'Neill, David Smith III, Michele Vigil, Mark Chrisman, Dan Gagliasso, Jeff Morey, Joseph Musso, and Phil Martin. Special thanks go to Leonard Maltin for his time and advice, to Leith Adams of Warner Bros. Studio Archives for his gracious help, and to Frank Thompson for his advice and assistance. And for inspiration and insight in the art of teaching philosophy, I thank my professors at the University of Copenhagen, Denmark.

There is, as well, a large group of people without whom this book might not have been written—in any case, it would have looked very different. I would like to thank my students for inspiring me to write *The Moral of the Story* and for making the daily task of teaching a continually joyous learning experience. Special thanks go to a class of students who graciously put up with being subjected to a first draft of Part 4, typos and all. I would also like to thank my niece, Jessica in Tempe, Arizona, and my young cousins Astrid and Ellen in Copenhagen, for providing a valid "reality check" for my personal evaluation of ethical problems.

Most of all I would like to thank the three people who are closest to my heart and who have put up with me while I prepared *The Moral of the Story*: my father, Finn Rosenstand, my mother, Gladys Rosenstand, and my husband, Craig R. Covner. I am grateful to my parents for having taught me to love stories and to think about questions such as what is the right thing to do and what is the right way to be. In addition, my father has been of invaluable assistance by conducting fact-finding research missions for me at the University of Copenhagen and by making available his knowledge of literature. My mother deserves a huge thanks for being the first person to read and proofread my manuscript and to submit suggestions. I simply can't thank my husband enough for his help—for his suggestions on the selection of art and film material for *The Moral of the Story* and for the use of his art library and collection. In addition, he assisted me with practical matters and provided valuable comments and thought-provoking questions while the manuscript was in progress. Thank you, Craig, for providing the best assistance anyone could possibly give a person writing a book on ethics: continuous *moral* support.

CONTENTS

Part 1

THE STORY
AS A TOOL
OF ETHICS

Chapter 1

Who Cares About Ethics?

Ethics, Morals, and Values

Somehow there is a general assumption these days that people have lost their moral sense, or at least that the pilot light of our conscience burns at a very low level. This view is supported by frequent media revelations of the low moral standards exhibited by people who should know better: A woman describes how her psychoanalyst abused her sexually; a young teacher is sentenced to prison for having her sixteen-year-old lover, one of her students, kill her husband; financial advisers go to jail for illegal transactions; politicians are indicted for drug dealing; police officers are convicted of serious crimes; and television evangelists show themselves to be morally corrupt. In addition, we constantly read and hear about terrorism, increasing gang violence, mass murder, and cannibalism.

Do these and other similar incidents indicate that we are on a downhill slide, morally? Before attempting to answer that, we must ask ourselves what we mean by a "downhill slide." Do we mean that, overall, everyone has less moral sense now than, say, thirty years ago? Or do we mean that some people (but not everyone) are becoming much worse than even the most morally corrupt individuals of the previous generation? Do we mean that *morality itself* has changed—that it no longer encompasses a set of more or less well-defined Christian values, but rather an ill-defined set of secular values? Or do we mean that its emphasis has shifted from altruism to egoism? Some people might say that we are on a downhill slide when we abandon certain older values (such as "humans are more important than other creatures," and "the land has been given to humans to develop") for newer values (such as "all creatures deserve respect," and "the land must be protected from abuse"). Others may view this change in attitude as an example of moral progress.

It may be that some people's consciences speak with a softer voice today than in the past, if they speak at all; it may be that some crimes of today are more cruel and demeaning to their victims than what we used to see in the past. However, it may also be that (1) we are witnessing a universal phenomenon; every generation seems to believe that the present, somehow, does not compare with what they believe was true years ago; (2) we are much more exposed to human suffering all over the world than any generation of the past has ever been; most of the news that is reported on TV, on the radio, and in newspapers concerns tales of human woe—wars, crimes, disasters, and bloodshed; (3) because of this exposure we have come to "expect the worst" from our fellow human beings. (Whether this is fair will be discussed later in this book.)

It's important to keep this misanthropic view of modern morality in perspective. Today, our general awareness of what kind of conduct breaks the moral rules has become increasingly enlightened. In times past, an abused woman patient might not report her psychoanalyst for any wrongdoing, for a number of reasons; today, we are aware of how doctors ought to behave with their patients, and we speak up if they don't live up to our expectations. We believe that teachers should generally avoid having affairs with their students, and lawyers with their clients, and so on. We expect people in official positions not to abuse their power, and people in leadership positions not to intimidate their employees through sexual harassment. In previous eras corruption and abuse of political power were, as we read in our history books, rampant. At least, so the argument goes, we are now more watchful. And although some books and films seem to say that life is cheap and brutality is fun, the majority of movies and novels today have a distinct moral point, which is not lost on the audience. (We will take up the moral impact of movies and books later.)

There is also the phenomenon of introductory ethics classes in schools. Courses such as Introduction to Values, Ethics, and Contemporary Moral Problems are offered by all colleges, with more classes being added all the time. Although some students do take these courses because they are genuinely interested in the issues raised, most students take them because they are required to do so. Why, though, are such classes required? Is it because university professors believe that students have such horrendous morals that they need to take a class before they can be let loose on society as lawyers, engineers, doctors, schoolteachers, and so on? That can hardly be the case, because these classes usually don't teach morals—they teach *ethics*. It also is not because students are seen to lack moral sense, but because they are assumed to *have* a moral sense that should be trained to work properly: not just to follow the rules, or decide to break them, but to question them and come up with a reasonable answer as to why they are good enough or not good enough.

So what is the difference between *ethics* and *morality*? Although we, in our everyday lives, don't distinguish clearly between morals and ethics, there is a subtle difference: Some people think the word *morality* has some negative connotations, and in fact it does carry two different sets of associations for most of us. The positive kinds are guidance, goodness, humanitarian attitude, and so forth. Among the negative associations are repression, bigotry, double standards, persecution—in other words, *moralizing*. Suppose the introductory ethics course on your campus had been labeled "Introduction to Morals." You would, in all likelihood, expect something different than you would from a course called "Introduction to Ethics" or "Introduction to Values." The word *morality* has a slightly different association than the terms *ethics* and *values*: that is because "morality" usually refers to *the moral rules we follow*, the values that we have. "Ethics" is generally defined as *theories about these rules*; ethics questions and justifies the rules we live by, and if ethics can find no rational justification for those rules, it may ask us to abandon them. Morality is the stuff our social life is made of—even our personal life—and ethics is the ordering, and the questioning, the awareness, the investigation of what we believe: Are we justified in believing it? Is it consistent? Should we remain open to other beliefs or not?

How, then, do we define *values*? In our everyday language, something we value is something we believe is set apart from other things that we don't value, or don't value as much. (Sometimes we simply mean that a thing is worth a lot of money; however, even if monetary value is a concept that is derived from our original definition of value, textbooks in value theory rarely tell us how to get a good bargain, that is, how to know whether something has economic value.) When do we first begin to value something? As babies, we live in a world that is divided into what we like and what we don't like—a world of plus and minus, of yes and no. According to some psychoanalysts, we never really get over this early stage, and some people simply divide their world into what they like, or approve of, and what they don't like, or disapprove of, and let it go at that.

If values have to do with people's likes and dislikes, why are they not studied only in the discipline of psychology? Why is philosophy involved with what values we have, what moral rules we follow, and what ethical justifications we give? Psychology can tell us only what people believe in, and possibly why they believe it; it can't make a statement about whether people are *justified* in believing it. Philosophy's job, at least in this connection, is to *question* our values; it forces us to give reasons, and preferably good reasons, for why we approve of one thing and disapprove of something else. We might approve or disapprove of something that is a matter of taste; in that case we talk about the values of *aesthetics*. However, the primary field where philosophers voice their approval or disapproval is in the field of morality. And when we are evaluating issues in morality, we are practicing ethics.

In today's world it is not considered enough for an adult person merely to divide the world into likes and dislikes; we are exposed to so many different values that we are expected to give reasons for our moral preferences. In other words, it is not enough just to have moral rules; we should, as moral, mature persons, justify our viewpoints with ethical arguments and, at the very least, ask ourselves why we feel this way or that about a certain issue. Ethics, therefore, is much more than a topic in a curriculum. As moral adults, we are required to think about ethics all the time.

Most people, in fact, do just that, even in their teens, because it is also considered a sign of maturity to question authority, at least to a certain extent. If a very young adult is told to be home at eleven P.M., she or he will usually ask "Why can't I stay out 'til midnight?" When we have to make up our minds about whether to study over the weekend or go hiking, we usually try to come up with as many pros and cons as we can. When someone we have put our trust in betrays that trust, we want to know why. All of these questions are practical applications of ethics: They question the rules of morality and the breaking of those rules. Although formal training in ethical questions can make us better at judging moral issues, we are, as adult human beings, already quite experienced, just because we already have asked "why" a number of times in our lives.

Do we have any guidelines for whether one viewpoint on morals is *morally better* than another? How would we know which one is superior? Centuries ago the answer would have been plain: Religion would have provided the answer. We would have looked for the answer to our moral problems in our religious texts or in the advice of our religious leaders; indeed, for some people, there is continuing comfort in the belief that answers can still be found there. More and more people in the western part of the world, however, live in a secularized universe, and although they may ask their God for guidance, they by no means believe that all of the answers are to be found in their religious tradition. Often, people find that our society today is more complex than that presented in their religious texts. For agnostics and atheists there can be no turning to religion for unquestioned moral guidance, because they view religion itself as an unknown or nonexistent factor. Agnostics claim that they do not know if there is a God, or that it is impossible to know. Atheists claim that there is no God. Both the agnostic and the atheist may find that religion suggests solutions to their problems, but such solutions are accepted not because they are from religion, but because they somehow make sense.

For now let us assume that for most people today in our part of the world, the connection between everyday duties and the word of God is unclear at best. In that case we must look to other general criteria to learn what makes one moral attitude better than another. As we shall see, those criteria may themselves depend on what we think is important in life: Our own selves and our personal happiness? The general well-being of all people? Taking care of the needy? Making sure that justice is done? Protecting people's rights? Keeping promises and avoiding breaking rules? Remaining tolerant towards the rules and ideas of others? Your basic approach to life will determine what you think is morally the most appropriate answer. We will discuss these and more approaches in the pages that follow.

Should schools teach values? Sometimes we hear that problems such as the crisis of the inner cities, the breakup of the family, crime, and general callousness might be

Family Values

On occasion, politicians and the media take on the topic of so-called "family values." During the presidential campaign of 1992 this was a major issue for the Republican party platform. But what exactly are family values? Some would say they are what American society is losing. The nuclear family is no longer the norm, with mother the homemaker, father the breadwinner, and children who are taught the difference between right and wrong. These days, the argument goes, such values are hardly taught at all in some homes, where the mother or father is permanently absent. Members of what has come to be called the "Religious Right," choose to identify family values specifically as what promotes the family in a traditional sense. Consequently, anything that is seen to threaten the traditional structure (abortion, women in the work force, homosexuality) is considered morally wrong. There are, however, those who see family values in a different light, who acknowledge that the *majority* of families today have a nontraditional structure (single parents, children with multiple parents because of divorce, and so on). In the opinion of some experts, about half of all children of the nineties will find themselves in single parent households during some part of their lives, and only 20 percent of families (some studies cite an even lower number) are now composed of a breadwinner father, a work-at-home mother, and their children. The other 80 percent are families with other structures. When asked what a family is, the Libertarian Party presidential candidate of 1992, Andre Marrou, answered, "any two or more people who identify themselves as being family, whether they live together or not." For someone with that viewpoint (aside from the fact that few libertarians approve of social programs), family values are those programs and policies that allow families to become and remain a support for their individual members: family leave programs, health care programs, child care for working mothers, and family planning programs. The term *family values* can thus have a very wide range of applications.

prevented if schools would just teach students the difference between right and wrong. There is no doubt that if children aren't taught at an early age that others can get hurt if people think only of themselves, then they may never truly catch on to the fact that they must learn to get along with other human beings. If children don't learn this kind of respect and consideration at home, then it probably will have to be taught in schools. We are talking about extremely basic values, the kind most cultures might agree on, the kind embedded in what we call the Golden Rule (Do unto others as you would have them do unto you). Problems occur, however, when schools begin to teach values with which not all parents agree. We live in a multicultural society, and although some parents might like religious faith to be on the school agenda, others would certainly not. Some parents want their children to have early access to sex education, while others consider the subject unthinkable as a school topic. There is nothing in the concept of values that implies we all have to subscribe to exactly the same ethics, no matter how strongly we may feel about our values. So, beyond teaching basic values such as common courtesy and manners, perhaps the best schools can do is make students aware of values and value differences, and let students learn to argue well for their own values as well as to question them. Schools, in other words, should focus on *ethics* rather than *morality*.

Who Thinks Ethics Is Important?

Obviously, college administrators find the topic of ethics most important—otherwise, there wouldn't be so many Introduction to Ethics classes. Historically, though, the topic of ethics has been considered vital by many cultural groups, and today it seems that even more voices are joining in. Here is a short list of some of the fields in our society that show an interest in ethical issues. These fields are significant for two reasons: Their interest in ethics is of interest to us, and, also, we may want to turn the tables and examine the ethics of the members themselves.

Philosophy

Philosophy was the first discipline in which ethics was considered a subject worth studying, and philosophers continue to dedicate curriculum hours, journals, papers, and conferences to its study. Ethics was first identified as a topic for intellectual scrutiny in the writings of Plato, in which Plato's teacher, Socrates, asked the all-important question, *How one should live?* From then on, and for over two thousand years, ethics has been one of the major branches of philosophical inquiry. Other key areas of philosophy are logic, metaphysics, aesthetics, and theory of knowledge, also known as epistemology.

The Church

Historically, the Catholic church has had a vested interest in ethics. To most Christians, the Church's brightest contribution to moral progress is the Christian emphasis on love for one's fellow human being. Its darkest hour was the time of the Spanish Inquisition (1237–1834), with its pattern of persecution, torture, and execution of nonbelievers. Throughout all of these events, the Church has been engaged in the question of right and wrong in the eyes of God. The Catholic church is not alone in

God and Values

For many people an obvious answer to the question, Which values are good? would be, Whatever God wants you to do. This answer has been sufficient for generations of humans of all cultures and religions; however, it presupposes a general agreement to accept the word of authority, and Western culture has come to identify as one of its key virtues the freedom to question authority. This doesn't mean people automatically end up turning their backs on religion, but if they choose the answers of religion it is because they have gone through a critical process of evaluating them and choosing them, and not because they have accepted a tradition of authority. This makes the authoritarian answer "because God says so" less appealing; indeed, such an answer carries no weight at all with atheists or agnostics. We might choose to say that in that case atheists and agnostics are immoral by virtue of their lack of faith, but many atheists as well as agnostics would insist that being a good citizen and neighbor, being a loyal friend, refraining from harming innocent people, and doing one's best to alleviate the pain of others all add up to a very high level of moral values regardless of what religion a person may have (or even if a person has no religion at all). It is possible that such an attitude of decency is brought about by fear of reprisals; it is also possible that people are decent because they would like others to be decent to them—in other words, they apply the Golden Rule. It is also possible that humans have the capacity to be altruistic (to do something good for others that doesn't necessarily benefit oneself). Some might even argue that if people live by God's rule only because they fear God, this may not say much for their moral values. As there is a preference for keeping the church and the state separate in our culture, there is a parallel tendency to view values and religion as separate, primarily because we may not agree on all religious concepts. Concepts involving basic decency, equality, tolerance towards one another, and other civic virtues are, however, at least in theory, appealing to everybody.

this interest; most religious institutions have an interest in the *mores* (moral customs) of their believers; indeed, it is often part of the identification of a believer that she or he follows a certain pattern of moral conduct. Historically, the politics of the religious institutions have often been the politics of the state; it was this way in Europe of the Middle Ages, and it is this way in certain countries today where fundamentalist Islam is the state religion. In this way the religious values have often come to determine the moral ideals of the population as such. With the separation of church and state, the justification for these moral ideals usually becomes questionable: Should the religious morality prevail, or is there a secular morality that can take its place? For many people morality is intrinsically connected with religion; the irreligious person is perceived as someone without morals. However, for many atheists and agnostics it is entirely possible to have high moral standards; in that case such standards are based not on religious doctrine, but on secular values such as fairness and justice, caring for those that are close to you, and working towards a better world. On page 9 you will find a discussion of whether it is possible to have values without accepting the concept of God.

Medicine

The field of medicine may not have shown an overwhelming interest in the field of ethics in the past; aside from the Hippocratic Oath, which all doctors still have to swear, the professional ethic of doctors is assumed to be obvious: to heal and comfort those in need of medical attention. However, today the issue is not so much the personal or professional morality of doctors so much as the ethics of the profession itself. This is because medical treatments that would have been unimaginable in earlier times are today possible. Life can be prolonged artificially, or terminated in the womb with comparative safety for the woman; fetal tissue can be used to cure diseases, and so on. In each of these cases, someone has to make the decision whether it is ethical to proceed. Medical science has entered into a brand new area in which there are no established rules on which to rely. For this reason, the medical profession has a vested interest in supporting the creation of a viable set of ethical procedures to follow in the grey areas of decision making. The ethical standards of the medical professionals involved in these procedures is another topic that is often raised. Ethics in the profession, regardless of which profession we are talking about, involve both an abstract interest in moral issues and a commitment to a certain professional standard that may not be so easy to define. Is the doctor who helps a terminally ill patient commit suicide doing a morally right thing or not? Is the doctor who refuses to help a terminally ill patient commit suicide doing the right thing or not?

Another element of the discussion of medical ethics is the attitude of society towards sick people—in particular, terminally ill people with communicable diseases. Should they remain part of society, or should they be locked away and forgotten? Do we as citizens remain ethical toward contagious fellow citizens, or do we send them to leper colonies or other such places?

Science

In the early years of modern science, that is, in the seventeenth and eighteenth centuries, the moral sensitivity that accompanied research seems to have been of a different nature than today. The main concern then was how to proceed with the research and at the same time not go against the values believed to be expressed in the Bible. At least once in modern times, science has digressed and deteriorated to a point where its ethics seemed warped to most people. In Nazi Germany the ultimate value was success for the Party and the realization of that abstract concept, "The Fatherland."

Is There Such a Thing as Value-free Science?

The question of whether or not science can be totally value-free has been a burning one throughout the latter part of the twentieth century. Especially in Germany, the debate has been led by the philosopher Jürgen Habermas, who in his book *Knowledge and Interest* (1968) claims that science may try to be objective, but there is always an element of vested interest present: Society will fund only those projects it deems "valuable" for either further scientific progress, prestige, or making money. Researchers often choose projects for much the same reasons. Furthermore, the process of data selection (selecting research material according to what the researcher finds is relevant to the research project) is influenced by the interests of the researcher whether we like it or not.

Scientific research (medical research in particular) engaged in painful, humiliating, and eventually fatal experiments on human subjects, primarily women and children.

Today we like to think that science will not transgress this way again, and yet we have a credo that says that science is "value-free": It is supposed to be objective, and not be swayed by personal ambitions and preference. But does that mean it is not supposed to be swayed by ethical values, either?

Medical and general scientific research now have capabilities that could only be dreamed of in previous generations. However, no set of ethical rules has developed by which to judge these capabilities. Genetic manipulation makes possible a future such as the one Aldous Huxley fantasized about in his *Brave New World*, one comprising a human race designed for special purposes. Already, agriculture is making use of genetic design to create experimental potatoes and strawberries that don't freeze, tomatoes that can be stacked, and other plants that glow in the dark. Although it may be to humankind's advantage to have access to these wonders, failure to *contain* such laboratory-generated genetic material could have disastrous results if no sense of ethics is instilled to guide the decisions of researchers. We have debates concerning scientific ethics; animal research is questioned, additives, fertilizers, and other agents harmful to the environment are limited, and above all, artificial ingredients—from food additives to drugs—are scrutinized for their harmful effects. It certainly is in the interest of the scientific community to further develop a sense of proper and improper projects.

Business

The business world, some might say, has not been particularly encumbered by ethical sensitivities for most of its existence—it is almost expected to be a "dog-eat-dog" type of environment. And yet the business world has both written and unwritten laws, ranging from rules that one should not take home pens and Post-it™ pads from the supply room or call long-distance on the company phones, to more serious rules against insider trading. Often colleges offer courses in business ethics, and often businesses themselves do the same thing for their employees. Is this because there is a general interest among business people to learn about issues in ethics—or is it because companies believe that their employees are in severe need of some moral training? Either way, the business world is interested in the questions that a study of ethics might raise, from issues such as drug testing, confidentiality concerning medical and other personal records, and sexual harassment on the job, to more general issues of the responsibility of large (and small) companies in society. Are businesses responsible to the community for creating jobs, keeping the environment clean, and so on, or are they just supposed to make money for the shareholders?

News Media

The media seem to be showing an increasing interest in reporting issues of moral controversy. This certainly reflects their interest in "good copy" (news that sells papers or commercial air time); however, if people weren't interested in hearing about such matters, it wouldn't be good copy. Usually what we hear about most is when someone of some social standing has transgressed. In recent years, though, general reporting of differences of opinion about what's right and wrong has become more common. Issues such as abortion and euthanasia are high on the list of media topics, and whenever someone is up for election to a high office, his or her opinions on such matters, as well as on matters of gender and racial politics, are closely examined. The question of moral standards in the news profession itself is an especially important one: Is it ethical, for example, for a journalist to make public a matter of national security? And does the public always have a "right to know?" Journalists who gain access to sensitive material and publish it may be said not only to report the news, but also to create conditions for more "news" to report. In other words, they may play an active role in situations that they supposedly are merely reporting.

Legislation

The relationship between morals and legislation is ancient. From the Code of Hammurabi (developed by Babylonians in approximately 2000 B.C.E.) to legislation of today, some laws exist that reflect the moral climate of the time. Not all laws do so, however. Some scholars argue that because laws tell us what we ought to do or ought not to do, all laws have a moral element to them; if nothing else, they promote the idea that it is morally good to uphold the law. However, sometimes the law does not seem to be morally right. When times change, what seemed right before may not seem right anymore, and if the legislative power is sensitive to that fact, the law will change. Sometimes it takes a civil war for such laws to be changed; sometimes it takes only a simple vote. We can't, therefore, conclude that all laws are morally just, because experience tells us that this is just not so. Some laws may not even have an obvious moral element, such as many traffic laws. A law that allows us to "go right on red" hardly addresses a moral issue.

Legislators, though, are naturally interested in the public's opinion of right and wrong, because, in general, this opinion will be represented by the laws of the country. However, not all moral issues are relevant for legislators; whether you come home for Thanksgiving may be an important moral issue in your family, but it is hardly the business of anyone else, let alone the state legislation.

The Entertainment Industry

The entertainment industry is interested in ethics, has always been interested in ethics, and will probably always be interested in ethics, at least in the sense of what happens when rules surrounding ethical issues are broken. There was a time in Hollywood (in the early thirties) when movies were free and loose, and things were said on the screen that would curl the toes of censors ten years down the line. Then in the mid-thirties came the Hays Office, a group of self-proclaimed moral watchdogs who eliminated most direct references to sex in movies until well into the fifties. During that same time, the stars of the entertainment industry were expected to lead model lives fit for consumption by their adoring audiences. (That not everybody lived up to this white-washed ideal was amply revealed by the industry itself in later years.) Regardless of whatever ideal has been established for films and their actors, however, the theme in the overwhelming majority of movies that have come out of Hollywood has been that of the breaking of moral rules.

An odd thing about the gigantic Hollywood industry is that throughout most of its 100 and some years of existence, it has equated bad morals with sex—a common equation, but odd nevertheless. Cruelty, callousness, criminal behavior, treason, and vicious gossip ought to be pretty good candidates for "bad morals," and, indeed, movies and soaps today have turned their eye to these topics, too. Talk shows, an integral part of the entertainment industry today, thrive on moral controversy, especially if sex is involved.

As with legislation, the entertainment industry reflects the changing moral climate. One decade of moviegoers idolizes the individualist, the loner; the next wants films about family values and friendship. It is a question of who influences whom: Do the movies and television shows mirror our values and show us what we are, or do we become what the movies and shows depict?

A question that is often raised is, does the entertainment industry display any consistent moral responsibility in the values it promotes? During the years of censorship, strict standards were established that defined what type of conduct films could depict, but since the fifties, Hollywood productions have become increasingly violent and increasingly sexually explicit. This has caused some viewers to long for the days of censorship. Others, who believe censorship should be a matter of self-regulation and moral responsibility, say it is about time Hollywood (and other producers of film and television) became aware of the message it sends to viewers. Is it truly necessary for the plot, or for the film as art-form, to show extreme violence, or is it done solely to attract a large, young, uncritical audience? Is it a good idea to show explicit sexual scenes in films, when a more subtle approach might be just as effective? There are several schools of thought on this matter, ranging from conservative to liberal. The most typical viewpoints are: (1) Hollywood should impose strict family values on its productions, and avoid showing explicit sex and extreme violence altogether; (2) Hollywood should understand what messages its films send and, above all, stop linking sex and violence, unless it is important for the story; (3) Hollywood should create more films in nonviolent, nonsexual categories, including family movies, so that those who don't enjoy films with explicit sex and violence can have quality entertainment; and (4) Hollywood is just responding to viewer demands, and if you don't like sex and violence, turn off your TV or don't go to the movie theater. Given that the views on the subject are so polarized, it may be a while before Hollywood responds.

Storytellers

In ancient times the primary teachers of morals were the storytellers. Of course parents have always had a hand in moral education, but in pretechnological cultures (what used to be called "primitive" cultures), those who knew the *legends* were the ones who, in effect, represented the social institutions of religion, school, legislation, and government. The myths surrounding the origin of the world, society, food, love, and death, as well as the stories about the important men and women in the tribe's past provided rules for the tribe to live by—moral structures that could be used in every-day life to make everyday decisions about crops, marriage, warfare, and everything else. The way to teach children how to become a good member of the tribe was to tell the old stories.

In our technological world we no longer have such a body of ready-made prescriptions for moral conduct—at least we don't think we do. In fact, however, we still tell stories, we still listen to stories, and we still take moral lessons from them. Some people read the Bible or the Torah and seek comfort in the stories of human frailty and perseverance. Some people keep their comic book collections from when they were kids, and dive into the old stories from time to time for some basic moral reinforcement (see the rabbit outwit the fox, see the bad guy get blasted, see Robin Hood be vindicated once again). Some people read biographies of remarkable men and women and are inspired by the stories of courage and bravery. Adults may not read fairy tales any more, but we read novels—classics, best sellers, or science fiction. And if we don't read novels, we go to the movies or watch TV. Wherever we turn we find *stories*. Some are real and some fictional, some are too outdated or too radical for us to relate to, but we find at least some stories that serve as our moral guideposts. Even if you are not a great reader or moviegoer, you probably can recall at least one story that has moved you at some time or other. In this book we will use such stories—both well-known ones and lesser known ones—to illustrate the moral problems we encounter in our lives, because *the moral of the story* provides one of the most enduring ways of relating to the question of what's right and what's wrong.

Why Have Rules of Moral Conduct?

Do we know *why* humans all over the world have an interest in establishing and following moral rules? An age-old answer that seems to be unsatisfactory to a large part of today's world is, Because the moral rules are decrees from God [the gods]. Philosophy has several answers, and, interestingly enough, some of them are mutually exclusive. Philosophy has traditionally looked for the origin of morality in the realm of *reason*: Somehow, applying rules for decent behavior makes sense, so rationality becomes a prerequisite for moral behavior. Some philosophers, however, reject that morality is a matter of the head—they claim that it is the *heart* that is involved, and the head just rationalizes whatever it is the heart wants. If this is the case, we will have a hard time persuading others that we are right, because no amount of rational argumentation will persuade people who just listen to their hearts and to their gut feelings. For those who adhere to this theory, there is no such thing as a "morally superior" point of view. All viewpoints are just subjective emotions.

There also are those who believe that morality is a built-in, fail-safe *biological* trait: We can't help being moral, because otherwise our species would perish. Genetically, we have an interest, in a limited sense, of looking after one another: It is to our own advantage, and it is to the advantage of our descendants.

Some philosophers go further in stressing the advantageous nature of ethics. Morality, they say, is nothing but playing it safe when you can't get away with doing what you want; it derives from *fear of being caught*. We stick to the "straight and narrow" because we are afraid of what may happen if we don't: we'll go to jail, or lose our friends, or go to Hell, or some other nasty prospect. If we can get away with something, however, we will do it—that is human nature. This view, a variety of egoism, will be discussed shortly.

Some of these attempts at explaining the nature of morality will be discussed in Part 2 of this text. There we will examine the ongoing human endeavor to answer the question, *What should I do?* When faced with a moral problem that requires our immediate attention, we often realize that deep down we know what we ought to do, but we just don't feel like doing it—perhaps we feel very much like doing the exact opposite. We may, for example, believe that it is our duty to be with our family for Thanksgiving, but we would rather accept an invitation to go to a mountain cabin with some good friends. Or we know we ought to work Friday afternoon, but the weather is so nice . . . Or we feel attracted to someone who already has a partner, so we know we ought to get out of the way, but . . . This conflict between what we ought to do and what we want to do—between duty and inclination—is perhaps the most common form of a moral dilemma; some people think it is the *only* form of

Some "Scruples"

We all face moral problems in our lives. Inspired by a game called Scruples, I have, on occasion, asked students to use their imagination to come up with some scruples for the class to discuss. Here is a selection of moral dilemmas written by college students in southern California. These moral dilemmas don't necessarily represent actual problems experienced by the students; they are, rather, excursions into the world of possible moral problems. Can you think of any possible solutions to these problems? Perhaps you have a scruple of your own to consider?

• Your new roommate is having emotional or mental problems and needs to seek professional help. He or she has worn you out by constantly fretting and complaining about the situation. Do you tell your roommate to seek professional help?

• You're married, and you go away on a business trip and have a one-night stand with a person that you will most likely never see again in your life. Do you tell your spouse about it?

• Your grandma is dying and tells you that all she wants is for you to carry on the orthodox religion she believes in. You are an atheist. What do you say?

• A woman is pregnant and tells the prospective father the news. He is excited but makes it clear he will not be able to provide any financial support to mother or child. He would, however, like to be involved with his child's life. Should the mother put "father unknown" on the birth certificate, thereby retaining 100 percent of the parental rights? (After all, she will be providing 100 percent of the financial support.) Or, should she reveal the father's name, giving him 50 percent of the parental rights?

• You and the person you've gone out with for three years decide to see other people. You end up back together, but *both* of you have slept with other people. A year later you're planning on getting married, and you find out your mate has contracted AIDS. Do you still get married?

moral conflict. However, there may also be another kind, one in which we have to choose between two things we should do, but we don't feel like doing either of them—or perhaps we don't mind doing them, but one just happens to preclude the other. We may be caught between a rock and a hard place in terms of needing to study for a final on the same night that our boss wants us to help take inventory at our part-time job. Tell the boss that school is more important, and chances are she won't agree. Tell the professor that work is more important, and he may be completely unsympathetic. Clearly, we need to do both, but we can do only one. We may even find ourselves in a situation where we have to decide whether to give up our car to a carjacker or put up a fight. We don't really want to do either, but we have to make a choice, because if we dawdle the carjacker will take that to mean we have chosen to refuse to give up the car, and we may be harmed. Such moral dilemmas fill our lives and can be either fascinating or extremely anxiety-provoking. Can moral theories help us decide what to do when we really need some good advice? That is the whole point; indeed, theories of moral conduct set out to do just that by giving us a basic value by which to measure the situation. With what are you most concerned? Your own happiness? Overall consequences down the line? Doing the right thing? Keeping a promise? Obeying the law? And what do you think your priorities *ought* to be? In Part 2 of this book we will look at various answers to these moral problems.

Ethics in Narratives

In the next chapter we will take a look at the phenomenon of storytelling in relation to questions of ethics. All cultures tell stories, and all cultures have codes for proper behavior. Very often those codes are taught through stories, but stories can also be used to *question* moral rules, and to examine morally ambiguous situations. We will look at a sampling of such stories in Chapter 2.

In this and other upcoming chapters we also will look at plot-outlines from stories of many kinds; some are from novels, some are from short stories and even poems, and several are from films. These outlines have two purposes. One is to supply a foundation for further debate about the application of the moral theories presented in the chapter; the other is to inspire you to experience these stories in their original form. In most cases the story is, of course, richer and more interesting than any outline can show, so I strongly suggest that you experience it for yourself. Most of the novels and short stories are available in libraries, and most of the films are available on videotape.

Some of these plot-outlines may be very familiar to you, and some are probably completely new. Some are considered classics, some come from the world of popular fiction, and some are relatively unknown stories that make a certain interesting moral point. On occasion an excerpt is presented instead of a full plot-outline.

In this section we will look at some stories that illustrate a few of the moral problems presented heretofore. It goes without saying that many other examples could be found to illustrate the same issues, and other issues discussed in this chapter but not represented by stories could also be illustrated. This selection simply represents a sampling of how ethics are discussed in stories, and this particular section uses films as discussion material.

Science and Ethics

The grandfather of all mad scientist stories surely must be the story of Frankenstein's monster. Invented by Mary Wollstonecraft Shelley as a contribution to a ghost story contest among friends in 1816, and pronounced a classic by Sir Walter Scott, it is the haunting story of a Westerner who wants to control nature and create artificial life. Mary Shelley's monster is not the hulking idiot of the movies, but an intelligent creature who is malicious because he is lonely; there is no one like him, and he has no purpose, since his creator, Dr. Frankenstein, denounces him. Shelley's subtitle for the story, *The Modern Prometheus*, gives another clue as to who the monster is. Prometheus was a legendary Greek figure credited with creating humans out of clay and giving them fire from the gods' hearth. Perhaps we all are Frankenstein monsters, abandoned by our creator, who didn't know quite what he was doing in the first place? Shelley was only nineteen when she wrote her story; perhaps she thought of it that way, and perhaps not.

Frankenstein's monster has become the archetype of an artificial being, but he was not the first one. The Jewish tradition contains stories of the Golem, a being made of clay and created to fulfill the wishes of its maker. Today, the evil computer-programmed android has taken over as the model for dangerous, artificial beings in a new age. We will look more closely at stories about artificial beings in the following chapter.

KEN RUSSELL (DIRECTOR) AND FRANKLIN COEN (SCREENWRITER), *Altered States*

Film (1980)

In this film, a variation on the artificial being theme, the scientist becomes his own monster. The scientist, a man who has trouble with commitments, withdraws from his family responsibilities. Immersing himself in theories about mind expansion, he becomes involved with drug-based experiments. Using a sensory deprivation tank, he succeeds in regressing to a prehominid stage of evolution and breaks out of the tank in the shape of an australopithecine (presumably). The prehominid goes on a killing rampage in the city but reverts to its human form before it is caught. The scientist manages to escape undetected, but he is far from discouraged. Excited by this result of his research, and not much dismayed by the fact that as a prehominid he displays nothing but violence, he enters the tank again, only to watch his personality dissolve into nothingness. Only the love and courage of his estranged wife bring him back to the world of the living. The moral? Don't let pure research entice you, because beyond the realm of human existence, there is nothing.

Study Questions

1. Do you think this film is hostile to science? Why or why not?
2. Can science work in a value-free environment, or does science have a duty to work within a system of moral values?

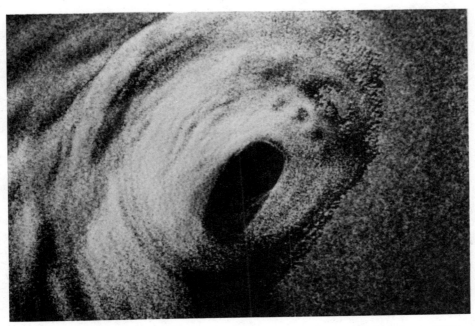

FIGURE I.I *Altered States*, Warner Bros. 1980. An experiment gone wild: the scientist (William Hurt) has gone too far in his experiment with mind expansion and feels himself being sucked into a maelstrom that is about to dissolve his very being. The lesson is that if you look for answers outside the human realm, all you will find is the horror of emptiness.

Business Ethics

Even though students may say, "I don't need to take an ethics class, because I'm going into business!" the topic of business ethics is an important one. Does the business world encompass duties and responsibilities, and if so, what are they? This story explores some questions of right and wrong in business.

MIKE NICHOLS (DIRECTOR) AND KEVIN WADE (SCREENWRITER), *Working Girl*

Film (1988)

Tess McGill, working-class New York girl, has her sights set on the business world. Eventually she lands a solid secretarial position under boss Katharine Parker, who tells her that

FIGURE 1.2 *Working Girl,* Twentieth Century Fox, 1988. Tess (Melanie Griffith) is about to learn a lesson in business ethics: As the assistant of Katharine Parker (Sigourney Weaver), she learns that despite Katharine's assurance that their work is a team effort, her boss has passed Tess's ideas off as her own. Here Jack (Harrison Ford) and Tess confront Katharine with the evidence that she stole Tess's ideas.

she wants Tess's input, because she wants their working relationship to be "a two-way street." McGill obliges by telling Parker of a business deal she envisions. The Trask Company, a major corporation, wants to buy into television, which is hard. Tess sees a way for Trask to break into the media world by buying a radio station first. Katharine brushes off the idea as only a "nice try" but insists that Tess keep up the good work, because, "You make it happen!"

Katharine goes on a skiing trip to Europe and breaks her leg; Tess goes to her apartment to take care of her affairs, and discovers that Katharine was in fact in the process of discussing Tess's idea (and passing it off as her own) with a business acquaintance, Jack Trainer (who is also Katharine's lover). Tess sets up a meeting with Trainer herself, passing herself off as Katharine's partner. Trainer likes the idea, and he likes Tess, too. Meanwhile, Tess's appearance and demeanor have changed from her former working-class style to a professional, Wall Street look. She takes over Katharine's office for meetings with Trainer. When they become lovers, she tries to tell him the truth. They are interrupted by a call from Katharine—she is on her way back from Europe. Tess and Trainer persuade a Trask executive to take a look at their deal. Katharine comes home and finds out what

Tess has been up to. During the final meeting between Tess, Jack, and Trask, Katharine shows up and denounces Tess as a fraud. Trainer suggests that the deal can be made nevertheless. Katharine fires Tess, who leaves the office with her files in hand, including the files showing how she first put the Trask material together. Later, Trainer stands by her as she tells Trask executives how the whole deal was her idea. Katharine cannot explain how she herself came up with the idea, so a Trask executive promptly fires Katharine and hires Tess. Tess has now arrived in the business world—she is no longer a secretary but rather an executive. She has won Trainer, too. But what has she become? A very small cog in the great wheel of the world of business.

Study Questions

1. What is this film trying to say about business ethics?
2. In your opinion, who is the worst transgressor, Katharine, who steals Tess's idea, or Tess, who lies to make a deal? Why?
3. Many believe that a good sexual morality demands that one never uses deception or coercion; it is morally wrong to lie to the person you are (or want to become) involved with, to withhold relevant information from that person, or to force him or her physically or with threats. When Tess meets Jack Trainer for the first time, he knows that she is seeking him for business reasons, but he doesn't reveal his identity to her. The next morning, she wakes up in his apartment, with no recollection of what took place the night before. Even though we learn that they didn't have sex, could Trainer still be faulted for "withholding relevant information" from Tess?

Ethics and the Media

The media often insist that the public has a "right to know," and that such a right overrides individual and collective wishes to keep things secret. But what are the ethical standards of the news media? Do journalists always stick to merely *reporting* events?

SIDNEY LUMET (DIRECTOR); WITH PADDY CHAYEFSKY (SCREENWRITER), *Network*

Film (1976)

The main topic of the film *Network*, now considered a classic, is the ordinary citizen reacting to social pressure and deciding that he is "mad as hell and not going to take it anymore." A subtheme in the film is that of media ethics: How far can the news media go in terms of seeking out news? We will not discuss the details of the film so much as its implications. What are the ethical standards of the news media? We already know that the media will sometimes hound victims of disasters and their relatives in times of grief and confusion, but what about when the media actually *creates* news items for the sake of ratings and viewer approval? In *Network*, a television executive makes a deal with a terrorist group to have exclusive interviews with them, and in turn provide them with coverage of their bank robberies and other terrorist acts. We soon find out there's more to it, however: The terrorist group becomes part of the network's programming plan; the network, in effect, *stages* acts of terrorism to put into their news slots. *Network* seems to have been the first film to suggest such a thing, but this theme has more relevance today than ever. What seemed far-fetched in 1976 has become possible reality with the advent of the video camera and the popularity of home video shows on television. The power of the video camera was made evident in the 1991 Rodney King case. The incident was taped by an amateur on a home video camera and broadcast on television stations nationwide. It later was shown to jurors during the subsequent trials of the four LAPD officers charged with the beating. It is now imaginable that networks might be in the market for home videos on issues with viewer appeal (sex and violence). Owners of home video cameras might even stage such events for the sake of selling them to television stations.

Two other films dealing with the news media and ethics should be mentioned: *Broadcast News* from 1987 (directed by James L. Brooks) and *All the President's Men* from 1976 (directed by Alan J. Pakula). In *Broadcast News* a television newscaster is the villain; he fakes a shot of himself in tears during an emotional interview. In *All the President's Men*, based on the Watergate affair, two journalists from the *Washington Post* are the heroes. They are the only persons in Washington with the courage, stamina, and intelligence to divulge the clandestine government actions that led to the Watergate scandal and subsequently brought about the downfall of Richard Nixon.

Study Questions

1. In an article in *TV Guide* on the TV series "I Witness Video," the writer expressed worry that networks might stage acts of violence for the sake of ratings. Do you think that this is a true problem?
2. Could you imagine scheduled programs involving real-life cases of violence on television? Would you approve or disapprove?
3. Under what circumstances would you approve of some form of media censorship? When and why? If you would not approve under any circumstances, explain why you would not.

Chapter 2

Stories in Our Lives

Learning Moral Lessons from Stories

We may think that the most powerful moral lessons are taught by events in our childhood (when we are caught doing something we aren't supposed to do, or when we *aren't* caught), but chances are that the most powerful lessons we carry with us are lessons we learn from the *stories* we have read, or that were read to us.

Many of you may recognize this typical, unpleasant event from when you were a child: Your authority figure takes you aside to tell you the story of The Boy Who Cried Wolf. Peter was tending sheep at the outskirts of town, and he thought it might be fun to give the village a scare, so he cried, "The wolf is here! the wolf is here!" And the villagers came running, but there was no wolf. Peter tricked the town again and again, until that fateful day when the wolf really did come. Peter cried for his life, "The wolf is here!" but nobody believed him anymore. The wolf ate the sheep, and Peter, too. At least this is the way I remember the story. Why are children told such a story? Because adults deem it necessary to teach children a moral lesson. Even a child understands the message: "Peter lied and suffered the consequences. You don't want to be like Peter, do you?" It is a powerful lesson.

Few of us who heard another story as children paid much attention to the lesson it taught. It is Hans Christian Andersen's story, "Little Fir Tree." Way out in the woods

FIGURE 2.1 "The Boy Who Cried Wolf" embodies one of the most effective early moral lessons in many people's lives: If we make a habit out of lying, the chances are that we will not be believed when we are finally telling the truth.

a little Christmas tree is growing. It is a pretty little tree, and it ought to be happy just being a little tree in the woods, but every time a rabbit jumps over it, it wishes that it were already fully grown, because it's not much fun to be little. Season after season this happens—the little tree wants to grow and be a mighty pine so that it can be cut down and travel to foreign lands and see exciting things. The wind and the sun whisper, "Be happy you're young! Be happy you're here in the forest with your friends. Don't wish for time to hurry." Finally the tree becomes a young adult. It is cut down for Christmas, purchased, and taken to a nice, middle-class home. It experiences a wonderful Christmas Eve, but that is it for the little Christmas tree. It keeps expecting other wonderful things to happen, but it has no future, and, finally, stuck in the attic with brown, drooping branches, it realizes that the wind and the sun were right—it should have been happy to be young and surrounded by its friends in the woods. I guess I don't have to spell out the moral lesson, but it's true that we often don't appreciate something until it is lost to us, and then we realize that we should have been more appreciative while it was still ours.

We can also learn, from stories, moral lessons about storytelling itself. There is a children's story about a young girl, Wendy, who has been told that she can no longer share the nursery with her two younger brothers because she is too old to play games, too old to tell them stories. Her father wants her to grow up, to stop believing in Peter Pan. For nineteenth-century readers of *Peter Pan*, it may have seemed appropriate that Wendy and the boys return from Neverland and grow up—after Wendy's one final flirtation with childhood—but for people who love stories it is profoundly disturbing: Does it mean that Wendy has to stop telling stories just because she is grown up? The Peter Pan story reveals an ambiguity in our attitude towards storytelling: On one hand telling stories is *intrinsically valuable*; it keeps us young, immortal, and with one foot in Neverland. In other words, we are doing something good by telling stories. On the other hand, storytelling is something we should lay aside if we want to be considered respectable and adult. Ethics scholars have, until recently, chosen the latter path. However, there a different attitude is on the rise: Stories and morals are now seen as somehow connected, and that can be good for the stories as well as for the moral theories, as this book will try to show.

The use of narratives or story outlines as illustrations of moral problems is by no means new, as we shall see, but it is a new addition to *contemporary* ethics. Philosophers have for a long time been suspicious of using stories as illustrations of moral problems, for several reasons. Some have felt that using stories would cause readers to be concerned with *specific* cases, rather than see the general picture. Others have worried that telling stories might manipulate readers' emotions instead of appealing to their reason; such stories would perhaps lead people to *do* the right thing, but they wouldn't lead people to *think* about moral issues, because a story is not a logical argument, but rather a persuasion—a story is not logic but rhetoric.

There is a difference, however, between stories that moralize and stories that discuss moral problems. In the past, philosophers seem to have assumed that stories illustrating moral problems are always of the moralizing kind. Now a different attitude seems to be growing among ethics scholars; they recognize that stories need not be moralizing in order to illustrate a moral point. Such stories may express a moral point of view, and then that point of view can be open for discussion. Or, a story may have an open-ended conclusion, one in which the moral issues are not resolved. Even moralizing stories may have their proper role to play from time to time, and stories are an excellent way to illustrate how difficult a moral problem can be. In other words, stories can serve as a "laboratory" where moral solutions can be tried out before any decisions are made. Medical students in many parts of the United States are now exposed to case studies that involve questions of medical ethics. Not only that, they are exposed to stories of *fiction* that deal with medical problems, and it appears that the students consider themselves to be better equipped to deal with real medical problems because of this exposure. Philosophy also is slowly warming up to the old idea that feelings are not all that irrelevant in moral discussions. The psychologist Carol Gilligan argues for the legitimacy of emotions in moral decision making. The philosopher Martha Nussbaum points out that emotions do not consist of uncontrollable events like hunger but instead involve decision making and rational choices. Another philosopher, Philip

Hallie, states that without feelings for the victims of evildoing, we can't hope to understand what a moral sense is all about. Jonathan Bennett, another contemporary philosopher, insists that our moral principles may be admirable, but they may just as well be warped: The Nazi exterminators (members of the National Socialist German Worker's party, 1933–1945) had firm moral principles, only they were principles most people don't approve of today. Without sympathy for other people, our principles may go astray. One of the ways in which we can engage both our sympathy and our moral principles is through stories.

In this book stories will be used to illustrate some classical and some more contemporary ethical problems. Some of the stories are *didactic* (they teach a lesson), and some of them are more open-ended. It seems that, usually, we enjoy learning from stories that were not written especially to teach a lesson—more so than we enjoy learning from didactic stories. This may be one of the secrets of literature: We may forgive a good story for preaching a little, but we can't forgive a bad story for preaching. In other words, we are most comfortable with a moral lesson if it is not too obvious, if it appears only "between the lines" and is subordinate to the plot and the characters. Perhaps, most of all, we enjoy learning a lesson from stories in which no lesson is intended.

On occasion during the last few decades we have heard that the novel is dead, that nobody reads books anymore. But people do write and read novels today, even if those novels are best sellers and not "serious fiction." Furthermore, people watch movies. Narrative theories rarely condescend to include films in the narrative category, but I believe they have their rightful place there, because they are certainly stories, usually having a beginning, a middle, and an ending. Historically, literature was drama before it became literature. And for some people, movies, not books, are the medium through which they are exposed to greater moral issues. It has been argued that books keep your attention for days, whereas you spend two hours watching a film, and then you forget it. That, however, was before the era of the videotape and the laser disc. Now people have their favorite films at home, and they review them ten or twenty times—more times than they might reread a book. We must conclude, therefore, that the moral lesson learned from a film can be as powerful as one learned from a book, even if the experience may be different, and I will include films among my examples throughout this book. (Some of the stories mentioned in this chapter can be found in later chapters as detailed outlines that serve as specific examples of moral problems.)

Telling Stories

It seems that humans are the only beings who tell each other stories. At least, we have no way, yet, to determine if other creatures also entertain each other with fictional accounts. The philosopher Alasdair MacIntyre finds the telling of stories so important for humans that he calls us "storytelling animals" (see Part 4, Chapter 19). There are many reasons for telling stories, for reading novels and short stories, and for making and watching films. It seems that in early, pre-technological cultures the purpose of storytelling was twofold: On the *human* side, the purpose was to knit the tribe firmly together by setting up the rules and boundaries that would establish a group identity. Besides, storytelling helped to pass the time on rainy days, and it kept the children occupied for a while. On the *cosmic* side, the purpose was to establish the story of the beginning of time, when everything was created, so if a symbolic re-creation seemed necessary (and it did, periodically), one could tell and enact the "beginning" stories and in that way "renew" the cosmos. Storytelling has never been more important than it was in those ancient times, for in telling the story people helped recreate the universe, put the sun in its right place, and make sure that the seasons followed one another in the proper order.

The strength of storytelling is no less apparent in many religions. Periodically (usually once a year), believers remind themselves of an important time in the history of their religion: the creation of the world, the creation of the religion itself, or the establishment of the believers' identity through a religious event. Usually a story is told about this event, and even if it is supposed to be a reminder rather than a re-creation, it is still a sacred and powerful vehicle.

Fact, Fiction, or Both?

In the secular world we usually tell stories of two kinds: those that we believe to be historically true, and those that we know never took place but that have their own special truth to them, a *poetic* truth. The fairy tale Little Red Riding Hood is not a historical account, but children may enjoy it if they are old enough to deal with their fear of the wolf, who comes to a gruesome end. Parents enjoy telling it, because they can smuggle home a lesson: Don't talk to strangers, and watch out for "wolves" in disguise.

What about accounts that we don't know to be either historical or poetic? The story of Robin Hood, for example, is not a historical account, although there may have been an outlaw in medieval England who resembled the Robin of Locksley character. Some readers feel cheated if they find out that a story is more legend than history, but others find it all the more fascinating, because it is a mixture of what we think happened, and what we wish had happened. It may not tell us much about the real Robin Hood, but it tells us a lot about people, including ourselves, who *wish* that Robin were real.

Even stories that we believe to be factual, such as the story of the battle of the Alamo, or the sinking of the Titanic, or the death of Marilyn Monroe, are not usually simple reports of facts; such stories must have a beginning, a middle, and an ending, and most often we choose the beginning and the ending according to what we feel makes the most *sense*. In actual life, the stream of events goes on, usually with little indication that here begins something new, or here a story comes to an end—except in the case of someone's birth or death. Even then, the story goes on, except for the dead person. So, even "true" stories have an element of *poetic creativity*, in that we choose what to include in the story, what is *relevant* to the story (not every meal or visit to the bathroom is important in order for us to understand the life and times of Ghandi, or James Dean, or Marilyn Monroe), and we choose where to begin and end the story. Even eyewitness accounts, often regarded as the one true record of events, are full of creativity. Two persons observing the same event will very likely come up with slightly different versions of it; they notice different things because they are standing in different spots, and because they are different people with different interests in life. If a considerable amount of time goes by and eyewitnesses are asked to tell about an event long past, some of their memories will be sharper than others; some will mirror exactly what they saw, and some will mirror what they felt, or what they feel now, which may be just as relevant, but definitely falls within the range of personal interpretation. At best, any account of a past event can only *approximate* what happened. We can never truly reproduce the event.

Religious legends reveal the same tension between fact and fiction. If believers suspect that events described in the legends never happened, or that they happened in a different and more "everyday" way than is described in the religious text, they may experience a general disappointment with their religion, feeling that it is based on stories that have no foundation in fact. Other believers, however, may see the stories as being rich with poetry and telling human truths that are on a higher, more spiritual level. Aristotle, who was intensely interested in the relationship between history and poetry, said that history may deal with facts, but poetry deals with Truth.

Stories with A Moral Lesson

Myths We don't know anything about the first stories ever told, but if we are to judge from ancient myths and legends, there is a good chance that they served as reminders of proper conduct. The Navajos tell of Grandmother Spider's way of making clay pots, and it seems to be (among other things) a lesson for Navajo women in how to make pots the correct way. Myths in general have two main purposes: to strengthen the social bonding among people, and to fortify the individual psychologically. *Traditional myths* work on both levels at one time by presenting stories of gods, goddesses, and culture heroes who tell their society about the ideal social behavior and individuals about the proper role models to follow. In a sense, traditional myths are a successful combination of *ethics of conduct* and *virtue ethics* (see Part 3). The philosopher Peter Munz calls myths "concrete universals," stories that in a very concrete form tell about the human condition and give us courage to deal with the troubles that being human usually entails.

The Trobriand myth of the loss of immortality is such a story; it tells us that once humans could rejuvenate themselves; they could shed their skins and become young again. A grandmother took her granddaughter to the river and then went off by herself to shed her skin. When she came back, the granddaughter didn't recognize her (she appeared to be a young girl) and shooed her away. Upset, the grandmother went back and put her old skin on again. Now the granddaughter recognized her and told her that she had chased a young girl, an imposter, away. The grandmother said, "Just because you refused to recognize me, nobody will be able to be young again. We shall all die of old age now." Aside from the fact that the story unfairly places the immense burden of causing humanity to die on an ignorant young girl—myths often blame a major disaster on a small event, as when Eve eats the fruit from the Tree of Knowledge—the lesson is that there is mortality and there is nothing we can do about it. The story also seems to say that humans, far from being victims, are very important beings since they can cause such a cosmic calamity as the loss of immortality!

Fairy Tales Another ancient category of stories with moral lessons are *fairy tales*. Grimm's fairy tales reflect what is probably a very old tradition of normative ethics, and not just for children; the stories were told, originally, to both young and old. The Trobriand people of New Guinea have a tradition in which they distinguish between three different kinds of stories. First there are the "myths," which are sacred stories about the beginning of the world and of society. They must be taken very seriously. Then there are the "true legends," semihistorical accounts of heroes in the past and their travels. They are supposed to be taken at face value, for the most part. Last, there are the "fairy tales," stories to be told in the rainy season, usually with some point of teaching the young about the customs of the people, but also with the intent of pure entertainment. (They are recognized as "never having happened.")

Most cultures recognize that there is a difference between stories where the good get rewarded and the bad get punished, and stories of everyday life. The fairy tale has been described by psychoanalysts as pure wishful thinking, but many fairy tales involve gruesome events that are hardly wish fulfillments, because they often happen to characters who don't "deserve" them. Such events do serve a purpose, though, in making the punishment of the bad characters seem justified.

Little Red Riding Hood, which was mentioned earlier, seems to be, in spite of its enormous popularity, a product of the literary elite and not of folklore, but that doesn't detract from its didactic power (the power to teach a lesson). Hansel and Gretl is a folklore classic with much the same lesson: Don't go with strangers, and don't let them feed you candy! There are also more obscure Grimm stories, such as The Maiden Without Hands, in which a pious girl's tears fall on her hands and prevent the Devil from taking her, so he chops her hands off, but she cries on the stumps, so he leaves her alone, and an angel gives her silver hands. When she is finally reunited with her beloved, she even gets her own hands back. What is the lesson here? That purity and piety carry their own reward. There are of course stories that teach a different lesson, such as The Juniper Tree in which the stepmother kills, cooks, and serves the baby brother up for dinner. His father loves the stew but doesn't know he is eating his own son. His older sister Marjory (who knows about the evil deed) gathers his bones and buries them under the big tree in the yard where his mother also lies buried; in the tree is a bird (the boy's spirit) who takes on the task of punishment and reward. Marjory receives a pair of red shoes; the stepmother, in her envy, wants something, too. She gets a millstone, which falls on her head. The baby brother comes alive again, after which the father, the sister, and the brother go in and finish their dinner. What do we have here? An untrustworthy, evil (step)mother, and a drastic revenge. Psychoanalysts today say that the real value of such stories—which, they say, children should not be protected from but rather exposed to—is that kids can get rid of their aggressions towards their parents through the stories. (As we shall see in an upcoming section, Aristotle would have agreed with this psychoanalytic point of view.) Also, the child is exposed to evil but at the same time acquires a dose of hopeful strength and learns that evil can be dealt with. In other words, the most horrible, gruesome, bloody fairy tales may be the ones with the most positive message for the impressionable reader: Yes, there are terrible things out there, but with fortitude we can vanquish them.

Parables For two thousand years, Christians have found moral support in parables such as the good samaritan and the prodigal son.

The *parable* is an allegorical story for adults; it is supposed to be understood as a story about ourselves and what we ought to do. Although the purpose of the fairy tale seems to be primarily to entertain and, secondarily, to teach a moral lesson, the purpose of the parable is *primarily* to teach a moral and religious lesson. Christianity is not the only religion with parables; the Islamic tradition contains such stories, as do the Hebrew and Buddhist traditions.

What fascinated the early readers of Jesus of Nazareth's parables was that they were so hard to live up to—not just because it was hard to be good, but because the moral demands of Jesus himself usually ran counter to what society demanded of its citizens, or what it viewed as proper moral conduct. What was so hard for Jesus' contemporaries to understand? Not only that we should be compassionate towards all in need, but that we should consider every person a fellow human being, not just those from our own village, country, or culture, and especially those who show compassion toward us!

The parable of the prodigal son has been an equally hard lesson for people with ordinary common sense and good manners to follow. The "bad" son who has squandered his inheritance comes home and is sorry. (The good son has been there all the time.) The father makes a fuss over the bad son and slaughters the fattened calf for him. The good son is upset, for he has never received any recognition of his stability from his father, and yet now it seems that the bad son is more important. And he is, to Jesus, for he has been on a longer journey than the good son: all the way to perdition and back. Christians, therefore, ask themselves if that means we should go on a binge and then repent, rather than never go on a binge at all. The answer may be that the story is not supposed to be judged from the point of view of the good or the bad brother, but from the father's point of view. Indeed, the secret to many of the parables is to find out whose viewpoint they express. The parable of the good samaritan is about a victim of highway robbery and mugging. As he lies wounded at the roadside, he is ignored by several upstanding citizens but is helped by a social outcast, the Samaritan. (The story is outlined in Chapter 13.) This parable is told from the

FIGURE 2.2 "The Trial of Abraham's Faith" (plate by Gustave Doré). Abraham, having received the command from God to sacrifice his only son, Isaac, dutifully takes Isaac up the mountain to the place of sacrifice. Isaac, unaware that it is he himself who is to be the victim, is carrying the firewood that Abraham will use to light the sacrificial fire.

wounded man's point of view ("who is my neighbor"), not from the point of view of the samaritan.

A Story of Sacrifice: Abraham and Isaac A story that does not count as a parable but that has had the same kind of effect on its listeners is the Old Testament story of Abraham being told to sacrifice his son Isaac. It is one of the hardest stories for a religion that believes in a loving God, be it from a Jewish or Christian point of view, to explain. Abraham and his wife Sarah are childless until they have Isaac very late in their lives, through God's intervention. God tells Abraham that his descendents will be as numerous as the stars in the sky and the grains of sand in the desert. When Isaac is a half-grown boy, however, God tells Abraham to take Isaac up the mountain and sacrifice him like a sheep. Abraham takes Isaac up the hill, heavy-hearted but obedient to God. The boy doesn't understand why they haven't brought a sheep if they are going to perform a sacrifice, and Abraham's heart is breaking. He ties Isaac to the sacrificial stone and is about to stab him the ritual way when God's voice stops him, saying the request was just a test of Abraham's piety. God supplies a ram for Abraham to sacrifice instead.

The implications of this story have confounded believers and nonbelievers for over two thousand years. A God who commands such a thing must be a cruel god, critics say, cruel and with a strange sense of humor. The philosopher Søren Kierkegaard (see Part 2, Chapter 11) sees the story as an illustration of the *limitations of ethics*: Ethically speaking, what Abraham was about to do was wrong; he had no business killing his son, because that is not how people are supposed to behave. But for Abraham, as for the believer, there is a law that is higher than the moral laws of society, and that is the law of *faith*—not faith that God will save his child, but faith that it really *is* God who is requiring him to sacrifice Isaac, and that we can't know God's purpose. Kierkegaard saw Abraham's ordeal as a test of his faith in God rather than of his morals, and a "leap of faith" is, for the lutheran Kierkegaard, a matter between the individual and God and nobody else. The opinion of society does not enter into the picture at all. Other interpretations of the story see no split between morality and faith, but view it as an illustration of God's absolute demands on his people. Yet others see it as justification for sacrificing everything one holds dear if a higher law demands it. With this last interpretation it really is irrelevant that God stopped Abraham at the last moment. For all Christians, the parallel to a later time when God did not stop himself from sacrificing his own son to save the world is a close one.

Fables and Counterfables In the eighteenth and nineteenth centuries adults finally were getting around to noticing that children were not just small and inadequate adults, and at this point in time children's literature was invented as a literary genre. The fairy tale was downgraded (and rewritten) to suit the nursery, and another kind of story, which had previously been enjoyed by adults as well, was introduced to children: the *fable*. Aesop's and La Fontaine's fables became very popular as moral lessons for children. The Mouse and the Lion taught that you had better not disregard someone unimportant, for he or she may be of help to you some day, and The Sour

Kafka's Abraham

Franz Kafka (1883–1924) gives a couple of interpretations of the story of Abraham and Isaac that are rather different from the traditional one. For one thing, he says, there was no need for any "leap of faith" in order for Abraham to accept the word of God, because if Abraham were to prove himself, then something precious to him had to be put on the line; if Abraham had so much—riches, a son, and a prophecy that he would become the father of the Jewish people—then he could be tested only by the threat of having something taken away from him. This is logical, says Kafka; it requires no leap of faith at all. What *would* require a leap of faith is if Abraham had been a different sort of person. Suppose he truly wanted to please God by performing the sacrifice but was a person of low self-esteem? He really wants to do what is right, like Cervantes's Don Quixote, but he can't quite believe that it can be him God was speaking to, because he believes he is unworthy. He is afraid that if he proceeds with the sacrifice, it will turn out that the command was just a joke, and he will be a laughing stock, like Don Quixote, who always tried to do the heroic thing but ended up fighting windmills. For this Abraham, being laughed at would make him even more unworthy of being called by God. It would be as though a worthy person had been called, but this grungy, unworthy Abraham showed up instead, foolishly believing himself to be the worthy one. Now this, says Kafka, would indeed require a leap of faith.

Grapes taught that if someone claims something is not worth having, it may be because they can't have it. The main reason adults told these fables to children was, of course, that the grown-ups wanted their children to become good adults, and the stories seemed a good way to press home the point. These early stories for children had more the character of "behave, or else"; they provided little opportunity for children's imagination to take flight. An important exception is the works of Hans Christian Andersen (1805–1875), who, throughout his fairy tales and stories insisted that children's imaginations should be left unfettered by the sour realism of grown-ups. In fact, Andersen's stories have a true poetic quality and also multiple meanings; they are not really children's stories at all. Children can enjoy them, to be sure, but they will enjoy them much more when they are older and capable of reading between the lines. For Hans Christian Andersen, it was not just the imagination of the children that was in danger of being stifled by adults: It was the imagination of the adults themselves that was in danger of withering away. Andersen's moral lesson is one of openness. He tells us to listen to the world and not just respond to it with preconceived notions; if we do, we will encounter only what we expect, and we will never again see the magic and splendor of the world the way children do.

Other stories with a moral lesson were being written for children during this same time period. Didactic stories took up the thread of the fables and taught children how to behave: to obey their parents, to be kind to animals, to finish their porridge, and to not make fun of people who looked different. Although today the lessons of these stories may seem, for the most part, quite inoffensive, the stories themselves often reveal sexism, racism, and a general naive belief that the writer has all the wisdom in the world. Like morality plays, these "moral stories" not only present a moral problem—they *moralize*. This tendency to teach moral solutions enraged Mark Twain to the extent that he wrote a parody called "About Magnanimous–Incident Literature" (to which *MAD Magazine* is in eternal debt). In Twain's parody we hear the "true" ending to the little moral stories. In one story, the little scruffy, homeless dog that the kindly village doctor cures comes back the next day with another scruffy little dog to be cured, and the doctor praises God for the chance to cure another unfortunate creature. End of moral story; here comes Twain: The next day there are four scruffy dogs outside the doctor's office, and the following week there are hundreds of howling mutts waiting to be treated. The original mutt is going crazy from all this philanthropy and bites the doctor, who wishes he had shot it in the first place.

Stories as Role Models

Who Are Our Heroes?

Who do we like to hear stories about? And after the story, do we go out and do the same thing as the hero in the book or the movie?

When we talk about fictional characters who somehow teach a moral lesson, we are talking about *role models*. Cartoon characters such as Superman and the Rocketeer may qualify as persons in a story who have certain qualities that we identify with and would like to emulate. But if we include Batman, we encounter an interesting twist: Batman is not a wholesome character; he has a psychological problem (which was, to some extent, explored in the 1989 film). Not all heroic characters are completely virtuous. If we look at fictional heroes in Western popular literature, from King Arthur, Lancelot, and Robin Hood to D'Artagnan and Scarlett O'Hara, we see that most of these people are morally flawed. The tendency today, in fact, is to depict them as being as morally flawed as possible, something that may reflect a certain sense of cynicism. A talk-show guest recently announced that she had learned her moral lessons exclusively from soap operas, and we know that soap characters are by no means morally without reproach.

This is not a new phenomenon; in the medieval churches of Europe, peasant congregations were spellbound by murals depicting biblical scenes that sometimes covered the entire inside of the church. The murals kept them occupied during the long hours while the priest spoke in Latin, which the peasants did not understand. The moral lesson of this artwork was obvious, but it was expressed not through depictions of good people as much as *bad* people; scenes illustrating people going to Hell are usually much more vivid and artistically interesting than scenes of people going to Heaven. Perhaps the artists thought it was more fun to depict horrors than bland happiness. It does seem to be a human trait that we dwell on stories with a dark element, rather than on those with happy endings. Yet these stories certainly can teach a moral lesson. We must conclude, therefore, that not all moral lessons involve role models to be emulated; rather, a considerable number of moral lessons teach: Don't do this! The moral lesson is negative rather than positive: *don't*. Sometimes characters who show themselves to be morally flawed become our heroes not because they are good, but because they are like us, or worse. Especially if these "bad good people" see the folly of their ways in the end (as when Scarlett realizes that she never really loved Ashley but does love Rhett, even if it is too late), we take them to our hearts. Perhaps that is because we hope that we will be loved, too, even if we make mistakes. It seems that, on the whole, we have the heroes we deserve, as it has sometimes been said. A cautious time has cautious heroes; a violent time has violent heroes. During the time that they are our heroes, we let their images guide our actions; when their day is done, we can still learn from them—they can teach us about the way we once were.

Some Contemporary Moral Lessons

Moral Noncommunication: *Brave New World* Sometimes the moral lesson in a story is hard to find; we may be blind to it, or it may be somewhat dated, having evolved in another era. There is a scene in Aldous Huxley's *Brave New World* where the young "savage," John, who has grown up on a nature reservation unaffected by the modern era of eugenics, total sexual liberty, and the industrialization of test-tube babies, introduces his friend, the Alpha-scientist Helmholtz, to Shakespeare. He reads from *Romeo and Juliet*, certain that the moral drama of the young lovers who can't have each other will move his modern friend. Helmholtz, however, doubles up laughing, because he can't for the life of him see that there is a problem: If Romeo and Juliet want each other, why don't they just have sex and let it go at that, instead of making such an embarrassing fuss about it? He is blind to the social and moral structures of the past, and the savage is very upset that ethical communication seems impossible in a new era that has done away with family relationships, birth, siblings, and spouses, and that refuses to recognize the phenomenon of death.

In a similar way, stories depicting unwanted pregnancies struck a deep chord in times past, but haven't had the same resonance since the advent of legal abortion and safe birth control. Old Hollywood films about the trials of two lovers who can't get a divorce from their spouses also sometimes require a bit of "stretching" in order for us to empathize with the characters. Stories praising the glory of war, which were quite successful until the early twentieth century, have not done well with the majority of modern readers and viewers for quite some time now.

War Movies with a Message

Most films and novels about war take place within a more or less historical context, though there usually is some artistic license taken. Although documentaries and actual combat footage can make a lasting impression on a viewer, works of fiction such as *War and Peace*, *The Red Badge of Courage*, *All Quiet on the Western Front*, *Twelve O'Clock High*, and *Platoon* often more effectively present the human experience in war. Some films, such as *A Bridge Too Far*, *Enola Gay*, and *Hamburger Hill* attempt factually to depict actual wartime events. Others, such as *Paths of Glory*, *Memphis Belle*, and *Glory* spin fictional elements and characters into a factual story in order to convincingly impart a message about war, its victims, victors, and survivors.

Wartime Ethics Wartime stories with moral lessons were very common in times past, when governments were less reluctant to embark upon war as a course of action than they are today. To be willing to die for your country was not a cliché, not a corny idea. Today we are inclined to say that the idea of the "glory of war" is mainly propaganda, invented by the leaders of the past in order to inspire their legions to march off to the front, unquestioning. However, the idea of a warrior's fate being something glorious has been important for so many people throughout history that we can't dismiss it as being merely the result of manipulation of the people by poets, propagandists, kings, and generals.

We should be careful to distinguish between the concepts of the glory of war, and honorable wartime conduct. Although the idea that war is a fulfillment of manly virtues vanished, by and large, from the Western mind-set with World War I, the concept of *honor* in war is as relevant as ever in discussions of ethical conduct, whether it is considered in terms of a war where the goals were unclear, as was the case with Vietnam, or a battle between good and evil, such as World War II and, for many people, the Persian Gulf War of 1991. In both "unjust" and "just" wars, there are demands that must be met and actions that call for bravery beyond the call of duty. Although war is, for most people, the last moral option for dealing with conflict (and no moral option at all for pacifists), we still can talk about the moral conduct of the soldier, both towards his or her comrades-in-arms, and towards the enemy. And even in peacetime, those virtues may still be used in fiction to illustrate both the difficulties of ethical wartime conduct, and, symbolically, the difficulty of making honorable decisions in any crisis situation. Even in stories with an antiwar message, the honor, decency, and heroism of the characters are emphasized by being contrasted with the meaninglessness of war. One such film is *Castle Keep*, in which a small band of Ameri-

FIGURE 2.3 *All Quiet On The Western Front,* Universal Studios, 1930. Katzzinsky (Louis Wolheim), the old "trenchhog," and Paul Baumen (Lew Ayres), the young idealist who is about to get his lesson in the realities of war. The Western world's image of war changed with World War I. No more shining swords and prancing horses—there was nothing glorious about dying in the trenches of the European battlefields, and few soldiers understood the purpose of the prolonged fighting. However, the virtues of friendship, courage, and loyalty seemed all the more important as a twentieth-century war ethic. (From the collection of C. R. Covner.)

can soldiers is given the task of guarding a European castle against the rapidly advancing Nazi army. If war has any fascination for the soldiers, it is only in the abstract; on a day-to-day level, each is obsessed with saving whatever remnants of civilization he can in the short time given to him. For one soldier, it is whatever love he can find in the village; for another it is the precious works of art in the castle. Yet another wants to live to write stories afterwards. In E. M. Forster's *Howards End*, the heroine Margaret says she hates war but loves soldiers. By this we see that it is entirely possible to disapprove of war while still recognizing the honorable qualities of those who fight it.

The Moral Universe of Westerns "*Westerns*," stories of the American West, have served as moral lessons for both the American public and a worldwide audience for more than one hundred years. In the 1970s and 1980s the public's interest in Westerns gradually waned, but in the nineties there seems to be a new interest in them. What is it about the Western that has for so long served so well as a moral lesson? Several factors may play a part.

All nations seem to go through periods where they "rediscover" their past, but the American West as a historical period is both recent and very short. The years of Western expansion that have become legendary are those from 1865 to ca. 1885—from the end of the Civil War to the end of the open cattle range, which came about with the advent of barbed wire and the bad winters of the 1880s. There have probably been more stories told about the Old West than could ever have had time to happen. Even when the Old West was still alive, those in the East were reading dimestore novels that glamorized the West, and the first Western films were being shot outside New York City. The process of creating a legend about the recent past was very rapid and involved even old cowboys and gunfighters who moved from the plains and deserts to Hollywood to lend a hand.

Making entertainment out of recent history was one way to draw people to the theaters. If that were all, though, the Western never would have lived as long as it has. Part of its allure seems to have been the draw of the *exotic*; the West is, still, quite different from the East. And then there is wishful thinking: Perhaps the Old West was never the way it appears in movies, but we wish it had been. An even greater appeal is the *moral potential* of a Western. The story usually is one we are familiar with, even if we see it for the first time; there has to be some gorgeous landscape, and good guys and bad guys, and horses, and they have to do a lot of riding back and forth among rocks. Then there is usually a good girl, and sometimes also a bad girl. And there is a threat, either from Indians, or the railroad, or rustlers, or (in later Westerns) big business, and it is warded off by the strength and wit of Our Hero, sometimes even reluctantly (he often has to be dragged into the fight). When the problem is solved, the hero rarely settles down, but rides off into the sunset so that he doesn't get entangled in the peace and prosperity of the society he helped stabilize. In later Westerns, the image of the good guys sometimes shifts, so that the good guys are Indians or Blacks, or a gang of outlaws, and the bad guys are the army, or other Indians, or the law, and the stable society becomes a negative rather than a positive image. Traditionally, though, the general pattern is the same: The power of the individual (the Good) rises above the threat of a larger force (the Evil).

FIGURE 2.4 The 1985 Western *Silverado* (Columbia Pictures) abandoned the seventies trend of depicting the Old West in its declining years and gave its audience a story set in a vigorous frontier setting with a happy ending. For this reason, the film is sometimes referred to as a "retro-Western." However, many of the themes incorporated in *Silverado* are anything but "retro"; for example, with this film the Western genre entered a new era of racial awareness. Here the four buddies (Danny Glover, Kevin Costner, Scott Glenn, and Kevin Kline) ride out to save the town of Silverado from corruption.

Why do people go to see Westerns if they already know what will happen? Because the movie experience (or TV experience) itself is a *moral event*. People take part in the story by watching it, and they feel that when the problems on the screen are solved, the general problems of life are, in some symbolic way, tackled at the same time. The moviegoer may not even be aware of this, but that is the psychological process that is in effect.

One might think that if the Western had a moral message, it would seem pretty dated, and sometimes even offensive, after a few generations. After all, the first generation of Westerns left the overall impression (though it was, perhaps, not entirely a fair assessment) that it was fine to kill Indians, that women were weak and had to be protected, that Blacks were nonexistent, that the land was there only to be developed, that animal life and suffering were irrelevant, and so on. However, the extraordinary thing that happened was that the ethics of the Western movie changed with the

The Changing Messages of Westerns

Western films have from the early days managed to integrate modern problems into the period plot. The Westerns of each decade tend to focus on the social and political issues of that particular decade, imposing them on the story and on the characters in the film, sometimes without much respect for the historical context. The Vietnam War era had its own "Vietnam Westerns," where massacred Indians symbolized the Vietnamese, and the army symbolized the American Army in Vietnam (*Soldier Blue*, *Little Big Man*). Post-Watergate Westerns showed corrupt politicians and greedy railroad tycoons (*Young Guns I* and *II*). With the recent return of the Western, there is a growing sensitivity not only for historical accuracy, but also for a multiethnic presence in the Old West. Recently, African-Americans have found a heroic identity in the Western landscape (*Silverado*, *Lonesome Dove*), and Native Americans have emerged from old stereotypes such as devils or angels to become real people with their own language and their own problems and jokes [*Dances with Wolves*, (outlined in Chapter 20), *The Last of the Mohicans* (outlined in Chapter 7)]. Strong female characters in Westerns are still few and far between, although there have been a number of them over the years in the films *Johnny Guitar*, *Rio Bravo*, and *High Noon* (outlined in Chapter 13), the television movie *Lonesome Dove*, and the television series "Dr. Quinn, Medicine Woman."

changing times. There were still good guys and bad guys and horses, but in each period they reflected the problems in the real world, at least in a symbolic sense. In the fifties the Western began to reflect a growing unease with the stereotype of townspeople conquering the wilderness; in the sixties there was an increasing sympathy for the outlaw. The Western of the seventies was influenced by the Vietnam war and began to address problems of discrimination, unemployment, overdevelopment, and pollution. In the eighties the Western seemed to have nothing more to say, but in the nineties it is beginning to have a voice once again; current Westerns often deal with cross-cultural and cross-racial issues in the American melting pot. The Western, being the one narrative genre that is truly American, shows an amazing potential for being able to deal with many kinds of social and moral problems in a simple framework where people have to make big, moral decisions in a land where they are dwarfed by rocks, mountains, and deserts. These stories of momentous decisions appeal not only to Americans, but also to people all over the world. This makes the Western much more than just a movie genre. It has become a transcultural story told in a universal moral language.

Science Fiction Although the Western may be able to deal with many modern moral problems such as racism and sexism, speciesism, ecology, crime, drugs, child abuse, and so on, it really cannot address such issues as genetic manipulation, environmental disasters, and so forth. Other genres are more popular and much better suited for such exploration. Such a genre is science fiction.

Like the Western, science fiction was born as a literary genre in the nineteenth century. The French author Jules Verne astounded the world with his fantasies of men on the moon, journeys to the center of the earth and the bottom of the sea. Even Hans Christian Andersen predicted, in one of his lesser known stories, that in "thousands of years" Americans would be flying in machines to Europe to visit the Old World. Verne's stories have always contained an element that has blossomed in modern science fiction: a *moral awareness*. There is an awareness of the possible repercussions of the inventions in his stories, as well as a general political awareness, which makes his books much more than mere entertainment. In England, the works of H. G. Wells fulfilled the same functions of science fantasy and social comment.

In the twentieth century, science fiction has become a major genre of entertainment, from pulp magazines and comic books to serious novels and films of high quality. Their themes range from pure fantasy of magical universes to hard-core thought experiments of exploratory science. Although science fiction need not always involve ethical issues, it has proved to be one of the most suitable genres for exploring moral problems, especially such problems as we believe may lurk in our futures.

In a category by itself is the "end of civilization" type of science fiction. The civilized world is destroyed by nuclear war, or a giant meteor strike, or pollution, or the advent of hostile aliens, or an epidemic disease, and so on. Although this type of science fiction affords the author a chance to present lots of stories of gruesome death or terrible disaster, the most serious problems usually occur in the relationships among the survivors. Will they revert to a "war of everybody against everybody," as the philosopher Thomas Hobbes would say, or does the human spirit of compassion for one's fellow beings triumph? This form also allows us to discuss how the characters got into such dire situations. If it is through human folly or neglect, such as global war or pollution, the stories can serve as powerful moral *caveats* or warnings.

Interestingly enough, there is a "counterfable" to the end-of-the-world scenario, which has proved to be even more popular. It is the story of the Happy Future—not a future without problems, but a future in which some of the pressing problems of the late twentieth century have been solved. Such stories present a world without nuclear threat, without racism or sexism, without nationalistic chauvinism, a world in which science has acquired a humanistic face, and politics on earth as well as in space are conducted with a democratic spirit and common sense. The original "Star Trek" television series pioneered this hopeful fantasy of the future, and the sequel, "Star Trek: The Next Generation," showed that the Happy Future scenario was as welcome as ever; not in a naive sense, but as a vision of a maturing humanity that, free from the fears, deprivations, and resentments of the twentieth century, may be able to turn its energy toward new frontiers and challenges.

Another science fiction category addresses the question, Who is a Person? Roger

MacBride Allen's *Orphan of Creation* (outlined in Chapter 20) describes the moral, political, and scientific problems that arise when a small band of Australopithecus Robustus are found in Africa—not human, not quite nonhuman animals. What will humanity do with them? Enslave them into forced labor, perform medical experiments on them, lock them up in zoos, or grant them human rights? Other stories explore the fate of altered chimps or harmless humanoid aliens. A typical science fiction slave revolt involves not human slaves, but genetically altered animals who have to fight for their right to be recognized as persons. This is the theme in *Norstrilia* and "The Dead Lady of Clown Town" by Cordwainer Smith.

A related category has as its focus the thinking computer or the android. The computer or android may think and speak, but can it feel? And even if it thinks, speaks, and feels, do we still have moral obligations to it, or is it just a machine, somebody's property? The issue of slavery also may be addressed, as it was in a *Star Trek: The Next Generation* episode, "The Measure of A Man" (outlined in Chapter 20). In some stories the thinking android may be hostile or simply without a moral notion of wrongdoing, and then it may resemble the Golem.

The *Golem* may be the oldest character in the science fiction tradition. It comes from the Eastern European Jewish tradition, where it was said that a man might create an artificial person out of clay, a Golem, but if he weren't careful to keep this creature in check with certain magical acts and formulas, the Golem would grow and eventually take over and kill him. One story tells of a rabbi creating a Golem to help the Jews protest false accusations of blood-sacrificing of Christians during Passover. This particular Golem helped the Jewish people for years by exposing Christian plots to plant dead bodies of Christians in Jewish homes. But the Golem became too strong and powerful for the rabbi to handle, so in the end the rabbi had to turn him back into the clay from which he had been created. (Another version of the story tells that the rabbi turned the Golem back into clay because his job was done and there was no reason to keep him around anymore.) In the early nineteenth century, Mary W. Shelley created a similar artificial person, Frankenstein's monster. As we saw in the introduction to this book, Shelley's theme was the same as that of the Golem story: Human arrogance and invention run wild. In a strange sense we might say that the Golem story is very conservative: If you exceed your boundaries, your creation will come back to haunt you. In a more progressive sense, though, the story teaches us to evaluate our actions from a moral perspective. In the movies, the artificial monster has taken on a number of guises, from the maniacal computer HAL in *2001, A Space Odyssey* to the Arnold Schwarzenegger character in *The Terminator*.

In any event, the artificial person serves well, not just as a topic for discussion about what to do if artificial beings become viable in our society, but also as a figurative image of ourselves. The artificial person makes us realize what it is to be human, and what we ought to be like to be *more* human; it provides an excursion into our own descriptive and normative concepts of humanity, and provokes us to explore how we should treat *The Other*. (In philosophy the person who is different from oneself is often referred to as The Other. It signifies that one is facing something or someone that one is fundamentally unfamiliar with. It can mean a stranger, a person of the other

The Nonhuman Who Wants to Become Human

Artificial persons in fiction and films often yearn to become human. Shelley's monster suffers from this yearning, but he is not allowed to become what he wishes to be. Data, the android in *Star Trek: The Next Generation*, does not have the capability to feel human emotions, but he is intellectually curious about what causes humans to act passionately or maliciously. He longs to be human the way a child longs to grow up. The replicants in *Blade Runner* are ready to kill for a chance to become full-dimensional humans. And the artificial human in Terminator II displays definite human characteristics; he bonds with a small boy and sacrifices him-self for the sake of humankind. Just as the monster side of the artificial person is symbolized by the Golem, the wanting-to-be-human side is epitomized by Pinoc-chio, the wooden puppet who wants to become a real boy. As the story of Pinoc-chio teaches, you don't become a "real" boy by doing the bad-boy things, but by doing the good-boy things. If you do the bad-boy things (have fun and skip school), you become what bad boys become: an ass. *Pinocchio* is for all intents and purposes a very moralistic fable. In Part 4 we will take a closer look at what it means to be human, and we will again encounter Data and Pinocchio.

sex or of another race, or it can mean other people or beings as such, as opposed to oneself and one's own experiences. Sometimes it signifies someone complementary to oneself, but it may also mean that The Other is not as complete, worthy, or impor-tant as oneself and one's own kind.)

Crime and Suspense Another category of popular stories today is crime fighting. From detective novels to "cop shows," these usually involve a "who-done-it" situ-ation. The range of moral issues is usually more limited than in science fiction, but the issues are often more tuned to the current problem of crime in the cities and what to do about it. The crime-fighting story, which has its roots in the nineteenth century, for the longest time depicted law enforcement as the good guys, and criminals as the bad guys. If the law wasn't the hero, at least the detective was. As cases of corruption among law officers have been made public, and as the general trend in the late twen-tieth century to question authority has grown, it has become not unusual to see the criminal portrayed as the antihero, or given heroic treatment. This is often the case in mobster movies.

Although some crime-fighting stories have little social or moral comment, most of the popular suspense stories in this category deal with solving crimes, and thus—like the Westerns—give their readers or viewers the feeling that some problems in the outside world have symbolic solutions. Often we get a glimpse of the underbelly of

The Good Guys and the Bad Guys

Does it make a big difference in crime stories whether we are supposed to sympathize with the criminal? As is the case with Westerns, there are several types of crime stories; also, there are classical "who-done-it" stories in the Agatha Christie mode (in which we usually approve of the apprehension of the criminal). Then there is the mobster genre, in which we may sympathize with some of the bad guys, such as in *Bonnie and Clyde*, *The Godfather I* and *II*, *Dillinger*, *Goodfellas*, *Bugsy*, and *Miller's Crossing*. In the last decades of the twentieth century there has been an increasing number of films that express some ambivalence toward crime fighting. The hunter often becomes the hunted, the cop becomes a criminal, the line between good and bad is blurred. Hollywood's recent response to such films? It's back to a defense of law enforcement, with mobsters and other criminals clearly the bad guys once again, and the good guys fighting both the underworld and the corruption of the authorities. This was the focus of the 1987 movie *The Untouchables*.

society, and the author speculates as to why things are the way they are: Is it because of misadministration, not enough police in the streets, or because of *human nature* itself? Why do some people commit violent crimes? Take drugs? Sell drugs? Have gang wars? What should be done about it? In the newer crop of crime-fighting stories there is sometimes a trend towards open-endedness, something you would never see in an old-fashioned cops-and-robbers story in which solving the crime is the whole purpose of the story. Today, the open-endedness (the crime was never solved, or someone knew but wasn't telling, or it was hushed up, and so on) reflects real life and the frustration that comes from living in the modern world. The much-acclaimed television series "Hill Street Blues" experimented with just such open-endedness. It is a dangerous thing for a genre of fiction to play around with, since readers and viewers traditionally wanted to see the crime solved and the criminal punished in the story precisely because they couldn't see it often in real life. Such closure gives us a feeling that evil things can be blamed on somebody, and they can be punished for it. The open-ended stories may have another moral point, though: "So you don't like it when we have no solution? Welcome to the real world"; or perhaps, less passively: "So you don't like it when the culprit isn't apprehended? Then help solve crimes in the real world."

In this section we have looked at examples of *popular fiction* that serve as moral comments or as forums for discussions. There are, of course, other genres that can serve as useful illustrations of moral problems. *Case studies*—situations from real life,

FIGURE 2.5 *The Untouchables,* Paramount Pictures, 1987. Federal Treasury investigator Elliott Ness (Kevin Costner) and his partners (Andy Garcia, Sean Connery, and Charles Martin Smith) fight to put a stop to Al Capone's reign of terror as well as police corruption in Prohibition-era Chicago.

such as those reported by the media—are for some people much more powerful than fiction. The lessons they teach may be somewhat more complex, but they are easier to relate to, because they are real. Other people prefer fictional stories because their message is clearer; all the irrelevancies of real life have been filtered away, and the problem is presented with the logic and emotion of an artist. Mainstream literature and films have a long tradition of presenting moral issues and, sometimes, suggesting a solution. In the next section we will look at some powerful stories from the history of literature.

Stories of Influence

Stories To Live and Die By

In the eighteenth century a novel, *The Sorrows of Werther* (1774), was published in Germany. The author was Goethe, who would also pen the definitive version of

Do Slasher Movies Teach a Lesson?

Is there a moral lesson to horror films and slasher movies, and if so, what might it be? Some might say that the overriding "moral rule" is for the studio to make as much money as possible. Such people might also say that the makers of such films have no moral sense at all, that they flood the minds of young people with dangerous garbage. However, there may actually be a sinister "moral" to these stories; perhaps unintentionally, the makers of slasher films are sending out the message that (1) life is cheap, and (2) somehow sex and violent death are intimately connected. What might an impressionable viewer conclude? For one thing, that individual life doesn't count for much, and for another, that if you fool around too much you will surely die. Although the first message is decidedly antisocial, the second has been taught for many, many centuries by teachers of the Christian tradition who believe that the wages of sin are death. Is this what the film makers intended to say? Slasher movies are an example of fiction sending out mixed messages that should be discussed responsibly among members of the film industry and the viewing community.

Faust, which we will discuss later. In the novel—incidentally, one of the first modern novels as we know it, with a story line involving the emotional development of a main character during the course of a happy or unhappy encounter—young Werther suffers so dramatically from unrequited love for the girl Lotte that he, in the end, takes his own life. In the wake of the book's publication, Germany, and later all of Europe, witnessed a rash of successful and unsuccessful suicides being committed by young readers of *Werther*. Why did they do it? Goethe certainly never intended for his book to be a suicide manual. This is one of the first examples in modern times where a work of fiction has inspired its readers to take drastic action. In order for you to view this in the proper perspective, I should mention that this was the Romantic Age, when the ideal person was perceived as an *emotional* rather than a *rational* being, and men as well as women acted on their emotions, often in public. The decision of young Werther was seen as a romantic option and had a powerful emotional effect; even some famous poets of the day chose to end their lives. Unfortunately for those following the example of Werther, they could derive little enjoyment from the effects of their act. However, the rest of Europe woke up to the dangers, and the thrill, of literature.

It was not the first time in Western culture that the topic had arisen: in Ancient Greece Plato and Aristotle had debated whether art was a good or a bad psychological influence. Plato claimed that art, especially drama, was bad for people, because it fanned violent emotions; people watching a play with a violent theme would be inspired to commit violence themselves. Aristotle believed art, and especially drama, was good for people, because it allowed them to act out their emotions vicariously; a good play would thus cleanse the spectator of disturbing emotions, and he or she could return home a calmer person. The debate is still with us, although it now takes a somewhat different form. We now must consider whether violence in movies and on television inspires people (and especially children) to commit violence, or whether it allows them to act out their aggressions in a safe environment. Psychologists who believe that violent fairy tales can be good for children clearly belong to the Aristotelian tradition, although they may not support the excessive violence portrayed in movies and on TV.

Whether we agree with Plato or Aristotle, the fact remains that stories—both the readable kind and the visual kind—affect us. Some societies have reacted by banning certain works, or by conducting one of the foulest displays of cultural censorship: book burning. Other, more enlightened societies support the right of their citizens to decide for themselves what they wish to read or view.

Most influential works were never intended as a moral guidebook for the public except in the broadest sense. Goethe didn't write his *Werther* in order to convince dozens of young, lovesick Germans to kill themselves—quite possibly, he intended for young Germans to examine their lives and loves more closely. Few authors would want their readers to imitate the actions of their fictional characters, although most would like to think their story has at least been food for thought. The many readers of Dante's *Divine Comedy* probably do not expect the afterlife to be designed according to the specifications of Dante, but many a reader who has traveled through Dante's circles of Hell probably has been caused to rethink the general course of his or her life.

Some stories are moral investigations of a flawed character, such as Joseph Conrad's *Lord Jim* (outlined in Chapter 13), whose main character makes a fatal, cowardly decision in his youth and tries to live it down for the rest of his life. In Victor Hugo's *Les Misérables*, Jean Valjean morally rises above the crimes of his youth only to be haunted by them until the end of his life. Fyodor Dostoyevsky's *Crime and Punishment* (outlined in Chapter 20) examines the philosophical deliberations of Raskolnikov as he imagines the right of the extraordinary individual to do whatever he wants. Gustav Flaubert's *Madame Bovary* (outlined in Chapter 7) traces Emma's deterioration through boredom and through fantasies (brought on by reading novels!). A work by the Danish author J. P. Jacobsen, *Marie Grubbe*, in some ways parallels *Madame Bovary*. It investigates the downfall of a noble lady through three marriages: to a nobleman, a soldier, and finally to a drunk. The cause of her deterioration seems to be the same as Emma's: sensualism and boredom. The last time we encounter Marie, she is tending the ferry that runs between two small towns, in order to support her drunkard husband. The irony of the story is that in this squalor, Marie finally finds the happiness that eluded her when she was a "fine lady."

Stories such as these are not written with the intention of sending their readers out on any heroic errands. They are, primarily, explorations of fascinating human characters. They also serve as moral evaluations by asking whether the characters redeem themselves somehow, even in their degradation. At times a character's redeeming act

FIGURE 2.6 From *The Divine Comedy;* plate by Gustave Doré. Dante follows his guide, the Roman poet Virgil, on a tour of Hell. Here they have reached the place of punishment for those who have sold off sacred items belonging to the Church. Their punishment is to be stuck head down in a hole while the soles of their feet are singed with flames.

Fictional Friends

Are there fictional characters you have felt close to, in the sense that you have carried them in your mind or heart long after you finished reading the book or watching the film? Many people have identified with Mowgli in *The Jungle Book*, Robert Jordan in *From Whom the Bell Tolls*, Celie in *The Color Purple*, or Michael in *Stranger in a Strange Land*. When we were kids we may have befriended Scarlett O'Hara and Rhett Butler, or Zorro in one of his many guises, or Robin Hood. We may have come to know ancient Israel through *Ben Hur*, and Old Spain through *El Cid*, and we may have felt perfectly comfortable in the company of the defenders of *The Alamo*. Viewers who have come of age in the late eighties may have learned about heroism while watching *Glory*. Even though many of these examples are Hollywood versions of history, they still have educated young viewers about a time long past.

We may measure our romantic interludes by those portrayed in *Casablanca*, *The Way We Were*, or *When Harry Met Sally*. We may rise to the call of duty by recalling what Will Kane had to do in *High Noon* (outlined in Chapter 7). We develop the courage to question authority by watching *Rebel Without a Cause* (outlined in Chapter 7). We know that life is worth living even when it stinks not because we have read Nietzsche, but because we've watched *It's a Wonderful Life* every Christmas. We view the battle between good and evil in the grand design of *Star Wars* (outlined in Chapter 13), where "the force is with you." And if we read *The Little Mermaid* when we were children, we may have learned about the great sacrifices that love may require of us.

or quality goes against mainstream morality, as in the story of Marie Grubbe, and then the story forces us to ask which value is the ultimate moral value. Do we agree with society that Marie's life was wasted, full of missed opportunities, or do we agree with the author that life, and morality, have many faces, and that there is some intrinsic value in staying true to yourself, no matter how much this sentiment may differ from the public ethos?

Stories give us a chance to ask such questions and carry them with us, for company. Most of us have read stories that impressed us, or affected us so deeply that they have somehow become part of our identity. Occasionally we acquire a new friend while reading a book, whether it be a classic or a best seller, and we feel a little bit sad when we have finished reading, because it is like saying good-bye (which is why authors write sequels).

The same can be said for movies. We often feel we know a film character and his or her experiences as well as any member of our family, and today, through video, these characters can become a lot more accessible to us.

Stories To Change The World

Before Karl Marx, philosophers had traditionally been content with *interpreting* the world. Marx, however, wanted to *change* it. Although Marx's writings certainly had a profound effect on the world, literature had effected change in the world for quite some time before Marx with the genre of *political satire* and that special literary genre that explores the idea of a perfect society, the *Utopia*. (U-topia means "no place" in Greek.) Sir Thomas More's *Utopia* (1516) was the first of many books to explore the prospect of an ideal society in fiction. The island of Utopia had none of the ills of More's sixteenth century society, and all the good things. Since More's time political fiction has become increasingly sophisticated. *Gulliver's Travels* (1726) by Jonathan Swift often is regarded as children's literature, but, like the stories of Hans Christian Andersen, the stories of Gulliver are multilayered. There is the story line for kids, in which Gulliver travels to the land of Lilliput, where tiny men and women make war on their tiny neighbors. Then there is the satire between the lines, where adult readers realize that everything that makes the Lilliputians look silly are the things that we take seriously in our own society.

The novels of Charles Dickens certainly contain elements of comedy, but also a heavy note of tragedy. They rank high among the books of political metaphor by being exposés of the social horrors of the mid-nineteenth century. In other words, the moral lesson is found in Dickens's criticism of the conditions described in the story: the debtor's prison in *David Copperfield* and in *Little Dorrit*, the child abuse in *Oliver Twist*, and the absolute cruelty shown by an employer to his employees (even on Christmas Eve), which we know so well from *A Christmas Carol*. These social facts of Dickens's England were presented for his readers to discover and criticize and had, perhaps, a more lasting effect than the writings of Marx himself.

In French literature there is a famous book of political satire by Anatole France: *Penguin Island*. A nearsighted monk lands on an island of very small people, and extends his blessing to them. In his nearsightedness, however, he doesn't see that they are not humans but penguins, and now he has blessed them, thereby giving them immortal souls. What is done can't be undone, and the penguins proceed to form a society, becoming more and more human along the way, and exposing all of the typical human faults and shortcomings. An even more ominous story was written by the Czech author Karel Čapek. It is *War with the Newts*, one of the first true science fiction novels written after H. G. Wells's *War of the Worlds*. It does not contain Wells's happy ending; the giant newts are taught to speak by humans, exploited by humans, bred by humans, and finally the newts take over and demolish the continents of the earth for their own purposes. The story has been analyzed as presenting an image of "the enemy within," the army of unfeeling creatures with no individuality that we might become under the rule of a totalitarian regime.

Obviously, writers of science fiction did not invent the idea of fantasizing about things far away in space or time. Mainstream literature has toyed with such ideas for a long time, especially in politically critical texts. George Orwell's *1984*, written in 1948, presents a misanthropic vision of what the future might become if we aren't careful, a future where everyone's every move is watched by the electronic "Big Brother," and where any kind of human deviance—anything the State does not approve of—is eradicated. Orwell's fable *Animal Farm* paints a dark picture of the deterioration of democracy into tyranny "for the sake of the citizens." In this Orwellian society everyone is equal, but "some are more equal than others." Another dark vision of the loss of human dignity and individuality in a world of bureaucracy is Franz Kafka's *The Trial*. On one level it is a satire of the red-tape society, but it works on many more levels, even focusing on the existential fear of losing control of your life. Perhaps the most frightening story about loss of control is Kafka's "The Metamorphosis," a short story about a young man who finds himself turning into a giant bug in his own bedroom, and loses not only his humanity but also the love and understanding of everyone who used to care about him.

A work of fiction does not have to be intended as a political satire in order to be read as one; at a later time a work may be viewed as a metaphor for contemporary conditions. During the Nazi occupation of Europe in the 1930s and 40s, the Nazis exercised a great deal of censorship, so the populations of resisting countries typically would look to their own classics for literature that stimulated their spirit of resistance. In Denmark, Hans Christian Andersen's fairy tales became the spirit-raising devices, unbeknownst to the Nazis, who thought of them as just stories for children.

Repressive societies know full well the effect of politically volatile fiction and usually proceed to ban such works. Often, in the twentieth century, such works have been published elsewhere rather than in the society described by the author, such as Alexander Solzhenitsyn's *The Gulag Archipelago*, which exposes labor camps for political dissidents in the Soviet Union but was published in Spain, and Salman Rushdie's *The Satanic Verses*, which takes place partly in the Middle East but was published in England and in the United States. The latter is an example of religious satire, directed against certain aspects of Islam. The religious satire is closely related to the political satire, especially because the religious satire most often does not attack a religion as such, but rather the policies and laws established by the religious powers.

Political satire may have an eye-opening effect, breaking up boundaries and causing changes for the better; however, we must not forget that satire can be used both ways: to open minds, and to close them. The Nazis spent a considerable amount of energy, especially in the thirties, prior to World War II, satirizing the ill-fated Weimar Republic (the elected government that preceded the Nazis) and ridiculing those population groups that the Nazis deemed inferior, such as the Jews. Before we let ourselves be carried away by a skillful satire, we should be careful to identify its ultimate political goal.

Some Fantastic Tales for Grown-ups

The stories that have affected Western culture are too numerous to count, but a few stand out as *archetypes*, models that we seem to return to over and over again. In this section we will look at three themes that keep showing up in the world of fiction: *the bargain, the good twin and the bad twin*, and *the quest*.

The Bargain There is a certain genre of stories that continually fascinates the adult imagination: the story in which someone bargains with fate (or with gods or devils) to gain some advantage—or doesn't literally bargain, but simply puts his life and happiness on the line to obtain what he wants most. Why do such stories continue to intrigue us? Perhaps it is because we recognize the single-mindedness of some individuals, and their success, and wonder what price they may have to pay (perhaps even hoping that they have to pay a price). Or perhaps it is because we, in desperate situations, also try to bargain with fate: If you let me live, I'll give up smoking/be kinder to my spouse/stop gambling/stop eating junk food, and so on. If you let me pass the test I promise I'll be a good student from now on. If you let me win the battle I promise you I will sacrifice the first living thing that approaches me when I come home. This is the bargain in the biblical horror story of Jephtha's Daughter. Jephtha thinks he will be met by his dog, but it is his virgin daughter who comes to greet him. What does he do? Does he resolve to cheat God and save his daughter? No, he gives her a month to grieve for her virginity, and then he sacrifices her. (In this case, God does not step in to prevent it as he did for Abraham.) Sometimes, like Jephtha, we keep our bargains with fate, but most often we don't. Stories in which a bargain has been made with the Devil, however, usually cast him as a reliable businessman: He keeps his end of the deal, and he expects you to keep yours.

The grandmother of all devil bargains is the story of Dr. Faust, the main character in Johann Wolfgang von Goethe's masterpiece, *Faust*. There was, in Württemberg, Germany, in the sixteenth century, an actual man named Johann Faust; he was an astrologer and magician at a time when science, astrology, and magic were only just beginning to be separated, conceptually and practically. "Alchemists" were undertaking experiments based in part on scientific evidence and in part on magical formulae; such practices usually were outlawed as heresy by the Catholic church. The Spanish Inquisition disposed of many an early scientist for being a heretic well into the seventeenth century. Even before *Faust*, though, stories appeared with the same motif: the necromancer (sorcerer) who sells his soul. These stories have been fused with the legend of Faust because of his frequent representation in literature. Around 1589 (some fifty years after the death of the actual Dr. Faust) Marlowe wrote the *Tragical History of Dr. Faustus*, but it was Goethe's version (1780–1833) that became the ultimate metaphor for the scientist who will do anything, including sell his soul, for pure knowledge (in Faust's case, to secure the formula for turning base metals into gold). (Goethe actually wrote two versions of *Faust*: the first one, *Urfaust*, was a draft but is considered the better work by some. The official, later version was written in two parts.) Goethe's story was made into an American tale by Stephen Vincent Benét, "The Devil and Daniel Webster," but with a twist: Webster outwits the Devil. (This is actually a whole subgenre by itself—the outwitting of the devil). In the 1940s, Nobel Prize winner Thomas Mann modernized the original story in his novel *Dr. Faustus*, which explores the mind-set of a man of the times; in Mann's book the obsession is not science, but art.

Through the Faust story runs a moralizing thread: *Faust does wrong in selling his soul.* There are folklore and fairy tale stories that are in complete accordance with this view.

One traveling story, a story that has traveled from country to country in different versions, is the tale of the boy who wanted to play the fiddle like no one else, and the Devil taught him to play so sweetly that the fish would jump out of the river to listen, the birds would stop singing, and all the girls the boy ever wanted would flock to him. The trouble was that every time he wanted to put the fiddle down, he couldn't. In other words, The devil made him do it, and he played himself to death. Some musicians might say it was worth it.

The Faustian theme also has been explored in films from time to time, as in *Angel Heart*, in which a character realizes something he had forgotten—that he sold his soul—and there is no help or redemption for him in the end. As we saw in Chapter 1, *Altered States* is another example of the Faustian myth. It is set in the drug culture of the early seventies, and again, the quest for ultimate knowledge is seen as a dead end, or at any rate a goal with too high a price tag.

There is another story that has the same bargaining theme, but with a completely different moral: the Nordic tale of Odin and Mimir. Odin, the Asa-god, wishes to be wise, and strikes a bargain with the giant Mimir, who owns the well of knowledge under the World Tree, Yggdrasil. One drink from Mimir's well in exchange for one of Odin's eyes, and Odin can gain wisdom. So Odin leaves his eye in Mimir's well. Both parties keep their bargain, and both are content—until, that is, Mimir becomes involved in a negotiation between warring gods, who subsequently chop his head off. They send the head to Odin as a sign that the negotiations fell through. But Odin reads magic words over the severed head, and it comes alive. After that Odin always keeps Mimir's head with him and consults with it before he makes any decision. Odin got the best part of Mimir, even if he had to leave his eye in the well. The moral of this story: Some things are worth a high price!

The Good Twin and the Bad Twin A story that is closely related to that of Dr. Faustus, but with an added element, is Robert Louis Stevenson's 1886 story of *Dr. Jekyll and Mr. Hyde* (outlined in Chapter 20). As with Goethe's story, Stevenson's is loosely based on a real person—in this case a nineteenth-century British scientist. The kindly Dr. Jekyll becomes the evil Mr. Hyde by drinking his own invention, a personality-changing drug intended, the story goes, to distill goodness from evil in the human character. Jekyll, who is not so kindly after all given that he throws away his life and *respectability* (a notion nineteenth-century readers found particularly problematic) for the sake of finding knowledge, parallels Dr. Faustus in this obsession—but here the story departs from the Faustian pattern. Not only is the Devil absent (he is manifested only in the "well-deserved" death of Jekyll/Hyde), but also another theme is introduced: the *double character*. After all, Jekyll and Hyde are the same man, and the symbolism is easy to read: We all have a beast "hyding" in us, an alter ego, and we must not let it loose no matter how much we would like to. The reason Jekyll keeps returning to his Hyde persona is because it feels good, it amuses him; he gets to do things that Victorian England frowned upon, like going out on the town. Of course, he exceeds even the tolerance of any time period when he tortures and kills. The moral lesson is broad and completely in tune with nineteenth-century Victorian

Twin Souls in Books and Films

The dual-character theme is used continually in books and films. The good/bad pair may be sisters, as in Bette Davis's debut film, *Bad Sister*, brothers (*Dead Ringers*, *Twins*), or androids ("Star Trek: The Next Generation"), but the theme is usually the same: Symbolically and psychologically the dual characters represent one person with two conflicting personalities. Usually, the bad tempered character is the more interesting one, and the one we are warned against. On the whole, traditional good twin/bad twin stories tend toward the conservative, with the bad twin as titillation which carries its own punishment in the end. The twin motif is one of the oldest and most-used themes in myths, legends, and fairy tales; the Romans believed that Rome was founded by the twins Romulus and Remus, who were raised by a she-wolf. Native American tradition tells of the Sacred Twins, one good and one evil, who nevertheless together rule the world as gods; their different personalities complement each other and keep the world in balance. Mayan religion teaches of the heavenly warrior twins. The African tradition has stories about holy twins, and twin sculptures are a favorite African folklore arti-

fact. Grimm's fairy tales tell of twins who part and meet again, experiencing parallel adventures in the meantime. A classic American tale of twins is John Steinbeck's *East of Eden*, in which Cal (the bad but misunderstood twin) and Aron (the good and innocent twin) take on the roles in the ancient Biblical drama of Cain and Abel. And the film *Dead Ringers* stars Jeremy Irons as twin gynecologists who gradually switch roles, socially and psychologically, with eventual tragic results: professional ruin and death.

Mark Twain, who always did things a little differently, presents another version of the dual-character theme in *The Prince and the Pauper*. The main characters are not twins, but rather identically featured boys, one the Prince of Wales and the other a poor boy from the lower end of society. The boys switch places, and each learns about the goodness and evil outside of them, in the inegalitarian society of Old England. This story exists in a multitude of versions, from Alexandre Dumas's *The Man in the Iron Mask* to Anthony Hope's *Prisoner of Zenda* to Disney's *The Parent Trap* (originally a very good German children's book).

mores, as well as with most of the Christian tradition: Keep your inner beast in check, and don't give in to your physical desires. Nietzsche, who saw this attitude as sheer repression of our life force (as we shall see in Part 4), might have rooted for Mr. Hyde and rewritten the ending of the story.

The Quest The first quest story that we know of is that of Gilgamesh, the king of Uruk. Gilgamesh loses his only friend, Enkidu, to a withering disease. This brings home to Gilgamesh the fact that all humans are mortal, and he is seized by a terrible fear of death. So he sets out to find the secret of immortality. This story has been told by Sumerians since at least approximately 1500 B.C.E. Gilgamesh goes to the ends of the earth and finds the oldest living humans, Utnapishtim and his wife, who survived the big flood by the grace of the gods (they were safe in a wooden box that floated upon the waters—an *ark*). Utnapishtim's rescue, however, was a one-time deal, and Gilgamesh must look elsewhere for his own rescue from death. In the end he finds the plant that gives immortality, picks it, and drops it in the water. Gilgamesh must go under the sea where the monster snake lives; into its gaping maw he must crawl to get the weed—but he can't retrieve it. Gilgamesh had immortality for a while, but then he lost it, for it is the fate of humans to be mortal.

Gilgamesh's quest was a failure, but it was heroic nevertheless, because it embodied a human longing to live forever, as well as the acknowledgment that we can't, even if we are the king of Uruk. The quest motif is one of the most moving in the history of literature and film, precisely because even if the hero doesn't find what he or she sets out to find, the search itself remains the most important part of the story. The quest forces the hero to mature and makes him or her realize the true importance, or lack of importance, of what he is looking for.

Myths and legends abound with quest stories. The Navajo goddess Grandmother Spider searches for the sun in the early days when the land is in darkness. She finds it and steals a piece, and puts it into her clay pot to bring home. In the Greek legend of Jason and the Golden Fleece, Jason and his argonauts go on a quest for a sheepskin made of gold. Egyptian legend tells of the goddess Isis, who searches for the remains of her husband, Osiris, who was murdered. Some searchers even go to the underworld to find what they are looking for: Ulysses goes to the realm of the dead to speak with the wise Teresias. Orpheus goes to the underworld to try to retrieve his beloved wife, Eurydice, from the dead. The Native American Modoc culture hero Kumokum goes to the land of the dead in search of his daughter. Ishtar, the all-powerful goddess of the Middle East, finds that her powers are limited when her young lover, Tammuz, dies, and she goes to the underworld to buy him back. The earth goddess Demeter goes to the kingdom of the dead to get back her daughter, Persephone, who has been abducted by the king of the dead.

These stories confirm what we know: that we would go to the ends of the earth and the land of the dead if it could bring back those we love. We also know that it would be to no avail; Gilgamesh's lesson is one that every human learns.

Some quests are of a happier nature. In the African folktale about the girl Wanjiru, Wanjiru's family sacrifice her so that the rains will come, but a young warrior goes to the underworld to fetch her back. He carries her on his back to the world of the living and hides her until she is strong again; then he displays her at the great dance. Her family is now ashamed of the way they treated her, and the warrior and Wanjiru are married.

One of Grimm's fairy tales has an unusual quest story: the quest for the feeling of fear and trembling. In The Youth Who Could Not Shiver and Shake, the protagonist goes through the most frightful horrors but still can't seem to shiver and shake properly, until his young bride throws a bucket of minnows at him: Now he knows what

Looking for Love

Stories of quests for love are innumerable. Characters may stay in one place and hope for love to come to them, as did Snow White and the Beast in Beauty and the Beast, or they may go out and search for love, like Cinderella. The Little Mermaid searches for human love, both in the tragic Hans Christian Anderson original version and in the upbeat Disney version. Madame Bovary searches for romantic love as a result of reading so many romantic novels, but because her life is romantically unfulfilled, she compensates by shopping for clothes and furniture, and ends up exceeding her credit line. In the film *Looking for Mr. Goodbar*, Diane Keaton looks for love in all the wrong places and ends up paying the ultimate price. Do such stories truly influence us in our own search for love?

it feels like to shiver and shake! There is more to this story than just a joke, for without the feeling of fear we are not complete humans. This quest, like the quest for love, is a search for something that will make the character a whole person. Indeed, most modern literature and films somehow involve a quest for oneself, a search for self-identity through encounters with The Other.

Two quest motifs have, each in its own right, come to epitomize the *search*. One is *Moby Dick*, and the other is the legend of the Holy Grail.

Herman Melville's *Moby Dick* (1851) (outlined in Chapter 13) has become the American model for the quest, but with a special angle: The searcher is mad, and the quest is meaningless, except to Captain Ahab himself. In many stories, although the object of the quest may be out of reach, it usually is something to which the reader can relate. In the case of *Moby Dick*, though, the reader identifies not with the searcher, but with an observer, Ishmael. The quest itself is seen as pointless, and quite mad. Eventually, Captain Ahab finds his white whale but he and the rest of the crew die, except for Ishmael, who alone "survived to tell thee."

Hollywood came up with a modern version of the whale search for a society that reveres whales but dislikes sharks. In *Jaws*, the symbolism is stronger than in the Melville story; the gigantic shark is a more obvious representation of inhuman evil. However, the sense of ambiguity present in *Moby Dick* is missing in *Jaws*. The Melville story makes us wonder if Ahab's quest was worth the passion and trouble; in *Jaws* we know the quest was ill-advised.

In a sense, there is one Hollywood story that is much more closely related to *Moby Dick* than *Jaws*. In one of its most superb productions, John Ford's film *The Searchers* (outlined in Chapter 13), Hollywood created a folklore version of the mad quest. As the title indicates, in the movie it is the search, more than the object of the search, which matters. For eight years Ethan and Marty look all over the western United

FIGURE 2.7 *Moby Dick,* 1956. Captain Ahab (Gregory Peck) in his quest for the white whale. He seeks to slay the giant whale, Moby Dick, who has already cost him a leg. For Ahab it is not a matter of a mere whale-hunt, but of supreme vengeance, and in his fanaticism he dooms his crew as well as himself. The story of Moby Dick is outlined in Chapter 13 as an illustration of the thirst for vengeance.

States for Ethan's niece Debbie, who was captured by the Comanche Indians. Marty is the observer we identify with, the "Ishmael" of the story. Marty tries to reason with Ethan, who is obsessed with revenge rather than rescue. Ethan finds his "white whale," the Comanche chief responsible for murdering Ethan's family and kidnapping Debbie, but he realizes, in the nick of time, that his motives were misguided. Ethan is redeemed and returned to sanity through human love. However, he has traveled too far on the road to obsession and human loneliness and is doomed to wander alone.

The search for the *Holy Grail*, part of the Arthurian Legend, is a quest that succeeds only symbolically, if at all. Several years after the glorious time of the Round Table, Arthur's knights become obsessed with finding the cup from the Last Supper of Christ, the Grail. They each go through trials to find the cup, but only Percival succeeds in seeing the Grail, and even he is denied any further access. Since the time that the tale was first told, the quest for the Grail has become a symbol of the search for a profound truth, a holy revelation, for the meaning of life, if you will. Even when the search is unsuccessful and even futile, as it is for Cervantes' Don Quixote, who searches far and wide for the "impossible dream," the search itself nevertheless lends

The Holy Grail in the Movies

The grail theme has been explored in films such as *Quest for Fire*, the hominid adventure story with gibberish dialogue by Anthony Burgess, and in out-and-out adventure stories such as *Raiders of the Lost Ark*. *Indiana Jones and the Last Crusade* is about the hunt for the Grail itself. The science fiction classic *2001, A Space Odyssey* is a grail quest for the ultimate mystery, the black, ancient monolith. *The Fisher King* is another film that uses the grail motif. It presents a realistic portrayal of homelessness and teaches the lesson that anything is worthy of being the object of a quest if that quest is undertaken in the spirit of love. In other films, from *Stanley and Livingstone* to *The Mountains of the Moon*, people traverse the jungles of Africa seeking out other people, the source of the Nile, or a better understanding of themselves and their role in the scheme of things.

Stories that involve a search for an antidote may incorporate both the grail element and an element of catharsis (a spiritual cleansing). Finding the Grail is the cure for the ailment, but it also may serve as a liberating, spiritual healing process. In *The Andromeda Strain*, scientists find out how to neutralize a killer plague from outer space, and they learn a lesson about human frailty. In *D.O.A.* (Dead On Arrival) a poisoned man tries to find his killer before the poison kills him, so that he can die knowing who killed him and why. In *Silence of the Lambs*, a young FBI agent seeks to apprehend a serial killer before he can strike again; however, she also is looking to plumb the depths of the human psyche in order to put an end to her own nightmare, in which she recalls childhood images of innocent lambs crying as they are led to the slaughter. She longs finally to hear "the silence of the lambs."

the searcher a cloak of heroism, no less than it did for Gilgamesh. The grail theme can encompass any kind of quest, not just a search for a cup or an item. Indeed, some scholars believe that the Grail itself was not a cup but a royal bloodline, the Sang Real, presumably the lost line of the medieval French Merovingian kings. In a controversial book, *Holy Blood, Holy Grail*, the authors speculate that the reason this bloodline seemed so important to some people in the Middle Ages is because they believed the bloodline could be traced back to a child born to Mary Magdalene and fathered by the man legend claims was her husband, Jesus of Nazareth!

If the Holy Grail is a symbol of the search for ideal truth, the Philosopher's Stone has become a symbol of the search for material riches. Some scholars believe that the Holy Grail and the Philosopher's Stone are one and the same thing. Originally, the Philosopher's Stone was a fantasy of the alchemists, the pseudoscientists of medieval Europe (attaining it also was the dream of Dr. Faust). These people had one specific

FIGURE 2.8 *Indiana Jones and the Last Crusade,* Paramount Pictures, 1989. The archaeologist Indiana Jones (Harrison Ford) and his father (Sean Connery) search for the ultimate treasure in Christian tradition: the Holy Grail, the cup used by Jesus Christ at the Last Supper. Here Jones and Jones are barely escaping with their lives from a fire in a Nazi stronghold.

goal: to find the chemical substance that would turn base metals into gold; this elusive substance became known as the Philosopher's Stone. It achieved a symbolic meaning as the agent that could transform life into a higher, spiritual existence, but on the whole the tie-in to gold proved to be the more vigorous one. Although there are few stories directly related to the Philosopher's Stone, there are plenty of stories about *treasure hunting.* The ultimate model for such stories is *Treasure Island* by Robert Louis Stevenson, but any story involving the search for hidden wealth can be viewed as a version of the legend of the Philosopher's Stone—the search for the item that will change your life and make you rich. From the epic film of the conquest of Mexico, *Captain from Castile,* to the Mel Brooks movie *The Twelve Chairs* (his version of a Russian comedy), to the marathon comedy *It's a Mad, Mad, Mad, Mad World,* the hunt is on for the treasures of the world.

The quest can thus be for something sublime, something ideal, or not of this world, or it can be for something as down-to-earth as money. Regardless of whether the story takes the high path or the low path, the quest as a story type seems to be very enduring.

This part of the book has examined some of the story types that seem to illustrate and affect our moral thinking most frequently. In the following chapters we will look at how thinkers of many eras, including our own, have approached these moral problems, and what solutions they have offered. Although these problems are often presented in abstract, general terms, and the solutions are presented as general principles, we will use stories (they come at the end of each major part of the book) to see how these principles can be applied and whether they provide us with acceptable solutions.

Part 2

WHAT SHOULD I DO?
Theories of Conduct

CHAPTER 3

Ethical Relativism

How To Deal With Moral Differences

On occasion we are forced to face this fact: Not everybody shares our idea of what constitutes decent behavior. You may wait at the movie theater for a friend who never shows up because she is on the phone with another friend, and it doesn't occur to her that it is important to keep her date with you. Such actions usually can be dismissed as merely bad manners or callousness; still, you probably will not want to make plans with that person again. *Moral differences* can run deeper than that, however. Suppose you are dating someone to whom you feel very attracted. During dinner in a nice restaurant, your friend casually mentions that he is supporting a white supremacist political candidate. The fact that your friend has a different idea about what constitutes moral behavior will probably affect the way you feel about him. Here we are assuming that you are against racism. If this example doesn't work for you, try imagining going out with someone who holds the opposite view on abortion, gun control, or some other issue important to you.

We constantly read and hear about actions that are to us morally unacceptable. A young, foreign girl is killed by her brother because she is pregnant and unmarried or perhaps merely going out with an American boy. To the Western mind the brother's act is an unfathomable crime. But the brother believes he is only doing his duty, as unpleasant as it may be; he is upholding the family honor, which the sister has squandered by her act of unspeakable immorality (according to the traditional moral code of his culture). The world is full of stories about people who feel duty-bound to do things you and I find repugnant. People in some cultures feel it is their moral duty, or moral right, to dispose of their elderly citizens when they become unproductive. Native cultures, in particular (where food is scarce) have a tradition for exposing their grandparents to the elements and leaving them to die when they believe it is time. Some cultures feel a moral right or duty to dispose of infants in the same way—usually cultures with no safe, medical access to contraception. Other cultures believe it is a sin to seek medical assistance—they believe life should be left in the hands of God. Some people believe it is a sin to destroy any life, even by inadvertently stepping on an insect. Some people think they have a moral duty to defend themselves, their loved ones, and their country from any threat; others think it is their moral duty to refrain from resorting to violence under any circumstances.

If we have led a sheltered life, we may have the impression that the only people whose morals are different from ours are those who live far away, in another culture, and we may grow up believing that people with morals different from ours are wrong, or wrongheaded. Then we wake up one day and discover that not only do our friends and neighbors have viewpoints on sex, politics, and justice that differ vastly from our own, but they look upon us as the wrongheaded ones and believe themselves to be in the right.

How do we approach this phenomenon of moral differences? There are at least four major paths to choose.

(1) We may choose to believe that *there are no morally right or wrong viewpoints*—that the whole moral issue is a cultural game, and neither your opinion nor mine matters in the end, for there is no ultimate right or wrong. This view is called *moral nihilism*, and at various times in our lives, especially if we are facing personal disappointment, we may be inclined to take this approach. This is a hard position to uphold, however, because it is so extreme. It is hard to remember, every minute of the day, that we don't believe there is any difference between right and wrong. If we see somebody steal our car, we are inclined to want the thief stopped, even if we don't feel like stopping him ourselves, regardless of how much our jaded intellect tells us that no one is more right or wrong than anyone else. If we watch a child or an animal being abused, we feel like stepping in, even if we tell ourselves that there is no such a thing as right or wrong. In other words, there seems to be something in most of us—instinct, or socialization, or reason, or compassion, or maybe something else altogether—that surfaces even when we try to persuade ourselves that moral values are but an illusion.

Related to the attitude of moral nihilism is *moral skepticism*, which holds that we can't know if there are any moral truths, and *moral subjectivism*, which holds that moral views are merely inner states in a person, and they can't be compared to the inner states of another person, so a moral viewpoint is valid only for the person who holds it. Both skepticism and subjectivism are more common than nihilism, but they seem to be equally difficult to adhere to in the long run, because at crucial times we all act *as if* there are valid moral truths that we share with others—we criticize a friend for being late, a politician for being a racist or sexist, a police officer for using unnecessary force. We praise a stranger for coming to our aid when we are stuck on the freeway, we praise our kids when they come home on time—so it seems that even if we believe ourselves to be nihilists, skeptics, or subjectivists, we still expect to share some values with others of our own culture.

(2) We may choose to believe that *there is no universal moral truth*, that each culture has its own set of rules that are valid for that culture, and we have no right to interfere, just as they have no right to interfere with our rules. This attitude, known as *ethical relativism*, is not as radical as skepticism, because it allows that moral truths exist but holds that they are relative to their time and place. Ethical relativism is viewed as an attitude of tolerance, and as an antidote to the efforts of cultures who try their best to impose their set of moral rules on other cultures. This theory will be discussed in detail later in this section.

(3) We may take yet another viewpoint. We may believe that deep down, in spite of all their differences, people of different cultures can still agree on certain moral basics. We may think it is a matter of biology—that people everywhere have basically the same human nature. Or, we may view it as a process of acculturation, whereby people adjust to the normal way of doing things in their culture. If the native peoples of harsh climates put their unwanted babies out in the wild to perish, it need not mean that they hate babies, but rather that they want to give the babies they already have a chance to survive, and they know that having another mouth to feed would kill them all. In this way we find a common ground in the fact that we, and they, do care for the children we are able to raise. If we believe that somehow, under the surface of antagonism and contradiction, we can still find a few things that we can agree on, even if we choose to act on them in different ways, we believe in the existence of a few universal moral truths. I will call this attitude *soft universalism*—universalism, because it perceives that there are some universal moral rules; *soft*, because it is not as radical as hard universalism, or absolutism.

(4) *Hard universalism* (sometimes called *moral absolutism*) is the attitude that most often is supported in ethical theories. It is an attitude toward morals in everyday life to which many people relate very well. Hard universalism holds that there is one universal moral code. It is the viewpoint expressed by those who are on a quest for the code ("I know there must be one set of true moral rules, but I would not presume to have found it myself"); by those who make judgments based on its analysis ("After much deliberation I have come to the conclusion that this moral code represents the ultimate values"); and by those who put forth the simple sentiment that moral truth is not open for discussion ("I'm right and you're wrong, and you'd better shape up!").

The first set of viewpoints will not be discussed much in this book. The second one, *ethical relativism*, has greatly influenced moral attitudes in the West in the twentieth century and is the main topic of this chapter. The third, *soft universalism*, and fourth, *hard universalism*, will be discussed in the remaining chapters of Part 2.

The Lessons of Anthropology

In the nineteenth century, cultural anthropology came into its own as a scientific discipline and reminded the West that "out there" were other cultures that were vastly different from Victorian Europe. Anthropological scholars set out to examine other cultures, and the facts they brought back were astounding to the nineteenth-century Western mind-set: There were cultures that didn't understand the male's role in procreation but thought that babies somehow ripened in the woman with the help of spirits. There were people who would devour the bodies of their enemies killed in war in order to share their fighting spirit. There were cultures that believed in animal gods, cultures that felt it appropriate for women to bare their breasts, cultures that felt it utterly inappropriate to let your in-laws watch you eat, and so on. It was easy to draw the conclusion that there were cultures out there whose moral codes differed substantially from that of the West.

This conclusion, the first step in what has become known as ethical relativism, was not new to the Western mind-set. Because people had always traveled and brought home tales of faraway lands, it was common knowledge that other cultures did things differently than we did. Explorers in earlier centuries brought home tales of mermaids, giants, and other fantasies. Some stories were truer than others. There really were, for instance, peoples out there who had a different dress ethic and work ethic. The lifestyle of the South Sea islanders became a collective fantasy for Europeans of the eighteenth and nineteenth centuries; imagine not wearing any clothes, not having to work all the time, living in perpetual summertime, and not having any sexual restrictions! Depending on their ethical predisposition, Europeans considered such peoples to be either the luckiest ones on this earth, or the most sinful, subhuman, and depraved. Reports of cultural diversity also were supplied by Christian missionaries over the centuries; they confronted more or less reluctant cultures with their message of conversion.

The idea of cultural diversity even in early historic times is well documented. The Greek historian Herodotus (485–430 B.C.E.) tells in his *Histories* of the great Persian king Darius, who from the borders of his vast empire—which at the time stretched from the Greek holdings in the West to India in the East—had heard tales of funerary practices that intrigued him. The Greeks were at that time in the habit of cremating their dead; Darius learned that a tribe in India, the Callatians, disposed of their dead by eating them. Darius sent for a delegation of Greeks and Callatians and asked them how much it would take to get them to switch practices—for the Greeks to eat their dead, and for the Callatians to burn theirs. Both groups declined with much vehemence, and Herodotus concludes that "custom is king"—we all prefer what we are used to.

When anthropologists point out that there is an immense variety of cultural differences in terms of moral codes, they are describing the situation as they see it. As long as those anthropologists make no judgments about whether it is *good* for humanity to have different moral codes, or whether those codes represent the moral truths of each

Descriptive and Normative Ethics

The terms *descriptive* and *normative* are important terms for any ethical theory, not just relativism. When we talk about a theory being *descriptive*, we mean that that theory merely describes what it sees as fact, such as: In the United States it is in general not considered immoral to eat meat. In other words, a descriptive theory describes what people actually do or think. A *normative* theory adds a *moral judgment*, evaluation, or justification, such as, It is okay to eat meat, because it is nourishing, or a criticism such as, Eating meat *should be* considered immoral. In addition

to descriptive ethics and normative ethics, there is a third ethical approach, that of *metaethics*. Metaethics is an approach that does not describe or evaluate, but analyzes the *meaning* of the moral terms we use. Some typical questions would be, But what do you mean by immoral? What do you mean by meat eating should be banned? Most ethical systems involve judgments, criticisms, evaluations, and justifications, and are thus normative, but many systems also require an awareness of the terms used to justify the theory. Such systems involve metaethics.

culture, they are espousing a descriptive theory usually referred to as *cultural relativism*. Let us look at an example. An anthropologist who was an acquaintance of mine came back from a field trip to Tibet and told me the following story: In the little Tibetan village where he had been "adopted" by a local family and was doing his fieldwork, the children worked hard and had very little leisure time. The concept of competition was totally alien to them. One day my friend thought he would give them a treat, and he arranged for a race. All the kids lined up, puzzled and excited, to listen to his directions: Run from one end of the compound to the other and back again, and whoever comes in first wins. The race was on, and the children ran like mad to beat each other and "win." As one beaming kid came in first, the anthropologist handed over a prize—some little trinket or piece of candy. There was dead silence among the kids, who just looked at each other. Finally one of the children asked, "Why are you giving a gift to our friend who won?" The anthropologist realized that because the children had no idea of competition, they had no knowledge that winning often is connected with a prize. To them, this new idea of "winning" was great all by itself, and there was no need to add anything else; indeed, the prize made them feel very uncomfortable. (My friend said it also made him feel very stupid.)

What the anthropologist was doing by telling this story was relating an example of cultural relativism—describing how customs differ from culture to culture. Suppose, though, he had added, "and I realized that they were right in their own way." (In other words, suppose he had made a *judgment* about the validity of the tribal way of

FIGURE 3.1 Ruth Benedict (1857–1948), American anthropologist and defender of ethical relativism. Her best-known work is *Patterns of Culture* (1935).

life.) In that case, he would have moved into the area of *ethical relativism*. Cultural relativism is a *descriptive* theory that states that different cultures have different moral codes. Ethical relativism is a *normative* theory that states that there is no universal moral code, and each culture's codes are right and valid for that culture. It is a subtle difference, but philosophically it is an important one. The cultural relativist sees the cultural differences and describes them: There are many moral codes in the world. The ethical relativist sees the cultural differences, and makes a judgment: We can never find a common code, and what seems right for one culture is right *for that culture.*

The anthropologist Ruth Benedict (1887–1948) did most of her writing toward the end of the era in which one could still speak of "uncontaminated" societies— cultures that hadn't yet been massively exposed to Western civilization. In general, cultural isolation was at that time coming to an end. The term *primitive* still was used for some cultures, and Benedict used it, too, but she was quick to point out that the attitude that Western civilization was at the top of the ladder of cultural evolution was—or should be—an attitude of the past. In a famous article, "Anthropology and the Abnormal," from 1934, she says that "modern civilization becomes not a necessary pinnacle of human achievement but one entry in a long series of possible adjustments." With this emphasis she establishes herself as an advocate of cultural and moral *tolerance*, implying that Western civilization has no right to impose its codes of conduct on other cultures. Ethical relativism has remained popular ever since, as a tool of cultural tolerance.

In the article mentioned above Benedict tells of a number of cultural phenomena that may seem morally odd, to say the least, to you. One example will have to suffice: Among the Northwest Coast Native American Indians of previous centuries, it was customary to view death, even natural death, as an affront that should be retaliated against in one way or another. In one tribe, a chief's sister and her daughter had drowned on a trip to Victoria. The chief gathered a war party. They set out, found seven men and two children asleep, and killed them. This made them all feel much better.

What intrigued Benedict about this story was not so much that the chief and the members of the war party viewed their actions as morally good, but that most of the tribespeople felt the same way. In other words, it was *normal* in the tribe to feel this way. Benedict concludes, "The concept of the normal is properly a variant of the concept of the good. It is that which society has approved."

Two things are worth mentioning here. First, Benedict is taking a giant leap from expressing *cultural* relativism to expressing *ethical* relativism. She moves from a description of what the people do, to the statement that it is normal *and thus good* for them to do it, in their own cultural context. Second, Benedict is saying that normality is culturally defined; in other words, cultures, especially isolated cultures, often seem to develop some potential human behaviors to an extreme. (For Benedict the range of possible human behavior is enormous, ranging from paranoia to helpfulness and generosity.) Those individuals who somehow can't conform (and they will always be the minority, because most people are very pliable) become the abnormals in that culture.

Is the behavior of the Northwest Coast people totally alien to us? Benedict thinks not, because it constitutes abnormal behavior in our own society, not unthinkable behavior. We might illustrate her idea with some examples. The postal worker who has been fired and who shows up the next day with a shotgun and kills a number of his coworkers is "crazy" to us, but he actually is following the same logic as the chief: His world has been torn apart by powers over which he has no control, and he is retaliating against the affront. The driver who cuts you off on the freeway because she had a fight with her husband is doing the same thing; so was the little girl who ripped a button off your coat in grade school because someone else ripped a button off of her coat. There is no question of vengeance, because neither the driver nor the little girl was looking to punish a guilty party. The seven men and two children had nothing to do with the deaths of the chief's relatives, and the chief never said they did. It is not a matter of seeking out the cause of the problem, of gaining *retribution*; it is rather an experience of healing a wound, so to speak, by making someone else miserable. (Suppose the strangers who were killed had been American or Canadian loggers who grew up in a culture that believes it is proper to find and punish whoever is guilty? Then we'd see retribution.) Perhaps we all "take it out" on someone innocent from time to time; some of us probably do it more often than others. The difference is that we've chosen to call what the Northwest Coast people did *abnormal*, whereas they, in the dawn of their tribal civilization, considered their actions to be normal. How do such choices evolve? Usually it is a matter of habits developing over time. If there is such a thing as a "normal" way for humans to behave, it is to adjust to the pattern of normalcy that prevails in their particular culture. Today, sociologists would call this process *acculturation*.

For Benedict there is no sense in imposing Western morals on another culture, because Western morals are just another aspect of the range of possible human behavior that we have chosen to elaborate; they are no better or no worse than anyone else's morals. Whatever is normal for us means that we think of it as good, and that is all there is to it. We have no right to claim that our choice is better than any other culture's.

The Psychology of Becoming a Moral and Social Being

How does a person develop and become like most of the others in his or her own culture in terms of moral values? Sigmund Freud would say that each individual internalizes society's rules and its morality; this process is the development of the *superego*—that part of our psyche that serves to reward and punish through a system of moral attitudes, conscience, and a sense of guilt. Freud, the founder of psychoanalysis, believed that we transform the moral voices of those in authority to that little inner voice called our conscience. Whatever the authority voices tell us, that is what our morality consists of.

(We will return to Freud in Chapter 19.) Ruth Benedict assumes that humans are extraordinarily flexible: Whatever is normal and accepted in a culture is the mold that most people will follow. However, in every group there usually will be some individuals who just don't fit the mold, either because they are not capable of adjusting, or because they don't want to, and those are the ones that the culture will label as the "abnormal." Of course, what is abnormal in one culture may well be normal and commendable behavior in another.

Is Tolerance All We Need?

Given the overwhelming intolerance for other cultures and customs that is displayed from time to time by Western civilization (a stance some refer to as "cultural imperialism"), for many people there is something very appealing and refreshing about ethical relativism. This is as true in today's United States, with its plurality of cultural and ethnic heritages, as it was in the early twentieth century when anthropology was only beginning to promote an attitude of open-mindedness. Certainly it is of doubtful virtue today to impose a particular brand of acculturation on another group who believes it is doing just fine with its own set of moral rules; indeed, having someone else's morality presented as one we have to conform to, even if it goes against our upbringing, usually feels demeaning and unpleasant. Cultural relativism teaches a useful lesson—that cultures are different, and "our way" is just one among many. Just because "our way" may prohibit eating certain foods, allows divorce, and condemns infanticide doesn't mean that we have a right to criticize cultures who look at such things differently.

Does this mean that it is always wrong to criticize another culture or group for what it does? If we are to follow the idea of ethical relativism to its logical conclusion, yes. We have no right to criticize other cultures, period. But on occasion things hap-

How to Test a Theory

What we are doing in this text is following standard philosophical procedure. We test a theory by pounding at it with hypothetical and actual situations until we see if it holds up logically. It is not unlike the procedure of testing a presidential candidate. When the going gets rough and all the nasty (but usually reasonable and relevant) questions are asked, we see what kind of character the candidate has. Is he or she arrogant? weak? capable of a sense of humor? vindictive? intelligent? stupid? lying? truthful? honest? strong? What is the breaking point of the candidate? In the same way, we seek the breaking point of a theory. As you will see, almost every theory does have a breaking point, but this does not always disqualify the theory (that is, render it invalid). If the breaking point comes late in the discussion, and only when the theory is attacked by an extremely unlikely hypothesis or by trifles, this speaks well for the theory and encourages acceptance or perhaps only a minor rewrite of the theory. Some theories, however, break early in the discussion and can be discarded. Ethical relativism is a theory with a fairly late breaking point; in other words, there are some good things to be said for the theory, which is a good reason not to discard it altogether.

pen in other cultures which we feel, either by instinct or through rational argument, we *should* criticize in order to maintain our own moral integrity. Curiously enough, at the time Benedict wrote her article (1934), one of the most offensive social "experiments" was being undertaken in the Western world. Europe was being overtaken by the Nazis, with their extreme racism and elitism, which was not kept secret by the Nazis, even though the existence of the death camps of later years was generally not known until after the war. A true ethical relativist would have had to stick to her guns and maintain that other countries had no right to criticize what was going on in Germany and Austria in the thirties. (As it happens, this pretty much mirrored the actual attitude of the rest of Europe at the time.) Benedict, however, mentions nothing about this issue in her paper.

People often say, in retrospect, that someone should have protested against or intervened in a particular situation while there was still time. Indeed, one of the arguments in support of the brief Gulf War of 1991 was that the world would have another Hitler and another genocide on their hands if Saddam Hussein's invasion of Kuwait was not stopped. Any attempt at armed take overs and genocide, even if it takes place within a country's own borders and is conducted by its own government, seems like a good candidate for justified intervention by the rest of the world—or at least like a good occasion for voicing the opinion that genocide is wrong. In the eyes of the relativist, though, we are against genocide only because it happens to be against the norms of our own culture; for another culture, genocide may be right. For most people, however, even those believing they ought to be tolerant, there are moral limits to tolerance, and any theory that doesn't recognize this is just not a good theory. We want to believe that we have the right to complain about governments who do not respect human rights and who abuse a part of their population, and in fact, pressure on such governments has at times yielded results. South Africa is not the bastion of segregation it was only a few years ago, and the concept of human rights is not alien to the Russian media or Russian leaders any more.

Not only are we prevented from criticizing another culture's doings if we accept the teachings of relativism, but also we cannot praise and learn from that culture. If we find that the social system of Scandinavia is more humane and functions better than any other in the world, the conclusion based on relativism has to be that this is because it is right for them, but we still can't assume that it is right for us. If we happen to admire the work ethic of Japan, we can't learn from it and adapt it to our own culture, nor can the nonviolence teachings of groups in the Hindu culture have anything to say to us. In short, ethical relativism, when taken to its logical conclusion, precludes learning from other cultures, because there can be no "good" or "bad" that is common to all cultures. Curiously, this doesn't mean that all ethical relativists would actually *forbid* us from learning from other cultures, or from criticizing others—on the contrary, ethical relativists think of themselves as very tolerant and open-minded. The problem is in the logic of the theory itself: When it is applied to real-life situations as a moral principle, it reveals itself to have certain limitations, like not allowing us to criticize and praise other cultures because of the viewpoint that what cultures do is good only for them.

The isolation of moral values to the conventions of specific cultural groups has another curious effect: It forces us to bow to *majority rule*. Remember that ethical relativism does not say that there are no moral rules—only that the rules of each society are proper and valid for that society. Suppose you live in a society and don't agree with the rules? Then you must, ipso facto, be wrong, because we know that the rules that are morally good in a society are those rules that are in effect. If you disagree with those rules, you must be wrong. This makes it impossible to disagree with any rules that are in effect, and therefore civil disobedience is out of the question. In Iran, if you disagree with the fundamentalist Islam rules of punishment, then you are wrong. It is, in fact, right and proper in Iran to amputate the hand of a thief. If you are an American and disagree with the general attitude against euthanasia and doctors who help patients commit suicide, then you are wrong, and the attitude of the majority is right—not because the attitude has been subjected to moral analysis, but simply because it happens to be the attitude of the majority. It does not work, either, to point to a historical precedent and say that it was not always so, because ethical relativism cuts through time as well as space. There are no universal values among different time periods, anymore than there are common values among different cultures of the same era. In other words, *that was then and this is now.* For an intellectual tradition such as ours, which prides itself in valuing minority opinions and promotes the idea of moral progress, the idea that the attitude of the majority is always right simply is unacceptable.

There is a further problem with the idea that a group's morality is determined by the majority or that a certain kind of behavior is normal, for what is "normal"? Is it the *professed* morality of the group or the *actual* morality? Imagine the following situation. The majority of a cultural group, when asked about their moral viewpoints, claim that they believe infidelity is wrong; however, in that particular society, infidelity is common practice. Everyone agrees that they shouldn't commit adultery, but most married couples engage in extramarital affairs anyway. Does that mean that the morality of the culture is what the majority say they ought to do, or what they actually do? We might simply decide that it must be the *normative* rules that define the morality, and not the actual behavior; however, Ruth Benedict assumed morality to be the same as majority *behavior*. In other words, her theory implies that the majority can be morally wrong in their behavior, according to their society's own standard. This seems to support our commonsense notion that high standards can be hard to live up to; Benedict's version of relativism, however, seems to leave little room for such commonsense ideas.

There is a practical problem involved with ethical relativism as well. Suppose the question of doctor-assisted suicide had been determined by a referendum and the law against it overturned in your state. The majority now believe it is right for doctors to help terminally ill patients die. It was morally wrong the week before, but today it is morally right. By next year people may have changed their minds, and it will become morally wrong again. There is something very disconcerting about moral rightness being as arbitrary as that and depending on a vote. Should moral rightness be determined by a margin of only a few percent? And what about the individual states? They obviously are part of a larger unit, the United States, and it would be the moral standards of this larger unit which would define the morals of each singular state. But not all laws and customs are the same from state to state, and what is considered morally wrong by the majority in one state may well be considered morally acceptable by the majority in another (such as abortion or doctor-assisted suicide). Therefore, might we instead want to allow for morally autonomous subgroups in which the majority within each group defines the moral rules, even if they are at odds with the larger cultural group? If we have large minority subgroups *within* a state whose moral values differ from those of the majority, should such groups constitute morally autonomous units that should not be criticized?

There are ethnic groups in the United States who differ from the majority in their views about male–female relationships, about using what Americans consider *pets* for food, about contraception and abortion, about the rights of fathers to punish their families. How large do such groups have to be in order to be considered morally right in their own ways? If we are generous and tolerant relativists, perhaps we'll say that any large, ethnic group should be considered morally autonomous. But would that mean that the Mafia could be considered such a subgroup, or neighborhood gangs? Would society then have to accept a plurality of "laws," each governing the subgroups, with no higher means of control? The relativist might accept that one set of laws—national ones, for instance—would be above all other laws, but it would still be an extremely complicated matter, with possible contradictions arising between what the national law says and what the gang law says. Could we eventually end up in a situation where acts such as looting are morally right for some because of their subgroup affiliation, but not for others?

One of the best qualities of ethical relativism is its tolerance, although we've now seen that it can lead to problems. However, there is something problematic about the very claim of tolerance, coming from a relativist, for is someone who believes in ethical relativism allowed to claim that tolerance is something everyone should have? In other words, can a relativist say that tolerance is *universally good*? If all values are culture-relative, then this condition must apply to tolerance as well: Tolerance may be good for us, but who is to say if it is good for other groups! This notion severely undermines the whole purpose of tolerance, which is not usually considered a one-way street.

Refuting Ethical Relativism

The Nature of Moral Truths

Now we have seen why many people believe that ethical relativism doesn't have enough to offer to be adopted 100 percent; it is a theory with immense theoretical and practical problems. For some critics, the *logic* of the key argument proposed by ethical relativism is faulty. Let us assume that the culture "up north" believes that abortion is morally wrong, while the culture "down south" believes it to be morally permissible. The relativist concludes that because there is a disagreement between the two groups, neither can be right in an absolute sense. But surely, the critics say, that is not so; some things are simply true or false. We may have had a disagreement in the past about whether the earth is round or flat. (Indeed, the Flat Earth Society today is upholding that tradition by claiming that all space reports and photos from space missions are fraudulent and were concocted in a movie studio.) However, that doesn't mean that there is no correct answer; the idea that the earth is round is a verifiable fact, and that is all there is to it. We may be able to verify that some moral codes are objectively right and others are wrong.

The trouble with this critique is that it is easy to verify that the earth is round; all we have to do is look at how things gradually disappear over a flat horizon. But how exactly would you go about verifying that abortion is objectively right or wrong? That would bring us into a much bigger discussion of the very nature of moral truths, which would be no help at all in determining whether ethical relativism is right. The flat earth example is, of course, not supposed to be taken that far. All it shows is that you can't conclude, on the basis of there being a disagreement, that both parties are wrong. It is never as easy to find out who is right in a discussion of moral issues as it is to settle questions of geography.

The Problem of Induction

Some critics believe that the very foundation of the ethical relativism theory is wrong; they believe it simply is not true that there is no universal moral code. If asked how they know that there is no universal moral code, relativists would answer that they looked around and found none, or possibly that given the diversity of human nature, there never will be one. This begs the question, though, because we might reasonably suggest that they should look around a bit longer and refrain from making absolute statements about the future. Blanket statements bring on their own undoing, because any theory based on collecting evidence faces a classical problem: the *problem of induction.*

Induction is one of two major scientific methods; the other is deduction. In deductive thinking we start with an axiom that we believe is true, and we apply this axiom to establish the validity of other axioms, or we apply the theory to specific cases. In inductive thinking we gather empirical evidence in order to reach a comprehensive theory. Ethical relativism is an example of inductive thinking; it bases its general theory that there are no universal moral codes on evidence from particular cultures. The *problem of induction* is that we never can be sure that we have looked hard enough to gather all possible evidence.

A recent report from the medical world serves as a very good example. Doctors and researchers have for years tried to find out how heart disease develops, and there now are several theories about the disease, plus a number of guidelines for how to avoid it and ways to cure it if and when it develops. This was considered a fairly well-researched area until information surfaced that revealed that all the research subjects over the years in every major study had been *male.* There was no sufficient available information on women and heart disease. This was a problem, because we can't assume that female biology responds to heart disease exactly the same way that male biology responds. (Now, studies that include women are underway.) Why were women excluded from the earlier studies? For many reasons, apparently: Men were easier to "keep track of," their schedules permitted them to become test subjects, they were the only ones invited, and so on. Here, then, was a series of studies believed to be comprehensive, but with one big problem: They excluded vital research material. This is typical of the problem of induction; whatever you are gathering evidence for or against, you'll never know for certain when you have gathered enough material, and you will never reach an absolutely certain conclusion, simply because it always is conceivable that something will come up in the future that will undermine your theory.

The induction used by the relativist to make up the theory that there are no universal codes suffers from the same problem. Can we know, with 100 percent certainty, on the basis of collected evidence, that there are no universal codes? No. We have to leave it open; perhaps some day a universal code will appear—or perhaps we will find that it had been there all the time, and we just didn't see it.

Soft Universalism

The clue to toppling ethical relativism actually lies very close, and perhaps that is why ethical relativists haven't seen it. Remember King Darius, who tried to get the Greeks to eat their dead and the Callatians to burn theirs? You may have asked yourself why anybody would want to eat their dead. You may have wanted to ask Benedict why the Northwest Coast Indians were so aggressive (she doesn't say). We all may wonder why some peoples approve of dismemberment as punishment, or approve of infanticide. *As soon as we ask why, though, we have left the realm of ethical relativism.* Relativists don't ask why; they just look at different customs and pronounce them fine for those who hold them. In asking why, we are looking for an *explanation*, one we can understand from our own point of view. In other words, we are expecting, or hoping, that there is some point where that other culture will cease to seem so strange. And very often we reach that point. For instance, disposing of the dead through cannibalism is not at all uncommon, and it usually is done for the sake of honoring the dead or sharing in their spiritual strength. It would seem, then, that the Greeks and Callatians had something in common after all: The Greeks burned their dead because they wanted to honor their spirits, and the Callatians ate their dead for the same reason. The nomad tribes of the Sahara consider it a grave faux pas to eat in front of their in-laws because they consider it to be bad manners. American couples rarely talk about sexual matters in the presence of their in-laws for the same reason—it often is considered bad manners. These cultures share some common values; both value good family relationships, and both express embarrassment when a transgression occurs.

The idea that all cultures have at least some values in common, even if they are buried beneath layers of different behavior patterns, is what I called *soft universalism* at the beginning of this chapter. The idea is not new; it was suggested by the Scottish philosopher David Hume in the eighteenth century. Hume believed that all people share a fellow-feeling, a compassion that may show itself in different ways, but that is present in all cultures nevertheless.

The philosopher James Rachels suggests that at least three values are universal:

1. A policy of caring for enough infants to ensure the continuation of the group
2. A rule against lying
3. A rule against murder

We may be horrified to learn about the custom of killing female babies in the old Eskimo culture, Rachels says, but we gain a better understanding when we learn that female babies were killed only for the reason that otherwise there would have been a surplus of females in the community, because there was a high death rate among male

FIGURE 3.2 James Rachels (b. 1941), American philosopher and human and animal rights advocate. He is the author of *Elements of Moral Philosophy* (1986) and is well known today for his contributions to the euthanasia debate.

hunters (Rachels doesn't tell us why having a surplus of females was a bad thing—it certainly wasn't because females were unproductive in Inuit [Eskimo] society. It is a fact that males were the sole providers of food—entire tribes subsisted on meat alone). Another important fact is that babies were killed only during hard times, and only if adoptive parents couldn't be found. In such times, if the babies had been kept alive, the lives of the older children would have been in jeopardy. In other words, the Eskimos killed some infants in order to protect the children they already had. Their culture valued what ours values: caring for the babies we already have.

Why do all cultures have a rule against lying? Because if you can't expect a fellow citizen to tell the truth most of the time, there is no use attempting to communicate, and without communication human society would grind to a halt. This doesn't mean, obviously, that humans never lie to each other, but only that, on the whole, the acceptable attitude is one of truthfulness.

The rule against murder derives from similar reasoning: If we can't expect our fellow citizens not to kill us, we will not want to venture outdoors, we will stop trusting in people, and society will fall apart (not, as some might think, because everyone will be killed off, but because of general mistrust and lack of communication). Rachels believes that even under chaotic circumstances small groups of friends and relatives would band together, and within these groups the nonmurder rule would be upheld. Again, Rachels is saying that if we have any kind of society, we also will have a rule against arbitrary killing.

The only trouble with the last two rules is that they seem to apply to "fellow citizens" only. As a member of society, you certainly are expected not to lie to or murder members of your own social group, but there really is nothing preventing you from being morally free to lie through your teeth to an outsider or to an enemy government. You may even be free to prey on and murder members of other tribes, gangs, or countries. Rachels has not provided us with any rules that apply universally, only with rules that all responsible people seem to be required to stick to *within their own societies.*

The New Relativism of Cultural Diversity

With the increasingly pluralistic character of modern Western society there is an increasing understanding that all cultural traditions and all viewpoints represented in the public deserve to be heard—at universities, in politics, in the media, and elsewhere. Sometimes this is referred to as "multiculturalism," sometimes as "cultural diversity."

Let us consider multiculturalism and its goals. America used to be called a melting pot, meaning that there was room for anybody from anywhere, that all would be welcomed, and that after a while all individual cultural differences would subside in favor of the new "culture" of the United States. To many Americans (those from many different ethnic backgrounds, in fact) this continues to represent a beautiful image as well as an accurate description of what America is all about. For many people around the world this is what America seems to be, a melting pot. For others, however, the idea of the melting pot is a travesty, an illusion, and an insult. America may have embraced immigrants from countries such as England, Sweden, Ireland, and Germany, but many other people still feel as though they are living on the fringes of American society; they have not been accepted the way others have been. For such people, who feel that they and their ancestors were excluded from the melting pot because they were too different or simply unwanted, there is no such thing as a *common* American culture, only a *dominant* American culture. Today there is a growing awareness even among those from the "dominant culture" that this damages the very concept of an American culture. The question is what to do about it.

Some proponents of multiculturalism believe that what we must do is begin to listen to each other. I call this *inclusive multiculturalism* (also referred to as *pluralism*). The general idea is to integrate everyone—by law, if necessary—into all aspects of our society; to break through the "glass ceilings" that prevent people of color (women and men) as well as white women from reaching top positions; to become sensitized to what others might perceive as slurs and innuendos (what one scholar calls *microinequities*, those little jabs that can hurt so deeply); and, if we are on the receiving end of such slurs, to learn to speak up for ourselves. An increased awareness of the multicolored pattern of our society will, the thinking goes, result in better working relationships, less of a sense that one cultural tradition dominates the country and that everyone who doesn't share it must be left out, and more tolerance and understanding between the groups. This awareness is supposed to begin in schools, where children should learn about as many cultural groups in American society as possible. This means there will be less time for some subjects that are usually taught, but proponents of inclusive multiculturalism believe that a growing cultural understanding is worth the price.

Some people believe that it is not enough simply to listen to each other. They believe members of each culture must regain their collective self-esteem, which was lost with the attempt to create a melting pot. They think the best way to do that is to occasionally *isolate* the children of each group so that they can be taught about the cultural advances of their particular group. I call this *exclusive multiculturalism* (also

FIGURE 3.3 *A Passage To India,* Columbia Pictures, 1984. A clashing of cultural differences and expectations: Adele from England (Judy Davis) and Aziz from India (Victor Bannerjee) at the Marabar Caves, immediately before the disaster happens. The story of *A Passage to India* is outlined in Chapter 7 as an illustration of the problems of cultural differences and ethical relativism.

referred to as *particularism*). This form of education is already taking place in American grade schools. African-American children are taught about the cultural contributions of other African-Americans, and Latinos are taught about Latino contributions. What if a Latino child wants to learn about African-American contributions or is interested in the "Eurocentric" mainstream culture? To those who believe in the in-

Cultural Diversity or Cultural Adversity?

The idea that moral viewpoints get their importance from the groups that utter them, rather than from their content, is, to some philosophers, a misguided attitude. In the old days of Western culture the dominant viewpoint was the one held by some but not all white males, and for most white males as well as for others that was enough to make that viewpoint "correct." Churches and political groups often take the same attitude: The identity of the group is enough justification for the correctness of its views. Today we also see this same viewpoint applied socially by certain groups: If you are a member of an oppressed group, your viewpoint on right and wrong is valuable *just because you are a member of that group, and if you are not, then your viewpoint is irrelevant.* This form of relativism, which grants the importance of a viewpoint on the basis of gender, race, and class, may be as misplaced as one that denies the importance of certain groups just because they are who they are. Such an attitude, the argument goes, reflects the logical fallacy of the *ad hominem argument*: You are right or wrong because of who you are, not because of what you say. Whether this attitude is assumed by those in power or by those who are dispossessed, it is equally faulty as a moral principle, according to the rules of critical thinking. Can you imagine situations where a person's identity alone would determine whether he or she were right or wrong?

clusive version of multiculturalism, this type of cross-cultural interest is a fine idea and should be encouraged. To those who advocate exclusive multiculturalism, it is not, because they do not believe children achieve self-esteem by hearing about what other groups have done. Critics of this method argue that children should be allowed to choose their heroes from among many cultures, not just their own, and that having cultural heroes from their own groups won't necessarily give them self-esteem—it takes more than that. These critics also argue that by practicing exclusive multiculturalism, different groups will never have a chance to learn about each other, and the ground will be laid for further "segregation," misunderstandings and enmity down the line. Whether inclusive or exclusive multiculturalism gives the greatest benefits to our American culture as a whole is something that schools and parents will have to decide on before too long.

How might multiculturalism affect our attitude toward basic values in ethics? That greatly depends on what we believe those values to be. If we think our values can't be disputed, that they are somehow determined by God or by Nature, then we will find it hard to accept other and different viewpoints. As we will see, such *absolutism* ("hard universalism") usually does not allow for any tolerance of other basic ideas.

If we adopt the attitude of ethical relativism, the result may surprise us, because ethical relativism doesn't automatically support multiculturalism. Ethical relativism states that there is no universal moral code—that each culture will do what is right for it, and no other culture has the right to interfere. This may work when cultures are separate and isolated from each other, because the moral code in that case is defined as the code of the *dominant population*. However, in our pluralistic society, this won't work, because the "dominant culture" (white society) is increasingly reproached for displaying cultural insensitivity. Can ethical relativism work, therefore, in a country as diverse as ours, where we often find opposing values ("looting is antisocial" versus "looting is a righteous act for the disposessed," for example) within the same neighborhood? Because a multicultural ethic asks us not to think in terms of one dominant set of rules, some might opt for an attitude of total *moral nihilism* instead: No values are better than any other values, because no values are objectively correct. Such nihilism might well result in the breakdown of the fabric of a society, and possibly in a greater cohesion within subgroups, with different groups battling each other. Rather than describe these battles as gang wars, we might call this phenomenon *balkanization*—when groups have nothing or very little in common except hatred for what the other groups stand for. It seems as though ethical relativism is not the answer to our new ethical problems of multiculturalism.

Suppose we look to soft universalism for the answer? If we are soft universalists we hope to be able to agree with others on some basic issues, but not on all issues. In the case of multiculturalism we may be able to agree on the promotion of general equality, tolerance, and cohesion in the nation (in other words, the will and ability to live together); we *have* to agree that what we want is a functioning society that we all share in. If we don't agree on this, multiculturalism is a lost cause, and so is the whole idea of a United States. According to soft universalism, values can't be allowed to differ dramatically, so we wouldn't end up with acts such as looting being morally right for some and not for others, nor would the killing of family members for the sake of honor be acceptable in one neighborhood and not in another. These questions of common values in the context of a multicultural society are particularly burning, for without some values in common we simply won't have a society.

Narratives That Explore Cultural Differences

Chapter 7 includes the following stories, which, in different ways, discuss the issue of cultural differences: Spike Lee's film *Do the Right Thing*, the 1992 film version of James Fenimore Cooper's classic *The Last of the Mohicans*, E. M. Forster's novel *A Passage to India*, David Lean's film *Lawrence of Arabia*, and Sheri S. Tepper's science fiction novel *Sideshow*.

Chapter 4

Myself or Others?

We usually assume that moral behavior, or "being ethical," has to do with not being overly concerned with yourself. In other words, selfishness is assumed to be an unacceptable attitude. Even among scholars, though, there is disagreement about what constitutes ethical behavior. Since very early in Western intellectual history the viewpoint that humans aren't built to look out for other people's interests has surfaced regularly. Some scholars even hold that proper moral conduct consists of "looking out for number one," period. These viewpoints are known as psychological egoism and ethical egoism, respectively. Both psychological egoism and ethical egoism are examples of absolutist theories; they hold that only one code is the norm for ethical behavior.

Psychological Egoism

Definition of the Theory

Some years ago an Air Florida plane crashed into the Potomac River in Washington. It was winter, and the river was ice-cold. The lives of many of the passengers were saved partly thanks to the efforts of a passer-by. When life jackets with rescue ropes were being lowered from the overhead bridge to the accident victims in the water (as part of a major rescue effort), he jumped in the water and kept passing jackets to the passengers. By the time rescuers got around to looking for him, he was gone from the surface, his life lost in the process of saving others. There is now a monument to him on the riverbank.

In the early nineties a woman in San Diego tried to get another woman out of the way of an oncoming train. She fell onto the tracks and was killed by the train.

In Calcutta and elsewhere around the world, Mother Teresa and her followers have striven to improve conditions for the poor and homeless without seeking any reward or advantages for themselves.

Such cases of what most of us would call selflessness are precious to most people, because they show us what some people are capable of—and perhaps what we ourselves are capable of in certain situations. We like to believe that humans have a built-in measure of courage that allows us to rise to the occasion and give up our life, or at least our comfort, for others. Of course few people perform heroic deeds with the *intent* of getting themselves killed, but if they lose their life in the process, we only seem to admire them more. (An exception is those who feel that losing one's life for someone else is stupid, useless, or even morally wrong. Such people may feel more comfortable with the theory of *ethical egoism*.)

If we ask a person who has done (and survived) a heroic deed why he or she did it, the answer is almost predictable: "I just had to do it" or perhaps, "I didn't think about it, I just did it." We take such comments as a sign that we are in the presence of a person with extraordinary moral character. But there are other ways of interpreting the words and actions of heroes. The theory of psychological egoism states that whatever it may look like, and whatever we may think it is, no human action is done for any other reason than for the sake of the agent. In short, we are all selfish, or at least we are all self-interested.

The term *psychological egoism* is applied to the theory because it is a psychological theory, a theory about how humans behave. A psychological egoist believes that humans are always looking out for themselves in some way or other, and it is impossible for them to behave any other way. As such, psychological egoism is a descriptive theory; it doesn't make any statements about whether this is a *good* way to behave. What does it take in order for a person to be labeled a psychological egoist? Not that he or she is a selfish person, but that he or she holds to the theory that all people look after themselves. As we will see later, it is entirely possible for someone to be kind and caring and still be a psychological egoist.

All People Look After Themselves

In Plato's *Republic* we find a discussion about morality and selfishness. Plato's brother Glaucon is trying to make Socrates give some good reasons for why it is better to be just than to be unjust. Glaucon insists that all people by nature look after themselves, and whenever we can get away with something, we will do it, regardless of how unjust

"Ought" Implies "Can"

Sometimes a philosophical text will state that "ought" implies "can." In the civil code of the Roman Empire (27 B.C.E.–395 C.E.) this principle was clearly stated, and Roman citizens knew that *impossibilium nulla est obligatio* (nobody has a duty to do what is not possible). Many philosophical and legal schools of thought today are still based on this idea, and one of these is psychological egoism. "Ought implies can" means that we can't have an obligation (ought) to do something, unless it is actually possible for us to do it (can). I can't make it a moral obligation for you to swim across San Francisco Bay to show your support of the Save the Whales program if you can't swim (but I might try to make it an obligation for you to donate a dollar, because most people can afford that). I can't make it a moral obligation for you to take home a pet from the pound if you are allergic to animals (but I might insist that you have an obligation to help in other ways). You can't tell me that I ought to be unselfish if in fact I was born selfish and can't be any other way because it is part of my human nature. This is the point that psychological egoism wants to make: It is irrational to keep wanting humans to look out for each other when, as a matter of fact, we aren't built that way.

it may be to others. Unfortunately, we may receive the same treatment from others, which is highly unpleasant, so for the sake of peace and security we agree to treat each other decently—not because we feel like it, but because we want to play it safe. Morality is just a result of us looking out for ourselves. If we can get away with something, it is in our nature to do so and to make the most of it.

What Glaucon is suggesting here about the origin of society is a first in Western thought. His theory is an example of what has become known as a *social contract theory*, and this type of theory became particularly influential much later, in the eighteenth century. A social contract theory assumes that humans used to live in a presocial setting (without rules, regulations, or cooperation) and then, for various reasons, got together and agreed on setting up a society. We will return to social contract theories in Part 4. Generally, social contract theories assume that (a) humans decide to build a society with rules for the sake of the common good or (b) for the sake of self-protection. Glaucon's theory belongs to the second category, because Glaucon claims (for the sake of argument) that humans primarily look after themselves. The theory that humans are by nature selfish is commonly known as psychological egoism.

To illustrate this, Glaucon tells a story of a man called Gyges, a shepherd in ancient Lydia. (The story was one of the local legends, probably well known to most Greeks at the time.) Gyges was caught in a storm and an earthquake, which left a large hole in the ground. He explored the chasm and found a hollow, bronze horse with a corpse of a giant inside. The giant was wearing only a gold ring on his finger. Gyges took the ring and left and later, wearing the ring, attended a meeting of shepherds. During the meeting Gyges happened to twist the ring, and he realized from the reaction of the other shepherds that he had become invisible. Twisting the ring back, he reappeared. Realizing the advantages gained by being invisible, Gyges arranged to be one of the elected messengers who report to the king about his sheep. Gyges went to town, seduced the queen, and conspired with her to kill the king. He then took over the kingdom, sired a dynasty, and became the ancestor of King Kroesus.

Glaucon's question is, Suppose we had two such rings? Let us imagine giving one to a decent person and one to a scoundrel. We know that the scoundrel will abuse the ring for personal gain, but how about the decent person? To Glaucon it is the same thing; their human natures are identical. Decent persons will do "unjust" things just as quickly as scoundrels if they know they can get away with it; furthermore, if they *don't* take advantage of such situations, they are just stupid. In the end, who will be happier, the unjust person who schemes and gets away with everything, or the just person who never tries to get away with anything but is so good that people think there must be something fishy about him? Why, the unjust person, of course.

Is Glaucon seriously implying that he believes it is foolish and unnatural to be just if you don't have to be? No, he is acting as the devil's advocate in order to make Socrates defend justice as something that is good in itself. However, Glaucon does imply that what he is describing is in fact the opinion of most people. He may have been right; a good two thousand years later Thomas Hobbes (1588–1679) agreed with Glaucon's theory of self-interest, on all three counts: (1) Humans choose to live in a society with rules because they are concerned with their own safety, and for no other reason; (2) Humans are by nature self-interested, and any show of concern for others hides a true concern for ourselves; (3) Furthermore, we would be fools if we didn't look after ourselves. (We return to this point in the next section.)

Surely we all can remember events in our lives that show that we don't always act out of self-interest. You may remember the time you helped your best friend move across town. The time you sat up all night preparing your brother's taxes. The time you donated toys to the annual Christmas toy drive. The time you washed your parents' car. Did their dishes at Thanksgiving. Or perhaps even helped a stranger on the road or saved the life of an accident victim. Was all that really for selfish reasons? The psychological egoist would say yes—you may not have been aware of your true motives, but selfish it was, somehow. You may have wanted to borrow your parents' car, hence the car wash and the dishes. You helped your friend move because you were afraid of losing her friendship. You may have felt guilty for not helping with your brother's taxes the year before, so you did them this year. The toys? You wanted to feel good about yourself. The stranger on the road? You wanted to rack up a few points in the Big Book of Heaven. Helping the accident victim? You wanted to get your name in the paper.

What about Mother Teresa and the other unselfish souls who spend their lives helping others? Maybe they want to get to Heaven, to atone for past wrongdoing, or

Hobbes and the Feeling of Pity

Hobbes believed humans feel pity for others in distress because they are afraid the same thing may happen to themselves. We identify with the pain of others, and that makes us afraid for ourselves. Therefore, helping others may be a way to ward off bad events. In actual fact we have no pity with others for their sake—only for our own. Hobbes was one of the first modern Western philosophers to ponder human psychology, and we might say that he put his finger on a sore spot: Sometimes we do sympathize with others because we imagine how awful it would be if the same thing were to happen to us. What exactly does Hobbes mean when he says we *identify* with others? It seems that if we ask ourselves, If this happened to me, how would I feel? This does not necessarily lead to concern for ourselves but rather to a concern for others, precisely because we know how they feel. Furthermore, isn't it possible to feel pity for someone or something with which you don't identify so easily? We certainly can feel pity for someone of the other gender, or someone of another race or culture, even if what happens to them wouldn't happen to us. But how about feeling pity for dolphins caught in gill nets? for animals caught in traps? for pets used in lab experiments? Some years ago a couple of whales were trapped in the ice off the coast of Alaska, and rescue teams and reporters came from all over the world to help free them. Even Inuit trappers and hunters joined in. One of them said, "This is kind of strange for me—I usually kill whales for a living!" It is hard to believe that in this case people cared only because they were afraid the catastrophe might happen to them. In a broad sense, perhaps we do identify with other creatures when their lives are in danger, and feel that we ward off our own demise by saving their lives. In the final analysis, though, that idea is rather far-fetched, because if Hobbes were right, and we fear "contamination" from the misery of others, wouldn't we rather turn our backs to them and flee, rather than expose ourselves to their suffering? Given that we don't, perhaps there are forces at work other than selfishness. An easier explanation is that we simply, on occasion, care for the well-being of others.

maybe they just want to feel warm and fuzzy inside. As far as the psychological egoist is concerned, they are, in the final analysis, doing it for themselves.

This theory, cynical as it may sound, has established itself firmly in the minds of many modern people. Somehow, it appeals to us. But what is so appealing? After all, this theory removes the halo from above the head of every hero and every unselfish person in the history of humankind. In fact, that may be part of its appeal: We like to think, in this day and age, that we are honest about ourselves, and we don't want to

FIGURE 4.1 In 1989 the attention of world media was for a few days focused on Alaska, where three whales were trapped in the ice. Because whales need open water to breathe, they were facing death. A joint effort by ice-breakers from what was then the Soviet Union, the United States, and other nations succeeded in creating a channel, guiding two of the three whales to open water. Sadly, it was too late to save the third whale. Afterward, many people asked themselves what it was in this incident that captured the world's attention and created a common goal for old political adversaries. Was it a media event, or genuine compassion, or both?

be tricked into thinking that we are better than we are, or that anyone else is, either. One reason, then, for this theory's popularity is its presumed honesty.

Closely related to the notion of honesty is our modern fascination with cynicism. Somehow, we have a hard time believing good things about people, including ourselves. Children who lived through the tragedies and disappointments of the sixties and seventies, and the children of those children, all have been affected by the assassinations of John F. Kennedy and Martin Luther King, by the Watergate scandal, by fuel shortages, and later by the fall of several televangelists, by the Iran–Contra scandal of the late eighties (the "weapons for hostages" deal), and by other covert government actions. All this has contributed to our tendency to believe the worst. This theory, called *revisionist* by some scholars (it revises what we thought about something), lets us rethink the stories we've heard and strip them of their heroics or sentimentalism; we are fools no longer, now that we know that true human nature is selfish. Remaining a skeptic and refusing to be sweet-talked may be the mature thing to do, but it

Hedonism

The search for pleasure, hedonism, is sometimes cited by psychological egoists as one reason people are selfish: Everyone wants pleasure, so we search for it. Searching and finding are two different things, however, and the paradox of hedonism often prevents us from finding what we are looking for. Suppose we set out to achieve pleasure on the weekend. We go to the beach, we take a walk in the woods, we hang out at the mall, we go to the movies, but we're just not enjoying ourselves that much; pleasure has somehow eluded us, and we face Monday with the sense of a lost weekend, telling ourselves that next weekend we'll look harder. Our friend, on the contrary, had a great time; he went with us because he likes going to the beach, loves the woods, wanted to look for a pair of jeans at the mall, and had been looking forward to seeing a movie for weeks. He even enjoyed our company. Why did he have a good weekend while we felt unfulfilled? Because we were trying to have a good time, and he was doing things he liked to do and enjoying being with someone he liked. The pleasure he got was, so to speak, a by-product of doing those things—it wasn't the main object of his activity. We, on the other hand, looked for pleasure without thinking about what we like to do that might give us pleasure, as if "pleasure" were a thing separate from everything else. The hedonistic paradox is this: If you look for pleasure, chances are you won't find it. (People who have been looking hard for someone to love can attest to this.) Pleasure comes to you when you are in the middle of something else and rarely when you are looking for it. Sometimes the "Don Juan syndrome" is cited as an example of the hedonistic paradox. A person (traditionally a man, but there is no reason it can't apply to women) who has a lot of sexual conquests very often feels compelled to move from partner to partner because he or she likes the pursuit but somehow tires of an established relationship. Why is this the case? It could be because such people are unwilling to commit themselves to a permanent relationship, but it also may be due to the paradox of hedonism: In each partner they see the promise of "pleasure," but somehow all they end up with is another conquest. If they had been setting their sights on building a relationship with their partners, they might have found out that pleasure comes from being with someone you care for, and you have to care in order to feel pleasure; you can't expect pleasure to appear if there is no genuine feeling—or so the theory says. . . .

also may harden our minds into accepting preconceived notions, something that is the opposite of having an open mind. By adopting this attitude we have decided beforehand that everybody is rotten at heart, so any sign indicating the opposite we are going to doubt.

A third reason psychological egoism is so popular has nothing to do with modern misanthropy (hatred or distrust of mankind). It has to do with saying, "I can't help myself—I was made that way," which is an easy way out. By using this excuse we don't have to worry about remembering Aunt Molly's birthday or calling the radio station about the mattress we saw blocking the number-two lane on the highway, because we are selfish *by nature*, and we can't worry about others even if we try—unless, of course, there is something in it for ourselves.

Shortcomings of Psychological Egoism

There is something beguiling about psychological egoism; once you begin to look at the world through the eyes of a psychological egoist, it is hard to see it any other way. In fact, no matter how hard we try to come up with an example that seems to run counter to the theory, the psychological egoist has a ready answer. This is due to several factors. For one, psychological egoism always looks for selfish motives and refuses to recognize any other kind. For any nonselfish motivation you can think of for doing what you did, the theory will tell you that there was another, ulterior motive behind it. It is inconceivable, according to the theory, that there might be other motives. This is in fact a flaw in the theory. A good theory is not one that can't be proven to be wrong, but one that allows for the possibility of counterexamples.

Biologically, psychological egoists have a forceful argument: the survival instinct. It seems a fact that all animals, including humans, are equipped with some sort of instinct for self-preservation. We might ask ourselves, though, whether this instinct is always the strongest instinct in all relationships, animal as well as human. There are cases where animals seem to sacrifice themselves for others, yet surely they don't have any underlying motives, such as the desire to be on TV or go to Heaven. Nor is it likely that they would be ridden by a guilt complex if they did not perform such deeds. There is, then, at least the possibility that some actions are not performed for the reason of self-preservation.

Is it true that we always do things for selfish reasons? Sometimes we do things we don't want to do, like going to the dentist, but even that is for our own good. Let us assume, for the sake of argument, that we do actually do what we want so that we may benefit from some long-term consequences. *But is doing what we want in order to benefit ourselves always a "selfish" act?* Abraham Lincoln seems to have agreed that it is. A famous story tells of him riding on a mud coach (a type of stagecoach) with a friend. Just as he is explaining that he believes everybody has selfish reasons for their actions, they pass by a mud hole where several piglets are drowning. The mother sow is making an awful noise, but she can't help them. Lincoln asks the driver to stop the coach,

Falsification Must Be Theoretically Possible

The inability of a theory to allow for cases where the theory doesn't apply is considered bad science and bad thinking. The *principle of falsification* is advanced by the philosopher Karl Popper as a hallmark of a viable theory. Let us look at an example: If someone expressed the psychological theory that any sign of emotional upset means that the person is yearning for a hot fudge sundae, that would be an example of a nonfalsifiable theory. There you are, weeping because you've lost a winning lottery ticket—7 million dollars just went into the washing machine because you didn't get the ticket out of the back pocket of your jeans. And a psychologist comes along, promising to end your troubles by buying you a hot fudge sundae. Much as you try to explain that this is not the cause of your concern, she refuses to believe you and tells you that you just don't understand your own emotions. After a while, who knows? Maybe you begin to believe her—what you really wanted was not 7 million dollars, but a hot fudge sundae. This is not a *theory*; it is a *prejudice*, a preconceived notion held by a narrow-minded, stubborn individual. It has no value as a theory because it doesn't say anything about the real world, but only about a concocted world. It doesn't stand up to Popper's principle of falsification. Psychological egoism is this type of theory.

gets off, wades into the mudhole, brings the pigs out, and returns to the coach. His friend, remembering what Lincoln had just said, asks him, "Now Abe, where does selfishness come in to this little episode?" Lincoln answers, "Why, bless your soul Ed, that was the very essence of selfishness. I should have had no peace of mind all day had I gone on and left that suffering old sow worrying over those pigs. I did it to get peace of mind, don't you see?"

So Lincoln saved the pigs in order to benefit himself (and here we thought he was just a nice man). That is of course the irony of the story: Lincoln is not known to us as a selfish person. But was he right? He may of course be lying in claiming that he did it for himself, but let us assume that he spoke the truth as he saw it—that he saved the pigs in order to gain peace of mind for himself. Was it still a "selfish" act? That depends on what you call selfish. Is doing things to benefit yourself always selfish, or does it perhaps depend on *what it is you want to gain*? Is there a difference between wanting to save pigs from drowning and wanting to hurt small animals (in order to watch them squirm)? They are both *wants*, but most people would say there is a substantial difference between the two. In other words, it is *what* you want that matters, not just the fact that you want something. If what you want is to save someone, that is surely different from wanting to hurt someone. Lincoln might, of course, interject

Lincoln: Humble Man or Clever Jokester?

We might ask how Lincoln could have been unaware of the distinction between caring and not caring that becomes apparent when we consider different kinds of behavior. For an intelligent man, his remarks seem unusually dim. It's possible, of course, that the pig story illustrates Lincoln's true nature: that of a very humble and honest man who does not wish to take credit for having done something good. The story makes him all the more endearing, if that is the case, for indeed we know him as Honest Abe. But there is another possibility—that he was joking. Lincoln had a fondness for jokes, and this may have been one of them. Knowing full well that he was doing a nice thing, he made use of *irony* by claiming that rescuing the piglets was nothing but a selfish act. Lincoln scholars may have to decide which version they like best. In any event, Lincoln was speaking as a psychological egoist, regardless of how unselfishly he acted, because he expressed the theory that everyone acts selfishly.

that saving the pigs was still in his own self-interest, so it wasn't done for them but for himself—but is that true? Why would it have been in his self-interest to know that the pigs were safe, if self-gratification was all he cared about? A selfish person hardly loses sleep over the misery of others, let alone that of drowning pigs. Let us suppose, then, that he did it just to feel "warm and fuzzy" inside, and let us conclude that people who help others because they enjoy it are as selfish as can be. Nevertheless, a person who enjoys helping others is not our *usual* image of a selfish person; rather, as James Rachels points out, that is exactly how we picture an *unselfish* person.

As we have seen, psychological egoism presents certain problems, because it does not always describe the world in a way that allows us to recognize it. One of its flaws may actually be a problem of *language*.

Suppose the theory insists that regardless of whether we want to help others or hurt them for our own gain, our desire to help or hurt them is a selfish want. In that case we may respond that we consider it less selfish to help others than to hurt them, and we may want to introduce some new terms: *less selfish* versus *more selfish*, terms that distinguish between acts done for yourself and acts done for others. This, however, is just another way of trying to distinguish selfish behavior from unselfish behavior. Psychological egoism seems to have overlooked the fact that we already have a concept for "less-selfish" behavior which is perfectly well understood: *unselfish*. Changing language to the extent that it goes against our common sense (by claiming that there is no such thing as *un*selfish, but that it is acceptable to use the term *less* selfish) does not make psychological egoism correct.

There is an even worse problem, known as the *fallacy of the suppressed correlative*. The correlative of the word *selfish* is *unselfish*, just as the correlative of *light* is *dark*, or *hot/cold*, *tall/short*, and so on. It is a psychological as well as a linguistic fact that we understand one term because we understand the other: If everything were dark, we wouldn't understand the meaning of *light*, and neither would we understand the meaning of *dark*, because it is defined by its *contrast* to something else, and without the contrast there is no understanding. In other words, a concept without a correlative becomes meaningless. If all acts are selfish, *selfish* has no correlative, and the statement "all acts are selfish" has no meaning. In fact, we could not make such a statement at all if psychological egoism were correct, because the concept of selfishness would not exist since any nonselfish behavior would be unthinkable. So not only does psychological egoism go against common sense and preclude a complete understanding of the full range of human behavior, but also it goes against the rules of language.

Ethical Egoism

Definition of the Theory

In Southern California in January 1992, a good samaritan stopped to help a man whose car had broken down on the freeway. The man shot and killed the samaritan, stole his car, and proceeded to lead the police on a high-speed chase. Eventually he ran out of gas and began a shoot-out with the police, who subsequently killed him. This, of course, didn't bring the samaritan back to life.

Although most people would admire the good samaritan for what he did and although we may deplore the fact that few people now would be inclined to follow his example, the ethical egoist would say that, in effect, the samaritan did the wrong thing. For ethical egoism there is only one rule: *Look after yourself.* You have no business stopping for anybody on the freeway; indeed, the ethical egoist would say, if you do stop you are throwing your life away.

Here we should make sure that we have our terms straight. This theory is called ethical egoism simply because it is an ethical theory, a *normative* theory about *how we ought to behave* (in contrast to psychological egoism, which claims to know how we actually *do* behave). The theory implies that we ought to be selfish. Or, to put it more gently, we ought to be *self-interested*. Calling the theory "ethical" does not suggest that there might be a decent way to be selfish; it just means that ethical egoism is a theory that advocates egoism as a moral rule.

You Should Look After Yourself

Glaucon insisted that if you don't take advantage of a situation, you are foolish. Hobbes claimed that it makes good sense to look after yourself, and morality is a result

Individual Ethical Egoism

A variant of this theory should be briefly mentioned: *individual ethical egoism.* This version, commonly held by small children and childish adults, holds that "everyone ought to do what I want," regardless of whether it is in the other person's interest. This view is rarely taken seriously as an ethical theory, because it doesn't have any good arguments to support it except that it's what the person wants. We can't expect everyone else to follow our whims or even look after our self-interests, if it in no way takes their own lives and human dignity into account. This is nothing but emotional tyranny. A moral theory, if it is to be accepted today, has to involve an important element of acceptance. It has to be imaginable that everyone, or at least most people, would be willing to adopt the theory for themselves. This phenomenon, which we shall discuss later, is known as *universalizability.* We can hardly imagine the world agreeing to serve our self-interests, because, after all, what makes us so special? However, it is a fact that some people choose to live their lives seeking to fulfill *someone else's* wishes or self-interests; such choices may be made by parents, spouses, grown children taking care of their parents, disciples following the way of their guru or leader, or devout believers trying to live the way God wants them to live. If you are a parent or a political or religious leader, you may claim that "everyone should do what I want because it is good for them." In that case, you are moving out of the realm of egoism; the main interest is no longer yourself, but everyone, and you just have the audacity to claim that you know better than anyone else how everyone's lives should be lived.

of that self-interest: If I mistreat others, they may mistreat me, so I resolve to behave myself. This is a rather twisted version of the Golden Rule (Do unto others as you would have them do unto you). It is twisted, because it is peculiarly slanted toward our own self-interests. The reason we should treat others the way we would like to be treated is that it gives us a good chance of receiving just such treatment; we do it for ourselves, not for others—so, do unto others so that you will be done unto in a similar way. The Golden Rule usually emphasizes others, but for the ethical egoist it emphasizes the self. With ethical egoism we encounter a certain phenomenon for the first time in this book: an ethical theory that focuses on the *consequences* of one's actions. Any theory that looks solely to consequences of actions is known as a *consequentialist theory;* the consequences that ethical egoism stipulates are good consequences for the person taking the action. However, we could imagine other kinds of consequentialist theories, such as one that advocates good consequences for as many people as possible. Such a theory will be discussed in Chapter 5.

Ethical egoists are themselves quite divided about whether the theory tells you to do *what you want* without regard for others, or *what is good for you* without regard for others. The latter version seems to appeal to common sense, because, in the long run, just looking for instant gratification is hardly going to make you happy or live longer. Saying that people ought to look after themselves need not, of course, mean that one should annoy others whenever possible, step on their toes, or deliberately neglect their interests. It simply suggests that one should do what will be of long-term benefit to oneself, such as exercising, eating healthy food, avoiding repetitive argumentative situations, abstaining from overeating, and so forth. Even paying one's taxes might be added to the list. In conjunction, it suggests that other people's interests are of no importance. If you might advance your own interests by helping others, then by all means help others, but only if you are the main beneficiary. It is fine to help your children get ahead in school, because you love them and this love is a gratifying emotion for you. But there is no reason to lend a hand to your neighbor's children, unless you like them or you achieve gratification through your actions.

This interpretation—that the theory tells us to do whatever will benefit ourselves—results in a rewriting of the Golden Rule, because, obviously, it is not always the case that you *will* get the same treatment from others that you give to them. Occasionally you might get away with not treating others decently because they may never know that you are the source of the bad treatment they are receiving. In such cases you would need not worry about being found out; it would be as though you had a magic ring of Gyges of your own. Ethical egoism tells you that it is perfectly all right to treat others in a way that is to your advantage and not to theirs as long as you can be certain that you will get away with it.

The Shortcomings of Ethical Egoism

Let us return to Glaucon and his rings for a while. He assumes that not only will the scoundrel take advantage of a ring that can make him invisible, but so will the decent man, and furthermore, we would call them both fools if they didn't. A theory of psychological egoism, therefore, can also entail a normative element: ethical egoism (which tells us how we *ought* to behave). Of course, it is hard to see what the point is if we can't help ourselves from doing other than what we do, anyway.

At the end of Glaucon's speech the reader expects Socrates to dispatch the theory of egoism with a quick blow. The answer, however, is a long time coming; as a matter of fact, Plato designed the rest of his *Republic* as a roundabout answer to Glaucon. In the end, Socrates's answer is: The unjust person can't be happy, because happiness consists of a good harmony, a balance between the three parts of the soul: *reason, willpower* (*spirit*), and *desire*. Reason is supposed to dominate willpower, and willpower desire. If desire or willpower dominates the other two, we have a sick person, and a sick person can't be happy by definition, says Socrates. We will return to this theory later in this book.

In considering the question, Why be just? it's important to understand that we must consider justice in terms of the whole society, not just the individual. We can't argue for justice on the basis of individual situations, but only in general terms. That makes the question of why be just more reasonable, because we don't look at individual cases but at an overall picture where justice and well-being are interrelated. For Socrates and Plato being just was part of "the good life," and true happiness could not be attained without justice.

To the modern reader there is something curiously bland and evasive about these answers. Surely unjust persons can be disgustingly happy—they may seem to us to have sick souls, but they certainly don't act as if they are aware of it or suffer any ill effects from it. The answer to this—that being selfish is *just plain wrong in itself*—is not addressed by Socrates at all. For a modern person it seems reasonable to be "just" out of respect for the law, or perhaps because that is the right thing to do, but Socrates mentions this only briefly—it is a concern that belongs to a much later time period than the one in which he lived. The highest virtue for the ancient Greeks was, on the whole, ensuring the well-being of the community, and this well-being remained the bottom line more than any abstract moral issue of right and wrong. And because justice was best for the state in the final evaluation, then justice was a value in itself. In the end, Socrates' answer evokes self-interest and urges us to discern truth from appearance: If you are unjust, your soul will suffer, and so will your community.

This attitude may not impress persons seeking self-gratification (who are unlikely to be concerned about the effects of their actions on their soul or on the people around them), but it may have some impact on persons seeking long-term self-interest. It still does rest on an empirical assumption, however: that sooner or later you must "pay the piper"—that is, atone for your wrongdoing. History, though, is full of scoundrels who have gone to their graves rich and happy. The religious argument that you will go to Hell, or suffer a miserable next incarnation if you are concerned only with yourself, is not really an argument against *egoism*, because it still asks you to look after yourself, even to the point of using others for the purpose of insuring a pleasant afterlife (treat others decently and you shall be saved).

The one type of argument against ethical egoism that has appealed to most scholars is one that insists that ethical egoism is self-contradictory. If you are supposed to look after yourself, and your colleague is supposed to look after herself, and if looking after yourself will mean stealing her floppy disks at work, then you and she will be working at cross-purposes: Your duty will be to steal her floppy disks from her, and her duty will be to protect her floppy disks. We can't have a moral theory that says that one's duty should be something that conflicts with someone else's duty, so ethical egoism is therefore inconsistent.

Few ethical egoists find this argument convincing, because they don't agree that we can't have a moral theory that gives a green light to different duty-concepts. Such a view assumes that ethical egoism benefits everyone, even when each person does only what is in his or her best interest. Occasionally, ethical egoism assumes just that: We should look after ourselves and mind our own business, because meddling in other people's affairs is an *intrusion of privacy*; they will not like our charity, they will hate our superiority, and we won't know what is best for them, anyway. So, along these lines, we should stay out of other people's affairs because it is best for everybody. The po-

FIGURE 4.2 *Madame Bovary,* MGM, 1942. Emma Bovary (Jennifer Jones, right) loves romantic novels and finds her own life unspeakably drab. She neglects her husband and her daughter, and in this scene she contemplates having an affair with the young man on the left, going shopping for new clothes, and buying new drapes and furniture—anything to make life a little more exciting. The story of *Madame Bovary* is outlined in Chapter 7 as an illustration of egoism.

litical theory resulting from this point of view is known as *laissez-faire,* the hands-off policy. Political theorists, however, are quick to point out that laissez-faire is by no means an egoistic theory, because it has everybody's best interests at heart, and that is precisely what is wrong with the idea that we should opt for ethical egoism for the reason that it will be good for everybody. It may be true that if we all look after ourselves, we'll all be happier—but who is the beneficiary of this idea? Not "I," but "everybody," so ethical egoism is, in fact, no longer a moral theory of egoism, but something else.

Another argument against the conceptual consistency of ethical egoism is this: Ethical egoism doesn't work in practice. Remember that the theory advocates that all people ought to look out for themselves—not merely that *I* should look out for *myself.* But suppose you set out to look after your own self-interests, and advocate that others do the same; within a short while you will realize that your rule is *not* going to be to your advantage, because others will be out there grabbing for themselves, and you will have fierce competition. The smart thing to do is to *pretend* that you are concerned about others, and continue to praise the virtues of looking after one another, while, on the sly, you proceed to look after yourself without being found out. In other words, you should not advocate that all people look out for themselves, but that everyone should look after one another, and you should keep quiet about your own intention of breaking the rule whenever possible. This would be the prudent thing to do, and it probably would work quite well. The only problem is that this is not a moral theory, because, for one thing, it carries a contradiction. It means you must claim to support one principle and act according to another one—in other words, it requires you to be dishonest. Also, a moral theory, in this day and age, has to have the capability to be extended to everybody; we can't uphold a theory that says it is okay for me to do something just because I'm *me*, but not for you just because you're *not me*—that would be assuming that I should have privileges based on the mere fact that I'm *me*.

Altruism: Ideal and Real

As an alternative to ethical egoism, altruism hardly seems preferable if we view it in its ideal, normative sense: *Everybody ought to give up his or her own self-interest for others.* In that case we might want to complain that we only have one life to live, and why should we let the moochers and leeches drain our life away? If we let them take advantage of us, they surely will, and our lives are not things to be thrown away. Only a few philosophers have ever held such an altruistic theory, and only a few religions. Usually there is a realistic recognition of the fact that humans are apt to ask what's in it for them.

And yet, as mentioned earlier, we do know of people who sacrificed themselves for others because "it was the least they could do." Some did it once, in a heroic situation, and others did it over the course of a lifetime, setting their own needs aside in order to help others. We already know what the psychological egoist will say to such deeds, but we also know now that psychological egoism does not have all the answers. Even if it were true that people do seek self-gratification, there are many examples of animals helping other animals, sometimes even those of a different species. Baboons sacrifice themselves to leopards so that their tribes can make a getaway. Dolphins carry drowning people to the surface and even to the shore. Dogs save us from fire, and cats curl up to comfort us when we are sad. Are these animals really thinking of us rather than of themselves? Biologists say no, they are thinking of themselves, but sometimes in a vicarious way: The baboon instinctively wants his genes to survive in his sister's children; the dolphin acts by instinct, because that is what she

David Hume: Humans Are Benevolent by Nature

The Scottish philosopher David Hume (1711–1776) believed that compassion is the one human natural feeling that holds us together in a society. For Hume, all of ethics can be reduced to the idea that reason acts as the handmaiden of our feelings; there is no such thing as an *objectively* moral act—nothing is good or bad in itself, not even murder. The good and bad lies in our *feelings* towards the act. For Hume, all morality rests ultimately on our emotional responses, and there are no "moral facts" outside our own sensitivity. This theory of *emotionalism* says that whatever we like to see happen we think of as morally good, and whatever we would hate to see happen we think of as morally evil. And what is it we would like to see happen? For Hume the answer is, whatever corresponds to our *natural feeling of concern for others*. Contrary to Hobbes, Hume believes that humans are equipped with not only self-love, but also love for others, and this emotion gives us our moral values. We simply react with sympathy to others through a built-in instinct—at least most people do. Having the virtues of compassion and benevolence is a natural thing to Hume, and if we are a little short on such virtues, it simply means that we lack a natural ability, as when we are nearsighted. Such people are an exception to the rule.

does when her baby is suffocating. The dog is well trained and afraid of punishment, and the cat is grateful that you're sitting down, presenting a warm lap.

Is there, though, anything inherently *wrong* about acting to benefit yourself? Ideal altruism seems to imply just that, and if that is the case, it will never become a widely accepted moral theory, because it will work only for saints. According to Peter Singer, the Australian philosopher, there is another way of viewing altruism, a much more realistic and rational way: Looking after the interests of others makes sense, because, overall, everyone benefits from it.

In *The Expanding Circle* (1981) Singer suggests that egoism is in fact more costly than altruism. He presents a new version of a classical example, known as the prisoner's dilemma. Two early humans are attacked by a sabertooth cat. They obviously both want to flee, but (let us suppose) they also care for each other. If they both flee, one will be picked off and eaten. If one flees and one stays and fights, the fleeing one will live but the fighting one will die. If both stay and fight, there is a chance that they can fight the cat off. So it is actually in their self-interest to stay together, and all the more so if they care for each other. Singer's point is that evolution would favor such an arrangement, because trustworthy partners would be viewed as better than ones who

FIGURE 4.3 David Hume (1711–1776), Scottish philosopher and historian. Hume believed that human beings are born with a fellow-feeling, a feeling of compassion and empathy for others. Even persons who are generally selfish will feel compassion toward others if there is nothing in the situation that directly concerns them personally.

leave you behind to get eaten, and they would be selected in future partnerships. If you are an egoist and you manage to get picked as a partner by an altruist, you will be the one who benefits from the situation (the altruist is sure to stay, and you'll be able to get away). However, this will work only a few times; after a while the altruist will be wise to you and your kind. In the end, then, it is in your own self-interest not to be too self-interested.

Why is this viewpoint not just another version of the ethical egoist's credo of looking after yourself? Because it involves someone else's interests, too. It says that there is nothing wrong with keeping an eye out for yourself, as long as it doesn't happen at the expense of someone else's interests. In other words, the solution may not be myself *or* others, but myself *and* others. This idea, incorporated in the moral theory of utilitarianism, will be explored in the next chapter.

Narratives That Explore the Issue of Egoism

Chapter 7 includes the following stories, which deal with questions of selfishness: Gustave Flaubert's *Madame Bovary*, Margaret Mitchell's *Gone with the Wind*, and Ayn Rand's *Atlas Shrugged*.

Chapter 5

Using Your Reason, Part 1: Utilitarianism

Whether through reason or instinct, many people will choose as their ultimate moral guideline a rule that encourages them to make life bearable for as many people as possible. Perhaps we can actively do something to make people's lives better, and perhaps the only thing we can do to make their lives better is to stay out of their way. Perhaps we can't *strive* to make people happy, but we can at least do our best to limit their misery. This way of thinking just seems the decent thing to do for many of us, and when we include ourselves in those who should receive a general increase of happiness and decrease of misery, then the rule seems attractive, simple, and reasonable. Small wonder this attitude has become the cornerstone of one of the most vital and influential moral theories in human history: the theory of utilitarianism.

A utilitarian is a hard universalist in the sense that he or she believes that there is one universal moral code, which is the only one possible, and everyone ought to realize it. It is the *principle of utility*, or the *greatest happiness principle*: when choosing a course of action, *always choose the action that will maximize happiness and minimize unhappiness for the greatest number of people*. Whatever action conforms to this rule will be defined as a morally right action, and whatever action does not conform to this principle will be called a morally wrong action. In this way utilitarianism proposes a clear and simple moral criterion: Pleasure is good and pain is bad, and whatever causes happiness and/or decreases pain is morally right, and whatever causes pain or unhappiness is morally wrong. In other words, utilitarianism is interested in the *consequences* of our actions: If they are good, the action is right; if bad, the action is wrong. This focus on consequences makes utilitarianism a consequentialist theory, one that strives to provide the best possible consequences for as many people as possible. This principle, utilitarians claim, will provide answers to all real-life dilemmas.

Are all theories that focus on the consequences of actions utilitarian? No. As we saw in Chapter 4, the consequences we look for may be happy consequences for ourselves alone, and in that case we show ourselves to be egoists. We may focus on the consequences of our actions because we believe that those consequences justify our actions (in other words, that the end justifies the means), but this does not necessarily imply that the consequences we hope for are good in the utilitarian sense that they maximize happiness for the maximum number of people. We might, for instance, agree with the Italian statesman Machiavelli (1469–1527) that if the end is to maintain political power for oneself, one's king, or one's political party, then this will justify any means that one might use for that purpose, such as force, surveillance, or even deceit. Although this famous theory is indeed *consequentialist*, it does not qualify as utilitarian, because it doesn't have the common good as its ultimate end.

Jeremy Bentham and the Hedonistic Calculus

Reforming the System of Justice

It is often tempting to say that history moves in a certain direction. For example, in eighteenth-century Europe and America there was a general movement toward greater recognition of human rights and social equality, of the value of the individual, of the scope of human capacities, and of the need for and right to education. We call this time period *the Enlightenment* to indicate that rulers as well as scholars were becoming enlightened in terms of modern human rights, and also in terms of their staunch belief that human reason, *rationality*, held the key to the future—to the blossoming of the sciences as well as to social change. This time period is, appropriately, also referred to as the *Age of Reason,* not so much because people were particularly rational at the time or society was so very enlightened, in a social or political sense, but because the social, scientific, and philosophical *ideal* was reason.

Perhaps, then, it is tempting to say that history moved toward an appreciation of human rationality, but it would be more appropriate to say that it was moved along by the thoughts of certain thinkers. Such a mover was the English jurist and philosopher Jeremy Bentham (1748–1832).

Bentham, author of *Introduction to the Principles of Morals and Legislation*, did not really set out to create a new moral theory so much as a hands-on principle that could

FIGURE 5.1 Jeremy Bentham (1748–1832), English philosopher and jurist. Bentham borrowed Hume's concept of a utilitarian philosophy—a philosophy of usefulness. With his friend James Mill, he created utilitarianism, a system of thought based on the principle of utility: Maximize happiness and minimize unhappiness for as many as possible. Bentham donated his body to medical research and his money to the University College of London, with the provision that after research ended he was to be preserved and displayed at university board meetings. He still sits in his glass case in the basement at the University College, but the case is apparently no longer on display.

be used to remodel the British legal system. Indeed, it was not Bentham but another philosopher, David Hume, who invented the term *utilitarianism*. Hume believed that it is good for an action to have *utility* in the sense that it makes yourself and others happy, but he never developed this idea into a complete moral theory. Bentham, however, used the term to create a moral system for a new age.

In Bentham's England the feudal world was all but gone. Society had stratified into an upper class, a middle class, and a working class, and the world of the industrial revolution was just beginning. Conditions for the lowest class in the social hierarchy were appalling. Rights in the courts were, by and large, something that could be bought, which meant that those who had no means to buy them didn't have them. The world portrayed in the novels of Charles Dickens was developing; if you were in debt, you were taken to debtors' prison, where you stayed until your debt was paid. Whoever had funds could get out, but the poor faced spending the rest of their lives, with their family, inside debtors' prison. There were no child labor laws, and the exploitation of children in the work force, which horrified Marx a hundred years later, was rampant in Bentham's day. He saw it as terribly unfair and decided that the best way to redesign this system of unfair advantages would be to set up a simple moral rule that everyone could relate to, rich and poor alike.

Bentham said that what is good is what is pleasurable, and what is bad is what is painful. In other words, *hedonism* (pleasure-seeking) is the basis for his moral theory. The ultimate value is happiness or pleasure—these things are *intrinsically* valuable. Anything that helps us achieve happiness or avoid pain is of *instrumental* value, and because we may do something pleasurable in order to achieve another pleasure, pleasure can have both intrinsic and instrumental value. In order for this basic rule to be useful in legislation, we need to let people decide for themselves wherein their pleasure lies, and what they would rather avoid. Each person has a say in what pleasure and pain is, and each person's pleasure and pain counts equally. We might illustrate this viewpoint by traveling back in our minds to old London. A well-to-do middle-

Intrinsic Versus Instrumental Values

An *instrumental* value is one that can help us get something else that we want, that can be used as an instrument or tool to get something else. If you needed to get to class or work on time, a car might be the instrumental value that would get you there. If you didn't have a car, then money (or good credit) might be the instrumental value that would get you the car that would get you to school or to your workplace. How about going to school? If you go to school in order to get a degree, then you might say that going to school is an instrumental value that will get your degree. And the degree? An instrumental value that will get you a good job. And the job? An instrumental value that will get what? More money. And what do you want with that? A better lifestyle, a better place to live, good health,

and so on. And why do you want a better lifestyle? Why do you want to be healthy? This is where the chain comes to an end, because we have reached something that is obvious: We want those things because we want them. Perhaps they "make us happy," but the bottom line is that we value them for their own sake, *intrinsically*. Some values can of course be both instrumental and intrinsic; the car may help you get to school, but also, you've wanted the car for a long time just because you like it. Exercising may make you healthy, but you also may actually like it. And going to school is certainly a tool that can be used to get a degree, but some people appreciate training and knowledge for their own sake, not just because they can be used to get them somewhere in life.

class couple may feel that their greatest pleasure on a Saturday night is to don their fancy clothes, drive to Covent Garden in their shining coach, and go to the opera. The girl at Covent Garden, who tries to sell them a bouquet of wilting violets as they pass by, would probably not enjoy a trip to the opera as much as she would enjoy the bottle of gin she saves up for all week. Bentham would say she has a right to relish her gin, as much as the couple has a right to enjoy the opera. The girl can't tell the couple that gin is better, and they have no right to force their appreciation of the opera on her. For Bentham, what is good and bad for each person is a matter for each person to decide, and as such, his principle becomes a very *egalitarian* one.

The Hedonistic Calculus

How exactly do we decide on a course of action? Before we decide what to do, we must calculate the probable consequences of our actions. This is what has become known as Bentham's *hedonistic calculus*. We must, he says, investigate all aspects of the proposed consequences: (1) How *intense* will the pleasure or pain be? (2) How long will it last? (*duration*) (3) How certain can we be that it will follow from our action? (4) How far away is it, in time and space? (5) How big are the chances that it will be followed by a similar pleasure or a similar pain? (6) How big are the chances that it will *not* be followed by the opposite sensation (pain after pleasure, for example)? (7) How many people will be affected by our decision? After considering these questions, we then must do the following:

> Sum up all the values of all the *pleasures* on the one side, and those of all the pains on the other. . . . Take the balance; which, on the side of *pleasure*, will give the general *good tendency* of the act, with respect to the total number or community of individuals concerned; if on the side of pain, the general *evil tendency*, with respect to the same community.

What do we have here? A simple, democratic principle that seems to make no unreasonable demands of personal sacrifice, given that one's own pleasure and pain count just as much as anybody else's. Furthermore, in line with the scientific dreams of the Age of Reason, the proper moral conduct is calculated mathematically; values are reduced to a calculation of pleasure and pain, a method accessible to everyone with a basic understanding of arithmetic. By calculating pleasures and pains one can presumably get a truly rational solution to any moral as well as nonmoral (morally neutral) problem.

This sounds very good, and yet there is a problem—actually, there are several. For one thing, from where does Bentham get his numerical values? Ascertaining that our pleasure from eating a second piece of mud pie will be intense, but will not last long, and very likely will be followed by pain and remorse will not supply us with any numerical values to add or subtract: We have to make up the numerical values! This may not be as difficult as it seems, though. It is surprising how much people can agree on a value system, if they just can decide what should count as top and bottom value. If they agreed on a system that goes from − 10 to +10, for example, most people would agree to assigning specific numerical values to the various consequences of eating that second piece of mud pie. What value would be assigned to the aspect of *intensity*? Not a 10, because that probably would apply only to the first piece, but perhaps an 8, right? The *duration* of the pleasure might get a measly 2 or 3, and the chance that it would be followed by pleasure or pain certainly would be way down in the negative numbers, perhaps − 5 or worse. As for evaluating how many people are affected by the decision, that could take into account friends and family who don't want you to gain weight, or the person who owns the second piece of pie (which you stole), who will be deprived of it if you eat it. All such hypothetical situations can be ascribed a value if people can agree on a value system to use.

What this rating system adds up to is what most people would call "pro and con" lists, those lists we sometimes make for ourselves when we are in severe doubt about what to do—what major field of study to choose, whether to go home for Thanksgiving or celebrate it with friends, whether to get married, whether to take a new job, and so on. The only difference is that in this system we assign numerical values to the pros and cons. Can such a list really help us make rational decisions? Bentham believed it was an infallible system for rational choice. For most people who have given the system a try, though, it is evident that it may help in clarifying one's options, but the results are not always persuasive. You may end up with sixteen items on the con side and four on the pro side and still end up getting married or taking a new job simply because you just want to so badly. There are parts of the human psyche that just don't respond to rational arguments, and Bentham didn't have much appreciation for that. Interestingly enough, his godson and successor, John Stuart Mill, did have just such an appreciation, and we will look at him shortly.

But suppose you actually make a detailed list of the consequences of your actions. How exactly do you decide on the values that you assign each consequence? If you want to decide, for instance, whether to stay in school for the duration or quit and get a job and make fast money, how do you choose what things to put on your list? Critics of Bentham's approach say that if we assign a higher value to getting an education than to acquiring fast money, then it is because we are operating within a system that favors higher education; in other words, we are *biased*, and our choice of values reflects that bias. To put it another way, we rig the test even as we perform it. If we were operating within a system that favored making money—for instance, if we already had left school to make money, then our values would reflect that bias. The values, therefore, are truly arbitrary, depending on what we would like the outcome to be, and we can't trust the hedonistic calculus to give us an objective, mathematically certain picture of what to do. This does not mean that such lists are useless; they can tell us much about ourselves and our own preferences and biases. However, they can do little more than that.

The Uncertain Future

Utilitarianism might still be able to make use of a less presumptuous system, one designed to give guidance and material for reflection rather than objectively calculated solutions. Even with that kind of system, though, there are problems to be dealt with. One lies in the concept of *consequences* itself. Of course we can't claim that an action has any consequences before we actually have taken that action. The consequences we are evaluating are hypothetical; they have yet to occur. How can we decide once and for all if an action is morally good, if the consequences are still up in the air? We have to (1) make an educated guess and hope for the best; (2) act; and (3) wait around for the results to come in. If we're lucky and wise, the results will be as good as what we hoped for. But suppose they aren't? You may intend to create much happiness, and your calculations may be educated, but your intentions still may be foiled by forces beyond your control. In that case, it is the *end result* that counts, and not your fine intentions and calculations. How long do we have to wait until we know if our actions were morally good or evil? It may take a long time before all the effects are known—maybe a hundred years or more. Critics of utilitarianism say that it is just not reasonable to use a moral system that doesn't allow us to know if what we did was morally right or wrong until sometime in the far-off future. Furthermore, how will we ever be able to decide anything in the first place? Thousands—perhaps millions—of big and small consequences result from everything we do. Do we have to calculate them all? How can we ever make a quick decision if we have to go through such a complicated process every time?

Answers to such criticisms were provided by philosopher and economist John Stuart Mill (1806–1873). For one thing, Mill says, we don't have to calculate every little effect of our action; we can rely on the common experience of humanity. Through the millennia humans have had to make similar decisions all the time, and we can make use of their successes and failures to decide on our own actions. (Because Mill had actually given up on calculating every action to an exact mathematical value, it was easier for him than for Bentham to allow for some uncertainty in future results.) What about having to wait a long time for future consequences to happen, in order to pass judgment on the morality of our action? Mill says that all we have to do is wait a reasonable amount of time—a short wait for small actions, a longer wait for bigger actions. Mill relies on us to know intuitively what he means, and perhaps we do. But the problems inherent in utilitarianism are not solved with these suggestions, merely diffused a little.

The Moral Universe of Utilitarianism: Advantages and Problems of Sheer Numbers

Initially, the thought of creating as much pleasure as possible for as many as possible seems a positive one. If we read on in Bentham's writings, we even find that "the many" may not be limited to humans. Bentham's theory was so advanced for its time that it gave the right to seek pleasure and avoid pain to all humans, regardless of social standing. Bentham went even further than this, however. He said that the criterion for who belongs in the moral universe is not who has the capability to speak or to reason, but *who can suffer*, and surely, suffering is not limited to human beings. The importance of this inclusion will be discussed in Chapter 14.

If we assume that the capacity to suffer (and feel pleasure) qualifies a living organism for inclusion in the moral universe, and if we believe that each individual's pleasure counts equally, we find ourselves with a dramatically expanded moral universe. Even today, the idea that all creatures who can suffer deserve to be treated with dignity does not meet with the approval of every policymaker. Moreover, if the decrease of suffering and the increase of happiness are all that counts for all these members of our moral universe, what does it mean for our decision if the happiness of some can be obtained only at the cost of the suffering of others? This is where we encounter the problem of sheer numbers in utilitarianism, because whatever creates more happiness for more individuals, or decreases their pain, is morally right *by definition*. If giving up using animal-tested household products causes human housekeepers only minor inconvenience, then we have no excuse not to do it, because major suffering is caused by such testing. However, if it could be shown that only a few animals would have to suffer (even if they would suffer horribly) so that an immense number of humans would find their housecleaning greatly eased, would it then be permissible to cause such suffering? Yes, if the pleasure gained from easy housecleaning in a large number of households could be added up and favorably compared to the immense suffering of only a very few nonhuman animals.

The argument for doing whatever benefits more living creatures, human or non-human, is usually advanced with regard to animal testing of medical procedures that could benefit humans. However, because sheer numbers are all we're concerned with, the housecleaning example works, too. (Curing human ailments is not intrinsically "better" than helping humans clean their houses—what matters is the happiness that is created and the misery that is prevented.) Suppose feline leukemia could be cured by subjecting ten humans to painful experiments? The humans would certainly suffer, but all cats would, from then on, be free of feline leukemia. For some, this type of example reveals the perversely narrow focus of utilitarianism; looking at pleasure and pain and adding them up is simply not enough. For others, examples like this one only confirm that all creatures matter, and no one's pain should be more, or less, important than anyone else's.

To focus on the problem, let's assume that we are faced with a situation in which some humans are sacrificed for the happiness and welfare of other humans. Suppose it is revealed that governments around the world have for years had a secret agreement with aliens from outer space—perhaps the ones with big, dark eyes and gray skin that the tabloids have entertained us with over the last few years. Suppose the governments have agreed to deny consistently that UFOs exist, and not to interfere with occasional alien abductions of humans for medical experiments. In return, at the end of their experiments, the aliens will provide humanity with a cure for all viral diseases. For a great number of people this would be a trade well worth the suffering of the "speci-mens" involved—provided that they themselves would not be among the specimens. Indeed, some humans might even *volunteer* for the experiments, but let us assume, as a condition, that the human subjects are reluctant participants. In fact, no volunteers are accepted. Although some people would gladly commit their fellow humans to death from suffering, others would insist that it is not right; somehow, these humans do not deserve such a fate, and the immense advantages of humankind forever do not really make up for it. In other words, some may have a moral sense that the price is too high, but utilitarianism can't acknowledge such a moral intuition, because its only moral criterion is one of sheer numbers. For many, the morality of utilitarianism is counterintuitive when applied to some very poignant human situations.

Still, the salvation of humanity is a forceful argument. Let us suppose, however, that we are not talking about salvation from disease, but about salvation from boredom. Television is already moving toward showing live or videotaped events involving human suffering and death; home movies are often the source of this footage, and this form of "entertainment" has become increasingly popular. A writer for *TV Guide*, supposedly the most read publication in the world, worried a few years ago that this kind of programming might start a trend toward "staged" real-life situations of suffer-ing and death, all for the sake of entertainment. (This concern was mentioned earlier, in Chapter 1.) The bottom line is, of course, ratings. Will viewers choose to watch real-time shows of criminals who are granted one television hour to run through a city or neighborhood, avoiding snipers and hoping to live through it all and win their freedom—as a part of a televised option to execution? The Romans watched Christians, slaves, criminals, prisoners of war, and wild animals fight each other, with much appreciation for the entertainment value of such events. If they had had the ability to televise the events, might we assume that they would have done so, having recognized that "bread and circuses" (food and entertainment) would appease the unruly masses of Rome? According to the utilitarian calculation a great number of people may be hugely entertained by the immense suffering of one or a few. How far are we allowed to "let numbers run away with us" in terms of disregarding people's inherent right to fair treatment?

A common utilitarian reply is that in the long run the utilitarian calculation does not provide for overall happiness; people start worrying about being victimized, and social unrest follows. Until that happens, though, utilitarians must conclude that there is justification in letting a large number of people enjoy the results of the suffering of a few (or even enjoy the suffering itself).

John Stuart Mill: Higher and Lower Pleasures

Some Pleasures Are Higher than Others

Bentham was not alone in designing the theory of utilitarianism. He and his close friend, James Mill, worked out the specifics of the new moral system together. Mill's son was John Stuart Mill, Bentham's godson (whom we have already mentioned). The young Mill was a very bright boy—today such precocious kids are sometimes called "Alpha-children"—and James Mill's ambition was to develop his son's talents and intelligence as much as possible, and as fast as possible. The boy responded well, learned fast, and was able to read Greek as well as Latin at an early age. Throughout his childhood he was groomed to become a scientist. He was privately tutored and performed marvelously until he came to a halt at the age of twenty, struck by a nervous breakdown. He took time out to reexamine his life and his future, turned his back on the sciences, and decided to go into his dad's business and become a social thinker. As a social thinker he became one of the most influential persons of the nineteenth century, laying the foundation for many of the political ideas in the Western world on both the liberal and the conservative side.

Mill's aim was to take his godfather's and father's theory of utilitarianism and redesign it to fit a more sophisticated age. What had seemed overwhelmingly important to Bentham—a more just legal system—was no longer the primary goal, due to the realization that without proper education for the general population, true social equality would not be obtained. Also, Mill realized that Bentham's version of utilitarianism had several flaws. For one thing, it was too simple; it relied on a very

FIGURE 5.2 John Stuart Mill (1806–1873), English philosopher and economist, and Bentham's godson. Believing that utilitarianism was the only reasonable moral system, Mill nevertheless saw Bentham's version as rather crude and created a more sophisticated version of the principle of utility, taking into consideration the qualitative differences between pleasures.

straightforward system of identifying good with pleasure and evil with pain, without specifying the nature of pleasure and pain. (Some say this was actually one of the strengths of early utilitarianism, but Mill saw it as a serious flaw.) Bentham's version also assumed that people were so rational that they would always follow the moral calculations. Mill pointed out, however, that even if people are clearly shown that it would give them and others more overall pleasure to change their course of action, they are likely to continue doing what they are used to, because people are creatures of habit, and our emotions often dictate what we do, rather than cool deliberation. We can't, therefore, rely on our rationality to the extreme degree that Bentham thought we could. (This doesn't mean, of course, that we can't *educate* children and adults to use their heads more profitably.) We will return to the education question in a while, but first let us look at how Mill decided to redesign the theory of utilitarianism.

Mill was a more complex person than his godfather, and his theory reflects this complexity. For Mill the idea that humans seek pleasure, and that moral goodness lies in obtaining that pleasure, is only half the story—but it is the half that is most frequently misunderstood. What do people think when they hear this idea? That all that counts is easy gratification of any desire they may have—in other words, a "doctrine worthy only of swine," as Mill says, repeating the words of the critics of utilitarianism. And because people reject the notion of seeking only swinish pleasures, they reject utilitarianism as an unworthy theory. They get upset, said Mill, precisely because they are not pigs and want more out of life than a pig could ever want. People are simply not content with basic pleasures, and a good moral and social theory should reflect this. Furthermore, says Mill, all theories that have advocated happiness have been accused of talking about easy gratification, but that is an unfair criticism when applied to utilitarianism. Even Epicurus (341–270 B.C.E.) held that there many things in life, other than than physical pleasures, which can bring us happiness, and there is nothing in utilitarianism that says we have to define pleasure and happiness as mere gratification of physical desires.

Why was Mill so uneasy about being accused of seeking gratification of physical desires? Perhaps he truly preferred other things in life, but perhaps we can seek further explanation by looking at the changing times in which he lived. By the time Mill wrote his book *Utilitarianism* (1863), the British Empire was already into the early years of the Victorian Era, and morals were subtly undergoing a change; preoccupation with physical pleasures was, on the whole, frowned upon in the middle classes, more so than in the previous generation—not that there was not as much pleasure to be found in physical indulgence as ever, but it was not considered proper to display such indulgence. For many this signifies an age of hypocrisy, of double standards, but it would be unfair to accuse Mill of such double standards, because several of his truly innovative social ideas stemmed from his indignation toward this preoccupation with the way other people choose to live (we'll get back to this in the next section). However, it may have been a sign of the times that Mill felt compelled to reassure his readers that they could be followers of utilitarianism without being labeled as hedonists.

What, then, does Mill propose? That some pleasures are more valuable, "higher," than others. That on the whole, humans prefer to hold on to their dignity and strive for truly fulfilling experiences rather than settle for easy contentment. *It is better to be a human dissatisfied than a pig satisfied, better to be Socrates dissatisfied than a fool satisfied*, says Mill. Even if the great pleasures in life require some effort—for instance, one has to learn to appreciate good music, or learn math in order to understand the joy of solving a mathematical problem—then it is worth the effort, because the pleasure is greater than if you had just remained passive.

Now the question becomes, who is to say which pleasures are the higher ones and which are the lower ones? We seem predisposed to assume that the physical pleasures are the lower ones, but need that be the case? Mill proposes a test: We must ask people *who are familiar with both kinds of pleasure*, and whatever they choose as the higher goal is the ultimate answer. Suppose we gather a group of people who sometimes order a pizza and beer and watch "Monday Night Football" but also occasionally go out to a French restaurant before watching "Masterpiece Theatre" on PBS. We ask them which activity—pizza and football, or French food and "Masterpiece Theatre"—is the higher pleasure. If the test works, we must accept it if the majority say that on the whole they think pizza and football is the higher pleasure. But will Mill accept that? This is the problem with his test—it appears that he will not:

> Capacity for the nobler feelings is in most natures a very tender plant, easily killed, not only by hostile influences, but by mere want of sustenance; and in the majority of young persons it speedily dies away if the occupations to which their position in life has devoted them, and the society into which it has thrown them, are not favorable to keeping that higher capacity in exercise. Men lose their high aspirations as they lose their intellectual tastes, because they have not time or opportunity for indulging them; and they addict themselves to inferior pleasures not because they deliberately prefer them, but because they are either

The Naturalistic Fallacy

Mill acknowledges that there is no proof that happiness is the ultimate value because no founding principles can be proved, and yet he offers a proof by analogy. This proof has bothered philosophers ever since, because it actually does more harm than good to Mill's own system of thought. The analogy goes like this: The only way we can prove that something is visible is when we know people actually see it. Likewise, the only way we can prove that something is desirable is when we know people actually desire it. Everyone desires happiness, so happiness is therefore the ultimate goal. Why does this not work as an analogy? It doesn't work because being "visible" is not analogous to being "desirable." When we say that something is visible we are describing what people actually see. But when we say that something is desirable, we are not describing what people desire. If a lot of people desire drugs, we do not therefore conclude that drugs are "desirable," because "desirable" means that something *should be desired*; we prescribe that it *should be* desired, not that it *is* desired. The problem, however, goes deeper. Even if it were true that we could find out what is morally desirable by doing a nose count, why should we then have to conclude that because a lot of people desire some

thing, there should be a moral requirement that we all desire it? In other words, we are stepping from "is" (from a descriptive statement that says something is desired) to "ought" (to a normative/prescriptive statement that says something ought to be desired), and as the philosopher David Hume pointed out, there is nothing in a descriptive statement that allows us to proceed from what people actually do to a rule that states what people ought to do. This step, known as the *naturalistic fallacy*, is commonly taken by thinkers, politicians, writers, and other people of influence, but it is nevertheless a dangerous step to take. We can't make a policy based solely on what is the case. For instance, if it were to turn out that women actually are better parents than men by nature, it still would not be fair to conclude that men ought not to be single fathers (or that all women ought to be mothers), because we can't pass from a simple statement of fact to a statement of policy. Although this idea is occasionally contested by various thinkers, it remains one of philosophy's ground rules. In Chapter 15 we will take a closer look at some problems associated with applying the naturalistic fallacy to the world of human affairs.

the only ones to which they have access or the only ones which they are any longer capable of enjoying.

What does this mean? It means if you vote for pizza and football as the overall winner, Mill will claim you have lost the capacity for enjoying gourmet French food and intellectual television (which demands some attention from your intellect). In other words, he has rigged his own test. This has caused some critics to voice the opinion that Mill is an intellectual snob, a "cultural imperialist" trying to impose his own standards on the general population. And the immediate victim of this procedure? The egalitarian principle that was the foundation of Bentham's version of utilitarianism—that one person equals one vote regarding what is pleasurable and what is painful—collapses under Mill's test. According to him, we have to go to the "authorities of happiness" to find out what it is that everybody ought to desire.

Mill's Political Vision: Equality and No Harm to Others

Did Mill achieve what he wanted? Certainly he wanted to redesign utilitarianism so that it reflected the complexity of a cultured population, but did he intend to set himself up as a cultural despot? It appears that what he wanted was something else entirely. Whereas Bentham wanted the girl who sold flowers at Covent Garden to be able to enjoy her gin in peace, Mill wants to *educate* her so that she won't *need* her gin anymore and will be able to experience the glorious pleasures enjoyed by the middle-class couple who have learned to appreciate the opera. What Mill had in mind, in other words, was probably the greater pleasure that can be derived from achievement, not elitism. We feel a special fulfillment if we've worked hard on a math problem, or a piece of music, or a painting, and we finally get it right. Mill thought this type of pleasure should be made available to everyone with a capacity for it. This Mill saw as equality of a higher order, based on general education. Once such education is attained, the choices of the educated person are his or hers alone, and nobody has the right to interfere. However, until such a level is achieved, society has a right to gently inform its children and childlike adults about what they ought to prefer.

This sounds today like paternalism, and there is much in Mill's position that supports this point of view. In order to look more closely at Mill's ideas of what is best for people, we must take a look at what has become known as the *Harm Principle*.

Although the principle of utility provides a general guideline for personal as well as political action in terms of increasing happiness and decreasing unhappiness, it says very little about the circumstances under which one might justifiably become involved in changing other people's lives for the better. Mill had very specific ideas about the limitations of such involvement; in his essay *On Liberty* (1859), he examines the proper limits of government control. Because history has progressed from a time when rulers preyed upon their populations and the populations had to be protected from the rulers' despotic actions to a time when democratic rulers, in principle, *are* the people, the idea of absolute authority on the part of rulers should no longer be a danger to the people. However, reality shows us that this is not the case, because we now must face the *tyranny of the majority*. In other words, those who now need protection are minorities (and here Mill thinks of political minorities) who may wish to conduct their lives in ways different from the ways of the majority and its idea of what is right and proper. As an answer to the question of how much the social majority is allowed to exert pressure on the minority, Mill proposes the "harm principle":

> That principle is, that the sole end for which mankind are warranted, individually or collectively, in interfering with the liberty of action of any of their number, is self-protection. That the only purpose for which power can be rightfully exercised over any member of a civilized community, against his will, is to prevent harm to others. His own good, either physical or moral, is not a sufficient warrant. He cannot rightfully be compelled to do or forbear because it will be better for him to do so, because it will make him happier, because, in the opinions of others, to do so would be wise, or even right. These are good reasons for remonstrating with him, or reasoning with him, or persuading him, or entreating him, but not for compelling him, or visiting him with any evil in case he do otherwise. To justify that, the conduct from which it is desired to deter him must be calculated to produce evil to someone else. The only part of the conduct of anyone, for which he is amenable to society, is that which concerns others. In the part which merely concerns himself, his independence is, of right, absolute. Over himself, over his own body and mind, the individual is sovereign.

This very radical point of view has had extremely far-reaching consequences; in combination with other social theories of the nineteenth century it, in effect, became the direct ancestor of two political lines of thought that, oddly, are now at odds with one another. We usually refer to Mill's view as *liberalism* because of its emphasis on personal liberty. This insistence on personal liberty and noninterference by the government has become a key issue in the political theory of *laissez-faire*, the hands-off policy that requires as little government interference as possible, primarily in private enterprise. The idea behind the laissez-faire policy is that if we all look after our own business, and no authorities make our business theirs, then we all are better off. This is today considered a conservative economic philosophy, expressed in its extreme form by the Libertarian party. However, the harm principle also has become the foundation of what Americans today refer to as liberalism, which encompasses the idea of *civil liberties*—the rights of citizens to, within their right to privacy, do what they want provided that it does no harm, and to have their *government* ensure that as little harm and as much happiness is created for as many people as possible. In a sense, Mill's harm principle has spawned inspirational ideas for the modern American political right as well as the political left.

The limitations of the right to privacy are more numerous than might be apparent at first glance. For one thing, what exactly does it mean that we are amenable to society only for conduct that concerns others? What Mill had in mind certainly included the right for consenting adults to engage in sexual activity in the privacy of

Mill and the Women's Cause

Mill is today recognized as the first influential male speaker for political equality between men and women in modern Western history. (In England, Mary Wollstonecraft published her *Vindication of the Rights of Women* in 1792, but already in 1673 the French author Poulain de la Barre, a student of Descartes, had published *De l'égalité des deux sexes*, in which he argued for total equality between men and women because of their equality in reasoning power. This book, however, was largely ignored for a long time.) Mill's book *The Subjection of Women* (1869) revealed to his readers the abyss of inequality separating the lives of men and women in what was then considered a modern society. His exposé of this inequality was a strong contributing factor in women's obtaining the right to vote in England, as well as elsewhere in the Western world. It is often mentioned in this context that Mill was inspired by his longtime friend and later wife, Harriet Taylor. Scholars now believe that Mill's fight for women's rights was not just a matter of subtle inspiration from Mrs. Taylor, but a direct result of their long and detailed intellectual discussions, for Mrs. Taylor was well educated and an intellectual in her own right.

their own homes, regardless of what any moral majority might feel about the issue. In such cases, only nosey neighbors might be "concerned," and for Mill their right to concern would be proportionate to the extent that they would be exposed to the activities of the couple in question. In other words, if it takes binoculars for you to become exposed to a situation (and hence become "concerned") then put aside your binoculars and mind your own business.

But what about, say, a teenage girl who decides to put an end to her life because her boyfriend broke up with her? Might that fall within the harm principle, in the sense that she is harming only herself, so society has no right to interfere? Here Mill might answer two things. First, she is not harming only herself, but her family as well, who would grieve for her and feel guilty for not having prevented it. Not only that, but there is the problem of role models. If other teens in the same situation learn about her suicide, they might think it would be a good idea to follow her example, and more harm would be caused. Mill also might add the following: This situation does not fall under the harm principle, because the girl is a) not an adult, and b) not in a rational frame of mind:

> This doctrine is meant to apply only to human beings in the maturity of their faculties. We are not speaking of children, or of young persons below the age which the law may fix as that of manhood or womanhood. Those who are still in a state to require being taken care of by others, must be protected against

their own actions as well as against external injury. For the same reason, we may leave out of consideration those backward states of society in which the race itself may be considered as in its nonage. . . . Despotism is a legitimate mode of government in dealing with barbarians, provided the end be their improvement, and the means justified by actually effecting that end. Liberty, as a principle, has no application to any state of things anterior to the time when mankind have become capable of being improved by free and equal discussion. . . . But as soon as mankind have attained the capacity of being guided to their own improvement by conviction or persuasion (a period long since reached in all nations with whom we need here concern ourselves), compulsion . . . is no longer admissible as a means to their own good, and justifiable only for the security of others.

With this addition to the harm principle, Mill certainly makes it clear that children are excluded, but so is anyone who, in Mill's mind, belongs to a "backward" state of society. Again, we see evidence of Mill's complexity: He is liberal, he wants to protect civil liberties, but he is also paternalistic: Whoever is not an "adult" by his definition must be guided or coerced to comply. Individuals as well as whole peoples who fall outside of the "adult" category must be governed by others until they reach sufficient maturity to take affairs into their own hands. Critics have seen this as a defense of not merely cultural but also *political* imperialism: There are peoples who are too primitive to rule themselves, so someone else has to do it for them and bring them up to Western standards. Who are these peoples? We may assume that it includes the old British colonies. This viewpoint, sometimes referred to as "the white man's burden," is very far from being politically correct in our era, but is it fair to accuse Mill of being an imperialist? Perhaps, but it must be added that what Mill wanted was for everyone to be educated to the extent that they could enjoy full civil liberty as well as the good things in life. Certainly the "good things" are defined by Mill as what *he* considers good (the "higher pleasures"), but his aim is still the utilitarian one of maximizing happiness for the greatest number and minimizing pain and misery on a global scale. If Mill was biased towards the British way of life, it may be understandable: That way of life was in many ways the best the planet earth had to offer in the nineteenth century for those with access to a good education. It was, in our terms, an extremely "civilized" culture, at least for the upper and middle classes. Perhaps, then, we can think of Mill not merely as an intellectual snob, but as an educator who wanted to see everybody get the same good chances in life that he got, and enjoy life as much as he did.

Act and Rule Utilitarianism

In the twentieth century it became clear to philosophers attracted to utilitarianism that there were severe problems inherent in the idea that a morally right act is an act that makes as many people as possible happy. One problem is that, as we saw previously, it is conceivable that many people will achieve much pleasure from the misery of a few others, and even in situations where people don't know that their happiness is achieved by the pain of others (so that it does not in any way constitute sadism), this is still an uncomfortable thought. It is especially so if one believes in the Golden Rule (which John Stuart Mill did), which holds that that we should do for others what we would like done for ourselves, and refrain from doing to others what we would not like done to ourselves. Mill himself was aware of the problem and allowed that in the long run, a society in which a majority abuses a minority is not a good society. That still means that we have to explain why the *first* cases of happiness occurring from the misery of others are wrong, even before they have established themselves as a pattern, with increasingly bad consequences. In a sense, Mill tried to address the problem. He suggested that utilitarianism be taken as a general policy to be applied to general situations. He did not, however, develop the idea further within his own philosophy.

Others have taken up the challenge and suggested that it is just that particular formulation of utilitarianism that creates the problem; given another formulation, the problem disappears. If we stay with the *classical* formulation, the principle of utility goes like this: *Always do whatever act will create the greatest happiness for the greatest number of people.* In this version we are stuck with the problems that we saw earlier; for example, the torture of innocents may bring about great pleasure for a large group of people. The Russian author Dostoyevsky explored this thought in his book *The Brothers Karamazov*. Suppose your happiness, and everyone else's, is bought by the suffering of an innocent child? (We will look more closely at this idea in Chapter 7.) It is not hard to see this as a Christian metaphor, with Jesus' suffering as the condition of happiness for humans, but there is an important difference: Jesus was a volunteer; an innocent child is not. In any event, a utilitarian, by definition, would have to agree that if a great deal of suffering could be alleviated by putting an innocent person through Hell, then it would be worth the suffering. It also would be worth putting nonhuman animals through Hell, or entire populations of humans. The glorious end (increased happiness for a majority) will in any event justify the means, even if the means violate these beings' right to life, or to fair treatment.

Suppose we reformulate utilitarianism. Suppose we say, Always do whatever *type of act* will create the greatest happiness for the greatest number of people. Then what is the result? If we try to torture an innocent person for the sake of others' well-being, we find that it may have worked for the first formulation, because that was a one-time situation, but if we view it as a *type* of situation—one that is likely to recur again and again, because we have now set up a *rule* for such types of situations—it becomes impermissible: The consequences of torturing *a lot* of innocent people will not bring about great happiness for anyone in the long run. Is this, perhaps, what Mill was trying to say? This new formulation is referred to as *rule utilitarianism*, and it is advocated by many twentieth-century utilitarians who wish to distance themselves from the uncomfortable implications of the classical theory, now referred to as *act utilitarianism*. If this new version is used, they say, then we can focus on the good consequences of a certain type of act rather than on the singular act itself. It may work once for a student to cheat on a final, but cheating as a rule is not only dangerous (the student herself is

FIGURE 5.3 *Abandon Ship!* Columbia Pictures, 1957. Facing a hard decision, Captain Holmes (Tyrone Power) surveys the situation after the shipwreck. Soon he must decide which passengers are fit to row to Africa and who must be thrown overboard, sacrificed so that the others have a chance to survive. The story of *Abandon Ship!* is outlined in Chapter 7 as an illustration of a utilitarian approach, but the discussion also includes elements from Kantian deontology (see Chapter 6).

likely to be found out), but it is also immoral to the rule utilitarian, because very bad consequences would occur if everyone were to cheat. Professors would get wise in no time, and nobody would graduate. Students would be miserable, and professors, too. Society would miss out on a lot of well-educated college graduates. The Golden Rule is in this way fortified: Don't do something if you can't imagine it as a rule for every-body, because a rule not suited for everyone can have no good overall consequences.

Some critics have objected that not everything we do can be made into a rule with good consequences. After all, lots of the things we like to do are unique to us, and why should we assume that just because one person likes to collect movie memo-rabilia, the world would be happier if everyone collected movie memorabilia? This is not the way it is supposed to work, say the rule utilitarians. You have to specify that the rule is valid for people *under similar circumstances*, and you have to specify what *exceptions* you might want to make. It may be morally good to make sure you are home in time for dinner only if you have a family to come home to, but not if you are living by yourself. And the moral goodness of being there in time for dinner depends on there not being something of greater importance that you should see to. Such things might be homework, a crisis at work, a medical emergency, extracurricular activities, walking the dog, seeing your lover, watching a television show all the way to the end, talking on the phone, or whatever you choose. They may not all qualify as good exceptions, but *you* should specify in your rule which ones are acceptable. Once you have created such a rule, the utilitarian ideal will work, say the rule utilitarians; it will make more people happy and fewer people unhappy in the long run. If it doesn't, then you just have to rework the rule until you get it right.

The problem with this is that it may be asking too much of people. Are we likely to ask ourselves about the consequences of whatever it is we want to do every time we are about to take action? Are we likely to envision everyone doing the same thing? Probably not, and we may even tell ourselves that not everyone is going to do the same thing, so we may as well go ahead and do it. Even if it is wrong to make lots of private phone calls from a company phone, it won't make much difference if one person makes private calls, as long as nobody else does. As long as most people comply, we can still get away with breaking the rule without creating bad consequences. Even so, we are in the wrong, because a healthy moral theory will not set "myself" up as an exception to the rule just because "I'm me and I deserve it." This, as philosopher James Rachels has pointed out, is as much a form of discrimination as are racism and sexism. We might call it "me-ism," but we already have a good word for it, *egoism*, and we already know that that is unacceptable.

The addition to utilitarianism, that one ought to look for rules that apply to everyone, is for many a major step in the right direction. Rule utilitarianism certainly was not, however, the first philosophy to ask, what if everybody did what you intend to do? Although just about every parent must have said that to her or his child at some time or other, the one person who is credited with putting it into a philosophical framework is the German philosopher Immanuel Kant. There is one important difference between the way Kant asks the question and the way it has later been developed by rule utilitarians, though. Rule utilitarianism asks, What will be the *consequences* of everybody doing what you intend to do? Kant asks, Could you wish for it to be a *universal law* that everyone does what you intend to do? We will look more closely at this difference in the next chapter.

Narratives That Argue for and Against Utilitarianism

Chapter 5 includes discussions of utilitarian solutions to moral problems in Johan Herman Wessel's "The Blacksmith and the Baker," a satirical poem; Dostoyevsky's novel *The Brothers Karamazov*; Ursula Le Guin's short story "The Ones Who Walk Away from Omelas"; and a film based on a true story, *Abandon Ship!*

Chapter 6

Using Your Reason, Part 2: Kant's Deontology

On the whole, we might say that there are two major ways in which we can approach a problem. We might either ask ourselves, What happens if I do X?, in which case we're letting ourselves be guided by the future consequences of our actions, or we might ask ourselves, Is X right or wrong in itself, regardless of the consequences? The first approach is utilitarian, provided that we are looking for *good* consequences for as many as possible. (We might have a perverted lust to create miserable consequences for as many as possible, perhaps even including ourselves, but that would, of course, not belong in the category of utilitarianism.) The version of the second type of question that has had the most influence is Kant's duty theory.

Kant's moral theory is often referred to as *deontology* (duty theory, from Greek *deon*, doing what you are supposed to). Kant believed that his theory was the very opposite

FIGURE 6.1 Immanuel Kant (1724–1804), German philosopher. This painting shows him second from the left, dining with friends. Perhaps the most influential Western philosopher of "modern times" (the seventeenth to the twentieth centuries), Kant was reportedly a popular guest at dinners and parties and equally popular with his students.

of a consequentialist theory and that his moral analysis was, in part, written to show how little a moral theory that worries about consequences has to do with true moral thinking. Let us look at an example to illustrate this fundamental difference.

To Do the Right Thing

The Good Will

Some years ago, newspapers reported an accident somewhere in the Pacific Northwest. A family had gone away for a short vacation and had left their keys with their neighbor so that he could water their plants and look after the place. On Sunday afternoon, a few hours before they were due to arrive home, the neighbor thought he would do them a favor and make sure they would come home to a nice, toasty house,

Kant: His Life and Work

Some famous and influential people lead lives of adventure. The life of Immanuel Kant (1724–1804) seems to have been an *intellectual* adventure exclusively, for he never did anything in his personal life that might in any other way be considered adventurous. He was raised in the town of Königsberg, Prussia, in an atmosphere of strict Protestant values, by his devout mother and by his father, who made a meager living as a saddler. He entered Königsberg University, studied theology, graduated, and tutored for a while, until he was offered a position at the university in his hometown. In 1770 he became a full professor in logic and metaphysics, and this was when the philosophical drama began, for Kant achieved an influence not only in Western philosophy, but also in science and social thinking—an influence that was never eclipsed by anyone else in the eighteenth century. He developed theories about astronomy that are still considered plausible; he laid out rules for a new social world of mutual respect for all citizens; he made contributions to philosophy of law and religion; he attempted to map the entire spectrum of human intelligence in his three major works, *Critique of Pure Reason* (1781), *Critique of Practical Reason* (1788), and *Critique of Judgment* (1790), as well as in smaller works such as *Prolegomena to Every Future Metaphysics* (1783) and *Grounding for the Metaphysics of Morals* (1785). When Kant calls a book a "critique," he is not implying that he is merely writing a negative criticism of a subject; he is, rather, looking for the *condition of possibility* of that subject. In *Critique of Pure Reason* he asks, "What makes it possible for me to achieve knowledge?" (in other words, what is the condition of possibility of knowledge?). In *Critique of Practical Reason* he asks about the condition of possibility of moral thinking, and in *Critique of Judgment* he examines the condition of possibility for appreciating natural and artistic beauty. In all of these fields his insights helped shape new disciplines and redefine old disciplines. Kant was never an agitator for his ideas, though; on the contrary, he was famous for living an extremely quiet and highly regulated life. He remained single throughout his life, and his life's interest seems to have been his work. His students have reported that he was in fact a good and popular teacher.

because the temperature was dropping, so he went in and turned on the furnace. You've guessed what happened: The house burned down and the family came home to a burned-out lot. This was the extent of the newspaper coverage, but suppose it had been reported by a classical utilitarian. Then the article might have ended something like this: "The neighbor will have to answer for the consequences of this terrible deed." Why? Because, given that only consequences count, the act of turning on the furnace was a terrible one, regardless of the man's good intentions. As it is sometimes said, the road to hell is paved with good intentions. In other words, only your deeds count, not what you intended to do.

Suppose, however, that a Kantian had written the article. Then it might have ended like this: "This good neighbor should be praised for his kind thought and good intentions regardless of the fact that the family lost their home; that consequence certainly can't be blamed on him, because all he intended to do was the right thing."

Let us continue speculating. Suppose the house didn't burn down, but instead provided a warm, cozy shelter for and saved the lives of the entire family, who (shall we say) had all come down with pneumonia. The utilitarian would have to say that the act of lighting the furnace was now a shining example of a morally good deed, but Kant? He would not change his mind: The neighbor's action was good because of the intention, and the consequences of the act don't make it any better or worse. For Kant the presence of a *good will* is what makes an action morally good, regardless of its consequences. Imagine a person who is rich, witty, and intelligent—those characteristics are worth nothing (and actually can be quite dangerous)—if the person doesn't have a good will. Therefore, even if you never accomplished what you intended, you still are morally praiseworthy provided you tried hard to do the right thing. In *Grounding for the Metaphysics of Morals*, Kant assures us that

> Even if, by some especially unfortunate fate or by the niggardly provision of stepmotherly nature, this will should be wholly lacking in the power to accomplish its purpose; if with the greatest effort it should yet achieve nothing, and only the good will should remain (not, to be sure, as a mere wish but as the summoning of all the means in our power), yet would it, like a jewel, still shine by its own light as something which has its full value in itself. Its usefulness or fruitlessness can neither augment nor diminish this value.

The Categorical Imperative

How do we know that our intentions are good? We put them to a test. In his book *Grounding for the Metaphysics of Morals* Kant says we must ask whether we can imagine our intentions as a general law for everybody. This means that our intentions have to *conform to a rational principle*. We have to think hard in order to determine if we're about to do the right thing or not; it can't be determined just by some gut-level feeling. However, we don't have to wait around for the actual consequences in order to determine if our intentions are good—all we have to do is determine if we could imagine others doing to us what we intend doing to them. In other words, Kant proposes a variant of the Golden Rule—but it is a variant with certain specifics, as we shall see—and it illustrates that Kant is also a *hard universalist*, perhaps the hardest one ever to write a text on morals.

For Kant, humans usually know what they ought to do, and that is almost always the opposite of what they feel like doing. Our moral conflicts are generally between our duty and our inclination, and when we let our desires "run off with us" it is simply because we haven't come up with a way for our sense of duty to persuade us to do the right thing. Kant therefore proposes a test for what is the right thing to do. He refers to this test as the *categorical imperative*. However, because it is a matter of "doing the right thing" not only in terms of the outcome, but also in terms of the intentions, we must look more closely at these intentions.

Suppose a store owner is trying to decide whether to cheat her customers. She might tell herself, "I will cheat them whenever I can get away with it," or, "I will cheat them only on occasion so nobody can detect a pattern." We can all tell, intuitively, that this merchant's intentions aren't good, although they certainly might benefit her and give her some extra cash at the end of the week. In other words, the consequences may be good, yet we know that cheating the customers is not the right thing to do. (We'll get back to the reason in a while.) Suppose, though, that the owner decides not to cheat her customers because she might be *found out*, and then she would lose their business and might have to close shop. This is certainly prudent, but it still is not a morally praiseworthy decision, because she is doing it only to achieve good consequences. What if the store owner decides not to cheat her customers because she *likes them too much* to ever do them any harm? She loves the little kids buying candy, the old ladies buying groceries, and everyone else, so how could she ever even think of cheating them? This, says Kant, is very nice, but it still is not morally praiseworthy, because the merchant is doing only what she feels like doing, and we can't be expected to praise her for just wanting to feel good. (If you want to reexamine this argument, go back to the section in Chapter 4 on psychological egoism, where a similar argument is analyzed in detail.)

The only morally praiseworthy reason for not wanting to cheat the customers would be if the store owner told herself, "It wouldn't be right," regardless of consequences or warm and fuzzy feelings. Why wouldn't it be right? Because she certainly couldn't want everybody else to cheat their customers as a universal law.

If the store owner tells herself, "I will not cheat my customers because otherwise I'll lose them," then she is not doing a bad thing, of course. She is just doing a prudent thing, and Kant says our lives are full of such prudent decisions; they are dependent on each situation, and we have to determine in each case what would be the smart thing to do. Kant calls these decisions, which are *conditional*, because they depend on the situation and on your own personal desires, *hypothetical imperatives—imperatives*, because they are commands: *If* you don't want to lose your customers, *then* you should not cheat them. *If* you want to get your degree, *then* you should not miss your final exam. *If* you want to be good at baking biscuits, *then* you ought to bake them from scratch and not use a ready mix. But suppose you're closing down your shop and moving to another town? Then you might not care about losing those customers. And suppose you decide to drop out of school—then who cares about that final exam? And if you and everyone you know hate biscuits, then why bother worrying about getting good at baking them? In other words, a hypothetical imperative is dependent on your interest in a certain outcome. If you don't want the outcome, the imperative is not binding. We make such decisions every day, and as long as they are based merely on wanting some outcome, they are not morally relevant. (They can, of course, be morally bad, but even if they have a good outcome, Kant would say that they are morally neutral). What makes a decision *morally praiseworthy* is if the agent (the person acting) decides to do something because it might be applied to everyone as a *universal moral law*. And in that case that person has used the categorical imperative.

What makes a categorical imperative *categorical* is that it is not dependent on anyone's desire to make it an imperative; it is binding not just in some situations and for some people, but always, for everyone. It is absolute, "categorical." That is the very nature of the moral law: If it applies at all, it applies to everyone in the same situation. Although there are myriads of hypothetical imperatives, there is only one categorical imperative, expressed in the most general terms possible: *Always act so that you can will that your maxim can become a universal law.* For Kant this realization was so breathtaking that it could be compared only to his awe of the universe on a starry night. How then does it work? Let us use Kant's own example to illustrate.

> [A man] in need finds himself forced to borrow money. He knows well that he won't be able to repay it, but he sees also that he will not get any loan unless he firmly promises to repay it within a fixed time. He wants to make such a promise, but he still has conscience enough to ask himself whether it is not permissible and is contrary to duty to get out of difficulty in this way. Suppose, however, that he decides to do so. The maxim of his action would then be expressed as follows: When I believe myself to be in need of money, I will borrow money and promise to pay it back, although I know that I can never do so. Now this principle of self-love or personal advantage may perhaps be quite compatible with one's entire future welfare, but the question is now whether it is right. I then transform the requirement of self-love into a universal law and put the question thus: how would things stand if my maxim were to become a universal law? He then sees at once that such a maxim could never hold as a universal law of nature and be consistent with itself, but must necessarily be self-contradictory. For the universality of a law which says that anyone believing himself to be in difficulty could promise whatever he pleases with the intention of not keeping it would make promising itself and the end to be attained thereby quite impossible, inasmuch as no one would believe what was promised him but would merely laugh at all such utterances as being vain pretences.

The structure of Kant's proposed test of right and wrong goes like this. What is it you're thinking of doing? Imagine that as a *general rule* for action that you'll follow every time the situation comes up. You have now expressed your *maxim*. Then imagine everybody else doing it, too; by doing this you *universalize your maxim*. Then ask yourself, could I want this? Could I still get away with it if everyone did it? The answer is no, you would *undermine your own intention*, because nobody would lend *you* any money if everyone were lying about paying it back. So it is not just the fact that banks would close and the financial world would be in chaos—it is the *logical outcome* of your universalized maxim that shows you that your intention was wrong.

Does this mean that the categorical imperative works only if *everyone* can accept your maxim as a universal law? Not in the sense that we have to take a poll before we

FIGURE 6.2 *Rebel Without a Cause,* Warner Bros., 1956. Jim Stark (James Dean) has been picked up by the police for drunk and disorderly conduct; here his father (Jim Backus) has come to take him home. Jim has trouble relating to his parents (as the picture symbolically indicates, there is much distance between them). He says to the understanding police officer, "If I only had one day where I didn't have to be confused. . . ." Jim is asking for absolute answers that will satisfy his search for what is right, and he discards his father's utilitarian problem-solving. The story of *Rebel Without a Cause* is outlined in Chapter 7 as an illustration of utilitarianism versus Kantian deontology.

decide to act; if everyone's actual approval were the final criterion, then each maxim would probably be bogged down in committee reviews, and the principle would lose its appeal as an immediate test of where one's duty lies. There is an element of universal approval in Kant's idea, but it lies in the reflection of an *ideal* situation, not an *actual* one. If everyone put aside his or her personal interests and then used the categorical imperative, then everyone would, ideally, come up with the same conclusion about what is morally permissible. Kant, who belonged to an era of less doubt about what exactly rationality means, believed that if we all use the same rules of logic and disregard our personal interests, then we all will come to the same results about moral as well as intellectual issues.

This immense faith in human rationality is an important factor in Kant's moral theory, because it reflects why to him humans are such privileged beings. We can set up our own moral rules without having to seek guidance by going to the authorities; we need not be told how to live by the church, or by the police, or by the monarch, or even by our parents. All we need is our good will and our reason, and with that we can set our own rules. If we choose a certain course of action because we have been told to—because we listen to other people's advice for some reason or other—we are merely doing what might be prudent and expedient, but if we listen to our own reason and have good will, then we are *autonomous lawmakers*.

Won't this approach result in a society in which everyone looks after him or herself and lives by multiple rules that may contradict one another? No, because if everyone has good will and applies the categorical imperative, then everyone will set the same, reasonable, unselfish rules for themselves, because they would not wish to set a rule that would be impossible for others to follow.

In this way Kant believes he has shown us the way to solve every dilemma, every problem where desire clashes with duty. When the categorical imperative is applied, we automatically disregard our own personal interests and look at the greater picture, and this action is what is morally praiseworthy: to realize that something is right or wrong in itself.

Kant's Critics

Perhaps, in the end, it comes down to a matter of temperament and personality. Some of us are immediately impressed by the idea that one's intentions count for more than the outcome of one's actions, and the question of right or wrong in itself is important; we can't consider only the consequences if it means violating the rights of others. Others of us claim that no matter how much you say you're not interested in consequences, they still end up being a consideration. One such critic was John Stuart Mill, who had some sharp things to say about Kant's example of borrowing money and not keeping promises. If this was the best Kant could do in showing that consequences don't count, he was not doing a very good job, said Mill, because what was he appealing to? By asking, "What if everybody does what you want to do," wasn't Kant worrying about *consequences*? What will happen if everyone borrows money and doesn't pay it back in spite of their promises? Then no one else can take advantage of promising falsely, either. In Mill's view, this is an appeal to consequences as much as regular utilitarianism. This caused Mill to conclude that everyone must include consequences in their moral theory, no matter how reluctant they are in recognizing their importance. This appears to be a valid point against Kant. The only thing Kant might say in response to this (he never did, of course, since he was long dead by the time Mill criticized his point of view) is that his viewpoint does not look at *actual* consequences, but at the *logical implications* of a universalized maxim: Will it or will it not undermine itself? Whether one is convinced that Kant has defended himself sufficiently or is instead persuaded by Mill is perhaps also a matter of temperament.

Other critics have pounced on other points when finding fault with Kant's theory. They raise the following questions: (1) Can we be so sure that the categorical imperative is always going to tell us what to do? (2) Might it not be possible to find a loophole in the imperative? (3) Who is to say when something is irrational? (4) Does it really seem right that we can never be morally correct in breaking a universal rule?

(1) Let us look at the first question. Suppose we have a conflict between two things we have to do—and we don't particularly want to do either of them. Kant's system assumes that a moral conflict is one between duty and inclination—between what we have to do and what we want to do. In that case it is entirely possible that we may be convinced to do the right thing by imagining our maxim as a universal rule for everyone. But suppose we have a conflict between *two duties*? Such as having to take inventory at our workplace the night before we have a final exam for which we should be studying. Certainly we can't say that we want to do one thing more than we want to do the other—anyone who has done both will probably agree that they are both rather unpleasant tasks. How might the categorical imperative help us decide what to do? All it can tell us is that failing to show up for the inventory would not be rational, but neither would skipping the final, because both are duties that everyone ought to do under the same circumstances. The amount of help offered by the categorical imperative is at best limited to cases where duties are not in conflict.

(2) What about the possible loophole? Suppose the categorical imperative tells us that it would be irrational (and thus morally impermissible) for anyone to even think about robbing a bank if he needs money, because we wouldn't want everyone in the same situation to take that course of action. But what exactly *is* the situation we're talking about? Suppose Joe is broke because he is out of work and has been for seven months. He is twenty years old and has a high school degree. He worked at a video arcade, but now it is closed because of gang violence. Joe likes to wear denim. His parents are divorced. He is dating a girl called Virginia who works at a supermarket and goes to the community college, and he needs money so that they can get married and rent a small apartment. Let's assume that Joe applies the categorical imperative, and his maxim is: Every time I (who am in a certain situation) am broke and cannot get a loan, I will rob a bank. Then he universalizes it: Every time someone who is twenty, and whose name is Joe, who has divorced parents, used to work in a video arcade, likes denim, and is dating a checkout girl called Virginia who goes to a community college—anytime he feels like robbing a bank because he is broke, it is all right for him to do so. Now is that rational? Will Joe's maxim undermine his intention because everyone else will do the same thing as what he is planning to do? No, because he has described his situation so that "everyone" is reduced to a group of very few people who are in his exact same situation. In fact, his description of "everyone" could apply to only one person—Joe himself. In that case it is perfectly logical for him to rob a bank, because he won't undermine his own intention. This is hardly the kind of ironclad philosophical proof of doing the right thing that we were looking for. This argument, which also works against rule utilitarianism, is of course not a valid defense for doing the wrong thing, and Joe shouldn't run out and rob the bank because he thinks philosophers have shown it to be okay. It is, however, an attempt to show that if we work with a principle that is as general as the categorical imperative, we just can't expect it to answer all our moral questions without a doubt.

(3) The question of who is to say whether something is irrational is an issue that might not have occurred to Kant. He, as a product of his times and a co-producer of the Age of Reason, believed that if we use our reason without looking to our self-interests, then we will all come up with the same idea and result. Actually, Bentham believed the same thing, even though his moral vision was quite different from that of Kant. Today, after garnering a century of knowledge about the workings of the sub-conscious mind, and realizing that people just aren't rational all of the time, or even most of the time, we are more inclined to believe that our individual idea of what is rational may depend greatly on who we are. If we use a very broad definition of rational, such as "realizing the shortest way to get to your goal and then pursuing it," we still may come up with different ideas about what is rational. Suppose our Joe is not only broke, but he also is a political anarchist who believes that the sooner society breaks down, the better for all humanity and for himself in particular. Why then would it be particularly illogical for him to rob a bank, given that the downfall of society, including banks, is what he is longing for? And why should we refrain from lying to each other if what we want is to create social chaos and alienate our friends? Why refrain from hurting each other, if we are sadomasochists and believe it would be great to live in a world of mutual harmdoing? Kant seems to assume that we all have the same general goals, which serve as a guarantee of the rationality of our actions. Change the goals, though, and the ideal of a reasonable course of action takes on a new meaning.

(4) Now let's consider the final objection: Can the categorical imperative always assure us that sticking to the rule is better than breaking it? Let us say that a killer is stalking a friend of yours, and the friend comes to your door and asks you to hide her. You tell her to go hide in the broom closet. (This is a slightly altered version of one of Kant's own examples). The killer comes to your door, and asks, "Where is she?" Most of us would feel a primary obligation to help our friend, but for Kant the primary obligation is to the truth. You are supposed to answer, "I cannot tell a lie—she is hiding in the broom closet." This is what is meant by an *absolutist* moral theory: A moral rule allows for no exceptions. But why? Most of us would assume that the life of our friend would at least be worth a white lie, but for Kant it is a matter of principle. Suppose you lie to the killer, but your friend sneaks out of the house, and the killer finds her; then it is your fault. If you had told the truth, your friend might still have escaped, and the killer could have been prevented from committing the murder (perhaps you could have trapped him in the broom closet). This farfetched argument follows Kant's own reasoning for why we should always stick to the rule: because if we break a rule we must answer for the consequences, whereas if we stick to the rule, we have no such responsibility. If we tell the truth, and the killer goes straight for the broom closet and kills our friend, Kant insists that we bear no responsibility for her death. But why should we accept Kant's idea that consequences don't count as long as you are following the rule (as long as you have good will), but they do count when you are not? Philosophers tend to agree that you can't make such arbitrary choices of when consequences count and when they don't.

If there are all these difficulties with the categorical imperative, why has it been such an influential moral factor? The reason is that it is the first moral theory to stress the idea of *universalizability*: realizing that you are in no different situation than other human beings. If something will bother you, it will probably bother others, too, everything else being equal. If you allow yourself a day off, you should not gripe when others do the same thing. Most important, however, you should think about it before you allow yourself that day off, and realize that it won't do as a universal rule. The problem is, on occasion we all encounter special situations when we might actually *need* a day off; perhaps we are sick or emotionally upset. Similarly, on the whole we should not kill, but in certain rare situations we may be called on to do just that, in war or as self-defense. On the whole we should not lie, but there may come a day when a killer is stalking a friend of yours, and you have a chance to save her. In that case you may need to lie. These are unusual situations, so why should Kant's generalizations apply to them? This issue has caused scholars to suggest that there really is nothing wrong with the format of the categorical imperative, provided that we are allowed to expand our maxim to include situations where we might accept certain *exceptions* to our rule. When this is done, we see that the universalization works just fine: We can universalize not killing, with the exception of self-defense and certain other specified cases. We can universalize not taking a day off from work unless we are sick or severely emotionally upset, and it doesn't happen very often. We can universalize not lying if it is understood that preventing the murder of an innocent person would constitute an exception. In Chapter 7 we will look at an episode from the television series "Star Trek: The Next Generation," in which this problem is nicely illustrated: Absolute moral rules may have their advantages, but a truly mature moral theory must allow for some exceptions to the rules.

Rational Beings Are Ends in Themselves

Never as Means to an End Only

In his book *Grounding for the Metaphysics of Morals*, Kant suggests two different ways to express the categorical imperative. The first one we have just looked at; the other goes like this:

> Now I say that man, and in general every rational being, exists as an end in himself and not merely as a means to be arbitrarily used by this or that will. He must in all his actions, whether directed to himself or to other rational beings, always be regarded at the same time as an end.

What does it mean to be treated as "an end in himself?" Let us first look at the opposite approach: to be treated as "a means to an end only." What is a means to an end? It is a tool, an instrument to be used to achieve some goal; it is something that has *instrumental* value in the achievement of something of *intrinsic* value. If someone is used as a means to an end, she or he is treated as a tool for someone else's purpose, in a very broad sense. If someone is being sexually abused, or kept as a slave, that person obviously is being treated as a means to an end, but so is the guy we befriend so we can get to know his sister, or the girl we befriend so we can get to know her brother. So is anyone who is being used for other people's purposes without regard for his or her *intrinsic* value and dignity as a human being. For Kant this is just another way of expressing the categorical imperative. What made him think this? For one thing, when you use the categorical imperative you are universalizing your maxim, and if you are refusing to treat others merely as means to an end, you are also universalizing a maxim, and a very fundamental one. Second, both maxims are expressions of the Golden Rule.

This statement about the immorality of treating other humans as a means to an end was, for the eighteenth century, a tremendously important political and social statement. In Kant's era (although not in Kant's country) slavery was still a social factor; abuse of the lower classes by the upper classes was commonplace; Europe was just emerging from a time when kings and warlords could move their peasants and conscripted soldiers around like chessmen with no regard for their lives and happiness. Then Kant clearly stated that it is not social status that determines one's standing in the moral universe, but one thing only: the capability to use reason. As one of the driving forces behind the Age of Reason, Kant stated that any rational human being deserves respect. Rich and poor, young and old, all races and peoples—all are alike in having rationality as the one defining mark of their humanity, and none deserves to be treated without regard for that characteristic. (Here it must be interjected, in case we get carried away with our praise, that Kant himself expressed doubt as to whether women were actually rational beings, or as rational as men; but here we will be generous and act as though Kant himself included both *genders*, though this is by no means certain.)

Why are rational beings intrinsically valuable? Because they can place a value on things. What is gold worth if nobody wants it? Nothing. Humans are value-givers; they assign a relative worth to things that interest them. However, as value-givers, humans always have an *absolute* value. They "set the price," so to speak, yet cannot have a price "set on them." We do, however, constantly talk about people being "worth money." A baseball player is worth a fortune, a Hollywood actress is worth millions. What does that mean? Have we set a price on humans after all? Not in the appropriate sense. It doesn't mean we can *buy* the Hollywood actress for a couple of million (well, we might, but in that case she is treating *herself* as a means to an end only, by selling her body). What we usually mean is that she has a lot of money. And the baseball player? He certainly can be "bought and sold," but hardly as a slave; he retains his autonomy and gets rich in the process. It is his talent and his services that are paid for. Under normal circumstances we don't refer to people as entities that can be bought for money; and if we do, we usually are implying that something bad is taking place (slavery and bribery, for instance). Thus people are value-givers, because they can decide rationally what they want and what they don't want. This means that rational beings are *persons*, and the second formulation of the categorical imperative is focused on respect for persons: *Act in such a way that you treat humanity, whether in your own person or in the person of another, always at the same time as an end and never simply as means.*

Notice that Kant is not just talking about not mistreating others. You have to respect yourself, too, and not let others step on you. You have a right to set values of your own, and not just be used by others as their key to success. But what exactly does it mean not to treat anybody simply as means to an end? We know that blatant abuse is wrong and that a subtler kind is no better. But what about using someone's services? When you buy your groceries, there usually is some person who bags your items. Truthfully, are you treating that person as a means to get your groceries bagged? Yes, indeed, but not simply as a means; he or she is getting paid, and you presumably don't treat them as though they were put on this earth just to bag your groceries. Everyday life consists of people using other people's services, and that is just the normal give and take of social life. The danger arises if we stop respecting people for what they do, and reduce them in our minds to mere tools for our comfort or success. As long as the relationship is reciprocal (you pay for your groceries, and the bagger gets a paycheck), then there is no "abuse" taking place. Indeed, students use their professors as a means to an end (to get their degree), but the professors rarely feel abused, provided that they receive a salary. Likewise, the professors use students as a means to their ends (to receive that salary), but the professors surely don't imagine that the students were put on this earth to feed them or pay off their mortgage.

Beings Who Are Things

Any rational being deserves respect. We assume that humans fall into that category, but suppose there are rational beings who are not human? It is not unthinkable that humans might encounter extraterrestrials who are rational enough to know math, language, and space science; how would they fare in Kant's moral universe? There is a common science fiction scenario of capturing aliens and dissecting them, without regard for their personal dignity, but would Kant allow for that? Never, since these beings are *rational*. They qualify as full members of our moral universe, and humans have no right to treat them as tools to achieve knowledge or power. The aliens likewise have no right to cart humans off for medical experiments, because all humans are generally rational beings.

There are beings on this earth who are not rational in Kant's sense of the word—animals, for example. Where do they belong in Kant's moral universe? They don't belong there at all; they are classified as *things* and can be treated any way that a rational person likes, because animals can't place a value on something—only humans can do that. And an animal is not worth anything in itself; it has value only if it is wanted for some purpose by a human. If nobody cares about cats, or spotted owls, then they have no value. Is it true, though, that animals can't place a value on things? Most people with firsthand knowledge of animals will report that pets are capable of valuing their owners above all, and their food bowl second (or is it the other way around?). And animals in the wild place extreme importance on their territory and their young. Many people today would probably categorize animal interests as just different in *degree* from human interests, and not different in *kind*. Although Kant and most of his contemporaries (with the exclusion of Bentham) believed that the moral universe is closed to nonhuman animals, it is just possible today that we not only might include animals as "creatures who deserve respect," but also might actively look for traces of *animal morality*. Might the self-sacrifice of a baboon to save her "tribe" from the leopard constitute a moral dimension? Are dolphins "morally good" when they help a wounded dolphin and prevent it from drowning? Or are we just witnessing automatic instinctual responses?

In Chapter 14 we look more closely at the animal issue and in particular at the exclusion of animals from Kant's moral universe. For now, suffice it to say that Kant did not condone cruelty to animals; however, he took this stance not for the sake of the animals themselves, but because someone who hurts animals might easily get used to it and start hurting people. We now have a broader understanding of animal intelligence than Kant could possibly have had, so for a modern Kantian it may be time to redefine what exactly a rational being is. The day may be near when dolphins, elephants, and the great apes may be the first to be included in a category of rudimentary rational beings. For our purposes here, we simply should remember that for Kant it was not just a matter of being able to think—a person must also be able to show that he or she has autonomy, and can set up universal moral rules for themselves and others; and although certain animals may have some thought capacity, it is doubtful whether they ever can be considered *morally autonomous* in the Kantian sense of the term.

Be that as it may, the last word certainly has not been said when it comes to Kant's own classification of *humans* as rational beings, for suppose someone who is genetically human can't think rationally? There are many humans who aren't good at thinking or can't think at all, either because they are infants, babies, Alzheimer's patients, or because they are mentally disabled or in a coma. Does this mean that all of these people aren't *persons* and should be classified as *things*? As some scholars have remarked, there are animals who are more like persons (that is, rational beings) than are newborn infants or severely retarded humans. Would Kant really say that such humans are no better than things? Probably not, if we could ask him, but the trouble is that Kant never made provisions for any such subcategories of "persons" in his writings. It is either or. His theory of personhood versus thinghood entails problems that he did not foresee.

There are, then, problems for animals and nonrational humans in Kant's theory. Still, the theory stands as Kant's most forceful contribution to a world of equality and mutual respect, because it is such a remarkable *expansion* of the moral universe described in previous moral theories, which tended to exclude social groups that somehow weren't considered quite as valuable as others. Furthermore, Kant placed the foundation of morality solidly with human rationality, and not with the state or the church.

This brings us to the third major theme in Kant's *Grounding*, the "Kingdom of Ends." Applying the categorical imperative is something all rational beings can do (and even if they can't do it exactly the way Kant uses it, the logic of it should be compelling for all people who can ask themselves, "Would I want everybody to do this?"). Kant calls this moral autonomy; the only moral authority that can tell us to do something and not to do something else is our own reason. As we saw previously, if all people follow the same principle and disregard their own personal inclinations, then everybody will end up following the same good rules, because everyone has universalized his intention. In such a world, with everyone doing the right thing and nobody abusing anyone else, a new realm will have been created: the *Kingdom of Ends*. "Kingdom" poetically describes a community of people, and "ends" indicates that the people treat each other as ends only—as beings who have their own goals in life—never as means to other people's ends. Every time we show respect and consideration for each other, we make the Kingdom of Ends a little more real.

Some readers of Kant believe that he shows a more humane side in his theory of ends in themselves, and indeed we might take this idea and apply it to the problem of whether to lie to the killer who has come to murder your friend. The categorical imperative tells you to speak the truth always, because then you can't be blamed for the consequences. But is this really the same as saying we should treat others as ends in themselves? Perhaps there is a subtle difference; if we apply this rule to the killer who is stalking our friend, would we get the same result? Might we not be treating our friend as a means to an end only if we refuse to lie for her, whether it is for the sake of a principle, or just so that we can't be blamed for the consequences? If we are sacrificing our friend for the sake of the truth, it might rightfully be said that in that case we are treating her as a means to an end only. So even within Kant's own system there are irreconcilable differences. This should not cause us to want to discard his entire theory, however; since the nineteenth century, philosophers have tried to redesign Kant's ideas to fit a more perceptive (or, as Kant would say, more lenient) world. Some of these ideas are working quite well—for example, allowing for general exceptions to be built into the categorical imperative itself, and allowing for animals to be considered more rational than Kant ever thought possible.

Narratives That Explore the Concepts of Duty and Dignity

Chapter 7 includes stories that discuss what it means to do the right thing on the basis of a sense of duty toward what is right. *Abandon Ship!*, which is included primarily as an example of utilitarianism, also can be viewed from a Kantian standpoint. Other stories are the James Dean film *Rebel Without A Cause*, the Western *High Noon*, and the episode entitled "Justice" from the television series "Star Trek: The Next Generation."

Chapter 7

Narratives of Right and Wrong Conduct

Certain types of moral conflicts have appealed to artists more than other types, so some themes, like utilitarianism, are very well represented in film and literature, while others, such as ethical relativism, have not been explored much at all. This chapter includes at least two narrative examples to illustrate each major ethical theory. I am certain the reader can think of many more examples, and I wish we had space to discuss more of them. Some examples can be seen as arguments in favor of the type of theory in question, and some can be viewed as arguments against it.

In most cases the ending of a story is important to the moral significance of that story, and in such cases I have included that ending, much as I dislike being a spoilsport and revealing a good mystery prematurely. In cases where the ending is not significant to the moral drama, I have done my best to avoid giving it away.

Dealing with Differences

The following stories all deal in some form with the issues of cultural differences and ethical relativism: Are there fundamental cultural differences between us? Can we bridge them if we try? And should all cultural practices be considered equally valid?

SPIKE LEE (DIRECTOR AND SCREENWRITER), *Do the Right Thing*
Film (1989).

In a chapter dealing with the question of what to do, I couldn't possibly pass up a film with the great title of *Do the Right Thing*. The question was, where to place it? The film can perhaps be seen as an argument for ethical relativism, or at least for cultural tolerance, and it perhaps cannot. I will leave that up to you.

It is a very hot summer morning in Brooklyn, in the predominantly African-American part of town called Bedford-Stuyvesant. Sal, an Italian, and his two sons are opening up their pizzeria on one corner; a Korean family is opening up their grocery store on the other. The police (all white) are cruising the streets. Most of the black population is out of work. Mookie, a young black man (played by Spike Lee), is delivering pizza to the neighborhood, and "Da Mayor," an old black man, is patrolling the streets, being friendly to everybody although not everybody takes kindly to him. He calls Mookie over and admonishes him always to "do the right thing."

As the day gets hotter, tempers flare. Sal likes the neighborhood and his customers (who all grew up on his pizzas). His youngest son is a good friend of Mookie. His oldest son, however, wants out; all he perceives is that his family are not welcome in the African-American community and should associate with their own kind in their Italian neighborhood. Squabbles erupt between the young Koreans and their customers and between the old black men and the young black men. Mookie quarrels with his girlfriend. One of Sal's young customers notices that Sal's wall is full of pictures of famous Italians and Italian-Americans and demands that Sal put up pictures of African-Americans, too. Mookie points out to Sal's oldest son that although he may not like blacks, all his heroes are African-American. Mookie becomes upset when his sister comes to visit the pizzeria and Sal appears to have a crush on her. The characters don't seem to be able to find a way to deal with their differences: The blacks hate the Italians, the Italians hate the blacks, the blacks hate the Koreans, and the Koreans are trying to get along with everyone and can't understand all the tension. Da Mayor is trying to smooth things out and eventually becomes a hero: He saves a little boy from being run over. The only one who thinks to thank him is a woman in the neighborhood who apparently has disliked him for years.

The sun sets, but tempers are still hot. More complaints about there being no pictures

FIGURE 7.1 *Do The Right Thing*, Universal City Studios, 1989. Mookie (Spike Lee) and Sal (Danny Aiello) are discussing issues of the neighborhood in Sal's pizza restaurant. On this hot day, tensions run high between the neighborhood groups of ethnic diversity: the Italians, the blacks, the Koreans, and the all-white police force.

of blacks on Sal's wall result in a riot: A young black man is killed by the police, and the others, led by Mookie, loot and set fire to Sal's pizzeria. They turn to the Korean grocery store next, but the young Korean storekeeper cries, "I'm just like you, I'm black, too!" That gets a laugh, and his store is safe for the time being.

The next day is another hot one. There is no solution to any of the problems in the neighborhood. Da Mayor is the only person who resolved anything; during the riot he managed to overcome the animosity of the woman he wanted to make friends with. Mookie resolves only to spend more time with his little boy.

The end of the movie? Two quotes appear on the screen, one from Martin Luther King, and the other from Malcolm X. A young, mentally disabled white man puts photos of the two leaders up on the burned-out wall of Sal's pizzeria. King says that violence never solves any problems. Malcolm X says that in general, violence is evil, but not in self-defense—in that case it is not even violence, but rather intelligence.

Study Questions

1. What do you think Spike Lee intended us to conclude?
2. *Did* Mookie do the right thing? Did anybody?
3. What did the Korean store owner mean when he said he was black, too?
4. Is this a film of racial tolerance?
5. Can there be different moral rules for different ethnic and cultural groups? Should there be?

MICHAEL MANN (DIRECTOR) AND CHRISTOPHER CROW (SCREENWRITER), *The Last of the Mohicans*

Film (1992); novel by James Fenimore Cooper (1826).

Cooper's novel is considered to be the first American novel and is in itself a landmark: In it, Cooper creates the romantic image of the "Man of the West," the frontiersman. Without the hero, Hawkeye, the white man of the forest, we might never have had Western movies or cowboy heroes at all. As far as being an illustration of ethical relativism, however, the novel works only as a negative image; it is tainted by the racist and sexist attitudes of the early nineteenth century. (The story itself takes place in 1757.) The 1992 film tells approximately the same story as the novel, but with a more modern and sensitive twist: Cora and Alice, daughters of Colonel Munroe, become prisoners of the Huron Indian Magua, and Hawkeye and his father and brother try to rescue them. During this process one of the women, Cora, comes to know and understand the ways of the new world and to value the wilderness spirit shared by pioneers and Indians alike. The film gives Hawkeye (who in Cooper's original series of novels is called Natty Bumpo) a new and modern identity; he is called Nathaniel Poe. He, his father, Chingachgook (the Mohican who raised him), and Chingachgook's son, Uncas, are a family unit. They live in perfect harmony with nature and with the new pioneer settlers, but not with the Huron Indians, nor with the French (who are employing the tribes in their warfare against the British troops), nor with the British troops themselves. The film shows us that although there was cultural intolerance among the British, there also were individuals who understood the importance of coexistence and cultural tolerance. The "enemies" in the film, be they the Huron Indians or the French, show themselves to be whole characters with reasons for doing what they do. The French captain shows sense and magnanimity by offering the British an honorable surrender; the arch-villain Magua is the enemy of the British because the British murdered his people. The British officers fare worst in this film; they are the intolerant ones. But Cora, the daughter of the British general, learns firsthand what it means to live cross-culturally, as she falls in love with Nathaniel (Hawkeye). The film does not follow the book in detail—some say there are things in the book that shouldn't have been left out in the movie—but as it stands, it is a film that illustrates a new American multicultural awareness. The British, French, and Native American tribes may not have tolerated each other in the frontier forests of the eighteenth century, but through the film we see that there is hope for a new era of understanding.

Study Questions

1. Do you think there is hope for multicultural understanding in our society, and do you think a film can help the process along?
2. Do you think the film would have made a stronger multicultural statement if the hero had been Chingachgook or Uncas, and not Nathaniel?

E. M. FORSTER, *A Passage To India*

Novel (1924). Film by David Lean (director and screenwriter), 1984.

This story takes place during the final decades of "the Raj" in India, the years of British rule. A young Englishwoman, Adele Quested, comes to visit her fiancé in India, accompanied by his mother, Mrs. Moore. Adele is acutely aware of the condescending manner in which the Indian population is treated by the majority of the British, including her fiancé, and both she and Mrs. Moore are instantly taken in by the colorful romance of the Indian world. At the house of a British schoolteacher who is intent on "bridging the gap" between his own culture and that of India, the two women meet two local Indians, the philosopher Professor Godbole and the physician Dr. Aziz. The meeting seems successful and the atmosphere is congenial, but it is apparent that in spite of everybody's goodwill some misunderstandings occur. Aziz feels compelled to invite the ladies on an outing—difficult and expensive—to the famous Marabar Caves, and Adele and Mrs. Moore happily accept the invitation. They do not realize that it was intended as a formal gesture of friendship, not as a serious invitation. Aziz may have had every reason in the world to expect Englishwomen to decline such an invitation, but these two prove to be different. Now he, to his horror and dismay, must go through with the preparations, which in the end include servants, chairs, tables, wines, and even an elephant to carry the British party from the train station to the caves.

At the caves something extraordinary takes place. After visiting the first cave, Mrs. Moore succumbs to an attack of claustrophobia, or perhaps premonition, and begs to be excused. Adele and Dr. Aziz continue on their own, striking up a conversation; Adele asks him if he is married, and he responds that he is, but he neglects to say that his wife is dead. As they talk, it is clear that each has different expectations of the conversation, based on their cultural backgrounds and preconceived notions about the other. All of a sudden, Aziz loses sight of Adele. The next thing he knows, she is joining her friends at the foot of the hill. Aziz is completely puzzled, and his confusion grows when he is subsequently arrested for assaulting the young woman.

What exactly happened at the caves? The story unfolds during Aziz's trial, where it becomes abundantly clear that the cultural gap between British and Indians is too great to be bridged even by well-meaning, educated persons such as the schoolteacher. Mrs. Moore has left for Britain in a state of mental anguish, so she can offer no supporting testimony. In a surprise move, Adele withdraws her accusations (which she never personally charged Aziz with, anyway), and Aziz is free. He turns his back on his former British friends, and only years later do he and the schoolteacher again reach a state of mutual friendship and acceptance.

Study Questions

1. How does this story illustrate ethical relativism?
2. Can we find any values in common for the Indian and British characters involved in this story?
3. If you have read the book or seen the film, you may want to discuss who really was to blame for what happened to Aziz.

DAVID LEAN (DIRECTOR), ROBERT BOLT AND MICHAEL WILSON (SCREENWRITERS), *Lawrence of Arabia*
Film (1962).

First a suggestion: If you plan to rent or buy this film on video or laser disc, make sure you get the "letterbox" version. Anything less than this near-cinemascope format will not do the magnificent imagery justice.

FIGURE 7.2 *Lawrence of Arabia*, Columbia Pictures, 1962. "El Awrence" (Peter O'Toole) rides with his friend, the Arab warrior Ali (Omar Sharif). Lawrence is dressed in a traditional Arab costume given to him by his friends among the tribal Arab leaders in recognition of what they believe is his loyalty to their cause, obtaining freedom from the Turks.

Perhaps it is no coincidence that two of the examples of ethical relativism in this chapter involve films directed by David Lean. Coming from a culture that encompasses examples of cultural intolerance as well as the most well-meaning attempts to counteract and combat such intolerance, Lean examines the theme of multicultural understanding in many of his films.

The story of Thomas Edward Lawrence, the main character of *Lawrence of Arabia*, is an example of the British duality towards other cultures. Lawrence is a historical figure credited, to a great extent and largely with justification, for uniting the Arab tribes in a fight against their oppressors, the Turks, during World War I, at a time when the British and the French were developing plans to partition the Turkish empire after the war. What makes Lawrence a very special British military man is that he, at least in the eyes of the British, "goes native." In the film we witness his development from small-time military observer in British uniform—a clown to his superiors (to which Lawrence answers, "We can't all be lion tamers")—into an adult and multifaceted, multicultural leader.

From his encounter with Ali, his first tribal warrior, and his meeting with Prince Faisal (where Lawrence impresses him with his knowledge of the Koran), to the moment where Lawrence succeeds in leading the Arab tribes in the taking of the seaport town of Aqaba and subsequently dons Arab clothing (because Ali burned his British uniform), Lawrence becomes "El Awrence" to the Arabs.

And yet, he is only a visitor. In his heart Lawrence thinks like an Englishman. When his Arab friends tell him there is something he can't do because "it is written," he tells them that "nothing is written." For the traditional Arab way of thinking, the future is already determined by Allah, "written" by his hand, whereas Westerners typically believe that they can shape the future through acts of willpower and decision making. Lawrence is no exception. The strength of his belief in his power to shape the future causes the Arabs to view him as a man of such power that "he does his own writing." It is Lawrence's idea to unite the Arabs, for otherwise they will remain a "silly little people" who approach each other with the utmost reluctance and suspicion. Lawrence is still an Englishman with the inspiration to save a non-English world—an attitude that reminds us of what used to be called the "white man's burden." And yet, in times of grief and hardship, Lawrence sides with the lowest of the low, his Arab servant boy; he drags him into the British officers' club and demands drinks and sleeping quarters for the boy, who has come out of the desert to tell the British about the victory at Aqaba.

What Prince Faisal realizes is that Lawrence's drive is passion, and as such it is unreliable. Whenever Lawrence has a particularly unpleasant and disturbing experience—such as when he has to execute one of his men, or when he is caught and beaten by the Turks (who never realize whom they have caught)—he wants out, not so much because the ordeal was unpleasant, or because he is a coward, but because he realizes something disturbing about himself: He somehow enjoyed the experience.

After the beating by the Turks (it appears that he was raped by Turkish soldiers, but the film is not explicit on that point), Lawrence no longer holds to the British belief that "nothing is written." He now thinks that it is his destiny to lead the Arabs. In an interesting turn, his British superior officer agrees that he is one of the few men with a "destiny." (This is interesting because Lawrence's Arab friends are convinced that only the select few have *no* destiny.) Lawrence explains it like this: "A man can do what he wants to do, but he can't want what he wants to do." Heritage is everything.

In the end Lawrence stands by his promise to lead the Arab forces to Damascus, believing that this will give them power over their own country. Naively, he doesn't want to believe that the English and the French already are thinking about taking over the Arab lands. After Damascus is won, Lawrence is terribly disappointed when the Arabs can't agree on setting up a government. He goes back to the British, dons a uniform, and says goodbye to Prince Faisal, who sees that the passion is spent—El Awrence has become Colonel Lawrence, British officer.

Shortly after his return to England Lawrence dies in a motorcycle accident (this is revealed at the beginning of the film). People who never knew him in life eulogize him, and those who knew him best refuse to make statements.

Study Questions

1. Can Lawrence be called a relativist?
2. Does the film function as an argument for or against ethical relativism?
3. What is the difference between the Arab and the British view of destiny? Do you agree with either of them?

SHERI S. TEPPER, *Sideshow*

Novel (1992).

Although *The Last of the Mohicans*, *A Passage to India*, and *Lawrence of Arabia* can be said to lean toward a view of cultural tolerance and possibly even noninterference, our last example of fiction that deals with differences is adamantly opposed to the tolerance praised by relativism. Sheri S. Tepper's *Sideshow* is a philosophical debate about misdirected tolerance; it is a philosophical story clad in a science-fiction cloak. The planet Elsewhere is the only place left in the galaxy that is not infected with the virus of the Hobbs Land Gods, a virus which, to the people of Elsewhere, is blasphemous; it abolishes war and enmity and cultural differences and creates a new kind of being by fusing humans and other sentient beings into *Fauna Sapiens*. Elsewhere is populated by humans who prefer to remain as they are, worship their gods, keep their slaves, sacrifice their children, and keep their men and women prisoners in their home the way they have always done, all in the name of holy diversity. Enforcers make sure that citizens of each country on the planet stay within their own borders (tourism is acceptable, but not emigration), that no one smuggles artifacts from a technologically higher culture to a lower culture, and that all rules that pertain to each country are strictly adhered to. Occasionally an Enforcer will let his or her human side show and will prevent some particularly gruesome tradition from taking place, such as the sacrifice of a child, but on the whole such interference is considered a criminal act.

Nela and Bertran, Siamese (joined) twins from earth in the distant past, take a tour with two of the Enforcers, Fringe and Danivon. The twins tell the Enforcers about political and social conditions on earth, of militarism, slavery, oppression of men and of women, and also of democracies and freedom-loving countries. They are told that equivalent societies to all of them can be found somewhere on Elsewhere.

"And this is the diversity you are sworn to preserve?" asked Nela.

"There are one thousand and three provinces," said Fringe. "We have mentioned only a tiny few of them. On Elsewhere, mankind is free to be whatever he can, or will."

The twins thought about this for a time before Bertran asked, "Let us suppose one of the women of Thrasis wishes to escape. Or one of the—what did you call them? The Murrey?—one of the Murrey from Derbeck? Let us suppose a civilian from Frick grows weary of being ruled by soldiers. What recourse do they have?"

"I don't understand," said Danivon. "Recourse?"

"Are they free to leave?"

"Of course not," said Fringe. "Persons must stay in their own place, in the diversity to which they were born. . . ."

"I'd call it a people zoo," [Nela] said. "Just like the zoos on Earth of long ago, with all the people in habitats."

Later the Enforcers apprehend a childkiller, and Nela and Bertram congratulate them on a job well done; however, the twins have misunderstood the Enforcers' mission:

"Our job is to protect diversity," [Danivon] said through gritted teeth, "the very diversity that is the essence of humanity! In that diversity children are always being killed for any number of reasons. If the killing is proper to that place, then it is proper. But this old man took children across *borders*! He *interfered* in the affairs of a province! Here on Elsewhere, we let one another alone."

As it happens, Fringe begins to doubt the Enforcer code herself when, on a river flowing from the country of Choire, where only children with perfect pitch fit for the choire practices are kept alive, they encounter a child in a basket. The child has been "exposed" by Choire parents, perhaps because they want a newborn child instead, or perhaps because the child is defective or doesn't get along with its parents. . . .

Following the extended finger, Fringe saw. A basket floated out in midstream, bobbing on the wavelets, carrying a child some three or four years old who held tight to the closely woven rim and cried silently, mouth open, eyes and nose streaming.

"You said babies . . . ," said Fringe to Jory [another traveler], surprised and offended at this event following so soon upon her catechism.

Jory corrected her, "I said children."

. . . The basket bobbed on the river waves. The child looked up, saw them, stretched out its arms, and cried across the water. "P'ease . . . p'ease . . . " The river flow swept the basket on past, the child's voice still rising in a wail of fright. "Oh, oh, pick Onny up, p'ease. Pick Onny up. . . . " Where the basket bobbed, something large and many-toothed raised itself from the water and gulped hugely.

Fringe turned blind eyes away from the water, shutting out the sight, driving out the memory of it. Such things were. Diversity implied both pleasure and pain, both justice and injustice, both life and death. That's the way things were.

Study Questions

1. Identify the elements in this excerpt that correspond to the debate about ethical relativism.
2. What is Fringe the Enforcer's problem?
3. What is Tepper trying to convey with this story?
4. Is this an argument against any kind of cultural tolerance? Why or why not?

Egoism

The following stories illustrate the issues of psychological and ethical egoism: Are we selfish by nature? How might a typically selfish person act, and should such behavior be condemned, or encouraged?

GUSTAVE FLAUBERT, *Madame Bovary*

Novel (1857). Film versions in United States (1949) and France (1991).

As a young girl in the country, Emma, the main character in *Madame Bovary*, devours sentimental novels and dreams about romantic love. She marries the first man ever to find her attractive, the decent and well-meaning but dull Dr. Charles Bovary. They have a little girl, but Emma finds no satisfaction in the tranquil life of a doctor's wife and a mother in a small French town. The fact that her husband is not even a mediocre doctor but is a downright bad doctor doesn't help any. Emma falls in love with a wealthy neighbor and embarks on a path that leads to her ruin. She has an affair with the neighbor, and she begins an extravagent shopping spree by mail order, on credit. After a while she prepares to elope with her lover, only to find that he already has eloped—without her. Devastated, she falls ill, but she recuperates when she meets a former acquaintance, a young man who has been secretly in love with her for years. They have an affair, and Emma reembarks on her shopping venture, sending her daughter to live with strangers. Eventually the merchant who has been supplying her with clothes, jewelry, and furniture confronts her with her enormous debt and demands immediate payment in return for promising not to tell Emma's husband of her affair. Emma, who is now desperate, begins selling off her own assets as well as Charles's property and his medical tools. In the end, forced to face her own degradation, she swallows poison and dies. Charles refuses to think evil of her and even when faced with the truth—Emma's love letters—sees only that she was a poor and desperate soul.

Study Questions

1. Can Emma's case be viewed as a case for psychological egoism?
2. Can Emma be considered an ethical egoist?
3. Emma gets her ideas about romantic passion from books. Does that mean that fiction can be morally dangerous?
4. Flaubert, the author, used to say, "Emma Bovary, c'est moi" (Emma Bovary, that's me). Do you think he viewed his protagonist in an overall negative or positive way?

MARGARET MITCHELL, *Gone with the Wind*

Novel (1936). Film version 1939.

The plot of the original story of Scarlett O'Hara is probably familiar to many readers, and I will mention only a few features of this very long novel in order to jog your memory or inspire you to read the book or watch the movie. Scarlett is a young girl of the antebellum South. She is secretly in love with Ashley, the son of a neighbor. Scarlett is a vivacious young woman, and most people would call her a flirt, but when she declares her love for Ashley (who is about to marry his cousin Melanie), she is very serious. Ashley, although he is attracted to Scarlett, lets her know that he intends to marry Melanie, and Scarlett becomes hysterical. Witness to this dramatic scene is Rhett Butler, an outcast and a cynic who sees Scarlett for what she is: a woman who is not unlike himself, with a strong will, a lust for life, and no scruples at all.

The Civil War breaks out. Scarlett marries Melanie's brother in order to spite Ashley, but she is widowed soon after. As the war proceeds, Scarlett attaches herself to Melanie in order to be close to Ashley when he comes home on leave. Melanie views Scarlett as a tireless source of help and support, especially when she undergoes a difficult childbirth, but Scarlett knows herself to be a hypocrite: She is only doing it for Ashley's sake. For Ashley's sake she cares for Melanie, for Ashley himself when he comes home from the war, and for their baby.

After the war, Scarlett is faced with having to pay enormous postwar taxes on the family estate, Tara. She resolves to come up with the money somehow. She offers herself as a lover to Rhett Butler, but he declines her offer because he has no money, and Scarlett is humiliated. She decides to seduce and marry her sister's boyfriend, who is getting wealthy running a sawmill. Tara is saved, for now. The remainder of the novel finds Scarlett in situation after situation in which she does what she thinks "she must," only to find that her efforts bring about unwanted consequences. In the end, alone, she seeks solace in her old motto: "I won't think about it today—I'll think about it tomorrow."

Study Questions

1. Is Scarlett a selfish woman?
2. Can you be selfish if you do things for someone you are in love with?
3. Compare and contrast Emma (from *Madame Bovary*) and Scarlett; do they have anything in common? Are there differences between them? Which of the two comes out as more morally tainted?
4. Do you think it is a coincidence that two famous fictional female characters (Emma and Scarlett) are both strong willed and self-serving, or do you think there is a pattern to such portrayals?

AYN RAND, *Atlas Shrugged*
Novel (1957).

Atlas, in Greek mythology, is the god who holds up the earth—and when Atlas shrugs, the world shakes. Ayn Rand's book is about the shake-up of the world by those who support it and hold up its economic foundation: the factory owners, the entrepreneurs, the railroad builders. It is not the workers but those who employ them who are the movers and the shakers of the world, and for Rand they have been abused by unions and "bleeding hearts" long enough. In this book she outlines her philosophy of objectivism "between the lines" of the novel, urging those people with creative powers to start thinking about themselves and be proud of what they do, for without them the world literally will come to a halt. In *Atlas Shrugged*, the movers and shakers go on strike, led by the mythic figure of John Galt and joined by the railroad tycoon Dagny Taggart, and in the end the common folk who have no talent or will to keep themselves going must perish because they simply don't have what it takes. This vision of ethical egoism sees the world divided between those who can think and create and those who are parasites on the creators; each person has a right to what he or she creates (and earns), and no one else has any right to any of it. The only duty we have is to look out for ourselves and not give our lives away to others who aren't willing to work for their own share. The following quote is from a conversation between Francisco d'Anconia, a railroad tycoon, playboy, and millionaire, and Henry Rearden, a steelworks owner and inventor who is beginning to understand that he has been letting people take advantage of him all his life:

"If you want to see an abstract principle, such as moral action, in material form—there it is. Look at it, Mr. Rearden. Every girder of it, every pipe, wire and valve was put there by a choice in answer to the question: right or wrong? You had to choose right and you had to choose the best within your knowledge—the best for your purpose, which was to make steel—and then move on and extend the knowledge, and do better, and still better, with your purpose as your standard of value. You had to act on your own judgment, you had to have the capacity to judge, the courage to stand on the verdict of your mind, and the purest, the most ruthless consecration to the rule of doing right, of doing the best, the utmost best possible to you. . . . But what I wonder about, Mr. Rearden, is why you live by one code of principles when you deal with nature and by another when you deal with men?"

. . . "What do you mean?"

"You have judged every brick within this place by its value to the goal of making steel. Have you been as strict about the goal which your work and your steel are serving? . . . Have you made any money?"

"No."

"When you strain your energy to its utmost in order to produce the best, do you expect to be rewarded for it or punished? . . . Now wherever there is a man who needs or uses metal in any way—Rearden Metal has made his life easier for him. Has it made yours easier for you?"

"No," said Rearden, his voice low.

". . . Did you want to see it used by whining rotters who never rouse themselves to any effort, who do not possess the ability of a filing clerk, but demand the income of a company president, who drift from failure to failure and expect you to pay their bills, who hold their wishing to an equivalent of your work and their need as a higher claim to reward than your effort . . . who proclaim that you are born to serfdom by reason of your genius, while they are born to rule by the grace of incompetence, that yours is only to give, but theirs only to take, that yours is to produce, but theirs to consume, that you are not to be paid, neither in matter nor in spirit, neither by wealth nor by recognition nor by respect nor by gratitude—so that they would ride on your rail and sneer at you and curse you, since they owe you nothing, not even the effort of taking off their hats which you paid for? Would this be what you wanted? Would you feel proud of it?"

"I'd blast that rail first," said Rearden, his lips white.

Study Questions

1. What is it that Francisco accuses Rearden of?
2. Can you identify Francisco's political standpoint and the standpoint he argues against?
3. Why is this considered an example of ethical egoism? Is it fair to call Ayn Rand's viewpoint egoistic?

Utilitarianism and Deontology

These stories are all, in some way, about evaluating one's actions from a basic principle that is either utilitarian (create as much happiness for as many as possible) or deontological (Kant's theory of duty: Do the right thing regardless of the consequences). Most of these stories are meant to be read from one of these viewpoints but can also be evaluated from the other, as the study questions will show.

JOHANN HERMAN WESSEL, *"The Blacksmith and the Baker" (1777)*
Poem. Loosely translated from Danish, from verse to prose.

Wessel is famous in his own country of Denmark for his satirical verses. This one may have been inspired by a real newspaper story or possibly by British fables of a similar kind.

Once upon a time there was a small town. The town blacksmith was a mean man. He had an enemy, and one day he and his enemy happened to meet at an inn. They proceeded to get drunk and exchange some nasty words. The blacksmith got mad and knocked the other man out; the blow turned out to be fatal. The blacksmith was carted off to jail, and he confessed, hoping that his opponent would forgive him in Heaven. Before his sentence was pronounced, four upstanding citizens asked to see the judge, and the most eloquent of them spoke:

"Your Wisdom, we know you are thinking of the welfare of this town, but this welfare depends on getting our blacksmith back. His death won't wake up the dead man, and we'll never find such a good blacksmith ever again."

The judge said, "But a life has been taken and must be paid for by a life. . . . "

"We have in town an old and scrawny baker who'll go to the devil soon, and since we have two bakers, how about taking the oldest one? Then you still get a life for a life."

"Well," said the judge, "that is not a bad idea, I'll do what I can." And he leafed through his law books but found nothing that said you can't execute a baker instead of a blacksmith, so he pronounced this sentence:

"We know that blacksmith Jens has no excuse for what he has done, sending Anders Petersen off to eternity; but since we have but one blacksmith in this town I would be crazy if I wanted him dead; but we do have two bakers of bread . . . so the oldest one must pay for the murder."

The old baker wept pitifully when they took him away. The moral of the story: Be always prepared to die! It comes when you least expect it.

FIGURE 7·3 "The Blacksmith and the Baker," illustration by Nils Wiwel, 1895.
Utilitarianism taken to an extreme: The baker is taken away to be executed for what
the blacksmith has done, because that is more useful to society. The policeman's belt
reads "Honest and Faithful," and the building in the background is the old Copenhagen courthouse with the inscription "With Law Must Land Be Built."

Study Questions

1. Do you think this is a fair picture of a utilitarian judge?
2. What might the utilitarian respond to this story?
3. What might a Kantian respond?

FYODOR DOSTOYEVSKY, *The Brothers Karamazov*

Novel (1881); film (1958).

(This excerpt should be read in conjunction with the outline of "The Ones Who Walk Away from Omelas," which follows.)

The two half brothers, Ivan and Alexey (Alyosha) Karamazov, are discussing an incident in which the powerful owner of a feudal estate has his dogs tear apart a little boy because the boy threw a stone at one of the dogs. Ivan asks whether the child's mother should ever forgive the tyrant.

> "Tell me yourself, I challenge you—answer. Imagine that you are creating a fabric of human destiny with the object of making men happy in the end, giving them peace and rest at last. Imagine that you are doing this but that it is essential and inevitable to torture to death only one tiny creature—that child beating its breast with its fist, for instance—in order to found that edifice on its unavenged tears. Would you consent to be the architect on those conditions? Tell me. Tell the truth."
>
> "No, I wouldn't consent," said Alyosha softly.
>
> "And can you accept the idea that the men for whom you are building would agree to receive their happiness from the unatoned blood of a little victim? And accepting it would remain happy forever?"
>
> "No, I can't admit it," said Alyosha suddenly, with flashing eyes.

URSULA K. LE GUIN, "The Ones Who Walk Away from Omelas"

Short story (1973).

There is a festival in the city of Omelas. The weather is perfect, the city looks its best, and people are happy and serene in their pretty clothes. This is a perfect place, with freedom of choice and no oppressive power enforcing the rules of religion, politics, or morality—and it works, because the people know they are responsible for their actions. This happy place is a Utopia, except for one thing: The happiness of the citizens is bought at a high price, with the full knowledge of every citizen.

In a basement under one of the public buildings there is a small, dark room, and here a child is kept prisoner. The child is never allowed out, it never hears a kind word, it has sores all over its body, it is malnourished, it is afraid of the dark and wants to go home.

All this is part of a greater plan. The child will never be let out—it will die within a short time—and presumably another child will take its place, for it is the suffering of this innocent being that makes the perfect life in Omelas possible. All the citizens know about it from the time they are adolescents, and they all must go and see the child so that they can understand the price of their happiness. They are disgusted and sympathetic for a while, but then they understand the master plan: the pain of one small individual in exchange for great communal happiness. Because the citizens know the immense suffering that gives them their beautiful life, they are particularly loving to each other and responsible for what they do. And what would they gain by letting the child go? The child is too far gone to be able to enjoy freedom, anyway, and what is one person's suffering compared to the realm of happiness that is achieved? So the people feel no guilt. However, a few young people and some adult visitors go to see the child, and something happens to them: They don't go home afterward, but keep on walking—through the city, through the fields, away from Omelas.

Study Questions

1. Where are they going, the ones who walk away? And why are they leaving?
2. How does Le Guin feel about the situation? Does she condone the suffering of the child, or is she arguing against it?
3. Develop a deontological critique of the people of Omelas (those who don't walk away).
4. Compare Le Guin's story with Dostoyevsky's story. Do they both illustrate the same idea, or is there a difference?

RICHARD SALE (DIRECTOR AND SCREENWRITER), *Abandon Ship!*

Film (1957).

The preceding three examples are antiutilitarian. This one, though, is perhaps intended as a defense of the theory of the Greatest Happiness Principle. *Abandon Ship!* explores such a complex problem that we might draw on other traditions, too, such as Kantian deontology, and Ayn Rand's ideas of self-reliance (see the study questions at the end of this example).

Based on a true story, this film opens during the aftermath of an explosion on a luxury liner far from shore. The ship sank so quickly that no S.O.S. signal was sent, and no lifeboats were lowered. Now, some twenty survivors are clinging to the one lifeboat that was launched. It is the captain's dinghy, and it can hold fourteen people maximum. The captain is dying, and he transfers his authority to his first officer, Alec Holmes (played by Tyrone Power), admonishing him to "save as many as you can." Holmes is hopeful that help may arrive, but when he realizes that no S.O.S. has been sent, he knows that their only option is to row for the coast of Africa, fifteen hundred miles away. An officer and a friend of Holmes, himself mortally wounded, tells Holmes that he won't be able to make it if he tries to keep everyone alive—he must "evict some tenants" in order to save others. To emphasize his point, the officer throws himself overboard, because he would only be a hindrance to the survival of the "fittest." Holmes at first will hear nothing of this plan, but when a storm approaches, he realizes that he must choose between the death of them all and the death of those who already are hurt and can't pull their weight. Under protest and at gunpoint, the others comply by forcing the wounded passengers and crewmen, who are wearing life preservers, overboard, and setting them adrift in shark-infested waters. One professor remarks, "This is an interesting moral problem," while another passenger insists that it is barbarism—the civilized thing to do would be to choose to die together.

A storm hits, and everybody on board survives because of Holmes's "weeding" process. In the morning, after the storm, one passenger tries to force Holmes to turn around and look for the ones that were adrift. Holmes kills the man in self-defense, but not before the man succeeds in wounding Holmes with a knife. Now Holmes applies his rule to himself and slips overboard so as not to be a burden, but the others rescue him and bring him back on board. Just as the passengers are getting ready to thank him for his foresight and effort, a ship is spotted on the horizon. Miraculously, help has arrived, "too soon," as a feisty woman passenger remarks—too soon for everybody to have decided to support Holmes in his plan to force some of the passengers overboard. The people on the boat are rescued (it is hinted that some of the evicted passengers are rescued, too), and Holmes goes on trial for murder. The film concludes with the question, "If you had been on the jury, would you have found Holmes guilty or innocent?"

Study Questions

1. How can this be seen as a defense of utilitarianism?
2. Do you agree that it would have been a more civilized thing for all of the passengers to die together?
3. Would you have convicted Holmes of murder? (In actual fact he was convicted, but he received a short-term sentence because of the unusual circumstances.)
4. How might Ayn Rand (author of *Atlas Shrugged*) have evaluated Holmes's solution?
5. Can you think of another way of solving Holmes's problem?
6. How might a Kantian evaluate Holmes's actions? (Remember that Kant's deontology involves not only "not treating people as means to an end," but also "universalizing one's maxim.")
7. What was Holmes's intention? Might a Kantian accept that as morally good?

NICHOLAS RAY (DIRECTOR) AND STEWART STERN (SCREENWRITER), *Rebel Without a Cause*

Film (1955).

This film is best known for being one of the only three films James Dean made before his untimely death at age twenty-four. Even if it is somewhat dated, depicting teen life in Los Angeles in the fifties, it is still eerily on the mark when it comes to depicting gang violence and the seductive nature of gang affiliation. We will look at two episodes in which the protagonist, Jim Stark, has problems communicating with his parents.

Jim and his parents have just moved to a new area, presumably because the family has a history of moving whenever Jim gets into trouble (Jim is prone to violence whenever he is accused of being "chicken"). Right away he tangles with the local gang and their leader Buzz; he also is on the verge of making friends with Buzz's girlfriend, Judy. He is challenged to a "chickie run," a stunt wherein he and Buzz will race stolen cars towards the edge of a cliff; whoever jumps out of the car first is "chicken." Jim goes home in a vain attempt to garner support from his father, a weak and indecisive man. Jim tells his father that he has to make a terribly hard choice, and he needs advice. His father tells him that he'll get pencil and paper, and together they will make a list of pros and cons. Jim, however, needs an absolute answer that reflects right or wrong, not an answer that depends on far-away consequences. He runs out and drives to the Millertown Bluff, where the chickie run is to take place.

He and Buzz meet and talk over the rules, and it is apparent that they have very similar personalities and might become good friends under other circumstances. The run takes place; Buzz's sleeve gets caught in the door handle, and he can't get out of the car. He plunges to his death, and the gang scatters in terror. Jim returns home to give his parents final chance to support him. He tells them everything. To his dismay, they don't support him in his intention to go to the police, but instead tell him that he "shouldn't have to suffer when nobody else is coming forth" and in ten years "will have forgotten all about it." Why ruin your future by becoming involved, they ask. He cries out to them, "But I am involved, and so are you!" What he needs from them—a moral rule that is absolute—he does not get, and so he leaves to find out what to do for himself.

The ending of the film involves more violence but also the discovery of Judy's love and, eventually, a kind of reconciliation with Jim's parents.

Study Questions

1. How can this film be seen as an illustration of a conflict between a utilitarian and a Kantian?
2. Is Jim being completely fair to his father?
3. Did Jim have to go through with the chickie run, or can you think of an alternative?
4. Should Jim have gone to the police or not?

FRED ZINNEMAN (DIRECTOR) AND CARL FOREMAN (SCREENWRITER), *High Noon*

Film (1952).

This film may be the most famous Western of all time, and yet it is not a "true" Western. There is very little riding, no troops or Indians, no cattle, no cowboys—but much talk about the right thing to do. This film was made in the early days of McCarthyism in Hollywood, and Zinneman (the director) has admitted that it is an allegory of the general attitude in Hollywood of 1952 of turning your back on friends who were accused (mostly falsely) of "un-American" (communist) activities, and who might have needed help. When it was produced, it was not considered to have any potential as a classic, but it has soared in public opinion ever since then, because, for one thing, it is a Western, but a Western of a different sort, a Western about the problems of budding civilization in the midst of an era of violence. The film also is very well crafted. The amount of time that elapses from the time that marshal Will Kane (portrayed by actor Gary Cooper) realizes he will have to face four gunmen alone because the whole town worries about the consequences of siding with him, to the time the actual gunfight takes place, is the exact amount of time you spend watching it in the theater or in front of your TV: 1-1/2 hours.

The plot is simple. Five years before, Kane brought a killer, Frank Miller, to justice. Miller was sentenced to hang, but "up North they commuted it to life, and now he's free," as the judge says. He is coming in on the noon train to have it out with Kane. Word of his intentions comes just as Kane is getting married in a civil ceremony (his wife, played by Grace Kelly, is a Quaker). He has already given up his job and is leaving town with his wife, when he turns around to face the gunmen coming in on the noon train. His wife, Amy, asks him why he is turning back—he doesn't have to play the hero for her, she says. He answers, "I haven't got time to tell you. . . . And if you think I like this, you're crazy."

In town, Kane tries to get his former deputies to join him, but everyone is afraid of Miller, except the deputy, who is the boyfriend of Helen Ramirez, Kane's former girlfriend. Helen is the only one who understands Kane's problem, because she has always felt like an outcast herself—and besides, she used to be Frank Miller's girlfriend, too. When Amy leaves Kane because she can't stand the threat of violence, she seeks out Helen because she thinks it is because of her that Kane is staying in town. Helen tells her, "If you don't know, I can't tell you." Helen's boyfriend looks up Kane and tries to force him to leave town so that he can take over as town marshal. He asks Kane why he is staying, and all Kane says is, "I don't know."

The mayor wants Kane to leave town so there will be no blood in the streets—such violence might deter investors from up North. The former sheriff wants Kane to leave town and says that keeping the law is an ungrateful business. Everybody wants him to leave, and at the train depot Frank Miller's three gunmen are waiting for the train that will bring Frank. But Kane feels compelled to stay, even with nobody to side with him.

FIGURE 7.4 *High Noon*, United Artists, 1952. Will Kane (Gary Cooper) has just been married and has resigned as marshal of Hadleyville, but a killer he helped put in jail is now looking for him with three other gunmen. He tries to get the townspeople to stand by him the way they did when he captured the killer five years earlier, but now everybody turns their backs on him because they would rather not get involved. Here a former friend, Herb (James Millican), is backing out of his promise to help Kane, having found out that nobody else is coming along.

The train arrives, a gunfight ensues in the dusty streets of the town, and two of Frank's gunmen are killed. In the end, Amy comes to Kane's rescue and kills the third of the gunmen; Kane kills Miller, and together he and Amy leave town—but not before Kane has thrown his tin star in the dust.

Study Questions

1. What makes Kane stay? Is he serious when he says, "I don't know"?
2. Is it fair of Kane to place Amy in a situation where she has to give up her own moral principles?
3. Why might we say that this is a "Kantian" Western?
4. How would a utilitarian judge Kane's feeling of conscience and duty?
5. Are the townspeople who refuse to help primarily deontologists, utilitarians, or ethical egoists?

James L. Conway (director) and Worley Thorne (teleplay), Star Trek: The Next Generation; episode entitled "Justice"
Television (1987).

The television series "Star Trek: The Next Generation" has supplied philosophy instructors with some superb examples of moral dilemmas dressed up as good entertainment.
This episode deals not only with a Kantian type of ethics, but also with its *shortcomings*.

The crew of the starship Enterprise are partaking of some rest and relaxation on what
seems like the ideal vacation planet: Everybody is friendly, sex is considered a nice way
for people to express their friendship (and it is, presumably, safe), and there is no crime.
For the adults this seems like paradise, but for Wesley, a young officer who is still in his
early teens, it is rather bewildering. He joins a group of children on the planet and shows
them how to play baseball, but he accidentally falls into some shrubbery that is marked
off by white bars. The other children become quite subdued when two uniformed officials show up. With a minimum amount of explanation, the officials tell Wesley that he
broke a rule—don't step on the grass—and now he must die.

The captain of the Enterprise, Picard, is alerted. The reason there is no crime on this
planet is because there is one overriding rule, and it is absolute: Do not break any rules
or you will die instantly. You never know when the attention of the "mediators" (the
execution squad) will focus on any of the forbidden zones (marked by white bars), but if
you are caught transgressing, you will die. Wesley has been caught; Wesley must die.

Picard's problem now is how to rescue Wesley. He can't use the "transporter," the
molecule disrupter beam that moves people from planet to ship, because a higher power
watching over this planet believes that he is interfering in their business and has frozen
the Enterprise's transport system. Furthermore, Picard must adhere to his own "prime
directive": Starfleet is not allowed to interfere with the internal affairs of nonspacefaring
peoples. And here is a population who is exceedingly moral—it is not a backward culture of immoral thugs. What to do? Picard is experiencing a conflict between his own
rules: "Keep the prime directive" versus "Do anything to save a crew member." At the
same time, he is threatened by the authors of the absolutist moral code, the higher beings
who are watching out for the people of the planet. Pleading that Wesley didn't know
doesn't do any good, because (as we all know) ignorance of the rules is no excuse. The
situation is put in focus for Picard when Data asks him, with his usual detached sense of
logic, if he is willing to sacrifice one member of the Enterprise for the safety of the rest.

In the end, Picard comes up with an answer that satisfies the higher beings, and with
the transporter functioning again, all the Enterprise crew members beam up and away.
What did Picard say to convince the higher beings to release Wesley? "Any mature moral
system must allow for exceptions." This may not seem very impressive, but in fact it is;
you may remember that it is the one major point brought against Kant's categorical
imperative.

FIGURE 7.5 *Star Trek: The Next Generation:* "Justice." Is it justice for Wesley or an inhumanly harsh sentence? Wesley (Wil Wheaton) has been caught trespassing on a planet visited by Starfleet, and only too late he learns that on this planet all crimes, big and small, are punishable by death. Here the lethal injection is being prepared for Wesley's execution, and we ask ourselves whether a system of laws that doesn't allow for exceptions is morally acceptable.

Study Questions

1. Can you think of another way Picard could have handled the situation, without violating the prime directive?
2. What is Kantian about the morality of the planet population?
3. Could you imagine a situation (perhaps this one qualifies) where it would be acceptable for a commander to sacrifice a member of his or her crew in order to save the lives of the rest of the crew? Under what circumstances might this be acceptable?

Part 3

HOW SHOULD I BE?
Theories of Virtue

Chapter 8

Socrates, Plato, and the Good Life

What Is Virtue?

Through most of Western civilization and most of the history of ethics, scholars have tried to answer the question, What should I do? Part 2 of this book explored this quest. Theories that consider what proper human conduct is often are referred to as *ethics of conduct.*

There is a more ancient approach to ethics, and in the past few decades this older approach has experienced a revival. This form of ethics asks the fundamental question, How should I be? In other words, it focuses on the development of certain characteristics, of a certain behavior pattern—in other words, on the development of what we call *character.* Because its foundation is in ancient Greek theories involving the question of how to be a virtuous person, this approach usually is referred to as *virtue ethics.*

The concept of virtue (Greek: *aretē*) is complex. For one thing, it carries certain associations, which it has acquired over the centuries; thus, in English, we may think of virtue as a basically positive concept—a virtuous person is someone you can trust.

We also may experience, however, a certain negative reaction to it; sometimes, a virtuous person is thought of as being rather dull and perhaps even sanctimonious (being called a "Goody Two Shoes" is not a compliment). In other languages, such as German, the term (*Tugend*) has all but lost its positive association in everyday language.

When we look back to the origin of Western virtue theory, ancient Greece, we find no negative associations, because the word *aretē* signifies a different kind of person altogether: not a person of untainted thoughts and behavior, but a person who does what he or she does best and does it excellently, on a regular basis. We still have a trace of the ancient meaning of aretē in the word *virtuosity*. Originally, a virtuous person was a *virtuoso* at everything he or she did, due to proper choices and good habits but, above all, because such a person had succeeded in developing a good character.

What Is Character?

Today we often take a deterministic view of the concept of character. It is something we are born with, something we can't help. If we try to go against our character, it will surface in the end. This viewpoint may or may not be correct, but in any event it is shaped by twentieth-century schools of thought in philosophy and psychology. Not everyone shares this view; it often is pointed out that we may be born with a certain character, but our character can be molded to a certain extent when we are young, and it certainly can be *tested* throughout our lives. This point of view comes closer to the prevailing attitude toward virtue among Greek philosophers: Character is indeed something we are born with, but it also is something that can and must be shaped. We are not the victims of our character, and if we let ourselves be victimized by our own unruly temperaments, then we are to blame.

The Case for Virtue Ethics

What happened to virtue ethics, and why has it been revived by scholars of ethics recently? By and large, what happened was Christianity—with its emphasis on following God's rules and conducting oneself according to the will of God. A chasm appeared between the teachings of the classical tradition and the moral and philosophical viewpoints of rising Christianity. Disagreements exceeded verbal argumentation and turned violent for the first time in Christian history (but unfortunately not for the last time).

To *do the right thing* became the main imperative of Christian ethics; however, the concepts of virtue and vice became main elements. Scholars of ethics point out, however, that it is not so much the question of *shaping your own character* that is important in this tradition as it is recognizing the *frailty of human character in general* and believing that with the help of God one may be able to choose the right thing to do.

Victims of Fanaticism

Two examples of Christians' early, violent reactions to the world of the classical tradition are both from the Egyptian city of Alexandria. In the year 415 C.E. a mob of fanatical Christian monks, possibly inspired by the Bishop of Alexandria, attacked and murdered one of the first women philosophers on record, Hypatia, leader of the Neoplatonic Institute in Alexandria. As far as we know, Hypatia lectured on Plato, Aristotle, and Pythagoras, and thus the Christians associated her with paganism. As she was riding through town in her chariot during one of the many religious riots, the mob dragged her out of her cart, tore off her clothes, and flayed her alive with clamshells. Hypatia had done her research in the great library at Alexandria. The library was founded by one of Alexander the Great's generals, Ptolemy I, who became the founder of an Egyptian dynasty (4th century B.C.E.). The library was expanded over the centuries and probably contained most of the works of Greek philosophy, literature, and science, either in the original or copied by hand. During the reign of Queen Cleopatra, one of Ptolemy's descendants, a part of the library was burned down by the Roman army, possibly by mistake. When another section of the library went up in flames in 391 C.E. (along with a pagan temple) there was no mistaking that the destruction was caused by Christian extremist fundamentalists. The final destruction of the library came at the hands of Islamic fundamentalist invaders in 646 C.E. Scholars estimate that science suffered a setback of perhaps a millennium from the loss of the library; humanity's loss of works of art—philosophy, literature, drama, and even artifacts—cannot be measured.

From the time of the Renaissance to well into the twentieth century, questions of ethics were less a matter of doing the right thing to please God, and more a matter of doing the right thing because it led to general happiness—because it was prudent, or because it was logical. However, present-day scholars interested in virtue ethics have put forth the following argument: You may choose to do "the right thing" to please God, or to escape unpleasant consequences, or to make some majority happy, or to satisfy your inner need for logic—but you may still be a less than admirable person. You may give to charity, pay your taxes on time, remember your nieces' and nephews' birthdays, hold the door for physically challenged people, and still be a morose and mean person. As we saw in the chapter on psychological egoism, you may be doing all these "correct" things just to get passport to heaven, or to be praised by others, or to make sure they owe you a favor. So "doing the right thing" doesn't guarantee that you are a good person, with a good *character*. However, if you strive to develop a good

FIGURE 8.1 Hypatia (370–415 C.E.), the leader of the Neoplatonic Institute in Alexandria and one of the first female philosophers that we know of, was driving through the streets of town in her chariot when she was intercepted, tortured, and killed by Christian extremists.

character—to be courageous, or protective, or tolerant, or compassionate—then, on the basis of this character trait, you will *automatically* make the right decisions about what to do, what course of action to take. In other words, virtue ethics is considered to be more fundamental than ethics of conduct, yielding better results.

In today's discussions on ethics, opinions are divided as to the merits of virtue versus conduct; however, no virtue theory is complete without recognition of the importance of conduct. We can have a marvelous "character," but if it never translates into action or conduct, it is not of much use, and how do we develop a good character in the first place if not through *doing* something right? Also, one of the most conduct-oriented ethical theories, that of Kant's deontology, has the question of character imbedded in it. For Kant, a good character in the form of a *good will*, a fundamental respect for other people, and respect for the nature of the moral law itself is essential to the moral decision process.

In this and the following chapters we will look at the classical virtue theories of Plato and Aristotle. We'll then move on to comparable theories in non-Western traditions, and finally we'll examine some examples of modern virtue theory. The section will conclude with narrative examples.

The Question of How to Live

The Good Teacher

The saying goes that a good teacher is one who makes herself or himself superfluous. In other words, a good teacher lets you become your own authority, so to speak; she or he does not keep you at the psychological level of a student forever. As a matter of fact, great personalities who have had considerable influence on their followers often have failed in this respect. For a teacher it is hard to "let go" and consider the job done (whether one is a professor or a parent), and for a student it often is tempting to absorb the authority of the teacher, because life is hard enough as it is without having to make your own decisions about everything all the time. This is what the good teacher or parent prepares the student for, however—autonomy, not dependence.

The teacher-student relationship between Socrates and Plato probably would not have become so famous if Plato had remained merely a "student," a shadow of the master. Indeed, we have Socrates's own words (at least through the pen of Plato) that the good teacher does not impose his ideas on the student, but rather serves as a *midwife* for the student's own dormant intellect. In many ways Socrates has become a philosophical ideal. As we shall see, he stood by his own ideals in the face of adversity and danger; he believed in the intellectual capacities of everyone; he strove to awaken people's sense of critical thinking rather than give them a set of rules to live by; and above all, he believed that "*the unexamined life is not worth living.*"

Socrates, Man of Athens

What do we know of Socrates? There is no doubt that he lived—he is not a figment of Plato's imagination, as much as Plato may have made use of poetic license in his writings. Aristophanes, the writer of comedies in Athens, refers to Socrates in his play *The Clouds* (albeit it in a rather unflattering way). The fact is that we don't have any writings by Socrates himself, for his form of communication was the discussion, the live conversation—what has become known as the "dialogue." From this word is derived the term for Socrates's special way of teaching, the *dialectic method* (sometimes also called the *Socratic method*). A method of teaching that uses conversation only, and no textbooks, is not exactly designed to affect posterity, but posterity has nevertheless been immensely affected by our indirect access to Socrates through the writings—the "Dialogues"—of Plato.

FIGURE 8.2 Socrates (470?–399 B.C.E), Greek philosopher and the first thinker to focus on the question of how one ought to live. Although Socrates didn't leave any writings when he died, his teachings have become part of the Western philosophical tradition through the *Dialogues* of his student Plato.

What we know of Socrates is that he lived in Athens from approximately 470 to 399 B.C.E. He was married to Xantippe and had children. He was one of several teachers of philosophy, science, and rhetoric in Athens at a time when internal politics were volatile (aristocrats versus democrats), and when Greece, which had experienced a golden age of cultural achievements in the wake of wars, was actually on the verge of decline. The single most important political element of the time was the city-state, the *polis* (the origin of the word *politics*). With the peculiar features of the Greek countryside—the inland features of tall mountains and the seaside features of islands—the stage had been set for centuries for a specific power structure: small, independent, powerful realms warring and/or trading with each other. Two of the main areas were Athens and Sparta. Each area, a state in itself, considered itself to be geographically Greek but politically specific to its particular *polis*. Thus it meant more to an Athenian to be a citizen of Athens than it meant to be Greek. Being a free citizen of a particular *polis* carried with it an inordinate pride. Today we might condemn such a pride as being nationalistic or even chauvinistic (in the original sense of the word); for a Greek of the time it was a reasonable feeling.

In one of Plato's Dialogues, *Phaedrus*, Socrates and a friend, Phaedrus, have ventured outside the city walls, and Socrates carries on about the beauty of nature, the trees and the flowers to such a degree that Phaedrus remarks that Socrates acts like a tourist. Socrates agrees, because he never ventures outside of Athens, not even for a walk in nature. The city of Athens is everything to him. It is the life among people, the communication, the discussions, the company of friends that is important to him—not nature, as beautiful as it may be:

> My appetite is for learning. Trees and countryside have no desire to teach me anything; it's only the men in the city that do.

It is not unusual to hear a big-city person say the same thing today—that New York, or Paris, or Rio has everything they could ever want. Most of us think such people are missing out on a few things, but Socrates's attitude becomes crucial to our understanding of his conduct toward the end of his life.

The Death of Socrates and the Works of Plato

In many cultures we find the attitude that we can't judge someone's life until it is over, that the ending helps define—sometimes even determine—how we think of the life spent. This may seem terribly unfair, for few of us are in full control over our lives, and we would prefer not to have our accomplishments judged primarily by circumstances beyond our control. In the case of Socrates, though, it seems fitting that his life is judged in the light of his death, for in the face of adversity, in the ultimate "situation beyond control," he seems to have remained in full control of *himself*. This is another reason that Socrates has become not just the philosopher's ideal, but a human role model: because he did not "lose his head" but instead faced injustice with courage and rationality.

After what in antiquity passed for a long life (he was nearing age seventy), Socrates found himself in a difficult political situation, brought about by several factors. First, Socrates had supported the aristocratic form of government of Athens, and the powers of the city were now democratic. Second, Socrates had great influence among the young men of Athens—those young men who might be of political influence in the future—and many were the sons of noblemen. Third, Socrates conducted his classes in public (this was customary at the time in Athens, prior to the formalization of classes, schools, and academy life), and his method was well known to his students as well as to any city council member who might cross the *Agora* while Socrates was teaching. Socrates used a certain method of *irony* to get his point across, and this often involved engaging politicians in a discussion under the pretext of ignorance in order to trick the speaker into revealing his own ignorance or prejudice. His students adored him for it, because this was the ultimate "questioning of authority." The fact that Socrates himself may have been serious, in a roundabout way, about claiming his ignorance was something his listeners may not have realized. Socrates did not adhere to any one conception of reality unless it could be tested by reason; in other words, he would not profess to "know" anything for certain before investigating it and discussing it. This attitude, which essentially was one of humility rather than arrogance, seems to have been lost on his enemies, and over the years he acquired a considerable number of such enemies.

Eventually his enemies took action; there was no way of getting rid of Socrates by political means, so they resorted to what appears to be a standard charge: that Socrates was "offending the gods and corrupting the young." Socrates was tried, and he declared himself not guilty—indeed, he declared himself deserving of a retirement paid by the city of Athens. The verdict was guilty, and the sentence was as standard as the charge: death by poison.

It seems possible that his enemies did not intend to get rid of Socrates by actually executing him. The standard reaction to such charges by accused citizens was to leave the city and go elsewhere within the Greek realm, and there were many places to choose from, because this realm extended from Italy well into the Middle East. However, because Socrates chose to stand trial, arguing that by leaving he would be admitting guilt, the verdict was inevitable. Even to the last minute there were powers working to free him; his friends, many of whom were of considerable influence, conspired to spring him from jail and bring him to exile in safety. In Plato's dialogue *Crito* we hear how Socrates's good friend Crito pleads with him to listen to his friends and take their offer of escape and life, because "otherwise people will say we didn't do enough to help you." Socrates answers:

> In questions of just and unjust, fair and foul, good and evil, which are the subjects of our present consultation, ought we to follow the opinion of the many and to fear them; or the opinion of the one man who has understanding?

. . . Then, my friend, we must not regard what the many say of us: but what he, the one man who has understanding of just and unjust, will say, and what the truth will say.

When Crito suggests that Socrates ought to escape because he has been convicted by unjust laws, Socrates replies that two wrongs don't make a right, and the laws of Athens have supported him throughout his life; even though unjust, they are still the laws of Athens. If he, Socrates, had been less of a faithful citizen of Athens, he might choose to leave, but because he never left the city, not even to see the Olympic games, he believes he has to live by his own rule of respecting the laws and the rules of reason and virtue, and not turn his back on them.

So Socrates, the citizen of Athens, could not envision a life away from the city, even when the alternative was death.

Plato tells us about the last, dignified minutes of Socrates's life, hereby giving history and philosophy the legacy of someone who chose to die for a rational principle. The scene is vividly described in the dialogue *Phaedo*. In the end, Socrates' friends and students are gathered to say goodbye. They are on the verge of breaking down, while Socrates does his best to keep their spirits up. Even the jailer who brings in the poison apologizes to the old philosopher for having to cause him harm and hopes Socrates will not hold it against him. Socrates assures him that he will not and swallows the poison, an extract of hemlock. He then lies down, and the end approaches quickly. His last words to his friends are to make sure they pay back a rooster he owes Asclepius, and they promise to do so. The meaning of this request has been discussed by philosophers ever since. Was Socrates driven by the memory of an unpaid debt, or was he talking in symbolic terms? Asclepius was a regular Greek name but also the name of the god of healing. Did he want his friends to sacrifice the rooster to the god because Asclepius had "cured" him, that is, released his soul from the prison of the body? We can only guess.

The effect of Socrates's death on Plato was profound. Born in about 427, Plato had been Socrates's student, in an informal sense, for over twenty years, and the death of his teacher caused him to take leave of Athens for a lengthy period. Eventually he returned to start his own school of philosophy, the *Academy* (thus named because it was the name of the building he was using). This school appears to have been the beginning of a more formalized teaching institution, with regular lectures and several professors associated with the school. As Plato took on the teaching mantle of his teacher, he began to reconstruct Socrates's intellectual legacy by writing his *Dialogues*. These books remain some of the most influential writings in philosophy, but they also are works of literature, as brilliant as any drama written in the antiquity. Socrates and his friends and students come alive. We understand their way of talking, and we gain insight into their way of thinking, which, on occasion, is rather alien to our own day and age. The early dialogues of Plato give a picture of Socrates that is very fresh and probably quite accurate. However, scholars believe that in later dialogues the image of Socrates changes into something that is more Plato's image of an ideal philosopher

FIGURE 8.3 Plato (427?–347 B.C.E). Greek philosopher. A student of Socrates for many years, he nevertheless developed a philosophical theory, the Theory of Forms, which seems to have gone far beyond the teachings of his master. Our knowledge about Socrates comes chiefly from Plato's *Dialogues*, where Socrates regularly appears as the main character and leader of the discussions.

than Socrates himself. Indeed, in the last dialogues, Socrates appears as Plato's mouthpiece for his own advanced theories on metaphysics—theories that Socrates probably never held himself. This may mean that Socrates was indeed a good teacher who did not hinder Plato from "graduating" intellectually.

The Good Life

We already have seen Socrates's answer to Crito: Some things are more important than life itself, such as being true to your principles, no matter how others may feel about it. This holds the key to what Socrates seems to have considered "the good life" or a life worth living—a life where one is not ruled by the opinion of others, or even by one's own "opinions," those ideas of ours that may or may not have some basis in the truth, but that we haven't bothered to examine any more closely. If we stop for a minute and examine such opinions, we will probably discover that they constitute the basis for the majority of our viewpoints: We think we live in a great country, or perhaps we think we live in a deceitful, oppressive country. We think that chicken soup is good for colds, or else we think that taking Dristan will make us fit to go to work when we're sick. Perhaps we think that premarital sex is bad in itself, or we think that it is the only way to find out whether two people are compatible. We may think that what scientists say must be true, as long as they are wearing white smocks. Perhaps we think that people who believe in UFOs are loons, or we think that UFOs abduct humans from time to time. We think a lot of things, and if we just allow ourselves to examine these opinions, we usually will find that they are based on very flimsy evidence. Of course, on occasion we feel strongly about something precisely because we *have* examined it, but in that case, Socrates would say, we are not talking about "opinion" (*doxa*) anymore—we are talking about knowledge (*epistēmē*). This, for Socrates, was the test of truth: Can it stand up to unprejudiced scrutiny? If so, it must override any sort of opinion we may have, even though it may hurt the feelings of others, because if they see the truth, they, too, will understand, because *only igno-rance leads to wrongdoing*. For Socrates as well as for Plato this is a truth in itself: No one is willfully evil, provided that he or she understands the truth about the situation. And if a person still chooses the wrong course of action, it must be because his or her understanding is faulty.

For a modern person the response to this seems inevitable: Suppose there is more than one way of looking at the situation? In other words, suppose there is more than one truth? We are so used to assuming that there is more than one way of looking at something that we sometimes assume that there is no truth at all. This, however, is very far from the intellectual attitude of Socrates. For Socrates as well as for Plato each situation has its Truth, and each thing can be described in one way that best captures its true nature, its essence. This does not mean that this was a common attitude among Greek thinkers. In Socrates' own time, contact with other cultures had brought about a certain amount of cultural relativism, and Greece was sufficiently heterogeneous to foster a tolerance of different customs. Accordingly, for many of Socrates' contem-poraries, such as the Sophists, relativism became the accepted answer to the search for absolute truth. For Socrates the theory that virtue might be a question of personal preference or relative to one's own time and culture was the epitome of misunder-standing, and much of the Socratic quest for the true nature, the essence, of a thing or a concept is a countermeasure to the prevailing relativism of Athens's intelligentsia.

Virtue for Socrates means to question the meaning of life and to keep one's integ-rity while searching, to not be swayed by one's physical longings, or fear of unpleasant situations, or concern for comfort. This ideal is attainable, because the Truth can be found—in fact, it can be found by *anyone* who has as a guide a teacher with integrity. In other words, Socrates says we can't hope to attain virtue without the use of our *reason*. Later on in history (in particular, during the Middle Ages) the link between virtue and reason was weakened, but for Plato and Socrates, as well as for Greek antiquity as such, the connection was obvious. Using our reason will make us realize what virtue is and will actually make us virtuous.

The good life, therefore, is not a pleasant life in which we seek gratification for the sake of having a good time. The good life is strenuous but gratifying in its own way, because one *knows* that one seeks and sees the Truth, and one is in control of oneself.

The Virtuous Person

Plato did not limit himself to describing the virtuous person in general terms; in his dialogue *The Republic* he presents a detailed description of what makes a person vir-tuous. He draws a parallel between a well-governed state and a well-balanced indi-vidual. In Part 4 we will take a closer look at that theory—one of the first theories of human nature in the Western tradition. For now, let us focus on what makes a person good. You may remember that Plato's brother Glaucon told a story about the Ring of Gyges, stating that if you had the chance to get away with something and you didn't, you had to be stupid. For Socrates this matter was of grave importance, and this was his answer: A person who does something unjust to others is either ignorant or sick. If we inform that person that he is being unjust, he may realize his ignorance and improve himself. But there is the chance that he will laugh in our face. In that case, Socrates said, he is simply not well—he is out of balance. (When I say "Socrates says . . ." it is the same as saying "Plato says," because the words assigned to Socrates in the dialogues are, as far as we know, the opinions of Plato, at least in most cases.) Glaucon's argument that an unjust person is happier than a just person carries no weight with Socrates, because an unjust person can't be happy at all; only a well-balanced person can be happy. But what is a well-balanced person?

Everybody has desires, and sometimes these desires can be very strong. We may want something to drink when we are thirsty, something to eat when we are hungry; we have desires for sex, for power, and for many other things. We also have desires to get away from things, as when we move away from a fire to which we're too close. These needs and wants Plato calls *appetites*, and these are what we must control if we are to achieve the good life. Appetites may rule a person's life, but that is not a good thing, because the things we desire aren't necessarily the things that are good for us. (As a matter of fact, Plato is not just talking truisms here; there are many philosophers who believe that what is natural for humans is good for them!) So sometimes we pull away from what we want because we realize that it will be bad for us. This power that pulls us back is our *rational element*, our *reason*.

There is a third element at play; Plato calls it *spirit*. Sometimes he also calls it *willpower*. We feel it when we sometimes let our appetites win out over our reason; afterward we feel disgusted with ourselves, and this anger directed at ourselves is our spirit. When we fall off our diet, our reason may have lost the battle, but our spirit will be angry at our weakness and will keep bothering us. What, then, should a person do? Establish a good working relationship between reason and spirit; let reason be clear about what it wants to do, and then "train" the spirit to help control the appetites. Reason and spirit will, side by side, keep the body healthy and the soul balanced. When reason rules, the person is *wise*; when spirit controls the appetites, that person is also *brave* (because it takes courage to say no to temptation and yes to a painful experience); and when the appetites are completely controlled, the person is *temperate*. Such a person is well balanced and would not dream of being unjust to anybody; on the contrary, he or she would be the very picture of *justice*, and justice is the virtue that describes the well-balanced human being who is wise, brave, and temperate. Only this kind of person can be happy in the true sense of the word; Glaucon's idea that an unjust person is happier than a just person can be discarded, because such a person is off balance.

How do we go about examining the nature of virtue in a practical sense? Socrates would begin with a concept, a word of common usage, such as *justice*, or *piety*, and ask his partners in the dialogue to define it, under the assumption that there would be one, and only one, description that would be the true one. At this point in the Platonic dialogues we begin to lose the sense that it is Socrates talking, for a theory develops that is uniquely Platonic: the Theory of Forms.

The Forms and the Good

What Is a Form?

When we ask about a person's view of reality, we generally want to know whether that person is religious or an atheist, pessimistic or optimistic about other people and events, interested in a historical perspective or mainly looking to the present and the future, and so on. Philosophically speaking, however, a person's view of reality is what we call *metaphysics*. What exactly is the nature of reality as such? In philosophy the answer will be one of three major types: Reality is made up of things that can be measured (*materialism*); or, Reality is totally spiritual, all in the mind (*idealism*); or, Reality is part matter, part mind (*dualism*). What, exactly, was Socrates' philosophical view of reality? Plato's early dialogues indicate that he seems to have believed in an immortal soul that leaves the body at death, which would make him a dualist. In later dialogues, though, Plato chooses to let Socrates speak for a theory—which was obviously Plato's own—that says that reality is very much different from what our common sense tells us. What we see, and hear, and feel around us is really a shadowy projection of "true reality." Our senses can't experience it, but our mind can, because this true reality is related to our mind: It is one of the Ideas, or *Forms*.

So what exactly is a Form? Today it is hard to grasp Plato's concept, but for the Greek mind of Plato's own day it was not so alien. In early times the Greeks saw each good thing as represented by some divinity; there was a goddess for justice, another for victory. There were "muses," lesser goddesses representing each form of art. The Olympic gods also had their own areas of protection. At the time of Plato many intellectuals, including Plato himself, had left traditional Greek religion behind. Some of the ancient tendency to personify abstract ideas, though, may have survived in his Forms. A Form is at once the ideal abstraction and sole source of each thing that resembles it. Let us look at an example. There are all kinds of *beds* today—double beds, twin beds, bunk beds, futons, waterbeds, hammocks. Plato would ask, What makes these things beds? We, today, would approach the question in a functionalistic manner and say something about them all being things "to sleep on." Plato would say they are all beds because they all participate in the Form of Bed, a kind of ideal "bed-ness" that they not only have in common as a *concept*, but that actually *exists* above and beyond each singular bed. It is this quality that gives the bed its share of reality, as a sort of dim copy of the true Bed Form. This realm of Forms is true reality, because the entire world in which we move around is only a dim copy of the ideal Form. Where exactly *is* this world of Forms? It is nowhere that you can see and touch it, because then it would just be another example of a copy. It has to be "out of this world," in a realm that our body does not have access to, but our *mind* does! So it is through our intellect that we can touch true reality, and only through our intellect. This is why Plato has Socrates tell Phaedrus that trees and countryside can't teach him anything—because there is nothing to be learned from the senses except confusion.

Three Theories of Metaphysics

In philosophy we encounter three major theories of the nature of reality, or of metaphysics: *materialism*, *idealism*, and *dualism*. Through the ages people have leaned toward one or the other, and today the prevailing theory in the Western world is overwhelmingly *materialistic*. This does not mean that people are overwhelmingly interested in accumulating riches, although this may be the case. Metaphysical materialism has nothing to do with greed; it merely means that you think reality consists of things that are *material*—they or their effects can be *measured* in some sense. This category includes everything from food to briefcases to brainwaves. It follows that a materialist doesn't believe in the reality of things supposedly immaterial, such as souls or spirits. Typical philosophical materialists are Thomas Hobbes, Karl Marx, and Paul and Patricia Churchland. *Idealism*, on the other hand, is the theory that only spiritual things have true existence, and the material world is somehow just an illusion. Again, this has very little to do

with the colloquial use of the word, which we associate with a person with high ideals. Few people in philosophy define themselves as idealists today, but this theory has had a certain influence in previous years. Bishop Berkeley was an idealist, and so was the German philosopher G.W.F. Hegel. The Hindu belief that the world we see is a mere illusion, *maya*, is also an example of idealism. The theory of *dualism* combines materialism and idealism in that a dualist believes reality consists of a matter-side and a spirit-side—in other words, that although the body is material, the soul/spirit/mind is immaterial and perhaps immortal. Although this theory seems to appeal to our common sense, it poses several logical problems, which philosophy has not been able to solve, for how exactly does the mind affect the body, if the mind is immaterial and the body is material? René Descartes is the most famous of the dualists, but Plato also is often counted among them, although some might prefer to call him an idealist because of his theory of Forms.

The only true lesson in reality we can have is when we let our mind, our intellect, contemplate the Forms, because the world we see changes constantly, but *the world of Forms never changes*. The Forms are eternal, and for Plato (and for many other philosophers), the more enduring something is, the more real it is.

Because the world of Forms is purely spiritual and immaterial, some philosophers choose to call Plato an idealist; however, more prefer to call him a dualist, because the world of matter is not "nonexistent," but merely of a lesser, shadowy existence than the world of Forms.

Does everything have a Form? Concepts like justice, love, and beauty have their natural place in the realm of Forms; they may be on this earth incompletely, but their

The Theory of Anamnesis

How do we know about the Forms if we can't learn about them by observing the world around us? Plato believed that we remember the Forms from the time before we were born, because during this time the soul's home was the realm of the Forms themselves. At birth the soul forgets its previous life, but, with the aid of a philosopher "in the know," we can be reminded of the nature of true reality. This is one of the functions of Socrates in the literature of Plato—to cause his students to remember their lost knowledge. The process is known as *anamnesis*, a re-remembering, or, literally, a nonforgetting. In Plato's dialogue *Meno*, Socrates shows that this knowledge is accessible to everyone, as he helps a young slave-boy "remember" truths of math and logic that he has never learned in this life. Plato, furthermore, believed in *reincarnation* (transmigration of souls). Socrates claims that the soul must undergo several cycles of life before it is purified sufficiently to go back to the Forms to stay forever. Scholars speculate that Plato may have been under the direct or indirect influence of Hindu theories of Karma and reincarnation, which had been influential in India for at least five hundred years prior to Plato's own time.

Forms are flawless. Cats and dogs obviously have Forms; things of nature have a perfect Form in the spiritual realm, which gives them reality. Manufactured objects have Forms, too, so in the realm of Forms there is a Form of a chair, a knife, a cradle, and a winding staircase. What about a Form of something that has not "always" been—like a computer, a videogame, or a microwave oven? Here we are moving into an uncomfortable area of Plato's theory, because even if microwave ovens are a new invention, presumably their Form has always existed. But what about Forms for dirt, mud, and diseases? Plato gives us the impression that the Forms are perfect and somehow closer to goodness than things on this earth; however, it is hard to envision perfect dirt, mud, and diseases, but this is certainly what the Theory of Forms implies. (A generation later, Plato's student Aristotle was to criticize the Theory of Forms for assuming that every phenomenon has a Form. Aristotle asserted that some phenomena are merely a "lack" or deficiency of something. A doughnut hole doesn't have a Form—it is just the empty middle of a doughnut.)

The Form of the Good

For Plato the world of Forms represents an orderly reality, nothing like the jumble of sensory experience. Forms are ordered according to their importance and according

FIGURE 8.4 In Plato's "Myth of the Cave," a group of prisoners is placed so they can only see on the wall of the cave reflections of objects carried back and forth in front of a fire behind them. Since this is all they see, they assume it to be reality. Had Plato been acquainted with movie theatres, he might have chosen the movie screen as a metaphor for the shadow-world of the senses.

to their dependence on other Forms. Certainly worms and dirt have Forms, but they are very low in the hierarchy; at the highest level are abstract concepts such as justice, virtue, and beauty. At the very top of the hierarchy Plato sees the Form of the Good as the most important Form and also as the Form from which everything else derives.

Is the Form of the Good a god, in the final analysis? Followers of Plato around the fourth and fifth centuries, the *Neoplatonists*, leaned toward that theory, but it is hard to say whether Plato himself had specifically religious veneration for his Forms; it is certain that he had intellectual respect and veneration for them and for the Form of the Good in particular.

The Form of the Good allows us to understand a little better what Plato means by saying that evil acts stem from ignorance only, because, according to the theory of Forms, if a person realizes the existence of the Forms and in particular the highest

The Cave

A brief outline of Plato's "Myth of the Cave": In a large cave a group of prisoners are kept chained to their seats so they can look only in one direction, toward a huge wall. Behind them there is a fire, and the fire is casting shadows on the wall. The prisoners, having never seen anything else, believe these shadows are all the reality there is. (So might someone believe who has grown up in a movie theater or in front of a big screen TV.) Suppose one of the prisoners frees himself and climbs out of the Cave. What does he see? At first nothing, because the light is too strong, but after a while he realizes the true reality of things and the pitiful existence of the others in the cave. He wants to stay out in the fresh air and the sunlight, but he knows his duty: to go back and tell the others. He does, and at first he can't see in the dark at all. His fellow prisoners ridicule him, but he persists. Who knows, perhaps some day he can get someone to listen to him.

Form of them all, the Good, it will be impossible for that person to deliberately choose to do wrong; the choice of wrongdoing can come only from ignorance of the Good. The choice to follow the Good is not an easy one, though, even when we have knowledge of it, because we have desires that pull us in other directions. Besides, the first time we hear about the Forms, the theory sounds so outlandish that we refuse to accept our own recollection of it. Plato tells a story to illustrate this, the "Myth of the Cave."

As the Cave is our everyday world of the senses, and as we are the prisoners who only see two-dimensional shadows instead of a multidimensional reality, so we have the same problems that the prisoners have when one prisoner stands up and claims that he or she has "seen the light" and knows that reality is totally different from what we think. How do we respond to such "prophets?" We ignore them, or ridicule them, or silence them and continue to live on in our illusion. And what is the duty of the philosopher who has seen "the light" of true reality, the Good and the other Forms, according to Plato? To return to the Cave, even if it would be wonderful to remain in the light of the Truth and forget about the world. The philosopher's duty is to go back and tell the others, and this, Plato believed, was what he himself was doing with his dialogues. For Plato, Truth was not something relative that differed for each person—it was an absolute reality beyond the deceptive world of the senses, a reality that never changes and that we, when we shed the chains of our physical existence—either intellectually or through death—will be able to see and be in the presence of.

As we will see in Part 4, this idea of a never-changing realm of goodness, light, and justice to which our soul can have access made its way into Christianity, along with the Platonic disdain for the physical world as an obstruction to this access. This disdain has been heavily criticized since the end of the nineteenth century by scholars such as Nietzsche who believe that it shows an abysmal contempt for the only true reality there is: the ever-changing reality of our physical existence on this earth.

Narratives That Illustrate Socratic Virtue

There is no separate section in this book containing stories that illustrate Socratic virtue theory, because Plato's dialogues are, in a sense, stories themselves—dramatizations of Socrates's life and ideas. "The Myth of the Cave" is even a story within a story; it is part of the dialogue of *The Republic*, and Plato was particularly interested in such myths, or fables, as he called them. They don't resemble classical myths of gods and heroes very much, but for Plato the best classical myths taught lessons worth repeating, and this is the sense in which he wrote myths. They are stories worth repeating, and they serve as shortcuts to his more complex metaphysical and ethical theories. Another famous myth illustrating the nature of reality and proper codes of behavior is the "Myth of the Charioteer" from the dialogue *Phaedrus*. We will take a look at it in Part 4.

Chapter 9

Aristotle's Virtue Theory

Aristotle the Scientist

Empirical Knowledge and the Realm of the Senses

After Plato's death in 347 B.C.E., leadership of the Academy fell to his nephew, Speusippus. History believes that another man had expected to take over, and with good reason, for he was by far the best student ever to be associated with the Academy. This man was Aristotle, and he had studied for twenty years with Plato. Scholars now think that because of the amount of traveling done by Plato, Aristotle may never have been especially close to his teacher; it seems certain that the closeness between Socrates and Plato was never repeated between Plato and Aristotle.

Because Aristotle was not a native-born Athenian but was born in Stagira in Northern Greece (in 384 B.C.E.), he did not have the rights of Athenians and had no recourse when he was not chosen as the new leader of the school. He left Athens, presumably in anger. He traveled to Asia Minor, got married, and began his studies in biology. In 343 he went to Macedonia, where he became a tutor for the young prince, the son of

FIGURE 9.1 Aristotle (384–322 B.C.E.), Greek philosopher and naturalist, here shown teaching the young Alexander. If one were to pick one scholar as the most influential person in Western cultural history, it would have to be Aristotle. Not only did he leave influential writings in a multitude of fields such as biology, metaphysics, logic, ethics, drama, and politics, he introduced the concept of empirical science to the ancient world. It is said about Aristotle that he knew everything there was to know at the time, and that may well be an accurate description. His school flourished for several hundred years after his death but closed with the advent of Christianity. In the Western world he was all but forgotten, while his influence remained strong in the Arab world. It was not until the time of the Crusades (12th–13th centuries) that thinkers such as Thomas Aquinas reintroduced him to the West.

King Philip. (In three short years, this boy would become the regent of Macedonia and later of an immense realm covering most of the classical world. He would come to be known as Alexander the Great.) By 335 Aristotle was back in Athens and the head of his own school, the Lyceum.

Making big claims about someone's influence on history can be risky business,

FIGURE 9.2 *The School in Athens,* painting by Raphael. During the Renaissance, Raphael painted a vision of Plato's Academy—not a true account of daily life in the school, but a highly symbolic image of two schools of thought. Two figures are approaching the steps in the center: Plato and Aristotle. Plato, the older man, is on the left, and on the left side of the painting are some of Plato's students; but most are historical figures, including those from Raphael's own day, who have subscribed to the Platonic way of thought. Plato is pointing upward to the world of Forms, his image of true Reality, whereas the younger man next to him, Aristotle, is stretching out his hand toward us, palm downward. "This world," he seems to say, stressing that it is in this world we can find true knowledge, not in any intellectual realm removed from the world of the senses. On the right in the painting we find the Aristotelians of history, the scientists. And on the far right, Raphael has chosen to place himself, peeking out straight at us.

because such claims tend to be exaggerated. In Aristotle's case, however, it is quite safe to say that he is the one person in antiquity who has had the most influence on Western thinking, and that even in modern times few people have rivaled his overall historical importance. As Plato left his legacy on Western philosophy and theology, Aristotle opened up the possibility of scientific, logical, empirical thinking—in philosophy as well as in the natural sciences.

It is no wonder that Plato made no mark in this area. He wouldn't have been interested in natural science, because its object is the world of senses, far removed from the Forms. Although Aristotle was a student of Plato and did believe in the general reality of Plato's Forms, he believed that Forms are *not* separate from the things of the world of senses; as a matter of fact, Aristotle believed the Forms have no existence outside their objects. If we're enjoying the view of a waterfall cascading off a cliff face, we are at the same time, Aristotle believed, directly experiencing the Form of cliff, of waterfall, and of falling. If we're in love with someone and think the person is beautiful, we are experiencing the Form of beauty right there in his or her face. And if we are studying a tree, or a fossil, the Form that gives us knowledge about the history of that tree or fossil is right there. In other words, knowledge can be sought and found directly from the world of the senses.

This turn in Aristotle's thinking—from Forms being separate to being inseparable from the thing or experience—is what made it possible for him to think in terms of empirical research (gathering evidence, making hypotheses, and testing theories on the basis of experience). Legend holds that Alexander the Great, on his exploits deep into Persia and Afghanistan, had samples of flora and fauna collected and sent to his old teacher. This may be a mere anecdote, but it serves a purpose: It confirms that Aristotle would have been delighted to receive such samples and would have studied them carefully, because he believed in the possibility of empirical knowledge.

Life, the Universe, and Everything

Aristotle was instrumental in founding the sciences—not the exact sciences as we know them today, but sciences in the sense that the concepts of *logic* and *observation* were combined. The extent of his influence, however, goes beyond that. It is hard for us to imagine that there was a point in time when a human being actually could "know everything," in the sense of having access to all available knowledge at the time, and yet it seems that Aristotle was in such a position. He was the author of what we know as classical logic; he laid down the foundations of the classifications in biology; he developed theories of astronomy; he was interested in politics, rhetoric (the art of verbal persuasion), and drama; he wrote books on the proper structure of tragedy and of comedy; he developed theories of the nature of the soul, of God, and of other metaphysical questions. Indeed, the term *metaphysics* derives from Aristotle: He supposedly wrote a book on physics and then another book without a title about the nature of reality. Because it came after the book on physics, his followers called it the "book after physics," *ta meta ta physica*. He also wrote a book about ethics, which may prove to have the most enduring influence of them all. He also wrote about the justification of slavery and the nature of woman as a lower being. Aristotle thus is hardly what has become known as "politically correct" for our time, but philosophers usually choose to read his more controversial writings as historical documents rather than as blueprints for how to live our lives. In many ways Aristotle was not what we call a critical thinker; indeed, Socrates would not necessarily have approved of him, for he often refrains from analyzing a viewpoint (such as the status and nature of women) but rather limits himself to mentioning it. He seems to assume that some things are obvious; most people who lived during his time probably agreed with him.

The Four Causes

For Aristotle every event has four causes, or four forces that work on it and bring it into being. First there is the *material cause*, or the "stuff" the thing is made of; next there is the *efficient cause*, the force that has brought it into being; then there is the *formal cause*, the shape or idea (the Form) of the thing, and last there is the *final cause*, the purpose of the thing. A good illustration (for which I give credit to one of my students) is: material cause: flour, water, and so on; efficient cause: me, the baker; formal cause: the idea of muffins; final cause: to be eaten!

A great many of Aristotle's writings are lost to us. Aristotle, like Plato, wrote dialogues, and the Roman orator Cicero held them in high regard, but only some fragments remain. The Aristotelian works we have today are, for the most part, lecture notes and course summaries that he used in his classes; some were written for general audiences and some for more advanced students. Some of the works are supplemented by notes taken by his students. Because these fragmentary writings are all we have left of Aristotle's work, he often has been considered less of a stylist than Plato. This reputation may be somewhat undeserved. Dialogues that might have greatly influenced early European philosophy (and that may have been written in a more elegant style) have not yet surfaced, nor has his treatise on comedy. Lost, too, are Plato's own lecture notes, which may have been very much the style of Aristotle's.

Teleology: The Concept of Purpose

One concept that is essential for understanding Aristotle's ideas on virtue comes from another branch of his philosophy, his metaphysics: the concept of *teleology*. In Greek *telos* means goal or purpose, and a teleological theory or viewpoint assumes that something has a purpose, or that the end result of some action is all-important. Examples of teleological theories exist even today, and we encounter them often in everyday discussions about "the meaning of life." Modern science, however, has preferred to leave the question of the purpose of the universe behind. Plato also believed in the purpose of things, but Aristotle built his teleology into a complete metaphysical theory of forces, or "causes."

For Aristotle everything that exists has a purpose, built into the fabric of reality from the very beginning. The idea of a purpose seems reasonable when we look at man-made objects, because these objects must surely have started with an idea, a purpose, in the mind of their maker. When we wallpaper our bathroom we do it for a purpose: to make the place nicer, or perhaps to get a better price for our house. If a

Teleological Explanations

We use teleological explanations quite often even today, although they generally are not acceptable as a scientific form of explanation. If we were to explain why giraffes have long necks, we might say something like, "It is *so they can* reach tall branches." Saying "*so they can*" implies that somehow giraffes are designed for that purpose, or else they have stretched and stretched over the ages until they can finally reach those branches. (There actually was such a theory in the nineteenth century, prior to Charles Darwin. Its proponent was Chevalier de Lamarck, and the theory is referred to as "inheritance of acquired characteristics.") Even though we all know that giraffes do eat leaves off of tall branches, it would not suit modern science to assume that that is their *purpose*. Darwin, with his theory of *natural selec-*

tion, proposed a new point of view: that giraffes don't come equipped with a purpose, nor does any other creature, but we all adapt to circumstances, and those who adapt the best survive and have offspring. We therefore must imagine the ancestors of giraffes as being rather short-necked, with some born with longer necks as a result of mutation. Because the ones with long necks could reach the leaves that the others couldn't reach, they were successful during times of hardship when many of the others perished. They gave birth to long-necked offspring, who gave birth to offspring with even longer necks, and so on. This is a causal explanation; it looks to reasons in the past to explain why something is the way it is today, instead of looking toward some future goal.

cutler makes a knife, its purpose is to cut well, not just to make a dent. When you bake muffins you intend them to be edible, whether they turn out that way or not. But can't we have human actions without a purpose? Aristotle would say no, especially if we are creating an object; its purpose is a given thing.

What about nature-made objects? Does a *tree* have a purpose, a *wolf*, an *ant*, a *river*? Today we would hesitate before saying yes, because after all, who are we to make such assumptions? If we say the purpose of a tree is to give us shade, or apples, we are assuming that it is here for us humans, and not just for its own sake in the order of things. Even if we say the wolf's purpose is to cull the herd of caribou, we still hesitate to say that someone "designed" it that way, with a purpose in mind. Few scientists, regardless of how they feel privately, would willingly mix up personal religious opinions and professional theories. Aristotle, however, had no such compunctions, not about making statements that reflected anthropocentrism (the view that everything happens for the sake of humans), nor about making statements about the general structure of the universe (for he believed he understood it). For Aristotle everything in nature does have a purpose, although it may not be easy to determine just what that purpose is. How *do* we go about determining what the purpose is? We investigate what the thing in question *does best*. Whatever this is will be the special characteristic of that thing. If the thing performs its purpose or function well, then it is *virtuous*.

Aristotle and the Virtues

Virtue and Excellence

In the introduction to Part 3 we saw that the Greek conception of virtue was slightly different from our colloquial use of the word. Although calling someone virtuous may for us imply a certain amount of contempt, no such meaning was implied by the ancient Greeks. If you were virtuous, there was no way you could be considered dull or withdrawn from life, because being virtuous meant, above all, that you managed your skills and your opportunities well. To be virtuous meant to act with *excellence*—we might even say with *virtuosity*, because this term retains some of what the Greeks associated with virtue.

For Aristotle virtue lies in the difference between doing something and doing it *well*. Virtue, therefore, is not reserved for humans; anything that fulfills its purpose with excellence can be said to be virtuous. Because everything has a purpose, including inanimate objects, we can talk about everything having *potential virtue*. There is virtue to a sharp knife, a comfortable chair, a tree that grows straight, and a healthy, swift animal. Most important to us humans, though, is the question, What makes a human virtuous?

The Human Purpose

In order to know what makes a human virtuous, we must ask ourselves what the specifically human purpose in life is. For Aristotle there is no question that there is such a purpose; each limb and organ of the body has a purpose, he says—the eye for seeing, the hands for grasping—so we must conclude that the person, as a whole, has a purpose above and beyond the sum of the body parts. (For Aristotle this was an obvious conclusion; today we are not so quick to conclude anything about purposes. See the box entitled "Teleological Explanations.")

The idea that humans are born for a reason and with a purpose is irresistible even to many modern minds. We ask ourselves, "What is the purpose of my being here on this earth?" "Why was I born?" We hope to find some answer in the future—some great deed we will do, a work of art we will compose, the children we plan to raise, the influence we will exert on our profession, or the money and fame we plan to acquire. Some believe their greatest moment has come and gone, like an astronaut who has been on the moon—how do you top that? Such people spend the rest of their lives searching for a new purpose.

Is There a Human Purpose?

In Part 4 we will look more closely at the question of whether there is such a thing as human nature and human purpose. Aristotle inspired an entire school of thought long after he was dead. The Catholic church came upon his writings some fifteen hundred years after his death, and Saint Thomas Aquinas (1225–1274) incorporated several of Aristotle's ideas into his Christian philosophy, including the idea that humans have a purpose. For Saint Thomas this purpose included life, procreation, and the pursuit of knowledge of God. Other thinkers are not so certain that humans have a purpose; Jean-Paul Sartre (1905–1980) believes there is no such thing as human nature, and anyone who believes so is only looking for an identity to hide behind so that he or she won't have to make difficult choices.

Our belief in destiny, in one form or another, influences our perception of the purpose of our lives. But this is only half of Aristotle's concept of *telos*, because it applies only on a *personal* level. Aristotle is talking not only about the person becoming what he or she is supposed to become, but also about the human being *as such* becoming what human beings are supposed to become. In other words, Aristotle believed not only that a telos exists for an individual, but also that it exists for a species as well. How do we know what the purpose of an individual as a member of a species is? We investigate what it is that that creature or thing does best—perhaps better than any other creature or thing. The purpose of a bird must involve flying, although there are flightless birds. The purpose of a knife must involve cutting, although there are movie prop knives that don't cut a thing. The purpose of a rock? To do whatever it does best: lie there. (This is true Aristotle, not a joke.) And the purpose of a human? To *reason*. We can't evaluate a person without taking into consideration the greater purpose of being human, which is to *reason well*:

Now if the function of man is an activity of soul which follows or implies a rational principle . . . [and we state the function of man to be a certain kind of life, and this to be an activity or actions of the soul implying a rational principle . . . and if any action is well performed when it is performed in accordance with the appropriate excellence: if this is the case,] human good turns out to be activity of soul in accordance with virtue, and if there are more than one virtue, in accordance with the best and most complete.

But we must add "in a complete life." For one swallow does not make a summer, nor does one day; and so too one day, or a short time, does not make a man blessed or happy.

Scholars are usually generous here in labeling reasoning the purpose of *humans*—for in Aristotle's terminology it is the "purpose of *man*." As we go deeper into Aristotle's works it becomes apparent that he is not using the word inclusively, to cover males and females, as was to become the intellectual habit in the eighteenth, nineteenth, and most of the twentieth centuries: He means *males*. For Aristotle men are the creatures who have the true capacity for reasoning; women have their own purpose (such as childbearing) and their own virtues. In this Aristotle seems to have joined forces with the public opinion of the times, although not with the opinion of his own teacher, Plato, who believed that the role of women depended on what they were well suited for, individually.

The purpose for man, as Aristotle would say, is to think rationally, on a regular basis, throughout one's life, as a matter of habit—in other words, to develop a rational *character*. And this, according to Aristotle, is the same as *moral goodness*.

For modern thinkers this is a surprising twist: that moral goodness can be linked with being good *at something* rather than being just good, period. Moral goodness seems for us to have more to do with not causing harm, with keeping promises, with upholding the values of our culture, and so on. For Aristotle, though, *there is no difference* between fulfilling one's purpose, being virtuous, doing something with excellence, and being morally good. It all has to do with his theory of *how* one goes about being virtuous.

Aristotle recognizes two forms of virtue, *intellectual* virtues and *moral* virtues. The intellectual virtues involve being able to think straight and act accordingly. The moral virtues also involve the use of the intellect, because the only way humans can strive for perfection is to engage their intellects in developing a keen sense of the needs of the moment.

The Virtues

Ancient Greece gave us the concept of moderation or the "Golden Mean." This is at the heart of Aristotle's idea of virtue: an action or feeling responding to a particular situation at the right time, in the right way, in the right amount, for the right reason—not too much, and not too little. By using the the Golden Mean, Aristotle believes he describes "the good for man"—where a human can excel, what a human is meant to do, and where a human will find happiness. We will return to the subject of happiness shortly.

In his *Nicomachean Ethics* Aristotle compares the Golden Mean with an artistic masterpiece; people recognize that you couldn't add anything to it or take anything from it, because either excess (too much) or deficiency (too little) would destroy the masterpiece. The mean, however, preserves it. This may remind some readers of a joke among artists: "How many artists does it take to make a great painting? Two—one to paint it, and the other to hit the painter over the head when the painting is done." Why the bash on the head? Because there comes a time, if the work is good enough, when more paint would be too much, and sometimes the artist doesn't recognize that moment. Aristotle would reply that the *virtuous* artist will know this moment—indeed, this is precisely what constitutes a great artist. If this is the case for art, then it must apply to moral goodness: We are morally good if we are capable of choosing the proper response to every situation in life, not too much and not too little:

> Virtue, then, is a state of character concerned with choice, lying in a mean, i.e., the mean relative to us, this being determined by a rational principle by which the man of practical wisdom would determine it. Now it is a mean between two vices, that which depends on excess and that which depends on defect; and again it is a mean because the vices respectively fall short of or exceed what is right in both passions and actions, while virtue both finds and chooses that which is intermediate.

Aristotle tells us that every action or feeling must be done in the right amount. In many ways this is quite modern and a very down-to-earth approach to our daily problems. We all have to make big and little decisions every day: How much gratitude should I show when someone does a favor for me or gives me a present I didn't ask for? How much is the right amount of curiosity to express about my friend's personal life? (I don't want to appear to be snooping, and I don't want to appear cold, either.) How much should I study for my final? (I know when I've studied too little, but what exactly is studying too much?) And how much love should I feel, and show, in a new relationship? All of these types of problems are things that we face every day, and we rarely find good answers to them. In this sense Aristotle shows a feeling for what we might call "the human condition," common human concerns that remain the same throughout the ages. Very few philosophers have done as much as he to try to give people some actual advice about these mundane matters. Thus, even though Aristotle's ideas derive from an ancient, alien world of slavery and other policies that are unacceptable to us today, there are features of his works that make his writings relevant for modern times and modern people.

Does Aristotle actually tell us what to do? Not really. He warns us that we each are prone to go toward one extreme or the other and that we must beware of such tendencies, but the only help we can find on the road to virtue is to try, and try again.

There are three questions one might want to ask. The first is, As this is supposed to be a theory of *character*, why does it seem to talk about actions and conduct and what to *do*? The answer is that for Aristotle this *is* a question of character, because he is not so much interested in our response to singular situations as he is in our response in general. If we perform a considerate or courageous act only once, he would not call us considerate or courageous; the act must be done on a regular basis, as an expression of the kind of person we strive to be. In other words, we have to acquire some good habits. This means we can't hope to be virtuous overnight—it takes time to mold ourselves into morally good people, just as it takes time to learn to play a musical instrument well. The second question one might ask is, What does this have to do with the specific human virtue of rational thinking? The answer lies in the fact

FIGURE 9.3 An application of Aristotle's theory of virtue: Three women on a bridge see a drowning child being swept along by the waters. One woman is rash and jumps in without looking; the other is too cautious and frets so much that the time for action is past. But the third one reacts "just right": She has developed a courageous character; she chooses an appropriate action and acts at the right time to save the child.

that the way we find out what the mean is in every situation is through reasoning, and the more times we have done it and acted correctly as a result, the better we can build up this habit of responding correctly. Now let's ask the third question: Does this mean that we are supposed to do *everything* in the right amount, not too much and not too little? It is easy to imagine eating in the right amount, and exercising in the right amount, but what about acts like stealing? Lying? Or committing murder? Must we conclude that we can steal and lie and murder too much, but also too little? That we will be virtuous if we steal, lie, and murder in the right amount? Hardly, and Aristotle was aware of this loophole; he tells us that some acts are just wrong by themselves, and you can't do them in the right amount. Similarly, some acts are right in themselves, and you can't do too much of them. Such a thing is justice: You can't be "too just," because being just already means being as fair as you can be.

How exactly do we find the mean? After all, it is not an absolute mean, where we can identify the exact midpoint between the extremes, the way we would measure the exact amount of calories allowed in a diet. It is far more complex than that, and

The Right Decision at the Right Time

Imagine three women on a bridge, Heidi, Jill, and Jessica. Below them a fast and dark river is rushing along, sweeping a little boy toward them, carrying him to certain doom. Heidi looks down at the swirling water and imagines all the things that could go wrong if she were to attempt a rescue: the submerged rocks, how heavy her shoes and jeans will get if she jumps in, the fact that she just got over a bad cold, and the fact that she doesn't swim well. Besides, she remembers, she has to make it to the library before closing time. While she has been doing all this thinking, Jill has already jumped in the river to save the boy. She jumped without thinking, however, and hit her head on one of the submerged rocks and knocked herself out. Jessica sees the boy, and fast as lightening she calculates the swiftness of the river, the position of the rocks, her own swimming prowess—and she runs down the little staircase to the riverbed, throws in the life preserver that is hanging on the wall, saves the boy, and pulls ashore the unconscious Jill for good measure. Or maybe she sheds her shoes and jumps in and saves the boy. Or shouts to some guys who are out fishing and asks them to give her a hand. Or whatever. The main thing is that she *thinks*, and then *acts*, at the right time, in the proper amount. That is courage to Aristotle. Jill acted rashly. Heidi may have had the right intentions, but she did not act on them. You must act on your intentions and succeed in order to be called virtuous.

Aristotle warns us that there are many ways to go wrong, but only one way to "hit the bull's-eye" in each situation. It takes a full commitment, involving the entire personality, over a lifetime of training. In his lectures Aristotle appears to have used a chart of virtues—not a full list of all possible virtues, but a sample list of right and wrong actions and feelings. Let us look at a few of them.

If someone is in danger, that person can react in three ways: with too little courage (in that case he is a coward), with the right amount of courage, or with too much courage (in that case he is being foolhardy).

Let's consider the act of pleasure-seeking. If you overdo it, you are intemperate—but suppose you are not capable of enjoying pleasures at all? That is not a virtue, and Aristotle doesn't know what to call such a person except "unimpressionable." The virtue is to know in what amount to enjoy one's pleasures; that Aristotle calls *temperance*. Thus for Aristotle there is no virtue in staying away from pleasures, for "temperance" does not mean "abstinence." The key is to enjoy them *in moderation*.

Suppose we look at the art of spending money? For Aristotle there is a virtuous way to spend money, too. If you spend too much you are prodigal, and if you spend too little you are a miser. Spending just the right amount, at the right time, on the right people, for the right reason, makes you *liberal.*

For the Greek mind, for the man of the polis, *pride* is a natural virtue, and so it is for Aristotle. You can, however, overestimate your honor and become vain, or you can underestimate it and become humble. The virtuous way to estimate yourself and your accomplishments is through *proper pride.*

Is there a virtuous way to feel *angry*? Absolutely—by having a good temper or, as we might say today, being even-tempered. Being hot-tempered is a vice, but so is being meek. If you have been wronged, Aristotle believes you ought to be angry in proportion to the offense against you.

Let us now consider the virtue of *truthfulness.* We probably would agree with Aristotle that this is a good thing, but what is his idea of a deficiency of truthfulness? Not *lying*, as we might expect, but *irony*, or as it is sometimes translated, "mock-modesty" (in other words, downplaying the situation). Aristotle obviously would not have enjoyed Socrates's ironical bantering. The excess of truthfulness? Bragging. To the modern reader the excess of truthfulness might be something different, like being *rude* by telling someone "You sure gained weight over the holidays!" But for Aristotle it is not a matter of not harming others by lying, or by being rude, but a matter of assessing the situation properly, not underplaying or overplaying the truth. Here we touch on a hidden element of Aristotle's virtue theory, for *who is the theory intended for*? Not necessarily young people who need to get their lives straightened out. It is, instead, directed at future politicians. The young noblemen and sons of wealthy landowners who had the leisure time to go to school were expected to become the pillars of Athenian society. What Aristotle is teaching them is, in many ways, to be good *public figures.* That is why it is necessary to know how much money to spend, in large sums. That is why it is important to know the extent of your pride and your anger. Of course Aristotle's virtues also are applicable to other people, but some of them—like the virtues of wit or humor—carry a direct message to those young men who plan to enter public life. Most of us probably would like our partners to have a sense of humor. But imagine how important it is for a public figure not to be a boor, not to be a buffoon, and to have a ready wit. Aristotle recognized this fact.

There are, then, three dispositions: two vices, one on either side, and virtue in the middle. How do we find the virtue? It may be hard, depending on our own personal failings. If we have a hard time controlling our temper, we might try for a while to be so cool that nothing makes us angry, just to get out of the habit of being irascible; in other words, we might shoot *past* the target of good temper until we feel we can control ourselves and find the mean. If we tend to overindulge in desserts, we might try to lay off sweet things completely for a while. This is not the ideal situation, but Aristotle advises us to experiment until we get it right. Besides, if we find ourselves at one extreme, it is hard for us to see the difference between the other extreme and the virtue: A chocolate-lover finds the chocolate-hater and the person who has just a few bites of chocolate each week equally dull and unsympathetic. Indeed, some extremes are closer to the mean, the virtue, than others. Being a coward probably is more opposed to being courageous than being foolhardy. So if you don't know what path

The Clash Between Classical and Christian Virtues

For a modern Western person the idea that it is legitimate to take pride in an accomplishment is not strange; we understand why Aristotle says we should not humiliate ourselves by making ourselves less than we are. But his idea that we have a right to feel proud about things that aren't our own doing, like being born of a certain class and race, is more problematic. To the traditional Christian mind, in fact, the entire idea of legitimate pride is a grave misconception. As much as Aristotle became an inspiration to medieval Christianity, there is a marked discrepancy between most of Aristotle's virtues and the Catholic lists of the cardinal virtues and the cardinal sins. For the Christian it is a cardinal sin to feel pride, because our accomplishments were done by the grace of God and are not our own doing. This is expressed in the Latin words *Soli Dei Gloria*, the honor (glory) is God's alone. The cardinal virtues are: justice, prudence, temperance, fortitude, faith, hope, and charity. The cardinal sins are: pride, lust, envy, anger, covetousness, gluttony, and sloth.

to choose, at least stay away from the extreme that is more opposed to the mean than the other extreme. We all have to watch out for our own personal failings, and we also have to watch out for temptations, because if we let ourselves indulge in too many pleasures we lose our sense of moderation and proportion. These matters are not easy, and Aristotle knew that we must judge each situation separately.

Is there such a thing as a perfectly virtuous person for Aristotle? Yes, it appears that he thought it was possible. Furthermore, he seems to have believed that if you are virtuous in one respect but fail miserably in another aspect, then you have lost out completely. If you only deviate slightly, though, you are still a virtuous person—a person who is good at being human and at realizing the human potential.

Happiness

Being virtuous makes you happy—this is Aristotle's sole reason for designing the development of a virtuous character. But if the goal is happiness, why does he warn us about indulging in too many pleasures? Because pleasure and happiness are not identical, as most ancient thinkers would agree. We have to ask what exactly Aristotle means by happiness.

Eudaimonia is the Greek word for happiness, and it is what's "good for man" according to Aristotle. For most of us a good life means a happy life, but a "good person" means a moral person. For Aristotle there was no conflict. We can be happy only if we're good, but in what way? The highest realizable goods are to live well, to be happy, to do well; what is good for man can't be something that harms him, and indulgence in too many pleasures certainly can be harmful. A further requirement of true happiness is that it must be steadfast; if we rely too much on pleasures we'll find that they cease to give us a thrill after a while, so pleasure can't be the same as happiness. Nor can fame or fortune, because those things are certainly ephemeral—we can lose both overnight. So what is the thing that can be ours forever, that nobody can take away, and that is not harmful but beneficial to us as human beings? Good reasoning, or as the ancient Greeks would put it, *contemplation.* This can be ours forever and, as anyone who has struggled with an intellectual problem and solved it knows, it can even be exhilarating. For Aristotle, then, the ultimately happy life is the life of the thinker. Aristotle is a realist, too, though—he adds that although the truly happy life may be a life of contemplation, it doesn't hurt to have friends, money, and good looks!

It appears that for a good deal of his life, Aristotle had all these things. With the death of his former student Alexander the Great in 323 B.C.E. at the age of thirty-three, it all came to an abrupt end. The anti-Macedonian feelings that were mounting in the realm controlled by Alexander's troops (including the city-state of Athens), no longer could be kept in check, and because Aristotle was considered pro-Macedonian, the Athenian city council decided to get rid of him. Ironically, their method was to charge him with the same charge that had been leveled against Socrates, of corrupting the young and offending the gods. But whereas Socrates chose to stay and die for his principles, Aristotle packed up and left Athens for good, so that "Athens wouldn't sin twice against philosophy." He died the year after of a stomach ailment.

Aristotle's school, the Lyceum, kept operating until well into the third century C.E., but with the advent of Christianity his works were by and large forgotten in the Western world. Primarily in Alexandria, it was the Platonic spirit that survived to put its mark on the new world religion. In the Middle East, though, Aristotle's works were studied continually. As the scientific spirit declined in the West, Arabic scholars kept Aristotelian research alive until the advent of another new world religion, Islam, and there Aristotle's philosophy has remained influential. It was not until well into the next millennium that an interest in Aristotle was rekindled in the Christian world. Eventually his theories found their way back into Western philosophy through the works of Saint Thomas Aquinas. In the late Middle Ages and through the Renaissance, Aristotle eclipsed Plato as a philosopher to the extent that he was known in European intellectual circles (as he had been for centuries in the Arabic world) as "The Philosopher."

Some Objections to Greek Virtue Theory

As mentioned earlier, the particular brand of ethical theory known as virtue ethics that we find in the Greek tradition by and large disappeared from view with the rise of modern philosophy. This was not merely because the texts were forgotten; this was a concerted effort by scholars to find a better approach to ethics, because as the centuries passed it was becoming clear, for a number of different reasons, that the Greek theories of virtue had several shortcomings. For one thing, Saint Thomas Aquinas found it difficult to reconcile Aristotle's virtues not just with Christian virtues, but also with the Christian respect for *God's laws*. In the Christian approach to morals, following commandments is far more important than striving toward virtues, and belief in the human ability to shape *one's own character autonomously* is considered to be a sin of pride. You become what you ought to be by God's grace, not merely by your own effort.

Philosophy, after parting ways with theology in the sixteenth and seventeenth centuries, began to look critically at virtue ethics from a secular point of view, for as we have seen, Aristotle was talking about the virtues of a ruling class, virtues that could not be disputed by someone with a different point of view. As we shall see in Part 4, the vision of equality does not enter into the Aristotelian moral theory, and from both a Christian and a social viewpoint an egalitarian approach had become indispensable for an acceptable moral theory by the eighteenth century. For those scholars believing in "natural rights" for all people, it was necessary to set up a moral theory that everyone could follow regardless of status, birth, or intelligence, and such a theory could be based only on laws that were clear and reasonable. Virtues were criticized as being too vague and logically problematic, because what happens if two virtuous people disagree about what to do? How can one persuade the other? There is no recourse to reason in that case except to declare one person less virtuous than the other. Such a problem does not arise if you have a clear set of moral and civil laws to refer to. This is what is needed if we regard each other as equals—not a theory with a static view of what makes a person virtuous. The rejection of virtue theory in favor of a rule- or duty-oriented moral theory was, therefore, considered a step forward in moral egalitarianism.

There is a more fundamental problem imbedded in classical virtue theory: its basis in *teleology*. It was natural for Plato and Aristotle to assume that as human actions had a purpose, so did humans themselves have a purpose, and that purpose was to let their rationality shine, because that was what human nature was all about. And because this is the human purpose, what is good for humans must begin and end with rationality. But must what is good for someone always be linked with what he or she does best? Suppose a man is excellent at forging paintings. Does that mean that his life should include this as a purpose, in order to make him happy? Aristotle and Plato would reject this on the basis that forging paintings is bad in itself, but that is surely a lame answer, because it assumes that we know beforehand which purposes are acceptable and which aren't. However, even if we stick to the idea of rationality, it is not all that obvious that this is the human purpose. For one thing, why must we talk about a human "purpose" at all? Science as well as philosophy today do not, as a rule, talk about purposes of nature, including human nature. A purpose requires that *someone* has that purpose; individuals may have purposes, but we hesitate to claim that nature has a purpose, or even that there is a higher power with a purpose. This is outside the realm of science and also of contemporary moral philosophy. Second, even if humans are very good at being rational, they are not excellent at it, at least not everybody, and even the select few geniuses can't be rational all the time. We are instead good at *being able* to act rationally some of the time, and with these qualifications it is hard to claim that rationality is our overriding purpose. And why should there be just one purpose for humans? A knife can be used to cut, to throw, to clean your nails (don't try this at home), to hang on the wall, and any number of other things. A tree surely has more functions than to supply humans with shade and fruit—it provides oxygen for the entire neighborhood, its leaves fertilize the ground, it provides a home for birds and squirrels and maggots, and it supplies a subject to paint for an art class. Why should we assume that each thing or species has one function that defines it? Humans surely have a multitude of functions. It is doubtful, then, whether a theory of virtue should, indeed, involve the question of function or purpose at all. Contemporary theory of virtue tends to steer clear of this ancient, problematic issue, as we will see shortly.

Narratives That Explore Virtue and Vice

The virtues of courage and honor were deeply admired by Aristotle, and in Chapter 13 we will look at some examples of these two virtues as they are explored in Joseph Conrad's *Lord Jim*, in the Icelandic epic *Njal's Saga*, and in the film *The Seven Samurai*. The virtue of compassion is illustrated by the story of the Good Samaritan and by Sir Walter Scott's novel *Ivanhoe*. Because no virtue theory would be complete without an investigation of vice, we also will look at the vice of jealousy in Shakespeare's drama *Othello*, in the Native American myth "The Faithful Wife and the Woman Warrior," and in the film *Fatal Attraction*. We also will look at the vice called "thirst for revenge" as it is explored in Alexandre Dumas's novel *The Count of Monte Cristo*, in Herman Melville's novel *Moby Dick*, and in John Ford's film *The Searchers*.

Chapter 10

Virtues and Values
of Other Traditions

The Greeks' philosophical awakening in the fifth and fourth centuries B.C.E. certainly can be said to have introduced formal critical thinking to the world. However, the Greeks didn't invent the idea of virtue or of correct conduct. All cultures have rules of behavior, and some of them seem close to being universal. In Chapter 3 we discussed the possibility of universal values; you may want to return to that discussion after reading this chapter. After looking at some of the great ethical traditions of the world that are either non-Western or nonmodern, it is tempting to conclude that most cultures do gravitate toward a few basic rules of behavior and ideal virtues, such as: "Do not harm the innocent (of your own culture)," and "Be respectful of the people in authority (who might harm you)."

It is questionable whether we can call all the ethical traditions we are about to discuss examples of *philosophy* in a strict sense, because many of them are developed as by-products of certain *religious* systems. We might say that this is where the Greek and Chinese traditions of ethics differ from most other moral systems, because both traditions have become more than mere commentaries to religious rules. Regardless of the origin of these rules of conduct, though, they are examples of how people have chosen to answer the question of *how one should live.*

Asian Traditions

Scholars in religious studies find it remarkable that the great religions of the world were established over a period of some six hundred years, from approximately 500 B.C.E. to 100 C.E. (except for Islam, which developed around 500 C.E.). It is equally remarkable that some of the great ethical systems of the world developed during the same time period. The Platonic school of thought and Aristotle's theories are contemporary with Buddhistic moral theory, Confucianism, and Taoism (Daoism)—all Asian religious or ethical traditions.

Confucius and Mencius

Chinese culture was already ancient in 551 B.C.E. when Confucius was born. When he died in 479 B.C.E., his thoughts on the *superior man* already had changed life and politics in his country, and they were to remain influential, even during periods of opposition, until the twentieth century in China. For centuries the common Chinese attitude toward virtue and right conduct had been to ask the advice of the spirits through divination. However, a certain practical vision had by and large replaced this view by the time of Confucius—a realization that human endeavor was more effective than spiritual guidance. The more important question became, What exactly is a good person, and what is the best kind of human endeavor? The question was important, because whoever was best—a "man of virtue"—was considered to be the person best equipped to rule the country. Prior to Confucius, such a man was presumed to be a nobleman, but Confucius redefined the man of virtue, the superior man, as someone who is wise, courageous, and humane; someone who thinks well and acts accordingly; someone who models his behavior after other virtuous men of the past; and someone who understands that life is a long learning process. The man of virtue exhibits his humanity by being benevolent, and he does not seek profit or revenge, but righteousness. His right conduct may show itself when he rectifies what is wrong or in particular rectifying *names*, or titles (in other words, use the proper words to address others, in particular your superiors). Studying proper conduct and developing proper character is the same as studying *the Way* (Dao, or Tao). The Way means the way to proper conduct and proper character—wisdom—and only through studying the Way do people become superior. How do we practice the Way? By developing good habits and continual good thinking. The evils to watch out for are, in particular, greed, aggressiveness, pride, and resentment. It truly is possible to become a superior man, according to Confucius, because people can be transformed by learning. Once we

FIGURE 10.1 Confucius (551–479 B.C.E), Chinese philosopher who defines the man of virtue as a wise, courageous, and humane person who studies the Way (Tao) to proper conduct by developing good habits and continual good thinking. Confucius's concept of virtue became a state religion in China for several hundred years.

Confucius and Aristotle

There are some extraordinary parallels between the virtue theory of Confucius and that of Aristotle; both greatly influenced posterity, each in his own way. For both thinkers, good habits are the proper way to develop a good character. Both Confucius and Aristotle emphasize the link between good thinking and subsequent action, and both believe that the virtuous human being is one who recognizes the *mean*, the middle state of moderation. But there are also considerable differences. For Confucius the superior man is one who shuns pride and strives for humility; Aristotle would consider such a man to have insufficient self-appreciation. Confucius also seems to have reached out to a more inclusive moral universe than did Aristotle, and this has caused some scholars to compare him to Christian thinkers. Confucius expresses a version of the Golden Rule: Don't do to others what you wouldn't want them to do to you. We don't find this attitude in Aristotle's writings, because the general ideal of *moral equality*, which is essential for the Golden Rule, is absent in Aristotle's code of ethics. Confucius's superior man also must appreciate *cooperation*—both between people and between people and Nature—whereas Aristotle stresses the hierarchy of rule. Both men, however, envision a state that is run according to the model of a well-functioning family, with the ruler as *pater familias* at the head, deciding what is best for his family.

have learned enough about the Way to recognize it, we will know that there is virtue in *moderation*. (Like the Greeks, Confucius believed in the virtuous nature of the *mean* between the extremes of deficiency and excess.)

Confucius's ideas of the virtuous man and the well-run state became so influential that they were adopted as state religion in China for a period of several hundred years (618–907 C.E.) in spite of the fact that Confucius didn't concern himself with religious questions. He believed that because we know very little about death and any life after death, we must focus our effort on this life and our relationships with other human beings.

Mencius (371–289 B.C.E.) followed in Confucius's footsteps but took Confucianism one step further. He believed that not only can humans learn to be good, but also that they are good from the beginning; they just have been corrupted by life and circumstances. Mencius thought that the proper method of finding our way back to our lost goodness is to look inside ourselves and recapture our nature—our conscience and our intuition. If we pay proper attention to our own good nature, it will grow and take over. Only through ourselves can we find the right way, and this process requires a certain amount of suffering. When we suffer, our character is devel-

Taoism

A contemporary of Confucius was Lao-Tzu. The two men knew each other and disagreed politely on several essential points, the most important one being the usefulness of social action. For Confucius the superior man must try to affect change, to make life better for others. For Lao-Tzu this is a useless endeavor, because humans can't affect changes. Nature is a complex duality of opposite forces working together, the forces of Yin and Yang. These forces work according to a pattern that can't be observed by most humans, and things happen in their own time. The best humans can do is to contemplate this fact. This is the only access to the Way, according to Tao: By doing nothing, by letting Nature take its course, we are not obstructing this course; we are emptying our minds of the constant wonder, "What should I do next?" and by letting our minds become still and perfectly empty, we are opening ourselves to the truth of the Way. The Tao of Lao-Tzu is far more mystical than that of Confucius, which is why his ideas have acquired their own label, Taoism. Virtue and proper conduct meld together in the concept of doing nothing, *wu-wei*, which entails unselfishness and mental tranquility. Interestingly enough, this doesn't mean that you deliberately should refrain from doing things like taking a box of matches out of the hands of a three-year-old; indeed, not to do so would be a selfish, willful act. You *should* take the matches away from the child but without congratulating yourself that you've saved her life; after all she may head straight for your medicine cabinet next. Do what you have to do, but don't think you can make a difference; eventually this will give you peace of mind. This is the hard lesson of Taoism.

oped. If someone has led an easy life, Mencius doubts that he or she can be truly virtuous. The virtues we are supposed to develop through suffering are independence, excellence, mental alertness, courage, and quietude of spirit. When one has reached such a mental equilibrium, one can help others achieve the same, because benevolence is the prime virtue. Humans should stop trying to improve on their fellow human beings before they have improved themselves.

The following admonishings are quoted from *The Book of Mencius*, a collection of sayings probably compiled by Mencius's followers. This excerpt shows that for Mencius the development of one's character is fundamentally the most important moral task. Although one has duties (which is why there are rules for one's *conduct*, which one ought to follow), one is not able to fulfill these duties without being *virtuous*—in other words, without having retained one's moral character.

What is the most important duty? One's duty towards one's parents. What is the most important thing to watch over? One's own character. I have heard of a man who, not having allowed his character to be morally lost, is able to discharge his duties towards his parents; but I have not heard of one morally lost who is able to do so. There are many duties one should discharge, but the fulfillment of one's duty towards one's parents is the most basic. There are many things one should watch over, but watching over one's character is the most basic. . . . Benevolence is the heart of man, and rightness his road. Sad it is indeed when a man gives up the right road instead of following it and allows his heart to stray without enough sense to go after it. When his chickens and dogs stray, he has sense enough to go after them, but not when his heart strays. The sole concern of learning is to go after this strayed heart.

Buddhism

For millions of people today, Buddhism is a religion; however, its founder, Siddhartha Gautama (563–483 B.C.E.), would have said that it is a philosophy of metaphysics and ethics, a system of thought exploring the nature of reality, and a subsequent system of rules of conduct with the overall purpose of diminishing the general suffering of human beings. Gautama is now referred to as "The Buddha," but within the tradition of Buddhism there are numerous Buddhas; in fact, anyone who has reached the ultimate level of enlightenment becomes *the Enlightened*, the Buddha.

Gautama began his life within the Hindu tradition. He was the son of a king and destined to rule. He led an extremely sheltered existence, far removed from the realities of human aging and suffering. At sixteen he was married to the princess Yasodhara, and they had a son. Legend tells that one day he, free of his usual supervision, visited a nearby town and received three jolts to his complacency, which changed his life; he encountered human suffering in three guises. First he saw an old man, next a terminally ill man, and last, a funeral procession. At that point he realized that there is suffering and anxiety awaiting all humans, and that even the most beautiful young body will one day grow old and die. But then he saw a fourth sight: a monk in meditation. This sight provided for him the answer to his anxiety. Like the monk, he would meditate about the nature of suffering; from that day on, he thought of this image. A few years later Gautama abandoned his family, leaving the palace in the middle of the night after first taking a last look at his sleeping wife and son. From then on he took on the life of a beggar-monk.

Renouncing worldly goods for the life of a monk was not very unusual in itself in the Hindu tradition at the time (and it still occurs to this day), but it was unusual for a young person of such social standing to make this commitment. After a period of self-denial and starvation, Gautama finally collapsed, and when he came to he realized that asceticism does not lead to enlightenment but only to fanaticism: A *middle way* between asceticism and self-indulgence must be found.

FIGURE 10.2 Siddhartha Gautama (563–483 B.C.E.), also called the Buddha, taught that the way to end human suffering is to put a stop to the craving for life.

Eventually Gautama found enlightenment as he sat meditating under a fig tree, later to be called a tree of enlightenment, a Bodhi tree. Sitting under the tree, he realized that the truth about life revolves around the concept of suffering. The wheel of *reincarnation* turns for everyone—from life through death to another life through another death to life again, endlessly—and each life is full of suffering. In a sense these endless cycles are a symptom of a disease that must be cured. The disease is desire for life itself, and the cure is to stop desiring life. This realization was formalized in the

Karma

A concept essential to both Hinduism and Buddhism is *karma*, the causal chain that leads inexorably from your actions in this life to their consequences in the next life. For the Hindu as well as the Buddhist, karma accumulates with human feelings and actions, good as well as bad. It is not a system of reward and punishment but rather an impersonal, automatic causal chain where one action inevitably has a result in this life or the next. In this manner the seeming injustices of life are explained: People who commit terrible crimes and get away with them will find themselves in their next incarnation living lives that correspond to their actions; they may live in poverty, be victims of abuse, or even come back in animal form. People who seemingly have done no harm yet still are victimized in this life are suffering the consequences of their own previous acts. People who do good without reaping the benefits in this life will achieve a higher existence in the next life: The beggar may be reborn as a Brahman (a member of the highest caste), the woman as a man (in traditional Buddhism only the male can achieve full enlightenment), and a Brahman as a wise man, a guru. Whatever actions we take, whatever good or evil deeds we engage in creates karma, and karma binds us to a next incarnation. For the Hindu it is the individual soul that travels from incarnation to incarnation; for the traditional Buddhist there is no individual soul but a series of aspects that we wrongly identify with and call "me." For the Buddha who reaches nirvana, the chain of karma itself is broken, and there is no craving for selfhood to carry over into a next life. In Part 4 we will look at the similarities and differences between the idea of karma and the Western concept of determinism.

Four Noble Truths: 1) Life is full of suffering; 2) Suffering is caused by *craving*—craving things in this life, but above all life itself; 3) If craving ceases, suffering will cease, too; and 4) The way to stop the craving is by following the *Noble Eightfold Path*. This path, the prescription to end the disease of recurring lifetimes, is a series of stages through which one seeks to reach a point where suffering has ceased. These stages are: right views, right aspiration, right speech, right conduct, right livelihood, right effort, right mindfulness, and right contemplation. Once one masters this path, one achieves *nirvana*, a state of mind where there is peace and insight. Only a few can achieve this goal, but once nirvana is reached, the wheel of reincarnation is broken for those individuals: There will be no more rebirth into more suffering, because the nature of suffering has been realized, and the wise person is not clinging to life anymore.

A Western person might feel relieved by the thought of reincarnation and not think of it as a terrible prospect, because Westerners generally are ridden by fear of death, either in the sense of oblivion (if you are an atheist or an agnostic) or in the sense of profound change (if you believe there is an afterlife with reward and punishment). Many Westerners, therefore, would feel mightily comforted if they could believe that after death there is just going to be another life much like the one they have been through. It might even appeal to them that such a life might reflect the way they behaved in the previous one—the idea of *karma*. So why does Gautama view the idea of rebirth as such a dreadful thing? Because he believes, according to Asian tradition, that life in essence is suffering, that we bring about the suffering by our very desire for more life, and that peaceful emptiness after a hard and busy life is blissful.

Who can achieve nirvana and escape the trap of rebirth after rebirth? Not ordinary people, because the world is "too much with them": They experience too many ties to their lives in the form of relatives, spouses and children, possessions, accomplishments, and memories and regrets. Only the person who has taken leave of the world can be expected to fully follow the Path; the layperson certainly should try to follow as much as he or she can, but they are not expected to devote their lives to the search for truth. Only the monks and nuns of Buddhism, who live in poverty and have no family ties, can be expected to attain enlightenment. And presumably the nuns will have to wait another incarnation until they reach it, for they cannot attain it until they are reborn as males. Aside from this traditional instance of gender inequality, Buddhism as a philosophy is more egalitarian than most others, because there is one great equalizer that is the same for both males and females: human suffering and craving for life in spite of the suffering. This ties both males and females equally to the wheel of reincarnation.

Other Traditions

As we mentioned before, each culture and each tradition has its own rules for conduct and its own conception of what a virtuous person is. Most often we find these rules embedded in the religious traditions of a country or a people; it is much rarer to find specific moral rules expressed outside the religious mainstream, as they are in Greek philosophy. Asian ethics, as in Confucianism, Taoism, and Buddhism, fall somewhere in the middle, for although the ideas of virtue and right living can be said to exist independent of any religious faith, these ideas still have been incorporated into religious movements. In this section we will take a brief look at some ethical traditions that are inseparable from their religious context, as well as at some that find moral rules to be a matter of secular importance.

Islam

The philosophical teachings of Islam are to a great extent based on the Greek tradition. The philosophies of Alexandria, which derived from the Neoplatonic school

FIGURE 10.3 Avicenna (Abu 'Ali al-Husayn ibn 'Abd-Allah ibn Sina, 980–1037), Arab court physician, astronomer, and philosopher. He was primarily influenced by Plato and Aristotle but also by the Islamic philosopher Alfarabi. Avicenna wrote books on medicine, science, metaphysics, logic, and politics.

and reflected an interest in Aristotle, were adapted by early Muslim thinkers. However, a similar legacy comes from the Hebrew tradition, which supplied the Qur'an (Koran, the holy book of the Islamic religion) with the stories of the Creation, of the Garden of Eden, of the Patriarchs, and of the prophets. The religion of absolute monotheism—of one God above all of His creation, Allah—was envisioned by Mohammed in the sixth century C.E. For the Muslim, Allah is immaterial and invisible but has created the visible world, and so the visible world must be good. In this sense the Muslim reality is far removed from Plato's disdain for the world of the body. It also is far removed from Plato's idea of the Form being separate from individual things. For the Muslim, reality consists of individual things, and it is precisely their individuality that makes things as well as humans special. The proper way to become virtuous, to achieve goodness and fulfillment, is to develop one's individuality—whatever makes one different from everyone else. The individual soul sees that the world is beautiful and praises Allah for it. Furthermore, each individual being has a rightful existence in the world, human and animal alike, because all beings are created by God.

Islam and the Protection of Women

Today most Westerners and an overwhelming number of Muslims view the traditional Islamic rules regarding the rights (or lack of rights) of women as barbaric. However, we should not forget that such rules were based, at least in part, on the idea that women needed *protection*—from men as well as from themselves. Avicenna believed that because women are not truly rational and are easily swayed by their emotions, it would be morally wrong to allow them to make major decisions, including the decision to get a divorce. In such a case, impartial judges must evaluate the matter. And because woman's character is by nature weak, according to Avicenna, she can and will arouse desire in many men if she is not protected against herself; otherwise she will cause great harm and shame to her husband. If, however, the husband has an affair with another woman, the wife will suffer only jealousy but no real harm, and because jealousy is an emotion that comes from the devil, it should not be taken seriously. For many reasons, then, women should be veiled, segregated from men, and forced to be dependent on their husbands for their own sakes. The man is obliged to take care of his wife, and his compensation for that is to be the only one with access to his wife's sexuality. He must own her, but not she him.

This means that the traditional Muslim not only avoids deliberate cruelty to animals but behaves considerately toward the animals in his or her care.

Islam hasn't been able to reconcile the idea of God's omniscience and the idea of human free will any better than any other religion with the same general belief. According to Islam, the virtuous person follows God's will, but humans also have a free will of their own. The problem is, if God knows what we will decide to do next and doesn't approve, why does He let us do it? And how can our wills truly be free if everything has been decided in advance by God? The attitude of fatalism and the idea of free will are continuously opposing forces in the Muslim tradition. (Fatalism will be discussed further in Chapter 15.) However, for the traditional Muslim man the concept of sin is not tied specifically to the idea of sexuality, as it is to the Christian. (Traditionally, the Christian religion has viewed sex outside of marriage as a particularly serious offense. We will take a closer look at the Christian view of human nature and the concept of *Original Sin* in Chapter 17.) For traditional Muslim women a sexual transgression is a more serious offense, because it reflects on the honor of her male relatives. The true sin is disobedience to Allah in the sense of *forgetting* Allah's commands, but Allah is understanding, too: If you are forced by circumstances to

FIGURE 10.4 Moses Maimonides (Moses ben Maimon, 1135–1204), Spanish rabbi, philosopher, and theologian. For Maimonides, wisdom is part of morality, but without the knowledge of God true morality can't be achieved.

forego part of the rituals that you are supposed to remember, a shorter version may be acceptable in order to show Allah that you haven't forgotten to perform them.

Most Westerners are familiar, in a more or less superficial sense, with the Muslim concepts of *Jihad* (holy war), the practice of punishment by mutilation (amputation), and the subjection of women. Although these traditions certainly are part of the classical Muslim system of values, one should be careful not to view them out of their cultural and historical context. Muslim values have their origin in rules that date back more than a thousand years, and if we look to Western systems of value from the same time period, we find remarkably similar thoughts on holy war, punishment, and women's status. Furthermore, not all Muslim countries adhere to such rules today. In fundamentalist countries where they are adhered to, Westerners would do well to examine the historical context before passing judgment.

Muslim thinkers such as Avicenna (ibn-Sina) (980–1037) and Averroes (ibn-Rushd) (1126–1198) worked on defining Islamic thought in relation to the Greek tradition. It is thanks to these philosophers that the translations of Aristotle eventually found their way into Christian Europe and into the European philosophical tradition.

Judaism

The West usually identifies its dominant value system as "Judeo-Christian," and yet many Westerners are not familiar with the Jewish value tradition. We will take a look at the ethical theory of Moses Maimonides (Moses ben Maimon) (1135–1204), who lived his life in the Jewish communities of Spain and Northern Africa at a time when Islam was spreading in these regions. In his book *The Guide of the Perplexed*, Maimonides develops his theory of virtue and wisdom.

Maimonides sees moral virtue as a subcategory to respect and understanding of the religious text, the *Torah*. Virtue is thus not so much valuable in itself as it is as an instrument for becoming a complete person capable of understanding the religious truths. For Maimonides *wisdom* is part of morality, but there is more to morality than wisdom. Through wisdom we realize that the law makes sense and must be obeyed. However, we can be wise in many different ways—wise in the sense of being rational, in the sense of being moral, in the sense of having skills, and also in the sense of using our heads to cook up evil schemes.

We can experience personal growth in four ways, according to Maimonides. We can learn to understand what everyday life consists of; when we have understood this, we have reached the first level of perfection. What *does* everyday life consist of? People owning things and laying claim to things—in other words, a "perfection of possessions." This level of perfection has no inner bearing on a person—the relation between persons and their possessions is purely external. This means that if you lose what was in your possession, you will not be a worse person, and if you are poor but manage to get rich, you will not be a better person for it.

The second level of perfection is that of the body. It consists of being of an even temper and in general good health. It is of course good to be physically fit, but we shouldn't think that this has any bearing on being a better *inner* person, because, after all, we share our physical nature with animals. It is good to be strong and fit, but we are still not above the level of animals.

The third level of perfection has more to do with the individual's self and more to do with our topic here: It deals with becoming morally virtuous. How do we accomplish that? By developing good habits; here Maimonides is in agreement with Aristotle. However, Maimonides says that our moral virtues are not an end in themselves; they function primarily in situations of human interaction. They really are just ways for us to be useful to others. Being morally virtuous can be a means of achieving the highest form of perfection, the fourth level.

The fourth level consists of perfecting the rational virtues, "the conception of intelligibles, which teach true opinions concerning the divine things." It is through these virtues that someone becomes truly human and an individual. This level of perfection belongs to no one but the person experiencing it, and it has no further instrumental purpose. How do we achieve it? By knowing and understanding God. This is the true wisdom, and it will come about by cultivating the acts of loving kindness, judgment, and righteousness, for those are the acts of God.

Within the Jewish tradition of the *diaspora* (Jews living outside of Israel), such acts of loving kindness were considered of the utmost importance, and a well-organized system of charity and welfare existed in most Jewish communities (this still is the case today). One rule of charity (of which I was informed by a rabbinical student in one of my classes) is that good deeds of charity are diminished in the eyes of God if the giver lets his or her identity be known. Gifts of compassion are supposed to be given anonymously; otherwise there is less virtue in giving.

Although we may assume that the virtue of charity is primarily directed towards needy *coreligionists* (members of the same faith), this was not always the case for the Jews. Talmud (the body of Jewish civil and religious law) prescribes that it is one's

Maimonides and the Death Penalty

Maimonides believed in strict adherence to the law. Only major crimes were to be punished by death, but among major crimes he counted "corruption of belief," such as profanation of the Sabbath, false claims of prophecy, and rebellious behavior on the part of elders. Kidnapping was punishable by death, and so was filial rebellion, because a rebellious son would grow up to be a murderer and therefore must be killed. Sexual transgressions could be punished by death, too, provided that they were easy to engage in or were very tempting. What can Maimonides have meant by that? Probably that very tempting situations were a test of human fortitude, and that people who gave in to such temptations and took advantage of a situation ought to be punished particularly severely.

duty to help the Gentiles and to visit their sick and bury their poor just as though they were Jewish, because "the tender mercies of God are over *all* his world" (Psalms 145:9). Scholar Cecil Roth speculates that this probably was more an ideal than an actual description of how charity worked in the old Jewish communities, but it is clear that compassion was supposed to be extended to anyone in need, coreligionist or not. In *Great Traditions of Religion: Judaism*, Roth speculates that a Jewish man in the Middle Ages might write a letter of ethical rules to his son much like this:

> My son! Make a point of visiting a sick man, for thus his suffering is eased. But do not fatigue him by staying too long, for his illness is enough for him to bear. . . . My son! Be considerate of the feelings of a poor man, by giving him alms in secret, and on no account before others. For this reason also give him food and drink in your own house—but do not watch him while he is eating. And do not overwhelm a poor man with words, for God will fight his cause.

The Virtues of the Vikings

Another example of a people who has become very much part of the Western tradition but whose prehistory is non-Christian is the Nordic people in Scandinavia. The Icelandic, Norwegian, Danish, and Swedish Viking tribes had their own brand of value theory before the advent of Christianity. It developed in about 800 C.E., and it is well preserved in those works of historical fiction known as the *Icelandic Sagas*. (In Chapter 13 we will take a brief look at one of the most famous ones, *Njal's Saga*.) The

FIGURE 10.5 Carved stone from Lärbro, Sweden. The scholar Else Roesdahl explains the images: "A stone three meters in height exhibits a drama in six parts, played out above a large ship design. The uppermost design shows a woman flanked by two men wielding swords—presumably the beginning of the story. Below are a horse, two swords, and two men with their arms upraised, apparently swearing solemn oaths. Next comes a scene showing a man hanged from a tree, surrounded by armed men. Below this is a group of men aboard a boat wielding swords in opposition to another group of similarly armed warriors, who are on foot and are led by a large woman; this perhaps represents a confrontation on a beach. The outcome of this action can be seen in the next scene where warriors surround a man lying on his back beneath a horse with an empty saddle. The ship at the bottom of the stone sailing in heavy seas make an appropriate close to the drama—the hero bound for the land of the dead." ("The Scandinavians at Home," *The Northern World*, ed. David M. Wilson. New York: Harry N. Abrams, Inc. Publishers, 1980.)

Sagas are not the only source of Scandinavian value theory, however. During the first centuries of Christianity in Scandinavia an unusual interest began to flourish among some monks: an urge to record and document the pagan world as it existed immediately before the advent of Christianity. Mostly this was a means of showing the advantages of Christianity by sheer contrast, but if it hadn't been for this propaganda feat from Christian scholars such as Snurri Sturluson, we would have known very little about the stories and morals of the Viking centuries immediately preceding Christianity.

What did the Vikings value above all else? *Justice* among equals (the Vikings had an institution called a "*Ting*," a meeting place where people took their quarrels to be judged by elected chiefs on a regular basis); *loyalty* among family and friends, especially in case of bloodfeud; and that elusive thing called *luck*, a good destiny. In *Culture of the Teutons,* Volume 2, Danish scholar Vilhelm Grønbeck describes the Viking people as full of a peculiar energy that comes together in the ideal person, male or female: "generous, brave, fearless, wise, merciless towards the enemy, faithful toward friends, and open toward everybody." Because many Viking men were often away performing exploits, Viking women enjoyed a certain amount of prestige and social, as well as personal, autonomy.

The Vikings' world view is dark; their myths foretell that the world will come to an end in earthquakes and great fiery eruptions, and that even their gods will die. The brave person will look his or her destiny straight in the eye without faltering, trust his or her luck, and strive to leave behind a glorious reputation. Honor in battle, loyalty

Rules of Viking Life

In an epic poem called *Havamal* ("The Word of the High One," the god Odin) we hear about the virtues and vices of the people who plundered and settled as far away as Turkey, Southern Spain, Greenland, and North America. Let's look at a few samples. What are you supposed to do when entering a door? Be on guard, because you never know if enemies are hiding behind the door. Don't have your guests sit on the firewood—they won't stay long that way. Drink well, because the soul gets reacquainted with itself when drunk. Remember that a fearful man thinks he never will die if he stays out of the way of enemies, but old age spares no man. A foolish man lies awake all night worrying; he is tired in the morning, and just as worried. The road to an enemy is a long detour even if he lives nearby, but the road to a friend is always a shortcut even if he is far away. Leave, and not be a guest in one place only; he who sits around another man's house all the time is loathsome. Middling wise is what a man ought to be; destiny is kinder to a man who has understood just enough. Don't praise the day until it's over, a woman until she is burned, a sword until it is tested, a maid until she is married, ice until you've crossed it, or beer until you've drunk it. The best things in life are fire, to see the sun, to have good health and power (if that be your fate), and to be spared shame. (And the most famous saying of *Havamal*): Cattle die, kindred die, you yourself will die. What never dies is the good name you have won for yourself.

at home, and respect for one's ancestors flavored the Viking morality, which was, in essence, not too different from the virtues of warrior castes all over the world.

African Virtue Theory

For the Akan people in West Africa (in the Ghana region) morality consists of having a good character. The scholar Kwame Gyekye describes the Akan ethics as solely focused on virtue and character; whenever a person commits an act of wrongdoing it is said not that "he/she did something wrong" but "he/she is a bad person." How does one become a good person? As in every theory of virtue, this is a difficult question, because "character" tends to be something we are born with. However, the Akan ethics assumes, like the Aristotelian theory of the Golden Mean, that we can work toward acquiring a good character through good habits. And the best way to teach those good habits is through *story telling*. Contrary to most traditional Western ethicists, the Akan thinkers have not forgotten that it is through stories that children get their first and perhaps their best exposure to the concepts of right and wrong. These stories and proverbs habituate the children to moral virtues. This doesn't mean that such children become indoctrinated robots, however. Gyekye points out that people still have a choice of behavior, and can be held accountable for that behavior, because if they act in a morally wrong way, it means that they have not built up their own character the way they should have.

This forms a link between an ethics of conduct and an ethics of virtue, says Gyekye: It is because of what you do that you become a good person; you don't start out doing good things because of who you are. Originally, a human being is born morally neutral.

What kinds of virtues are favored by the Akans? Kindness, faithfulness, compassion, and hospitality are among the key virtues. Akan values are utilitarian in the sense that anything that promotes social well-being is a good thing. Even if God approves of virtue, the bottom line is that it is good for the people.

The Akan view of virtue, with its emphasis on story telling, comes close to the premise of this book: that we, as socialized humans, can explore our ethical systems by listening to and making up stories. This is the way we learn about what is right and what is wrong when we are little, and it is one important way that our sense of morals is fortified when we are adults. Thankfully, it also is one way we are able to *question* our moral systems: by being exposed to or making up stories that force us to reevaluate what we believe to be right and wrong.

Native American Values and the Environment

The value system of North American Indian tribes has itself acquired a rather mythological status in America and indeed around the world. The values of the Native American have come to stand for *ecological virtue*, because it commonly is believed that these tribal people lived in harmony with nature, without abusing their own resources.

Is this true? Is there actually a value system available that might teach a person of the twenty-first century to preserve that which we are in danger of losing, our livable environment? Should we look to the American Indian for a functional environmentalism? As with all mythologies, there is fact but also much romantic fiction in this viewpoint. It does appear that most Native American tribes had a quite different relationship with their environment than did the settlers from Europe, or even from Asia. It is common knowledge that the hunter would evoke the spirit of the animal before the hunt, asking its permission to kill it and promising it some kind of sacrifice in return; that the hunter would not kill in excess; that the hunter would not let anything of his prey go to waste; that the women of the tribe would utilize every bit of material from the kill; that the women would supply a large percentage of food for the tribe by gathering tubers, berries, and so on; and that because theirs was a nomadic existence, they would not stay in one place long enough to deplete its resources. There is evidence of a close spiritual relationship between the tribal people and their environment, of an understanding of the seasons, of animal movements, and of inter-relationships between animal and human spirits—an understanding that humans have only a small part to play in the general order of things and are by no means all-important. There is evidence of a reverence for the mother of all (the earth) in the rejection of plowing by nineteenth-century Indians on the grounds that you don't plow furrows in your mother's breast. A Navajo song praises the beauty of this world, "beauty before me, beauty behind me," not just empty land ripe for development.

These values are, to be sure, sorely needed in a world where there is little appreciation of the environment as an autonomous whole, and where the word *development* seems to indicate that before the housing area there was "nothing," or at least "nothing of value." We are, however, not doing our Native American legacy any favor by elevating the tribal people to the status of ecological saints. We are just adding to the many misunderstandings and building on the romantic myth of the "noble red man" that was so much loved by intellectuals in the eighteenth century. A realistic view will serve everybody much better; there certainly was occasional ecological mismanagement among the Native American tribes. It now seems clear that the reason the Anasazi tribe of Arizona and New Mexico abandoned their cliff cities after several hundred years was partly because of a drought but also because they had exhausted the environment: There was no more wood, no more topsoil, and so they had to move. It also is a fact that although the Plains Indians did not hunt more animals than they could process (and the animal population did not suffer as a consequence), part of their success was due to the fact that the hunters were not very numerous. Had they been *able* to process large numbers of prey, we might have seen a decline in the animal population back then. It is now speculated that the woolly mammoth disappeared from the face of the earth because of very well-organized human hunting in North America as well as in Eurasia. Humans, regardless of their tribe, have the potential for great care and great greed; we should be careful not to label whole populations "saints" and others "sinners." But if we look to the Native American tribes today, in the southwest United States and elsewhere, we find an attitude toward life and the role of humans in nature which indeed is based on a system of values that looks to the *balance* of things: Humans can be physically and mentally fit only if they are in harmony with their surroundings, and nature has to be in similar harmony in order for humans to stay healthy. The idea of internal and external harmony, which at one point in time seemed to be disappearing with the decline of Native American culture, is on the rise again, along with an interest and pride in cultural traditions. If we choose to focus on the environmental values of the Native American tradition, we might find a weapon with which to battle our own ecological nightmare—a set of universal virtues that have, in all probability, been cherished before in a bygone culture and that still is cherished among Native Americans. Such a system could be brought to new life as a shared virtue system for the entire population of the earth.

Narratives That Explore Virtue in Other Traditions

Chapter 13 contains stories that illustrate how non-Western or noncontemporary cultures might view the issue of virtues and vices. Some of these titles were mentioned in connection with Aristotle, too, because they are equally relevant for discussing his virtue theory. *Njal's Saga* represents the Viking virtue of courage; the film *The Seven Samurai* illustrates the traditional Japanese virtue of honor; and "The Faithful Wife and the Woman Warrior" shows one Native American attitude towards the emotion of jealousy. For a look into Islamic values you may want to reread the outline of *Lawrence of Arabia* (Part 2, Chapter 5), even though it is written from a Western point of view. The Jewish focus on compassion is illustrated in the novel *Ivanhoe*.

Chapter 11

The Modern
Perspective

A Revival of Virtue Theory

In the introduction to Chapter 8, I mentioned that the idea of a good character as one of the key elements in a moral theory was eclipsed by the general notion that all that matters is *doing the right thing.* With the advent of what we call modern philosophy, virtue ethics was rejected in favor of *ethics of conduct*—asking the kind of questions introduced in Part 2 of this book. As we saw earlier, this was in part a result of a greater social awareness: There is more fairness in asking everybody to follow rules of conduct than there is in trying to make people adapt to vague principles of how to be, and there is a greater chance of developing rational arguments for your position regarding rules of conduct than there is of getting others to agree to your viewpoint concerning what is virtuous. In recent years, though, philosophers have turned their attention to the ancient thoughts about character-building, and virtue theory is now experiencing a revival. This trend has been hotly contested by scholars such as J. B. Schneewind, who believes that the original reasons for adopting ethics of conduct are still valid.

The revival of virtue theory has been primarily a British and American phenome-

Can We Change Our Spots?

Opponents of virtue ethics often claim that in order for people to be praised for what they do, or blamed for it, it must be assumed that they are *responsible* for their actions. (The issue of moral responsibility and free will is discussed in Part 4.) But are we responsible for our character and disposition? Virtue theory asks us to look primarily at people's character. Suppose we ask someone to give to charity, and she doesn't have a generous disposition. Can we then blame her for her lack of virtue? If we can't, then virtue ethics is useless as a moral theory. It may praise people for dispositions that they already have, but it doesn't tell us how to improve on ourselves. Virtue theory's response to this is that certain people have certain dispositions, and in that respect some are more fortunate than others, morally speaking; some people are just naturally thoughtful and generous, or courageous, or truthful. The rest of us have to work on these things. Just because we lack a strong disposition doesn't mean that we can't work on improving it, and just because we have a tendency toward a certain disposition doesn't mean we can't work on controlling it.

non, and we will look at some of the proponents of this new way of approaching ethics. However, a version of virtue theory has been in effect in continental philosophy ever since the nineteenth century, and we will take a look at this tradition, too. Because virtue theory is now associated with the new British/American theory, we will call its continental counterpart the "Quest for Authenticity."

As we have seen before, there is a subtle difference between morality and ethics, and in the debate about virtue this difference becomes very clear. In *ethics of virtue* the issue is to ask yourself what kind of person you want to be, to find good reasons to back up your view and to listen to possible counterarguments, and then to set forth to shape your own character, all the while being ready to justify your choice of virtue rationally, or change your mind. An ethics of virtue doesn't specify what *kind* of virtue you should strive for, although it is usually assumed that it will be something benevolent or at least nothing harmful. The important thing is that you realize that you *can* mold your character into what you believe is right. The question of whether your chosen virtue really is a morally good choice is not necessarily part of the issue.

However, a *morality of virtue* focuses precisely on this issue: Which virtue is desirable to strive for, and which is no virtue at all? We touched on this subject briefly in the introduction to this book. In the neoconservative environment of the late twentieth century, the question of virtue entered the public arena not as an abstract issue but as a very concrete one; many people felt that somehow the times are without values, and that it was time to reintroduce not just the concept of virtue, but *specific*

Negative Role Models

Virtue theory usually focuses on heroes and saints that are to be emulated, but little attention is given to those characters who perhaps teach a deeper moral lesson—the negative role models. Whether we look to real-life figures or fictional characters, moral lessons can be learned if we follow the destiny of a bad person, provided that he doesn't get away with his wrongdoing. (Twisted souls can of course learn a lesson from the evildoer who does get away with it, but that is another matter.) From childhood we hear of people who did something they were not supposed to do and suffered the consequences. Most of these stories are issued as a "caveat," a warning: Don't "cry wolf," because in the end nobody will help you. Look what happened to Adam and Eve, who ate the fruit of the one tree they were not supposed to touch. Look what happened to the girl who stepped on a loaf of bread so she wouldn't get her feet wet. She was pulled down into the depths of Hell (a Hans Christian Andersen story). When we grow up we learn the lesson of politicians who turned out to be crooked, of televangelists who didn't practice what they preached, of rich and famous people who have serious drug problems. Movies and novels also bombard us with negative models: Darth Vader (*Star Wars*) sells out to the Dark Side, so we learn to beware of people who have lost their integrity. Charles Foster Kane (*Citizen Kane*) forgets his humanity and dies lonely, his heart longing for the time when he was a small boy. The Count of Monte Cristo loses his own humanity through an obsession with revenge. Madame Bovary loses control of her life because she fantasizes too much. Through exposure to such characters we get a warning; we live their lives vicariously and find that bitterness lies at the end. There are, however, works that fail to bring home the moral lesson because they are either too pompous or simply misinformed. Such a film is *Reefer Madness*, which is now a cult classic and which elaborates on the brain damage awaiting marihuana smokers. Another antidrug film but with a far superior story and impact is *Drugstore Cowboy*: It doesn't preach, but it shows us in terrible and detached detail the downhill slide of addicts and dealers of dope. In Chapter 13 we will look at a number of stories with both positive and negative role models.

virtues, such as "family values" (not a very clear concept in itself), sexual abstinence, and religious faith. Although such virtues may indeed be desirable, at least to a certain part of the population, it is by no means certain that they can be deemed desirable for everybody, or that those people who may have a different idea of what virtue is are necessarily "bad people." Although the idea of character-building may be a positive one, we have all too often seen the idea of virtue used as a weapon in witch-hunts, religious as well as political ("If you don't share our idea of virtue, you must be evil").

This chapter will focus on the approach of *ethics of virtue* rather than on morality of virtue, because ethics of virtue leaves open for discussion, at least to a degree, which virtues you want to have shape your life.

Have Virtue, and Then Go Ahead

Bernard Mayo

In 1958 the American philosopher Bernard Mayo suggested that Western ethics had reached a dead end, for it had lost contact with ordinary life. People don't live by great principles of what to do ("do your duty" or "make humanity happy"); instead, they measure themselves according to their moral qualities or deficiencies on an everyday basis. Novelists have not forgotten this, says Mayo, because the books we read tell of people who try hard to be a certain way; sometimes they succeed and sometimes they fail, and we, the readers, feel that we have learned something.

Ethics of conduct is not excluded from virtue ethics, says Mayo—it just takes second place, because whatever we *do* is included in our general standard of virtue: We pay our taxes, or help animals who are injured in traffic because we believe in the virtues of being a good citizen and fellow traveller on the planet earth. In other words, if we have a set of virtues we believe we should live by, we will usually do the right thing as a consequence. However, ethics of conduct without virtue may not be benevolent at all; it is entirely possible to "do your duty" and still be a bad person—you do it for gain, or to spite someone. You can do something courageous without actually being courageous, says Mayo (although Aristotle would insist that if you do it often enough you actually *become* courageous, and utilitarians would insist that it doesn't matter why you do something, as long as it has good results).

So how should we choose our actions in an everyday situation? Mayo says we shouldn't look for specific advice in a moral theory (do such and such); we should, instead, adopt a more general one (be brave/lenient/patient). This will ensure that we have the "unity of character" that a moral system of principles can't give us. The best kind of advice we can get is the type that involves a role model, either an ideal person or an actual one. Be just, be a good American—or be like Socrates, Jesus Christ, Buddha, or perhaps Robin Hood. There are heroes and saints throughout history from which we can choose, not necessarily because of what they have done (for that is usually not so easy), but because of the kind of person they were.

So when Mayo suggests that we learn from factual *exemplars* like Martin Luther King, Mother Teresa, or perhaps our parents, he is not saying that we should emulate their actual doings, but rather that we should live in their "spirit" and respond to everyday situations with the strength that a good character can give. This is a much more realistic approach to morality than is reflected in the high ideals of principles and duty that ethics of conduct has held up for people. People have felt inadequate because nobody can live up to such ideals, says Mayo, but everyone can try to be like someone they admire.

Kant and His Rejection of Role Models

Mayo points out that Kant rejected the idea of imitating others as a moral rule and called it "fatal to morality." For Kant this meant taking the "low road" and just holding up an example of an ideal, rather than striving for the ideal itself. Mayo thinks striving for the ideal itself is too much to ask of ordinary people. But if we read Kant's *Lectures on Ethics* we find an interesting argument for why it is not a good idea to point to *people* as worth emulating: If I try to compare myself with someone else who is better than I am, I can either try to be as good, or I can try to diminish that other person; this second choice actually is much easier than trying to be as good as the other person, and it invariably leads to *jealousy*. So when parents hold up one sibling for the other to emulate, they are paving the way for sibling rivalry; the one who is being set up as a paragon will be hated by the other one. Kant suggests that we should recommend goodness as such and not proffer individuals to be emulated, because we all have a tendency to be jealous of people we think we can't measure up to. So the Kantian rejection of role models is not merely an abstract preference for an ideal, but a realistic appreciation of family relationships and petty grudges. It may even serve as a valid psychological explanation for why some people have a profound dislike for so-called *heroes* and make consistent efforts to diminish the deeds of all persons regarded as role models by society. Such an attitude may just be another reaction against being told that someone else is a better person than you are.

Philippa Foot

Opponents of virtue theory ask how we can call beneficial human traits "virtues" when some humans are *born* with such traits while others don't have them at all. In other words, human responsibility for these dispositions doesn't enter into the picture at all. Good health and an excellent memory are great to have, but can we blame those who are sick and forgetful for not being virtuous?

The British philosopher Philippa Foot counters this argument in her book *Virtues and Vices* by stressing that virtues aren't merely dispositions that we either have or don't have. A virtue is not just a beneficial disposition, but a matter of our *intentions*. If we couple our willpower with our disposition in order to achieve some goal that is beneficial, then we are virtuous. So having a virtue is not the same as having a skill; it is having the proper intention to do something good—and being able to follow it up with an appropriate action.

For Foot, virtues are not just something we are equipped with. Rather, we are equipped with some tendency to go astray, and virtue is our capacity to *correct* that tendency. Human nature makes us want to run and hide when there is danger; that is why there is the virtue of courage. And we may want to indulge in more pleasure than is good for us; that is why there is the virtue of temperance. Foot points out that virtue theories seem to assume that human nature is by and large sensual and fearful, but there actually may be other character deficiencies that are more prevalent and more interesting to try to correct through virtue, like the desire to be put upon and dissatisfied, or the unwillingness to accept good things as they come along.

But what about people who are *naturally* virtuous? The philosophical tradition has had a tendency to judge them rather oddly. Suppose we have two people who make the decision to lend a hand to someone in need. One person likes to do things for others and jumps at the chance to be helpful. The other really couldn't care less about other people but knows that benevolence is a virtue, so he makes an effort to help in spite of his natural inclination. For Kant the person who makes an effort to overcome his or her inclination is a *morally better person* than the one to whom virtue comes easily. But surely there is something strange about that judgment, because in real life we appreciate the naturally benevolent person so much more than the surly one who tries to be good for the sake of a principle. As a matter of fact, those are the people we *love*, because they *like* to do something for the sake of other people. Psychological egoism, however, claims that these people are still doing virtuous deeds because they enjoy it (that is, because they *themselves* get something out of it). And many other schools of thought agree that it takes a greater effort to overcome than to follow your inclination, so it must be more morally worthy. Aristotle, on the other hand, believed that the person who takes pleasure in doing a virtuous action is the one who is truly virtuous.

Foot sides here with Aristotle: The person who likes to do good, or to whom it comes easily, is a morally better person than the one who succeeds through struggle. Why? Because the fact that there is a struggle is a sign that the person is *lacking in virtue* in the first place. Not that the successful struggler isn't good, or virtuous, but the one who did it with no effort is just a little bit better, because the virtue was already there to begin with. Foot's own example, from her book *Virtues and Vices*, is honesty:

> For one man it is hard to refrain from stealing and for another man it is not: which shows the greater virtue in acting as he should? . . . The fact that a man is *tempted* to steal is something about him that shows a certain lack of honesty: of the thoroughly honest man we say that it "never entered his head," meaning that it was never a real possibility for him.

In addition, Foot offers a solution to another problem plaguing virtue ethics: Can we say that someone who is committing an evil act is somehow doing it with virtue? Say that a criminal has to remain cool, calm, and collected in order to open a safe, or has to muster courage in order to fulfill a contract and kill someone. Is this person virtuous in the sense of having self-control or courage? Curiously for someone who argues for virtue-ethics, Foot borrows an argument from the one ethicist who is most often identified with ethics of conduct, Kant: *An act or a disposition can't be called good if it isn't backed by a good will.* Foot interprets it this way: If the act is morally wrong, or rather if the *intentions* behind the act are bad, then cool-mindedness and courage *cease to be virtues*. Virtue is not something static; it is a dynamic power that appears when the intention is to do something good. The "virtue" value is simply switched off when the good intention is absent. This holds for other situations, too, in which there may not be any evil or criminal element. Hope, for example, is generally supposed to be a virtue, but not if someone is being unrealistic and daydreams about wish fulfillment; in that case hope is no longer a virtue. And temperance may be a virtue, but not if a person is simply afraid to throw herself into the stream of life. In that case it is a shield and not a virtue.

Christina Hoff Sommers

Which, then, are the virtues to which we should pay attention? Foot leaves the question open to an extent, because people tend to differ about what exactly is good for others and desirable as a human trait. Another ethicist, however, prefers to be more direct; her aim is not so much to defend virtue ethics as such, but to focus on specific virtues and moral failings in our Western world. Christina Hoff Sommers tells of the woes an ethics professor of her acquaintance would experience at the end of a term. In spite of the multisubject textbooks they have read and the spirited discussions they have engaged in, the professor's students have somehow got the impression that there are no moral truths. Everything they've studied about ethics has been presented in terms of rules that can be argued against and social dilemmas that have no clear solutions. More than half of the students cheated on their ethics finals. The *irony* of cheating on an ethics test probably did not even occur to these students.

What is lacking in our ethics classes? asks Sommers. It can't be lack of good intentions on the part of instructors, because since the 1960s teachers have been very careful to present the material from all sides and to avoid moral indoctrination. (Even this text, as you have noticed, contains sporadic mention of the difference between doing ethics and *moralizing*.) Somehow, though, students come away with the notion that because everything can be argued against, moral values are a matter of taste. The teacher may prefer her students not to cheat, but that is simply her preference; if the student's preference is for cheating as a moral value ("cheat but don't get caught"), then so be it. The moral lesson is learned by the student, and the chance for our society to hand down lessons of moral decency and respect for others has been lost because of a general fear of imposing one's personal values on others.

What does Sommers think should be done? She suggests that instead of teaching courses on the big issues like abortion, euthanasia, and capital punishment, we should talk about the little, everyday, enormously important things, like honesty, friendship, consideration, respect. These are virtues that, if not learned at a young age, may never be achieved in our modern society. Sommers mentions that in ethics courses of the nineteenth century, students were taught how to be good rather than how to discuss moral issues. When asked to name some moral values that can't be disputed, Sommers answered:

> It is wrong to mistreat a child, to humiliate someone, to torment an animal. To
> think only of yourself, to steal, to lie, to break promises. And on the positive

FIGURE 11.1 Christina Hoff Sommers (b. 1950), American philosopher and co-editor of *Vice and Virtue in Everyday Life* (1985). Sommers argues for a return to virtue ethics in order for people in modern society to regain a sense of responsibility rather than leaving it to social institutions to make decisions on moral issues.

side: it is right to be considerate and respectful of others, to be charitable and generous.

For Sommers it is not enough to investigate virtue ethics—one must practice it and teach it to others. In this way virtue theory becomes virtue *practice*. If we study virtue theory in school, chances are that we will find it natural to seek to develop our own virtues. Sommers believes a good way to learn about virtues is to use the same method that both Mayo and philosopher Alasdair MacIntyre (whom we will meet in Chapter 19) advise: to read stories in which someone does something decent for others, either humans or animals. Through stories we "get the picture" better than we get it from philosophical dilemmas or case studies. Literary classics can tell us more about friendship and obligation than can a textbook in moral problems. For Sommers, there are basic human virtues that aren't a matter of historical relativism, fads, or discussion, and the better we all learn them, the better we'll like living in our world with each other. These virtues are part of most people's moral heritage, and there is nothing oppressive about teaching the common virtues of decency, civility, honesty, and fairness.

Too often we tend to think that certain issues are someone else's problem; the state will take care of it, whether it is pollution, homelessness, or the loneliness of elderly people. For Sommers this is part of a virtue ethics for grown-ups: *Don't assume that it is someone else's responsibility.* Don't hide from contemporary problems—take them on and contribute to their solution. Do your part to limit pollution. Think of how you can help homeless people. Go visit someone you know who is elderly and lonely. These are the kind of virtues that will benefit us all, and the kind we must learn to focus on if we are to make a success out of being humans living together.

This vision of personal virtues is probably the most direct call to a resurgence of moral values that has been produced so far within the field of philosophy. Of course, it doesn't even come close to the call for a revival of values that is heard every day in our contemporary society, usually from religious groups. However, Sommers doesn't

MacIntyre and the Virtues

Alasdair MacIntyre believes that our moral values would be enriched if we followed the examples of older cultures and let *tradition* be part of these values. We don't exist in a cultural vacuum, he says, and we understand ourselves better if we allow a historical perspective to be part of our system of values. This doesn't mean that everything our ancestors did and thought should become a virtue for us, but a look back to the values of those who came before us adds a depth to our modern life that makes it easier to understand ourselves. And how do we understand ourselves best? As storytellers of stories of history, of fiction, and of our own lives. We understand ourselves in terms of the story we would tell of our own life, and by doing this we are defining our *character*. So virtue, character development, is essential to being a moral person and doing what is morally good. But virtues are not static abilities for MacIntyre any more than they are for Foot. Virtues are linked with our aspirations; make us better at *becoming* what we want to be. It is not so much that we have a vision of the good life; rather we have an idea of what we want to accomplish (what MacIntyre calls "internal goods"), and virtues help us accomplish these goals. Whatever our goal, we usually will be more successful at reaching it if we are conscientious and trustworthy in striving for it. Whatever profession we try to excel in, we will succeed more easily if we try to be courageous and honest and maintain our integrity. With all the demands we face and all the different roles we have to play—in our jobs, sexual relationships, relations to family and friends—staying loyal and trustworthy helps us to function as one whole person rather than as a compilation of disjointed roles. We will take a closer look at MacIntyre's theory of storytelling in Chapter 19.

argue for a revival of religious values, but for a strengthening of basic concepts of personal responsibility and respect for other beings. Her claim is that few ethicists dare to stand by values and pronounce them good in themselves these days for fear of being accused of indoctrinating their students. For Sommers the list of values cited above is absolute: They can't be disputed. But we still might want to ask a fundamental question: *How exactly does Sommers's call to virtuous living differ from old-time moralizing?* Perhaps she is right that most people would agree her values are good, but there still seems to be something missing: the little safety valve that *reason* provides—in other words, a way to convince others who disagree with you about virtues and values. *How* do we convince those students that cheating is a bad thing? It can't be done simply by teaching them that honesty is a virtue; we can rely on the *obviousness* of virtues and values only to a certain degree. A moral story may teach that self-sacrifice is a far better thing to practice than anything else, but I can easily disagree and dismiss it as propaganda. What has seemed indisputable at other times in history may seem unacceptable now. What seems indisputable to us may seem unacceptable to another culture. What Sommers still needs is to show that reason can provide evidence for *why* something is a virtue, even if it may seem obvious to most of us.

The Quest for Authenticity

Within what is called "contemporary continental philosophy"—by and large European philosophy after World War I—there is one school of thought that holds that there is only one way to live properly, and only one virtue to strive for: that of *authenticity*. This school of thought is *existentialism*. Although existentialism developed primarily at the hand of Jean-Paul Sartre (1905–1980) as a response to the experience of meaninglessness in the day-to-day struggle of World War II, it has its roots in the writings of the Danish philosopher Søren Aabye Kierkegaard (1813–1855), and it achieved a distinct philosophical definition from the German philosopher Martin Heidegger (1889–1976).

Kierkegaard

During his lifetime, Kierkegaard was known locally, in Copenhagen, as a man of leisure who had a theology degree and spent his time writing convoluted and irritating attacks on the Danish establishment, including officials of the Lutheran church. Few people understood his points, because he was rarely straightforward in his writings and hid his true opinions under layers of pseudonyms and irony. The idea that there might be a great mind at work, developing what was to become one of the most important lines of thought in the twentieth century, was obvious to no one at the time, in Denmark or elsewhere. As a matter of fact, Kierkegaard was working against the general spirit of the times, which focused politically on the development of socialism, and scientifically on the ramifications of Darwinism. People weren't ready to listen to ideas such as the value of personal commitment, the psychological dread that accompanies the prospect of total human freedom of the will, the relativity of truth, and the value of the individual. As it happened, though, such ideas were to become key issues for French and German existential philosophers a couple of generations after Kierkegaard's death.

There are two major, very different ways of approaching the strange writings of Søren Kierkegaard. You can dismiss him as a man who had a difficult childhood and as a consequence developed an overinflated ego with no sense of proportion as to the importance of events. In other words, you can view his writings as simply the product of an overheated brain that pondered the "great mystery" of Søren Kierkegaard's life and times. Or, you can view his writings as words that speak to all humanity from a uniquely insightful point of view, which just happens to have its roots in events in

FIGURE II.2 Søren Kierkegaard (1813–1855), Danish philosopher, writer, and theologian. Kierkegaard believed that there are three major stages in human spiritual development: the aesthetic stage, the ethical stage, and the religious stage. Not everyone goes through all stages, but true selfhood and personal authenticity can't happen until one has put one's complete faith in God.

Kierkegaard's own life. Among scholars this second approach has become the prevailing one in the twentieth century.

What was so eventful about Kierkegaard's life? Nothing much, compared to the lives of other famous people, but contrary to most people, Kierkegaard analyzed everything that happened to him for all it was worth and with an eerie insight. He was born into a family of devout Lutherans (Lutheranism is the state religion in the Scandinavian countries and has been since the Reformation) and was the youngest boy born to comparatively old parents. Several of his older siblings died young, and for some reason both Søren and his father believed that Søren would not live long either. His father's opinion had an extreme influence on the boy—an influence that Kierkegaard later analyzed to perfection, years before Freud had described conflict and bonding between fathers and sons.

When his father was young and a shepherd in rural Denmark, he was overcome by hunger and cold one bleak day on the moors, and he stood up on a rock and cursed God for letting a child suffer like that. Shortly after this incident his parents sent him to Copenhagen as an apprentice, and his hard life was over. This was a psychological shock to him, because he had expected punishment from God for cursing him, and he waited for the punishment most of his life. He grew rich while others lost their money, and for that reason he expected God to punish him even more severely. The first tragic thing that happened to him was that he lost his young wife; however, two months later he married their maid, who was already pregnant at the time!

When Søren's older siblings died, his father thought that God's punishment had finally struck, but otherwise his luck held while his guilt grew. It is possible that he then got the idea of letting his youngest son somehow make amends for him—take on the burden and strive for a reconciliation with God. In the Lutheran tradition there is no such thing as making a confession to your minister in order to "get things off your chest"—you alone must face your responsibility and handle your relationship with God. This means that you have direct access to God at any time, in your heart; you have a direct relationship to God. Your faith is a personal matter, and for Kierkegaard in particular the concept of faith was to become extremely personal.

Søren turned out to be an extraordinarily bright child, and his father devoted much time to his education, in particular to the development of his imagination. The two made a habit of taking walks—in their living room. Søren would choose where they were going—to the beach, to the castle in the woods, down Main Street—and his father would then describe in minute detail what they "saw." It was intellectually and emotionally exhausting for the boy, and scholars have ridiculed the father for his fancy, but today it is recognized by many that the combination of imagination and intellectual discipline is just about the best trait a parent can develop in a child, although one might say that this was a rather extreme way of going about it.

Kierkegaard was a young adult when his father died, and he understood full well the immense influence that his father had on him. He wrote the following in *Stages on Life's Way*, though he didn't let on that he was writing about himself:

> There was once a father and a son. A son is like a mirror in which the father beholds himself, and for the son the father too is like a mirror in which he beholds himself in the time to come. . . . the father believed he was to blame for the son's melancholy, and the son believed that he was the occasion of the father's sorrow—but they never exchanged a word on this subject.
>
> Then the father died, and the son saw much, experienced much, and was tried in manifold temptations; but infinitely inventive as love is, longing and the sense of loss taught him, not indeed to wrest from the silence of eternity a communication, but to imitate the father's voice so perfectly that he was content with the likeness . . . for the father was the only one who had understood him, and yet he did not know in fact whether he had understood him; and the father was the only confidant he had had, but the confidence was of such a sort that it remained the same whether the father lived or died.

So Kierkegaard *internalized* the voice of his father; as Freud would say, he made his father's voice his own *superego*. This had the practical effect of prompting Kierkegaard finally to get his degree in theology (which his father had wanted him to get, but which he hadn't really wanted himself). Kierkegaard also internalized his father's guilt and rather gloomy outlook on life. Kierkegaard believed that everyone, even children, have an intimate knowledge of what anguish feels like; he believed that you feel dread or anguish when you look to the future; you dread it because you realize that you must make choices. This feeling, which has become known by its Danish/German word—*Angst*—is comparable, Kierkegaard says, to realizing that you're way out on the ocean and you have to swim or sink, act or die, and there is no way out. The choice is yours, but it is a hard choice, because living is a hard job. Suppose you refuse to make your own decisions and say "society will help me" or "the church will help me" or "my uncle will help me"? Then you have given up your chance to become a real person, to become *authentic*, because you don't accomplish anything spiritual unless you accomplish it yourself, by making the experience your own. Each person is an individual, but only through a process of individuation—choosing to make your own decisions and be responsible for them in the eyes of God—can a person achieve selfhood and become a true human individual. The truth you experience when you have reached this point is *your truth alone*, because only you took that particular path in life. Another person can't take a shortcut by borrowing "your truth"—he must find the way himself; otherwise his insight is not worth anything at all. We can't, then, gain any deep insights about life from books or from teachers. They can point us in the right direction, but they can't spoon-feed us any truths.

This attitude is reflected in Kierkegaard's cryptic and disturbing assertion that *truth is subjective*, an idea that is vehemently disputed by scientists and philosophers alike. Some philosophers believe Kierkegaard meant there is no objective knowledge at all; we can never verify statements such as "2 + 2 = 4," "the moon circles the earth," and "it rained in Boston on April 6, 1990" because all such statements are, presumably, just a matter of subjective opinion, or what we call cognitive relativism. This would mean that we could never set any objective standard for knowledge. Although other philosophers, like Friedrich Nietzsche, actually have worked toward such a radical viewpoint, Kierkegaard is not among them. He never says that *knowledge* is subjective, and to understand what he means we have to look closer at what he says. His actual words are "*Subjectivity is Truth*," and Kierkegaard scholars believe this to mean the following: There is no such thing as "Truth" with a capital *T* that we can just scoop up and call our own. The "meaning of life" is not something we can look up in a book or learn from anybody else, because *it just isn't there unless we find it ourselves.* There *is* no "objective" truth about life, only a *personal* truth, which will be a little bit different for each individual. It will not be vastly different, though, because when we reach the level where we are truly personal, we will find that it corresponds to other people's experiences of individuation, too. In other words, the personal experience becomes a *universal* one—but only if you have gone through it yourself. This is the ultimate meaning of life, and the ultimate virtue: to become an authentic human being by finding your own meaning. If you settle for accepting other people's view of life, you are no better than the evil magician Noureddin in the story of Aladdin (or Jaffar, in the Disney movie version); he has no personal magic or talent himself, so he tries to steal it from the one who has, Aladdin.

For Kierkegaard himself, truth is a religious truth: One must take on the concept of sin and responsibility and seek God's forgiveness directly, as an individual. But this is hard for most people to do, because we are born with quite another character. Typically humans are born into the *aesthetic stage*: the stage of sensuous enjoyment. Children obviously have a very strong interest in the joys of their senses, but if this persists into adulthood it can result in unhealthy character development, symbolized by the Don Juan character who can't get enough of conquests. He loves to pursue the girl, but once he has seduced her he loses interest; she wants to get married, and he wants *out.* He leaves, only to fall in love with and pursue some other girl, and on it goes. Today we would say that this is a person who *can't commit.* Kierkegaard makes the same basic observation but explains that this happens because the Don Juan type is steeped in sensuous enjoyment, which sours on itself: Too much of the same is not

A Kind of Love and a Marriage That Wasn't: Regine Olsen

One event of great importance in Kierkegaard's life was when he fell deeply in love for the first and only time. The girl's name was Regine Olsen, and she was the daughter of a minister. Regine and Kierkegaard became engaged, and Kierkegaard engaged himself in a new intellectual scrutiny: What was this feeling? Was it constant or a fluke? What might go wrong? Was it right for him to try to do something "universal" that everybody did, like get married and have children, or would it somehow interfere with his father's plans for him to be a sacrifice to God? Regine, a kind and loving girl, was utterly puzzled at Kierkegaard's reluctance to accept that they were just young people in love. When they were together he was in a good mood and was confident about their future together, but when he was alone, the doubts started closing in on him. It appears that he felt he was not quite worthy of her, for some reason—perhaps because in years past he had visited a brothel, or perhaps because he couldn't quite explain his father's influence on him to her. Mostly, though, it was the shock of the physical attraction he felt toward her that distracted him, he thought, from becoming truly spiritual. During this period he began to understand one aspect of the Don Juan character: He realized that he loved Regine the most *when he was not with her* but was fantasizing about her. Once they were together his love cooled considerably. Eventually he decided that it was better for both of them if they broke up, but because nineteenth-century mores demanded that the girl, not the boy, break off the engagement if her character were to remain stainless, he had to try to force Regine to break the engagement. This he did by being as nasty to her as he could, even though he still loved her. For a long time he persisted in being rude to her, and she continued to forgive him, because she was very much in love with him. In the end he himself broke up with her, however, and she appears to have talked about killing herself. Kierkegaard wanted her to despise him, and a short time later she actually became engaged to a friend of theirs. After that Kierkegaard never tired of talking about woman's fickle, stupid, and untrustworthy nature.

a good thing, but a person who is stuck in the aesthetic stage doesn't have any sense of what is morally right or wrong. Such knowledge usually comes as people mature (although some people are stuck in the aesthetic stage forever), as they enter the *ethical stage*.

In this stage people realize that there are laws and conventions, and they believe that the way to become a good person is to follow these conventions. A fictional character from nineteenth-century middle-class Copenhagen becomes Kierkegaard's prototype for the ethical stage: Judge William, the righteous man who tries to be a

FIGURE 11.3 Regine Olsen, Søren Kierkegaard's fiancée, a gentle Copenhagen girl who did her best to understand the intellectual scruples of her boyfriend, who could not reconcile his devotion to God with the idea of physical attraction to a woman and a subsequent bourgeois marriage. This photo was taken only a few years after Kierkegaard finally broke up with her. (Photo of Regine Schlegel [*née* Olsen] courtesy of The Royal Library, Copenhagen.)

good judge and a good husband and father. Scholars don't quite agree on how to evaluate this good and kind man, because the fact is that we are rarely certain when Kierkegaard is being serious and when he is being sarcastic, since Kierkegaard also cites Socrates (whom he greatly admired) as an example of an ethical person. Although Socrates is commonly recognized as a truly courageous and virtuous man who strove to live (and die) the right way, Judge William doesn't come across as a heroic person; we even get the impression that he is actually a pompous, self-righteous, bourgeois bore who has his attention fixed on "doing the right thing" merely because society expects it of him. So it seems that Kierkegaard wants to tell us that it isn't enough to follow the rules and become what everyone else thinks you ought to be; that way you exist only in the judgment of others. You have to take on responsibility for judging yourself, and the way you do that is by making a *leap of faith* into the *religious stage*. It isn't enough to judge your own life in terms of what makes sense according to society's rules and rational concepts of morality; what you must do in order to become an authentic person is leave the standards of society behind, including your love for reason and for things to make sense, and choose to trust in God, like Abraham, who made that same choice when he brought his son Isaac to be sacrificed, even though it didn't make sense to him. Reason and the rules of society can't tell you if the insight you reach as a religious person is the truth.

So why is Socrates not a perfect person? Why did he stay within the ethical stage and make no leap of faith to the religious stage, according to Kierkegaard? Because the leap was not available to him, presumably since he didn't belong to the Judeo-Christian tradition. Socrates is an example of how far you can reach if you stay within the boundaries of reason. However, in the religious stage there is no objective measure of meaning. At this stage you take responsibility for yourself, but at the same time you give up your fate and place it in the hands of God. Finally you can become a true human being, a complete individual and person, because only in the religious stage can you realize what it means to say that "Subjectivity is Truth."

Heidegger's Intellectual Authenticity

Martin Heidegger is a controversial and enigmatic philosopher. He is enigmatic, because he aims to make people break through the old boundaries of thinking by inventing new words and categories for them to think with. This means that there is no easy way to read Heidegger; you must acquaint yourself with an entirely new vocabulary of key concepts and get used to a new way of looking at reality. In spite of his rather inaccessible style, though, Heidegger has become somewhat of a cult figure in modern European philosophy. He is controversial because he was a member of the Nazi party during World War II.

Heidegger sees human beings as not essentially distinct from the world they inhabit, in the same sense that traditional epistemology does: There is no "subject" on the inside of a person, nor no "object" of experience on the outside. No, humans are "thrown into the world" at birth, and they interact with it and in a sense "live" it. There is no such thing as a person who is distinct from his or her world of experience—we *are* our world of experience. This idea of interaction with the world from the beginning of life is one that Heidegger took over from his teacher and mentor Edmund Husserl, but he adds his own twist to it: What makes humans special is not that they are on the inside and the world is on the outside, but that they experience their *existence* differently than do all other beings. Humans *are there* for themselves; they are aware of their existence and of certain essential facts about that existence, such as their own mortality. So Heidegger calls humans "Being-there" (*Dasein*) rather than "humans." Things, on the other hand, don't know they exist, and presumably neither do animals; an animal may know that it is hungry, or in pain, or in heat, but it doesn't know that its days are numbered, and that makes the difference. Our humanity consists primarily of our continuous awareness of death, our "Being-towards-death" (*Sein-zum-Tode*). On occasion we let ourselves get distracted, because this awareness is quite a burden on our minds, and we let ourselves forget. We become absorbed in our jobs, our feelings, the gossip we hear, the nonsense around us. According to Heidegger, we often refer to what "They" say, as if the opinion of those anonymous others has some obvious authority. We bow to what "They" say, and believe we are safe from harm and responsibility if we can get absorbed by this ubiquitous "They" (*Das Man*) and don't have to think on our own. In other words, we try to take on the safe and nonthinking existence-form of things—we objectify ourselves.

This does not make an authentic life, however, and in any event it is doomed to failure, because we just can't forget that completely. Humans just can't become things, because they are the ones who understand the relationship between themselves and things. When we do the dishes we understand what plates are for, what glasses are for, and why they must be cleaned. We understand the entire "doing dishes" situation. When we prepare a presentation on our computer we understand what a report is, what a computer is, and why the two have anything to do with ourselves, even if we may not understand what the report is for or how the computer works. In the end, humans are different because they can ask, What is it for? and understand the interconnections of the world in which they live. We are asking, thinking creatures, and

FIGURE 11.4 Martin Heidegger (1889–1976), German philosopher and poet and a member of the National Socialist party. An authentic life is, for Heidegger, a life open to the possibility of different meanings. The feeling of *angst* can help jolt us out of our complacency and help us see the world from an intellectually flexible point of view.

in order to regain our awareness of that fact, we must face our true nature. We may pretend to be nothing but victims of circumstances (I have to do the dishes; there is no other choice), but we also can choose to realize that we interact with our world and affect it. In *Being and Time* (written in his exasperating style), Heidegger calls this phenomenon "An-already-thrown-into-the-world-kind-of-Being who is existing-in-relationship-to-existing-entities-within-that-world" (*Sich-vorweg-schon-sein-in* [*der-Welt*] *als Sein-bei* [*innerwelt-lich begegendem Seindenen*]). But he also describes it, in another and slightly more down-to-earth fashion, as the structure of "*care.*" "Being-theres" always "care" about something, Heidegger says. This doesn't mean humans care *for* others, or *for* things—it merely means that they are always *engaged* in something (the state of being engaged in something Heidegger called *Sorge*—care). Sometimes this involves caring for others, but mostly it involves engaging in your own existence: We fret, we worry, we look forward to something, we're concerned, we're content, we're disappointed—about something—our health, our promotion, our parents' well-being, our new kittens, or the exciting experiences we anticipate on our next vacation. We are always engaged in some part of our reality, unless we get caught up in another and deeper element of human nature: a *mood*, like anguish.

Heidegger's concept of anguish (*Angst*) is related to Kierkegaard's: It does not involve fear of something in particular; it is, rather, the unpleasant and sometimes terrifying insecurity of not knowing where you stand in life and eventually having to make a choice—perhaps with little or no information about your options. For Kierkegaard this experience is related to a religious awakening, but for Heidegger the awakening is metaphysical: You realize that all your concerns and all of the rules you live by are *relative*, in the deepest sense; you realize that you have viewed the world a certain way, within a certain frame, and now for some reason the frame is breaking up. A woman may feel angst if she loses her tenured job at a university, not just because she is worried about how she will provide for her family, but because her worldview—her professional identity and the security of her tenure—has been undermined. A young

Heidegger and the Nazi Connection

At the time of Hitler's takeover of Germany in 1933, Heidegger's philosophy professor, Edmund Husserl, was head of the Philosophy Department at the University of Freiburg. Husserl was already a famous philosopher, having developed the theory of *phenomenology*, a philosophical theory of human experience. Its main thesis is that there is no such thing as a consciousness that is empty at first and then proceeds to order and analyze the objects of sense experience; instead our mind is already engaged in the process of experiencing the world from day one. We can't separate the concepts of the experiencing mind and the experience of the mind, and because it is impossible for philosophy to say anything about a nonexperiencing mind and an unexperienced object-world, phenomenology sees its primary task as describing, as clearly as possible, the phenomenon of experience itself. Husserl had been the essential inspiration for many of Heidegger's writings; in fact, he had taken Heidegger under his wing when Heidegger was a young scholar. Husserl was Jewish, though, which meant that he was targeted for persecution by the new Nazi leaders. He was fired from his university position and eventually died as a result of Nazi harassment. Heidegger, his former student and protégé, profited from these events by taking over Husserl's position as department chair; indeed, it seems that he never raised any protest against the treatment of his old professor. At this time Heidegger joined the Nazi party for, as he explained later, purely professional reasons: He couldn't have kept his university position without becoming a party member. This appears to be stretching the truth, for Heidegger never did anything even to distance himself from the Nazi ideology during the war years. Today people are divided in their views on Heidegger; some feel that because of his Nazi association, Heidegger's philosophy is tainted and must somehow contain elements of Nazi thinking. Others believe that Heidegger was essentially apolitical, although he was not very graceful about it; they think his philosophy should be viewed independent of his personal life.

man may feel angst if he learns he has an incurable disease—not just because he is afraid to die, but because "this isn't supposed to happen" to a young person. Children may feel angst if they are drawn into a divorce battle between their parents. A hitherto religious person may feel angst if he or she begins to doubt the existence of God, because this is the breakup of the ultimate framework. And humans may feel angst when they realize that their worldview is somehow not a God-given truth.

People whose attitude towards the world is *inauthentic* may experience the most

FIGURE 11.5 Edvard Munch: "The Scream." This image, which exists in more than fifty original versions, is the epitome of the feeling of *angst*. Munch himself described in his diary the moment that inspired him to do this work: "I was walking along the road with two friends—the sun was setting—all of a sudden the sky turned crimson—my friends walked on, and I froze, shaking with anguish—and I felt that through nature was passing a vast, endless scream." (Ulrich Bischoff, *Edvard Munch 1863–1944*, Köln, Benedikt Taschen GmbH & Co, 1989. Translated by the author.)

Henri Bergson: Let Your True Self Emerge

The French philosopher Henri Bergson (1859–1941) is not considered an ethicist per se, but his theories of consciousness and time perception involve an unusual concept of authenticity. For Bergson humans live most of their lives subject to the demands of circumstances and customs, and subject to the internalized opinions of others. Once in a while, however, their true selves break through. We can't live our lives without a certain amount of custom and regard for immediate circumstances, but if we are to remain true to what we really are, we need to listen to the murmurs of our own self that are hiding behind the facade of our civilized lives. And how do we know there is such a true self? We all have agonized over some decision, weighing the pros and the cons, coming up with the most logical answer or the one that will please us or seems to be the morally right thing to do. Then, sometimes, to our own surprise, we end up doing something else entirely. Afterward, when we are asked why, we answer that we just "had to do it"—we "couldn't help ourselves." This, says Bergson, is our true self emerging. It may happen to a person who has decided to marry someone, received all the gifts, ordered all the catering, and is standing at the altar—the person says NO! when she meant to say yes. If you experience, in the midst of your everyday life, that all of a sudden there is *something you must do before it is too late*, like running away with the circus, learning the art of fencing, going to Paris, or having a baby, this, says Berg-son, is your true self trying to get your attention, and this is true authenticity—all the rest is a veneer. There are two major problems with this. The first is that we have no assurance that this "deeper self" is actually a *good* self; the urge that comes over us may be to kill or betray someone. So it is doubtful that Bergsonian authenticity can actually be called a "virtue." The second problem is that Bergson thought this deeper self was proof that we have freedom of the will, but the whole point is that we have *no control* over what that self wants, and this is hardly what we normally mean by having a free will. (The question of free will is discussed in Part 4.)

As a private person Bergson seems to have been a man of much integrity; in 1917 he went to the United States in order to fulfill a moral duty, as he saw it—to put an end to World War I. He also was utterly devoted to his daughter, who was hearing-impaired. In 1941 he lined up in the rain to be registered as a Jew by the Nazis during the Paris occupation; he contracted pneumonia, and it caused his death. He had wished to convert to Catholicism, but in view of Hitler's persecution of the Jews he decided to remain a member of the Jewish faith as a gesture of solidarity. These are the deeds of what we would call a person of moral virtue, so let us suppose we asked Bergson if he did these things as a conscious, free decision. We might receive the answer that other people of moral virtue have given in similar situations: I did what I did because I could not do otherwise.

fundamental form of angst. Heidegger himself states that if a Being-there is open to the possibility of different meanings in his or her reality, then he or she is living an authentic life. If, however, a Being-there does not want to accept the possibility that something may have a different meaning than he or she has believed up until now, then he or she is inauthentic. A typical trait of those who are inauthentic is that they become absorbed in just reacting to the things in their world—in driving the car, loading the laundry into the dryer, working on the computer, shopping, watching TV. Such persons think that the predigested opinions of others or of the media are sufficient for getting by; they let themselves become absorbed in "The They," Das Man. But what does authenticity mean? Is it a call to "get in touch with yourself" by pulling away from the world? Or is it just a banal reminder to "stay open-minded"? Even worse, is it a built-in feature of being human, something we can't escape? Some Heidegger scholars see it not just as a call to reexamine yourself or to avoid hardening of the brain cells; to them authenticity is a fundamentally different attitude from one by which we allow the readily available worldviews of others to rule our lives. Being authentic means, for Heidegger, that you stop being absorbed by your doings and retain an attitude that "things may mean something else than what I expect." Only through this kind of of intellectual flexibility can we even begin to think about making judgments about anything else, be they facts or people. So authenticity is, in a sense, remaining "open-minded," but it also involves performing a greater task by constantly forcing yourself to realize that reality is in flux, that things change, including yourself, and that you are part of a world of changing relationships. And *this* causes angst, because this means you have to give up your anchors and security zones as a matter of principle. In the end, angst becomes a liberating element that can give us a new and perhaps better understanding of ourselves and the world, but it is hard to deal with while it is happening.

Sartre's Ethical Authenticity

For some people angst is simply an existential fact, something we have to live with all our days as humans. Jean-Paul Sartre (1905–1980) is one of those persons. Sartre is the best known of the French existentialists of the mid-twentieth century; others include the writer Albert Camus and the philosophers Gabriel Marcel and Simone de Beauvoir.

Sartre studied phenomenology (the study of the phenomenon of human consciousness and experience) in Berlin during the years separating the two world wars, and he was well acquainted with the theories of Edmund Husserl and Martin Heidegger. During World War II Sartre was held by the Nazis as a prisoner of war, but he escaped and joined forces with the French resistance movement. These experiences in many ways influenced his outlook on politics and on life in general: His political views were socialist and at times even Marxist, to a certain degree. Always politically

FIGURE 11.6 Jean-Paul Sartre (1905–1980), French philosopher and writer. Recognized as the most influential thinker in the existentialist movement, his best-known works of philosophy are the lecture "Existentialism as Humanism" (1945) and the much larger, much more intellectually challenging *Being and Nothingness* (1943).

active, Sartre may well be considered the most influential philosopher in twentieth-century Europe and possibly elsewhere, too—perhaps not so much because of his philosophical or fictional writings (for Sartre was also a dramatist and novelist), but because of his intellectual inspiration. The existential movement may not have reflected a completely faithful version of the Sartrean philosophy, but it is certain that in his own century Sartre inspired the most extensive philosophical movement ever to reach people outside the academic world—the movement of existentialism.

Although existentialism as a fad in the 1950s became stereotyped as the interest of morose young people who dressed in black, chain-smoked late at night in small cafes, and read poems to each other about the absurdity of life, Sartre's existentialism had a whole other and more substantial content. Partly inspired by his experiences during World War II, Sartre came to believe that there is no God, and because there is no God, there are no absolute moral rules, either. The concept that God's nonexistence makes everything permissible was not new at the time; it was well known to Western readers of Dostoyevsky and his book *The Brothers Karamazov*. However, it was given a new twist by Sartre. Instead of saying, as did many other atheists, that we can find our values in our own human context and rationality, Sartre held that without the existence of a God, there are no values, in the sense that there are no *objective* values. There is no master plan and, accordingly, nothing in the world *makes sense*; all events happen at random, and *life is absurd*. So what do we do? Give a shrug, and set about to make merry while we can? No, we must realize that because no values exist outside ourselves, we, as individuals in a community, become the *source* of values. And the process by which we create values is the process of *choice*.

When a person realizes that he or she has to make a choice, and that the choice will have far-reaching consequences, that person may be gripped by *anguish*—Sartre uses the image of a general having to choose whether to send his soldiers to their death. It is not a decision that can be made lightly by a person of conscience, and such a person may worry about it a great deal, precisely because he doesn't know beforehand if he will make the right decision. If he realizes the enormity of the situation and still makes his choice as best he can, shouldering whatever consequences may develop, he is living with *authenticity*. However, suppose the general says to himself, "I *have* to send the soldiers out, for the sake of my country/my reputation/the book I want to write." Then he is acting inauthentically: he is assuming that he *has no choice*. But for Sartre we always have a choice. Even the soldier who is ordered to kill civilians still has a choice, even though he may claim that he will be executed if he doesn't follow orders and thus "has no choice." For Sartre there are some things that are worse than death, like killing innocent civilians. So, claiming that one's actions are somehow *determined* by the situation is inauthenticity or, as Sartre calls it, *bad faith*. But bad faith can be displayed in another way, too: Suppose the general is so distraught at having to make a choice that he says, "I just won't choose—I'll lock myself in the bathroom and wait until it is all over." In that case, Sartre would say, the general is deluding himself, because he is already making a choice—*the choice not to choose*—and in that case he is in even less control of the consequences of his choice than if he actually had chosen a course of action. In our hearts we know this, and for Sartre we can never deceive ourselves 100 percent: There will always be a part of us that knows we are not like animals or inert things that can't make choices, simply because we are human beings, and human beings must make choices, at least from time to time. (Sartre believes animals can't make conscious, free choices, as do most other philosophers. In Part 4 we will take a closer look at Sartre's theory of human nature and the concept of choice.) Animals and things can exist without making choices, but humans can't, because humans are aware of their own existence and their own mortality; they have a relationship to themselves (they exist "for themselves" [*pour soi*]), whereas animals and things merely float through existence (they exist "in themselves" [*en soi*]).

How does bad faith manifest itself? Sartre presents his famous example involving a young woman on a date. The woman's date makes a subtle move on her—he grasps her hand—and she doesn't quite know what to do. She doesn't want to offend him or appear to be prudish, but she really doesn't know whether she wants to have a relationship with him, either; she just doesn't know what to do. So she does nothing. She somehow manages to "detach" herself from the situation, as if her body really doesn't concern her, and while he moves in on her, her hand seems not to belong to her at all. She looks at his face and pretends that she has no hand, no body, no sexuality at all. This, says Sartre, is bad faith: The woman thinks she can turn herself into a thing by acting thinglike, but it is an illusion, because through it all she knows that sooner or later she has to say yes or no. What should she do in order to be authentic? She should realize that she has to make up her mind, even if she can't foresee if she will want to have a relationship or not. Making up her mind will then create a new situation for her to react to, even though it is essentially unforeseeable. This openness to the unforeseen is part of being authentic. Like Heidegger, Sartre sees endless possibilities as part of the universe of an authentic human being. But contrary to Heidegger, Sartre sees them as an *ethical challenge.* For Heidegger, remaining open to that which is unforeseen is mainly a question of remaining a good intellectual; for Sartre it is a question of remaining or becoming a good person. When we make a choice, Sartre says, we are taking on the greatest of responsibilities, for we are choosing not only for ourselves and our lives, but for everyone else, too. Whatever choice we make sends out the message to everyone else that This is okay to do. Therefore, through our choices we become role models for others. If we choose to pay our taxes, others will notice and believe that it is the right thing to do. If we choose to sell drugs to little children, somebody out there will see it and think it is a good idea. (Interestingly, doing something just because someone else is doing it is not enough for Sartre; true authenticity must come from personal choices and not just from following role models.) Whatever we choose, even if we think it will concern only ourselves, actually will concern all of humanity, because we are endorsing our action as a general virtue. This is why choices can be so fraught with anxiety—and for Sartre this anxiety never goes away. We must live with it, and with the burden of the choice, forever. We are free to choose, but we are not free to refrain from choosing. In other words, *we are condemned to be free.*

But how can we make a choice if the world is absurd and all of our actions are meaningless? When we first experience the absurdity of existence we may feel nauseated, dizzy from the idea that reality has no core or meaning. But then we realize that we must create a meaning, we must choose for something to matter to us. For Sartre the social conditions of France became a theme that mattered to him, but you might choose something else—your family, your job, or your Barbie Doll collection. Any kind of life project will create values, as long as you realize that the world is still absurd in spite of your project! If you think you are "safe" with your family or your job or your doll collection—if you think you've created a rock-solid meaning for your life—then you've fallen back into bad faith. This is the case with the waiter (another of Sartre's examples) who wants so badly to become the perfect waiter that he takes on a "waiter identity" that provides answers to everything: how to speak, what to say, how to walk, where to go. The waiter has not chosen a project; he has turned himself into a thing, an "In itself" that doesn't have to choose any more. Living authentically means living in anguish, always on the edge—facing the absurdity of life and courageously making choices in the face of meaninglessness. When something you care about appears, then you will know what to do. The French philosopher Simone de Beauvoir, Sartre's close friend and collaborator on the subject of existentialism, puts it like this: "Any man who has known real loves, real revolts, real desires, and real will knows quite well that he has no need of any outside guarantee to be sure of his goals. . . . " We will look more closely at Beauvoir in Part 4.

Suppose you decide that you'll do something about your life *tomorrow*? That *next year* you'll write that novel? Or go back to college? Suppose you decide that you *should have* married someone else, had children, gone to see the Pyramids, or become a movie actor? Then there is not much hope for your authenticity, says Sartre, because your virtue lies only in what you accomplish, not in choices you make about things you are *planning* to do. If you never try to write that book, you have no right to claim you are a promising writer. If you never tried to become an actor, then you can't complain that you're a great undiscovered talent. We are not authentically anything but what we *do*, and we are hiding from reality if we think we are more than that. Like Aristotle, Sartre links the value of our virtue with the success of our conduct: Intentions may be good, but they aren't enough.

The Art of Being Human

So what is an authentic person today? Some people believe it has something to do with "ego integrity." This idea has been advanced in American psychology by the influential American analyst Erik Erikson (born in 1902). Erikson believes that a psychologically mature human being has gone through several stages of personality development. In passing from stage to stage, a person may experience a sense of loss of self, an "identity crisis" (a term also coined by Erikson), especially during adolescence. If the person can resolve the crisis successfully, he or she is on the way to becoming a stronger and more balanced human being. If the crisis remains with the person, he or she will develop psychological problems later in life. People who have managed to emerge successfully from each crisis eventually will obtain "ego integrity," an inner harmony and balance of the mind that gives the ego a sense of meaning and fulfillment. Persons with ego integrity don't agonize over "what might have been." Such persons don't dwell on how their parents did them wrong, how bad choices were made by others that affected their lives, or how short life is. Such persons take responsibility for their actions but aren't weighed down by guilt about things over which they have no control. Persons who lose their ego integrity experience fear of death, despair at lost chances, and start up new projects in their panic over the brevity of life. A person doesn't need to be well educated in order to achieve ego integrity—people who have achieved it can be found in all cultures—but cultures can help individuals through their crises by supporting their transition and welcoming them on the other side. Erikson says that healthy children will not fear life if their elders have integrity enough not to fear death.

It is conceivable that the concept of ego integrity might change with changing times and places. In some cultures we might find it to mean a reconciliation with *fate*—accepting what life has handed you and learning to love it, as hard as that might be. Or it might mean putting your faith in the will of God and not asking why. In other cultures, though, this might be considered "bad faith." True ego integrity would then consist of a courageous realization of the unpredictability of everything, and of not losing courage when facing an uncaring universe. As we saw in Chapter 10, virtue may mean different things to different cultures. In Part 4 of this book we will look at the question of whether there is one way to be human that is more normal or more acceptable than any other way—in other words, whether there is such a thing as human nature and what role such a concept might play in a moral system.

Narratives That Explore Angst and Authenticity

Chapter 13 contains a discussion of virtues in a modern perspective, illustrated by stories dealing with the phenomenon of angst and the achievement of authenticity. The angst-ridden stories include Jean-Paul Sartre's *No Exit*, Woody Allen's film *Hannah and Her Sisters*, and Bertil Malmberg's short story "The Tail." Stories of authenticity include Karen Blixen's novelette *Babette's Feast*, the film *Star Wars*, and Iris Murdoch's novel *The Good Apprentice*.

Chapter 12

Case Studies
in Virtue

This chapter presents two classical virtues for closer examination: *compassion* and *gratitude*. We will look at how they have been perceived by some past and present philosophers, and how they may affect our lives.

Compassion: Are We Born with It?

You may remember Thomas Hobbes's view that humans are by nature self-centered, and compassion is something humans show towards others in distress because they are afraid the same calamity might happen to them. In other words, when people show sympathy and pity towards one another it is either to make sure that others will help them if the same thing should happen to them, or else it is a kind of superstition, a warding off of the fate of others by showing you feel sorry for them. There are scholars who think Hobbes's viewpoint was flavored by the political unrest of the seventeenth century, which might well have caused a thinker to focus on his own survival and to believe that self-love is the primary driving force. In the eighteenth century, the Age of Reason, two philosophical giants shared a different idea. Both the Scottish philosopher David Hume and the Swiss philosopher Jean-Jacques Rousseau believed that humans are naturally compassionate toward one another. Hume held that even a selfish person will feel benevolence toward strangers whenever his self-interest is not involved. Rousseau claimed that the more we are steeped in civilization, the more we tend to forget our natural inclination to help others and sympathize with them, because it is not an aberration of nature that makes people selfish—it is *civilization* itself. Rousseau certainly agrees that there are people who show compassion only because they are afraid something might happen to them, and because they have only their own interests at heart, but this is not a natural thing, he says; it is caused by human culture. If we would seek only the natural capacities in ourselves, we would find the natural virtue of compassion still intact. The best way to reestablish contact with our original nature is to educate children as freely as possible so that they don't become infected with the evils of civilization. (We shall return to Rousseau in Part 4). Philosophers in the Western tradition were not the only ones to speculate about human nature and compassion; in the third century B.C.E. the Chinese philosopher Mencius claimed, as Rousseau would some two thousand years later, that humans are compassionate and benevolent by nature but have been corrupted by the circumstances of everyday life.

Philip Hallie: The Case of Le Chambon

Could Rousseau be right that civilization is the cause of evildoing, or does "civilized" mean "compassionate"? The American philosopher Philip Hallie doesn't answer this directly, but he gives a concrete example of compassion that occurs in the midst of a civilization under the heel of barbarism. In the southern part of France there is a small village called Le Chambon-sur-Lignon. The population of this little town has had a long history of persecution because of their Hugenot faith. During World War II the people of the village came to the aid of Jewish refugees from all over France in a rescue effort that was matched only by the massive efforts of Danish citizens to save the Danish Jews by smuggling them across the water to neutral Sweden during World War II. The people of Le Chambon saved about six thousand lives (more than twice the number of their own population). The majority were Jewish children whose parents already had gone to the extermination camps. This took place all through the German occupation of France, even when southern France ceased to be a "free zone" governed by French collaborators.

The village of Le Chambon has become a well-known case study of compassion primarily because of Hallie, who himself was a soldier in World War II. As a professional philosopher, Hallie was profoundly disturbed by the evidence of malice throughout world history and in particular during the Nazi reign. The Nazis regularly humiliated their prisoners; during marches prisoners were not allowed to go to the bathroom and had to perform their physical functions while on the march. Hallie describes this as an "excremental assault" and calls it an example of *institutionalized cruelty*. Hallie defines this type of cruelty as not only physical but also psychological. When a person's or a people's self-respect and dignity are attacked on a regular basis, the victims often begin to believe that somehow this cruelty is *justified*, and that they really are no better than dirt. This is especially true when one population group commits this offense against another group. Thus cruelty becomes an institution, approved by the victimizer and tolerated by the victim. Such instances of institutionalized cruelty can be seen not only in oppressive war-time situations, but also in race-relations throughout the course of history, in relations between genders (which Hallie doesn't get into), and in certain parent-child relations. The general pattern is a demeaning and belittling of one group by another, so that soon such behavior becomes routine.

Why does institutionalized cruelty occur? Because one group is more powerful than the other, either in terms of physical power (it is bigger, it is more numerous, or has more weapons) or in terms of economic, educational, or political power (as when one group can hold property, get an education, and vote, and the other group can't). Power can even be verbal, as when one group has the monopoly of using slurs against the other.

How can it be helped? By changing the power balance, says Hallie. This, of course, is hard—it is hard to acquire the rights to vote, to own property, to get an equal education. It is hard to build up physical strength. And it is hard to reverse the trend of slurs and other insults. Even if all this happens, though, the insidious effect of institutionalized cruelty is that it is not over just because the cruelty ceases, because *it leaves scars.* The prisoners who were liberated from Nazi extermination camps never were truly "free" ever again; they carried their scars with them forever. And just being "kind" to a victim doesn't help—it only serves to remind him how far he has sunk. What truly helps is what the people of Le Chambon did for the Jewish refugees in the face of the Nazi occupation.

Hallie heard of Le Chambon and went there to talk to the people; most of them didn't think they had done anything exceptional. What these people did for the refugees, though, was to show them compassion in the form of *hospitality*. They showed the refugees that they were equal to the villagers themselves, that they deserved to live in the villagers' own homes while their escape to Switzerland across the mountains was being planned. This, says Hallie, is the only effective antidote to institutionalized cruelty: hospitality offered as an act of compassion, in a way that makes it clear to the victims that their dignity is intact.

The story of Le Chambon has a twist that makes it even more exceptional. The rescue effort was indeed a noble effort, but how did it succeed in an occupied country with Nazi soldiers everywhere? It wasn't that the villagers were tremendously discreet—no group of people can hide six thousand people who pass through over a five-year period. It was because of the courage of the town minister, André Trocmé, that Nazi curiosity was deflected for the longest time. When the Nazis finally became suspicious and decided to investigate, Trocmé was deported and executed. This still did not stop the rescue effort, though, because the villagers had an ally in a very

Is It Better to Cry Over Your Victim than Not to Feel Sorry?

In a celebrated paper the philosopher Jonathan Bennett claims that it is better to be a person of wrongdoing who has compassion than it is to be a person of no wrongdoing who has no compassion. An example of the first kind of person is Heinrich Himmler, who, as head of the Nazi SS (an elite guard), developed stomach troubles because of what he felt he had to do. The American minister Jonathan Edwards was the other type of person; although he presumably served the needs of his flock, he believed everybody deserved to go to Hell. Philip Hallie responds to Bennett's point of view by referring to an incident in Lewis Carroll's *Alice in Wonderland*. The Walrus and the Carpenter lure some little oysters to take a nice walk with them along the beach.

After a while they all sit down on a rock, and the Carpenter and the Walrus begin to eat the oysters. The Walrus feels sorry for them and weeps, but he eats them nevertheless. The Carpenter couldn't care less about the oysters and is just concerned with eating them. Hallie asks, Are we really supposed to believe that the Walrus is a better creature than the Carpenter because he has sympathy for his victims? The Walrus ate as many oysters as he could stuff into his mouth behind his handkerchief. Likewise, Himmler killed over thirteen million people even though he was "feeling sorry" for them. For Hallie sympathy is no redeeming quality at all if it isn't accompanied by compassionate action.

unlikely person: the Nazi overseer of the village, Major Schmäling. Despite being a party member, Schmäling chose to ignore the steady stream of refugees and did not report the incidents to his superiors. In a paper read at the University of San Diego in 1985, Hallie told the emotional story of the trial at Le Chambon: After the war, when all of the Nazis who had been captured were standing trial for war crimes, Le Chambon was the site of trials, also. The entire village was crammed into the courthouse when the time came for Major Schmäling to be tried. As he walked up the aisle toward the judge, everyone rose to pay tribute to this man who had saved so many at the risk of his own life. The judge asked him why he had not reported the refugees and whether he was against the Nazi philosophy. He answered, paradoxically, "No, I believe in Nazism—but I could not stand by and watch innocent blood be shed."

This, to Hallie, is virtue: the compassion one shows in reaching out to save others at the risk of one's own life. It is not as easy nor as passive as just avoiding any wrongdoing, and it is not necessarily the result of any logical thinking. It is an act of the heart.

Richard Taylor: Compassion Is All You Need

In Chapters 3 through 7 we looked at a number of rules and principles regarding the nature of moral goodness and the proper conduct of human beings. Even in this section on virtue, most of the theories we have discussed involve using *reason* to evaluate the proper moral action. For some people, the answer to doing the right thing and having virtue is much more simple: We do the right thing *when our heart is in the right place*; moral goodness is simply a gut feeling that we all have, a conscience that speaks without words, a fellow-feeling that leads us to reach out in compassion to others. If we don't have that, we have no morality at all. For Richard Taylor, an American philosopher, reason has *no* role to play in making the right moral choice; he believes the eternal focus in ethics on reason needs an antidote, and he finds it in an analysis of *malice versus compassion.*

Imagine a series of atrocities. A child pins a bug to a tree just to watch it squirm. Boys set fire to an old cat and delight in its painful death. Soldiers make a baby girl giggle before they shoot her, and they force an old man to dig his own grave before they beat him to death. What is so awful about these stories? It is not just that these people did not live by the categorical imperative, says Taylor (referring to Kant). It is not that they didn't try to maximize general happiness for everyone involved (referring to utilitarianism). It is not that they were ignorant (Socrates) or didn't follow the Golden Mean (Aristotle). The horror we feel—and for Taylor it is the *same kind of horror* in all three cases—stems from the fact that these incidents are simply malicious. The acts are horrible not because the consequences are so terrible (the death of one bug, one cat, and two war victims may not have widespread effects) but because the intent was to cause suffering for the sake of someone else's pleasure or entertainment. These are not crimes against *reason* but crimes against *compassion.*

True moral value, then, lies in compassion, and Taylor illustrates this with three more tales. A boy comes up to an attic to steal something and rescues some pigeons that are trapped there, despite his father's strict command to leave the birds alone. A white sheriff beats up a black rioter during the race riots of the 1960s and then, breaking down in tears, cleans the man up and takes him home. An American soldier who is trapped on an island with a Japanese soldier during World War II finally finds the Japanese asleep but is not able to kill him. In each of these cases, Taylor says, the *reason* of these people told them to do one thing, but their hearts told them something else, and *their hearts told them right.* In the final end we can't trust our reason, but we can trust our hearts; compassion is all we need in order to be moral human beings, compassion toward all living things. Even people who do the right things can't be called moral if they don't have compassion—in other words, if they don't have the right intention.

This is a much more radical view than Hallie's, because it tells us to *disregard* our reason. Let us look at how that might work in practice. Taylor assumes that we all have this compassion in us—he appeals to our *moral intuition.* But what about the boys who set fire to the cat? Where was their natural compassion? And what about soldiers

Carol Gilligan: Compassion Is What Men Need

In her 1985 book *In a Different Voice*, which recently has been gaining influence in the field of ethics, psychologist Carol Gilligan argues that ethical standards in our culture all have been set by male scholars. There is an overwhelming tendency to look toward *rules of fairness* in our moral system, and for Gilligan this corresponds to a particularly male orientation toward ideal conduct; even small boys incorporate the idea of rights, justice, and fairness into their childhood games, and this tendency never changes in adulthood unless a man is exposed to another system of values that is primarily female—an ethics of *care*. For little girls the rules of the game become subordinate to the friendship between the players; if there is a disagreement, girls will more often abandon the game for the sake of friendship, while boys will argue about the rules until they have reached a solution. In adult life these two ethical visions are regarded differently. One, the male vision, is viewed as the "proper" approach to moral thinking—thinking in terms of rights and rules of conduct. The other, the female vision of harmonizing relationships and making things "work out" for everybody, is seen as a more confused and less relevant ethic. But, says Gilligan, it is not a lesser or more illogical approach; it is just different, and equally relevant. What ethics needs is for men to appreciate the compassion inherent in an ethics of care, and to realize its relevance and benefits. Women, who in caring often lose their concept of rights and self, need to establish a sense of selfhood as well as legitimate rights for the caretaker. In Part 4 we will take a closer look at Gilligan's theory of human nature—the ethics of justice and the ethics of care.

who kill defenseless civilians? Obviously, not everyone has this compassion, not even the people in Taylor's own examples. What can we do about people who have no compassion? Well, we can try to tell them stories about malice and compassion, but chances are that they will think it is a great idea to set fire to a cat, and that the boy in the attic should have left the pigeons trapped. How can we appeal to people who are not responsive to compassion? If we were to ask Kant, Mill, Aristotle, or just about any moral thinker, he or she would say we must try to appeal to their *reason*. If we all had compassion there might not be any need for reason, but as we have seen, not everyone has it, and not everyone has it at the right time, at the right place, and for the right people. Therefore we must have something that might convince people who are lacking in compassion, and this is where reason has to come in. What arguments can we use? We might say, "How would you like it if someone did that to you?" In other words, we might appeal to their logical sense of universalizability, and invoke the Golden Rule (whatever you do to others may come back to haunt you). Or we might say, "If you do this you will get caught and punished." In this way we appeal to their sense of logic and causality; they can't possibly "get away with" any wrongdoing. If these two arguments don't convince them to do right, we might just lock them up—protect them from themselves, and us from them—until they display enough rationality to understand our arguments. Reason, then, is not a substitute for moral feeling (compassion), but it becomes the necessary argument when the moral feeling is absent or deficient. A moral theory that leaves room for only compassion is powerless when it comes to enforcing moral values and virtues.

There is one more problem with Taylor's idea that compassion is all we need, and to illustrate it we will turn to Mark Twain and the story of *Huckleberry Finn*. In the story Huck, a young boy, helps Jim, a slave, escape from his owner, Miss Watson. Jonathan Bennett analyzes this famous literary incident—and Bennett is a philosopher who believes in reason as an important part of ethics. He concludes that Huck certainly did the right thing in helping Jim, but it still wasn't good enough, because he did it for the wrong reason. Let's review what happens in the story. Huck's problem is that he wants to help his friend Jim, but he realizes that by doing so he goes against the morals of the town, which require him to return stolen property (slaves). Because nobody has ever told Huck that owning people is wrong, he has no principle of equality to hold up against what Bennett calls the "bad morality" of the nineteenth-century town. So in the end Huck ends up lying to protect Jim without understanding exactly why, and he resolves not to adhere to any moral principles from then on because they are too hard to figure out. Bennett's conclusion is that Huck did the right thing, but for the wrong reason; he should have set up a new principle of his own, such as "It is wrong to own people" or merely "Jim is my friend, and one should help one's friends." This way Huck's sympathy for Jim would have been supported by his *reason*, and he would not have had to give up on morality because it was too puzzling.

To this we might add something: Mark Twain himself probably wouldn't have shared Bennett's conclusion, because for Twain Huck is a hero who does the right thing for the best of reasons—because he has compassion for a fellow human being (a human being whom many educated readers of Twain's own day and age might have chosen to turn in). Huck has virtue, even if he doesn't think very well. So Twain and Taylor would be in agreement there. But that doesn't make Huck's attitude any better, philosophically speaking, because it is just a stroke of luck that Jim is a good guy and worthy of Huck's compassion. Suppose the story had featured not the runaway slave Jim, but a runaway chain-gang prisoner, Fred the axe murderer? Huck still might have felt compassion for this poor, frightened man and decided to help him go down the river and get rid of his irons. But later that night, Fred might have repaid Huck by killing him and an entire farm family farther down the river in order to get money and take possession of Huck's raft. This, tragically, is the fate of many a good samaritan. What Huck lacked was not compassion but *reason* to shape it, reason to help him choose when to act and when not to act—because surely not everyone is deserving of our compassion to the extent that we should help them escape what society has

FIGURE 12.1 Huck and Jim on the raft, from Mark Twain's *The Adventures of Huckleberry Finn*. A professor of American studies, Shelley Fisher Fishkin, has recently suggested that the character of Huck was actually modeled after an African-American boy, Jimmy, whom Twain had written about in an essay, "Sociable Jimmy."

determined is their rightful punishment. We may sympathize with mass murderers and understand that they had a terrible childhood, but that doesn't mean we should excuse their actions and help them go free. This example serves another purpose, too. Not only does it show that we can't dispense with reason, but also it shows that there is something else missing in virtue theory: If we focus solely on building a good character and develop the right virtues, like loyalty, compassion, and courage, we still have to decide *what to do* once we've developed the virtues. We may have a wonderfully virtuous character but still be stuck with deciding between several, mutually exclusive courses of action. Huck might ask himself (once he has decided to be loyal to Jim) what exactly is the best way to enact that loyalty: Is it to take Jim up north where nobody can own slaves, or is it to hide him until his owner stops looking for him? Might it be to help him escape with his family, hire him a lawyer, or what? Philosophers who object to virtue theory complain that even if we are virtuous, we still may not have a clue as to what to do in specific situations. A possible answer is that virtue

Reason and Feeling

Is it possible to be moral without having any emotions, or at least without letting those feelings interfere with reason? Hallie and Taylor would say no; Hume would claim that morality is nothing but emotions; and Kant would claim that true morality is a matter of reason alone, because feelings usually focus on our own private preferences. Fiction actually has furnished our moral universe with a race of people who are highly moral but who have no feelings at all—or at least are 100 percent in control of their feelings—the Vulcans of the television series "Star Trek." In episode after episode we see that it is indeed possible for a people to maintain a high moral standard that is based on the virtue of total rationality and on rules of conduct that advocate doing the most logical thing, with no allowance for the human tendency to let feelings of compassion "interfere." Whether this is a moral system we would want to adopt is another matter, but the system seems to be logically valid. In fact, when the half-Vulcan, half-human Mr. Spock experiences lapses in which his human side emerges, we realize that without that *humane* element of emotion, a moral attitude seems cold and insufficient. This doesn't mean, however, that reason has no role to play in a moral system.

ethics need not necessarily stand alone; even Aristotle talks about finding the right course for one's *actions*, not just for one's character. But if virtue ethics needs some rules of conduct in order to be a complete theory, then surely an ethics of conduct would do well to include elements from virtue ethics. We will take another look at the possibility of a combination of theories at the end of this chapter. *264 ff.*

Gratitude: How Much, and When?

Gratitude as a virtue usually implies that it is something that is *owed* to someone. A religious person may believe we always owe God gratitude for our life. A despot may think that we owe the state gratitude for letting us live, work, and eat. Aunts and uncles may believe that their nephews and nieces owe them thank-you notes after Christmas. Your best friend may think you owe her a favor because she gave you a ride last week, and your parents may think you owe it to them to come home for Thanksgiving because they raised you. The question is, are we obliged to feel or show gratitude just because someone expects it, or are there guidelines for when we should express gratitude?

Love as a Virtue

When we talk about love as a virtue, we usually are not talking about passionate love. Passionate love does involve virtue; the passionate lover should not be self-effacing or too domineering, for example. However, that is not the issue here. The issue is love that we can *expect* of someone, and we usually can't expect to receive passionate love on demand. During the marriage ritual, when we promise to love and cherish one another, are we promising our partner that we will be passionately in love with him or her forever? Some undoubtedly see it this way, and they often are in for terrible disappointment if the passionate love of their relationship turns out not to last forever. Of course there are fortunate couples who remain passionately in love over the years or whose passion develops into even deeper feelings, but this is not something every couple can count on. The promise to love one another is rather a promise to *show* love, to show that you care about the other person's welfare and happiness and are 100 percent loyal to that person. This we *can* promise to do, even if passion might not last. So love can be a virtue between people who love each other. The Christian virtue of love does not imply any marital promises but is rather an impersonal reverence for other people. Because it also does not involve romantic passion, it can be a requirement in an ethical system, too.

For one thing, gratitude is a feeling, like love. Either you feel love or you don't, and nobody can make you feel it if you don't. (This is something that is known by all those who have experienced unrequited love.) Similarly, we can't make someone feel grateful toward us for something we have done for them; indeed, the more we point out how grateful they should be, the more distant and uncooperative they may become. So perhaps we should not talk about making people *feel* gratitude; perhaps we should talk instead about encouraging them to *show* it. Even if you don't *feel* grateful for the socks you got for Christmas, it would be virtuous to *show* gratitude to the person who gave them to you. Not everyone agrees with this viewpoint—I knew a European pedagogue who taught his children that they never had to say thank you or show gratitude for presents given to them, because they had not asked for those presents and to show gratitude without feeling was, in his view, hypocrisy. He may be right, but life must have been hard for those children when they realized that few others played by the same rules as their father. There are limits to how far you can place yourself and your family outside the mainstream of your culture without getting your nose bloodied from time to time.

We Owe Our Parents Everything

Confucius taught that making one's parents happy is the highest duty of the grown child. One person whose ideas are consistent with this tradition is the Chinese writer Lin Yutang (1895–1976). Aside from Mao Tse-Tung, Lin Yutang is the most influential of all modern Chinese writers in the West. He traveled extensively in the United States but never lost touch with his Chinese heritage and values. Even more than Confucius, Lin Yutang was inspired by the ancient Chinese philosopher Mencius (see Chapter 10), who believed that humans are basically good, and that there is much joy to be found in life if one follows the Way. Lin himself believes that Western philosophers have been too fixated on the idea of reason and have forgotten what the ancient Greek thinkers saw as the most important element of their philosophy: human happiness. In his 1937 book *The Importance of Living*, he mentions with much modesty that he is uneducated in philosophy. His knowledge of both Chinese and Western philosophy is considerable, however. What *is* the importance of living? Knowing when to take things seriously and when to laugh at the solemnity of life; being so fortunate, and living so long that one can become a serious intellectual and then return to a higher level of simple thinking and simple ways.

In several books Lin Yutang has attempted to bridge the gap between East and West, especially at a time during the first half of the twentieth century when there wasn't much understanding between the two worlds. Writing about family values in a transitional period in which Chinese values were changing (the later Communist takeover forced a transfer of authority to the people as the feudal system was dissolved), Lin Yutang saw the greatest difference between East and West not in the area of politics or gender issues, but in the way we treat our elderly—our parents in particular.

Whereas a Western man might think most about helping women and children, a Chinese man would think primarily about helping his parents and other elderly people. This is not because the elderly are thought of as being helpless; it is because they are *respected*. In the Chinese tradition, the older you are, the more respect you deserve. Lin Yutang describes this in *The Importance of Living*:

> In China, the first question a person asks the other on an official call, after asking about his name and surname, is, "What is your glorious age?" If the person replies apologetically that he is twenty-three or twenty-eight, the other party generally comforts him by saying that he still has a glorious future and that one day he may become old. But if the person replies that he is thirty-five or thirty-eight, the other party immediately exclaims with deep respect, "Good luck!"; enthusiasm grows in proportion as the gentleman is able to report a higher and higher age, and if the person is anywhere over fifty, the inquirer immediately drops his voice in humility and respect.

Just as people under twenty-one in our culture may lie about their age in order to get into clubs that serve liquor, Chinese young people may pretend to be older in

FIGURE 12.2 Lin Yutang (1895–1976), Chinese philosopher and writer. The author of *The Importance of Living* (1937) and *The Wisdom of China and India* (1955), Lin may be the best-known modern Chinese author in the Western world. He worked hard to create a cross-cultural understanding between East and West, but he himself believed that some traditional Eastern values, such as respect for the elderly, are fundamentally different from modern Western values.

order to gain respect. In the West there is a point at which most people don't want to seem older than they are; in fact, they might like to appear *younger* than they are. When they are in their late twenties or older, Westerners actually may feel flattered about being "carded." The Chinese traditionally want to appear *older* throughout their lives, because it is to their advantage. Lin Yutang saw the quest for youth in the American culture as alien and frightening—and he was writing in the thirties, when American teens still attempted to dress and act as "adults." Today, in the exaggerated youth cult of the baby boomer legacy, the phenomenon has become even more extreme. As respect grows with age in the Chinese traditional culture, it seems to *diminish* with age in the West: Somehow we perceive ourselves and others as less powerful, beautiful, and valuable as we get to be "over the hill" and reach the far side of fifty, or even forty. Lin Yutang quotes an American grandmother who says that it was the birth of her first grandchild that "hurt," because it seemed to be a reminder of the loss of youth.

Self-Worth and Retirement

Lin Yutang chastises the West for its "throwaway" attitude toward the older generation. He praises respect and love for one's parents and grandparents as a virtue that has to be learned. The West, however, has not always discarded its citizens at the onset of old age. In the old farming communities in particular, the older generation not only was respected but also was considered an important part of the community because of their *usefulness*. Perhaps they couldn't knead bread or plow the field anymore, but they still could look after the children and share their wisdom. In some parts of the Western world we still can find this type of relationship within a community. But as most people would agree, this is not the case in the larger cities of the West, where it is not customary for grandparents to live with their children. The general attitude seems to be that showing signs of aging is somehow a flaw. A British writer once wrote of Americans that they think death is optional—that if you die you must have done something wrong, like not eaten enough vitamins. It would appear that part of our problem with accepting the aging process is that as Westerners we have developed the attitude that when we stop being *productive*, we stop being *valuable* as human beings. When a person retires, this feeling often is reinforced, be-cause the person is all of a sudden excluded from part of his or her habitual environment—the workplace. Especially during the beginning and the middle years of the twentieth century, when people would stay in their jobs for over forty years, retirement forced a reevaluation of the person's identity, and all too often the retiree felt that he or she had been *reduced* in value, had been deemed useless by society. This may be one reason it is not uncommon for people to fall ill and even die a short time after retirement, even if they had initially looked forward to retirement. There are signs that this trend may change; there is a growing awareness that older people are still people, and because nowadays people usually don't stay at the same job as long as they did in previous generations, they may depend less on their jobs for their sense of identity. Also, many retirees re-enter the work force part-time, either because they want to or, sadly, because they can't afford not to. In ten or so years the oldest members of the so-called baby boomer generation will be approaching retirement; perhaps they will refuse to be "thrown away." Either way, we may see more emphasis on the autonomy, competence, and worthiness of the retired or older person in the future.

American parents are afraid to make demands on their children, says Lin Yutang. Parents are afraid of becoming a burden, of meddling in their children's affairs, of being nosy. But in whose affairs would we meddle if not in those that are closest to us, he asks? Parents do have a right to make demands of their children, he says; they do have a right to be cared for by their children. This is because *their children owe it to them.* We owe a never-ending *debt of gratitude* to our parents for raising us, for being there when we were teething, for changing those diapers and taking care of us when we were sick, and just for feeding and clothing us.

According to the Chinese conception of virtue, letting his parents grow old and die without his support is the gravest sin a man can commit. This is true for a woman, too, but less so, because it is the duty of the firstborn boy to take care of his parents. Who is the daughter supposed to take care of? Her *husband's* parents. Herein lies the secret as to why it is so important for Chinese families to have male offspring—even today when restrictions call for only one child per family. The state may take care of you in your retirement, but even so, life is not complete without a son to lean on in your old age. The pressure to have male babies is so intense that occasionally female babies are killed at birth so that the parents can try again to have a male child. If parents choose to keep a little girl, the response from friends and colleagues is quite different than it would be if they had a boy. A boy is cause for celebration; a baby girl may prompt friends and colleagues to send cards of condolence to the parents. These strains on modern Chinese are the result of a centuries-old tradition, and there is no modern psychological alternative. Even among Chinese who immigrated to the United States, the guilt over not being with their parents in China is enormous, even if they have brothers and sisters who can perform the duty in their homeland.

In Communist China, because of the restrictions on having children, it is today hard for older people to rely on receiving care from their own daughter, especially if they have a married daughter. Her prime duty is not to her parents but to her in-laws. The system, however, does provide for older people. Much to the shame of traditional Chinese, there are now some nursing homes for the elderly in the villages of China, and they are more humane than the "human storage tanks" we have in our Western civilization. The elderly are still part of the community, and the problems of the village are presented to them in their capacity as advisers. In this manner the traditional respect for the older people is maintained, at least on a symbolic level, even though the family patterns have been disrupted.

We Owe Our Parents Nothing

A young American philosopher, Jane English (1947–1978), suggested a solution to the constant and very common squabbles between parents and their grown children. It seems rather radical: She suggests that we owe our parents nothing. This suggestion is not as harsh as it appears, however. English thinks the main problem between grown children and parents is the common *parental* attitude that their children somehow are indebted to them. This "*debt-metaphor*" can be expressed in a number of ways, such as, "We are paying for your schooling, so you owe it to us to study what we would like you to study"; "We've clothed you and fed you, so the least you could do is come home for Christmas"; or "I was in labor with you for thirty-six hours, so you could at least clean up your room once in a while." The basic formula is, "You owe us gratitude and obedience because of what we have done for you." For English this attitude undermines all filial love, because the obvious answer a kid can give is the following: "I didn't ask to be born." And there is not much chance of fruitful communication after that. (As one of my students remarked, a parent can always fire back with "And you weren't wanted, either," but that would surely be the end of any parent-children friendship.)

So what should parents do? English said they should realize that there are appropriate and inappropriate ways of using the debt-metaphor, and that applying it to a parent-child relationship is inappropriate. An appropriate way to use the debt metaphor would be the following:

> New to the neighborhood, Max barely knows his neighbor, Nina, but he asks her if she will take in his mail while he is gone for a month's vacation. She agrees. If, subsequently, Nina asks Max to do the same for her, it seems that Max has a moral obligation to agree (greater than the one he would have had if Nina had not done the same for him), unless for some reason it would be a burden far out of proportion to the one Nina bore for him.

English labels what Nina does for Max a "favor"—and favors incur *debts*. But once you have paid your debt—once Max has taken Nina's mail in—then the debt is discharged, and the matter is over. This is *reciprocation*, and it means that you must do something of a similar nature for the person you are in debt to. But suppose Nina never goes out of town, so Max never has an opportunity to take in her mail and pay off the debt? Then he might mow her lawn, give her rides to work, or walk her dog. If she has no lawn or dog and likes to drive to work, then he might figure out something else to do for her, and chances are that they might become friends in the process. In that case another type of relationship kicks in, one that no longer is based on a reciprocal system of favors and debts. Instead, the relationship is based on a system of duties relating to *friendship*.

In friendship, according to English, the debt-metaphor ceases to be appropriate, because friends shouldn't think they owe each other anything. Although debts are discharged when a favor is reciprocated, friendships don't work that way; just because you do something for your friend, who has done something for you, doesn't make you both "even," and you shouldn't be worrying about that anyway. Friendships aren't supposed to be "tit for tat," and if they are, then the people involved aren't real friends. Friendship means that you are there for each other when needed, and that you do things for each other because you *like* each other, not because you owe each other. The fact that there can be no debts doesn't mean that there are no obligations, however; on the contrary, friendship carries with it the never-ending obligation to be there for each other, at least while the friendship lasts. It implies a mutual sense of duty toward each other. With friendship, instead of reciprocity, there is *mutuality*.

Let us speculate a bit. Suppose you borrow fifty dollars from a friend, and then you have a falling-out with her. Because there are no debts in a friendship and because obligations last only as long as the friendship does, you don't have to pay it back, right? Wrong, because owing somebody money is a true debt and must be paid back regardless of whether it is owed to friends or strangers. Similarly, you have to fulfill your part of a contract, regardless of whether it is with a friend, business partner, or stranger. Such transactions come under the proper use of the debt-metaphor and persist beyond the extent of friendships. (In fact, they often are the cause of the ending of friendships.)

We often fall into the trap of regarding friendship duties as debts. Most couples find themselves saying things like, "We've been over to Frank and Claire's four times now, so we owe them a dinner." For English this is a gross misunderstanding of what friendship is all about. You can go visit Claire and Frank a hundred times, and you still don't owe them a thing because they aren't doing you a "favor"; they ask you over because they like you. To most readers this may seem a trifle idealistic; after the twentieth dinner, Claire and Frank surely will think something is wrong and won't ask you over again. But English's idea is that you will be there if they need you, and that you should contribute to the friendship in *some way or other*—she doesn't say with how much you should contribute or in what way—how you contribute is up to you. We'll get back to the question of "how much" in a little while.

Let's return to the relationship between parents and grown children. English says this relationship should be molded after the "friendship" pattern, and not after the debt-metaphor pattern. Parents don't do their children a "favor" by raising them, and, accordingly, children don't owe any debt to them. But this doesn't mean grown children don't have *obligations* to their parents—they have the same obligations as they have to their friends. Those obligations are limitless as long as the relationship lasts; they cease when the relationship ends. No reciprocity can be evoked, such as, "You fed and clothed me for eighteen years, so I'll take care of you for the next eighteen but not a minute longer." However, *mutuality* is expected at all times.

What is the basis for a good parent-child relationship, then? Above all, love and friendship. If this is present, all that must be considered are 1) the need of the parents, and 2) the ability and resources of the grown child. The parents may be sick and in need, and their son may love them, but he also may be out of work and unable to help with the medical bills. In that case, helping to pay the bills would *not* be part of his obligations, but other things would, such as providing cheerful company, taking the trash out, or whatever.

Suppose the parents need help, but there is *no friendship* between the parents and the child? Then, essentially, the grown child is not obliged to help, especially if the end of the friendship (if in fact it ever existed) was the parents' choice. One might imagine that this would be the time for the parents to approach their estranged child and ask for a favor in the hope of reestablishing the friendship. English seems to assume that all the parents have to do is announce that they are sorry and would like to be friends again—but suppose they follow this approach with immediate requests for support? Then their son or daughter might soon get the idea that there is a calculated reason behind this renewal of friendship. (This works both ways, of course; if the son

What About Relatives?

English's main concern is for parents and grown children to realize that their relationship ought to be like that between good friends, and in such a relationship there are limitless obligations. But do we have any obligations to people who aren't yet our friends (we may hardly know them) but aren't strangers, either, because they are more distant relatives? Should they rank as friends or strangers? English has no category for them, and yet many people are concerned about how much we can and should rely on the support of relatives other than those in our immediate family. When they come to visit, should we give up our bedroom to them? Can I, as a student, ask my mother's cousin in Paris if I can stay with her for a year while I study at the Sorbonne? How can we tell our aunt and uncle from Sweden/Los Angeles/Idaho/Mexico that it really is not convenient for them to stay six weeks in our apartment? Am I obliged to find a lawyer for my half-brother who

is in trouble? And so on. Many times we might *choose* to help, just as we might help a stranger, but often the old line that "blood is thicker than water" makes us feel that we do have a specific *duty* to our extended family. One solution might be to think of this duty as a "duty to do small favors"—like finding your relatives a good, cheap hotel, or showing them around town and taking them out a few times—but not as a duty to provide very large favors, like letting them have the run of your home for six weeks. Instead of finding a lawyer for your half-brother who is in trouble, you might provide him with the number of a good legal agency but let him choose a lawyer himself, and let him be financially responsible. By doing these small favors, a small debt to reciprocate now rests with the relative. If this debt is discharged to everyone's satisfaction—through reciprocal hospitality or perhaps through an annual Christmas card—you can all proceed to becoming friends.

or daughter has left home in anger and later decides that he or she needs help from home, an approach of remorse and offers of renewal of friendship followed by requests for support will look equally suspicious to the parents.) For a solution we may want to turn to the American philosopher Fred Berger (whose theory we will discuss in more detail shortly). In assessing the extent of the gratitude you ought to show others for acts of kindness towards you, Berger says you should look for the *motivation*. Were these acts of kindness done for your sake, for the doer's, or both? If done for your sake alone, you should show gratitude; if done for the doer's own sake, you have no obligation; if done partly for your sake and partly for the doer's own sake, you should show some gratitude, but there is no need to go overboard. In a similar manner, we might ask, why are the parents approaching their grown child (or the children their parents)? Is it because of a genuine wish to reestablish contact, is it solely because they want assistance, or is the truth somewhere in between? If the approached party can determine the motivation with reasonable accuracy, then he or she can decide how to react.

What should parents say if they very much would like their grown child to take a certain course of action but realize that he or she does not owe it to them to do so? Not "You owe us" but something like "We love you, and we think you'd be happier if you did x." Or, suggests English, "If you love us, you'll do x." But is this second example a very good one? To most people this alternative would set off a tremendous guilt trip, because it plays on the notion that if you don't comply, you don't love your parents. Few people are able to follow their parents' advice all the time, no matter how much love and friendship there may be between them. One alternative approach, which was suggested by a student at San Diego State University, is for the parents to explain the whole situation: "Because of our past experience, we believe it is best for you, but it's your choice."

Jane English never lived to develop her theory further, because she died at the age of thirty-one while on a mountaineering expedition in Switzerland. In her short life she published several other thought-provoking papers, and one might wonder how this bright person might have felt about the same issue had she lived to become a parent of grown children.

Friendship Duties and Gratitude

English supplies some guidelines for how we should consider *friendship* as a virtue that applies to the relationship between parents and grown children; Lin Yutang believes the virtue that should be applied to such relationships is *gratitude*. But what about both friendship and gratitude in other types of relationships, like those between friends, or lovers, or neighbors? How far do our duties of friendship go? Are we obliged to help our friends in every way, to help them cheat on their tax returns, lie to their spouses about where they were last night, hide them from the police, buy them drugs? The answer is of course no—even if they would do those things for us. This is because, presumably, this is not the way to be a good friend; it allows you to be incriminated by your friend, and a good friend does not ask that of another. So if your friend asks you to do these things, he or she is not being a good friend *to you*. But this doesn't mean you can't do *something* for your friends when they are in trouble, like be there for them to talk to, or find them an appropriate counselor.

A more mundane but equally tricky situation arises when someone does something nice for us that we didn't ask for, and then expects something in return. Jane English states that such "unsolicited favors" do not create any debt, so we don't have to do anything. However, the situation may be more complex than that. For one thing, we may feel that the person truly was trying to be nice; in that case, doing nothing seems a little rude, even if we didn't ask for the favor. Here the philosopher Fred Berger answers that certainly we have an obligation, and that obligation is to to show *gratitude*.

Does the Golden Rule Always Work?

The Golden Rule has been mentioned several times in this text, and it is certainly one of the most widespread rules of ethics in existence, finding expression in religions and moral teachings throughout recorded history. But is it always the best solution to do unto others as you would have them do unto you? Suppose a friend wants you to put her up for a few weeks. She tells you she has been involved in a hit and run accident, and now she wants to hide from the police. You are reluctant to let her stay, but she assures you that she would do the same for you, or even that you would want her to do the same for you if you were in her shoes. But that may not be the case; you may see the situation in quite a different light. If you were in her shoes you might need a friend, but you might not ask that friend to hide you; chances are you wouldn't have left the scene of the accident in the first place. (Staying at the scene is of course the only ethical course of action—besides, it's the law.) Your friend's perception of what she wants done for her is not the same as what you might want a friend to do for you. In everyday life we find lots of examples of this type of situation: Maria gives Cheryl a bread machine for Christmas because that's what Maria would like to get. But she didn't think to find out whether Cheryl might also like one, and in fact Cheryl doesn't like kitchen gifts. Paul and Lisa stay at Lee's and Chi-Wah's house while they are abroad, and as a gesture of gratitude they mow the lawn, tear up all the wildflowers, and make the yard look "neat," because that's the way they would like it to look. However, Lee and Chi-Wah love the wild and unkempt look and are heartbroken at the sight of their tidy, trimmed yard, but, being polite, they pretend to be grateful for all the yardwork. Often, such misplaced acts of kindness are caused by a self-centered attitude, a lack of perception, but they also may happen due to a fundamental difference in the approach to life. In her book *That's Not What I Meant*, the linguist Deborah Tannen describes a classic situation of misapplied Golden Rule approaches between partners who have different visions of correct behavior (or what Tannen calls different "styles"):

> Maxwell wants to be left alone, and Samantha wants attention. So she gives him attention, and he leaves her alone. The adage "Do unto others as you would have others do unto you" may be the source of a lot of anguish and misunderstanding if the doer and the done unto have different styles.

It appears that if we are to evoke the Golden Rule, we have to make certain that the others really want to "be done unto."

A plain thank-you, verbal or written, may be all it takes. In some situations the person who did us an unsolicited favor (offered to give us a ride or gave us a present) may *insist* that we show gratitude and reciprocate by doing business with him, going out with him, or even having sex with him. In that case, Berger says, we have to look at the giver's *intentions*: Did he give us something or do us a favor just so that we would be indebted to him? In that case, we don't owe the person anything, not even gratitude, because he did it for *himself*, not for us.

So how do we know when we owe people gratitude? Certainly we owe it when we have *asked* them to do us a favor. As far as unsolicited favors go, though, we should express gratitude when we can be reasonably certain that they did it for our own sake—because they like and respect us, as Kant would say, as "*ends in ourselves*"—not because they viewed us as the "*means to an end.*" We also should make certain that they did help us *on purpose*, and didn't just blunder into the situation. Moreover, we have to ascertain that they did it *voluntarily*, that no one else forced them to do it. In Berger's words, gratitude should be a response to benevolence, not benefits, and this applies to all relationships, even those between parents and children. We should express gratitude in proportion to the things that are done for our sake (to be sure, not everything parents do is done for the sake of the child). If something is done for other reasons, our duty to show gratitude diminishes proportionately. And, says Berger, when we do show gratitude to people who have done something for us, we show that we appreciate *them* as intrinsically valuable persons—as ends in themselves and not just as instruments for our well-being.

Suppose the people who do things for us like us and respect us but still hope to get something out of being nice to us? This is one of those borderline situations where we have to decide for ourselves how much part the personal advantage played in the decision to do something for us. We shouldn't disqualify others from deserving our gratitude just because they were hoping for some little advantage themselves; it is when we were considered solely a means to an end that our duty to show gratitude disappears.

Suppose you have good reason to feel grateful for something someone has done. Let's assume you are a poor student and your neighbors have seven kids. They cook up a huge dinner every night, and at the end of the month, when you are broke, they always invite you over for dinner. They say, "We have to cook anyway, so come on over." And you do, month after month. You keep waiting for the moment when the family may need your invaluable assistance with something, but the time never comes. So you keep eating their food and feeling like a moocher. What can you do? Well, you might do the dishes once in a while, or help with the laundry. In other words, you can contribute to the mutuality of a friendship even if you aren't specifically asked to do so.

To return to the question of, How much gratitude should I feel? the answer, even if it is vague, lies in Aristotle's theory of virtue: Just enough—not too much and not too little. As vague as it is, this still is the guideline most people instinctively use when they try to figure out how to respond to an act of kindness. We know that enslaving

Dating, Debt, and Friendship

Many of the problems of dating stem from a difference in attitude, says Jane English. One person thinks of the date in terms of a friendship, and the other one sees it as a debt-metaphor situation. Suppose Alfred takes Beatrice out for a dinner and a movie, and at the end of the evening Alfred expects "something" in return for his investment. Alfred has chosen to view the situation as a favor-debt situation; he sees Beatrice as being indebted to him. Beatrice, however, is upset, because she viewed the situation as a "friendship" situation, with no favors and debts. In essence, Beatrice doesn't owe Alfred a thing, because Alfred's gesture was not presented as a "tit for tat" situation to begin with, but as an overture to friendship. The situation would have been more complex had Beatrice *agreed with Alfred* in the beginning that the dinner and movie were to be a "business arrangement" to be "paid off" later in the evening. A recent survey has shown that, shockingly, a majority of California high school students, females as well as males, feel that dating is in fact a favor-debt situation. In that case we must say that if both participants agree, then so be it. There is, however, a good old word for when someone sells physical favors for material goods; that word is *prostitution*. In such a situation the one who is "bought" becomes merely a means to an end. What can you do if you want to make sure to avoid a favor-debt situation on a date? For one thing, you can insist on going Dutch. Both of you probably make the same kind of money these days, so why should one of you pay for the other? Remember, nobody should expect payment for doing someone an unsolicited favor (if the people involved aren't friends), and nobody should expect payment for doing any kind of favor (if the people involved are friends). So either way you shouldn't expect anything of your date, and you shouldn't feel pressured by your date to repay anything. Be careful not to abuse this rule, though. One girl commented that "it's great to be able to be taken to a dinner and a movie and not have to do anything in return!" By taking this attitude, she reduces her date to becoming merely the means to an end, and that's not the idea.

ourselves for the rest of our natural lives, giving up our firstborn, and other such measures would be "too much." We also know that being rude and doing or saying nothing to show our appreciation is "too little." But where exactly lies the right amount? This is, as with all the Aristotelian virtues, a case-by-case matter. Sometimes the right amount consists of a thank-you note, a bottle of wine, or a batch of chocolate-chip cookies. Sometimes it is house-sitting for six months, and sometimes it is going across country to give someone a helping hand. If we manage to "hit the bull's-eye" and find the right response, perhaps Aristotle is right, and we are on the way to becoming virtuous.

Virtue and Conduct: Ethical Pluralism?

In Chapters 3–7 we explored the most influential theories of what has become known as ethics of conduct, and in Chapters 8–12 we looked at classical and contemporary versions of virtue ethics. The majority of ethicists over the years have perceived their task as defining in the simplest terms possible, and with as few rules as possible, a moral theory that would have universal application, one that would be valid in all situations. As we have seen, no theory so far can be said to work equally well in all situations; all theories, when put to the test, show some flaws or problems. For all its positive elements, ethical relativism has a problem with allowing for a tolerance that objects to nothing, not even crimes against humanity; egoism, while recognizing the right of the individual to look after one's own interests, fails to recognize that humans may actually be interested in serving the interests of others; utilitarianism, while seeking general happiness for all sentient beings, seems to allow for the few to be used, and even sacrificed, for the sake of the many; Kantian deontology wants to do the right thing but is so focused on duty that it may overlook bad consequences of doing one's duty—consequences that otherwise could have been avoided. And virtue ethics, which is intended as an alternative to these theories of conduct, hasn't quite solved the problem of when and how to use one's reason and rational argumentation in terms of defining moral standards, and it hasn't succeeded in coming up with a theory of action in which the general ideas of virtue can be brought into play in particular situations. For those who look for a good answer to moral problems, this can be more than discouraging, and some might even decide, like Huck Finn, that moral speculations are too confusing and it's better just to follow their gut-level feelings. But this would be taking the easy way out, and actually it is not a very satisfying solution. On occasion we all may have to justify our action, and "it seemed like a good idea at the time" is just not a good answer. Furthermore, we may decide that ethicists haven't come up with a complete solution to moral problems, but that doesn't mean we don't have to keep on trying to solve moral problems on an individual basis. Just because the experts haven't given us all the solutions on a silver platter doesn't mean we're exempt from seeking solutions on our own. There *are* alternative answers, and we will look briefly at the most important one in ethics today, ethical pluralism.

Most of the theories we have looked at originated in time periods when it was assumed that humans would some day know all the answers to everything. It also was assumed, from a scientific viewpoint, that a simple explanation was better and more pleasing than a complex one. To a great extent that is still true: A theory gains in strength if unnecessary elements are cut away (this phenomenon is often referred to as *Occam's Razor*, from the British medieval philosopher William of Occam). But the late twentieth century has also taught us that simple solutions may not always be available, or even desirable, because there may be many possible ways of looking at each situation. (A case in point is Deborah Tannen's example of different "styles" of behavior.) So we are not focused on seeking simple answers to complex issues in ethics any longer.

As I often hear students remark, why do all these philosopers have to be so single-minded about everything? Why can't their theories allow for nuances? It is a good question—but it is a question that is possible only because we have become a culture that allows for nuances and different perspectives. This culture probably wouldn't have arrived at such an openness had it not been for the progression in moral theory (the phenomenon the Australian philosopher Peter Singer referred to as "the expanding circle," as you may remember from Chapter 4). Elements in theories that may now seem too narrow and absolutistic have at some point in time expanded or broken a narrower and more rigid system of values. It seems that we are now ready for something of a more complex nature: an expansion that allows for assuming the possibility that we can have certain basic values in common, and at the same time allows for a relativistic tolerance of other values. We may be looking for what was introduced in Part 1 as *soft universalism*. However, this is not going to be easy, because we have to find a common ground where we can agree on *which* values are supposed to be the ones we have in common, and here our different cultural upbringing and ethnic diversity may come into play.

Some philosophers have already been trying for a long time to redesign the traditional theories (such as utilitarianism, deontology, or virtue theory) to make them more logical, more responsive to present-day sensitivities, or more tolerant of exceptions. But we can choose another path: the path of *ethical pluralism*. The approach of Fred Berger to the question of compassion is an example of ethical pluralism at work: He uses both Aristotle's theory of the mean between extremes, and Kant's theory of ends in themselves, in order to explore the subject of compassion. In other words, he allows for several different theories to be used at the same time, letting them work together to achieve a functional solution. This is a very pragmatic approach, and some might even call it a very American approach, because Americans are (presumably) typically interested in whether or not something *works*.

Ethical pluralism may work if we don't expect too much. The term itself stands for many things, and holds much promise. We are reminded of the pluralism of multicultural education, where all ethnic groups learn from each other without having to sacrifice values that are important to them. The term also evokes the pluralism of moral values and opinions in a contemporary society—even a so-called monocultural society (because even when a large majority comes from the same ethnic background there usually is a wide variety of viewpoints)—and it evokes the political pluralism of present-day democratic societies. If we add to this the plurality of ethical traditions worldwide, we begin to approach the philosophical concept of ethical pluralism: letting the vast spectrum of ethical viewpoints and traditions become available as options. But this will certainly be no easy road, primarily because we can't just decide to take the best of all theories and lump them together in the hope that they may work. For one thing, they may well contradict each other, and for another thing, if we choose a theory for its advantages, we're stuck with its disadvantages, too. We can't just decide to add deontology to utilitarianism, for example, and assume that a smooth theory will emerge; we may have doubled our range of solutions, but we have also doubled our problems.

Ethical pluralism is, however, probably the only viable solution for a future theory of ethics. We need theories of conduct, and we need theories of virtue, from more than just a few cultural groups; besides, most of us already use a pluralistic approach on a day-by-day basis. Sometimes we consider consequences as vitally important (especially in matters of life and death); sometimes we think keeping promises and other obligations are more important than looking to consequences; sometimes we feel we're entitled to look after ourselves and our own interests; and sometimes we are focused on developing a good character—compassion, courage, or another virtue. Often we do combine these views in specific situations. What ethical pluralism may do for us is help us decide when one viewpoint or aspect is more appropriate than another and prevent us from contradicting ourselves. But ethical pluralism must address the task of evaluating this diversity of values by setting up a system of justification for which moral values should be considered valid at all times (like the United Nations list of human rights, for example), which values should be considered a matter of cultural preference and tradition, and which values should be considered globally unacceptable (such as "some people are born to be free, and others are born to be slaves"). A new theory of ethics must comprise all such elements if it is to offer genuine solutions to the problems of a highly complex world.

Narratives That Explore Compassion and Gratitude

Because this section of the text contains so many factual and fictional narratives, only two stories about compassion and gratitude are presented in Chapter 13. Both of them, however, are classics of the Western literary tradition: the parable of The Good Samaritan from the New Testament, and Sir Walter Scott's *Ivanhoe*.

Chapter 13

Narratives of Virtue and Vice

Virtue theory is much better represented in fiction than is theory of conduct. Stories of people who show or develop strength of character in light of hard times and hard choices come to mind much more easily than do stories that illustrate specific problems of conduct. The stories that the Western world has been most familiar with since the eighteenth century—stories that tell of *character development*—usually are less concerned with how the hero actually solves a problem than with how the problem affects him or her. Often the stories deal with a young man or woman who is rather shallow to begin with but through a series of hardships develops into a "real person," a person of good, strong character or, as we might say, a *person of virtue.*

As I mentioned earlier, virtue ethics consists of not only the good examples, the role models that embody a good character, but also the negative models, and as an educational device the negative role models are perhaps more effective. We all know that virtue is supposed to be its own reward, but hearing about vicious people coming to a gruesome end is a mighty strong incentive to behave well.

Some Traditional Virtues

In this section we will take a look at narratives that explore three virtues: courage, honor, and compassion. Not all cultures place the same importance on these virtues, but most cultures now and in the past have recognized them as part of what constitutes a good character.

Courage

Is courage the same as never feeling fear, or is it doing what you feel you must do in spite of your fear? The following two stories, each a classic in its own way, explore the relationship between courage and fear: Joseph Conrad's *Lord Jim*, and *Njal's Saga*, an Icelandic epic that takes place in the late Viking era.

JOSEPH CONRAD, *Lord Jim*

Novel (1900); film by Richard Brooks (director and screenwriter), 1965.

Lord Jim is one of the finest explorations of a human soul trying to do the right thing, at the right time, for the right reason. Conrad's novel tells the story of a young man named Jim who dreams of doing great deeds. As a newly appointed officer in the British Mercantile Marine, he spends quiet moments on board his ship fantasizing about saving damsels in distress and suppressing mutinies. During a storm he hurts his leg and is taken ashore so that he can recuperate in a harbor somewhere in Southeast Asia. By the time he is well again, his ship is long gone, and only one ship has a position for him: the rusty old ship Patna, which is to take a group of local pilgrims to a holy city. Jim takes the job as chief mate to a crew of drunken, raucous white sailors with an equally unpleasant captain. Once at sea, a storm approaches, and Jim inspects the ship's hull. It is so rusty it is on the verge of breaking up. Back on deck Jim sees that the crew is lowering a lifeboat into the water—just one, for themselves. No measures are being taken to save the hundreds of pilgrims on the ship. Jim insists to the others that he is staying on board, but at the last minute, as the storm hits and Jim's vivid imagination takes in the situation, he comes face to face with his greatest fear, the fear of death. Overwhelming fear of imminent death causes him to push aside all dreams of heroic deeds, and he jumps into the lifeboat after all.

Believing that the Patna is lost already, the men in the lifeboat set course for shore. When they arrive, they see that someone got there ahead of them; in the harbor lies the Patna herself, safe and sound. She was salvaged and towed to shore by another crew, and all the pilgrims are safe. Jim is relieved that no one was hurt, but his dreams of valor have

FIGURE 13.1 *Lord Jim*, Columbia Pictures, 1965. To stay or to jump? Jim (Peter O'Toole) is about to make the decision that will ruin his life: During a storm, he abandons the ship Patna and the many pilgrims who had put their trust in him.

been shattered—he is tormented by guilt. Everywhere he goes from now on, the memory of Patna will haunt him; somebody will recognize him, or mention the scandal, and he will have to go somewhere else, to another port and another odd job.

Is Jim a coward? Were all the dreams of noble deeds just fantasies? He doesn't know. He finally meets a man who knows the story of the Patna but is willing to give Jim a second chance to prove himself. Jim goes to the Malay Archipelago, to the village of Patusan, to help the local people fight against a tyrant. He becomes the hero of the people, respected and trusted. They call him *Tuan Jim*, Lord Jim. He now believes that he finally has proved himself, but in fact the real test is yet to come. A band of pirates land in Patusan, and with the help of a traitor from the village they trick Jim into believing that they have good intentions. They are white, they promise that they will sail away without harming any of the villagers, and Jim chooses to believe them; he lets them go without disarming them, trusting their word. He promises the chief of the village that if anyone is harmed because of his decision, he will forfeit his own life. As it turns out, the chief's own son is killed in a fight between the pirates and the villagers. The villagers expect Jim to flee to save his life, but this time Jim stands fast; he goes to the chief, who is mad with grief over his son, and offers him his life. The chief shoots him.

Study Questions

1. Is Jim a coward, or is he courageous? Is it possible to be both?
2. Is Jim a virtuous man, or is he just preoccupied with himself and with his own feelings?
3. Do you think we all are like Jim in the sense that we all have a moral breaking point which, when we reach it, reveals the frailty of our character?

Njal's Saga

Prose epic (ca. 1280 C.E.); author unknown.

This story is set in the latter part of the Viking Age. It isn't a story of Vikings, however, but of their relatives, who stayed in Iceland to farm the land. The area was settled by the Norsemen (mostly Danes and Norwegians) in about 800 C.E., and by the time *Njal's Saga* was written it was a land of great unrest; blood feuds and various intrigues led to the Danish takeover of the country, which for four hundred years had been independent. *Njal's Saga* is one of many Sagas, which are historical epics about past life in Iceland.

Nordic mythology teaches that the world as well as the gods eventually will perish in a natural disaster. Thus the Norsemen (the farmers as well as the Vikings) held to the belief in a gloomy fate looming ahead. Even though Christianity was by that time the official religion, the old view of life being ruled by Fate still had a hold on people's minds.

This very brief outline cannot explain the complex plot of the saga but can only hint at the inevitable tragic ending. Njal, his wife, Bergthora, and their four sons are carrying on a blood feud with neighbors, not because either party is evil but because over the years events have led in that direction. Through misunderstandings and marriages, the enmity between Njal's family and their neighbors grows, even though Njal does his best to avert it by talking sense to everybody. His negotiations backfire, though, and things get worse. At the *Alting* (the place of arbitration) it becomes clear that all hope of peace is lost, and Njal goes home and prepares for a siege. His adversary, Flosi, arrives with 100 men, and Njal asks his sons to help him defend the house from inside. The enemy are quick to take advantage of the situation and set fire to the farmhouse.

There was an old woman at Bergthorsknoll called Sæunn. She knew a lot about many things and had second sight. She was very old by this time, and the Njalssons called her senile because she talked so much; but what she predicted often came true. One day she snatched up a cudgel and made her way round the house to a pile of chickweed that lay there, and started beating it and cursing it for the wretched thing that it was. Skarp-Hedin laughed at this, and asked her why she was so angry with the chickweed.

The old woman replied, "This chickweed will be used as the kindling when they burn Njal and my foster child Bergthora inside the house. Quickly, take it away and throw it into some water or burn it."

"No," said Skarp-Hedin [one of Njal's sons], "for if that is what is ordained, something else will be found to kindle the fire even if the chickweed is not here."

The old woman kept nagging them all summer to take the chickweed indoors, but they never got round to doing it. . . .

. . . They [Flosi and his men] brought the chickweed up and set fire to it, and before those inside knew what was happening, the ceiling of the room was ablaze from end to end. . . .

Njal said to them, "Be of good heart and speak no words of fear, for this is just a passing storm and it will be long before another like it comes. Put your faith in the mercy of God, for He will not let us burn both in this world and the next."

. . . Now the whole house began to blaze. Njal went to the door and said, "Is Flosi near enough to hear my words?"

Flosi said that he could hear him.

Njal said, "Would you consider making an agreement with my sons, or letting anyone leave the house?"

"I will make no terms with your sons," replied Flosi. "We shall settle matters now, once and for all, and we are not leaving until every one of them is dead. But I shall allow the women and children and servants to come out. . . ."

. . . Flosi said to Bergthora, "You come out, Bergthora, for under no circumstances do I want you to burn."

Bergthora replied, "I was given to Njal in marriage when young, and I have promised him that we would share the same fate."

Then they both went back inside.

"What shall we do now?" asked Bergthora.

"Let us go to our bed," said Njal, "and lie down."

Then Bergthora said to little Thord, Kari's son, "You are to be taken out. You are not to burn."

The boy replied, "But that's not what you promised, grandmother. You said that we would never be parted; and so it shall be, for I would much prefer to die beside you both."

She carried the boy to the bed. Njal said to his steward, "Take note where we lay ourselves down and how we dispose ourselves, for I shall not move from here however much the smoke or flames distress me. Then you can know where to look for our remains."

The steward said he would.

An ox had recently been slaughtered, and the hide was lying nearby. Njal told the steward to spread the hide over them, and he promised to do so.

Njal and Bergthora lay down on the bed and put the boy between them. Then they crossed themselves and the boy, and commended their souls to God. These were the last words they were heard to speak. The steward took the hide and spread it over them, and then left the house. . . .

Study Questions

1. Do you think Njal, Bergthora, and the little boy display courage, or are they just giving up?
2. Would removing the chickweed have prevented the arson?
3. For the old Norsemen and women, the name and reputation you leave behind when you die is all-important. How do you think Njal and Bergthora were regarded after they died?

Honor

The virtue of honor has helped shape the identities of most societies, although the definition of honor may vary from culture to culture. Some definitions focus on honorable trade relations (and interpret as honorable anything from fair trade and keeping contracts to haggling or even getting a good deal by misleading the other party); some focus on honor in family relations (such as honoring one's elders, or accepting responsibility for the actions of relatives); and others place great value on honor in battle (hence the expression "field of honor" for a battlefield). Here we will look at the meaning of honor in medieval Japan: the honor of the samurai warriors.

AKIRA KUROSAWA (DIRECTOR), SHINOBU HASHIMOTO (SCREENWRITER), *The Seven Samurai*

Film (1954).

The scene is Japan in the sixteenth century. The country has been torn apart by civil wars. Warlords and bandits roam the countryside, preying on the farming population. They swoop down from the hills at harvesttime and take everything they can from the village. Then they bide their time until the next harvest, when there will be more plunder. The villagers are desperate, but they also are aware of their low social standing. They consider themselves cowards because others consider them cowards. The Old Man of the village remembers far back to time when the country was in a similar situation; only one village in the region survived, and it survived because the people of the village hired help: samurai warriors. But samurai are expensive, so the Old Man and his village can only hope to find some down-and-out samurai or some who would agree to fight just for the fun of it.

The villagers have ambivalent feelings about samurai, for they have killed deserter samurai themselves and taken their expensive equipment. Nevertheless, a delegation sets out to find willing samurai. At first the task seems impossible, but then one samurai becomes the first to enlist. He is shrewd and compassionate and understands how to appeal to the honor of other samurai in order to recruit them: They can't expect pay other than food, but they will be doing something honorable. After a while seven men have lined up. Five of them are regular samurai, one is a novice who hopes to qualify, and one is a buffoon (we are not sure he is a samurai, although he would like us to believe that he is). What traits is a samurai supposed to exhibit? He must display the true samurai spirit: He must be gentle, fearless, skillful, and modest, and he must understand *teamwork*, the idea that you don't win a war on your own.

When the samurai arrive at the village, the villagers are too frightened to meet them and hide their daughters or dress them up as boys. There is general mutual mistrust, especially when an outfit that was stolen from a murdered samurai is brought forth. But harvest is approaching, and everybody knows that the enemy will strike shortly thereafter; the samurai set out to train the male villagers in combat and to fortify the town. When the harvest is secured, the samurai post guard, and they sight an army of forty men marching toward the village.

During the battle that ensues, the samurai and the villagers prove themselves; even the "buffoon" and the novice fight courageously. The enemy is strong, however, and several of the samurai are killed. In the end, with the danger past, the surviving samurai agree that *they* really did not win the battle—the farmers did—not because the farmers fought harder or better than the samurai, for without the warriors the villagers would have been ruined, enslaved, or perhaps dead, but because, in the end, the farmers stood to gain something tangible from their victory: They are the ones with the land, the harvest, the livelihood, the homes, and the families. And what do the samurai have? They have each other, and they have the knowledge that they have accomplished something honorable. But they have no home, no family, and no sense of belonging. The samurai, assured that there will be peace in the village now, drift on, their honor intact.

Study Questions

1. Describe the samurai sense of honor. Is there an equivalent sense of honor as a virtue in contemporary Western society?
2. Is there something that is more important than honor? What would a utilitarian answer?

Compassion

The virtue of compassion has by many scholars been praised as the one truly universal human virtue. Philosophers such as Mencius, David Hume, and Jean-Jacques Rousseau believe that humans are born compassionate. This does not necessarily mean that all humans are born with an equal amount of compassion; the theory of virtue encourages those who fall a bit short to work on developing this and other virtues further.

The Russian author Ivan Turgenev tells in his book *Senilia* (*Prose Poems,* 1883) a fable about a party in heaven. The Most High had invited to the party all the virtues (that means ladies only, because all the virtues were ladies). Big and small virtues arrived, and everybody was having a good time, but the Most High noticed that two beautiful virtues didn't seem to know each other, so He went over and introduced them: "Gratitude, meet Charity." The two virtues were very surprised, because, says Turgenev, this was their first encounter since the creation of the world, which occurred a long, long time ago.

In the following two stories we will look at compassionate and charitable heroes, male and female, who shine against the background of their fellow human beings who are lacking in compassion. The stories are the parable of The Good Samaritan and Sir Walter Scott's *Ivanhoe.*

The Parable of The Good Samaritan

(*from the* New Testament*)*

For readers with a Christian background, the story of the Good Samaritan is the archetypal story of compassion. The Good Samaritan is one of the parables of Jesus of Nazareth, and it is intended to be taken as an allegory. A man was traveling from Jerusalem to Jericho and was mugged and left for dead by thieves. People in high religious positions passed him by without helping, but one person stopped and felt compassion for him. He was a Samaritan (from Samaria). He dressed the injured man's wounds, brought him to town, and paid for his stay at the local inn. To the modern reader, the story illustrates that the Good Samaritan is the one who is truly good, because he acts with compassion while others, who are supposed to know the difference between right and wrong, do nothing. For contemporaries of Jesus, however, the story may have meant something slightly different. For one thing, a Samaritan was, for the Jews of Israel, a social outcast; the Samaritans were a population politically and ethnically distinct from the Hebrews, and people from Samaria had hardly any standing at all. To the Jews, then, Jesus' purpose in telling the story was not so much to tell us to be compassionate, but to tell us to recognize who our *neighbor* is (our neighbor is any person who acts with compassion toward us). The lesson is: "Even" a Samaritan can be our neighbor. But of course the overriding lesson is to "go and do likewise."

FIGURE 13.2 "Arrival of the Good Samaritan at the Inn" by Gustave Doré. The good Samaritan has rescued a victim of a highway assault and here is taking him to be cared for. The Samaritan pays for the victim's keep and treatment out of his own pocket and lets the innkeeper know that if the costs add up to more, he will pay for that, too.

SIR WALTER SCOTT, *Ivanhoe* (1820), novel.

Film by Richard Thorpe (director), 1952. Film made for television by Douglas Camfield (director), 1982.

The novel *Ivanhoe*, one of the first novels in the Western literary tradition, is a very exciting story of handsome knights and beautiful, strong-willed women, of kings, usurpers, outlaws, battles, castles, and all that good stuff—even Robin Hood plays a minor part. All kids should have a chance to hear the story before they are too old and jaded to enjoy it. *Ivanhoe* contains many different story lines, but what we're going to look at here are two examples of compassion—two examples of "good Samaritan" behavior that transcends racial prejudice. We will follow the relationship between Ivanhoe, Isaac, and Rebecca.

Ivanhoe is returning home from the Crusades (a series of military expeditions in the late middle ages instigated by European and Christian leaders in order to recapture the "Holy Land," Palestine, from the Muslims). He comes to his father's estate in England. He is in disguise. His father has previously disowned him for being in love with the father's ward, Rowena. Ivanhoe is invited to dinner at his father's house; he arrives dressed like a pilgrim, and his father does not recognize him. His father, Cedric, is generous and believes in extending hospitality even to one's political enemies (Cedric is an Anglo-Saxon, and the country is ruled by the Normans). There are Normans at the dinner table and also an elderly Jew, Isaac. Ivanhoe overhears the Normans plotting to kidnap Isaac in the middle of the night and hold him for a ransom (a common pastime in those days). When the house is asleep Ivanhoe warns Isaac of the planned attack. (He is still dressed in his pilgrim's outfit.) Isaac, however, notices that underneath the pilgrim's cloak, Ivanhoe is carrying a sword, and Isaac guesses correctly that he is a knight in disguise. The old man is moved by Ivanhoe's gesture, because most people of the time discriminated against Jews. In order to repay Ivanhoe for his kindness, Isaac helps him get together a jousting outfit for the great jousting match that is coming up.

At the match Ivanhoe bests his enemy from the Holy Land, Bois-Gilbert, but he is also wounded. His father, Cedric, and Rowena rush to his side, but Cedric remembers his oath to disown his son and turns away from him. Isaac shows up to take matters in his own hands; with him is his daughter Rebecca. Together they care for Ivanhoe until he is better, and Rebecca falls tragically in love with Ivanhoe. Why tragically? Because Ivanhoe is still in love with Rowena, and anyway it is unthinkable that Ivanhoe, a Gentile, and Rebecca, a Jew, might actually marry.

Dramatic things happen: Ivanhoe, Rebecca, and Isaac are captured by Bois-Gilbert and his friends; together with Cedric and Rowena, they are imprisoned in a castle. Friends of the group (including Robin Hood) besiege the castle and eventually rescue them all, but Bois-Gilbert is now in love with Rebecca and kidnaps her. That is something he should not have done, for he belongs to the order of the Knights Templar and is supposed to be chaste. (The Knights Templar were an order of warrior monks who, during the Crusades, were assigned the task of protecting what was supposedly the tomb of Christ in Jerusalem. According to legend, a considerable treasure was hidden there.) His superiors now accuse Rebecca of having bewitched him. She is about to be burned at the stake when she claims her right to a trial by combat. The others agree. If she finds a champion who can battle for her and win, it means God has spoken: She is innocent. Bois-Gilbert wants to fight for her, but his order appoints him as their own champion. In the nick of time a champion for Rebecca shows up—Ivanhoe. Still weak, he jousts with Bois-Gilbert; he is wounded again, but Bois-Gilbert falls from his horse, dead. Rebecca is free, but she still cannot have Ivanhoe. He returns to Cedric and Rowena, and Rebecca returns to her father and dedicates her life to healing the sick.

Study Questions

1. Why is it important to the story that it is Isaac and Rebecca who tend Ivanhoe, not Cedric's people?
2. Do you think a popular novel such as *Ivanhoe* can make a difference in people's attitudes towards different population groups?
3. Can Scott be said to use the Samaritan parable in his book? If yes, how?

Vices We Love

As we've seen, lessons in virtuous living are often told through negative examples, through stories about vice and about people of frail or evil character. In this section we will look at some of literature's favorite vices and failings of character. Such themes might easily fill an entire book, and space allows us only a couple of examples. Please feel free to discuss more vices and more examples on your own!

Jealousy

"O, beware, my lord, of jealousy! It is the green-eyed monster, which doth mock the meat it feeds on." The all-time classical exploration of the pangs of jealousy in Western literature is Shakespeare's *Othello*, but the theme also is found in other cultures. We will look at an example of an Othello-type story from the Pueblo Indians of New Mexico. And we'll explore a modern twist to the theme—the woman who is jealous of her lover's wife—in *Fatal Attraction*.

WILLIAM SHAKESPEARE, *Othello*

Play (1604–05); film (1952, 1965).

In Venice a beautiful young woman, Desdemona, falls in love with Othello, the Moor. ("Moor" usually stands for Arab or Muslim but can also mean "black," and Othello is described as a black man; however, he often has been played by white actors wearing makeup.) Desdemona's family is against the match, but Desdemona prevails and marries Othello, who meanwhile has been promoted to a high military position. Enter Iago. Iago is in love with Desdemona and jealous of Othello's success. He bets that the two will tire of each other because they are so different, but he thinks of ways to help the situation along. What if Othello could be made to believe that his wife is being unfaithful to him? A young lieutenant of Othello's, Cassio, seems to fit the picture. Desdemona, who wants to be a good friend to Othello's friends, is kind to Cassio; Iago begins to drop hints to Othello that there is foul play going on. Without knowing of her husband's plan, Iago's wife, Emilia, who is a good friend of Desdemona, lends a helping hand by obtaining from Desdemona a handkerchief that Othello has given her. Iago plants the handkerchief among Cassio's possessions. Othello refuses to believe Iago's assertions, but when Desdemona can't produce the handkerchief he considers it proof that Iago is telling the truth. He becomes increasingly distant and critical toward his wife, who doesn't understand the change that has come over him. Desdemona begins to think her parents were right—that perhaps she and Othello are too different to have a successful marriage.

Othello persuades Iago to kill Cassio. Iago succeeds only in wounding him seriously, but Desdemona grieves when she hears of Cassio's misfortune, because she thinks of Cassio as a good friend. Othello takes Desdemona's reaction as further proof that Cassio is her lover and decides, at Iago's urging, to kill Desdemona. Why would Iago suggest this, when he is himself in love with her? Because she is not interested in him, and if he can't have her, he vows that nobody else will.

As Emilia discovers the truth about the situation and rushes to Othello to tell him, he is already in the process of murdering his wife. She insists that she is innocent and begs for a little more time, begs to live for half an hour, just long enough for a prayer, but he will not listen and strangles her. Emilia bursts in and tells Othello the truth; Iago is right behind Emilia, however, and he kills her. Officials show up and arrest Othello. Cassio himself tells the truth about the handkerchief—that he merely found it among his possessions one day, but never was given it by Desdemona. Othello, full of despair over his lack of faith in his wife, stabs himself and dies. Iago is taken away to answer for his crimes.

"The Faithful Wife and the Woman Warrior"

Tiwa (Pueblo) Indian tradition, reported by Elsie Clews Parsons (1940).

Two Apache warrior friends are going off on a raid against an enemy tribe. Blue Hawk is married to the chief's daughter, and Red Hawk is single. Once they are away from the village, Red Hawk suggests that Blue Hawk's wife sleeps around when he is not there, because that's how women are. Blue Hawk insists that his wife is true to him. Red Hawk says he'll bet that if he goes back alone, Blue Hawk's wife will sleep with him. Blue Hawk accepts the bet, and the two return to the vicinity of the village, where Blue Hawk hides while Red Hawk rides in alone.

Red Hawk tries to make Blue Hawk's wife interested in him, but she just ignores him. He turns to an old woman of the village and asks if there is any way she can help him see the girl when she has no clothes on. The old woman complies and goes to Blue Hawk's wife, pretending to be poor and in need of shelter. The young woman feels sorry for her and takes her in. During the night the old woman observes that the young woman's anatomy is peculiar: She has a long, gold braid coming out of her stomach, and a black spot on her backbone. The old woman returns to Red Hawk and tells him what she saw. Red Hawk rides out to Blue Hawk and confronts him with the details of his wife's body as proof that he slept with her. Blue Hawk believes him and is depressed. The two men return to the village. Blue Hawk gives Red Hawk all his possessions, much to the surprise of his wife. He then fills a big trunk with supplies and asks his wife to jump in the trunk, too. He explains that they are going on a trip and the trunk will protect her skin from the sun. Once they are away from the village, Blue Hawk dumps the trunk in the nearest river and goes back to the tribe with no explanation of where his wife has gone. This upsets her father, who guesses that foul play has occurred. He arranges for Blue Hawk to fall into a deep hole.

Blue Hawk's wife is not dead, however; she is rescued by a fisherman and enters a new phase of her life. Disguised as a man, she becomes a famous warrior. With the help of witchcraft she kills all the enemies of her tribe and returns to her father's village. She reveals her true identity and asks for Blue Hawk, who is still in the hole and near death from starvation. She embraces him, tells her side of the story, and asks that Red Hawk and the old woman, as well as two wild ponies, be brought forth. Red Hawk and the woman are tied to the ponies; the horses are then let free, and the two culprits are torn to pieces.

ADRIAN LYNE (DIRECTOR), AND JAMES DEARDEN (SCREENWRITER), *Fatal Attraction*

Film (1987).

The two previous examples featured husbands who falsely suspected their wives of being unfaithful. Here is the story of a married man, Dan Gallagher, who has a brief affair with a woman, Alex Forest, one weekend while his wife is out of town. Gallagher's marriage is one of intimacy and friendship but not much sex; his wife is more involved with being a good mother to their little girl. Gallagher is quite content to let the weekend affair remain a closed chapter, but Alex is not. She begins to move in on the family, claims to be pregnant (perhaps truthfully), and demands that Gallagher take responsibility for his actions. Her persistence becomes so unnerving to him that he looks for another place to live with his family, but Alex shows up as a prospective new tenant of the apartment they are vacating and makes friends with his wife. Alex's plan seems at first to be to persuade him to tell his wife the truth and leave her; she begrudges his wife the life she has with Dan and their child. When Alex realizes Dan is not going to leave his wife, her plans change and she becomes intent on destroying him, even if it means destroying his family. Because the film has several different endings, depending on what version you watch, I will not reveal what happens in this gripping and suspenseful story.

Study Questions

1. Is jealousy an evil character trait in itself? Why or why not? Is jealousy ever appropriate, and what kind of action might it suggest?
2. Contrast *Othello* and "The Woman Warrior." Is there a difference between Shakespeare's vision of jealousy and that of the Native American storyteller? Are there any similarities?
3. Do the visions of jealousy in *Othello* and *Fatal Attraction* differ? Are there similarities?
4. Who is worse in *Fatal Attraction*—Alex Forest, who hounds and torments the family, or Dan Gallagher, who began it all by cheating on his wife?
5. The French writer La Rochefoucauld once said, "*Il y a dans la jalousie plus d'amour propre que d'amour*" (there is more of self-love in jealousy than love). Do you agree?

Thirst for Revenge

With *Fatal Attraction* we have already encountered the theme of revenge. Why is thirst for revenge an evil thing, when our justice system allows for punishment? Briefly, because revenge is not an acceptable reason for punishing people. We can accept reasons such as *deterrence*, *rehabilitation*, and *protection of the public*, because they are reasonable and effect desirable consequences. We also can accept *retribution* as a reason for punishment: We punish people because they have committed a crime, and we punish them accordingly. But what is the difference between retribution and revenge? For one thing, retribution is exacted by society, as a logical measure. Revenge is undertaken by the individual, and is a matter of emotion. Also, retribution ensures that the punishment does not exceed the crime, but revenge takes no such precautions. Furthermore, retribution ensures that only the guilty person is punished. Revenge can easily spill over into a blood feud, resulting in the killing of innocents. In the following story, the Count of Monte Cristo believes that he has been appointed by the Lord to carry out his heavenly retribution, but in the end he realizes that he has engaged in revenge only. (If we look to the Bible, we find the words, "Vengeance is mine, sayeth the Lord" (Rom. 12:19).

ALEXANDRE DUMAS, *The Count of Monte Cristo*

Novel (1844); film (1934, 1954, 1961); television film (1975).

This story has been made into a film numerous times by French and American filmmakers, but as yet no film has succeeded in capturing the *entire* plot of the book. Neither will this outline, for the plot is extremely intricate.

The story begins in France, where Napoleon is in exile for the first time. Edmond Dantes is a young man, handsome, in love, and about to become captain of a ship, the Pharao. On the day before his wedding all his plans come to an abrupt halt: He is arrested for a crime he is not aware of and transported to Castle If, the prison island in the harbor of Marseille. There he stays, and stays; he almost goes mad trying to figure out what happened to him. Several years into his incarceration he meets another prisoner, the mad Abbe Faria, who, trying to escape, managed only to dig his way into Edmond's cell. The Abbe is a learned man, and upon meeting him Edmond's true education begins. The Abbe teaches him languages, chemistry, history, science, politics, economics, and intrigue. Through the Abbe's insight Edmond learns who is to blame for his downfall: Fernand, who wanted Edmond's girlfriend, Mercedes, for himself; and Danglars, who didn't want Edmond to become captain because he wanted the job for himself. These two men put together a letter denouncing Edmond as a Bonapartist (supporter of Napoleon). Villefort, the prosecutor, also was part of the plan; he knew that Edmond was innocent but condemned him to oblivion, because if he let Edmond go, it would implicate Villefort's father as a Bonapartist and put an end to Villefort's own career.

Faria dies, but just before his death he tells Edmond why everyone considers him, Faria, to be mad: It is because he claims to know of a treasure on the island of Monte Cristo. Edmond escapes from prison by donning the burial garments meant for the Abbe and pretending to be him. He figures he can dig his way out of the soft earth, but to his surprise he is not buried in a cemetery; he is thrown into the ocean. He is picked up by smugglers, and he embarks on a new life. First he visits Monte Cristo and finds the treasure, which does exist. Then he sets out to gain his revenge (or what he sees as divine retribution), fourteen years after having been thrown into prison.

It takes years and careful planning. Certain that God has chosen him as his instrument of retaliation, Edmond (who is now the Count of Monte Cristo) seeks out his old enemies, who have all done well for themselves. Fernand has married Mercedes and is a war hero. Danglars is a rich banker, and Villefort holds a position close to that of attorney general. Piece by piece the Count's revenge falls into place. He inflicts defamation, ruin, and death on the the three culprits and their families, until he realizes that in the process he has caused innocent lives to be lost. He understands that no man can play God, and he tries to make amends to the blameless survivors. One of these is Mercedes, who recognized him from the start. She tells the Count that she is as guilty as any of the three, because she didn't wait for Edmond but believed him dead. Edmond, however, is through with revenge; he lets Mercedes and her grown son go, and he awards them a pension and a small house—his own home in Marseille, the very house they were to have been married in.

Study Questions

1. Do you believe that Edmond's actions were justified? How might Edmond's approach be criticized?
2. If you can't expect society to retaliate against a crime on your behalf, is it all right to take matters into your own hands? Why or why not?
3. Some scholars claim there is a difference between revenge and retribution. Are they right? Why or why not?

HERMAN MELVILLE, *Moby Dick*

Novel, (1851) Films by Lloyd Bacon (director), 1984, and John Huston (director), 1956. The 1956 version is available on videotape and is highly recommended.

The plot of *Moby Dick* probably is known to most readers: Young Ishmael gets a job on board a whaling ship, the Pequod. Her captain is Ahab, and Ahab has an artificial leg, not made of wood but of whalebone. When Ishmael asks about the accident that caused Ahab to lose his leg, his shipmates tell him that the captain lost it in a battle with an immense white whale, Moby Dick, and that catching this whale has now become an obsession for Ahab. Just as Ishmael is about to board the ship, he is approached by a wreck of a man who utters a strange prophecy of doom for the ship and its captain, but

Ishmael dismisses it as the ravings of a madman. The whalers continue their voyage, killing and stripping whales (this was long before the movement to "Save the Whales" got underway). We get to know Ishmael's shipmates as good, solid people, especially his friend the headhunter, who is a marvel with a harpoon. Only Ahab holds himself aloof from the crowd.

As they enter the waters where Moby Dick can be found, Ahab becomes excited. He promises a gold coin to the first man who sings out when he sees the white whale blow, and he constructs special harpoons to pierce the heart and soul of his enemy. A ship approaches the Pequod; its crew begs Ahab to help them search for a boat that has been captured by the white whale. But all Ahab says is, "You haven't killed it, have you?" (meaning Moby Dick). He wants the revenge for himself. One day the great whale appears; Ahab orders the boats in the water, and the hunt begins. It becomes clear that this is no ordinary whale; it is intelligent, and the hunters become the hunted. The whale attacks the boats, and all of them go down except the one carrying Ishmael and Ahab. Ahab hurls the harpoon at his enemy, but his foot gets tangled in the rope, and he goes over the side of the boat. Moments later the old prophecy is fulfilled: Tangled in the ropes of the harpoon, and stuck to the side of the giant whale, Ahab reappears—dead, but still beckoning for others to follow him (his arm has fallen loose with the movements of the whale and appears to be gesturing). Now the whale goes after the Pequod herself; the ship is destroyed, and in her wake she sucks down the last remaining boat. Miraculously, Ishmael survives by clinging to some driftwood—a coffin, which was requested by his friend the headhunter, who had a premonition. Ishmael is picked up by the other ship, which is looking for survivors of her own catastrophe. And Moby Dick? Like all good monsters, it too lives on, somewhere.

Study Questions

1. What is so inappropriate about Ahab's obsession with the whale?
2. What is Ishmael's role in the story?
3. Is it reasonable to want to take revenge on an animal? Why or why not?

JOHN FORD (DIRECTOR), FRANK S. NUGENT (SCREENWRITER), *The Searchers*

Film (1956).

Ethan Edwards returns from the Civil War to his brother's ranch and to his brother's wife, Martha, with whom he has been in love for a long time. He gets reacquainted with his brother's family, two daughters and a son, and with the grown foster son, Marty, who

FIGURE 13.3 *The Searchers*, Warner Bros. 1956. Ethan Edwards (John Wayne) discovers that his brother and sister-in-law have been murdered and that his niece Debbie has been kidnapped by the Comanches. He vows to find her, no matter how long it takes. He is sure that he will find her, "just as sure as the turnin' of the earth." It soon becomes apparent, however, that Ethan not only wants to find his niece, he wants vengeance for the murders. As time goes by, he plots to kill Debbie herself because, in his view, she has been "contaminated" by living with the Indians.

is part Indian. An Indian raid lures Ethan and Marty away from their home the following day; they realize too late that it was a trick. In the meantime the Comanches have killed the family and taken the youngest daughter, Debbie, prisoner. For eight years Ethan and Marty look for the girl all over the western United States. The search changes Ethan: Now he wants to find Debbie in order to kill the Indians as well as to kill Debbie, who he believes has been "contaminated" by living with the tribe (this reflects the general opinion of the community of the time). Marty tries to reason with Ethan, to no avail. After years of obsessive searching they finally catch up with Debbie and the Comanche tribe, who are by now quite aware of the two searchers. Debbie comes to warn them of an ambush, and Ethan tries to kill her, but Marty prevents it. Debbie escapes, and the two find her again only after staging a raid on the Indian village and killing the chief, Scar, who was responsible for the murder of Ethan's brother, the rape and murder of Martha, and the abduction of Debbie. Ethan completes his revenge by scalping Scar, who is already dead (Marty has killed him). Ethan then sees Debbie and rides toward her to intercept her. But in the end, when Ethan finally is face to face with Debbie, he can't kill her. Instead he lifts her up and says gently, "Let's go home, Debbie." The French film director Jean-Paul Godard calls this one of the most moving moments in movie history. Ethan brings Debbie home. She is welcomed by her parents' old friends and neighbors (we are wondering if they will share Ethan's prejudice toward her), and when everybody is too busy to notice, Ethan turns around and leaves. His job is done, and he has been estranged from civilization too long to belong anywhere now. He has no home anymore.

Study Questions

1. Is Ethan Edwards a racist?
2. What is he really avenging?
3. What happens to him in that moment when he can't kill Debbie?

Virtue in a Modern Perspective: Angst and Authenticity

What is it to be virtuous, in the modern perspective? Perhaps authenticity is one of the most important character traits in a modern virtue theory, whether we approach it from the point of view of virtue theory itself, or from the point of view of existentialism. Being virtuous means remaining true to yourself in spite of challenges, temptations, and hardships, and taking responsibility for your actions.

Angst, Dread, Anguish, Anxiety, and So On

For existentialism, the phenomenon of angst (anguish) can serve as the gateway to authenticity if it is approached responsibly and courageously, so we will look at some stories of anguish. Although angst is not a virtue, facing up to angst can be, and at any rate the feeling of anguish illustrates the profound problem of living in the face of absurdity. In this section we will look at three twentieth-century stories that discuss the feeling of angst: Sartre's *No Exit*, Woody Allen's film *Hannah and Her Sisters*, and a short story by the Swedish author Bertil Malmberg, "The Tail."

JEAN PAUL SARTRE, *No Exit*
Play (1944).

For Sartre there is no life after death, for there is no God to send the soul to one realm or the other. But as a dramatist and a novelist Sartre played with the idea of Hell nevertheless. In the drama *No Exit* three characters find themselves in a locked room with no windows: a middle-aged man, Garcin, a young woman, Estelle, and a lesbian woman, Inez. They all know that they are dead and in Hell, and they are highly surprised that there is no torture chamber—merely a room decorated in bad taste. They don't know each other, but they are forced to spend an unforeseeable amount of time together in this room, interrupted only occasionally by a prison guard, the "valet." For a while they can "glimpse" the life of the living, but that soon fades, and all they have are each other. Each pretends to wonder what the others have done to be sent to hell, but as Inez says, they are all "murderers." Estelle killed her baby, Inez killed her lover's husband (or at least drove him to his death), and Garcin killed the spirit in his wife by his cruelty to her. What tortures Garcin most, though, is that he is a deserter. He, who always thought he would live and die bravely, never had a chance to prove himself, he says—he died too soon. But Inez corrects him:

> One always dies too soon—or too late. And yet one's whole life is complete at that moment, with a line drawn neatly under it, ready for the summing up. You are—your life, and nothing else.

Estelle is beginning to find Garcin attractive (she is used to men fawning over her). Inez is falling in love with Estelle, and Garcin is himself attracted to Estelle but prefers that each of them stay in their own corner rather than hurt each other. But the stage is set, and they can't help interacting. All three try to manipulate each other; they team up, two against the third one. They constantly scrutinize each other (for in Hell you have no eyelids you can close). They need each other for comfort and support, but they have no trust in each other. They realize that there is no need for torture instruments and devils—they are each other's torturers. The room and the other two people in it *are* Hell for them: Their punishment is spending an eternity with each other in a hostile triangle. In the end Garcin succeeds in opening the locked door to their room, but now all three are reluctant to leave, because that would mean the other two had won the dominance game. All three stay to torment each other, forever.

On the symbolic level Sartre is—probably—not talking about any real life after death, but about the human condition. He is saying we make life a hell for each other, because we are so very good at manipulating each other, and every human relationship, even that between lovers, has at its core a battle for power and dominance. Sartre concludes with one of his most famous lines: "Hell is—other people."

Study Questions

1. Would you agree with Sartre that "Hell is other people"?
2. Do you think Garcin, Estelle, and Inez might apply Sartre's own principles of existentialism to cope with their life in Hell? How?

WOODY ALLEN (DIRECTOR AND SCREENWRITER), *Hannah and Her Sisters*

Film (1986).

Can a comedy deal seriously with issues such as angst and the absurdity of life? Absolutely, at least when the director is Woody Allen. We will look primarily at the character played by Allen—Mickey, a hypochondriac who is always running to doctors believing he has some form of terminal illness. While his friends engage themselves in stealthy extramarital affairs and other self-realization projects, Mickey finds that he is experiencing some dizziness and has lost some hearing in one ear, so he goes to see his doctor. He fully expects the doctor to shrug it off as an imagined disease as usual, but this time the doctor suggests X rays, because, although it might be just a minor problem, it also might be a brain tumor.

Mickey is plunged into the abyss of despair; he tries to make deals with God. He can't believe it is happening, and yet he believes it. On the X ray there is an ominous spot, and the doctor schedules him for a CAT scan. The idea of death, as often as he has played around with it, now seems both real and unfathomable: "You're in the middle of New York City, this is your town, you're surrounded by people and traffic and restaurants—how can you just one day—vanish?"

Finally, in the doctor's office, the doctor has all the charts and X rays out and shows him with clinical exactitude where the tumor is, saying there is nothing that anyone can do about it. His worst nightmare is coming true for the hypochondriac.

And yet—a split second later—we find that he has just *imagined* the doctor speaking the words of doom; now the doctor comes in and says what Mickey was hoping to hear, that they can't find out why he has a minor hearing loss, but it is not a tumor. Mickey should be revived and elated, right? At first he is, but the close call has profoundly disturbed his equilibrium; he comes to the realization that life is absurd and meaningless because it can be threatened, and regarded, so casually. If we can be gone in an instant, what's the point of living, he asks? His release from *fear* has actually deepened his existential *angst*, for now he sees that there are no guarantees, no master plan, and no ready-made meaning for him to hold on to. If life is going to come to an end anyway, why bother doing anything? Nothing is worthwhile anymore; the hypochondriac has become a *nihilist*.

If only he could believe in God. . . . Mickey seeks help from religious experts, from Catholic priests to Hare Krishna converts (much to his mother's chagrin—couldn't he just give his own religion a try? His family is Jewish). And yet one day Mickey is feeling better. He meets an old acquaintance, his ex-wife's nutty sister, and tells her the story: Recently he had reached the bottom of the abyss and was toying with the idea of killing himself; he actually held a rifle to his head, pondering the question of life and death, when the gun went off, shattering a window! He had held the trigger so tightly that it just went off, but because of his sweaty palms it slipped out of his hands. In a state of total confusion he went out, walked the streets of New York, and ended up in a revival movie theater where they were showing an old Marx Brothers comedy. Here he recaptured the meaning of life: "What if the worst is true—there is no God and you only go around once. Don't you want to be part of the experience?"

So Mickey finds meaning in absurdity, and he finds marriage and children with his ex-wife's nutty sister.

Study Questions

1. Do you think such an experience as Mickey's is common?
2. Has Mickey learned Sartre's lesson about living with absurdity, or hasn't he?
3. Compare Sartre's and Nietzsche's approaches to the idea that life is absurd. (A section on Nietzsche appears in Part 4, Chapter 17.)

BERTIL MALMBERG, "The Tail"

Short story, (1937). From the book Åke and His World.

The story of the transformation of a human being into something else is a familiar theme in fiction. Sometimes the human is transformed into a werewolf or a vampire, sometimes into a bionic creature (like in *Robocop*), and sometimes into a godlike being (like in *Star Trek: The Movie*). These stories sometimes symbolize that we have all of these things within us, and sometimes they illustrate the anxiety of change and loss of control. The most frightening story of transformation may be Franz Kafka's "The Metamorphosis," which is about a young man who finds himself slowly being turned into a giant bug. We feel his disbelief, his anguish, and his slow loss of humanity as he loses the love and caring of his family, who no longer recognize or acknowledge him. A Swedish counterpart, which takes a much milder form but which deals with the same phenomenon, that of angst, is the short story of Åke (pronounced "Ohka"), who thinks he is turning into a monkey.

Åke is a little boy who lives with his mother and father and big sister in a small Swedish town. His father is a quiet country doctor; his mother takes care of the home, and she is wise, young, and understanding. Åke's sister Aja (pronounced "Eye-ya") is a brat who can be a good playmate at times but is otherwise a pain in the neck. Åke lives a life of worry-free security, guarded by his parents and his own lack of knowledge of how hard life can be. Everything he hears is wondrous, and he loves stories; he doesn't yet know there is a difference between fact and fiction.

One night Åke's grandmother is visiting, and she is reading a children's story for Aja. At first Åke is not listening, but all of a sudden the story catches his attention. It is about a small boy who is slowly becoming a monkey. A tail begins to grow, then fur, and finally his friends and family chase him away—even his mother won't have anything to do with him. Åke feels sorry for the little boy, and then Aja jumps up and pinches him at the tailbone, proclaiming that Åke is growing a tail, too! He shrugs it off, but later on, at night, his hands steal to his tailbone, and he feels it, too: He really is becoming a monkey!

This is the end of Åke's innocence; he has no more feeling of security, no more naive trust that tomorrow will be like today. He already envisions himself being thrown out in the snow, a pathetic little furry creature with a tail. For days he tries to hide his feeling of anguish, but in the end his mother can't help noticing the state he is in, and she drags the truth out of him. She restores his world by reassuring him that he is not growing a tail at all—and besides, if he did, he could be sure that his mother would never abandon him. Because Åke is a child, this is enough to restore his world, and now he has an idea:

"Mom," he asks, "if I get a long tail . . ."

"You won't."

"But if I do—do you think I can wave it around?"

Study Questions

1. Is it reasonable to call the worries of a child a case of angst?
2. For an adult, is there anything that can alleviate a case of angst? Does Sartre have a suggestion?

Authenticity

What does it mean to obtain authenticity? The following stories explore the idea of being true to oneself and maintaining (or regaining) one's self-esteem. We will look at Karen Blixen's "Babette's Feast," George Lucas's film *Star Wars*, and Iris Murdock's *The Good Apprentice*.

FIGURE 13.4 The Danish storyteller Karen Blixen (1885–1962) originally published her works under the pseudonyms of Isak Dinesen and Pierre Andrézel. She married baron Bror Blixen-Finecke and went with him to Africa, where she ran a coffee farm in Kenya from 1914 to 1931. Natural disasters and lack of business success forced her to leave Africa and return to Denmark, where she began to write short stories. The author of *Out of Africa* (made into a film in 1985 starring Meryl Streep in the role of Blixen herself), Blixen became one of the greatest writers of short stories in the twentieth century. This photo was taken at about the same time she wrote *Babette's Feast*. (Photo courtesy of The Royal Library, Copenhagen, Denmark.)

Karen Blixen (also known as Isak Dinesen), *Babette's Feast*

Novelette (1953). Academy-Award-winning film by Gabriel Axel (director), 1988.

The book takes place in Norway, but the film moves the locale to the Danish West Coast, a culturally similar location.

To a community of fundamentalist Christians in a remote Norwegian community of the late eighteenth century comes a refugee of the French Revolution, a woman. Two unmarried sisters take her in as a deed of charity, offering to pay her a token sum for becoming their cook. In time the woman, Babette, learns some Norwegian and becomes a pleasant companion for the two sisters. She has learned to cook the rather bland Norwegian food the way the sisters like it, and life seems to be good. The sisters, who are the daughters of the deceased religious leader of the community, concentrate on the spiritual task of keeping the elderly community members from bickering.

Through flashbacks we learn that the sisters have both had opportunities to experience the world outside their tiny village. One had great promise as an opera singer but gave up a career because she was in love with her instructor, a great opera singer, and because the idea of her going out into the profane world disturbed her father the minister greatly. The other sister has known love, too; a young lieutenant passed through town in her youth, and they fell in love but the lieutenant decided he could not give up his career for her.

How did Babette end up in this forsaken place? By recommendation of the opera singer, now a very famous man and an acquaintance of Babette. As the story unfolds, we understand the magnitude of destiny. After living with the sisters for many years, Babette learns that she has inherited a small fortune. She asks one thing of the sisters: that she be allowed to cook a good French meal for them on the day that they are to celebrate their deceased father's birthday. The sisters are skeptical, but because Babette has never asked for anything before, they agree. Strange foods begin appearing at the house; they have been sent directly from France. On the day of the feast, Babette cooks the dinner. The congregation, who have caught wind that they will be served pagan and inedible things, resolve not to mention the dinner but merely eat it so as not to embarrass the sisters. One guest is not in on the arrangement, however; the former lieutenant, now a military commander, is back in town, and he immediately appreciates the exquisite food, the wines, the sauces. Only once, he says, has he had such a meal, and it was at a very expensive, very elegant restaurant in Paris before the Revolution.

The celebration over, the sisters expect Babette to leave them and go back to France. But she has no such intention, for she has no more money. As she explains, the money has all been used to pay for the exquisite meal. She then reveals to the sisters that she is the former master chef of that very elegant French restaurant, the one the general used to dine at before the Revolution. The sisters then understand that like them, Babette was destined for something greater than what she got. All any of them can do is hold on to their integrity and act with dignity no matter what the circumstances. In Heaven their talents will be appreciated.

Study Questions

1. Is this a sad story? It may seem like it, but if you read the story or watch the film you may have a different opinion.
2. How might we say that Babette maintains her ego-integrity?
3. Blixen believed that in order to be a mature and virtuous human being you had to come to terms with your destiny. Do you think that is an appealing or an unappealing thought? Why?

GEORGE LUCAS (DIRECTOR AND SCREENWRITER), *Star Wars*

Film (1977).

The *Star Wars* trilogy has reached a level of popularity that warrants calling it a modern myth—a term that the mythologist Joseph Campbell first assigned to it. Why is it a "myth"? Not because it is "wrong" or "false" but because it tells an archetypal story

FIGURE 13.5 *Star Wars*, 20th Century Fox, 1977. Darth Vader (the voice of James Earl Jones), was once a Jedi Knight, but he let himself be taken over by the dark side of the *Force*, which leads to personal power and ruthless abuse of others.

about human endeavor in a format that can be understood by humans at all times. Expressions such as "may the Force be with you" and "the Dark Side" became household words for a whole generation of kids; they became a powerful metaphor for making the right choice, doing the right thing, and being the right kind of person.

In *Star Wars* good and evil forces battle each other, and who will win no one knows (except the audience, of course—we all know that good will triumph in the end, don't we?). Luke Skywalker and his two teachers, Obi Wan Kenobi and Yoda (*The Empire Strikes Back*), represent the Jedi Knights (the good guys); the arch villain with the marvelous voice, Darth Vader (voice by James Earl Jones), stands for the Dark Side, the powers of darkness. What makes the story interesting is that the Dark Side seems good and right to those who have chosen it; to a Jedi Knight, the Dark Side is tempting because it lures with power and pragmatism: Join the winning side or you will die. Those who do choose the Dark Side, of course, show themselves to be of weak character. Everyone in the audience understands this conflict, especially because Luke has problems remaining on the shining path himself. We are all tempted by power and pragmatism.

Study Questions

Warning: If you know Darth Vader's true identity and your fellow students don't, please don't reveal it to them . . . let them watch the trilogy for themselves!

1. If we see *Star Wars* as a metaphor for "learning to be the right kind of person," can anybody truly live up to such an ideal? If not, should we stop trying?
2. Do you know of anybody you would perceive as having "sold out to the Dark Side"? Might that person disagree with your assessment? Why?
3. Would Aristotle have any useful advice for Luke Skywalker?

IRIS MURDOCH, *The Good Apprentice*

Novel (1985).

Edward is either a tragic hero or a pitiful fool; he causes the death of a friend, through stupidity and callousness. He tricks his friend Mark to take drugs and then leaves him alone in his room. When he returns, he finds the window open and Mark lying dead on the ground below. This event sends Edward off into his own "private hell," and it is then that he is transformed into a hero. Through taking on the ultimate guilt and responsibility, Edward remakes himself into a whole person. This sounds like a dud of a story, but in fact it is not only full of suspense, but also it is awfully funny, because Edward's life has become so dreadful that it is comical. The lives of those around him fall apart all by themselves; his step-brother tries hard to find something to do in life that will allow him to become a saint, but he must face the fact that he doesn't qualify because he has no passion (and, presumably, saints are passionate people, in a spiritual sense). Edward's step-father has an affair with Edward's dead mother's sister, who happens to be Edward's therapist's wife, and their relationship is exposed under the most humiliating and ludicrous circumstances. Meanwhile, Edward's natural father, the great artist Jesse Baltram, who has never expressed an interest in him before, draws Edward to his out-of-the-way farmhouse by means that may be supernatural. Once in the presence of his father, now a mental invalid, Edward redefines himself as his father's rightful son—but this redefinition doesn't have the healing properties we expect. On the contrary, Edward's healing begins when he *repeats* his fatal mistake; he leaves his father alone, with devastating consequences. As a result, however, Edward has now become a whole person to such a degree that he can, unwittingly, inspire his step-father, his step-brother, his therapist, his aunt (the therapist's wife), and even dead Mark's sister to "do the right thing." From being the morally guilty person he has emerged as a moral catalyst. His quest was for peace of mind, but he never truly achieves it, for Mark continues to be dead, and Edward continues to be guilty. He wanted absolution, but no one can give that to him except himself, and that is a cheap solution that he is constantly fighting against. In the end he and his step-brother drink to the good things in life—only they are not sure what they are. Edward's quest has yielded something—another identity—but it wasn't what he expected or hoped for.

Study Questions

1. Has Edward found a solution? Do all problems have to have solutions?
2. Is this a Say No-to-Drugs story? Why or why not?
3. Can we say that Edward has developed his character at the end of the story?

Part 4

ETHICS AND HUMAN NATURE

Chapter 14

What Is a Person?

We all know what it is to be human—at least until we're asked. Then we may find that an exact definition is not that obvious. Some traits, which once were considered specifically human, like being tool users or even toolmakers, turned out to be shared by many other animals. Other characteristics, such as "free will," turned out to be doubtful altogether. In this part of the text we will explore what we might call the "human condition" from points of view ranging from classical philosophy to existentialism, psychology, and gender theory.

There is no such thing as a present-day consensus of how to define a human being. Some nations still have not determined when a human being stops being a human being—in other words, the criterion of death. In this country we have decided on a certain criterion—brain death—but that doesn't mean everybody automatically agrees on when life ceases. We don't even agree on when exactly a fetus becomes a human being. The arguments on all sides hinge less on scientific facts than they do on personal beliefs and commitments—in other words, *viewpoints* of human nature. On these we base our rules of how others are supposed to live. Members of some nations seem not to be sure if members of other nations are humans at all; we may ourselves be ready to pronounce that someone has transgressed to such a degree that he or she has stopped being human or has lost the right to live in a human community (as if being human is a state of honor).

When we try to define what human nature is, we can choose one of two basic

What Does It Mean to Be Human?

Most classical definitions of a human being can be questioned in the light of new knowledge. We always must ask, are these specifically human characteristics, or are they shared by other creatures? Are they in fact human characteristics at all? If so, are they shared by *all* humans? Let us look at some popular definitions: A human being is *two-legged*, with upright posture and free hands; has *language*; is *rational*; is a *social* being; has *warfare* with its own species; can *laugh* and *cry*; can *remember* and *plan* for the future; *uses tools*; *makes tools*; has a *soul*; has a *free will*; uses *symbols*; tells *stories*; creates pictorial *art* and *music*; can *lie*; is *self-aware*; is *conscious*; can *blush* (Mark Twain liked to point out this fact and added that humans probably blush because they are the only creatures with a reason to do so); has *values*; is aware of *death*. You can add to the list endlessly. Humans also have opposed thumbs, play at politics, write books, invent computer games, are fascinated by the universe, make love facing each other, have a long childhood, have psychological repressions, can feel guilty, and so on and so forth.

approaches, the *exclusive* method or the *inclusive* method. The *exclusive* method concentrates on one aspect or definition and tries to explain human nature from that. The *inclusive* method tries to give an explanation of human nature as a mixture of all or some of these features. The tendency among scholars today is toward the inclusive method; we can't begin to understand what humans are if we aren't willing to look at the whole picture and even leave some space open for knowledge that may become available to us in the future. Regardless of whether we prefer an exclusive or an inclusive method, we will be dealing with theories of either a *normative* or a *descriptive* type.

Faced with a puzzling example of human behavior, we often resort to the stock answer, "It's human nature." We might even dig up the old excuse, "I'm only human." But what do we mean by that? What we are usually saying is something akin to (a) "I couldn't help myself," (b) "I really don't have a strong character, but neither do you," (c) "We humans are very versatile," (d) "We humans really are incredibly stupid sometimes." On occasion we do apply the stock answer to a laudable situation, in which case we mean (e) "We humans really can be great when we put our minds to it." On the whole our use of the answer depends on our intent: If we are expressing an ideal of what we believe humans can do at their best, then we are *prescribing* what we think human beings ought to be like. We are thus expressing a *normative* theory.

Usually a normative theory of human nature tends to idealize human characteristics. However, because we live in a time that focuses on "facts" and "evidence," we often find that a theory of human nature, even one that is on the level of a stock

What Is a Fact?

A note about the nature of facts: Sometimes it is not that easy to determine what a "fact" is. Is it a fact that humans are the only creatures that use tools? That apes can be taught to speak? Is it a fact that it rains in the autumn? Or that freedom is a good thing? What we call facts are part of a theoretical method. We collect certain data based on a preconceived notion that those data are relevant for our research, but often we forget that this is a selective process. Some data are considered irrelevant and don't get considered—but to a rival theory they may appear to be important "facts." To an eyewitness of an accident it is a "fact" that the hit-and-run car was a blue sedan, even though in actuality it was a gray van. Such facts can be checked, but how about checking eyewitness "facts" when the eyewitness ac-count is two hundred years old? To the believer it is a fact that there is a Heaven—but what about for the nonbeliever? Besides, "facts" can be manipulated to create a theory. The German philosopher Nietzsche said, "There are no facts, only theory," by which he meant not that we can't know some things, but that everything we state as a "fact" goes through a process of evaluation and selection and is ultimately dependent on the perspective of the human who has an interest in the matter. So when a descriptive theory claims to deal with "facts," we should take this claim with a grain of salt: What it means is that it believes itself to be factual and not normative, but there is no reason for accepting its "facts" as the truth without examining them.

answer, tries to be *descriptive*—it describes what we perceive human nature actually to be rather than what we hope it might achieve. Thus we say that "it's human nature" when we mean that humans can't help looking after themselves, are greedy, are self-glorifying, and so on.

Why is a descriptive theory of human nature so often negative or apologetic? Often the tendency today is, as we saw in the chapter on psychological egoism, to be as honest about oneself as possible. There is also a modern, cynical tendency to view one's fellow human beings, oneself included, in a less than favorable light, believing that the worst is probably true. Finally, a negative or apologetic theory serves as a good excuse for when we or others do something we shouldn't have done: We just couldn't help ourselves—"we're only human." (In all fairness we should mention that a descriptive theory of human nature need not be cynical at all—one certainly can express the idea that humans are hopeful, are survivors, care about each other during hard times, and so on.)

A descriptive theory need not be correct in its description in order to be called descriptive—it is enough that it *believes* it is expressing a theory that corresponds with the factual situation. Therefore, two rival theories that describe human nature as inherently decent versus inherently evil both can be descriptive.

Who Qualifies as a Human Being?

The Ethical Connection

Why is there a connection between ethics and theories of human nature? Because our very morality—how we believe humans should be treated, and how we actually treat others—usually reflects our view of human nature. Do we believe humans are basically good, or basically bad? Do we believe they are incompatibly male or female, are endowed with a soul, or have freedom of the will? Any theory of human nature will answer these questions: (1) Who qualifies as a human being? (2) How should we treat this being? and (3) How should we treat those that don't qualify? In this way a connection is established between a view of human nature, a general morality, and politics, because if we for instance happen to believe that human beings are generally weak and untrustworthy, we will develop not only a personal ethic that says not to trust your friends too much, but also a general politic of mistrust: Because citizens can't be trusted to do what is good for the state (or perhaps even what's good for themselves), the state must control them. In a benevolent society this can happen through rigid standards of education and legislation; citizens are taught to do the right thing, and when they lapse the law is there to get them. In a less benevolent society, this theory of human nature may translate into *totalitarianism*: Citizens can't be trusted to do what is good for the state, so they must be forced to and chastised if they don't. If we think people are basically quite decent, then we give them a lot of political and personal leeway. If we think people are basically evil, selfish, and stupid, we will either try to guide and steer them through their lives through some political and social system of limitations, or we simply will try to control them with strict political and military means. We may even *agree* to be oppressed, if we think we are evil and selfish and stupid. As a result, a great deal of political propaganda has to do with installing a certain view of human nature into citizens. As an intellectual exercise one could take a political statement or a statement of legislation and from that derive the underlying view of human nature. We will return to this later in connection with Aristotle and Hobbes.

The Issue of Physical Criteria

Let us look at the three basic questions posed by a theory of human nature: (1) Who qualifies as a human being? (2) How do we treat those who qualify? and (3) How do we treat those who don't? The first question looks plainly descriptive; we describe what a human being is, and then it should be fairly easy to see who qualifies. But it is not as easy as that, for how do we describe a human being? Are the criteria physical? Does a being have to look human in order to be human? How detailed must we get? A traditional answer is "a featherless biped"—in other words, a creature that walks upright on two legs but is not a bird—but that is hardly a sufficient criterion. Nowadays, if we want to use physical criteria, we include not only physical appearance, but also genetics. But with this type of explanation we're faced with two problems. One is that genetically, there are creatures that are 99 percent identical to the human but are obviously not human: chimpanzees. On the other hand, there are individuals born of human parents who may not have all the human physical characteristics—for instance, persons with multiple physical disabilities (here we're not even talking about *mental* disabilities). So a being born of humans who happens to have some physical aberration—from missing limbs to minor abnormalities such as extra toes and fingers—is it human? For most people today, the answer is obviously yes, but this was not always so. A worldwide tradition in pretechnological societies has been to dispose of newborns with physical "handicaps" ranging from missing limbs to unwanted birthmarks, and not all of those disposals can be explained by saying that a tribe isn't able to feed someone who can't feed himself. People with birthmarks or cleft palates can usually fend for themselves just fine. So today we don't follow that practice, but we do screen the fetus for severe disabilities and perform abortions if we deem these disabilities to condemn the child to a less than dignified life. This is not a discussion of the merits and problems of abortion, any more than it is a discussion of infanticide, but it does point out that a good deal of our policy-making in ancient times as well as today depends on what we consider to be a human being, including what a human being, and a human life, *should be like*—a normative concept.

The Person as a Moral Agent

A mere physical description, or even a prescription, is usually not sufficient for describing what is human and what is not. We must look to psychological and social criteria, and this is where the concept of a *person* begins to take over. A human being usually is identified as one born of human parents, regardless of what might be different about the infant, physically or mentally. But a *person* is someone who is capable of psychological and social interaction with others, capable of deciding on a course of action and being held responsible for that action. In other words, a person is considered a *moral agent*, and as such, a person can be considered to have certain rights and obligations (at least in our type of society). It is for this reason that the issue of "human nature" is not just an academic question but a very real and very nasty problem, for we also must answer the question, To whom do we wish to grant "human rights"? Or at least "rights"? Whom do we wish to welcome to the club of responsible individuals, treat with respect, grant the right to life, liberty, and property?

The Expansion of the Concept "Human"

There was a time when people distinguished between friend and foe by calling friends humans and foes beasts, devils, or such. At the tribal level of human history it always has been common to view the tribe across the river as not quite human, even if a member of your tribe marries their sons or daughters. (In fact, the usual word that tribes use to designate themselves is their word for "human," "the people," or "us.") In any geographical area there are people who remain skeptical of those from "the other side" (the big city or the country) because their habits are so different that it seems there must be something "strange" about their general humanity. At the gender level, from the time of the Ancient Greeks until quite recently, a common assumption has been that women are not quite human. Interestingly enough, this idea has been held not only by men but also by women, who took the men's word for it. (Some still do.) At the nationalistic level, it still is common practice to view foreigners as less than human, not in a physical sense, but rather politically and morally. And the humanity of a people's wartime enemies almost always is denied, usually because it becomes easier to kill an enemy, either soldier or civilian, if you believe he or she really is not quite as human as you or I. Thus the term *human* sometimes evolves into an honorary term reserved for those with whom we prefer to share our culture. Historically, the meaning of the term in the Western world expanded to include not only "our people" but "all Europeans" and, with the advent of the Enlightenment, all free white males of any nationality. In the nineteenth century the term was expanded again to cover women as well as people born into slavery. The abolition of slavery was a natural result of the new idea as to who qualifies for personhood. Philosophically, it can be described as the recognition that all beings capable of rational thinking deserve respect, because they have the capacity to weigh a problem rationally, decide on a course of action, and take responsibility for their choice.

Today we in the Western world assume that all humans are persons with inalienable rights. However, this is not a recognized truth all over the world (and even in our own society we may have doubts about our landlord, our professor, or the neighbor's noisy kids, though such feelings usually are rather tongue-in cheek). A more serious problem of recent years is the reemergence of *racism*, which can be seen as a reduction of the human fellow-feeling, a return of the reluctance to call other humans "persons." Perhaps this reluctance was always there, at a primitive level, but lately it seems more persistent, for whatever reason, be it the increasing crime in our cities, our need for scapegoats, or whatever. Still, we view the term *human* as an honor badge, even if we hide behind it, claiming "we're only human." It seems it's only human to be self-contradictory, too.

The question of what constitutes a person is, within the realm of ethics, a normative question. In other words, we're asking not about genetics but about a moral standard: Who actually counts as a person, and who do we wish *should* count as a person? Who counts morally, and who doesn't? In this section we cannot hope to solve the problem, but we can perhaps come closer to understanding why it is a problem.

The Beginnings of Slavery

Slavery seems to have been invented when warring tribes in pretechnological times captured prisoners of war (soldiers and captured civilians). They had to decide what to do with them, and the logical answer was to make a profit and sell them. Because the prisoners (the enemy) already were viewed as not quite human, and because the idea of human rights was several millennia in the future, no moral problem arose from the concept of slavery during those early times.

Kant Revisited: Humans Are Ends in Themselves

As you may remember from Part 2, Immanuel Kant cut across the feudal hierarchy of "who's who" in terms of civic importance when he declared that whoever is capable of rational thinking possesses moral dignity and should be treated accordingly. It was not the conditions of birth, nor wealth, nor geographical placement that were the determining factors; the sole qualification was the human capacity for rational thinking. As a product of the early Enlightenment and a gigantic influence in the development of the concept of human rights, Kant is to be credited with being the author of a major expansion of the idea of "who counts":

> Now I say that man, and in general every rational being, exists as an end in himself and not merely as a means to be arbitrarily used by this or that will. He must in all his actions, whether directed to himself or to other rational beings, always be regarded at the same time as an end. . . . Beings whose existence depends not on our will but on nature have, nevertheless, if they are not rational beings, only a relative value as means and are therefore called things. On the other hand, rational beings are called persons inasmuch as their nature already marks them out as ends in themselves, i.e., as something which is not to be used merely as means and hence there is imposed thereby a limit on all arbitrary use of such beings, which are thus objects of respect. . . . The practical imperative will therefore be the following: Act in such a way that you treat humanity, whether in your own person or in the person of another, always at the same time as an end and never simply as a means.

What exactly is an "end"? For Kant it meant that you, as a rational being, are your own goal and purpose in life, and nobody has the right to use your life for his or her own purpose—merely as a means to an end. (In Part 2 we looked in detail at the difference between people being treated (1) as means to an end, (2) merely as means to an end, and (3) as ends in themselves.)

Kant's ethical proposal meant the expansion of our social politics and of our concern for humans as persons: All people count, as long as they have a rational nature. However, some problems still remained. For one thing, Kant was not quite sure whether women had a rational nature—and without a rational nature, they would not qualify as persons. We might ask further, are children rational beings? We might agree that a twelve-year-old certainly is quite rational, and perhaps even an eight-year-old, but what about a four-year-old or someone even younger? Should we treat them as beings with dignity because they will *become* rational one of these days? Kant doesn't say, but it's hard to believe that he would call infants "things" just because their rational capabilities aren't yet developed. But what about those unfortunate infants whose mental capabilities never will develop because they are mentally disabled? Kant has no place "in the middle" for beings who are genetically human but who lack rational capacities. Does that mean they fall into the category of things? Kant doesn't say. And what about those "irrational beings"—animals—which Kant thought should be classified as things? To most people today it seems preposterous that we should treat animals as mere things, and we will get back to this question soon. We may choose to view the lack of a moral "middle section" as an oversight in Kant's theory and a positive sign that our sensitivities as to "who counts morally" are further developed than his own, but the fact remains that there is a serious flaw in Kantian moral theory.

The Question of a Soul

Christians and Others

In the Christian tradition the question of who has moral standing is answered with a counterquestion: Who has a soul? The answer given by Christianity is that *man* has a soul; *animals* do not. Some religious traditions, including Christianity and Islam, have found it problematic to decide whether *woman* also has a soul, but the exclusion of animals is clear. Although Christians believe animals have been put on this earth for man's sake and can be put to any use man desires, Muslims believe animals should not be abused by man (however, they too believe that men are the rulers of creation). A Christian lesson in noncruelty is taught by Saint Thomas Aquinas, who points out that it is not good to be cruel to animals, not because the animal will suffer, but because it predisposes man toward cruelty against other men. This argument, by the way, was taken up by John Locke and Immanuel Kant and was predominant in Western philosophy until the time of Jeremy Bentham (see Part 2).

No one in the Western religious traditions has claimed that an animal has a soul—not even Saint Francis of Assisi, who preached love for animals because they have God in them (as does the entire creation for Saint Francis, whose teachings were very much opposed to church policy of the day). However, the idea that animals do have souls is a belief that is commonly shared by Hindus and Buddhists; it is based on the theory of transmigration of souls, or reincarnation. As we saw in Part 3, the spiritual life of many Native Americans includes the moral stature of animals as a part of everyday life. It probably is not the case that the Native American sees all living creatures as equal—that idea is the result of a massive romanticizing of Indian culture. However, Native Americans' respect for animals most likely ties into their realization that "what goes around, comes around"; in other words, the way you treat the animals you depend on for your livelihood will determine your own fate. This is a pragmatic version of the Golden Rule, Lakota style.

In general, anthropology has given us ample evidence that for pretechnological (what used to be called "primitive") cultures, humans do not constitute a class apart from other animals. This does not necessarily mean that humans and animals are considered "one big happy family," an idea that belongs to our present-day ideology of environmentalism. It more likely reflects the life experience of a people on the fringe of existence, where life is as dangerous for the hunter, the woman in childbirth, and the infant as it is for the hunted animal. It is a feeling that "we are all in this together, and it doesn't hurt to ask the animal for forgiveness when I kill it, for then I may be safe from its spirit." The key concept is that for most pretechnological cultures it is natural to imagine both humans and animals in possession of a spirit; indeed, spirits are not confined to animate objects but may reside in natural objects such as rocks, trees, rivers, waterholes, and so on. We usually call this attitude *animism*, the belief that spirits are everywhere. But it is for only a few cultures that this attitude translates into a veneration for nature and commands against killing fellow creatures (like the Hindu *ahimsa* [nonviolence] rule).

Within the Western tradition the view of animals as not having souls has condemned them to thousands of years of sanctioned use by humans, and to considerable abuse—what some people have called the human reign of terror on earth. Why did this happen? There are several possible reasons. One is that some people believe such actions can be justified on the basis of biblical authority. Another is that it is convenient. We can't discount the fact, though, that occasionally killing animals has been perceived as *necessary* for self-defense and the preservation of *human* life. The fact that we usually no longer *need* to kill any animal larger than a roach or the occasional rat should not make us forget that there was a time when animals posed a real danger to people and crops. However, that is no excuse for the wholesale extermination of a species, now or then.

New Christians and Animal Rights

Among contemporary Christians there is a new interest in reviewing the attitude toward animals so as to include them in the moral and religious universe of humans. The following quote is taken from a report issued by the World Council of Churches in September 1988.

> An ethic for the liberation of life is a call to Christian action. In particular, how animals are treated is not "someone else's worry," it is a matter of individual and collective responsibility. Christians are called to act respectfully towards "these,

the least of our brothers and sisters." This is not a simple question of kindness however laudable that virtue is. *It is an issue of strict justice.* In all our dealings with animals, whether direct or indirect, an ethic for the liberation of life requires that *we render unto animals what they are due, as creatures with an independent integrity and value.* Precisely because they cannot speak for themselves or act purposively to free themselves from the shackles of their enslavement, the Christian duty to speak and act for them is the greater, not the lesser.

If we ask ourselves where in the Christian tradition we can find the basis for these thoughts, the English theologian Dr. Andrew Linzey will tell us no place—but, he says, Christianity has the capacity to rethink an issue, as it did the slavery issue. Christianity used to condone slavery, believing that it's better to have a Christian slave than a free heathen, but now Christianity opposes slavery. For Linzey, the animal rights concept is due for the same shift in Christian opinion. He says if one asks, What can the church do for animal rights? then the first answer has to be, "What it can do is repent."

From an ethical and political point of view those interested in animal rights generally steer clear of the soul issue, for who is to say what a soul is and who has one, if indeed souls exist? Ethicists prefer not to cloud the issue with further unknown components. Instead they turn toward the question of what the results will be if we expand the concept of personhood to include certain nonhuman groups. We like to think we treat other persons with respect and dignity, and we might believe that some nonhumans deserve the same treatment. In order for such a policy to be morally valid, the proper thing to do would be to grant personhood to these groups.

Rights and Personhood

Who Is a Person?

The question of who is a person is a very modern question; as we saw earlier, until two hundred years ago, not all human beings were automatically considered persons. Being a person entails certain duties and privileges—in other words, it is a normative concept: what a person *ought to be* and do in order to be called a person. Personhood implies that one has certain social privileges and certain social duties, and that under extreme circumstances these can be revoked. What was a person to the Greeks? To the Romans? To Medieval Europe? To these groups a person was usually a male adult landowner or tribesmember. Different societies have excluded some or all of the following people from their concept of a person: slaves, women, children, foreigners, prisoners of war, and criminals. Usually the list of exclusion extended to animals, plants, and inanimate objects, but other beings might well be granted personhood, such as gods and goddesses, totems (ancestor animals), and dead ancestors.

In our type of society we usually identify persons with human beings—at least legally. Morally it remains a question. Do we treat every human being as a person with rights and personal dignity? AIDS patients might think not, and so might some retired people—there is considerable age discrimination in our society. There also is still the problem of racism and sexism. Mentally disabled citizens also may experience discrimination, and another large group in our society is only now coming under the scrutiny of social philosophers in terms of their status as persons: *children*. In previous times—in fact, as recently as the nineteenth century and, in some places, the twentieth century—the father of the household had the supreme right to treat his family (including his wife) any way he pleased. This might very well include physically punishing all the family members, even unto death. This right, *patria potestas*, is still in effect in certain societies in the world. The thought of protecting children against abuse, even abuse from their own parents, actually is quite a new idea in the Western world; but an even more novel idea is the thought that children have interests and wishes that they are capable of expressing and that should be heard, such as which parent they wish to stay with after a divorce. A landmark case in 1992 allowed a twelve-year-old boy to sue his natural mother for separation so that he could be adopted by his foster parents. He was granted that separation on the basis of parental neglect, and he now has a new life and new identity with his new family.

We are now at the point where the conscious interests of children (which can include everything from having enough food, shelter, love, and education to refusing to go to school and instead play videogames or watch TV) must be balanced against what conscientious adults deem to be in the children's best interests, best *in spite* of themselves. In other words, we must remember that what children want is not necessarily good for them. The idea that children are minors who have neither the legal rights nor the legal responsibilities of adults is not about to disappear, even when their interests are taken into consideration. We tend to forget that when a group is excluded from having rights, it also usually is excluded from having *responsibilities*. In other words, such a group must be given legal protection so that its members, who are incapable of taking on civil responsibilities, will not be treated unjustly.

Historically, the responsibility for animals and children has shifted back and forth. Until the mid-nineteenth century, animals could be held legally responsible for their actions (although they had very few recognized rights); all through the European Middle Ages rats, roaches, and other pests were put on trial (usually in absentia) for the damage they caused to human lives and property. Even in the United States, animals were put on trial for hurting their masters or their own offspring, and they were "executed" if found guilty. Today, when a pit bull attacks a small child and is put to death, do we consider ourselves to be "executing" the dog? Some might argue that that is exactly what we are doing—we are punishing the dog for transgressing a human law. But legally we simply are disposing of the dog's owner's property not as a punishment against the dog, but as a precaution against the public. Who *does* get punished? Not the dog, but the *owner*, who receives a fine or even a jail sentence. This is what happened a few years ago in California when a woman told her dog to attack another person. She was sentenced for using a deadly weapon. Today we don't consider animals to be legally responsible for their actions, because we don't consider them to be moral agents. A dog who fails to wake up her owners when the house is on fire will not be blamed for it afterward, though her owners might be blamed for not training her properly. (In previous times, when animals were put on trial, the issue of whether they were moral agents still was not solved, because it was commonly considered that they had no soul and thus had no free will. So were the people who put them on trial contradicting themselves? Yes. But so do we sometimes, and one of the objectives of discussing these issues is to get into the habit of thinking more consistently.)

The case of the legal responsibility of children parallels that of animals. It is only within this century that we in the Western world have agreed not to hold minors responsible for criminal acts. The famous German legendary figure Till Eulenspiegel was a mischievous kid who played one too many tricks on decent citizens, and the decent citizens hanged him. Herman Melville's *Billy Budd* faced the same fate. Billy, a young sailor, was falsely accused of wrongdoing by a vicious officer. Because Billy had a problem articulating and could not speak up to defend himself, he acted out his frustration by striking out at the officer. Unfortunately, this resulted in the officer's death, and the captain, although aware of Billy's problem, had to follow the law of the sea: mandatory death for anyone who strikes and kills an officer. In the end, Billy had to submit to the traditional execution method by climbing up the rigging and slipping a noose around his own neck. Today a crime committed by a person under the age of eighteen must reveal an extraordinary amount of callousness and "evil intent" in order for the court to try the minor as an adult. This is because childhood is considered to be a state of mind and body that doesn't allow for the logical consistency that we assume is available, most of the time, to adults; therefore children aren't held accountable for their actions to the degree that adults are.

In the past, women's rights have followed a course similar to that of animals and children. Women had very few rights until the late nineteenth century—no right to hold property, no right to vote, no right over their own person. This went hand in hand with the common assumption that women were not capable of moral consistency and thus were not responsible (mention of women and children in the same breath was no coincidence). This view often coincided with a male *reverence* for women and their supposedly higher moral standards, but such reverence often was combined with an assumption that women were idealists and had no conception of the sordid dealings and practical demands of the real world.

When it applied to women, the practice of holding only those with rights legally responsible was not strictly adhered to. Many, many women were put on criminal trial. Even so, the general idea was that withholding rights from women *protected* them from the harsh world of reality, whose demands they weren't capable of answering. A similar kind of argument kept slaves from having rights throughout most slaveholding societies—rights were denied in order to provide "protection" of these people because they were "incapable." This did not preclude punishing slaves, of course, as anyone who has read *Huckleberry Finn* knows. In *On Liberty* (see Chapter 5), John Stuart Mill argues that the right to self-determination should extend universally *pro-*

Is a Fetus a Person?

The debate over whether or not abortion should be generally available often focuses on the question of whether or not the fetus is a person. In some cultures the fetus is not a person at all; even the newborn infant is not considered a person until after a waiting period that usually is imposed to see if the baby will live. The view adopted by the Catholic church (but not by all churches or religious communities) is that the fetus is a person from conception. However, this has not always been Catholic dogma. The idea underlying this viewpoint is that the soul is present when the fetus *looks* human; thus, in earlier times, a fetus was not considered a person until well into the pregnancy. Saint Augustine specifically states that terminating a pregnancy before the fetus is able to *feel* anything should not be considered homicide, because until that point in time the soul is not present. However, in the late seventeenth century, a primitive microscope seemed to show that a tiny, fully formed person (a *homunculus*) could be seen in the spermatozoon, and so the church policy to consider the fetus a person from conception was established. The church policy remained unchanged even with the advent of better microscopes, which conclusively refuted the previous theory. One can of course choose to view the beginning of life as the beginning of personhood regardless of church policies and misunderstandings about microscopes. But there also are people who believe that it takes more to be a person than just having human genetic material. The philosopher Mary Ann Warren argues that a person has to have *language*, *self-motivation*, and *self-awareness*, among other things, to be considered a person; thus even the most developed fetus does not qualify. Another philosopher, Judith Jarvis Thomson, argues for the right to an abortion by saying that it does not matter whether the fetus is a person: what matters is that a woman has a right to *defend her body* against invasions—even if the fetus qualifies for personhood.

vided that the individuals in question have been educated properly, in the British sense, so that they know what to do with the self-determination. Until then, they are incapable of making responsible decisions and should be "protected"—children by their guardians, and colonial inhabitants by the British. (Today, an animal rights activist would argue that we see the same pattern repeated with animals: We don't believe them to be fully developed moral agents, and so we "protect" them—by withholding rights from them.) An interesting concept evolves from these arguments—namely that it is possible for someone to be considered a person, but a person with *limited* rights, duties, and privileges, whose rights are assigned to a guardian.

The Question of Interests and Rights

The philosopher Joel Feinberg suggests that whoever has *interests* should have *rights*. But what does it mean to have interests? Is an interest something that someone really *wants* (like quitting school, watching TV, or wanting drugs), or is an interest something that is *good* for someone (like being given vitamins)? Obviously, we can assess that a lot of things are good for living beings, humans and nonhumans alike: Clean water is good for wildlife, a safe environment is good for people, reading to small children is good for them, setting a curfew for adolescent children is good for them, and fertilizer is good for our tomatoes. But do our tomatoes *want* fertilizer? Do our children *want* a curfew, even if it is good for them? Do we *want* to go to the dentist, even if it is good for us? What we want and what is good for us are not always in agreement. And if interests include rights, does that mean that people have a right to anything that interests them, be it something they want *or* something that is good for them? It is preposterous to claim that just because someone *wants* drugs, or wants an item that does not belong to her, she has a *right* to that item (contrary to what some children and people with childish minds often believe). But if something is *good* for someone, is it preposterous to say that she has a right to it? And who decides what is good for someone? And shouldn't that someone's own wishes be taken into consideration?

These problems don't mean that the idea of interests should be thrown out—only that it must be discussed further. Like most interesting ideas, it is not a simple one; it does bring us closer to a recognition that just because you can't express what you want, it still may be possible for you to have some rights protected. So persons need not be only those people who are capable of protecting their own interests. Besides, the law grants person status to other entities, such as corporations, and religious people usually grant God (or several gods) person status. And given that there is legal and moral precedence for granting personhood to abstract entities, perhaps it someday will be granted to other entities, including animals. (We'll talk more about this later.)

Suffering as a Moral Criterion

Human Suffering

You may remember that Jeremy Bentham asked why we should focus just on humans when deciding who "counts" in a moral sense. In *Principles of Morals and Legislation*, he writes, "The question is not, Can they *reason*? nor Can they *talk*? but *Can they suffer*?" If Bentham's idea of suffering as qualification for moral attention is the one we want to follow, then the next question must be: Who can suffer, and how do we know?

One thing you know for a fact is that *you* can suffer. Your memory reminds you of the time you were inoculated, the time you broke your foot, the time you gave birth.

The Donner Party—Survival Statistics

In 1848 a party of immigrants coming to California became trapped by the winter snows in the high passes of the Sierra Nevada. The ill-fated Donner party is known mostly for having resorted to cannibalism. What is rarely told is that the majority of women and girls survived. Approximately one-fourth of the men, and three-fourths of the women lived through the ordeal. The women did not get special treatment, and some managed to pull through without eating human flesh.

Your senses tell you when your shoes are too tight, when you have a headache, when you have stomach cramps. Personal experience is the clearest evidence of suffering that anyone has. Unfortunately, it also is the only certain piece of evidence. How do we know that *others* are in pain? They usually tell us; their capacity for speech is our warrant. However, I know when I have a headache, but when you tell me you have a headache, how do I know you are telling the truth? The capacity for speech does not provide certain evidence of suffering. Our own pain is the only direct evidence; any other evidence of suffering is indirect. What if the sufferer's face goes white, she clenches her fists, she grinds her teeth, she moans, she clutches our hand. Do we believe her now? Usually, yes—and sometimes more so than if she had simply *told* us that she was hurting. But in the end, we *conclude* that the other human being is suffering—we don't *experience* it, and we can't *measure* it, at least not yet. Historically, people have been known to cast doubt on the suffering capacity of other people. Newborns were thought to have no or little sensation of pain, which is why circumcisions generally were administered without anesthetics (anesthetics also are dangerous to the newborn brain). A doctor recently performed an experiment in which she recorded the cries of a boy infant when he was hungry and when he was circumcised without anesthetics. There was a remarkable difference in the quality of the infant's screaming, so the doctor concluded that the infant was in considerable pain. Her conclusion probably was right, but it still was based on conjecture, not measurable evidence. Women were once thought to have a "lower pain threshold" than men and thus to be more fragile creatures. We now know that in spite of men's statistically greater physical strength, men and women have about the same general pain threshold, and it seems that women have slightly more endurance than men.

In earlier times, people of the lower classes were thought to have a less refined mind and thus less awareness of physical pain, than people of the higher classes. Similar arguments have been advanced about people of different races.

So the answer to the question, Who is suffering, and how do we know? is less obvious than it looks. In any case our answer reveals our view of the subject's moral standing: Does it count morally, or doesn't it?

FIGURE 14.1 René Descartes (1596–1650), French philosopher, mathematician, and naturalist. Descartes is known as the founder of modern philosophy, and he is particularly famous for having said "*Cogito, ergo sum,*" or "I think, therefore I am." Descartes believed that a human consists of a body and a soul; thanks to the soul, humans can be self-aware and conscious of their bodies, including physical pleasures and pains. But since Descartes couldn't imagine that animals have souls, he had to conclude that animals couldn't be aware of their physical condition, either, so the inevitable conclusion was, for him, that animals can't feel pain.

Animal Suffering

The follow-up question to who is suffering is: *Can animals suffer?* Anyone who has witnessed an injured animal has no doubt that they can. Anyone who has had a pet is equally certain. Of course animals can suffer—we might witness it every day of our lives if we put our minds to it and sought out places where animals are made to suffer for the convenience of human beings: labs, slaughterhouses, factory farms. Sensitivity to this issue is increasing, and some scholars have predicted that just as we have become sensitive to the predicaments of slaves, of women, of the poor, and of children, so we will become sensitive to the plight of the "slaves" of the twentieth century, animals. Such sensitivity is reflected in recent developments. In 1993 a judge sentenced a man to one year in prison for deliberately stepping on his girlfriend's kitten and crushing its spine. (The kitten had to be put to death.) And in Sweden a few years ago, a nationwide referendum was passed to ban all factory farming. (Factory farming involves raising animals for maximum yield and profit. Little concern is given for the welfare of the animals.) By law all farm animals have to spend at least three months of the year in the fields. This means that the Swedes pay more for their meat, but at least they know that the animals they eat for food were not mistreated. (For *vegans* [people who don't use animal products in any form], this is a paradox, because the law doesn't say anything about not *killing* farm animals. Indeed, the question of whether or not to kill animals has become an altogether different issue from that of preventing their suffering—and it is an issue that divides animal activists themselves.)

A counterargument to all of this can be voiced: It is all very well to say we should protect animals against suffering, but nature itself makes animals suffer, and in nature animals kill animals, often inflicting great pain. Humans are Homo sapiens; they eat meat, which allows them to occupy themselves with things other than finding food. So why change a natural thing that has worked for so long? One might answer that nature does a lot of things that we might not want to do, and don't have to do. Nature kills its weakest members—but that doesn't mean it would be a good idea for us to do the same thing. The Nazis took this approach in World War II, and their legacy reminds us of the atrocities committed for the purported purpose of strengthening what nature created. We are beings of culture; we can reason. We can decide whether to follow nature or not. If we think now is the time to distance ourselves from the "natural" path, we can do so. Animals can't decide that. (We will return to this question in Chapter 15.)

There are scholars who have doubted the suffering capacity of animals. Descartes (1596–1650), known as the founder of modern philosophy, believed that animals cannot feel pain, because they have no spirit (soul) that can tell them that they are in pain. In other words, they have no self-awareness, and without self-awareness there can be no pain. Pain is a state of mind, and if you have no mind, you have no pain. This is far from a crude and insensitive argument; indeed, it is the result of a complex theory of mind and matter, which we can't get into here. And Descartes is not alone. Other philosophers have arrived at the same conclusion: Because animals don't know they are in pain, they feel no pain. So what about the wretched animal that has been run over by a car? To Descartes, the screams and the frantic movements are not signs of pain but merely a mechanical reaction, as though the animal is a windup toy, or a clockwork. (In today's terminology he would probably have used terms such as *robots* or *computer hardware*.) How do we know that an injured *human* feels pain? The human has a "spirit," says Descartes, and is thus self-aware. For Descartes, the world is divided into spirit, which interacts with matter, and matter without spirit. Animals belong to matter without spirit and thus feel no more than a rock on a well-traveled road.

Other scholars have dismissed animal suffering based on a less sophisticated argument. They say that ascribing suffering to animals complicates the issue; it is easier to *assume* they can't feel pain. Today this argument does not hold up. As Australian utilitarian and animal activist Peter Singer points out, we now know so much about physiology that we can conclude that human and nonhuman animal nervous systems are very similar, to such a degree that it would complicate the issue if we assumed that animals feel radically *different* than humans. Besides, it is unthinkable, in an evolutionary sense, that a species would survive without the capacity for feeling pain. Imagine a totally insensitive creature being stalked and attacked by a predator. After being bitten, what would the prey do? Nothing, for it would feel no pain. Consequently, it would be eaten, and thus would bring no more of its own kind into the world. The end result would be that the species would become extinct. Evolutionarily speaking, it is to any living being's advantage to be able to feel pain so that it can escape danger and live to propagate its own kind.

It seems certain, then, that animals do feel pain. But how much pain do they feel? And should we let their moral relevance be determined by how much pain they feel? There could be some sense to that. Peter Singer suggests that we have some inkling as to the *amount* of pain felt by other animals (a horse can stand more pain than a human baby, for instance), and our concern for their well-being should reflect their relative capacity for suffering. Obviously fish don't feel as much pain as mammals, because they have a more rudimentary nervous system. This seems to be a sufficient argument for some vegetarians, who will not eat meat, but will eat fish. For a while there has been a vivid consumer campaign against certain tuna fish companies whose fishing methods cause dolphins to become accidentally captured in the nets; the dolphin meat and tuna meat are then combined in the canning process. When asked why they boycott the tuna companies in question, most consumers answer that dolphins shouldn't be eaten. Most people tend to agree with this, but the question is, why? It is not because dolphin meat is taboo (as is pork for Jews and Muslims) or is considered a nonfood, as are snakes and lizards. It is rather because we tend to "respect" the dolphin as a higher animal. But is it the dolphin's intelligence or its capacity for suffering that we respect? If we say that it is its capacity for suffering, some bright person will usually ask, "Well, how about feeling sorry for the tuna?" We still are faced with the problem of having no real way to measure pain.

The Capacity for Pleasure

A utilitarian criterion of moral relevance naturally includes not only suffering, but also the capacity for pleasure. Because our concern for animals usually has to do with protecting them from suffering, we rarely consider their capacity for pleasure. However, this topic must be included in any general discussion of moral criteria. Here again we are hampered by lack of knowledge: How great is the joy a gorilla experiences in a new, spacious zoo exhibit compared to what it might feel if it lived in an old, cramped exhibit or in its natural habitat? As we saw before, we can ask other people what they are feeling, but they may lie—to please us, or to save themselves, or for whatever reason. Even if animals seem to have the capacity to fool other animals deliberately, their reactions of pain and pleasure seem genuine. What it comes down to is the old utilitarian problem of what pleasure or happiness is. Is it simply the absence of pain? Or is it some specific warm and fuzzy feeling? The easiest explanation might be to conclude that human and nonhuman animals aren't that different in terms of what they need for their physical well-being, and all we need to do is ensure that they experience nonconstraint and freedom from starvation in their everyday lives. Anyone who has had pets knows that at certain times animals display something akin to "happiness" or ecstasy, as do humans. However, it has never been the object of utilitarianism to promote that idea—that would be much too complicated an objective. Freedom from pain, and general contentment are the highest obtainable goals for most utilitarians.

Who Should Be Saved?

What guidelines for making moral decisions can be drawn from the knowledge of animal suffering and the knowledge that not all animals suffer or rejoice to the same extent? Peter Singer has suggested a method: Look to the capacity for pain and joy in the animal in question, and make your decision based on what you find. We can elaborate on that with a rather extreme example inspired by Singer. Suppose you come across a house on fire. You know that inside the house is a three-year-old golden retriever and a three-year-old boy. You have time to save only one of them. Who would you save, taking Singer's criteria into consideration? The boy, for he has a greater capacity for suffering and joy than the dog (if not now, he will have it when he grows up). But suppose the occupants of the burning building are the dog and the boy's comatose granddad, who, the doctors say, will never regain consciousness. Whom should you save? The dog, who has a much higher capacity for pain and joy than the granddad at this point in his life. Now, what if all the people are out of the building, but in the house are the dog and the little boy's goldfish. Who should be saved? The dog, for the same reason: He has a much higher capacity for pain and joy. Finally, what if the only creatures inside the house are the goldfish and the little boy's collection of slugs. Why bother to save any of them? Because they are living creatures, and if you can help without great risk of injury to yourself, you should. So save the goldfish if you imagine them to have more capacity for pain and joy than the slugs. (Of course you really can't *know* about that.)

This hierarchy gives us some practical guidelines, to be sure, but it still is controversial; *we* are the ones deciding how much pain and joy the others can get out of life. It probably is the best we can do under the circumstances, though.

Rationality as a Moral Criterion

What Is Rationality?

If Kant's idea suits us better and we choose *intelligence* as the criterion for who counts morally, then we are faced with a different question: What exactly is "rationality"? We may say that it has two components: (1) the logical thinking process, and (2) its expression in action and/or speech. A bottom-line definition states that rationality is the recognition of the most cost-efficient way of achieving a goal, and then choosing to put that method into action. In other words, we might know what we want and realize that there are several ways we can get it, but we know some are difficult and some are uncertain. Rationality would then consist of choosing the most *effective* way of getting what we want. Many philosophers of the Enlightenment thought that if only people would put their minds to it, they could achieve perfect rationality at all times. Unfortunately, if we apply this criterion to people's everyday actions, we must conclude that what many people do is not exactly "rational." As J. S. Mill complained about Bentham's faith in the brain as a logical mechanism, humans aren't all that logical. Sometimes we know we should drive straight to work, but we get sidetracked and end up getting in late. We know we ought to write our term paper on time, but we procrastinate. We know we should shop early for Christmas, but we run around in circles on December 23 anyway. Psychoanalysis has taught us that the mind has its own "logic," which takes into consideration old habits, psychological repressions, and personal inclinations—and all of these may sidetrack us from following the most cost-effective path. Fortunately this doesn't mean that we are not rational beings, for we still have the *capacity* for rational thinking.

Who Is Rational?

As we have discussed, the Kantian criterion for granting someone respect and dignity is their capacity to think rationally in a practical sense—in other words, to apply the *categorical imperative* to any given situation. If we take this literally, precious few people would qualify as rational beings, but if we interpret the categorical imperative in a broader sense, it does seem like a fairly reasonable standard. If someone can decide on a course of action by asking, "How would I like it if this became a general rule?" or "What if everybody did this?" then that person has enacted the principle of *universalizability*, which says that I can't allow myself to do anything I wouldn't let you do under the same circumstances. (The "sour grapes" version is: If I can't do it, I won't let you do it, either.) We use this method to teach children about proper behavior. But can all humans actually perform this thought process? What about mentally disabled persons? What about infants? As we've seen, Kant's inherent problem is that he divides the world up into those who can—they are called persons—and those who can't—they are called things. But infants are hardly "things." Animals, who by Kant's definition can't perform this mental feat, are automatically classified as things.

It is fashionable these days to engage in a certain amount of "Kant-bashing" whenever animal rights are on the agenda. We should realize, though, that Kant was extremely conscientious when it came to gathering evidence, and proper evidence regarding animals' mental capacity simply wasn't available to him or to any scholar expressing theories about animal intelligence prior to the 1960s. We can blame him for not focusing on the capacity of animals to suffer, but not for being unaware that animals can think. Animal research has established beyond the doubt of most scholars that animals do have a rudimentary practical rationality, especially so-called "higher" animals. They understand quite well the cost-efficiency of a chosen course of action, and they can even be observed to calculate the best response to a given situation. A mother bear who is threatened can decide whether to hide or pick up the cubs and move them. A hungry dog whose master is away can decide to wait by the door or by the refrigerator. A hungry cat can decide to stay under the table during dinner, even if nothing is offered, because there may be scraps on the floor. A pet dog can decide to bark when there is smoke in the house. Knowing whether any of these actions is altruistic or basically self-centered is not essential for determining that the animals certainly are rational. But are animals always rational? Probably no more than people are, but that shouldn't disqualify them. Of course animals don't have the higher intellectual capacities of humans, but dolphin, gorilla, and chimpanzee experiments have established that at least some animal intelligence embraces a certain understanding even of grammar and of hypothetical situations.

Most higher animals can be trained to fetch hoops or balls, especially if the correct action is rewarded with food. B. F. Skinner's theory holds that even complex human actions are nothing but *reward-oriented* actions (we will take a closer look at Skinner in the next chapter). However, one experiment has attempted to show that dolphins not only can be trained to perform tricks but also can understand certain linguistic concepts. The dolphin is presented with a sentence of three words, such as "fetch hoop ball," which means that the hoop is supposed to go over the ball. The dolphin performs the trick accordingly. Then the command is changed to "fetch ball hoop." To creatures with no sense of grammar, the two sentences will mean the same—but the dolphin grasps that now the ball is supposed to be brought to the hoop and thrown through the middle. This and other experiments like it have been used as evidence that dolphins have some sense of grammar.

When told of this experiment, disbelievers might remind us that once there was a horse in Germany (in the early twentieth century) called Clever Hans. Clever Hans was supposed to be very clever, for he could do math, or so his owner said. Ask him any question of math, said the owner, and Hans will stomp the right number with his front leg! And Hans did, to the astonishment of the crowds in Germany, and again to the astonishment of German scientists, who decided to put him to a test: They took the trainer aside and asked Hans the questions *themselves*. The horse still got the answers right. Then, after having almost agreed that Clever Hans could do math, they tried one last experiment—they blindfolded Hans. And that was the end of Hans's cleverness in math. He literally didn't have a clue as to what the answer was. What had happened was this. As Hans stomped out the answer, he kept an eye on his trainer, and by the time he reached the right number of stomps, the trainer imperceptibly *cued* him, with a slight nod of his head and blink of his eyes. The trainer may not even have been aware of it; it is obvious that the scientists who asked Hans the questions did the same cuing without even knowing it. Any question-answer situation follows the same pattern: If the questioner knows the right answer, he or she will unconsciously give a physical cue when the answer is right. (Even college professors do this—watch their eyes!) So was Hans clever? Yes, he was very clever at understanding human psychology. But he was never credited for that. And some scholars, like Thomas Sebeok, have for years been saying that dolphins and other lab animals involved in intelligence experiments are just a bunch of Clever Hanses. In order to disprove this, the trainers go through rigorous training themselves and wear masks that hide their eyes and facial features in order to avoid the Clever Hans syndrome.

Especially controversial these days are the cases of apes who use sign language to communicate. The most famous one is probably Koko the gorilla. Koko was taught sign language and was able to communicate with her trainers. Not only was she able to let them know she'd like some more fruit and cookies, but also she was able to let her trainers know about her feelings. Her trainers realized that she was capable of feeling joy and sorrow, and she even displayed a sense of self-awareness. She could recognize herself in photographs and identify herself as a gorilla, not a human, because she had seen pictures of other gorillas. There are video recordings of her toying with

FIGURE 14.2 The gorilla Koko with her kitten. Koko has been taught sign language, and her level of awareness has surprised researchers. She recognizes herself in the mirror and in photos, and this has led some researchers to the conclusion that animal intelligence may not be different in kind from human intelligence, merely different in degree.

a red cap in front of a mirror; she seems to be absolutely aware that she is seeing herself. For a short while she had a Manx kitten in her care, and she treated it the way a child would who had a pet. The kitten died, and Koko expressed signs of severe grief and an understanding that the little cat was dead. After a while she requested another cat, preferably a Manx.

Another example involves Bonobo chimpanzees, presumably the most intelligent animals on this earth aside from humans. A mother chimp, Matata, was taught written language (using lexigram, not our alphabet) while her tiny son, Kanzi, was in the room. Over a period of time not only did Kanzi pick up on the lexigram himself, without being taught by the staff, but he also kept expanding his vocabulary even when his mother lost interest in the game. This has been interpreted as direct evidence that nonhuman animals can display linguistic behavior even when no reward is involved. Kanzi is now an adult and part of an extended research program. He is involved with experiments that have to do with inventing tools, and according to a *Time* magazine article (March 1993) he has successfully solved the problem of how to open a locked box containing foodstuff. First he figured out how to open another box, which contained the key: He manufactured a sharp implement (a "knife") by smashing some

FIGURE 14.3 *Blade Runner*, Warner Bros., 1982. Even a replicant wants to live: Batty (Rutger Hauer) and Deckard (Harrison Ford) in the dramatic conclusion of the film. Batty, dying because of a built-in self-destruct mechanism, shows that even with only four years of life, an artificial intelligent being can develop a sense of wonder and emotion—in a sense, develop a soul. And Deckard is left wondering about the nature of his own humanity. The story of *Blade Runner* is outlined in Chapter 20 as an illustration of the question of personhood and human rights.

flint pieces until he had made a cutting edge (much the same as prehistoric humans used to do). Then he took his flint knife, cut the cord that kept the box with the key closed, took the key, and unlocked the box with the food.

More and more, scientists seem to be ready to accept the possibility that rationality is not a matter of a difference in *kind* between humans and nonhuman animals, but rather a difference in *degree*. Human intelligence is of course on a different scale than any other animal intelligence, but that doesn't mean that some nonhuman animals can't use their minds to make rudimentary logical conclusions. If intelligence counts, even in its most rudimentary form, then animals can't be excluded from having some standing in the human moral universe. We should remember, though, that Kant is not just concerned with the capacity for *thinking*, but with the kind of thinking that can envision living by a *universal moral law*. Because Kanzi, now in his prime, has reached the intellectual level of only a 2-1/2-year-old child, there is not much chance that he or any other nonhuman animal might qualify as a person on Kant's terms anytime soon. However, Kant is more generous about what beings he includes in the category of "ends in themselves" than most humans would be. All he requires is that a being is able to think logically. If we were visited by extraterrestrials who revealed themselves to us and turned out to be rational beings, Kant would welcome them as persons with all the rights and duties of humans. He might even include the hypothetical super-computers of the future or the cyborgs and robots that we know well from science fiction—*2001's* HAL, the robots in *The Terminator*, *Blade Runner's* dying replicants, and the android Data from *Star Trek: The Next Generation*.

Trees and Other Elements of Nature

In Hans Christian Andersen's fairy tale of Little Ida's Flowers, a little girl, Ida, is upset that the flowers in the vase, which were so beautiful the day before, are now all wilted, but a college student living with her family comforts her: The flowers are just tired, because they have been to the King's Ball all night; flowers have a life of their own at night, he tells her, and sometimes they even leave their stalks and fly off to seek new adventures—butterflies are really flowers in flight! A sour old government official grumbles, "Why teach the child a lot of nonsense?" But the student insists that flowers are alive, have feelings, and can communicate, not with words, but with gestures. That night, Ida sneaks into the living room and watches to see if the flowers come alive, and they do! They are joined by all the flowers in the yard, and all night they are dancing. Her own flowers, which have come back to life, ask Ida to bury them in the yard next day, for then their life will be over, but they will come back next sum-mer. The next morning, when Ida wakes up, she knows the student was right. And we, the readers, know that Ida was dreaming, because we (or most of us) have turned into cynics, just like the sour old government official.

As adults, we know this story to be a metaphor for the magic of childhood, which should be the birthright of any child. But suppose the story were true? Suppose the flowers could tell us whether they wanted to be in the sun or the shade, and suppose the tree communicated that it would prefer that we not lower the waterline, or else it will die. In a sense these things do happen; plants do "communicate" with us to let us know their needs—not in a conscious sense, but quite mechanically. When they need water they droop; when they need sun they look pale and get long and scraggly. So it seems that plants do have interests, even if they aren't aware of it. Does that mean we should think of including them in our moral universe as beings with some standing?

This is a question that some scholars predict will be bothering us long after we've settled the question of animal rights—and, as with animal rights, it will have far-reaching consequences. It provokes the same question we asked before when considering our treatment of animals: If we decide not to be cruel to these living things, for whose sake are we doing it? For the sake of people or animals? If we decide to grant the right to life to plants, are we doing it because people like to look at trees or because trees like to continue to grow?

In 1974 Christopher D. Stone wrote a paper, "Should Trees Have Standing? Towards Legal Rights for Natural Objects." Many dismissed the paper as complete nonsense at the time. However, it has gained in influence since then. In the paper Stone states that every time we have opted to include another group in our welfare concern, such as slaves, women, minorities, children, or animals, the decision has been met with ridicule before it has achieved common acceptance. He proposes that we now expand our moral universe to cover not only individual animals, but also species and natural objects such as lakes and streams, mountain meadows, marshes, and so on (who really can't be said to have interests since they are not "alive"):

> Wherever it carves out "property" rights, the legal system is engaged in the process of *creating* monetary worth. . . . I am proposing we do the same with eagles and wilderness areas as we do with copyrighted works, patented inventions, and privacy: *make* the violation of rights in them to be a cost by declaring the "pirating" of them to be the invasion of a property interest. If we do so, the net social costs the polluter would be confronted with would include not only the extended homocentric cost of his pollution [. . .] but also cost to the environment *per se*.

What Stone suggests here is a grand solution not only to the problem of whose rights should be protected, but also to the problem of *how* they should be protected. He proposes fining polluters because it is *bad for nature*, regardless of whether there are people who want to go there or not. It would take us too long to discuss in detail the concept of giving rights to plants and natural objects such as rocks and streams (and of course we'd want to include cultural objects such as historical buildings, old baseball fields, statues, favorite movie locations, and so on). The question is, how far do we want to go, not in assigning protection for the environment—because we can take that as far as we want to go—but in assigning rights per se, regardless of human interest in the subject? If nobody cares about a certain meadow, or about the building in downtown Los Angeles where they filmed *Blade Runner* (the Bradbury building, incidentally), then should we give it rights on the basis that someone may someday care, or because it has acquired those rights just by hanging around?

If we do want to assign rights to plants, where do we stop? It is all well and good to preserve a good-looking row of trees, but what about preserving a scraggly row of carrots on the grounds that they have a right to life? What we have here is a *slippery slope argument*. There are three paths we can take: (1) Abandon our original position of granting rights to trees, because the consequences now seem ridiculous; (2) Admit that we must take the consequences seriously and stop eating carrots or any other plant that we kill by eating it (cucumbers and tomatoes are all right, because the plant doesn't die when the cucumber is eaten); (3) Look for a good place on the slippery slope and dig in, because, in your opinion, "there is a difference between trees and carrots." If we choose the third path, we had better have convincing arguments ready.

Regardless of whether we choose to view the environment as ethically relevant for the sake of humanity (an *anthropocentric* approach), or for the sake of the environment as such (a *biocentric* approach), it is now becoming clear to many people that we must include environmental considerations in our contemporary concept of ethics. Such an approach, involving questions of the environment, is sometimes referred to as *bio-ethics*, and it is likely that the role of bioethics will increase considerably in the years to come.

Some Solutions

In a book called *Can Animals and Machines Be Persons?* (1985) Justin Leiber toys with the idea that a future panel of counselors has to decide whether or not to close down a space station. The station costs too much, and the private business that has been footing the bill is not willing to continue to do so. But on the station are two beings whose "lives" are dependent on the station: the chimp Washoe-Delta and the super-computer Al. They are not humans, but are they "persons" in the sense that they should have certain rights? Washoe can't display human intelligence, but she has been a nice companion for the station crew, she can feel pain and pleasure, and she certainly is more rational than a human infant or a severely mentally disabled human. Al, on the other hand, feels no pain or pleasure, but Al can think rationally and is aware of itself and its situation. The book leaves the question open, although the author has a clear bias toward granting personhood to both beings. Washoe can suffer, so we should grant her rights (this corresponds to Bentham's ideas). Al can think, so we should grant it rights (this harkens back to Kant's ideas). Who pays? The book does not say. It merely stands as an example of *applied ethical pluralism* (see Chapter 12); it applies different theories to different parts of the same problem, and because it does not pretend to solve all other problems, it gets away with it.

The idea of granting rights to artificial persons can be relevant for only two reasons: (a) because artificial persons actually exist (and they don't—yet); and (b) because the

Do Humans Always Count for More?

The whole debate about displaying moral responsibility in our treatment of animals hinges on whether one believes there is a good reason for doing so. One might believe that because the Bible ensures that humans are the masters of the earth, there is no reason to take animal suffering into consideration. Or one might believe that even though animals do have a capacity for suffering, humans are more important per se because of their higher capacity for reasoning or for feeling pleasure and pain. In each case the basic argument is the same: Because we are humans, we have an inherent right to put humans first. Philosophers such as Peter Singer would label this *speciesism*. Other terms for the same attitude are *homocentrism* and *human chauvinism*.

debate reveals something about our efforts and failings in granting rights to humans and other creatures now and in the past. The Leiber debate is relevant for the second reason. Usually the debate over the right to person status has centered more on the rights of animals and "marginal" humans (a group that once included women, children, slaves, and minorities, and that still includes children, to some extent, mentally disabled people, sick people, and so on). In a paper called "Persons and Non-Persons" the philosopher Mary Midgley has suggested that we look less toward the Kantian criterion of rationality and more toward the Benthamian solution, and ask about (1) the animal's capacity for suffering, and (2) its capacity for bonding with other individuals, either of its own species or another species, including humans. The greater the awareness of suffering, and the deeper the sense of bonding, the sooner we should be ready to grant at least some rights of personhood to that animal. Does this mean that animals should be considered our "equals"? Not in the sense that they should be treated *the same way* as humans (and be given the right to vote or assigned a drinking age). There are factual differences that warrant different treatment. It seems evident that humans have a greater capacity for certain pleasures than animals do— partly in terms of what J. S. Mill would call the "higher pleasures," but also in terms of *anticipating* pleasure. Similarly, humans have a higher capacity for suffering in terms of *dreading* the future. Animals presumably can't visualize the future, but they can experience extreme fear in situations where adult humans would know that the discomfort is temporary. The fear of danger is as vivid in an animal caught by zoologists for tagging purposes as it is in an animal caught in a hunter's trap. A policy of animal rights must take the full range of animal consciousness into consideration: Animals wouldn't enjoy being granted human privileges such as access to a good education, but they are capable of enjoying a clean and reasonably safe environment. Our efforts to promote animal happiness or prevent animal suffering must result in consequences that the animals are capable of experiencing and benefiting from.

A practical outcome of this debate might be to appoint a guardian or legal counsel to humans or animals who can't defend their own rights in the courts, and to appoint similar human guardians to individual animals or species whose interests need looking after. In a legal sense, these humans and animals would then become "persons" in the same manner that corporations are (unless legal minds would insist that corporations are "persons" only because they *consist of* persons). So it seems that it might be possible to have a responsible ethic with an expansion of the term *personhood*, provided that we add a set of guidelines for responsible treatment of those who do not qualify as persons.

Narratives That Explore the Concept of Personhood

Chapter 20 includes a selection of narratives that illustrate the subjects discussed in Part 4. Several stories discuss what it means to be a person with a person's rights and privileges. *Orphan of Creation* explores the possibility of a species of prehominids still existing on this earth, and the moral and political problems such a finding might entail. The film *Blade Runner* envisions a future of humanity in which intelligent and physically perfect "replicants" are denied human rights. Jorge Luis Borge's "The Circular Ruins" tells of the power of imagination and the difficulty of telling dream from reality. The classic story of *Pinocchio* asks what it takes to become a real boy if you are a wooden puppet who has no conscience. The episode "The Measure of a Man" from the television series *Star Trek: The Next Generation* asks whether an intelligent android should be considered a person with human rights, or merely a machine, a piece of property.

Chapter 15

Can We Decide Our Own Actions?

DETERMINISM VERSUS FREE WILL

As we discussed previously, the term *human nature* generally implies a set of characteristics that human beings can't help displaying. If we can't behave any differently from what our nature allows, there is no sense in trying, or in blaming ourselves or others when we don't change. The ultimate logical conclusion of this concept is known as *determinism*, which is the idea that if we knew enough about people (about human nature), we could predict their every move.

Fatalism, Predestinarianism, and Karma

Conceptually, determinism is related to two other theories of predetermined human behavior: fatalism and predestinarianism. But there are major differences in both the origin and the scope of these theories. Fatalism is a religious theory that assumes that everything happens according to *fate*, or *the Fates*. Both Greek and Scandinavian mythology embrace the image of three old women (the "Fates" or "Nornes") who measure out the threads of life for every human being, without regard for the individual actions of any human being. Whatever will be, will be, and nothing humans can do will have any effect upon the destiny of each individual. The British author Somerset Maugham tells the story of one man's fate:

> Death speaks: "There was a merchant in Bagdad who sent his servant to market to buy provisions and in a little while the servant came back, white and trembling, and said, 'Master, just now when I was in the marketplace I was jostled by a woman in the crowd and when I turned I saw it was Death that jostled me. She looked at me and made a threatening gesture: now, lend me your horse, and I will ride away from this city and avoid my fate. I will go to Samarra and there Death will not find me.' The merchant lent him his horse, and the servant mounted it, and he dug his spurs in its flanks and as fast as the horse would gallop he went. Then the merchant went down to the marketplace and he saw me standing in the crowd and he came to me and said, 'Why did you make a threatening gesture to my servant when you saw him this morning?' 'That was not a threatening gesture,' I said, 'it was only a start of surprise. I was astonished to see him in Bagdad, for I had an appointment with him tonight in Samarra.' "

Fatalism, then, holds that we cannot escape our destiny; no one can have any effect on the course our lives will take. Predestinarianism, on the other hand, holds that God is not only omniscient but also all-powerful. (He also is supposed to be all-good, but predestinarianism tends to play down that element.) It is a Christian theory held primarily by certain Protestant groups. From the beginning of time God has known what will happen in the future, who will be a sinner, and who will be a saint. *Everyone* is tainted by the *original sin* and deserves eternal punishment. It is only by God's grace, which He grants at random or at least according to rules known only to Him, that some sinners are allowed to share eternity with Him. Whether a person will end up in Heaven or Hell has nothing to do with his or her good or bad deeds. (So, you might ask, what is the point of being good? The believer in predestinarianism has two answers: (1) Do you only do good in order to be rewarded? How selfish of you; and (2) Do good anyway—God may decide to take your good deeds into consideration.)

The Hindu and Buddhist concept of *karma* may look like another version of fatalism, but actually it is quite different and much more closely related to mechanistic determinism. As we discussed in Part 3, karma is a theological concept that has its place in a religious worldview that embraces reincarnation. It teaches that your actions in this life will determine your status in your next incarnation, just as your status in this life was determined by your actions in previous lives. You may be working your way toward an existence as a worm or as a high priest. Whatever you do will have consequences. Hindus believe you can work on accumulating good consequences for your next life—a better status of living, or freedom from poverty and disease. However, classical Buddhists believe *any* concern for future incarnations further ties you to the "wheel of life," where you will be doomed to incarnation after incarnation. Total disdain of future incarnations is just as bad, because a negative attitude will tie you to life just as much as a positive one will. The solution is to remain in mental equilibrium and not let things disturb you in any positive or negative sense. Eventually you will reach a full understanding of your previous incarnations, and will escape the wheel of life for good.

What makes the theory of karma so different from fatalism is that there is no higher power who decides your fate. *You* decide your fate through your actions. Your fate is a purely mechanistic result of whatever your actions are. What makes karma different from mechanistic determinism is that it assumes that at any time we are free to change our course. The present has been determined by the past, but the present also allows us to determine our own futures. So karma represents a form of causality sometimes known as *self-determination*. The psychological as well as social consequences of a theory of karma are profound. Because your social situation has been determined by what you yourself have (or have not) done in the past, there is little room for pity from others; you have made the bed yourself, and now you're lying in it. Thus, social programs designed to improve on the conditions of those in need are not prompted by the theory of karma, which holds that each *individual* is responsible for his or her own condition. On the other hand, giving help to the needy may be part of improving one's own karma.

Mechanistic Determinism

Prediction and Behavior Control

Both fatalism and predestinarianism are theological theories, that is, they believe that some divine power has decided the fate of the world in this life and the next. Determinism, on the other hand, is primarily a result of eighteenth and nineteenth century science. Although the ancient Greek philosophers Leucippus and Democritus speculated on the predetermined movements of particles, and other philosophers have in the past viewed human nature as a response to physical forces, it was not until Western scientific theory developed the idea of causation to its fullest extent that the idea of determinism emerged as a compelling definition of human nature—a purely mechanistic theory of cause and effect, based on scientific insight. Science tells us that same causes give same effects, and the more we know, the better we can predict and control the effects. Therefore, according to determinism, *100 percent knowledge would yield 100 percent accuracy in predicting future events and understanding past events*. Nothing is generated out of nowhere; everything has a cause. Thousands of years of believing that old rags and dirt *spontaneously* generate mice and fleas came to an end once science demonstrated a clear cause-and-effect relationship that proved that mice and fleas come from other mice and fleas.

Science today generally is based on the principle of causality: The more knowledge we have, the better we can understand geological events, climatic events, and biologi-

FIGURE 15.1 B. F. Skinner (1904–1990), American psychologist, associated with the school of behaviorism. Skinner, a materialist, held that there was no such thing as a mind or mental life but that all experiences were a result of physical stimuli and responses.

cal events of the past, present, and future. Science doesn't necessarily assume that we have that kind of knowledge, or that we will ever have it, but it assumes that it is *logically possible* to achieve it and to make accurate predictions on that basis. A theory of ethics has no problem with scientific causality. The problem arises when scientific causality is applied to the *human world*, to the realm of human decision making.

Imagine a barbecue party on a canyon rim in Southern California. There is lots of scrub down below in the canyon, and on the rim a lot of beer is flowing. Foolishly, the partygoers have placed a barbecue on the rim. Someone knocks it over, and the result is predictable: The canyon burns, causing loss of homes on the other side, the death of countless coyotes and rabbits, and so on. What happened? Scientifically, the grill caused the ignition of some bushes; the fire spread; the houses burned; the animals died, and so on. Fire investigators use this line of reasoning in order to establish responsibility—*who* started the fire, and why? Suppose a partygoer kicked over the grill *on purpose*—just to be mean. He or she will get a bill from the fire department in addition to a jail term, because he or she obviously is responsible. What if the grill got knocked over by accident? Suppose the partiers were horsing around or were drunk. Will the fire investigator still hold them responsible? Yes, because they should have behaved themselves and thought of the consequences of horsing around and drinking. But suppose a partygoer had a seizure and fell against the grill, which then tumbled down into the canyon. Then we would not hold the person responsible, because he or she couldn't help what happened. This is where determinism becomes philosophically interesting. The determinist takes the causal chain one step further and claims that *none of the three cases is significantly different, because in none of the cases did the people involved have any free decision or free will.* In each case there is a cause that explains the ensuing action, and thus what we believed to be a matter of choice becomes simply one link in a predetermined chain of events.

The most influential proponent of this theory in the United States was B. F. Skinner (1904–1990), professor of psychology at Harvard University. Working on the

What Is Free Will?

In moral philosophy "free will" is not the same as "free choice"—free choice is a political concept. But the political concept of being able to choose freely whom to marry, where to live, or what education to get provokes the same basic question we've been asking about freedom of the will: We think the choices we make are ours—we think they are made freely—but are they really? Our common sense tells us that we are free to choose, at least most of the time, and that we will be held responsible for what we do. We don't blame people for actions beyond their control, though. You may remember the saying "ought implies can"—that we can't be expected to do what is impossible for us to do. Believers in freedom of the will usually claim that although humans may not be free to choose all the time, they have that freedom at least some of the time. However, there are indeterminists who believe we *always* have a choice, and thus we always can be held responsible. If you are late for a final exam and your tire blows on the freeway, you may think you are the victim of circumstances and should be eligible for a makeup test, but if your instructor is an indeterminist he or she may point out that you still had options— you could have left home earlier, you could have hitched a ride, you could have *tried something*. Most instructors are not so unyielding, but Jean-Paul Sartre's followers, who hold an *existentialist* viewpoint, would insist that there are no excuses, good or bad: You always retain responsibility.

assumption suggested by psychologist J. B. Watson that mental states really don't exist but are merely a function of physical behavior, Skinner further developed the branch of psychology known as *behaviorism*. The key element of behaviorism is that it views human behavior as primarily a matter of environmental influences (stimuli) and physical responses to these stimuli. In this manner human behavior can be controlled through *conditioning*. If a certain behavior produces unpleasant results over a period of time, it can be negatively reinforced; the negative reinforcement will cause the subject to stop that behavior. If a behavior produces pleasant results, it can be positively reinforced; the positive reinforcement will cause the subject to continue the behavior. All behavior can be explained by such primarily environmental conditioning. The more we know about stimuli and responses, the better we can predict and control behavior: We can raise well-behaved children, make people stop smoking, explain why people get angry or fall in love or perform heroic deeds. For Skinner we never need to take recourse in any talk about "mentalistic" concepts such as intelligence, dreams, personalities, virtues, memories, wishes, or interests, for they all can be reduced to physical responses to physical stimuli, and they all are subject to increasingly effective prediction and control. Accordingly, there is no such thing as freedom of the will.

The problem is: If our behavior is determined by heredity or the environment, can we then ever be held *responsible*? If we can't, the entire objective of ethics is undermined: We never can strive to be better, we can't be held accountable for what we do, and we can't hold others accountable. For a theory of human nature this means that the more we know about people, the more accurately we can predict their behavior. The freedom we think we have to make decisions is just an illusion—we can't help being as we are and doing what we do. For some thinkers this idea is intolerable, because human freedom is considered an inherent part of what being human means.

Nature or Nurture?

We often ask ourselves whether our character is shaped by "nature" or "nurture"—by heredity or environment. Both theories are of course deterministic, if we mean that either one is the *only* factor that makes our character the way it is. Usually, when we discuss whether heredity or environment is the most important factor, we imply that a certain amount of choice also goes into determining our character. Determinism doesn't allow for that possibility. But if we look at a child's development and forget about the aspect of free will for a while, is there a scientific consensus as to whether nature or nurture is the strongest factor? Most people agree that the environment plays an important part in a child's development, but research now seems to show that genetic factors can be very significant, too. A child with a resilient genetic heritage can emerge unscathed from years spent growing up in a dysfunctional family; another child, who is less resilient, may be emotionally scarred for life. Children of alcoholics apparently have to watch their own drinking habits as adults, even if they have grown up in nondrinking foster families; this is because there is now thought to be a genetic component to alcoholism. Not everything is a matter of genes, but genes seem to play a more important role in our behavior than scientists used to think.

Recent research with twins separated from birth has yielded fascinating results. Often, twins who have been separated for decades not only look alike but also work alike and even taste alike. (Two brothers who had been separated were both heavy and mustached; both were fire chiefs; both preferred the same brand of beer; and both were bachelors.) The proposed explanation for this is that although twins who grow up together make a point of being different (because children and young adults usually don't enjoy being dressed alike and considered one of a pair), twins who are unaware of each other have no such pressure to differentiate themselves, so their natural tendencies develop freely, and similarly. This theory assumes that such twins have some choice in the matter. Determinism would say it is all heredity and environment; in the case of the brothers who grew up apart it is more heredity than environment and in the case of twins who grow up together it is more environment than heredity—what Skinner calls *counter-control*: You feel a pressure from your environment, and you respond by trying to control it.

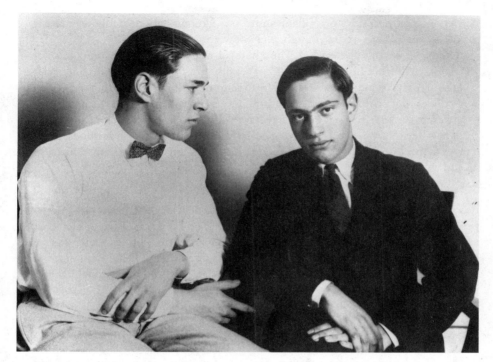

FIGURE 15.2 In the early twenties Leopold and Loeb killed Loeb's 14-year-old cousin, Bobby Franks, just to see if they could commit the perfect crime. However, they were soon found out. Because of their lawyer Clarence Darrow's defense, based on the theory of determinism, they were sentenced to life in prison instead of to death by hanging.

Determinism in Court: Leopold and Loeb—and Others

Determinism has had a marked influence in validating the concept of no responsibility in the courts.

In the early 1920s two boys decided to commit murder just to see if they could commit "the perfect crime." The boys' names were Nathan Leopold and Richard Loeb, and their victim—whom they chose by accident, because he happened by— was Loeb's fourteen-year-old cousin, Bobby Franks. They bludgeoned him to death and left him in a storm drain. Then they went home and mailed a ransom note, typed on a stolen typewriter, to Bobby's parents.

Bobby was soon found. The police had no problem tracing the letter to the typewriter, and the boys were arrested. It was a surprise to the community, because both boys were from "good families." The boys' families asked the famous lawyer Clarence Darrow to defend their sons. This was part of his defense of Richard Loeb (there was no jury, only one judge):

I know that there are no accidents in nature. I know that effect follows cause. I know that, if I were wise enough, and knew enough about this case, I could lay my finger on the cause. . . . The child, of course, is born without knowledge. . . . Dickie Loeb was a child of wealth and opportunity. . . . But, Your Honor, it is just as often a great misfortune to be a child of the rich as it is to be a child of the poor. . . . Here was a boy at a tender age, placed in the hands of a governess, intellectual, vigorous, devoted, with a strong ambition for the welfare of this boy. He was pushed in his studies, as plants are forced in hothouses. He had no pleasures, such as a boy should have, except as they were gained by lying and cheating.

So, Darrow continued, the boy turned to detective stories, and because of what Darrow called "childhood delusions," he and Leopold developed the idea to commit the perfect crime. (We should mention here that throughout the trial Leopold and Loeb are referred to as "boys" or "children," although at the time of the crime they were eighteen and nineteen years old, and both were attending college. The diminutive terms used by Darrow are a clever lawyer's trick.) So, Darrow contended, Dickie can't be blamed for his actions—he is a victim of circumstances. Can we, then, blame the governess? No, she did what she thought best, and besides, it logically follows that she was part of a causal chain, too, as were the parents (and as is Darrow himself, and the honorable Judge):

Nature is strong and she is pitiless. She works in her own mysterious way, and we are her victims. We have not much to do with it ourselves. . . . What had this boy to do with it? . . . He did not make himself. And yet he is to be compelled to pay.

The judge sent the boys to prison for life. Loeb died there in his thirties; he was stabbed to death in the shower by another inmate. Leopold lived until 1971. So, Darrow didn't win the case? In a way he did—because the boys could have been sentenced to hang; there was no hesitation about trying adolescents as adults in 1924. Darrow suggested that if the boys had been taken to a hospital for a psychiatric evaluation, the doctors would have found that they were not to blame. Today, a psychiatric evaluation is performed on any juvenile offender—it is standard procedure at trials for serious crimes.

Can we be certain that Darrow was a true believer in determinism? That he left the courtroom firmly convinced that he did not have the freedom of will even to choose his next case? Actually, yes. His defense, which utilized determinism, was not just a lot of rhetoric; he was a firm believer in the new deterministic theory of psychiatry. The Leopold and Loeb defense opened the door for a number of similar defenses with which we are quite familiar—the type of defense that points to the violence encountered by a murderer, or the childhood abuse suffered by a child-molester. One of the most famous of such defenses has come to be known as the "Twinkie defense." In 1978 the mayor of San Francisco, George Moscone, was killed by a man named Dan White. White's lawyer claimed that he was not to blame because he was on a sugar "high" from eating too many Twinkies. The court took this factor into consideration, giving him a lenient sentence. Another version of the same defense was attempted in the eighties during the aftermath of the San Ysidro, California, massacre at a McDonald's restaurant. The widow of the accused mass murderer, James Huberty, tried to take the fast food chain to court, claiming that her husband had suffered from a chemical imbalance due to eating too many Big Macs. The case was never brought to trial.

Darrow opened a can of worms when he offered his "victim of circumstances" defense, because it raised the question, If nobody is responsible, can we ever punish anybody? A determinist might actually agree to punishment even without responsibility; as the philosopher W. T. Stace explains it, the punishment could be considered an added "cause" to make the person behave better next time or to deter others from committing the same offense.

Everything Has a Cause

Few people doubt that there is such a thing as bad influence—or good influence, for that matter. Such an influence usually is regarded as a push in a certain direction, but it certainly is not the sole determinant of an action—one's *decision* to follow the good or bad influence is the most important part of a human action. For determinists, though, there is *only* influence, and one's decision is either an illusion, or else the final inevitable link in a causal chain (depending on which determinist you ask). The determinist argument is quite forceful: Is there, it asks, any action in your past or present that has not had a cause based either on your genetic makeup (your *heredity*) or on what you've been taught or exposed to (your *environment*)? Your decision to go on a diet—do you think that was a free decision? No, it was determined by societal pressures, combined with your doctor's advice and the product ads on TV. It is all manipulation, and even the manipulators do not manipulate freely; they too are victims of their heredity and their environment. Your decision to go to Europe, to explore the streets of Seville, to go see the statue of the Little Mermaid in Copenhagen—wasn't that free? No, it was determined by the stories you heard, reports of friends who had gone there, ads for cheap fares, and perhaps a genetic Wanderlust. Our decision to change our major, to date, to marry, to have children—all are determined by our heredity and environment. And when we look at it that way, it becomes downright impossible to think of any action that did not have a preceding cause. This is what the determinist relies on—and this, strangely enough, is what contributes to the downfall of the theory. The theory tricks us into thinking that because we can't think of any action without a cause, no action reflects freedom of the will.

But what exactly is freedom of the will? Can freedom of the will pertain even when an action has no "cause"? Imagine a crowded movie theatre. The lights are out, the movie is just starting, and all of a sudden a moviegoer starts singing "Louie Louie" as loud as he can. The other moviegoers gag him. When he is asked why he did it, he says, "I couldn't help myself; I don't know what came over me." Is that a case of free will in action? No, because the person clearly did not make a conscious decision to start singing; probably the singing had some psychological cause. (You may remember that the French philosopher Bergson seems to have believed that such outbursts were a sign that one's inner self is free—but most psychologists today would call such actions examples of compulsory behavior. We will get back to Bergson shortly.) The point is, when we claim that something was our free decision, we usually mean that we know why we did it—that after a certain deliberation, based on whatever knowledge we had, we made the choice that seemed to make the most sense to us. The *cause* of our decision may forever elude us, because we can't remember everything in our heredity and environment that might have affected our behavior; however, the *reason* for our decision is clear to us, and that reason is part of our free decision. So for a moral agent who is responsible for his or her actions, it is not the physical cause of the action that is important as much as it is the *reason* behind it. The reason is the overriding element in the decision process. It therefore may be true that no action is without a cause, but this does not preclude the concept of free will.

When Can We Be Held Responsible?

The problem of deciding when someone should be held responsible for his or her actions is accentuated by the growing precision with which science can determine cause-and-effect relationships. However, Aristotle outlined his ideas about when we can rightly assume that someone has exercised freedom of the will and should be held responsible for his actions. These guidelines, outlined in *Nicomachean Ethics*, still can serve us well today:

> Those things, then, are thought involuntary, which take place under compulsion or owing to ignorance, and that is compulsory of which the moving principle is outside, being a principle in which nothing is contributed by the person who is acting or is feeling the passion, e.g., if he were to be carried somewhere by a wind, or by men who had him in their power.

There are, of course, borderline situations, such as when a soldier is ordered to kill civilians. Some might say that he has no choice, but others—like Jean-Paul Sartre—would most emphatically say that the soldier can say no, even though he may be punished for disobedience. Let us look at a few other dilemmas.

Case of Ignorance #1: "Gee, I Didn't Know"

Scenario: A friend offers to take you to the airport, and you accept her offer. On the way you run into heavy traffic, and you miss your plane. Should you blame your friend? No, because she couldn't have known the streets would be blocked.

Scenario: Your friend drives you to the airport on a street she goes by every day. There has been construction going on there for the past six months. You miss your plane. Now can you blame your friend? You could consider it her fault, because she didn't take precautions, and she wasn't ignorant of the situation.

Scenario: You rent a car in a foreign country and get stopped by a policewoman, who informs you that you failed to stop at some white stripes painted on the road. She calls them "shark's teeth," and they turn out to be the local version of a stop sign (this happens to be the case in Scandinavia). Can you plead ignorance? No, because you were supposed to know the traffic rules before you started driving.

Case of Ignorance #2: Lack of Skill

As we know, "ought implies can." We have no duty to perform what is impossible for us to perform. Here are some cases to illustrate that.

Scenario: Your friend asks you to help him with a math problem, but your mathematical skills stop at about the third grade level. You can't help, but he can't blame you for not helping, because you don't have the skills to help him.

Scenario: Your friend needs help with math, and you're good at math, but you have a date, so you tell your friend you're sorry but you can't help him. Now he can blame you for not helping.

Scenario: You are walking along the shore of a lake, and you see a child fall out of a rowboat. You can't swim. Can you be blamed for not jumping in to save the child? No, but you can be blamed if you don't try to help in some other way. And, just possibly, you can be blamed for not having learned to swim; after all, you never know when you might need it.

Scenario: Same lake, same child, but you are now the only person around for miles, and you are in a wheelchair, so there is no way you physically can help. This certainly is a case of "lack of skill," but in this case the lack of skill is not due to ignorance. You may very well know how to swim, but you can't swim. So what does that mean? For one thing, you of course cannot be held accountable, even if you are familiar with the skill that is needed. Ought still implies can. For another thing, perhaps lack of skill is not the issue here; perhaps the issue is *compulsion* (another category proposed by Aristotle). Compulsion means a situation is dictated not by what you *don't know*, but by what you *can't do*.

Let us look at some cases of compulsion.

Case of Compulsion #1: Outside Forces

Scenario: You are kidnapped and forced to join a gang that robs banks. During one of the robberies you are filmed by a hidden camera, and the police catch you. You claim that you were abducted and threatened—that if you didn't join in, the gang would kill you. The gang members, however, claim that that was the case only in the beginning—later on, you seemed to enjoy taking part in the robberies. This you explain by saying that the gang leaders brainwashed you to the point where you didn't know what was right or wrong anymore. Sound a bit farfetched? Not at all. This description fits the Patty Hearst case of the 1970s, in which the daughter of a newspaper magnate was kidnapped by a group of anarchist revolutionaries, or so the story goes. The jury believed that she sufficiently established that she acted under compulsion, both of an external kind (she was held at gunpoint) and an internal kind (she was brainwashed).

Case of Compulsion #2: Inside Forces

Scenario: Chuck decides to try drugs and ends up wrecking a stolen car. Can he claim that he was under some sort of internal compulsion and couldn't help himself from wrecking the car? No, because he took the drugs voluntarily in the first place, so he is to blame and will be held responsible.

Scenario: Ramon is at a party and someone puts drugs in his drink without his knowledge. He, too, ends up wrecking a stolen car. Can he be blamed? If he can establish that he didn't take the drugs voluntarily (that can be hard to prove), then he will not be blamed.

Scenario: Sandy suffers from kleptomania (the compulsory urge to steal). She steals air fresheners, light bulbs, and a dog collar from the supermarket. (She has no dog; there is no sense to the items she steals.) She is caught shoplifting. Will she be held accountable? Not if she can produce a valid doctor's statement that she is sick. She will not be able to go free without therapy, however.

Scenario: Neil shoplifts from the supermarket because he is hungry and he can't afford food for his baby. Is he to be held accountable? *Absolutely*. Hard times are no excuse, and he is not sick, nor is anybody forcing him to steal. He might say that he "had no other choice," but a social worker would tell him otherwise and inform him of the options.

Case of Compulsion #3: Unforeseen Circumstances

Scenario: You are on your way to a midterm, and your car breaks down; or, you were supposed to send in your tax return, but you got tonsillitis. Such situations may be considered "bad excuses," but sometimes we truly are the victims of circumstances beyond our control, and we need all the understanding we can get. How can we be sure other people will understand our unfortunate predicaments? We can't, but we can be careful not to offer up poor excuses in cases where the predicament really is our own fault; otherwise our explanations may never be taken seriously.

Aristotle's two excuses, ignorance and compulsion, can be elaborated on and specified, but the thought behind them remains the same: When you are *ignorant* about something (including math or swimming) you can't be blamed for not taking action that is dependent on the proper knowledge. If you are under some *compulsion*, of internal or external nature, you can't be blamed for what you do. At all other times, however, you can be held accountable for your actions. This corresponds to both our common sense and our legal sense, and the determinist who claims that you can *never* be held accountable for anything is at odds with both.

Answers to Determinism

Compatibilism

In his book *Religion and the Modern Mind*, the philosopher W. T. Stace suggests that determinism has wrongly defined free will. It does not mean, he says, "uncaused," but rather "not directly caused by any agency outside myself." As long as the "cause" lies in a person's own reasoning, we can safely retain the concept of free will. This viewpoint, which Stace shares with many other twentieth-century philosophers, is that of "soft determinism," or "compatibilism," which views determinism (causality) and free will as compatible.

In soft determinism the premise of causality remains, as does the belief that everything is caused by heredity or environment. That doesn't mean, though, that we don't have free will, because as long as we're not constrained, our will is free. (For Stace *constraint* means being physically forced to do something, or prevented from doing something.) Free will has to do with weighing pros and cons, which are based on our character and our wishes. If we think an "out of the blue" decision like singing in the movie theater constitutes free will, we're wrong. That's not free will, that's madness. There are problems with this approach, though. The kleptomaniac is hardly "constrained." Neither is the parent who beats her child because she herself has a background of being beaten. Yet we still can point to a clear influence from the past as one factor in these people's actions.

Self-Determination

Scholars who otherwise embrace the causal principle of determinism, both of the physical and the mental realm, suggest that mental causality represents a kind of "self-determination." In our minds we have so many options that they constitute a kind of freedom in itself. The options are so complex that our actions become totally unpredictable. Thus the complexity results in the phenomenon of choice, even if our choices are causally determined. The causality translates into mental freedom in the sense of self-determination.

Freedom as Lived Experience

Some philosophers have suggested that although it may be true that every single decision we make has causes over which we have no control, most of the time we are unaware of those underlying causes; we know only that we have reasons for our de-

The Indeterminism of Quantum Physics

A fascinating argument against determinism has been derived from subatomic science. The classical deterministic argument of 100 percent predictability is based on Newtonean physics and concerns items we can see and touch. However, at the subatomic level the principle of causality doesn't hold: We can't determine both speed and position of a given subatomic particle. If we know *how fast* it is, we can't tell *where* it will hit. If we know *where* it will hit, we can't tell *when*. Some scientists see this as an argument that we can't achieve total prediction at the subatomic level, which is at the very core of every human being, so why should we assume that we can predict human behavior?

cisions. Ethics, then, must focus on decisions resulting from reasons of which we *are aware*, because those are the decisions for which we are responsible and for which we *feel* responsible. So whether or not free will is a scientific fact, it is something we experience, and that is what counts. It affects us psychologically and morally, and that is the sign of true reality for us.

This solution appeals to people who believe that natural science does not have all the answers about the human mind, and that the world of the mind determines human reality.

Indeterminism

Another related solution is so-called indeterminism, or libertarianism. Causality rules the physical realm, say indeterminists, but not the mental realm. Psychologically we are completely acausal and thus completely free to *choose any path we like*. (One of the most famous versions of indeterminism was proposed by Jean-Paul Sartre, and we will look more closely at his theory in a later section of this chapter.) Indeterminism today must fight a hard battle against deterministic psychoanalysis, which views everything in our mental life as caused by conscious and unconscious factors. But there also are problems with the logic of indeterminism. Suppose it is true that there is no causality in the mental realm. In that case I can make a decision to cook a dinner for some good friends, but the chicken never will get fried because my decision doesn't cause anything to happen—and I can't be sure my guests will turn up, either, because I can't predict their behavior. Chaos rules the mental realm, and I can't predict my own or anybody else's behavior. With indeterminism as well as with determinism, free will disappears.

FIGURE 15.3 Henri Bergson (1859–1941), French philosopher. Bergson strongly believed that humans have a willpower that cannot be predicted on the basis of past events. Bergson was Jewish, but at the end of his life he was considering converting to Catholicism. He never followed through, though, because at that time Jews were being increasingly persecuted all over Europe as a result of the spread of Nazi thinking. As a gesture of solidarity, he decided to remain a Jew for the remainder of his life. This was not to be long, however; he was forced by the German Nazi forces occupying France to stand in line for hours to register as a Jew. It was raining hard, and as a result Bergson caught pneumonia. He died shortly thereafter.

I Am Not You: Bergson's Solution

The French philosopher Henri Bergson (1859–1941) was strongly opposed to the concept of determinism, which he thought pacified people into thinking that they existed in the world in the same manner as things do: merely to occupy space. For Bergson, human nature is unique in being *temporal*—humans have a sense of time. Not just clock time—which in reality is nothing but the objective monitoring of seconds, minutes, and hours—but the time we live and experience, and which has a subjective component. Sometimes it moves slowly (as when our date is late or when we wait for the roast to be cooked or our car to be fixed), and sometimes it moves fast (like when we're having a great time with a friend or are concentrating on a test). In these situations time is something we *feel*, rather than something we measure.

Bergson believes that although we certainly can predict what will happen in the world of objects, we can't possibly predict human behavior, because the human willpower is a force that will, on occasion, cast aside all previous influences and deliberations. But Bergson does not believe in indeterminism either, because just as it is wrong to think there is only *one* path to follow (determinism), so is it wrong to think that we can choose between *different* paths in the future (indeterminism). The future has no paths at all—it has only decision-making—and after a decision has been made, we look back and think we see a path. Bergson has an unusual solution to the problem of deterministic prediction: We can never predict the actions of others with certainty, because then we would have to know everything there is to know about the other person. We would have to have lived with that person always and have shared everything with him or her, including all acts of the conscious and unconscious mind. But if we were that close to someone, we would be *identical* to that other person! And that other person certainly doesn't know what he or she will do next. So it's logically impossible, as well as practically impossible, to predict other people's actions.

This doesn't mean we can never predict anything about each other, of course.

Knowing someone well means being able to predict—with probability, not with certainty—what they are likely to do. Predicting that my friend will not talk behind my back and give away what I have told her in confidence is not a matter of predicting what she will be forced to do by heredity and environment, but what she will choose to do, based on her good character. I may of course be wrong. But whatever my friend does will still be a matter of choice.

Sartre: There Is No Human Nature

The Issue of Free Will

Although most thinkers faced with the question of what is human nature try to come up with an answer, at least one thinker has refused to answer the question at all. Jean-Paul Sartre believed that the question is unanswerable, because *there is no human nature.* Sartre read Bergson in his youth and was influenced by Bergson's radical opposition to determinism. If we believe there is a human nature, we become determinists; we believe we have to become what we think we are supposed to be. But there is no specific way that humans are supposed to be. *Things* are supposed to be what we intend them to be when we make them or when we buy them. *Nonhuman animals* don't have any choice as to what they are supposed to be, because their minds are ruled by instinct (at least this was the common way of viewing the animal mind during the middle years of the twentieth century, when Sartre developed his philosophy). But if *humans* assume that they have a "nature," they reduce themselves to the status of things and of animals—of beings *who have no free will.* Sartre labels the existence of such beings an existence "in itself" (*en soi*): Such things exist without any awareness *that* they exist. But Sartre labels the human form of existence, with its capacity for self-awareness, "for itself" (*pour soi*), which means living with self-awareness and the responsibility for one's actions.

In a sense, Sartre is close to Kant in that he divides the world into those who can make up their mind about things (humans) and those who cannot (things). But although Kant firmly believes that humans have a specific nature (they can reason) and purpose (they ought to use their talents and reason appropriately), Sartre denies that humans have any predetermined nature. For most philosophers, human nature is an unfolding of characteristics laid down by nature or by God. Just as the idea of a paper knife exists in the mind of the artisan before it is manufactured, so does the idea of a human being exist in the mind of God, according to the traditional view. In other words, for most philosophers, a thing's *essence* precedes its *existence*, and this also is true with humans; the idea of what they are or will be (their essence) precedes their coming into being (their existence). But for Sartre, human beings are different from all other beings in that *their existence comes before their essence.* For Sartre, humans make their own "essence" or characteristics, and we are therefore *responsible* for what we are—we never can blame our shortcomings on God, nature, our parents, fate, or anything else. If there were a God, we might be able to talk about human nature pre-existing in the mind of God, but Sartre is an atheist and believes that, tragically, there is no God to uphold our values (see Chapter 11); therefore life is essentially absurd, in the sense that there is no meaning to be found anywhere outside ourselves.

As we discussed previously, Sartre's celebrated existentialist philosophy was developed during World War II; it clearly was colored by the wartime experience, in which huge populations faced annihilation. The special wartime ethic that grew out of this experience—to take on responsibility and do what you decide is necessary, even in the face of meaninglessness and annihilation—has become a legacy of existentialism and its view of human nature and human action.

Bad Faith, Anguish, and Choice

For Sartre, the ideal is for everyone to acknowledge that there is no predetermined destiny for anybody, and that we determine our own direction in life every moment of the day. If we fail to realize that, we reduce ourselves to something less than human. Of course, most people don't go around consciously deciding what they want to be at each moment—we all are caught up in the web of everyday life. But once we realize that whenever we seek support for our actions in the idea that "it can't be otherwise" we are fooling ourselves into thinking that there is a destiny, or a pattern we have to follow, then we realize that we are, in a sense, *condemned to be free*. We have to make decisions, and we have to be responsible for them. If we choose to hide behind "it can't be otherwise," or "I was just following orders," then we make ourselves victims of *bad faith*, the illusion that we can view our own existence as that of a thing: We have no choice, we have to be what our parents want us to be/what the church wants us to be/what our country expects us to be. As you may remember from Chapter 11, bad faith happens when we try to fool ourselves into thinking that we don't have to make a decision—but of course then we make the decision to have others decide for us. And with that decision we tell the world that that is an appropriate way to behave, because any decision we make sends out a signal to others that we believe this kind of decision is appropriate. Whatever we decide, Sartre says, we are setting ourselves up as role models for everyone else:

> When we say that man chooses himself, we do mean that every one of us must choose himself; but by that we also mean that in choosing for himself he chooses for all men. . . . To choose between this or that is at the same time to affirm the value of that which is chosen. . . . Our responsibility is thus much greater than we had supposed, for it concerns mankind as a whole.

What makes our decision the right one? Sartre says we don't know, because since God is not there to tell us what is right or wrong, there really is no right or wrong decision. The young man who has to decide whether to join the French underground during World War II or stay at home and help his mother can hope for no sign from Heaven as to what to do (Sartre tells of a student of his who had exactly that problem).

He can't ask the resistance movement or his mother, because they can't give him any absolute answers. The only thing he can do is make a decision and follow up on it—and then he will know what was most important to him. Before he decides, he can't know. If he tries not to decide, he will be trying to transform himself into a thinglike existence without responsibility. This is a common phenomenon and is quite reassuring, for a while. We can identify so strongly with playing a certain role that we forget that it is just a role; it makes us forget, for a while, that we have to make major decisions that determine our life, and that we can't seek advice anywhere. But the anguish over decisions and the despair at not having access to absolute answers will find us, eventually, for this is the existential *angst* with which we all have to live. We always must contend with a lack of firm values and meaning, and the necessity of making decisions in the face of this meaninglessness.

For many, this means that the existentialist theory of free will is quite pessimistic: We have to make choices in an absurd world with no absolute values. But for Sartre, it is the ultimate, optimistic freedom: We are bound by nothing—no masters, no values. Contrary to Nietzsche, Sartre doesn't conclude that everything is permitted to the man with the will to power; on the contrary, Sartre says we have an absolute responsibility to ourselves and each other, because the only values that exist are set by humans, for other humans as well as for themselves.

How Free Are We?

The question now is this: If humans really aren't determined by anything in the outside world but can decide, at any time, to escape the causal chain and its demands, how can that be worked out in a practical situation? Given that we are stuck in an unhappy situation, how can we decide to "do something else"? Sometimes there truly seems to be no way out, other than some obvious, unpleasant solution. The soldier who is ordered to kill civilians and who will be shot if the order is not followed will wonder about Sartre's claim that we, at any given time, can choose to do something else. So will the prisoner on Death Row who is scheduled to be executed in the morning. So will the homeless person who is sick and without a job. So will the student who is about to take a final exam. So will the person waiting in the dentist's office or the person filing a tax return. And all of us must watch ourselves and the ones we love grow older and gradually lose our powers, and we certainly would rather that these things *didn't* happen. So isn't there some destiny in life, when it comes down to it?

Sartre would answer that in some of these cases we do choose what we want: We choose to go to the dentist and to file our tax returns and even to take a final because we would rather not deal with the alternatives—toothaches, legal action, and a failing grade. But Sartre is no advocate of psychological egoism; he doesn't believe we always choose what we want. He does believe, however, that we always make a choice. The soldier who is ordered to kill civilians cannot claim that he or she is "just following orders" and thus escape responsibility, *because we can always refuse an order.* "But then they will kill me!" the soldier protests. And Sartre would answer: "So let yourself be killed; there are worse things than that, like taking the life of an innocent person." Sartre has no moral inhibitions about advocating death and suicide when he sees it is the only honorable way out.

But what about the Death Row inmate who can't escape and who can't commit suicide in order to avoid being executed by, say, lethal injection? Wouldn't Sartre agree that this person is locked into his or her fate? No, because the *spiritual freedom* of the prisoner still exists. When faced with something inevitable, we can choose for it not to consume our personality, not to get us down. We may not have much control over being poor, sick, or plain-looking, but we can choose to retain our integrity and dignity as long as we have a mind that can choose. (Like other existentialists, Sartre would be adamantly against choosing suicide just because life is becoming too hard to face. This, for Sartre, would be nothing but an evasive action, an attempt to avoid facing up to one's responsibilities, the ultimate gesture of bad faith: making an inert thing out of oneself. Sartre doesn't seem to have much sympathy for people who can no longer cope with life.)

This freedom to choose how to respond to any given situation has far-reaching consequences because not only can it change our present and our future, but also it can change our past. Not in terms of changing the facts of the past but in terms of changing our *interpretation* of the past. (For Sartre most "facts" are a matter of inter-pretation, a result of hindsight.) In this way the past can be viewed in an entirely new light. Many people perform this feat several times in their lives. A typical time for "reinventing the past" is during a breakup, especially if longtime partners are divorc-ing. It is common for people to reconsider key moments in a relationship and seek a new and usually ominous meaning in them. "So that was why he did such-and-such," we may say. (This practice may do a giant disservice to oneself and one's partner, because those moments may be better left to memory and regarded fondly, rather than dragged into a reevaluation of the relationship.) Another time when people typically reinvent the past is when they change careers. Elements relating to one's new career are suddenly viewed as particularly meaningful, while anything relating to one's old career is reinterpreted as "a waste of time." All of the major events in a person's life—change in residence, marriage or divorce, the arrival of children, completion of a job, illness or recovery, or simply the transition from one stage of life to another (adolescence to adulthood, for instance)—can spark a reinterpretation of one's past. Of course we are not always accurate in our reinterpretations, but Sartre may be right that we are masters of how we choose to view ourselves.

Narratives That Explore the Nature-Nurture Question

Chapter 20 includes several stories that examine the issue of heredity versus environ-ment. The famous children's story "The Ugly Duckling" is contrasted with "Flight of the Eagle"; one claims heredity is all that counts, and the other insists that you will become what your environment has determined, regardless of your heredity. In addition, the film *The Wild Child* explores the phenomenon of *feral children*—children who have been raised by animals in the wild. What is the determining factor for them—their heredity or their environment?

SOCIOBIOLOGY: DETERMINISM APPLIED

The Principle of Sociobiology

Our expanding base of knowledge in the sciences, especially in biology, has inspired theories of human nature to the point where a new school of thought has developed: the school of *sociobiology*. Sociobiology is a theory of human social life based on biological theory. It holds that human social structures and traditions have biological grounds. The idea seems inevitable; after all, biology draws conclusions about animal populations based on their biological makeup. Animals defend territories, migrate, choose mates, raise offspring, and hunt and forage all in response to biological needs, so why not also humans?

Darwin's Legacy

Natural Selection

The biological equivalence of human and nonhuman animals is a legacy of Darwinistic evolutionism. Before the publication of *On the Origin of Species by Means of Natural Selection* (1859), it was unthinkable to place humans and animals on the same scale when examining their behavioral patterns. This was true despite the fact that the theory of evolution was advanced well before Darwin came along (Darwin contributed mainly his theory of *natural selection*), and anybody with the capacity for observation could see that humans and animals sometimes engage in similar types of behavior.

The one factor that allowed for not only a theory of human behavior based on biological factors and related animal behavior, but also a certain *interpretation* of that behavior was the Darwinian concept of *survival of the fittest*, a term coined by his friend and staunch defender, Julian Huxley. According to this theory, living organisms evolve gradually according to a principle of competition in nature: Whoever is capable of surviving long enough to have healthy offspring who can carry one's genetic code into the future is "fit," and the "fittest" are those species that fill their biological niche successfully and manage to have equally successful offspring. Because humans

FIGURE 15.4 Charles Darwin (1809–1882), English naturalist. The influence of Darwin on the modern worldview can't be measured. His theory (and the "blow to human self-assurance" that it dealt) is still hard for many people to accept: that humans and all other animals have evolved to their present form through natural selection, not through a once-and-for-all act of creation. However, some religious minds have no trouble reconciling Darwin's theory of evolution with their faith in God; they see evolution as a process begun and supervised by God.

are living organisms, they too engage in this fight for survival. Human evolution has favored certain traits in human nature, such as human sociability. Thus, Darwin gave us a key to human social life that was biological, and our social life was basically reduced to a fight for the survival of one's own kind.

Charles Darwin (1809–1882) was a naturalist, not a philosopher. However, since the publication of his book, *On the Origin of Species by Means of Natural Selection*, which put forth his hypothesis regarding the gradual evolution of species, Darwin's theory of the survival of the fittest has proved an inspiration and challenge to philosophers as well as to naturalists. If Darwin is right, are we then destined always to selfishly promote our own genes? Is psychological egoism right after all—is it biologically impossible for us to think of anyone but ourselves? Darwinism even supplies a self-oriented explanation for seemingly altruistic acts of self-sacrifice. The baboon who sacrifices himself in order to lure the leopard away from his "tribe" is not doing it because he loves his fellow baboons, but because he "loves" his own genes and wants them to live on in his offspring and his siblings' offspring. We can't attribute such reasoning to his conscious mind, but here nature speaks through the baboon's unconscious actions. The same factor may be at play when soldiers give their lives to defend their homeland; they don't get any offspring themselves, but their relatives do, and that is the next best thing, biologically speaking.

Criticism of Darwin's Ideas

Darwin came under attack right from the start of the publication of his theories, not only from the church and other religiously oriented circles, but also from other scientists. It now has been firmly established that evolution is a fact, not just a hypothesis (although science is still studying whether evolution happens gradually, or in spurts, or both), and that humans and apes have a fellow ancestor. Incidentally, Darwin never claimed that humans descended from apes—that idea came out of the propaganda of anti-Darwinists. Attacking evolutionism as a preposterous or ill-founded theory is hardly reasonable or profitable any more. However, questions still arise concerning the scientific and philosophical implications of Darwin's theory, such as, What exactly is meant by "survival of the fittest"? Some scholars claim that it is actually a tautologous argument—it is true by virtue of its logical form alone: Who survives? Those who are fit to survive. It is a circular definition. Should we simply call it "survival of the strongest"? No, because sometimes the big, strong creatures die out, while the little ones survive. Case in point: the death of the dinosaurs and the rise of the mammals. So perhaps we should say, "survival of the best adapted." But however we phrase it, how do we use this one principle to explain all animal evolution and all human biological and social evolution? Sometimes an animal population survives because no one has challenged its niche, and not because it is particularly well adapted to that niche. Sometimes well-adapted animals mutate and die. The last chapter in evolutionism has not been written yet.

The theory seems even more questionable when it is applied to human evolution. We certainly are not very well adapted—our esophagus is right next to our windpipe, and because we walk upright it is very easy for us to choke. Our spine doesn't hold up well to a seventy-to-eighty-year life span, and neither do our feet or knees. So perhaps we are still adapting. However, here human *culture* comes into play, and decides that not just the ones with especially strong spines and good feet can have children who survive until adulthood. Human culture often chooses to keep alive members who might otherwise be at a biological disadvantage. It appears, perhaps, that natural selection has given way to cultural selection. Humans have some natural advantages, of course: We have excellent temperature regulation, which allows us to adapt to most climates on this earth, and we have a rapid population replenishment system because our females can bear several children, whereas apes, as a rule, care for only one child until that child can fend for itself. (The human characteristic *was* an advantage to a sparse human population—it is hardly an advantage anymore.) And we can eat almost anything organic except cellulose. We also have a unique social structure, which may be responsible for the human success story more than any other factor: We have vast organizational abilities, from food-sharing to raids, and we can conceptualize "friend" and "foe." We take care of our friends. (What do we do about our foes? We will consider that problem shortly.)

Modern scholars have pointed out that Darwin's theory of evolution, when applied to humans, may explain the evolution of small groups, but it can hardly explain the evolution of individuals nor the evolution of large groups such as nations. Factors other than a simple survival principle surely play a part. Darwin also has been viewed as an implicit supporter of the idea of a *master race* that evolves and looks out for itself—a concept that was promoted by the Nazis during World War II but had its roots, at least in modern times, in the writings of Nietzsche. It seems certain that Darwin believed humanity was evolving—but he saw it evolving toward a higher *moral goal*: Humanity was becoming *nicer*, kinder, and Darwin believed in an expansion of natural family affection that would extend, eventually, to the entire human race. As hopeful as that sounds, evolutionism always has had a hard time explaining why it is biologically *advantageous* to be nice, or to display affection for your family. If you are too nice, others may take advantage of you; you may spend so much time taking care of others that you never marry or have offspring of your own. We might conclude that affection is a bad investment. However, we also might conclude that if Darwinism seeks to explain every human act and emotion from a survival standpoint, then Darwinism is too simplistic. (Perhaps affection is not always survival-oriented, but it serves valuable social and personal functions nevertheless.) You may want to return to Chapter 4 and reread the section on altruism that deals with the "Prisoners' Dilemma"; sometimes, it seems, it can be to our advantage to not just think about ourselves all the time. Teamwork has a survival value of its own.

One complaint that has been voiced against Darwin is that he was so much a child of his day and age (nineteenth-century capitalist England) that it not only flavors his theory but gives it a unique metaphoric structure. Individual competition and the need to fight to get ahead—that is not just a biological description but an *economic* metaphor. Marxists used to say that Darwin tried to justify capitalism ideologically by claiming that the urge for competition is grounded in human nature! Whether or not Darwin had any wish to justify capitalism, the fact remains that his description of the motives behind human actions evokes images of selfishness, competition, and hostility—just like Marx's analysis of the psychology of the capitalistic system. (However, it was not Darwin, but one of his readers, the British philosopher Herbert Spencer, who argued that unrelenting competition is a human survival mechanism. This theory is now known as *social Darwinism*.) Modern evolutionists have occasionally suggested that new metaphors be explored, such as the metaphor of *cooperation*.

Philosophers in particular have a problem with Darwin's predilection for drawing moral values into his theory of human development. Darwinism is a deterministic theory, and, as we saw previously, when applied to the nonhuman realm, the theory of cause and effect yields much knowledge. However, when it is applied to humans Darwinism enters the realm of ethics, and most philosophers consider this to be an area that is better left untouched by biologists. If we choose to see morality as a purely biological development, with biological reasons for every decision, we lose sight of the fact that *human reason*—at least in the way most philosophers see it—allows us to detach ourselves from our natural inclinations, and judge them. We can choose to follow them, but we also can choose to control them. That control may have a biological basis, but it also may not. The assumption that every cultural occurrence can be explained biologically is known as *sociobiology*.

Cain's Children: Konrad Lorenz and Robert Ardrey

In the 1960s one man published a series of books about human aggression, and each became a best-seller. The author's name was Robert Ardrey. He had majored in natural sciences at the University of Chicago and since then had become a playwright and a Hollywood screenwriter. He understood better than many scientists the *language* of popular scientific books. His style was colorful, and he became immensely influential in the general population. Within the science community he was never recognized as an influence, but that community had its own writer of human aggression. He had a more distinguished scientific background than Ardrey, and a similar talent for popularization: the Austrian Konrad Lorenz. The two men shaped the opinion of the time with their assertion that *humans are by nature aggressive*. They will defend their territory for sexual reasons—in order to gain the right to mate—just like other animals.

Lorenz and Ardrey were not the first to make this claim; Freud had thought pretty much the same thing after witnessing World War I and believed that "we are descended from an endlessly long chain of murderers whose love of murder was in their blood as it is perhaps in our own." Lorenz, through his fascinating reports of animal observations, illustrated animals' territorial tendency and the importance of imprinting and bonding of the baby animal. Ardrey coined the term *the territorial imperative* (compare *categorical imperative*) and explored other people's research on animals primarily to draw conclusions about humans.

Whereas Lorenz's conclusions about human culture were by and large developed as an afterthought, Ardrey's theories represented sociobiology in its popular form; they were deterministic theories of human culture based on human biology and couched in survivalist jargon.

Why was Ardrey so preoccupied with human aggression? We might surmise that it was simply a sign of the times: Ardrey wrote his first major book, *African Genesis*, during the Korean War, and the issue of human aggression loomed large in the nation's mind. But other wartime theories of human behavior, such as Sartre's, do not emphasize any innate human aggression. (Ardrey seems to have sought inspiration from two sources in particular, aside from the Korean War: Darwin and Nietzsche. We shall take a look at Nietzsche in Chapter 17.)

For Ardrey humans are what early human evolution made them: hunters and killers. It is their *weapons*—in combination with the upright stance, which gave their hands freedom to grasp, hit, and throw, and allowed the males' eyes to scan the plains in search of prey, females, and a good fight—that made humans what they are today. Had humans not encountered hard times, they would not have developed the brains to use their hands to make weapons. So the "aggressive imperative" liberated humans from their earlier animal ways, even though we still have those earlier animal tendencies of fear and dominance. Man, says Ardrey, has "an overpowering enthusiasm for things that go boom." Does that mean, then, that we are "evolution's most tragic error," or is there hope for the human race? For Ardrey the hope does not lie in abolishing war, for humans must have war in order to stay intellectually fit; if we abolish violence we will lose the ability to defend ourselves, he says. All human advances have been won through the use of violence; the advance of Christianity, the rule of law, the concepts of material and individual worth—all have been won through war. War hones the human mind for new and splendid achievements, and without war we'd be no better than the peaceful gorilla, whose life is full of empty rituals and who is destined for extinction. If we become morally special creatures, with goodness and wisdom, we will perish. If we remain "beasts" we will instinctively

The Lion as Metaphor

Ardrey uses the metaphor of a male lion to illustrate the early human hunter—but does the analogy hold up? In a pride of lions, it rarely is the male lion who hunts and kills prey—the lioness does this. And the lion as a rule gets killed defending his territory only when he is too old and weak to defend it any longer; attackers usually are not killed, but merely bullied away. Young male lions, however, who are cast out from the pride and are in search of their own females, may display behavior such as Ardrey describes. Young male outcast apes and monkeys display a very similar behavior, too, and it is possible that early hominids behaved in a similar fashion.

know how to survive. But how can we have wars without annihilating ourselves? Ardrey says it is not likely that we will all be annihilated—only a large number of us will perish. As if that makes anybody feel better.

So, humans are aggressive by nature, and being aggressive is not only acceptable but also the proper way to behave, for the sake of humanity's future. Most of Ardrey's theories are discussed in one chapter of his book *African Genesis*—the final chapter, entitled "Cain's Children." The implications are that *mythologically* or symbolically speaking, humans are the children of Cain, who was the first murderer. (The Bible teaches that Cain, the firstborn son of Adam and Eve following their expulsion from the garden of Eden, killed his younger brother Abel because God preferred Abel's sacrifice to Cain's; Abel was a shepherd and had sacrificed a lamb, while Cain, a farmer, had sacrificed ripe grain. Because Abel's death was the first death of a human being, according to the biblical storyteller, we might ask whether Cain was truly committing *murder* since he didn't know the nature of death when he struck out at his brother. Perhaps it was, instead, *manslaughter*.) Ardrey and many others have labeled Cain a murderer, and because he was (according to legend) the father of the human race, we are all Cain's children. (Ardrey does not mean we are Cain's children in the genetic sense; he does not profess any belief that we are actually descended from the biblical character.) Ardrey also likens the early human to the proud lion who roams freely, hunts its prey, and kills in order to defend his territory.

What is Ardrey really saying—that it is wonderful to move about, do what you want, have sex with whomever you want, and then go off in search of new adventures? This is hardly a description of the tightly knit hominid family groups we now believe populated the savannah, but it is perhaps a good description of the *outcast young hominid males* who strived to form a group of their own.

It is somewhat unfair to blame Ardrey for omitting facts that were unavailable to him at the time. But he does commit a grave logical error that has nothing to do with

FIGURE 15.5 *2001, A Space Odyssey,* MGM, 1968. The mental connection is made between killing a tapir with a weapon and killing other prehominids. The great black monolith teaches the prehominid tribe to use their intelligence to make weapons; in the introduction to the film, which depicts "the Dawn of Man," human nature is being formed by the invention of the weapon. The story of the dawn of man in *2001, A Space Odyssey* is outlined in Chapter 20 as an illustration of Robert Ardrey's theory of human aggression.

the facts available to him: He implies that violence and war are the same. If we try to imagine a world without violence, then even *justified* violence, such as that committed in self-defense, cannot exist, and as a result humanity will fall victim to whoever has no compunctions about using violence. However, Ardrey then takes a giant leap in claiming that this is the same as saying that we must have wars. Surely war and violence are two different things. A police action may be considered justifiable violence, but usually not "war." If you defend yourself or someone else against a mugger, you are not going on the warpath. What Ardrey is concocting here is known as a *straw man argument*: He sets up a weak and implausible argument that is supposedly in opposition to his own theory and then knocks it down as easily as you would knock down a straw dummy.

Another thing we might question is why we should accept Ardrey's word that war is necessary for inventions. Even if this has been true in the past, why should it continue to be so in the future? Space research has yielded more inventions than war, lately.

On the whole, Ardrey's ideas are valuable to us because they represent a point of view that was so prevalent a generation ago that it was rarely questioned: that humans are prone to use weapons, and that that has been a major factor in developing human intelligence. The opening sequence of the science-fiction film classic *2001, A Space Odyssey* is pure Ardrey: The monolith (a large, black slab of rock that is supposed to be a thought-enhancer, among other things, from outer space) makes a certain ape population *use their reason*—and what do the apes do with their new brains? They use them to figure out how to kill their neighbors and gain possession of a waterhole—by wielding an animal thighbone and using it as a weapon. (We will take a closer look at *2001, A Space Odyssey* in Chapter 20.)

The Naturalistic Fallacy

What makes Ardrey's theory an example of sociobiology is not merely that he develops a hypothesis of human behavior based on biological research, but that he proceeds to make *value statements*. He tells us not only what people do (which would be descriptive), but also whether it is all right for them to do it (which is normative).

The danger in this approach is that sometimes thinkers slip from one kind of statement to the other without being aware of it. We might think we describe human nature when we say humans are by nature aggressive, and therefore it is okay to be aggressive. But this is a major fallacy, sometimes called the *naturalistic fallacy*: We can't move from an "is" statement to an "ought" statement without making a value statement. We have encountered this idea before: Just because something *is* the case, doesn't mean it *should be* so or can't be otherwise. David Hume brought this to the attention of philosophers some two hundred years ago, and the principle has been regularly violated before and since.

If we can prove that something is the case, why not incorporate that fact into our policy-making? Let us see how it works. If, for instance, we could prove biologically that Asians statistically are smarter than Caucasians, then should Caucasians be excluded from certain types of intellectual endeavors? If it turns out that women statistically are better parents than men, should single fathers be forced to give up their children? If men statistically are better at spatial comprehension than women, should woman be prohibited from becoming pilots? It is very easy to use factual statements as a basis for *discrimination*—to progress from saying *it is this way* to saying *it has to be this way*. Even if women should happen to be better parents than men statistically, there always will be male individuals who are excellent parents, just as there will be women who have superb spatial comprehension, and there will be smart Caucasians. A sociobiological theory that assigns tasks to certain groups and withholds them from other groups on the basis of biology can't help but discriminate against individuals who would rather do (and might be good at doing) something else. Sociobiologists may insist that they only want to assign different tasks to different groups, not create a *hierarchy* in which some groups are viewed as more important than others. But what they intend and what the end result will be are two different things. If one group is assigned parenting and housekeeping duties, and another is assigned work outside the home, it is very likely that the group that is favored with additional power (in our society the group that makes money outside the home) will come to think of itself as more valuable.

Criticizing Ardrey for moving from a biological "is" to a moral "ought" does not imply that we never can use biological or other scientific facts in our moral theories;

the very idea that we shouldn't take advantage of scientific results to form our moral and political policies is preposterous. However, we can't go *straight* from those facts to a policy about how things should be, because in between the statement of fact and the statement of policy we have to insert a statement about our *moral values*, because values can't be derived from scientific facts. We then will have a bridge between fact and policy, and those who don't like our policy can criticize our values without having to criticize our facts. Let's look at an example. If you believe it is a fact that humans tend to have children, you can't conclude that they therefore *ought* to have children; you have to insert a statement that you believe having children is a *good thing*. After inserting this value statement, you then can conclude what people ought to do. In this way people who accept your statement of fact are still free to agree or disagree with your values.

Ardrey uses biology to justify problematic human traits such as aggression, rather than viewing them as appropriate or inappropriate responses depending on the situation. (Sometimes aggression is an appropriate response; sometimes it isn't.) He is selective about whatever biology and prehistory he chooses as evidence, and he commits the naturalistic fallacy by using a description of what (he thinks) we are to predict what it is okay to be. But as we saw in the section on personhood, just because nature does something, like kill its weakest creatures, doesn't mean we have to do it, too. It is natural to scratch ourselves, but we don't do it in public (this is true of most other physical functions). It may be natural to be promiscuous, but that doesn't mean we can't or shouldn't control ourselves. It may be natural to eat meat, but that doesn't mean we shouldn't decide to become vegetarians.

The Weapon or the Basket?—Leakey and Goodall

Contemporary objections to Ardrey's theory of the weapon's importance for human culture come from the fields of paleoanthropology (the study of fossilized humans and humanoid primates) and biology. The works of Richard Leakey, paleoanthropologist, and Jane Goodall, naturalist, both indicate that aggression is not the cultural catalyst we thought it was—at least it is not the only factor in human cultural evolution. In his book *The People of the Lake* (1978), Leakey suggests that warfare is far from being biological—it is a purely political device. Fossilized skulls that were thought to have been bashed in now seem to have been damaged by natural forces, after the death of the individual. And Ardrey's idea that hunting was what allowed humans to have the time to advance culturally has been refuted by findings indicating that humans ate all kinds of things, including what they could *gather*. (This is something we can tell by looking at human teeth.) Indeed, some anthropologists suggest that the term should be *gatherer-hunter societies*, not *hunter-gatherer societies*. According to Leakey, anthropologists such as Nancy Tanner and Adrienne Zihlman make much sense in suggesting the following:

> Compared with males . . . females have a tremendous investment in the offspring. . . . The females' pivotal position in the protohuman social group . . .

FIGURE 15.6 Ninety-nine percent genetically identical to humans, chimpanzees are now known, thanks to Jane Goodall, to display complex social behavior that includes organized aggression as well as caring and close bonding.

put into their hands the power to exploit technological innovation. The first tools . . . were invented "*not for hunting* large, swiftly moving, dangerous animals, *but for gathering plants*, eggs, honey, termites, ants, and probably small burrowing animals."

So was the cultural catalyst the male's hunting and his invention of *weapons*, or the female's social bonding with her child, and her invention of—the *basket*? The first use of a gourd, or a skull, or any kind of container to bring home supplies for the entire tribe or the immediate family may have occurred prior to the development of the weapon. At any rate, scholars now believe that humanity is not built on aggression alone. The caring instinct is present, too, and not just in the females; sharing seems to be a trait both genders have in common. Whether hunting and sharing of the kill occurred prior to gathering and sharing of the harvest is of little matter. In pretechnological cultures of this century the hunters' contribution to the overall diet is no more than 25 percent at the most—the rest is supplied by harvesting and gathering. What is clear is that both hunting and gathering were part of the early human experience, male and female, and we all have been shaped in our values by both activities.

A broader and more conciliatory view of human cultural origins has come out of the field of biology. Jane Goodall's study of the chimpanzee population of Gombe, which spanned several decades, has made an extraordinary impact on our understanding of chimps. Goodall undertook the study not with the goal of writing sociobiology, but with the aim of acquiring solid knowledge about chimpanzee life without flavoring it too much with anthropomorphisms. Her book *In the Shadow Of Man* revealed to an astonished world that the chimpanzee is far from being a peaceful creature; both males and females conduct raids on neighboring groups, killing them mercilessly (even the infants) in order to take over their territory. The occasional murder happens even within the home group. This sounds as if Ardrey has been vindicated. But at the same time, Goodall insists, the chimps show a highly developed sense of community; they care for each other, give food to injured family members, and spend hours grooming each other just for the sake of good company. When a group member dies, the relatives grieve for long periods of time, even to the point of dying of sorrow.

When Goodall was asked some years ago what implications these studies have for understanding human nature, she smiled a little smile and replied that they have very few implications. Chimps have certain tendencies, and we must assume that humans have those same tendencies—but that does not mean we can't help being aggressive, or that we all are caring, loving creatures. These are potentials, nothing more. It is good science to acknowledge tendency and relationship, and bad science to see characteristic traits as inevitable.

Goodall might add that although we may use the chimps as working metaphors for what we are, we should never confuse what we learn with determinism. Biology may be part of what we are, but it is not all that we are.

A Narrative That Explores Territorial Imperatives

Chapter 20 includes an outline of the film *2001, A Space Odyssey.* We will look not at the entire story, but at the beginning sequence, in which the monolith serves as an intelligence-enhancer.

Chapter 16

Different Gender, Different Nature, Different Ethic?

What Is Gender Equality?

Gender and Language

Throughout the Enlightenment and on into the twentieth century it has been customary to use words of the masculine gender to refer to both males and females. It is even surprising to realize that some statements referring to "all men" in fact do not (and were never intended to) refer to women at all, such as the American Declaration of Independence, which asserts that all *men* are created equal.

It is not true, of course, that the term *men* can *always* be used to indicate women; it doesn't make any sense to say, for instance, that half of all men have ovaries and half don't. Today, however, the use of the terms *he* and *man* are considered by many to be

The Issue Is Manhole Covers

The objection is sometimes heard that we are getting too radical in our eradication of gender-specific terms. It may make sense to do away with words such as *chairman* and *fireman*, and use *chairperson* and *firefighter* instead, but what about all the words in the English language that just happen to include a gender-specific term but for which there is no graceful substitute? Will *freshman* now be *freshperson*? Do we have to say *personhole* cover instead of *manhole* cover? How about *manpower*? And *manned space missions*? (And, jokesters might ask, how about *man*-ipulate? and *his*-tory?) Other languages present similar problems, but some languages have less of a problem finding a common word for humanity. German has a specific term for "man" (both genders)—*Der Mensch*—which is different from the terms for man and woman but which still includes a gender-specific term (*Mensch*, which is masculine in gender). In Danish the word for "man" (both genders) is a gender-neutral term, *Et Menneske*. And in Sweden, the term for "man" (both genders) is *En Människa*, a grammatically feminine word! To make matters even more interesting, there is a word in ancient Icelandic, *man*, that means slave/maid/mistress! Apparently that word has no connection with the ancient Germanic word for man (*Maðr*), which is the source for the term *man* in English.

So, getting back to the manhole covers, what should we do? Change some words and not others? Leave *manhole covers* alone, but change *manned mission* to *crewed mission*? Change them all? Leave them all the way they are? Two things are at stake here: the self-esteem of half the English-speaking population versus the comfort of those used to an established language. We can choose between four major courses of action: (1) Forcibly change language to some degree (and we have seen that this can be done within a generation); (2) Wait until a new gender-neutral terminology evolves by itself, in response to the changing times; (3) Make a distinction between sexist and nonsexist terms and change only the blatantly sexist ones; or (4) Insist on keeping the traditional terms no matter what. What would you suggest?

discriminatory whenever they are used to include women. And despite the fact that very few men or women ever intended discrimination by using the word *he* for a man or a woman and *man* (for all humankind), we now are moving away from what is known as "gender-specific" language toward "gender-neutral" language, because many believe that even when used with the best intentions, gender-specific terms subconsciously tell us that being male is somehow more important than being female, and that certain social roles are best performed by men. The real reason for being sensitive about gender and language is, of course, to achieve gender equality.

Textbooks and cultural documents continually are reworded to accommodate our new sensitivity toward gender and language. The Catholic church has officially endorsed the use of non-gender-specific language in religious documents and biblical translations. Gender-specific words such as *mailman, chairman, housewife,* and *maid* are being changed to *mail carrier, chairperson, homemaker,* and *maintenance assistant* in order to signify that these terms cover both genders. Writers and speakers alike are instructed to avoid the use of *he* as a generic term and instead use "he or she," "they," "one," or "you." (This is not always easy, especially in philosophical discussions about "the individual . . . *he.*" In instances like this, we need a gender-neutral third person pronoun to solve the problem.) College students are urged to avoid gender-specific language in their term papers. Perhaps you think that this is a subject of little importance—that it is merely a matter of semantic misunderstanding. But consider this. If you are male and you hear a statement such as, "Now is the time for every man to stand up for what he believes in," there is a good chance you will feel somehow compelled to think hard about what you believe in. If you are female, you *may* feel the same way, but chances are you will feel, subconsciously, that somehow this statement does not apply to you; you may even think, "Yes, it is about time *they* pulled *themselves* together!" If even a few women feel excluded when they read or hear language that uses the masculine gender—excluded either in the sense of feeling left out, or in the sense of not having to get involved—then that is enough reason to change the way we phrase things.

Is Biology Destiny?

When we ask whether or not there is sexual equality, we really are asking one of two questions: (1) Is there a cultural and social equality? or (2) Is there biological equality? The first question is relative to the historical time period: Today we have reason to say that we have not reached total equality yet, but we hope to do so in the future. (In the past, in Western society, the answer would have been a flat no.) But if we ask the second question, we have to ask a follow-up question: What do we mean by "biological equality"? Do we mean that men and women are the same? Or similar? That they will do similar things in similar situations? Or perhaps that they have a similar genetic makeup, even if there are cultural differences?

The bottom line is the difference between a descriptive and a normative approach. A descriptive theory of equality compares capabilities and pronounces people to be "similar" or "dissimilar." A normative theory of equality may or may not look at the "facts" presented by the descriptive theory, but states that people *ought* to be treated a certain way—either (a) the same, or (b) similarly under similar conditions, or (c) differently. And if a normative theory asserts that equality is a good thing, it will present a theory for how to achieve it.

Sexual equality, as an idea, is a complex issue (the same is true of racial equality). We must ask, Is sexual equality a biological fact? What does that mean? And is that important for an ethical policy? We must remember that a policy based purely on a biological theory is *sociobiology* and may result in discrimination, as we discussed in the

Sex or Gender?

By consensus, the term that is most commonly used today when people talk about sexual differences that go beyond mere biological functions is *gender*.

Although this used to be a strictly grammatical term, it now is used instead of the biological term *sexual* as a sociopolitical term.

preceding chapter. But that doesn't mean that we can't take biology into *consideration* when we establish policies. The idea of sexual or *gender* equality is so important to us now that we have antidiscrimination laws against "sexism." In other words, we believe that regardless of whether or not equality between the genders is a natural fact, it should be a cultural and sociological institution. This is a *normative* idea.

Past Views on Women

Women's Role in the Public Sector

Gender equality is, of course, a novel idea in terms of Western history. Until the mid-nineteenth century it was common practice in Western culture to assume that male and female natures were essentially different in their functions, aspirations, and potential, and that male nature was somehow more *normal* than female nature. It was not thought of as necessarily *better*, for many men seemed to believe that women had higher moral standards, but it was considered more important in the sense that male nature was more representative of the human species than was female nature. What was this assumption based on? Today we might say *prejudice*, but it can't be dismissed as easily as that, because for a great many thinkers, objectivity was an important ideal. They tried to describe things as they saw them, not as they believed things ought to be, nor as they might appear to an undiscerning eye. And what they saw was that few women had any role to play in public life: There were few women politicians, few women artists, few women scientists. (It would be easy to progress to stating a naturalistic fallacy: Because there are no women in public life, women can't, or should not, be represented in public life.) But why were there so few women in public life? The answer is tentative; not all the facts are in yet. It seems obvious, though, that a person's contribution to what we call public life is greatly dependent on that person feeling called or welcome as a contributor. If no one expects or wants you to become a good politician, or mathematician, or sculptor, you might not think of trying. Encouragement and expectation are major factors in such choices. On the other hand, if it appears that you are *destined* for a certain task, you might not question that, either. For most women (until the arrival of dependable birth control), motherhood, several times over, was their destiny. And for those familiar with the demands of large families, it does not come as news that for the person in charge of the *private sphere*, the home, there is precious little time for anything else, unless you can afford domestic help. Indeed, throughout history—Western history as well as world history—most cultural contributions by individual women were made by those who either did not play the role of homemaker or else somehow managed to "do both."

An interesting question is why women's contributions to the *private sphere* are rarely discussed. It's certainly true that although women could not own property, had no right to vote, could not hold a job without the permission of a guardian, and had no legitimate influence in the world of affairs, many women still had considerable power within the four walls of their home. They managed the bookkeeping and purchases, planned and prepared meals for the household, educated the children, and kept things running on the farm—a full-time job in itself. Why were these management skills not considered important? In an odd way, they were; it is probably our modern-day prejudice to think that they weren't. A young woman chosen as a spouse was expected to have these qualities, and "woman's work" was a vitally important social factor. But in terms of the public sphere women had no place and were not considered potential contributors until almost the end of the nineteenth century. Even today, many people accept the idea that the public sphere is the vital one—perhaps because work in the public sphere is *paid for*, and work in the private sphere generally is not.

Another factor must be mentioned here. In early times having women remain outside the public sphere was thought by most men (and women, too) to be a way of *protecting* women; they were spared the unpleasantness and insecurity of the world of affairs. This is the viewpoint of the Arab fundamentalist world, where much the same pattern prevails today. This may be a genuine concern, but some critics believe it can be interpreted more realistically as a way of treating women as *property* (namely the property of their husbands and fathers)—as an investment in the next generation and as a working resource.

Some Philosophers on the Status of Women

Traditionally, philosophy has supported the view that women have a separate function from men; on occasion it becomes clear that individual philosophers are implying that this function is somehow less important than that of men, or that women's rational capabilities do not quite measure up to those of men. In this section we will examine some of the more famous viewpoints (several of the philosophers mentioned here will show up again later in this part of the book).

Plato's famous vision of the ideal state in *The Republic* allows for both men and women to perform whatever function they are best at. However, in a later dialogue, *The Laws*, he seems to have drifted toward a more traditional view of women. We already have had a brief encounter with Aristotle's view of women; in his text "Generation of Animals" he states that it is the male who supplies the soul during the act of conception (and thus the male is the formal cause of the fetus) while the female merely supplies the material: "The female is as it were a deformed male."

For St. Augustine it is evident that both men and women have souls, and both are as likely to be saved by grace, or eternally condemned. And because God created them both in his own image, woman, too, is in the image of God—but only when she is married to a man. When she simply fulfills her function as his helpmate, she is not in the image of God; only the man is.

Few philosophers before the nineteenth century spent time discussing the male-female issue in detail. Kant, although he expanded the concept of "moral agent" to include all who can think rationally, expressed severe doubts about whether women actually count as rational persons in the same sense that men do. Kant represents the classical attitude of *adoration* of the woman as civilizer and guardian of beauty. In his essay "On the Distinction of the Beautiful and Sublime in the Interrelations of the Two Sexes," Kant describes the dangers of allowing women to think too hard:

> Laborious learning or painful pondering, even if a woman should greatly suc-ceed in it, destroy the merits that are proper to her sex, and because of their rarity they can make of her an object of cold admiration; but at the same time they will weaken the charms with which she exercises her great power over the other sex. A woman who has a head full of Greek . . . or carries on fundamental controversies about mechanics . . . might as well even have a beard.

What is revealed here is that even though it may not have seemed proper in Kant's day and age for a woman to have intellectual or mechanical interests, it was not en-tirely unthinkable. This was the age of the Enlightenment, when so many concepts of social and personal limits and proprieties were redefined. Still, the ones who benefited from the Enlightenment's emphasis on the values of education and human rights were primarily members of the male population.

Jean-Jacques Rousseau (1712–1778), a contemporary of Kant, believed children ought to be raised the natural way, with as few rules and regulations as possible. Such an ideal would apply to girls as well as boys—but with a slight qualification: Although the young boy is supposed to be raised with few restrictions and allowed to roam barefoot in the woods, the girl must wait for him at home and be his proper playmate and friend; she must learn to inquire about his interests. In his book *Emile*, Rousseau writes about a boy, Emile, and a girl, Sophie. The boy becomes a "natural" man, while the girl becomes in turn a "natural" woman:

> The faculties common to the sexes are not equally shared between them; but take them all in all, they are well balanced. The more womanly a woman is, the better. Whenever she exercises her own proper powers she gains by it; when she tries to usurp ours she becomes our inferior. . . . A man does not want to make his companion a servant and deprive himself of the peculiar charms of her company. That is quite against the teaching of nature, which has endowed women with quick pleasing minds. Nature means them to think, to judge, to

French Salons: An Important Influence

We must add a historical footnote to this vision of the properly educated girl. In Rousseau's own place and time—in France just prior to the French Revolution—women intellectuals were not at all uncommon. A Parisian tradition known as *Le Salon*, society clubs for intellectuals and politicians, most often were presided over by a hostess who was as skilled and well versed in the current literary and philosophical trends as any of her male guests. Salon hostesses such as the famous Madame de Staël often were the active force "behind the scenes" of important power changes in French society. Indeed, Rousseau owed much to the Salons for advancing the popularity of his own romantic philosophy.

love, to know and to cultivate the mind as well as the countenance. This is the equipment nature has given them to compensate for their lack of strength and enable them to direct the strength of men.

So Sophie must be guided toward the life *nature has intended for her*—as a clever housekeeper and helper to her husband. She must be kept busy, never idle; she must learn to read and count; she should learn art (still lifes only, not landscape or figure painting); she must learn to preserve her sweetness and seductiveness even in the face of being wronged. As for religion and philosophy, there is no need for Sophie even to think about them, for girls can't understand these subjects. All they need to know are the basic dogmas. However, girls should not neglect their reason, because reason allows them to understand their duties as wives and mothers.

Generations later, Friedrich Nietzsche (1844–1900), the ultimate misogynist, described his view of women in *Thus Spoke Zarathustra*:

Man shall be trained for war, and woman for the recreation of the warrior: all else is folly. . . . Surface is woman's nature, foam tossed to and fro on shallow water. . . . Thou goest to women? Remember thy whip!

In *Beyond Good and Evil* Nietzsche elaborates on these sentiments:

Woman wants to become self-reliant—and for that reason she is beginning to enlighten men about "woman as such"; *this* is one of the worst developments of the general *uglification* of Europe. For what must these clumsy attempts of women at scientific self-exposure bring to light! Woman has much reason for shame; so much pedantry, superficiality, schoolmarmishness, petty presumption, petty licentiousness and immodesty lies concealed in woman—one only needs to study her behavior with children!—and so far all this was at bottom best repressed and kept under control by *fear* of man.

Early Feminism in France

A very early speaker for the rights of women was the Frenchman Poulain de la Barre, who in 1673 argued that men and women are fundamentally similar because they have the same powers of reasoning. Poulain believed women should have access to all occupations in society, even as generals in the army and leaders of Parliament. However, few people paid much attention to Poulain; he remained both unique and unknown as a seventeenth-century feminist. In the 18th century, Rousseau's view of the fundamental difference between men and women became the popular view. During the French Revolution things changed considerably in France. Many sided with the thinker Madame d'Epinay, who believed that women and men have the same nature and the same constitution, and will display different virtues and vices only if they are brought up that way; any differentiation is due to social pressure, nothing else. Her thoughts inspired the politician Concordet, who in 1792 suggested that education should be available to women because both men and women were, primarily, members of the human race. Concordet's opponent, Talleyrand, who was inspired by Rousseau, managed to put a stop to these ideas, which, it seems, were too radical even for members of the French Revolution.

Is there nothing, then, for Nietzsche to admire in women? Besides voicing his appreciation for their ability to "bear strong sons," he makes the following observation:

> What inspires respect for woman, and often enough even fear, is her *nature*, which is more "natural" than man's, the genuine, cunning suppleness of a beast of prey, the tiger's claw under the glove, the naivité of her egoism, her uneducability and inner wildness, the incomprehensibility, scope, and movement of her desires and virtues.

One might ask why Nietzsche displayed such scorn for female nature. The usual explanation, which has its roots in psychoanalysis, is that growing up in an all-female household gave him much to ponder. However, this seems to assume that any boy living under women's rule would come to the same conclusions, which is another way of saying that Nietzsche was right. We don't know what exactly prompted his misogynistic attitude, but it did reflect a certain nineteenth-century misgiving about the growing women's liberation movement. In a sense Nietzsche merely was voicing what many other men, and some women, felt at the time. Another fact that must not be forgotten is that Nietzsche had harsh words for many other groups besides women—for Christians, Platonists, Germans, and Englishmen—as well as for many of his old friends and teachers, whom he conceived of as having disappointed him. In short,

FIGURE 16.1 Mary Wollstonecraft (1759–1797) English philosopher and writer of *Vindication of the Rights of Women*, which was much ridiculed at the time by male scholars but which was to have a lasting influence. Wollstonecraft died in childbirth, giving life to a second Mary Wollstonecraft, who, under her married name Shelley, was to give life to another kind of creature with the story of Frankenstein and his monster creation.

Nietzsche was a man of much passion and little delicacy in his writing. As is the case with Aristotle, if we wish to partake of Nietzsche's more profound insights, we must accept the fact that much of his writing is quite offensive by today's standards.

There were, in the eighteenth century, voices—male as well as female—that argued for the possibility of a different order. The British philosopher Mary Wollstonecraft (1759–1797) was one of the few women of the eighteenth century who directly addressed the women's situation. In *Vindication of the Rights of Women* she suggests that not only is it not fair to women to train them to be uneducated, unthinking creatures who are only eager to please, but also it is unfair to men, because although a man may fall in love with that kind of woman, he certainly won't want to live with her. After all, what will the two have in common once the seduction is over and they are married? No, women should have the same opportunities as men. If they don't measure up, men will have reason to claim superiority—but to apply two different value systems, one that says what is proper for men, and one that says what is proper for women—is to make a mockery out of the concept of virtue itself:

> I wish to persuade women to endeavor to acquire strength, both of mind and body, and to convince them that the soft phrases, susceptibility of heart, delicacy of sentiment, and refinement of taste, are almost synonymous with epithets of weakness, and that those beings who are only the objects of pity and that kind of love, which has been termed its sister, will soon become objects of contempt. . . . Besides, the woman who strengthens her body and exercises her mind will, by managing her family and practicing various virtues, become the friend, and not the humble dependent of her husband.

In the nineteenth century John Stuart Mill, inspired by his intellectual, longtime friend (and later wife) Harriet Taylor, wrote about how women's as well as men's characters are molded by society:

> All women are brought up from the earliest years in the belief that their ideal of character is the very opposite to that of men; not self-will, and government

by self-control, but submission, and yielding to the control of others. All the moralities tell them that it is the duty of women, and all the current sentimentalities that it is their nature, to live for others.

Under different social circumstances, Mill says, we would see women acting no longer as the full-time slaves of their husbands, but as independent individuals with original intellectual ideas to contribute to society. If women are capable of fulfilling social functions, they should be free to do so. If women can't fulfill certain functions, there is no need to prohibit them from doing it (this is again the concept "ought implies can"). Even if only a few women are capable of certain tasks, the opportunity should be open to them. Mill does believe that male and female qualities in general are not the same—men and women usually are good at different things—but from a moral point of view these qualities should be considered equally important. So what might Mill say about the current controversy as to whether women soldiers should be allowed in combat? Probably that most women would prefer not to, and would not qualify, but that those who want to and who do qualify should be allowed to do so.

For proponents of early Marxism, women's situation was directly determined by the economic conditions of society. In a capitalist society, where every consideration revolves around property, women are under the control of men because they are considered property (and in the capitalistic society of the nineteenth-century middle class, women could rarely own property, either). Friedrich Engels writes that "the modern individual family is founded on the open or concealed domestic slavery of the wife. . . . Within the family [the husband] is the bourgeois, and the wife represents the proletariat." But when property is abolished in communist society, both men and women will stand forth as equal individuals, with monogamy abolished as a form of capitalistic ownership.

Contemporary Views on Gender Equality

The Two Facets of Gender Equality

The moral demand for gender equality has changed complexion several times in the twentieth century: Early movements for equality were focused on very tangible things, such as the right to vote, the right to own property, the right to live without a guardian, the right to marry as an adult without parental consent, the right to divorce, and so on. As these issues were resolved, the focus shifted to other concrete issues: the right to hold previously "male" jobs, the right to partake of higher education, and the right to receive equal pay for equal work. Most people today consider these demands right and just. It may come as a surprise to those who are wary of the term *feminism* that these demands are what classical feminism defines as its goal: not "women's rule," but simply equal treatment and opportunity for both genders.

During World War I, when so many "household providers" were at the front, women all over the Western world took on men's jobs, partly so that they and their families could stay alive, but also in order to meet the needs of society. This was a major revelation both to women and to the political powers, because it conclusively proved that women could hold technical and intellectual jobs that previously had been thought of as "male." In the twenties and thirties what we call "women's liberation" was quite significant for this reason. The World War I phenomenon repeated itself in the forties with World War II. But after World War II there was a gigantic push to get women out of the job market and back in the home in order to provide jobs for returning servicemen. Indeed, many of the ideals of gender equality were all but forgotten with the birth of the baby boomer generation. In the sixties and seventies "women's lib" was revived; the main thrust was to get the traditionally male job market open for women so that women could become doctors, lawyers, truck drivers, and so on. In the eighties and early nineties certain women's rights have become law; affirmative action and laws prohibiting sexual harassment have passed, although the ERA legislation (Equal Rights Amendment) has not yet passed.

In the eighties another issue took on importance. With a large percentage of women back in the job market, new questions arose. Should women mold themselves to fit the job market, or should the job market adjust to accommodate women? The job market had been a "man's world" for a long time, and some people felt that women were expected to take on "masculine" qualities in order to fit in. The question was, Is that desirable? Or might "feminine" qualities actually *benefit* the job market? Today the thinking is that women definitely can contribute something of their own to the public sphere; in fact, many believe the working world has suffered from being without women's special talents for so long.

Today, then, the idea of gender equality has two facets. One is related to classical feminism, which calls for men and women to be considered as *persons* first, and sexual beings second. The other is the belief that men and women possess *fundamentally different* qualities, and that both sexes should learn from each other and respect what the other can contribute.

Men and Women Are Persons

For those taking the view that men and women should be considered as persons first, the gender differences are primarily cultural. Biological differences are significant only in terms of procreation; apart from birthing and breastfeeding infants, which can be done only by women, the sexual differences are irrelevant. Culture has shaped men and women, and a cultural change could therefore allow for another type of gender: the *androgynous* type.

The French philosopher Simone de Beauvoir, one of the most powerful voices for equal education and equal opportunities in the twentieth century, accuses the philosophical tradition of seeing woman as the atypical human. Woman, she says, is considered a deviant human being, by men as well as by women. Somehow, psychologists and philosophers have come to believe that man is the "typical" human being, so woman thus becomes "atypical." For man woman becomes "the Other," an alien

FIGURE 16.2 Simone de Beauvoir (1908–1986), French philosopher and writer. Beauvoir viewed gender inequality as primarily a matter of upbringing. If you teach girls and boys that they are fundamentally different and exclude girls from doing what the boys are allowed and expected to do, you will have a society of gender inequality. Men and women will live up to their expected roles; compared to man, woman will appear to be a different and not-quite-successful human being, "The Other." But Beauvoir teaches, with existentialist theory, that there is no such thing as human nature and that women as well as men must be taught to free themselves from preconceived cultural gender images.

being who helps man define himself through her alienness, and with whom he communicates on an everyday basis, but who never becomes "one of the boys." Woman, who has been placed in this situation for millennia, also has come to believe that she is atypical. The female anatomy is seen as a psychologically determining factor, while the male anatomy is not. In other words, women do what they do because they are women; men do what they do because they are normal. This is a *cultural* fact, not a natural one, says Beauvoir. And the only way a woman can become *authentic* is to shed her role as "deviant" and become a true human being by not being locked into the traditional female role. Society can assist in this process by treating little boys and girls the same—by giving them the same education and the same subsequent opportunities.

Until women begin to think of themselves as a group, Beauvoir says, they will believe that they are abnormal human beings. And as long as men and women receive different educations and different treatment from society, the situation will remain the same, and woman will not feel responsible for the state of the world, but will regard herself as men regard her—as an overgrown child. Of course women are weak, Beauvoir says. Of course they don't use male logic (here we must remember that she is talking about uneducated women of pre-World War II). Of course woman is religious to the point of superstition. Of course she has no sense of history, and of course she accepts authority. Of course she cries a lot over little things. She may even be lazy, sensual, servile, frivolous, utilitarian, materialistic, and hysterical. She may, in short, be all that Rousseau and Nietzsche thought she was. *But why is she all these things?* Because she has no power except by subterfuge. She has no education, so she never has been taught about the cause and effect of history, and the relative powers of authority. She is caught up in a never-ending stream of housework, which causes her to be practically oriented. She nags because she realizes that she has no power to change her situation. She is sensual because she is bored. In her book *The Second Sex*, Beauvoir says, "The truth is that when a woman is engaged in an enterprise worthy of a human being, she is quite able to show herself as active, effective, taciturn—and as ascetic—as a man."

The Other: Simone de Beauvoir

Simone de Beauvoir (1908–1986), a feminist and existentialist, was long considered a minor thinker by the philosophical community. One reason was that she was Jean-Paul Sartre's "significant other," and her books, such as *The Second Sex*, show a considerable influence from Sartre's ideas. However, most philosophers now recognize that many of the fundamental ideas of existentialism came about through discussions between Sartre and Beauvoir, and many ideas first published by Sartre may well have originated during these discussions. There is even some suspicion that Sartre occasionally may have published ideas by Beauvoir under his own name. True or not, this new attitude reveals a changing perspective on women in philosophy. At the end of the twentieth century, Beauvoir's influence in the area of gender inequality has turned out to be just as viable as Sartre's philosophy. Beauvoir is primarily interested in the existence of woman as a cultural phenomenon; she analyzes woman's situation in a man's world (which was far more the case in the mid-twentieth century than at the time of writing this book). She hopes that instead of a world where woman is considered deviant and man normal, we will have a society of *human beings*, not just males and females, and people will interact with each other equally as productive, authentic beings. Beauvoir has come under heavy criticism by some feminists for not realizing that she herself regards man as the norm, and wants women to be treated and act like men, rather than rejoice in their inherent female nature. It appears that Beauvoir herself decided to live a childfree life in order to escape the female stereotype.

So, if we change our culture, we will change what has for so long been considered female nature—and with it, probably also male nature. We will create people who are responsible human beings above all, and who will respect each other for that reason. This philosophy has been adopted by many late-twentieth-century feminists, including Germain Greer, Gloria Steinem, and Joyce Trebilcot.

The quest for *androgynism* has taken on several shapes. A moderate, modern viewpoint advocates a common upbringing for all children, one that avoids using pink for girls and blue for boys, and makes use of toys that don't perpetuate typical male/female roles. Proponents of this viewpoint advocate a general change in language from gender-specific terms to gender-neutral terms.

Two versions of androgynism as a political goal currently are being advocated, and Joyce Trebilcot analyzes both. One proposes a society in which men and women *share* all the best characteristics of the traditional sex roles, and if a woman *doesn't* want to hold a job (typically a male role) or if a man prefers *not* to care for his sick children (typically a female role), then society must teach them the necessity of sharing these

Can Gays Choose Not To Be Gay?

In talking about the possibility of choosing gender roles, it is reasonable to discuss the issue of homosexuality and the gay lifestyle. There still is considerable political and moral opposition to homosexuals in Western societies, in some more than in others. In some societies homosexuals can now marry; in others homosexuality is still illegal. Why is there a traditional opposition to homosexuality in Christian countries? It is because of several traditional Christian assumptions, such as (1) Homosexuality is a *moral choice*, and one that goes against nature (nature calls for procreation), so homosexuality is morally wrong; and (2) Homosexuals are primarily seducers of adolescents, who then will become homosexual. In the early nineties scientists have reached the *tentative* conclusion (based on brain autopsies) that male homosexuality is not a matter of choice, but of biology. In that case both of the above objections would be invalid, because (1) Gays don't choose their lifestyle or sexual orientation but are born with it (so it is *natural* for them); and

(2) Boys can't be seduced to become homosexuals; they either are born that way or are not. (Besides, being gay does not imply that one is primarily interested in young boys.) But there is as yet no extensive research about lesbianism, nor about bisexualism. The advantage for homosexuals of a conclusive result pointing to biological factors is obvious: There could be no more reason for discrimination based on the belief that homosexuality is an "immoral choice." But such a finding might open the door for new areas of discrimination: Might we see parents take their young children to the doctor to have them "screened" for homosexuality, and if they test positive, ask to have them "cured"? In this way homosexuality would be labeled a *defect*, a disease. Some homosexuals might say that they would prefer to be heterosexual if that were possible, but certainly not all would. Joyce Trebilcot would say that in a polyandrogynous society the question of what your sexual orientation ought to be would never come up in the first place.

duties. This version is sometimes referred to as *monoandrogynism*. The other version, *polyandrogynism*, suggests that gender roles be left as open as possible, with no demand that the duties be shared. If a man wants to fulfill the traditional male role, he is free to do so. If a woman wants to live the life of a traditional male, she can. If a man wants to stay home and care for the kids, fine. If a woman wants to do the same thing, so be it. Both theories assume that gender roles are cultural artifacts; however, polyandrogynism allows for the possibility that people just might be biologically different from one another. Trebilcot herself opts for polyandrogynism.

An ultraradical version of androgynism assumes that there are profound biological differences between men and women, and suggests that we eradicate them. Thus, if women are the only humans capable of giving birth, we must *change human biology* so that this becomes an option for men also.

The question is, can we choose our gender at all? Obviously we can't choose our *sex* (not without going through major physical operations, anyway). But the term *gender* also encompasses our *social roles* as male and female. Can we, then, decide which social role we wish to adapt—which gender we wish to be—or do biological factors exist which prevent people from exercising gender choice? In other words, is our gender determined by our biology to a greater extent than people who advocate androgyny realize?

Recent experiments with androgynous training of infants and children give conflicting results. A recent *Newsweek* article states that in spite of the efforts of egalitarian parents, their children still end up playing "boys' games" and "girls' games," still prefer blue if they are boys and pink if they are girls, and generally conform to the old patterns of assuming that most Moms stay at home and most Dads go to work, even if their own parents both work outside the home. This, the article said, is probably not a sign that gender is determined by biological factors; it is more a sign that children are influenced by a lot of factors and not just by their well-meaning parents: TV programs, including cartoons and commercials, influence their perceptions. So do their playmates, whose parents may not be so intent on gender equality. The author of the article adds that if young children are placed in an environment where there is no pressure to play with toys specifically made for their own gender, then both boys and girls will be perfectly happy playing with gender-neutral toys like model farms and building blocks. In such an environment some boys will choose to play with dolls, and some girls with guns, but it is a fact that most children, when presented with gender-specific toys, will conform to the traditional pattern. The issue of androgynism is thus not closed, but rather suspended on the grounds of "insufficient evidence."

Men and Women Are Fundamentally Different

By the beginning of the eighties women had been in the work force long enough for people to begin to evaluate the situation, and although some women felt good about working in what used to be a "man's world" and conforming to its standards (to a greater or lesser degree), others felt that somehow those standards were damaging to their female identity. Few provisions for childcare existed, there was little understanding of maternal (or paternal) duties at home, and the overriding atmosphere was one of competition and isolation rather than networking and teamwork. For these women survival in the male-dominated public sphere was possible only if they were willing to give up some of their female values. Although this doesn't entirely explain the rise of the "new feminism," it serves as a clue to why the focus of the movement changed from seeking equal opportunity and equal pay for both men and women to questioning whether women want something different than men do, and whether some of women's capabilities lie in other areas from those of most men.

Interestingly enough, it is not the first time such ideas have been advanced—we already have encountered theories of Aristotle, Rousseau, Nietzsche and others which state that women and men have different abilities and thus different places in society. However, these theories were not advanced with any notion of gender equality. John Stuart Mill was the first influential philosopher to suggest that although men and women have different capacities, they should nevertheless be given equal opportunities and equal respect for their abilities. It is this concept toward which the new feminism looks.

Research into "human nature" has until recently focused primarily on male nature, say the new feminists, and they support this claim with overwhelming facts. As we shall see, the theories of the "state of nature" focus on the male. Freud's psychoanalysis focuses on the boy's development more than the girl's. In general, the values we've celebrated for so long as good human behavior have been predominantly male values, because the male person has been considered the "real" person, while women have been thought of as slightly deviant. The man is the typical human being. In older textbooks on human development, the earlier forms of hominids, such as *homo habilis* and *Neandertal*, have usually been depicted as males (the "Neandertal man"). Only recently in textbooks and articles have humans been symbolized by both male and female figures. Even recent theories of psychology seem to use boys and men as their research material rather than girls and women, and the medical industry must now face the problems resulting from years of conducting research with primarily male subjects. The statistics regarding women and certain diseases (heart disease, for example) are unreliable, and the administration of medicine to women has been decided on the basis of research on male subjects. This is not just a matter of a slanted ideology; it is a very practical problem. Women have for a long time been judged by the standards of men, as though women were what Aristotle claimed so long ago—deficient males. The new feminism wants to replace the image of one of the genders being more "normal" than the other with an image of both genders, with all their differences, being equally representative of the human race. This involves upgrading the "female virtues" of motherhood, housekeeping, caring for family members, and so on, virtues that for some people seem to fall by the wayside in the first rush to get women into the workforce. The values that typically have been considered male are: justice, rights, fairness, competition, being independent, and living by the rules. Typical female values, on the other hand, are: generosity, caring, harmony, reconciliation, and working to maintain close relationships.

Psychologist Carol Gilligan has been a major inspiration in the gender debate. Her book *In a Different Voice* (1982) analyzes different reactions of boys and girls, men and women, and concludes that there is a basic difference in the *moral attitudes* of males and females. In one of her analyses she uses an experiment by a well-known contemporary psychologist, Lawrence Kohlberg; it is called the *Heinz dilemma*. Kohlberg asked two eleven-year-old children, Jake and Amy, to evaluate the following situation: Heinz's wife is desperately ill, and Heinz can't afford medication for her. Should Heinz steal the medication? Jake has no doubts; he says yes, Heinz should steal the medication, because his wife's life is more important than the rule of not stealing. Amy, though, is not so sure. She says no, he shouldn't steal the medication, because what if

FIGURE 16.3 Carol Gilligan (b. 1936), American psychologist and author of *In A Different Voice*. Like Beauvoir, Gilligan believes that throughout Western history men have been considered the "normal" gender and women have been viewed as not-quite-normal. However, Gilligan does not argue for a monoandrogynous society as does Beauvoir but believes that men and women are fundamentally different in their approach to life—different but equal.

he got caught? Then he would have to go to jail, and who would look after his sick wife? Perhaps he could ask the pharmacist to let him have the medication and pay later. Kohlberg concluded that Jake had a clear understanding of the situation: It would be just that the wife should receive the medication, because her rights would override the law of not stealing. However, Kohlberg thought that Amy's comprehension of the situation was fuzzy at best. Jake understood what it was all about: rights and justice.

Gilligan returns to the Kohlberg example, rereads Amy's answer, and comes up with another conclusion entirely: Although Jake answered the question, *Should Heinz steal the drug or not?* Amy heard it differently: *Should Heinz steal the drug, or should he do something else?* In effect, the children were answering different questions, and Amy's makes as much sense as Jake's. But Amy is not concerned with the issues of rights and justice as much as she is with what will happen to Heinz and his wife; she even takes the humaneness of the pharmacist into consideration. In other words, she thinks in terms of *caring*. She acknowledges that there are laws, but she also believes people can be reasoned with. Kohlberg, Gilligan says, didn't hear this in Amy's answer because he was looking for the "justice" answer. Gilligan concludes that there is a tendency in boys and men to focus on an *ethic of justice*, while girls and women look toward an *ethic of care*. The whole point of Gilligan's book is to open our eyes to the advantages of a combination of the two ethics, and a recognition that both have their place in our social life. Gilligan's aim is to reevaluate the so-called female characteristics and see them not as illogical, irrelevant, and emotional, but as following their own, very sensible logic. In the end, the ideal situation will be not only for men to learn about women's ethics, but also for women to learn about the male way of thinking, for without it a woman may forget that she, too, has rights and isn't merely a "means to an end."

Consequences of the Gender Debate

For a philosophical analysis, the all-important question now is: If there really is a male tendency toward justice and a female tendency toward caring, *why is that?* Is it biological, or is it cultural, or is it a little bit of both? Gilligan herself answers that she doesn't know, and that the question doesn't interest her very much. But it is a vital one for a philosophy of human nature, because knowing the origin of a certain trait enables us to discuss what to do about it. If the difference is biological, many changes will need to be effected in our society so that the values of two genders can be accommodated. But if it is cultural, we must discuss whether it is a difference we want to perpetuate, or one we want to try to eradicate.

Gilligan's theory has been an eye-opener for thousands of women and men, and has fostered a new cultural debate. One result of this debate is linguist Deborah Tannen's book *You Just Don't Understand*, which analyzes male and female speech and behavior patterns and which may prove to be another milestone in understanding the psychological nature of men and women. Tannen argues that men and women grow up with different speech patterns and different body language, and this is one reason some men and women find it hard to communicate: They simply expect a different kind of answer than the one they are getting. A woman may say to her partner, "Let's go to the beach," and what she intends is to suggest an action that both parties can agree on, a cooperative effort. Her partner, however, may hear something else entirely: "I want to go to the beach and you have to go, too." In other words, he is hearing an order, and he therefore reacts negatively, believing he is being bossed around. A woman may tell her male boss, "I'm sorry that X cancelled the account," and her boss may answer, "Well, it wasn't really your fault," or worse, "That's all right—I accept your apology." The woman intends to share a feeling of sympathy, but her boss thinks she is taking blame and apologizing. Tannen believes that such differences are primarily cultural in origin, and that although we perhaps can't do away with them entirely, we can at least learn to listen to each other—to what we are saying and what we are intending to say.

Other consequences of the gender debate are being felt in the corporate world. Until recently, women have been working according to "male" values. Now, however, female executives are beginning to favor networking, showing "caring" feelings at work, talking about problems, and so on. Indeed, these "female values" are coming to be viewed as *corporative assets* instead of as "soft" and unprofessional behavior. So changes are underfoot, and they are supposed to be beneficial for men, too, because now men supposedly can allow themselves to develop closer relationships.

What does the Gilligan theory add up to? For many women it means that their experiences of attachment and their important relationships are normal and good and not "overly dependent," "clinging," or immature; it means an upgrading of what we consider traditional female values. The point of Gilligan's book is to prompt the mature woman to understand rights, and the mature man to understand caring, so we all can work and live together in harmony. Her hopes may not be realized for decades to come however, for although some may argue that they know some very caring men

FIGURE 16.4 *Thelma and Louise,* MGM, 1990. Victims of circumstances and past traumas, Thelma (Geena Davis) and Louise (Susan Sarandon) try to escape not only the police, but also their past roles and self-images, on a trek from Arkansas to New Mexico and their ultimate destiny. The story of *Thelma and Louise* is outlined in Chapter 20 as a portrayal of women struggling to find their identity.

and some very justice-oriented women, it seems that Gilligan is right in claiming that most women in the United States grow up believing that caring is what is most important, and most men grow up believing that individual rights and justice are the ultimate ethical values.

There are risks involved in Gilligan's theory. Some think we may end up elevating female values *far above* male values. In that case we will have reversed an unfair system but created another unfair system by declaring women "normal" and men "slightly deviant." Another, more pressing problem is the following: If we say that it is in the woman's nature to be understanding and caring, we may be forcing her right back into the private sphere from where she just emerged. Men (and also women) may say, well, if most women aren't able to understand "justice," then we can't use them in the real world, and they'd better go home and do what nature intended them to do: have babies and care for their man. Similarly, if a job calls for "caring" qualities, employers may be reluctant to hire a man, because men are not "naturals" at caring. So instead of giving people more opportunities, Gilligan may actually be setting up new categories that could result in policies that exclude women from "men's work" and men from "women's work." It is not enough to say that the qualities of one gender are not supposed to outweigh the qualities of the other, because we all know that even with the best intentions, we tend to rank one set of differences higher than the other. We may all be equal, but remember George Orwell's *Animal Farm*? In this book, which is a metaphor for political despotism, Orwell warns against some being considered "more equal than others." Critics have claimed that what Gilligan is doing is throwing a monkey wrench into the philosophy of gender equality, and her "ethics of care" theory may result in statements such as this: "We need a new executive with a good head for legal rules—but we can't hire a woman, of course, even though she seems otherwise qualified, because science says that women have a lousy sense of justice." In short, there is a danger that a psychological theory of gender may turn into a theory of sociobiology, that it may move from describing what seems to be the case to prescribing a set of rules about who ought to do what.

Narratives That Explore Women and Men and Their Worlds

Chapter 20 includes stories from several cultures about women and men. Some are told through the eyes of men, and some through the eyes of women. A Pueblo Indian myth called "Men and Women Try Living Apart" is almost but not quite identical to a Navajo myth, "The River of Separation." Alice Walker's *The Temple of My Familiar* contains a "pseudomyth" about how men became religious. *Foucault's Pendulum*, by the philosopher Umberto Eco, sees women as having privileged access to the Truth. And the film *Thelma and Louise* spins a tale of female bonding.

Chapter 17

Are We Good or Evil from the Beginning?

What is your gut feeling? When all artifice is stripped away; when there is no longer any pretense, deception, fabrication, or falsehood, what is the human animal *really* like? Are we by nature good and compassionate, or are we uncaring, self-centered, aggressive, and even vicious?

As we have seen, today biology tells us that we are both, but this information was not known in earlier centuries, when philosophers and laypersons struggled with the question. Even today the biological answer to the question seems insufficient for many people. We don't really want to hear that we have tendencies for both good and bad behavior; we'd much rather hear that we are basically bad, or basically good—then we could set about to demonstrate that the theory is wrong. In other words, we'd rather grapple not with a biological issue, but with a *moral one*. Perhaps this skeptical struggle with descriptive and normative theories of human nature is simply a part of modern human nature.

This section explores four major contributions to the human nature debate: one from the days prior to the age of descriptive science, two from the dawn of science as we know it, and one inspired by Darwin himself. Before we begin, we must make one distinction. In Chapter 4 we examined the theory of psychological egoism, which assumes that humans are selfish, or at least self-interested. The two terms are different: One contains a *value judgment* (being *selfish* is being bad) while the other is more *value-neutral* (being *self-interested* is neither bad nor good). Accordingly, theories that claim that humans are bad by nature often mean that humans are *selfish*, and theories that claim that humans are selfish often are interpreted as meaning that humans are *bad*. As we will see with Thomas Hobbes, this interpretation may not always be appropriate.

The Christian Viewpoint

The Original Sin

The classical Christian view is that humans are bad by nature—but not necessarily "selfish." The story in Genesis of the Fall of Man is taken to illustrate that not only do humans have an inherent tendency to be disobedient to God, but also the original act of disobedience (when Adam and Eve ate the forbidden fruit from the tree of knowledge and thus acquired a sense of right and wrong similar to God's) is inherited by every single human being ever born. This is what is known as the original sin. For some theologians, the sin was primarily the act of disobedience itself, but for many others, such as Saint Augustine (354–430), the sin was really that *Adam and Eve had sex*, or at least felt sexual desire for each other. This interpretation makes it easier to understand how the original sin can be passed on to descendants, because we all are conceived during intercourse, and we all have sexual desires. For Augustine, Adam was free to choose not to sin, and he chose to sin; therefore human beings are not free any more—we are destined to sin. And because it was Eve who tempted Adam, tradition has been quick to put the blame on her.

This is the main source, at least in the Western world, of the idea that sexuality is evil, devilish, and must be controlled by all means available—an idea that has haunted people throughout the centuries, and to which Nietzsche reacted very strongly (as we will see). But scholars disagree about whether Augustine thought that sexuality itself was bad, because this idea doesn't match the Catholic view that because God created nature, natural things must be good; and because God invented genitals (and God doesn't invent anything evil), sex can't possibly be considered bad or unnatural in itself. Indeed, early Christianity before Augustine, between the first and fourth centuries, seems to have agreed with Judaism that all of God's creations are good, including the physical nature of humans. But for Augustine there really is no such thing as human "nature," because all the suffering inherent in the human condition is the result of one human who chose to sin. As Elaine Pagels says in her book *Adam, Eve, and the Serpent*, "For Augustine, natural and moral evils collapse into one another." Saint Augustine's view of the original sin became dogma for the church.

Where did Augustine acquire his view of the human condition, if it wasn't from the book of Genesis? The answer may lie in his early intellectual training. Before he

Manicheism and Neoplatonism

Manicheism, a Persian religious philosophy, taught that good (the soul) and evil (the body) are locked in battle throughout creation; Neoplatonism—the school of Plotinus (205–270)—revived Plato's idea that the physical world is less valuable, and even less real, than the spiritual realm. For Plotinus, true reality is that of God, the *One*. In the beginning the One was alone in the universe, but as It began contemplating, It evolved into a second stage, called *Reason* by Plotinus. In this stage the One has, so to speak, become a twosome, carrying on a rational dialogue with Itself. As the process of reasoning expands, however, the One turns Its attention outward. This is the stage of the *Spirit*, and is represented as a triad.

Now Spirit continues to divide itself into smaller pieces, endowing individual creatures with a soul. This emanation ("flowing forth") of the One does not extend to the material world, however, because according to Plotinus the material world is not important. It is actually characterized as "nothing," because it has no presence of the One. If the individual soul preoccupies itself with the material aspect of the world, it loses itself in worldly matters. It is far better to focus one's soul on spiritual things in order to begin the journey to join with the One—a journey Plotinus believed could be completed in this life, through a mystical experience. Plotinus believed that he himself had had such a reunion with the One several times.

became a Christian, he was intensely interested in two philosophical schools: manicheism, and Neoplatonism. Both theories hold contempt for the material world and believe that the soul ought to shun it. Scholars assume that the presence of antiphysical sentiment in Christianity comes from these sources, courtesy of Saint Augustine.

Whatever the nature of original sin, the punishment for it has been for all people to suffer the human condition of living, aging, and dying on this earth, experiencing sexual desire, giving birth to children (a painful experience and Eve's punishment for her sin), and scratching out a living under harsh conditions (Adam's punishment for his sin).

So even if an individual never has done anything wrong in his or her life (and babies have done absolutely nothing in their lives, good or bad) all humans are considered guilty of that first sin, and are thus tainted. According to Augustine, if humans are evil from birth, it is their own fault—they could have behaved when they had the chance. If we view this idea in a greater historical context, we see that many mythologies have had the same idea that some advantage, like immortality, is lost through the stupidity, carelessness, frailness, or willful disobedience of one person—most often a woman.

Loss of Immortality: Placing Blame

Part of being human is knowing that life is a temporary thing. Many cultures believe that immortality was lost through the fault of one or two human beings. The Christian tradition talks about the original sin of Adam and Eve and puts the blame on Eve for listening to the serpent's words of temptation. You may remember the story in Chapter 2, from the Trobriand culture in Melanesia, about the grandmother who shed her skin and appeared again as a young woman. Her granddaughter refused to recognize her, so the grandmother put on her old skin and blamed her granddaughter for causing humanity to be doomed to grow old and die. A Native American Indian myth from the Blackfoot tribe blames mortality on First Old Woman, who disagreed with First Old Man about whether humans should be dead for four days and then come back to life, or remain dead forever. Old Man wanted to decide the matter with a buffalo chip: If it floated when thrown into the water, then humans would come to life again. But Old Woman didn't like the idea of a buffalo chip; she wanted to throw a rock in the water. If it floated, then humans would live again. She thought it was better for people to die, because in that way they would develop sympathy for each other. Later, when her daughter died, Old Woman changed her mind, but it was too late—Old Man did not want to change the rules. So in this story both man and woman share the responsibility for death, and the story even argues that death is meaningful. An African myth puts a twist on the theme of immortality. Hare (the character who represents a mischievous god, a prankster who shapes the fate of humans), brings some humans a message from the Moon Goddess, but he tricks them—it is the wrong message. What he tells humankind is that they shall all die and never come to life again. The original message from the Moon Goddess was, "As I die, and dying live; so you shall also die, and dying live."

Redemption

Must Christians, then, reconcile themselves to the idea that life is terrible and all is lost from the start? No, because the presence of Christ in the history of the world makes all the difference: Adam's sin has been redeemed, as have all of Adam and Eve's descendants, provided that they believe in Jesus. "Mainstream" Christianity—Catholicism as well as Protestantism—generally believes that faith, which must come from God (we can't *decide* to believe) is the "saving grace" in itself. Therefore the original sin does not condemn the believer to an eternity in hell. But suppose you have trouble believing in God? Then you must decide to open yourself up to His grace, and you will receive it.

FIGURE 17.1 Albrecht Dürer, "Adam and Eve in the Garden of Eden." Tradition blames the woman and the snake for the Fall of humans from the Garden of Eden. But mythologists speculate that the blaming of Eve was a device to keep women in their place, especially since women had a somewhat higher status in the non-Jewish cultures surrounding ancient Palestine. Similarly, the snake may have become the voice of the devil in the Judeo–Christian tradition because it was common for non-Jewish cultures in the region to venerate the snake as a sacred animal of the Mother Goddess.

What about nonbelievers who are decent people? And all the generations who lived after Adam but prior to Jesus? Are they condemned? Theoretically, yes. The traditional Catholic view of the afterlife reserves certain not-so-bad sections of Hell for such unfortunates.

The Fall as Metaphor

Whether the Christian chooses to regard the Genesis story as something that truly happened, or as a good story that should be viewed as an *ethical metaphor* for how one should live one's life, the lesson is clear: Humans are weak and untrustworthy, with a clear tendency to do what they are not supposed to do. They are tainted with evil, and their only hope is to be receptive to God's grace. Once humans were immortal— in Eden before the Fall—but that immortality was lost through a human act of disobedience. Immortality of the soul can be achieved only through faith and grace.

Another example of the Fall as a metaphor relates to the idea that original sin is identical to sexual activity. There is a time in every human's life when we are asexual, or at least not sexually active: the time of "innocence" known as childhood. The Fall represents the period of adolescence, when the sexual drives awaken and childhood becomes "paradise lost." Strangely enough, this interpretation is at odds with the dogma that even babies are tainted with the original sin and are thus not "innocent"—but the Judeo-Christian story of Genesis has been around for a long time and has inspired many different interpretations. (We will return to the idea of childhood as the lost paradise in the upcoming section on Sigmund Freud.)

Consequences and Criticism

From the Augustinian view of human nature we should expect a certain type of policy-making. At best such policies would support the idea that people must be guided, trained, and educated to understand their own weakness of character so they don't transgress. At worst, such policies would maintain that because people are weak and evil, they must be controlled in the strictest manner by a force that receives its authority from a higher source, from God. Historically, both policies have been in effect in the Christian realm, from times when the church played the part of parent and educator, to periods when the church was in effect police, judge, and legislator at the same time, as happened during the Spanish Inquisition. Pagels, in *Adam, Eve, and the Serpent*, has this to say concerning this approach:

> The "social control" explanations assume a manipulative religious elite that *invents* guilt in order to dupe a gullible majority into accepting an otherwise abhorrent discipline. But the human tendency to accept blame for his misfortunes is as observable among today's agnostics as among the Hopi or the ancient Jews and Christians, independent of—even prior to—religious belief. For quite

apart from political circumstances, many people need to find reasons for their sufferings.

When asked in an interview why she thought Christians have embraced the notion that they are guilty, Pagels answered that seeing humans as guilty and sinful allows us also to conclude that humans in fact have a *tremendous power*. They have lost Paradise all by themselves—not a bad feat for such "weak" creatures. So the immense guilt of the Christian is in direct proportion to his "illusion of power." There is a "human need to imagine ourselves in control, even at the cost of guilt." In other words, Pagels sees the story of the Fall and Redemption as an example of *anthropocentrism* (putting humans at the center of things): We may be sinful, but we are very, very important! In view of the many ways human importance has been diminished—both *astronomically* (the geocentric view is no longer valid), *biologically* (we know humans are not the purpose and pinnacle of evolution), and *psychologically* (we may think we are in control, but really our unconscious mind rules us)—the Christian view of the importance of humans holds considerable attraction for the shrinking human ego.

Narratives That Illustrate the Battle Between Good and Evil

Chapter 20 does not include any stories covering the specific topic of original sin, but you may want to spend some time comparing the biblical story of Adam, Eve, and the Fall with the Trobriand myth of the loss of immortality. Chapter 20 does include many stories that explore the issue of whether humans are born good or evil; some of these stories explore the battle between good and evil by using the the alter-ego story format. Stories included are: Robert Louis Stevenson's *Strange Case of Dr. Jekyll and Mr. Hyde* (the original short story), Hans Christian Andersen's "The Shadow," and two sections from Dostoyevsky's *Crime and Punishment*.

Hobbes: Self-Interested Humanity

A Short Digression into the Concept of Metaphysics

Chapter 8 included a box on the topic of metaphysics ("Three Theories of Metaphysics"); here we will talk in a little more detail about the subject. Metaphysics deals with theories of the nature of reality. This topic has been discussed since the beginning of philosophy, and in earlier times—prior to the eighteenth century—it was the primary topic of philosophical discussions. It is still being discussed, but since the eighteenth century it has taken a back seat to ethics and epistemology (theory of knowledge).

There are three major forms of metaphysical theories: *materialism, idealism,* and

FIGURE 17.2 Thomas Hobbes (1588–1679), English philosopher. Hobbes was one of the first modern materialists, claiming that all of human psychology consists of the attraction and repulsion of physical particles. As such, the natural human approach to life is one of self-preservation. The natural life of humans outside the regulations of society (the state of nature) is for Hobbes a filthy and frightening war of everyone against everyone.

dualism. Materialism and idealism are known as *monist* theories, which means they both believe reality has only *one* component. Materialism believes that reality consists of *matter*; idealism believes reality is "all in the *mind*" (the mind of God, or of people, or both). Dualism, on the other hand, believes that reality is a mixture of mind and matter. There also are hybrid forms of dualism, which hold that reality is mainly physical but with some mental elements, or mainly mental but with some physical elements.

Materialism (which is only distantly related to the modern, popular concept of acquiring material goods and placing a high importance on money) has enjoyed periodical popularity. It was in vogue among the ancient Greeks, it resurfaced again in the eighteenth century with the blossoming of the natural sciences, and it is by far the most predominant theory of reality today. Thomas Hobbes and Karl Marx, among others, are representatives of materialism in philosophy. One modern version of materialism is the *identity theory*, which holds that the mind and the brain are identical, and there is no soul or mind aside from neural transmissions. The identity theory is much favored by scientists working with artificial intelligence. The theory of *epiphenomenalism* is another modern metaphysical theory, sometimes classified as a materialistic theory and sometimes as a dualistic one. It holds that the mind or consciousness is merely a by-product of brain activity and disappears when the brain ceases to function. One can argue that it is a dualistic theory because it recognizes two phenomena, mind and brain activity, but one can also argue that because epiphenomenalism views the mind as a kind of nonproductive echo of brain activity, it is a monist, materialistic theory.

Idealism (which in this case must not be confused with an attitude of high ideals) can be found in a pure form in the Hindu philosophy that the world we see around us is nothing but an illusion, *maya.* The British philosopher George Berkeley is a Western idealist. He finds that existence depends on the observer: The world we know exists only when it is being observed; when there are no people to observe it, God is still watching, so it still exists. Although idealism has been increasingly unpopular in the West during the twentieth century, scientific research is now being conducted which implies that the mind, which observes, may actually have tremendous influence on what it observes, if it does not actually *create* its own observations.

Dualism, which seems to many people to be the preferable solution, half spirit and half matter, also has several versions; the most influential ones are *interactionism* and *parallelism*. Interactionism holds that the mind interacts with matter. In other words, the mind tells the body what to do, and the body does it. Parallelism claims that there is parallel synchronicity between mind and matter, so that the body does what the mind wants, and the mind registers physical sensations, but there is no actual connection between the two. How then do the two keep pace with each other? Through God's intervention. In dualistic theories, the idea of a soul that lives on after the death of the body is a conceptual possibility. Dualistic philosophers are Plato (who has a leaning towards idealism) and Descartes and a large number of others.

None of these metaphysical theories has succeeded in presenting itself without logical flaws. Idealism seems to fly in the face of common human experience, and it requires quite a lot of faith to be accepted. Materialism seems well suited for an age of science but somehow has failed to explain why our mental experiences don't *feel* as though they are just brain activity. Dualism, which was supposed to be the solution to both problems, inadequately explains exactly *how* mind and matter interact—for if the mind is totally noncorporeal, how does it influence the corporeal world? The British philosopher Gilbert Ryle called this problem "the ghost in the machine," and fictional stories of spirits and ghosts reflect the problem: How does a ghost affect the world of the living when it has no substance? This problem is intriguing because we can draw a parallel between the incorporeal ghost who is unable to affect the material world of the living, and the incorporeal spirit who is stuck somewhere in the human brain. If the ghost can't affect the material world, then how can the mind affect the body? For interactionist dualism it is as much a mystery that you can will your own hand to move as it would be if you were able to will a book to move across the room without touching it.

Hobbes the Materialist

Thomas Hobbes belongs to the school of thought which recommends social control over people because of their inherent natural tendencies. However, he does not advocate this practice for any theological reasons. Rather, he believes that his viewpoint is purely descriptive and scientific, based on a *materialistic* theory of reality—one that says reality consists of what we can see, touch, and measure. Consequently, all of reality is material (consists of matter, not spirit), and all human emotions have their basis in physiology. Humans are driven by instincts and by the natural tendency to seek what they enjoy and stay away from what they dislike, and as such, humans can't

The Life and Times of Thomas Hobbes

If we wish to consider different theorists in light of the period of history in which they lived—Freud, with his gloomy view of human nature, which reflected his experiences during World War I, and Ardrey, with his predictions of human destiny, which may have been based on the Korean war—then Hobbes makes an excellent subject. The time in which he lived was violent beyond belief, and one might ask why everybody of his day and age didn't reach the same conclusions he did concerning human nature. He was born around the time when Mary, Queen of Scots was executed by Queen Elizabeth of England. In his lifetime the Spanish Armada attacked England and was defeated, and piracy and buccaneering were rampant in the oceans of the world. In the 1640s England witnessed a civil war that ended with the execution of Charles I. London was hit repeatedly by fire and plague; women and men were accused of witchcraft and burned at the stake; and there was continual strife between England and France. Hobbes traveled in France, met Galileo, and corresponded with Descartes. In 1640 he took refuge there because he was a royalist, but after they beheaded Charles I, he came back to England to live.

help being oriented toward their own self-preservation and comfort. This viewpoint makes Hobbes not only a psychological egoist, but also a determinist and, presumably, an atheist (although it was not politically wise to make such a statement in his day). Indeed, materialism, psychological egoism, and determinism often go hand in hand. (Atheism may or may not be part of the package—at any rate, it is entirely possible for an atheist not to share any of these theories.)

This doesn't sound too far removed from what we have heard from Darwin and Ardrey, but Hobbes expressed his opinion a good two hundred and fifty years before Darwin and three hundred and fifty years before Ardrey, so in effect he was the originator of the idea that the "fittest"—those who can look after themselves—survive.

The State of Nature and the Social Contract

Hobbes translated his world situation (which included the budding phenomenon of science) into the view that humans always will do what is to their advantage. Thus, if there are no restrictions, humans will be aggressive toward each other to the point of murder, in order to gain an advantage or simply acquire property. Physically, humans are "created equal"—not in a normative, political sense of having equal rights, but in a descriptive sense: Humans are equal in their *capabilities*. The strong can kill the weak, but the weak can band together and kill the strong, so we all are in danger of each other.

This is why social control is necessary. However, such control does not bind people together *against their will*. Hobbes believes that because people are generally intelligent, they know an intelligent idea when they hear it. For instance, I know that if I can take what belongs to someone else, he or she can do the same to me, and I will suffer. So it's better that I am restricted in my doings, because it means that others are restricted, too, and that means we all can live in peace. This is Hobbes's version of the *social contract*, a hypothetical theory that says that early human society was instituted by people who agreed to a set of rules for communal living.

Humans who have not entered into such a social contract are considered by Hobbes to live in the *state of nature*—a "natural condition" in which morality has not yet come into being, where there are no families or social bonding, and where there are no rules except those inherent in human nature. Hobbes sees this situation as a "war of every man against every man" and describes it vividly in his book *Leviathan*:

> In such condition, there is no place for industry, because the fruit thereof is uncertain; . . . no arts; no letters; no society; and what is worst of all, continual fear, and danger of violent death; and the life of man, solitary, poor, nasty, brutish, and short.

Did Hobbes really believe that society started out this way? It is hard to say. Sometimes he claims that perhaps this never really happened, but at other times he presents it as historical fact and insists that at least the situation between nations reflects a state of nature with no rules and perpetual war. At any rate, there is no evidence that any society prior to that in which Hobbes lived ever was founded in this manner, but since Hobbes's day a social contract has become reality with our adoption of the Constitution of the United States (although we can't say that *all* citizens were cosigners).

Incidentally, Hobbes was not the first thinker to view the birth of society as a grim necessity forced upon selfish people by their own aggression. Plato's brother Glaucon expressed the same theory a good two thousand years earlier, in Plato's *Republic*:

> They say that to do wrong is naturally good, to be wronged is bad, but the suffering of injury so far exceeds in badness the good of inflicting it that when men have done wrong to each other and suffered it, and have had a taste of both, those who are unable to avoid the latter and practice the former decide that it is profitable to come to an agreement with each other neither to inflict injury nor to suffer it. As a result they begin to make laws and covenants, and the law's command they call lawful and just.

For Hobbes this type of social contract is not binding forever. You never give up your right to defend yourself and your property, and if others don't abide by the terms of the contract, you are not obliged to, either. But who is to make sure that the contract is kept? The *sovereign*. For Hobbes the only solution is to give up your freedom to a sovereign, a monarch, who in turn promises to protect you. If the sovereign fails, the contract is dissolved, and everyone reverts to the state of nature. But as long as rulers are doing the job they are supposed to do, you have no right to self-determination beyond the right to protect your life and property.

The State of Nature as Political Theory

Scholars have suggested that what Hobbes is doing is not so much expressing a theory about the beginning of society, as defending the institution of absolute monarchy—and indeed, Hobbes the royalist had tutored children of the nobility in his younger days. What matters to us, though, is that although he views human beings as intensely self-oriented, it is doubtful whether Hobbes would call this "evil." In the state of nature there are no moral rules, and thus there is no good and evil. There is only self-preservation, a fact of nature. Value judgments arise *after* the establishment of a social contract—but even *within* a society humans never stop being selfish; it's just that once they are part of an organized society, it is in their own self-interest to behave themselves. The question of "good" or "evil" does not enter into the picture. What is evil is living in fear, so for Hobbes society is at least a better choice than the state of nature.

What interests Hobbes is the social aspect of human nature, not as it affects the state, but as it affects the individual. As we approach modern times and its emphasis on the rights of the individual, we see that this is one of its beginning points—the period after the Reformation and before the Enlightenment. Hobbes's influence was felt later in philosophy as well as in politics: The theory of *political libertarianism* (everyone has a right to life, liberty, and property; and everyone ought to look after himself—no one owes a helping hand to anybody) has in him one of its spiritual progenitors.

Hobbes's speculation about the state of nature is reflective of his time period—not as a historical theory, but as a political one: Why are we the way we are, and what should we be? State of nature theories therefore usually have a normative purpose and supply an argument for a certain political structure—in Hobbes's case, an argument for *monarchy*. True historical interest in human prehistory was only just awakening, and seventeenth- and eighteenth-century scholars didn't have access to the knowledge that has emerged in the twentieth century. Today we know that humans have lived in groups for at least four million years—and animal studies suggest we did this even before we became humans (baboons, chimps, and gorillas all live in social groups). The paleoanthropologist Don Johansen and his crew discovered what has become known as "the first family" some years ago: a number of fossils from Australopithecus Afarensis, a type of prehominid that existed approximately four million years ago. The bones all were found at the same spot, which indicates that the group all perished together in some disaster. In the group were young people, old people, and mature individuals. Scientists take that as evidence that we always have lived in groups, never in the loneliness of Hobbes's state of nature. But of course we don't know if such groups may in fact have been living in a "state of nature," a perpetual war of group against group.

A Narrative That Explores Evil Nature

One of the most pessimistic, and most famous, stories expressing the idea that human nature is evil and that humans, if given a chance, will revert to a war that pits everybody against everybody is the novel *Lord of the Flies* by William Golding. An outline of it appears in Chapter 20.

Rousseau: Back to Nature

Arrival of the Enlightenment

Another hundred years or so have passed. We are in the middle of the eighteenth century; more wars have been fought in Europe, science has progressed, Europeans are listening to the music of Johann Sebastian Bach, and a new spirit is forming in intellectual circles: the ideology of the *Enlightenment*. The concept of the individual as a valuable person is increasing in acceptance, and consequently the fate of "ordinary" people is becoming a political question. Whereas citizens previously were viewed as little more than tools, without rights or dignity of their own, the question now being posed is, to what extent is the ordinary man capable of deciding his own fate, and how much political freedom should be granted?

In the eyes of the Enlightenment, education was the key. Given the opportunity to learn, the ordinary man could develop the talents and capabilities necessary for political and personal self-determination. Once it was recognized that individuals had such capabilities, the democratic election of officials became a genuine possibility. The general goal was to break up the feudal patterns that had become established in many parts of Europe, and give the right to self-determination back to people who had been victimized by increasing social inequality. (It is no coincidence that here the individual is referred to as "man" and not "human." The interest in extending education and the right to vote to ordinary citizens was, in the first phases of the Enlightenment, directed toward the male population only.)

Rousseau the Traveling Man

Jean-Jacques Rousseau (1712–1778) was born in Geneva, Switzerland, and spent much of his youth on the move, first fleeing the profession of engraver, for which he had no taste, and later traveling to France, Italy, and then back to France, occasionally tutoring children in music. Several times in his life he changed his religious affilia-

FIGURE 17.3 Jean-Jacques Rousseau (1712–1778), French philosopher and novelist. Contrary to Hobbes, Rousseau believed that humans in the state of nature were peaceful creatures without much interaction. Rousseau by and large introduced to the Western cultural tradition the idea that what is natural is good in itself, and this idea has grown more successful over the centuries. Today we see the latest example of Rousseau's influence in concepts such as Earth Day and commercial ploys such as "no artificial ingredients."

tion—from Protestant to Catholic and back again—but these changes seem to have been politically motivated more than anything else.

Rousseau entered the philosophical scene with an award-winning essay on arts and sciences in 1750, but he achieved more fame with his next essay, the "Discourse on the Origin of Inequality." This essay, written in Paris, won no awards but is the one for which he is remembered. After writing the essay Rousseau went back to Geneva but then returned to France, where he began to write the books for which he was to become famous: the novel *La Nouvelle Héloise*, a love story between a strong-willed woman and her lover, whom she discards for marriage to an older man; *The Social Contract*, a philosophical analysis of the relationship between the citizen and society; and *Emile*, a blueprint for a new, natural approach to the education of children. Rousseau felt great hostility in France, and he went back to his hometown of Geneva again. However, he could find no refuge. His good friend in England, the Scottish philosopher David Hume, invited him to come and stay with him, but after a while this relationship turned sour, too. Rousseau somehow developed the idea that Hume was not the friend he thought he was, and he began publicly ridiculing Hume's work. Although Hume was a very easygoing man, he did not take lightly to these actions, so Rousseau had to leave and return to France. Twelve years later he died there; those who knew him described him as "emotionally disturbed."

What kind of a man emerges from this description—someone who cannot find peace, and who mistrusts his friends and everybody else? There is medical evidence that Rousseau actually had a touch of paranoia, and physically he was never very strong—he seems to have suffered continually from bladder problems. He had a deep mistrust of doctors, didn't particularly like living close to people, and saw enemies everywhere. Nevertheless this troubled, intelligent man still managed to usher in a new era, the Romantic Era.

The Eighteenth Century: A Time of Persecution

As the saying goes, "Just because I'm paranoid doesn't mean they're not out to get me." This seems to fit Rousseau's case very well, because on occasion he feared for his life with very good reason—they *were* out to get him. Who? Astonishingly enough, the Inquisition. The Roman Catholic Inquisition was a court for the discovery, examination, and punishment of heretics (often the secular authorities were in charge of the punishment, though). Begun in the thirteenth century, it continued its persecutions through the centuries until 1834, when it was abolished. The branch known as the Spanish Inquisition was responsible for the deaths of thousands (some even say millions) of men and women accused of heresy. Many, especially women, were burned at the stake for witchcraft. Although we usually associate such barbarism with medieval times, the persecution of heretics went on throughout the sixteenth, seventeenth, and eighteenth centuries and continued well into the nineteenth century. In general the Inquisition of the eighteenth and nineteenth centuries did not follow the patterns of medieval times, when those viewed as heretics were tortured or put to death.

However, people who expressed theories that went against the dogmas of the church were still a major problem for the Catholic church of the eighteenth century (certain Protestant groups also were known for their intolerance of scientific endeavors, for that matter). What was it in Rousseau's books which earned him the attention of the powers that be? Primarily, his view of nature, and the "natural human being." Rousseau knew his theories might result in his works being banned. This made his existence extremely uncomfortable, if not downright precarious; he knew he might be excommunicated, or possibly even killed. At this point in time certain "secret societies," such as the Freemasons, were thriving in Europe. Members of these societies worked "underground" as a sheer precaution; had they gone public the lives of their members would have been endangered. Such societies still exist today. However, they remain "secret" only in the sense that their teachings are disclosed only to members. Their function is mainly to create a bonding experience for members rather than to protect members from a repressive society.

Before Rousseau: "Natural" Equals "Evil"

It would be preposterous to say that before Rousseau people didn't enjoy nature; of course people have forever taken walks under budding trees, listened to the birds, hiked a mountain trail, taken a rowboat out on the lake, and done the kinds of things

Nature in Art

Historically we know when a person in Western civilization first climbed a mountain just for the fun of it (at least this is the earliest account of it). In his book *Landscape into Art*, Sir Kenneth Clark tells about a man named Petrarch, who in 1340 climbed a mountain in the French Alps. While he was enjoying the view, he took out the book by Saint Augustine that he was carrying (the *Confessions*) and read a random page about people who abandon their own self-scrutiny for the wonders of the world. This made Petrarch feel terribly guilty, and he hurried back down the mountain. In the fifteenth century Italian and Dutch painters begin to explore the beauty of the wilderness, but it wasn't until the seventeenth century that artists expressed a real joy of nature; in fact, the nature paintings of the seventeenth and eighteenth centuries very quickly became symbolic—they were viewed as metaphors for "moods." Did Rousseau, then, inspire a new painting style with his praise of all things natural? No, because painters of the eighteenth century already were expressing their admiration for pastoral nature. However, as the saying goes, artists don't paint nature the way we see it; instead, we learn to see nature the way artists paint it, and it is possible that Rousseau is the first philosopher to have made the intellectual connection between artistic love of nature and a moral love of everything natural—an idea that heralded the movement of Romanticism.

everybody enjoys doing. But until Rousseau, nobody in the Western world saw nature as anything intellectually worthwhile in itself. In *An Enquiry Concerning the Principles of Morals*, David Hume, Rousseau's contemporary and onetime friend, found that:

> The eye is pleased with the prospect of corn-fields and loaded vineyards, horses grazing, and flocks pasturing, but flies the view of briars and brambles, affording shelter to wolves and serpents.

The general attitude of the Western world towards nature, from the time of Augustine to the time of Rousseau, is reflected in typical medieval art. Paintings and drawings usually show a lush little garden, walled in. Inside the wall there may be a unicorn or a beautiful maiden. There are uniform rows of trees and flowers, well cultivated. But outside the stone wall lurks nature, a chaotic realm of darkness—trees with eerie branches, thorny thickets, and wild animals, usually wolves. This view of nature controlled versus nature uncontrolled works on several levels. The first is a *practical* interpretation of nature and of the precarious status of civilization. We tend to forget it today, but for long periods of human history, nature was the enemy against which people wrestled to build their homes and grow their crops. It was dangerous to travel from town to town because of the threat of wild animals and outlaws, and it became easy to view nature, and thus all things natural, as something dangerous. The second level is a *theological* interpretation: Humans are the rulers of creation, and the wilderness is there to be pacified and ordered. It presents a task, and a challenge, because before the wilderness acquires a "human" characteristic—it is really a "nothing." It becomes a "something" only through human control, through human *development*. This is why today, companies who bulldoze a naturally balanced habitat for the sake of human business or habitation are known as *developers*, which implies that nature is not "developed" in its own way, but is nothing, or worse, is something vile that must be tamed. This leads to the *economic* interpretation: Nature is meaningful only if it can be used to make a profit, or to serve humans in some other sense. In this viewpoint, development means *economic* development. The fourth level on which this view of nature works is as a *psychological* interpretation: Just as ordered nature is good, and chaotic nature is evil, so too are the controlled human passions good, and the uncontrolled drives evil. The evil ones may be tempting and fascinating, but they are bad by nature. Traditional fairy tales like Little Red Riding Hood teach this lesson over and over again: Beware of the greedy wolf who lives in the woods and of the greedy wolf who lives *inside you*. It is customary in symbolic art to have animals represent the unrepressed drives (usually sexual) of human nature. Watch for the pooch or the kitty next to the proper young lady in a seventeenth-century painting—it has a deeper meaning! Augustine would have added: It also may represent the original sin.

Rousseau: "Natural" Equals "Good"

Legend has it that Rousseau was taking a walk along a lake one lovely day, and was all of a sudden struck by a revelation: The beauty of nature was not only representative of God as creator, but also was beautiful *in itself*, and furthermore, it was beautiful because humans had not messed around with it. What nature has created on its own is good, and needs no improvement from humans; on the contrary, humans can learn from the uncorrupted innocence of everything natural.

With one stroke of his pen, Rousseau wiped away centuries of intellectual disdain for nature. His writings influenced the entire Western world and announced the advent of the *Romantic Movement*. In place of fear and disdain came *reverence* for nature and everything natural. The term *back to nature* was coined in those years, and with this reversal of values came a whole intellectual and artistic program. Rousseau inspired a quest for the original natural state of humans and of civilization; Rousseau believed humans originated in a paradisiacal state of nature where humans were content, healthy, and in harmony with each other and with their surroundings. *Psychologically*, emotions were considered to be more genuine than reason, and thus more "natural" and valuable. For this reason an entire generation of writers, composers, and painters gave us a legacy of art that emphasized the drama of human emotions. *Ethically*, animals and children came to represent moral innocence. Animals now are no longer symbols for "sinful drives," but metaphors for "sound natural instincts." When an animal kills, the action is viewed as an action that is necessary for survival, and not as an expression of a dangerous nature. The pooch in the Romantic painting may have quite another meaning than the one it had in the seventeenth-century painting! *Historically*, the interest focused on the early populations of Europe and their myths and legends, because it was assumed that they were less corrupted than later European populations. The term *the noble savage* was born of Romanticism. (American pioneer stories and works of art are drenched in the view of nature as an enemy, a force that must be subdued—but at the same time they also are inspired by Rousseau's Romanticism, so they represent a marvelous contradiction. Intellectuals among the pioneers expected the Indians to be noble savages; ordinary pioneers expected them to be godless creatures hardly worthy of being called humans. Both attitudes created much misunderstanding.) *Politically*, Rousseau's positive attitude toward humans who are uncorrupted by civilization had widespread consequences. We'll explore this idea shortly.

Today the influence of Rousseau can hardly be overestimated, on all levels. In a sense we are still living with the legacy of romanticism and its view of nature. When a commercial tells us that a product has no additives and is full of "natural goodness," we are impressed partly because we have come to believe, on the basis of scientific studies, that such things are healthier for us, but our attitude also reflects the latest resurfacing of Rousseau's worship of nature. The quest for the "natural look" (which is to be achieved by using as many artificial aids as needed), the research into "natural behavior," and finally the increasing seriousness of the "Save the Earth" movement all have modern reasons for existing, but their common philosophical parent is Rousseau.

Humans in the State of Nature

How does Rousseau view the human being in its natural state? He adopts the same hypothesis of the "state of nature" that Hobbes and many others did, but he has his own version: Because humans are basically nonaggressive, he says, and will attack others only if provoked, then we must imagine early humans as solitary, content individuals who got together only occasionally, for sexual reasons. They were more hardy than people today because they were well adjusted to the climate; their eyesight was better because it wasn't clouded by chimney smoke; their sense of smell was better for the same reason; and they rarely got sick. As he writes in *Discourse on the Origin of Inequality*, living was easy:

> When I consider [man], in a word, as he must have left the hands of nature,
> I see an animal less strong than some, less agile than others; but, all in all, the
> most advantageously organized of all. I see him satisfying his hunger under an

FIGURE 17.4 A romantic vision: the human being alone with untouched, uncorrupted nature. While Western art in the centuries between the Middle Ages and the advent of the Romantic era had been fascinated with cultivated nature—in particular the pastoral, peaceful scenery of Greek and Roman Antiquity—artists of the Romantic era turned their attention to the wilderness as the ideal metaphor for true human nature, partly due to the influence of Rousseau. (*Scribner's Monthly, Conducted by J. G. Holland, from Nov. 1873, to April, 1874*, vol. VII, No. 3. New York: Scribner & Co., 1874.)

oak tree, quenching his thirst at the first stream, finding his bed at the foot of the same tree that supplied his meal; and thus all his needs are satisfied.

Of course his wants are few, because he hasn't been corrupted by civilization. And it is easy for him to be nonaggressive, because he rarely encounters other human beings. On those occasions when he does encounter other humans, says Rousseau, it may be in circumstances where the other party is injured. What does our noble savage do in such situations? He does his best to help, because human beings are *naturally compassionate*. This compassion manifests itself in animals (in nature), and it manifests itself in grown men who cry in theaters over the sad fate of good people. So compassion is a *prerational foundation for morals*. It is the basis of all other social virtues, because we identify with whoever suffers, regardless of whether it is a person or an animal. It is *thinking* that makes us selfish; naturally, and emotionally, we are unselfish.

In the state of nature there is certainly *physical inequality*, because some are stronger than others. However, the stronger ones never use their strength to disturb the peace of the others. *Social inequality* doesn't exist, because there is no society yet. Inevitably, though, human *reason* manifests itself, and humans draw together to own things, build things, and improve themselves and their lot. This, says Rousseau, is the loss of paradise:

> The first person who, having enclosed a plot of land, took it into his head to say *this is mine* and found people simple enough to believe him, was the true founder of civil society. What crimes, wars, murders, what miseries and horrors would the human race have been spared, had someone pulled up the stakes or filled in the ditch and cried out to his fellow men: "Do not listen to this impostor! You are lost if you forget that the fruits of the earth belong to all and the earth to no one!"

From this time on disasters happen. It is during this time period that Hobbes's war of all against all occurs, says Rousseau. Eventually tyrants take over, making life miserable for people forever after.

The Social Contract and Beyond

A few years after formulating his state of nature hypothesis, Rousseau published his famous book *Social Contract*, which viewed the fate of civilization in a slightly less hopeless light. In this book Rousseau theorizes that at an early point in time, after humans left the state of nature, they formed a social contract. Unlike Hobbes's version of the beginning of society, though, Rousseau's people never gave away their personal freedom to any sovereign. For Rousseau, humans can't be asked to give away their *sovereignty*—it is an *inalienable right*. So how should we conduct our society? We should make decisions together with the group, and rule ourselves. Although Hobbes's social contract was an apology for monarchy, Rousseau's version praises the general principle of *democracy*—and the philosophical basis for this idea lies in his view of human nature: Because humans are good by nature, they can be trusted to rule themselves, provided that society hasn't corrupted them too much.

We all know that power corrupts, though, so how does Rousseau say democratic citizens can stay focused on what is good for everybody? He says they they should leave their personal wishes and ambitions at home when they go to vote, so that when they arrive, they will be filled with civic conscientiousness, and all their opinions together will form the *general will*, which can't be wrong, because it always has everybody's welfare in mind.

What if you feel tired, or would rather stay at home and play with the kids—can you get somebody to go and vote for you? *Never*, says Rousseau. A true democracy cannot allow representation. We can't vote for or pay people to make the decisions for us—that makes a mockery of democracy. Accordingly, any country that has representational democracy—like most democracies in the world, including the United States—are not true democracies. Rousseau's native Switzerland is, though, because it is divided into small groups of people who show up to vote (at least they are supposed to), defend themselves with a militia, and govern themselves. It seems that if

Rousseau's democratic ideal is to work, his society must be small enough for every citizen to have a direct influence on decisions.

What if you leave your personal ambitions at home and vote in all earnest, thinking only about the common good, but find yourself in the minority? Then, says Rousseau, *you must be wrong*, because the general will, which is the majority, can never be wrong. This is one of the truly problematic elements of his political theory: It does not allow for valid minority opinions. If a minority of people take a view that differs from that of the majority, it is because they somehow are thinking about their own advantage. Rousseau's democracy has no place for legitimate minority dissent or discussion, and if you don't agree with the decision of the majority, you have no right to rebel—the majority are right by definition. Hobbes gave his citizens the right to take matters into their own hands if their monarch lets them down, but there is no legitimate recourse to civil disobedience in Rousseau's utopian democracy. Another morally vague aspect of Rousseau's principle of the "tyranny of the majority" is when exactly something constitutes a majority. Does 51 percent of the votes constitute a majority, or must there be a *significant* majority? Suppose a majority of 51 percent votes against a proposition, but over the next twenty-four hours 2 percent change their mind, so now it is 49 percent against and 51 percent for. Was yesterday's decision made in everybody's best interest then, even though it would seem not not to be in everybody's best interest today—even with a difference of only 2 percent? The problem is that this approach can make decisions regarding right and wrong quite *arbitrary*, depending on how the votes stack up. There is nothing wrong with making *decisions* by majority votes, but determining their *moral correctness* by vote is quite another matter.

History and Politics

Did Rousseau believe that society really got started with a state of nature and a social contract? It appears that he did, because he regarded "primitive" tribes as living on the edge between the two states. There is a peculiar passage in the introduction to his *Discourse* where he says that we must *put aside all facts*, "for they have no bearing on the question." This is a strange thing for a scholar who is about to talk about early human history to say. But Rousseau was not a modern historian, so he may have meant that his is not a descriptive account, but a normative one: He is not interested in how it really was, but in how it *should be* for a theory of true democracy. He is doing what Hobbes was doing: giving good reasons for why one should accept a certain political system. But he also may be saying something else, for if we read more closely, we find that the "facts" he asks us to put aside are those included in the *biblical interpretation of Genesis*, where Adam and Eve are social beings from the start! Rousseau wants to dispense with these because they aren't important to his political theory. This may very well be one of the reasons he worried about the wrath of the Catholic church.

Is there *anything* factual in Rousseau's description of the state of nature? We know that humans weren't solitary. Rousseau seems to have had the notion that women, with their infants, roamed around by themselves in the forest like foxes and bears; adolescents were on their own. We think we know better—you'll recall the anthropological discovery of the fossil remains of the "first family." But does Rousseau's idea that pretechnological people were generally healthy and happy, and had lots of free time, come closer to the truth than does Hobbes's view that life for these people was "nasty, brutish, and short" (in *Leviathan*)? As a matter of fact, it does. Although today there is no such thing as people who live in a "complete state of nature," we have ample evidence of "primitive people" who live in small groups and engage in hunting and gathering. If they haven't been exposed to "white" civilization, they are generally quite healthy. Their average life span is short, but that is partly because they have a high infant mortality rate. If they live past the age of five and don't die in childbirth later on, they may live almost as long as people in the civilized world. Rousseau didn't know about germs and the spread of disease in densely populated civilizations, but the healthy conditions he describes are typical of isolated populations such as those of pretechnological societies.

Were the first human beings happy, and did they have lots of free time? Most people think that the tribal existence was a miserable one and that members toiled dawn to dusk just to get enough food. However, the evidence now indicates that pretechnological groups actually had a pretty good time (just as we always secretly suspected). They worked a couple of hours each day—the women slightly longer than the men—collecting food. The rest of the time they were free to sit around, tell stories, repair broken tools, and sleep. As new research has shown, the life of toil came about later, with the invention of agriculture (which was supposed to have made life easier for people). Crops demand much more attention than is required for a hunting-gathering existence, and crops can feed more mouths, so a more elaborate social structure is needed to keep the growing population under control, and stress is a result of the ensuing social hierarchy.

Should We Stop Thinking?

Because Rousseau believes thinking is what makes people selfish, and emotions are naturally unselfish, does he suggest that we should stop thinking? That would be an odd suggestion for any philosopher to make—and that is not Rousseau's solution, either. We can't stop thinking once we have started, but we can remind ourselves that too much thinking is bad, and we were better off before we began thinking so much. We can, though, use our thinking to strive toward becoming more natural. As happens with so many things Rousseau doesn't like, he sees thinking as a necessary evil: We can't avoid civilization, or thinking, or language, but we can make the most of them and try not to let them corrupt us. Rousseau sees our natural past as a constant lesson in *awareness*. We can never return to Nature, but we can incorporate natural things in our everyday life, especially in our way of *raising children*. Instead of disciplining them at an early age, making them read and write, keeping them in closed school-rooms, or worse—making them work from the time they are little—we should let them run barefoot in nature and allow them to pick up on nature's own wisdom. We can teach them the rules and necessities of civilization when they are older and can better understand them. (As we saw earlier, Rousseau here thinks primarily of the education of boys.)

This theory of natural child caring was quite revolutionary for the time. Along with Charles Dickens's stories of child abuse and child neglect, it created a wave of attention toward the situation of children, as well as the realization that childhood is not simply a nonsensical, irritating form of preadulthood that should be gotten over as soon as possible, but a most valuable time all in itself. This idea preceded Freud's realization of the psychological importance of childhood by a century and a half, and it fueled people's conception of childhood as the lost paradise, the only true "state of nature" ever known to an individual—a state of goodness and innocence. From this conception arose the notion that there is nothing bad in children, that children are morally innocent by nature, and an unruly child just has to be met not with punish-ment and restrictions but with the right understanding in order to become a social being—a notion with which modern theories of child-rearing have had a mighty struggle. Today, though, it is generally recognized that you can discipline a child with-out resorting to punishment (although some *restrictions* may still be necessary). (As it so often happens, we cannot look to the author of the theory for an example of the theory in action: Rousseau was the father of five children, but they all were raised by others, in foster homes, and presumably not according to Rousseau's ideas of natural childhood.)

A Narrative That Explores Natural Goodness

A film from the early nineties presents an excellent example of how Rousseau's idea of uncorrupted nature lives on in our imagination, and how it even can be used as a cultural and political statement. The film is Kevin Costner's *Dances with Wolves*. You'll find an outline of it in Chapter 20.

Nietzsche: Beyond Good and Evil

The Masters of Suspicion

The French philosopher Paul Ricoeur (b. 1913) says there are three thinkers who have developed the art of suspicion to the point of mastery: Friedrich Nietzsche, Karl Marx, and Sigmund Freud. What is the art of suspicion? In a sense it is what we do when we think critically: We question the logic, the evidence, and the motives of

Ricoeur: To Suspect and to Listen

Paul Ricoeur believes that these three masters of suspicion have given Western thinking some jolts that have forced us out of a state of complacency forever; we can't think in terms of the mind, economics, culture, or ethics, without taking these men's theories into regard. But for Ricoeur it is not enough for a philosopher to "suspect." For him, pointing out problems in our assumptions is only half the task. In order to understand an idea we also have to truly listen to what it has to say. A full understanding of something— a text we read, a cultural phenomenon we investigate, a person we talk to—involves two activities: an "unfriendly" one, the suspicion, and a "friendly" one, the listening. These two activities, says Ricoeur, combine to form the proper approach to understanding. For those who spurn Nietzsche, Ricoeur would suggest a bit of listening, and for those who adore Nietzsche, Ricoeur would serve up a healthy dose of suspicion.

whatever text we are studying. But in a more specific sense it means questioning our basic cultural assumptions. Freud questions our assumption that the human consciousness controls human life. Marx questions the assumption that culture is independent of economics. And Nietzsche questions the underlying assumptions of Western moral values.

Nietzsche's Background

Friedrich Nietzsche (1844–1900) is as extraordinary a character in Western philosophy as Rousseau, and some might argue that his influence eventually will match that of Rousseau. He was born in Leipzig, Germany, and several of the male members of his family were Lutheran ministers. His father was a minister, but he died when Nietzsche was young, and the boy and his sister Elisabeth were raised by their mother and other women in the family. His upbringing was of the Christian variety, in which the pleasures of this life are considered sinful, and life after death is regarded as the true goal of this life. As a young man Nietzsche studied theology for a while; he then switched to philology, for which he proved to have a true talent. He was made professor in Switzerland when he was just twenty-five. He served as a medic during the Franco-Prussian war of 1870, but during that time he became ill (he presumably had contracted syphilis a few years earlier), and bad health followed him for the rest of his life. He was forced to retire from his professorship, and in a sense he retired from life, too, living a secluded life with his mother, who tended him. It was during his retire-

FIGURE 17.5 Friedrich Nietzsche (1844–1900), German philosopher and writer. Nietzsche's teachings of the master morality and his scorn for the weakness and petty resentment of what he calls "the herd," the Christian working and middle class, have alienated many readers. What Nietzsche advocated, however, was not a "master race" but the right of humans to rediscover talents such as strength and heroism in themselves. To Nietzsche, such talents make a superior person, and such a person should be able to pursue life with zest, using others where possible, without being hindered by the herd morality of mediocre people.

ment, when he was still a young man, that he wrote the works that were to shake up the Western intellectual world, and, tragically, inspire the ideology of the Nazi movement some fifty years hence. When he was forty-five his mental health deteriorated to such an extent that he had to be institutionalized, and he lived with severe insanity until his death eleven years later, tended by his mother and sister.

It has sometimes been said that the theories of a man whose mind was deteriorating shouldn't be taken for anything more than the ravings of a mad person. But the fact is that Nietzsche's mind was quite healthy and vigorous when he wrote most of the works that were to become so influential after his death (only a few European intellectuals were aware of his philosophy during his lifetime). Besides, a theory must be able to stand on its own, and if it seems to make sense, or at least make interesting observations, it can't be dismissed because of the condition of its author. Nietzsche's works have stood the test of time with eery brilliance.

Nietzsche's Suspicion: Beyond Good and Evil

What is Nietzsche's view of human nature? Are we, from the start, good, or evil? He would choose to answer that question with a counterquestion: What do you mean by "good" and "evil"? This is an important question, because our viewpoint is determined by our cultural and historical background. If you are a nineteenth-century person, if you belong to the Judeo-Christian tradition, or if you are inspired by Plato, you might say that a good person shuns physical pleasures, because they are sinful, and concentrates on the afterlife, because that is when life really begins. If you are a socialist, you might say that a good person is not offensive or willful, but subordinates his or her will to that of the community. A good person is meek, helpful, kind, and

FIGURE 17.6 Friedrich Nietzsche's younger sister Elisabeth (1846–1935) appointed herself curator and editor of Nietzsche's works after his death and was responsible for much creative editing of her brother's philosophy. The Italian dictator Benito Mussolini read some of these edited works with much enthusiasm, and Elisabeth succeeded in getting her brother's name associated with the ideology of the German National Socialist party as well. Here her idol, Adolf Hitler, pays a visit to the 87-year-old Elisabeth.

turns the other cheek. An evil person is selfish, gives orders, thinks he is better than others, will not help others in need, looks to this life and disregards the afterlife, and wallows in physical pleasures. If this is your view of good and evil, says Nietzsche, then clearly you are a child of your times, and you must re-evaluate those values, for their nature is now becoming apparent: Their true nature is *repressive*, and this realization calls for a *transvaluation of values*. What should be the focus of such a transvaluation? The one that was common in ancient times, before people began to value weakness: the moral value of strength, of *power*.

In Nietzsche's view, the way we value human characteristics depends on who we are, and there is no "ultimate truth." It all depends on our perspective, which is why Nietzsche gives this view the term *perspectivism*. What Nietzsche intends is neither a descriptive nor a normative approach, but rather a metaethical approach: an analysis of how Western values have arisen in people's minds, and how, under other circumstances, the values would be different. There is, however, in the midst of his metaethics a normative ethic: There *is* a value that is better than others, and that is the value that *affirms life*.

Elisabeth Nietzsche and the Nazis

Elisabeth Nietzsche's role in her brother's life has long been recognized as an extremely powerful one, but only recently has her full role in connection with Nietzsche's writings become known. As children Friedrich and Elisabeth were close, but for a number of years they were not on the best of terms; Nietzsche loathed Elisabeth's husband and did not approve of her frequently expressed anti-Semitic views. Eventually Elisabeth traveled with her husband to Paraguay, South America, where they founded a colony of "racially pure" Germans. (The colony still exists, a small, largely inbred, nineteenth-century German village frozen in time.) During a time of trouble Elisabeth's husband killed himself, and she went back to Germany to care for Nietzsche, who by this time was quite ill. During Nietzsche's final years she proclaimed herself curator of his works, and frequently invited scholars to come view her severely insane brother. After his death she took on the task of editing his unpublished works, and it now appears that her editing was quite creative: some of the material she wrote herself and passed off as her brother's. Toward the end of her life, in the early years of German Nazism, she managed to get the attention of Adolph Hitler and other prominent Nazis. She inspired them to use her brother's philosophy, which she had edited to conform to her own anti-Semitic, totalitarian views, as a blueprint for their Nazi ideology. Hitler regarded her very highly, and when she died, he gave her the funeral of a "mother of the Fatherland."

We can't look to Nietzsche's writings for a systematic account or a point-by-point criticism of the Western value system: His viewpoints are scattered around in his writings, and one must play detective to get the whole picture. Some material is in his novel *Thus Spoke Zarathustra*, and some is in his *Genealogy of Morals*, but it is the title and topic of his book *Beyond Good and Evil* that gives us the clearest picture of his cultural critique.

Who is beyond good and evil? In the past, the *Masters*. In the future, the *Overman* (or *Superman*).

The Master and the Slave

People of Nietzsche's time believed in the value of the scientific method, and by the late nineteenth century few people took the idea of a state of nature seriously. Nietzsche's theory does not have any hypothetical *state of nature*. But in a peculiar way, his theory is related to those of Hobbes and Rousseau in that he, too, goes back to what

Perspectivism and Postmodernism

Nietzsche's theory of perspectivism can be said to have inspired the movement of *postmodernism*, in which all historical viewpoints are considered to have equal value because they all are part of the general picture. Your own description (as Caucasian, Asian, Latino, black, or male or female) is just a part of the whole, and no dominant mode of interpretation carries more weight than any other.

he thinks is a historical period to find the proper argument for how things should be today. The period he chooses is early Greek history, before the time of Socrates and Plato. (At that time similar types of societies existed all over Europe and probably in many places throughout the world: small communities of warlords and their serfs, some in alliance with each other, and others fighting each other.)

Nietzsche's task, as he saw it, was not to comment on the atrocities of slavery. His task was to analyze the two moralities that grew out of the two strictly separated and yet in some ways intertwined communities of the masters (the warlords) and the slaves (their serfs). In the mind of the feudal warlord, a good person is one who can be trusted and who will stand by you in a blood feud. He is a strong ally, a good friend, someone who has pride in himself and who has a noble and generous character, someone who is able to arouse fear. If the warlord wants to help the weaker ones through his own generosity, he can choose to do so, but he does not have to: He creates his own values. The warlord respects his enemy if he is strong, and values honor in his friends as well as in his enemies. Those who aren't strong are not deserving of respect, for they are put on this earth to be preyed upon (the resemblance to Darwin's concepts of competition in nature and survival of the fittest is no accident—Nietzsche had read *On the Origin of the Species*). Someone who is not willing to stand up for himself, who is weak, and afraid of you, who is of the "common folk"—that is a bad person:

> Let us acknowledge unprejudicedly how every higher civilization hitherto has *originated*! Men with a still natural nature, barbarians in every terrible sense of the word, men of prey, still in possession of unbroken strength of will and desire for power, threw themselves upon weaker, more moral, more peaceful races. . . . At the commencement, the noble caste was always the barbarian caste; their superiority did not consist first of all in their physical, but in their psychical power—they were more *complete* men (which at every point also implies the same as "more complete beasts").

The slave, on the other hand, hates the master and everything he stands for, which for the slave are identified with *evil*: strength, the will and the power to rule, and the

Hegel and the Master-Slave Dialectic

Years before, the German philosopher Hegel (1770–1831) had formulated an analysis of the abstract relationship between the master and the slave which to this day is still being praised for its logic. The slave is dependent on the master (for food, clothing, and, above all, his good-will), but the master also is not free—he is dependent on the slave. There are things the slave has control over, but the master does not (like keeping house). Moreover, the slave has to be kept in check by the master, so the master constantly has to be aware of the slave, whereas the slave is free to scheme and connive as long as he stays clear of the master. In a sense, the master is as much "enslaved" as the slave, if not more. Nietzsche must surely have read this famous analysis, and one interesting point to discuss is whether or not his own analysis shows any trace of the Hegelian dialectics.

arousal of fear. *Good* is the fellow slave who helps out—the nonthreatening person, the one who shows sympathy and altruism, the one who acts to create the greatest good for the greatest number of people. (Thus, the morality of "utility" is for Nietzsche a "slave-morality.") The slaves feel tremendous *resentment* toward the masters, and this resentment ends in revolt. Historically, the slaves gained power over the masters, says Nietzsche, and the "master-morality" was reversed to the status of evil, while the slaves' own morality was raised to become a common ideal. Their morality became the morality of the *herd*, where no one is supposed to raise his head higher than the rest of the herd. So in a sense, for Nietzsche, the meek have inherited the earth already. But the herd has retained their feelings of resentment toward the idea of the master, and everything the master stood for is still considered evil (even though the herd allows for no new masters):

> The noble type of man regards *himself* as a determiner of values; he does not require to be approved of; he passes the judgement: "What is injurous to me is injurous in itself"; he knows that it is he himself only who confers honor on things; he is a *creator of values*. . . . It is otherwise with the second type of morality, *slave-morality*. Supposing that the abused, the oppressed, the suffering, the unemancipated, the weary, and those uncertain of themselves, should moralize, what will be the common element in their moral estimates? Probably a pessimistic suspicion with regard to the entire situation of man will find expression, perhaps a condemnation of man, together with his situation.

For Nietzsche this dichotomy between slave and master can be found in every culture, sometimes even within the same individual. The situation initially developed in early European cultures, as well as in the Judeo-Christian tradition, which, in Nietzsche's eyes, clearly displayed the herd mentality of the slave, with its requirement that you must turn the other cheek and refrain from doing harm if you wish to partake of "pie in the sky when you die." This mentality has been carried on by Christianity (described by Nietzsche as the "mass egoism of the weak"), by utilitarianism, and by socialism, and it has the effect of reducing everything to averages and mediocrity, because it advocates general happiness and equality. For Nietzsche that is the same as a herd mentality, which fears anything that is different, even if what is different is grander, stranger, and more magnificent.

The Overman

If a pessimistic view of human nature is the outcome of a slave-morality, Nietzsche must conclude that his own view is a positive one—and he does. For him, the slave-morality *says nay to life*; it looks toward a higher reality (Heaven), and it is mirrored in traditional Western philosophy, which, inspired by Plato, looks toward a world of ideas far-removed from the tangible mess of sensory reality. This *Hinterwelt* (world beyond) is for Nietzsche a dangerous illusion, because it gives people the notion that there is something besides this life, and thus they squander their life here on earth in order to realize their shadowy dreams of a world to come or a higher reality.

This, for Nietzsche, is to live wrongly. A proper existence consists of realizing that there is nothing beyond this life, and that one must pursue life with vigor, like a "master" who sets his own values. If one realizes this, and has the courage to discard the traditional values of Christianity, one has become an Overman (*Übermensch*), or "Superman." The Overman is the human of the future—not in the sense of a biological evolution in terms of Darwinism and natural selection (not all men of the future will be Overmen)—an automatic, natural selection, but as an aggressive taking of power. What the Overman realizes is that there is one feature of human life which is overriding: not reason, and not fellow-feeling, but *will to power*. The slave-morality will do its best to control or kill it, but the man who is capable of being a creator of values will recognize it as his birthright, and will use it any way he sees fit. His right lies in his capacity to use the power, because that power is itself the force of life.

Again, the use of *man* instead of *human* is intentional here: Nietzsche, for whatever reasons, mistrusted female character and female capabilities, and did not count women among his future Overmen. Although many thinkers have omitted women from their theories either because it didn't occur to them to include women, or because they assumed that the terms *man* and *he* would cover both genders, Nietzsche is a true misogynist who deliberately excludes women from any significant moral existence. One might wonder how his sister felt about that.

Two reactions to the Overman concept have occurred over the years. One has been an intellectual rekindling of the joy of life (in spite of what theologians and philosophers preach about the sadness and incompleteness of life). This reaction brought with it a critical evaluation of the *double standard* that existed in Western culture in the past—a standard that may have been applied to Nietzsche himself, and against which he argued as aggresively as he argued against the Christian tradition: the verbal condemnation of physical pleasures combined with tacit acceptance of those pleasures when experienced on the sly. The Victorian era was particularly infested with this type of hypocrisy, and Nietzsche fought it whenever he saw it.

We may want to call this reaction against hypocrisy the *positive* legacy of Nietzsche. Unfortunately, there is a negative outgrowth of his ideas: the Nazi ideology. As we have already mentioned, Nietzsche's Overman was adopted by Hitler's Third Reich as the ideal of the new German culture. Picking upon Nietzsche's idea that power belongs by right to he who grabs it (an idea that was taken out of context and also was marred by Elisabeth's editing), the Nazis saw themselves as a new race of Overmen, destined to rule the world. The weak would have no rights, and their sole purpose in life would be to provide fuel for the power of their masters.

Would Nietzsche have approved of Hitler? Absolutely and emphatically not. Nietzsche would have seen in Hitler something he despised: a "slave" full of resentment against others in power. And, strangely enough, Nietzsche was filled with contempt for the Germans; that is why he moved to Switzerland. Furthermore, he was a sworn enemy of totalitarianism, because he viewed it as just another way to enslave a few capable people and prevent them from using their own will. The fact remains, however, that Nietzsche's writings include elements that unmistakably lead to the abuse, or at least the neglect, of the weak by the strong, and because of Hitler's use of his writings, Nietzsche was a closed subject in philosophy for almost twenty years after World War II—he was considered too controversial to touch. Today we can view his writings with more detachment, but when we read his fighting words, the tension still comes through. Liberation of the body and the spirit, coupled with a disdain for the weak—what can we make of this mixture of free thought and contempt?

The Eternal Return and the Value of Life

Nietzsche is famous for having said "God is Dead." (Some student joker has inscribed another famous line in the wet concrete at the University of California, San Diego: "Nietzsche is dead, signed: God.") But what did Nietzsche mean by saying that God is dead? The opinion of an atheist (which Nietzsche called himself) is usually that God has never existed, not that he is *dead*. This tells us something about Nietzsche's view of reality: In earlier times people believed in God, and that made him alive. Now we don't believe anymore, so God is dead. For most people this means that morality has lost its sanction, so they lose faith in everything and become *nihilists*.

The word *nihilism* is often mentioned in connection with Nietzsche. It comes from the Latin word (*nihil*, or nothing), and usually means that there is no foundation for believing in anything, and that existence is senseless and useless. On occasion Nietzsche himself is called a nihilist by critics, but is that correct?

There seem to be two differing views of what Nietzsche *really* meant by this concept: (1) If everything is permitted, you soon despair because there are no values, and you become a nihilist. (2) Even if you realize that there are no objective values or truth, you make your own values. By doing so you affirm life and your own strength, so you are *not* a nihilist. To many Nietzsche scholars it seems that this is exactly what he is saying, not that there is nothing to believe in. Above all, Nietzsche believed in the value of life itself, and of affirming life, saying yes to life.

Nietzsche's idea, in fact, is to say yes to life no matter what it throws at you (because to many people life doesn't seem particularly wonderful). It is easy to love life when it treats you well, but Nietzsche wants us to love life even at its worst. And what is the worst that Nietzsche can imagine? That everything that has happened to you will happen again, the very same way. This is the theory of the *eternal return*. There is a legend of Nietzsche taking a walk one day and being struck by the awful truth: history repeats itself, and all our fears and joys will be repeated. We have experienced them before, and we will experience them again, endlessly. The idea horrified him, and he was forced to consider the question: Even if you know that you will have to go through the same tedious, painful stuff over and over again, would you choose to, willingly?

As with the theory of nihilism, there are two interpretations of this problem. One holds that Nietzsche actually believed that everything repeats itself. We're doomed to live the same life again and again, life is absurd, and our existence is pointless. The other suggests that Nietzsche had simply come up with the ultimate way of testing a person's affirmation of life: *What if* everything repeats itself? Would you want it all over again? If you can answer, "Let's have it one more time," then you truly love life, and you have passed the test. (In Chapter 20 we will take a closer look at how Nietzsche himself expresses this idea.)

Which interpretation is correct? Is the "eternal return" real, or is it a *thought experiment*? (A thought experiment is a method often used by thinkers. You imagine a set of premises, and then you use your reason to calculate their consequences, thus performing an experiment in your mind.) Nietzsche experts disagree, but either way, it serves as a true test of our love of life. The same exams, the same driving tests, the same falling in and out of love, the same tax returns, the same vacations and children and illnesses—would you do it all over again? If yes, Nietzsche congratulates you. You have won the battle against doubt, weakness, and nihilism, and you will experience the ultimate joy in the face of meaninglessness.

Narratives That Explore the Eternal Return of the Same

Chapter 20 includes a section that explores the idea of time repeating itself. You may find it relevant partly for a discussion of existential concepts, and partly for a discussion of Nietzsche's idea of the eternal return. The stories selected are Camus's *The Myth of Sisyphus*, Nietzsche's own *Thus Spoke Zarathustra*, and Ken Greenwood's novel *Replay*.

Chapter 18

The Soul and
the State

This chapter covers four classical philosophical theories about human nature. They have one major feature in common: the viewpoint that humans don't necessarily know what is good for them, or know their own nature, and that informing them about these issues is the task of the philosopher (or, as the case may be, the psychoanalyst). Aside from this feature, all of the theories are concerned with the connection between the individual and his or her social world.

Plato's theory of human nature looks partly at the organization of the *psyche* and partly at the organization of the *state*. Because of these elements one might be tempted to call it a psychological theory, or a theory of sociology, but Plato is not very interested in how humans—both individually and politically—actually are, but how they ought to be. Thus, his is primarily a normative theory. The same is the case with the political theory of Aristotle. You may remember that Aristotle focuses on the cultivation of human virtues in order to build a good character, and his theory is linked to his concept of man as a social creature. Aristotle says that humans are by nature social beings, and he proceeds to outline a normative theory about what humans ought to do as social beings. In this way a political theory grows out of Aristotle's concept of what is natural for humans.

The third and fourth theories take us into modern times with Karl Marx and Sigmund Freud. Marx's social theory takes a view of human nature that contains a strong normative element. He believes human society ought to change from one structure (capitalist) to another (socialist), and that human nature will undergo a similar transformation when political conditions change.

For Plato and Aristotle, as well as for Marx, there is a strong connection between the concepts of ethics, human nature, and political theory, and for all three, the key to understanding this connection is acquiring knowledge of what humans are, and what their potential is. For Sigmund Freud, however, the political connection is not important—at least not as a key feature of his theory. (Other psychology scholars, like Wilhelm Reich and Herbert Marcuse, have been inspired by Freud to create a political theory on the basis of Freud's psychological theory of human nature.) Although scientifically descriptive, Freud's theory has a definite normative element in that it assumes there is a healthy condition versus a pathological one. The healthy condition thus becomes the ideal norm to strive for (although Freud himself thought this was an ideal that could only be approximated).

Plato, the Soul, and the State

The Nature of Reality: Changing or Unchanging?

The dichotomy we saw in Saint Augustine between the world of flesh and the world of spirit has its foundation not in the words of the Old or New Testament, but in Plato's *theory of Forms*, to which Augustine was introduced through Plato's own dialogues as well as through the teachings of Neoplatonism.

As we saw in Chapter 8, Plato's philosophy is based on his theory of Forms and their underlying concept of reality: whatever is unchanging has true reality, and whatever changes is less real. The human being, a victim of the physical and spiritual changes wrought by time, would thus do well to focus on those of his or her abilities that show the most permanence: the abilities of *reason*. It is reason that directly accesses the Forms by paying less attention to the external world, and so it is through Reason that we acquire knowledge of the everlasting truths (through the senses we gather only *doxa*—opinion). Although the beliefs originating in our sense experiences are uncertain (because we can't trust our senses 100 percent) Forms are objects of certain knowledge (*epistēmē*). This means that although we can never gain certain knowledge about the world of the senses, we *can* obtain certain knowledge about the world of Forms. Here is an example: We can't ever experience a perfect circle through our senses, but intellectually (by way of the Forms) we can understand and visualize a perfect circle. The world is thus divided into two kinds of reality: a tangible but shad-

Metaphysics and Human Nature

What has all this got to do with human nature? Any view of human nature is based on metaphysics, on a theory of reality. If you think *reality is change*, then you may believe that humans change, too, or that nothing is permanent or absolute. You may become a *skeptic* (you don't believe absolute certainty can be obtained, either in terms of every kind of knowledge or in terms of certain kinds of knowledge) or a *nihilist* (you don't believe in anything, at least not until it is proven). You may become a *relativist* (you believe that truth is a relative thing, depending on cultures and viewpoints), or a *revolutionary* (you believe it is time for a change). Some people might add that you may also become a *pragmatist*, one who takes things as they come and regards those things that *work* as true. If you think *reality is unchanging*, then you look for permanent elements beyond the change. You place emphasis on contemplation or think about a world beyond this one, and perhaps you become politically *withdrawn*, or you become a *conservative*. Either way, our view of human nature is based on our personal metaphysics, our view of reality.

owy material world, which most people mistake for being the true one (remember *Myth of the Cave*?), and an intangible but truer reality beyond the world of senses—the spiritual world of the Forms. This metaphysical theory makes Plato a *dualist*, someone who believes that reality consists of both matter and spirit. Plato's brand of dualism, however, leans toward the world of spirit as the truer one.

Where did Plato get the idea of looking for permanence beyond the flux of tangible reality? From Parmenides of Elea, Italy (ca. 515 B.C.E.). For Parmenides *true reality is unchanging reality*. Whatever changes is not real or is only a minor reality, or an illusion. And because we, as well as the physical world around us, seem to change, true reality must lie beyond what we see; true reality must lie in the intellectual realm.

Heraclitus supplied another answer to the question of the nature of reality at about the same time as Parmenides. He said *reality is change!* If you look at a river, Heraclitus said, you cannot bathe in it twice. In other words, you may think you are still you, and the river may still be where it was yesterday, but you have changed, and so has the river.

These two schools of metaphysics came to determine the Western tradition. The one we know best is the Parmenidean legacy, because that is the one Plato took up, and the one that, through Plato, became part of the Christian tradition. The view of Heraclitus became an esoteric view that surfaces occasionally in Western philosophy through philosophers such as Bergson, Whitehead, and Nietzsche.

The Soul

Our main source of Plato's theory of human nature is the dialogues *The Republic* and *Phaedrus*. They both were written in the mature years of Plato's life and are believed to reflect at least as much of Plato himself as they do Socrates' thoughts. When asked why people do things that are morally wrong, Socrates' answer was that it is *not* due to an evil human nature, but merely to *ignorance*: Had they known better, they would not have done the wrongful act. For both Socrates and Plato this means that the better education people receive, the better their moral character will be. Eventually—once people realize that good behavior brings about peace of mind—they will be reasonable about their actions and will avoid striving toward anything that would disrupt that peace of mind. In other words, the theory of Forms serves as a foundation for a moral theory of virtue: the realization of the nature of true reality will turn one's mind from the unstable world of the senses and sensual desires to the unchanging and true world of knowledge.

Plato also was gifted with common sense. He realized that our "knowing" what is right doesn't automatically make it happen, because we are more than just reason: our *psyche* (or soul) consists of two additional elements: physical *desires* or *appetites*, and spiritual willpower. In the harmonious person these elements work well together, but they always present a conflict that needs to be kept under control. In his dialogue *Phaedrus*, Plato illustrates how hard it is for a person to achieve spiritual balance and harmony: A human being is like a charioteer with two horses. One horse is well trained and well behaved, but the other is wild and unruly. So what must the charioteer do? Make the "good" horse help control the "bad" horse (those of you who know about horses will know that this is an old technique that actually works). In the end the charioteer will be the one controlling both horses. What does this symbolize? The charioteer is our reason, the good horse is our spirit and our willpower, and the bad horse symbolizes our desires and appetites. Why don't we just turn out the wild horse (our physical desires)? Because of human destiny. We are stuck with both our unruly desires and our headstrong willpower. We can't cut the horses loose—we must learn to steer them for the purpose of harmony. If we don't let our reason be supported by our willpower—if, instead, we let our desires control our willpower—then our soul will become corrupted, and we will not achieve harmony.

The principle of the soul being tainted by physical desires is known not only in the Greek and Christian traditions, but also in the more ancient Hindu philosophy. The idea that the body is a prison for the soul, and that at death the soul will fly free, is known as *soma sema* (the body is a prison), and it usually implies that the material world is evil. Can Plato possibly have been influenced by Eastern ideas regarding the relationship between the mind and the body, and the notion that the soul exists before the body? It is not impossible at all. Trade routes ran through the entire Persian realm (which reached from Greece to India at its height, during Plato's childhood), and it is not inconceivable that Hindu teachings reached Athens. But Plato also was inspired by the mathematician Pythagoras, who believed that the body was unimportant compared to the life of the soul (Pythagoras also is supposed to have believed in reincar-

Socrates on Self-Control in All Things, Including Love

Interestingly, the follow-up to the story of the charioteer in *Phaedrus* is rarely mentioned, probably because it has very little to do with the virtues of reason in general: Socrates is not so much concerned with reason for its own sake, but with the proper way to approach someone with whom you are terribly in love. (Socrates assumes that the person in love is an older, more experienced male; the one he is in love with is a young man. As you may know, sexual relationships between men and in particular between older and younger men were common in Ancient Greece and carried no stigma whatsoever.) What must one do in matters of the heart? Socrates says one must control one's wild desires, and approach the person one desires with self-control! It will be better for the entire relationship.

nation). In *Phaedrus* Plato expresses his own brand of reincarnation theory: Before we are born we exist in the realm of the Forms and have full knowledge of the eternal truths. Then we are born, and we forget what we knew—but a good teacher can help us remember. (This is the theory also known as *anamnesis*. See Chapter 8.) When we die we go back to the Forms, but then after a while it is time to be reborn again. It seems that Plato thought the purpose was to be born into a life where you finally remembered what you knew in between existences (the truth of the Forms); when that happened you would not have to be reborn again.

In different dialogues Plato gives slightly different accounts of the fate of the soul and its general structure. In his dialogue *Timaeos* he even states that reason resides in the head, passion in the stomach, and appetite in the genitals—but this should probably be taken as a metaphor and not as a physical description.

The State

Just as there is a proper way for the psyche to be in harmony, so is there a proper way for society to function, and for Plato those two ideas are interrelated. The same three parts that make up the psyche also make up society. There are the people who represent, or ought to represent, *reason*—the Guardians; there are the people who represent *spirit*—the Auxiliaries (soldiers, the police force, and civil servants); and there are people who represent *desires*—the working population. Justice in the city-state means the same as justice in an individual: harmony between the three parts, and contentment at doing one's share. Translated into politics, this means that if you belong to the working population, you must be content to let others (the Guardians)

A Mind Divided: Other Views of the Soul

Plato's theory of the tripartite soul is by no means the only ancient theory that states that the soul consists of parts. This is in fact a common notion. The ancient Egyptians believed that the soul consists of several parts that can act independently. One part is closely attached to the body and stays with it after death; another part is able to travel in dreams, and may, after death, haunt the living. The most important part of the soul is the *Ka*, which is of divine origin. After death, and after a court process in which the deeds of the past life are judged, the Ka returns to the gods.

Shamanism also incorporates theories of soul parts. Shamans (men and women who are believed to cure or cause diseases with the help of supernatural powers) are found throughout most of the world in pretechnological societies. There are shamans (once referred to as "medicine men") among the indigenous populations of North, Central, and South America, as well as among the Inuit (formerly known as Eskimos) and the peoples of Siberia, Tibet, China, Japan, and India. There is evidence that shamanism was also widespread in Old Europe.

The shaman, in a trance, may send his or her power soul on quests to seek information or affect events, but the body stays alive. (In some American Pacific coast tribes, illness was considered to be caused by soul loss, and shamans often were called to recover the souls of sick people. In other words, tribe members believed that some mental or spiritual part keeps the body alive, and the important part of the soul is missing in the sick person.)

Looking toward scientific theories of the modern Western world, we find a curious parallel to Plato's theory of the tripartite soul: It is commonly recognized in biology that the human brain consists of three major parts, each reflecting a stage in human evolution. There is a primitive part of the brain usually referred to as the reptilian part, a brain structure which we share with the reptiles; next comes a more advanced mammalian part, shared by other mammals and testifying to our past as prehominids; and last comes the neocortex, which is the location for the thought processes we usually identify as specifically human. We might speculate how Plato would relate his theory to this scientific view of the structure of the human brain (and here we should remember the dualistic metaphysical theory that "brain" and "soul" or "mind" need not be the same thing).

In the last section of this chapter we will look at an immensely influential modern theory of divisions in the human mind: the psychoanalyst Sigmund Freud's theory of the *Id*, the *Ego*, and the *Superego*.

think for you, and let others (the military) control you. Plato uses a mythic image to illustrate this concept: There are people of "gold"—the Guardians. There are people of "silver"—the Auxiliaries. And the working people? Brass and iron. As with the charioteer and his horses, the Guardians achieve harmony by keeping the Auxiliaries and the working people under control. This does not correspond to our modern idea of justice, which is that everybody should be given equal consideration; rather, it is based on the notion that everybody must *know his or her place* in society.

Today this blueprint for the ideal state seems less than ideal. We have a word for the *organic* theory of the state, the belief that everyone has his or her given place, and that the limbs exist basically to keep the head going, and the head rules absolutely over the limbs: We call it *totalitarianism*. The state takes precedence over the individuals, and as long as there is harmony the Guardians' might makes right. Still we might consider that Plato's state is not the same as the organic state devised by Mussolini, the fascist Italian despot of World War II, because Plato assumes that this arrangement is best for every citizen, while Mussolini apparently had no such notions.

Plato envisions the Guardians to be none other than *philosophers*—people who are so far advanced that they know the truth of the world of Forms, and the lower status of the material world. The best way to choose a guardian is to find someone who is capable but doesn't want the job. This should ensure that he or she will do the job efficiently, without allowing personal ambitions to influence the task. People who give up their individuality to become philosophers have already conquered the lust for power. Therefore, they will not become corrupted by power once they are in the job. (This solves the worry of "who guards the Guardians.") (People who nominate themselves for the job are automatically disqualified, because they have demonstrated a lust for power.) Other features designed to eliminate personal ambition include a ban on private property, and a rule for male Guardians that wives and children must be shared.

The usual problem with a hierarchical society of castes is that it suffocates itself because it doesn't allow for movement between the classes. Or rather, you can usually move *down*, but you can't move *up*. How does Plato's ideal state fare in comparison? Suppose you are a soldier's son, but your true talent lies in toolmaking. Or you are a farmer's daughter, but you show a clear talent for administration and thinking in general. Or you are a Guardian's daughter, but you want to be a soldier. Surprisingly enough, Plato says if that's what you want, so be it—if you have the talent, you should perform that function regardless of your background or sex. (If women can also become Guardians, we must assume that they are required to share their husbands, just as the male Guardians share their wives; however, Plato neglects to fill in that detail.) However, on the whole Plato believed that the hierarchy would be better off if everyone stayed within his or her class.

Plato thus shows considerable faith in the power of reason, the strength of harmony in the psyche and in the state, and individual talent. But what about faith in the ordinary person's character? Plato was no democrat; he was skeptical of the ability of the masses to rule themselves or control their own appetites. It is inevitable that such a view of human nature leads to a policy of control and regulations. Plato doesn't see human nature as evil, but rather as weak and easily influenced by the physical world if not imprinted by reason. Thus the "people" can't be left to govern themselves, and philosophers have a moral duty to infuse them with as much reason as they can—for their own sake, but most of all for the sake of the harmony of the state.

Aristotle: Man Is a Political Animal

Teleology and Theory of Causation

Aristotle, although influenced by Plato and subjected to the same general acculturation process of the city-state as Plato, has his own theory of how human nature and the state should fit together. As we saw in Chapter 9, his key question when investigating a subject is, What is its purpose? This *teleological* assumption that everything has a purpose, a necessary condition for being what it is, is clarified in his famous theory of *causation*, which you may remember from Chapter 9. For Aristotle everything has four types of causes, and once we know them, we can understand the nature of that thing. They are (1) the *material* cause, (2) the *efficient* cause, (3) the *formal* cause, and (4) the *final* cause.

How are we supposed to apply these four causes? Think of a house. What is its *material* cause? (In other words, what kind of matter does it consist of?) In Aristotle's day, timber and stonemasonry. Today, usually wood slabs and concrete. Either way, the building material is the material cause. What is the *efficient* cause of the house? In other words, what or who made it into what it is? The builders and carpenters. And the *formal* cause? This is the element most closely related to Plato's theory of Forms, because it means the *idea* of the house, its Form, which for Aristotle existed nowhere other than in the house itself, not off in some intellectual realm. So if we translate this idea into meaning the house's *physical appearance*, we are close to what Aristotle intended. And the *final* cause? This was possibly the most important question for Aristotle. We must read the word *final* as meaning the *end* or *goal* of the house—in other words, its *purpose*, or *telos*. The purpose of a house is to provide shelter. Together these causes give us the essence of the house.

For Aristotle everything, not just intentional actions, has a purpose. Natural objects have a telos, and so do humans. But for Aristotle the state is a natural object, too, and so it must have a purpose given by nature, not merely a human purpose. Its purpose, however, is not necessarily *permanence*. Even though Aristotle is a student of Plato, he says that just because something *lasts*, that doesn't automatically make it *good*. The more important question is, Has it fulfilled its purpose? Only then can we say it is good. So here we see a significant departure from the ideal of unchanging reality.

Man, the Political Animal

Aristotle is famous for having said that man is a "political animal." To us this implies a warning; the modern person can hardly help associating politics with a certain ele-

The Virtuous Person Recalled

The question, What makes us human? is for Aristotle the same as asking, What is our final cause? What can we do better than other creatures? In other words, what is our purpose as human beings? You may remember that Aristotle believes that our purpose is to use our reason, think well, and act accordingly. We may apply our intellect to abstract issues, or we may use it to solve practical problems. Virtue lies in modifying our actions and emotions so that they are neither excessive nor deficient. The soul is as important for Aristotle as it is for Plato, but Aristotle doesn't seem eager to attribute a separate existence to the soul, even if the soul is immaterial. For him the soul represents the ultimate telos of the body, and there is no emphasis on the soul existing before or after the life of the body. Thus there is no fundamental negativity attached to the life of the body, other than what Aristotle has already told us in his theory of the Golden Mean—that too much of a good thing is bad for you.

Our purpose is, then, a rather down-to-earth one. Our goal is to achieve a state of *well-being* (Eudaimonia)—not through physical contentment alone, but by leading a life of moderation and practicing good, clear thinking. How do we achieve that? By being taught well, and by developing good habits. It is not something that happens overnight, so for Aristotle the human being closest to perfection is not a young person, as nice as that person may seem. It takes years to acquire good habits, and with those habits you acquire true appreciation of the many facets of life. In fact, you can't really be happy if you are young, and very young children can't be happy at all—their laughter is just outbursts of immaturity and maladjustment, if one is to believe Aristotle. Virtue is something we must learn, and it is the duty of the state to teach us—because what we want is not always what we need. For Aristotle we certainly have freedom of the will, as a moral choice, but that doesn't mean we are *politically* free. Just as humans can't choose their telos because it has been given to them by nature, so they can't choose their political purpose. That is determined by their status, their talents, and their destiny (whether they were born male or female, a free person or a slave, a Greek or (horror of horrors) a barbarian. Part of being virtuous is to know oneself, that is, to conduct a proper self-assessment: How do I come across to others? What are my limitations and problem areas? Am I performing my actions at the right time, to the right degree? Once we know this much about ourselves, we may be able to call ourselves virtuous, but it is a matter of both intelligence and maturity.

ment of ruthlessness. But is this what Aristotle meant? It seems not. In Book I of
Politics he says:

> If the earlier forms of society are natural, so is the state, for it is the end of them,
> and the nature of a thing is its end. For what each thing is when fully developed,
> we call its nature, whether we are speaking of a man, a horse, or a family. Be-
> sides, the final cause and end of a thing is the best, and to be self-sufficient is the
> end and the best.
>
> Hence it is evident that the state is a creation of nature, and that man is by
> nature a political animal. And he who by nature and not by mere accident is
> without a state, is either a bad man or above humanity. . . . Further, the state is
> by nature prior to the family and to the individual, since the whole is of neces-
> sity prior to the part. . . . The proof that the state is a creation of nature and
> prior to the individual is that the individual, when isolated, is not self-sufficient,
> and therefore he is like a part in relation to the whole. . . . A social instinct is
> implanted in all men by nature.

We have to go back to the Greek origin of the word *political* to understand Aristotle's intention. It means "*of the polis*," the city-state. So "man is a political animal"
means that for humans it is natural to live a social existence in close proximity to
others, and to be organized into a hierarchical society for the sake of the common
good. Humans are dependent on each other and are naturally inclined to live together
in families and communities. So in a sense people are social by choice, but this choice
is not based on self-directed concerns (as Plato's brother Glaucon claimed for the sake
of argument, and as Hobbes claimed in all earnestness some two thousand years later).
The true basis for being "civilized"—for being a decent city dweller—is the natural
love between family members and between *friends*. In his *Nicomachean Ethics*, Aristotle
spends much time discussing friendship as a virtue. On the political level, this virtue
is what keeps the state together.

What does this political theory mean? That human beings have no social contract.
We have no "state of nature," because *society is a natural phenomenon*, and humans have
never lived outside of it. In fact, it is impossible to live outside of society; if you do,
you are either a beast or a god. The human community is made possible by the human
capacity for *speech* and for *reason*, and this can be either good or bad, because with the
ability to *conceptualize* comes a sense of justice and injustice, of good and evil. Speech
thus makes us both social and moral beings, so ethics and politics are closely related
historically as well as in each individual.

The state is thus a given, and so is its *structure*. What already exists must have a
purpose, and should not be altered. (You might say that Aristotle shows us one of the
first examples of the *naturalistic fallacy*, by moving from what *is* to what *ought to be*).
People must find their place in society and not look elsewhere. And Aristotle had very
specific thoughts about people's proper place:

> For that some should rule and others be ruled is a thing not only necessary, but
> expedient: from the hour of their birth, some are marked out for subjection,
> others for rule. . . . The living creature . . . consists of soul and body; and of

these two, the one is by nature the ruler, and the other the subject. But then we must look for the intentions of nature in things which retain their nature, and not in things which are corrupted. And therefore we must study the man who is in the most perfect state both of body and soul, for in him we shall see the true relation of the two. . . . The soul rules the body with a despotic rule, whereas the intellect rules the appetites with a constitutional and royal rule. And it is clear that the rule of the soul over the body and of the mind and the rational element over the passionate, is natural and expedient; whereas the equality of the two or the rule of the inferior is always hurtful. The same holds good of animals in relation to men; for tame animals have a better nature than wild, and all tame animals are better off when they are ruled by man; for then they are preserved. Again, the male is by nature superior, and the female inferior, and the one rules, and the other is ruled; this principle, of necessity, extends to all mankind. Where then there is such a difference as that between soul and body, or between men and animals (as in the case of those whose business is to use their body, and who can do nothing better), the lower sort are by nature slaves, and it is better for them as for all inferiors that they should be under the rule of a master.

What can we make of such blatantly supremacist and sexist (and even speciesist) talk today? We might of course discard Aristotle altogether for not being "politically correct," but we would deprive ourselves of a marvelous body of interesting writing, of a sense of history, and, perhaps most important, of a chance to brush up on our arguments about why supremacism, sexism, and speciesism are wrong. We might instead choose to say that Aristotle didn't know any better, for these were the thoughts of his day and age. And Socrates himself would be the first to say that there is no evil intent, only ignorance. That is not quite sufficient, however, because Aristotle's own teacher, Plato, didn't quite share his views on what women can and should do in the perfect society. But Aristotle is not as hardened in his views of political hierarchy as it may seem, because who were the slaves of ancient Greece? They were prisoners of war, always, and any offspring they might have in captivity. Many of the prisoners, of course, weren't "born to be ruled," and were good for many things other than physical work. Indeed, Aristotle believed that some of them never should have been enslaved, particularly if the war in which they had been fighting was unjust. So there are slaves *by law* (and a great number of them ought not to be slaves), there are slaves *by nature* (people who are good at following orders and doing physical work), and there are *free men by nature* (people who are good at giving orders and using their mind). Ultimately, it is supposed to be *good* for the natural slaves to be slaves. All humans have a chief purpose in life, even slaves. That purpose is to to be happy although slaves never can be as happy as a free Greek male who thinks rationally. If the master has abused his slaves to the point where they have no contentment and don't feel their lives have been well-spent in perfection of their purpose, then the master is to blame. In the end, the social structure Aristotle envisions is one that is supposed to be to the advantage of everyone involved, based on their individual talents and telos.

It is still difficult to view Aristotle's position on slavery with much sympathy. We

Natural Law and Natural Inclinations

When Supreme Court Justice Clarence Thomas had just been nominated to the Supreme Court, some members of the media, as well as members of the Senate Confirmation Committee, were interested in whether or not he was a *natural law theorist*. His previous work seemed to indicate that he might be, but because media attention quickly focused on other matters during the Thomas hearings, the question was never fully discussed. Many wondered at the time what a natural law theorist was, and why it was relevant to the hearings. Because we have talked about Aristotle's idea of teleology, it is appropriate here to discuss the phenomenon of natural law. You can then judge for yourself whether it is relevant to ask a Supreme Court nominee whether he or she supports that theory.

Natural law has nothing to do with laws of physics. Such laws, such as the law of gravity, describe how natural objects behave, and natural objects can't help but behave according to the laws of physics. This means that laws of physics are descriptive. Natural law, however, is a normative theory about how humans ought to behave, based on a theory about human nature. Thomas Aquinas (1225–1274), an Italian religious authority and philosopher who got his inspiration from Aristotle's theory of teleology, developed a version of this theory that influenced the Catholic Church. For Aquinas the idea of purpose meant God's purpose, and if God gave humans a purpose, then anything corresponding to that purpose must be what is natural for humans. *Natural inclinations* thus become the basis of a moral theory, but not just any natural inclinations. *Self-preservation*, *procreation*, *intellectual curiosity*, and *social existence* are the four key inclinations. This means that humans ought to strive to preserve life (their own as well as others), to have children and raise them, to seek knowledge (especially knowledge about God), and to be good citizens (who only in extreme circumstances have the right to civil disobedience). Humans have freedom of the will to decide whether or not they want to follow this natural law, but if they decide not to, they are choosing the path of sin. The practical consequences of such a theory can be considerable. Natural law regards not only abortion, but also contraception, as impermissible under most circumstances. Critics have pointed out that natural law theorists are committing the naturalistic fallacy by jumping from an "is" to an "ought," but some natural law theorists don't recognize this as a fallacy.

should realize, though, that Aristotle is talking not so much about the ideal state (as Plato was), but about the state as he saw it with his own eyes. The society he describes is only a perfected version of what he believed already existed. Furthermore, he was fairly convinced that he was, by and large, expressing the opinion of the majority of educated men, with perhaps the exception of the issue of slavery, which he acknowledges as a touchy subject. There were those who, despite the fact that the entire Athenian economy was based on the work of slaves (or perhaps because of it), argued that slavery is a crime against nature.

Democratic theories have wrestled with these various ideas ever since. We may all agree that man is a political animal, but we may not agree with Aristotle's conclusion that some are born to rule and others to be ruled. A more modern reading might sound like this: *Some are born leaders, others are born followers.* If this were all Aristotle had intended to say, many people today might agree with him (although such a theory also would suffer from the problems of the naturalistic fallacy). The trouble is that Aristotle actually talks about people *owning* other people, and this runs counter to our sense of democracy and justice.

Karl Marx: Human Nature Will Change

Regardless of whether the world has seen the last of Marxism as a social experiment, there is no denying that Karl Marx has been the greatest political influence of the twentieth century, either in the way societies have been shaped according to the rules of communism, or in the way societies have defined themselves in contrast to communism, and have taken precautions to prevent its spread. This is not a textbook of political theory, and we will not go into detail about Marxism as such, but Marx developed a distinct theory of human nature that goes hand in hand with his visions of the communist society of the future. As you may remember, Ricoeur pronounced Marx one of the "masters of suspicion" (the other two were Nietzsche and Freud). Let's take a look at the Marxist brand of "suspicion."

Marx as a Materialist

It is common knowledge that Marxism requires the end of private property, the end of profit-making businesses—in short, the end of the capitalist economic system. Why is it, then, classified as a *philosophical* theory, and not simply a politico-economic one? The reason is that the foundation for the Marxist social structure is a philosophical, even metaphysical, one—a theory of the nature of reality. For Marx, reality is what you can see, touch, and measure. In other words, he is a *materialist*; he believes that reality is material, and not spiritual. But he also believes that *reality is change*, that it changes through a process of development known as *dialectics.*

Karl Marx (1818–1883) was born in Trier, Germany, into a Jewish family that had converted to Protestantism. Marx himself became an agnostic. He studied philosophy and economics in Bonn, and there he was introduced to the ideas of the German philosopher G.W.F. Hegel, who at that time was at the height of his influence in European intellectual circles. Hegel believed that reality is *spiritual*, and he developed a kind of "absolute idealism." He said that as history develops, the World Spirit evolves. Any natural item or cultural movement is a manifestation of the World Spirit, and it becomes more and more rational through a certain pattern of development, through *opposition*. Any idea will, like a pressure, create its own opposition, or counterpressure. This opposition also, then, creates its own opposition, which is thus related to the original idea. (The process follows a yes-no-yes pattern.) This pendulum pattern, in which each new opposition absorbs some of the previous oppositions into itself, is what Hegel calls a *dialectic movement*. (It is sometimes referred to as "*thesis-antithesis-synthesis*," but Hegel never used that expression; it came from his colleague J. G. Fichte.) Reality is a dialectic movement of the spirit, because at every new movement, the spirit becomes more rational. As time progresses, World Spirit will become completely rational, and the world will reach its maximum, glorious potential, which is a state of complete human self-realization. Hegel seems to have believed that reality had reached its peak with the Prussian state of the early nineteenth century, and thus the Prussians were the most rationally developed people in the world.

This theory, strange as it may sound, nevertheless swept Europe in the nineteenth century, and Hegelianism became a way of life among intellectuals. Why? It may be because it was one of the most *positive* theories in terms of human progress. The nineteenth century saw a tremendous boost in technology and science in general, and intellectuals and laypeople alike wanted to believe that the world was getting better—that scientists were becoming more knowledgeable, and that people in general were becoming wiser. This positive metaphysical view of life met its defeat during World War I: No longer could Europeans believe that things were getting better, or that humans were becoming wiser.

Just as the Renaissance followed the Middle Ages, and just as neoclassicism followed the rococo, so too did the dialectic movement follow a movement that seemed in most respects to be its opposite—romanticism. How would Hegel explain the development of the spirit through these eras? He would assume that somehow the development reflected people's growing rationality. However, few people accept this idea any more, mainly because another explanation came along which seems more viable. Marx decided that Hegel was right that historical developments are the result of a pattern of back-and-forth movement between opposite beliefs, but he wasn't right in assuming that this process marked the evolution of World Spirit. No, Marx thought, such developments were simply the result of *economics*; the dialectic movement was a *material* development, not a spiritual one. The cultural developments of the world, the intellectual and moral state of affairs, are for Marx directly dependent on the economic system. His "suspicion" consists of suspecting that society is not what it appears to be on the surface—a collection of *independent* cultural institutions. Your churches, your libraries, your theaters and hospitals, your defense system, your rules for moral behavior, for retirement, for education, for marriage and divorce—all

The Fail-Safe Nature of Hegel's Theory

Because Hegel believes that all intellectual development has its own place in the dialectical process, even *philosophical opposition* to Hegel's theory would have a place in his dialectical theory. Such opposition would be absorbed by a better understanding eventually, when Hegel's critics realize that they are wrong, or when time proves them wrong! This tricky argument often has been used by Hegelians to bash philosophers who disagree with his system, such as the Danish philosopher Søren Kierkegaard.

of this (what Marx calls the *Superstructure*) is directly related to the economic system to which your country subscribes. For Marx, mind does not determine society; rather, society determines one's state of mind. Even religion is created and perpetuated by economic forces, and is nothing but the "opiate of the people," a pacifying influence designed to make them believe that life has to be miserable, and that they should look to the afterlife for comfort instead of trying to do something about their miserable conditions while they are still alive. (In this respect Marx and Nietzsche would fully agree on the oppressive legacy of Christianity for ordinary people.)

Believing that culture is independent of economics is a *false ideology* for Marx, and such faulty notions must be exposed. Thus, in essence, any cultural idea conceived during the years when the Western world was ruled by profit-making should be subject to critical examination, and most likely dismissed. (This is why the argument that communism neglects *human rights* has never had much effect on hard-line Marxists; for them "human rights" is a concept that emerged from within the capitalist middle-class consciousness, and is just another economy-dependent notion that must be critically examined.)

Marx believes society developed according to the pattern reflected in Hegel's dialectics; this is why Marx refers to his system as *dialectic materialism*. Just as feudalism was replaced by capitalism, so will capitalism, in time, inevitably be replaced by socialism.

Why Communism?

In 1843, after completing his studies, Marx went to Paris, where he met German socialist Friedrich Engels (1820–1895). This was to be a friendship that lasted for the rest of his life. Engels was the manager of a factory in Manchester, England, and through him Marx became acquainted with the effects of industrialism on society and

FIGURE 18.1 Karl Marx (1818–1883), German philosopher, politician, and social critic. For Marx, human nature could not be deduced from conditions in nineteenth-century Europe, because these were tainted by the presence of capitalism. According to Marx, when an economic system changes, all cultural features will also change, and with them human nature. After the communist revolution, everything would be different; gone would be the selfish greediness of the capitalist world and a contentment with life and meaningful work would flourish instead.

its individuals. Together they coauthored *The Communist Manifesto* (1848). Marx and Engels took part in both the French and German revolutions of 1848, but after these failed, Marx went to England, where he spent the rest of his life. Here he worked part-time as a journalist, and wrote his most famous work, *Das Kapital* (1867).

Today it is a common assumption that the world can be made a better place without resorting to a ban on private property and profit making. We tend to think in terms of providing better health care and child care, giving food and education to starving nations, or raising ecological awareness. This is generally because the problems we face are of a different nature than those with which Marx was familiar. Who is to say that if we were faced with the conditions that so enraged Marx, we might not also suggest a curbing of the capitalist spirit?

What Marx saw in the cities of nineteenth-century Europe was poverty—not just the problem of making ends meet from paycheck to paycheck, but *extreme* poverty, such as we see today in the slums of certain cities in the Third World. In Marx's time people worked to death, literally. There was no protection of the working population, and no support for those who couldn't find work—they and their children faced starvation. The children worked in the factories themselves, ten to sixteen hours a day, with no health insurance and no minimum wage. Industrialization had created jobs for millions, but it had also, as Marx perceived it, robbed the working class of its spirit and given a life of bare existence in exchange. How had it done this? By taking the *time* of the worker, making him or her work for as low wages as possible, and then *selling the finished product for more than the worker was paid*. This we call profit. Marx calls it *surplus value* and views it as exploitation of the worker.

The process Marx calls the *realization of labor* is one in which the worker's own work time is made into a product that is bought and sold (an "object") and the product itself takes on an existence apart from the worker, because he or she has no control over the whole production process, only over a small part of it. The worker thus experiences a "loss of reality"—he doesn't control his own time or products anymore. The result? *Alienation.* You can't possess the things you produce (they cost too much, and you're making them for others who make money off of them, money that they don't share with you). You never really know what happens to the finished product of your work, because you are not in charge of the whole process, so what you've worked on at the assembly line leaves your hands without you ever having a feeling that you had anything to do with it. This is damaging to your sense of self.

The result is that you, as a worker, don't enjoy working, and you look forward only to the time that you can go home. But what do you go home to? Barely enough time to eat and sleep (and not much money for anything else). Then it's back to work. The only enjoyment in life is procreation. You are thus reduced to an animal existence of food, sex, and sleep.

Why did this happen? Because of *private property* and *division of labor*. The factories, the farms, the tools (what Marx calls *productive forces*) are in private hands, and workers each have their own separate task. They have no sense of the whole, and no fellow-feeling for others in the same situation.

Human Nature and Capitalism

Work wasn't always exploitative and demeaning, says Marx. At one time, humans enjoyed working—when they were in charge of the whole process and got to keep their own product, or trade it themselves, or give it away—in other words, when they had control over their product. Then people experienced *self-activity*—work pleasure. And humans can't be happy unless they experience self-activity. For Marx, humans need food, clothing, shelter, and meaningful work; without it, we are not fully human. Under the capitalist system there is no hope for the working classes to ever become "fully human," because their self-activity has been made impossible. And in a sense, the owners of the productive forces (the employees) are suffering, too, because exploiting their fellow human beings reduces their own humanity. So what happens? Human nature itself becomes warped. Humans begin to think in terms of *ownership*. They begin to view work versus free time as an example of evil versus good, and they develop what many in the Western world see as a typically human trait—a selfish concern for taking care of Number One, and an overwhelming concern for the accumulation of material goods. All of this is a result of the economic system of capitalism.

So what must we do? We can't just sit back and *interpret* the world anymore, as philosophers have done for so long, says Marx. Now is the time to *change* things. And the way to change them is not by changing the cultural institutions, but by altering their base: the economic foundation.

Human Nature and the Socialist System

Thus things have now come to such a pass that the individuals must appropriate the existing totality of productive forces, not only to achieve self-activity, but also merely to safeguard their very existence. This appropriation is first determined by the object to be appropriated, the productive forces, which have been developed to a totality and which only exist within a universal intercourse. From this aspect alone, therefore, this appropriation must have a universal character corresponding to the productive forces and the intercourse.

What is Marx saying with these words from *The Communist Manifesto*? That now is the time for the *revolution*. The working classes, the proletariat, must take over the productive forces—the factories, farms, distribution centers, and so on. Furthermore, because commerce is complex and multinational, the revolution ought to be *universal*. In other words, "Workers of the world, unite." In this way nationalism will become a thing of the past. It is futile to try to improve capitalism from the inside; it has to be abolished altogether. But this change must be effected by the workers in the big cities, whose misery has reached the extreme proportions that warrant the dialectic change to the opposite kind of system. Farmers, be they ever so miserable, can't undertake the revolution, because they haven't gone through the experience of alienation; they aren't ready. In the new system, all productive forces will become common property for the workers, and a new era will arise: the era of communism.

"To each according to need, and from each according to ability" is Marx's creed for the new society. In the beginning of the new society wages must be paid for work, but no profit will be made. This is the socialist phase. The eventual goal is to establish a communist society in which wages are abolished, because they are not necessary: Each individual receives what he or she needs—food, clothing, shelter—and is given the opportunity to work at whatever he or she enjoys doing. From then on, humans can be trusted not to exploit each other because *human nature will have changed*. As we know, Marx believes human nature is determined by the economic system, and selfishness is a result of the capitalist system. In the new world people will have no desire to accumulate money and things, because they will be given what they need, so they will not want more. What they want will coincide with what they need. When this condition exists, the communist era will have arrived.

Objections to Marx's Theory

Critics of Marx have used the term *millennium* to describe the communist era, because *millennium* has religious overtones, and it seems to them that Marx is promising the same kind of thing that religion promises—salvation for the believers. Unbelievers—capitalists—are promised only perdition, eternal damnation, until, that is, they get "reeducated" and realize the benefits of communism.

There are other questions one might want to ask of Marx, and we will consider them systematically. The one objection to communism which would occur to most people who witnessed the fall of the Berlin Wall in 1989 is: Communism has been tried, and it didn't work, so Marx was wrong. We might imagine the following answer from Marx: The Eastern European and Soviet social experiment called communism was never what I intended. First of all, it was not begun by workers in the cities alone, but also by the feudal population of farmers (and that goes for the Chinese and the Cuban Revolutions, too). As such it was doomed, because it never could reach the proper dialectic turning point. In addition, the communism of the Eastern Block was never true communism: Wages were paid, and there was social inequality. At best these countries reached an intermediate stage between capitalism and communism. True communism has never been tried.

Other objections are not as easy to dismiss. For one thing, if the revolution occurs through the process of dialectical determinism, that is, if it is automatic, why work for it? And if people's state of mind is determined by whatever economic system they live in, how can we ever get to a point where we can be critical of the system we live in? Furthermore, if reality is change, and history moves dialectically, why should the communist stage necessarily be the final one? Why shouldn't the dialectic process just go on and on? (Ironically, some might say that this is precisely what has happened in the former Soviet Union. The dialectic movement has caused the states of the former union to move away from from hard-line communism toward a system that is as yet undefined.) Such paradoxes exist in Marx's thinking, and various answers have been suggested, but most non-Marxist thinkers find that no truly satisfactory answers have been given.

Marx did attempt, in his own texts, to refute certain other objections. One of these is reflected in the question, If the Marxist society gives everybody meaningful work according to their own wishes, then who does the dirty work? It is hard to believe that someone should want to empty bedpans or collect garbage as part of their self-activity, so how do we get those things done? Well, says Marx, we must take turns: You fish on Monday while I empty the bedpans, and then I'll teach school on Tuesday while you empty the bedpans.

Another question seems obvious: If you get only what you *need*, what is the incentive to get a better education and work harder, if you won't make more money? Marx would answer: You speak from capitalist presuppositions. In the new society, people *will want to work hard* for the satisfaction of it. Doing what you're good at is a reward in itself, so you will not want further rewards. (Remember, in the new world human nature supposedly will change.) But can we be sure that human nature will change? A wicked parody of the communist dream has been proposed by the author Ayn Rand in her book *Atlas Shrugged*. In the book those in charge of a factory decide to shift to the system of "to each according to need, from each according to ability." The end result? Not a change in humans from exploiters to saints, but a dehumanizing split of the working population into those with ability and those with needs (which continually grow and result in the exploitation of those with ability). A more detailed outline of this story is presented in Chapter 20.

Some critics object that Marx failed to take human *biology* as well as *psychology* into consideration. They argue that there is a certain element of self-preservation in everyone, even if we may not all be 100 percent selfish. But for Marx human nature is primarily culturally determined. Humans create a certain form of society, and, in turn, that society will create a changed human population who will create a new society (this is the dialectic process). Other than agreeing with Aristotle that humans are social by nature, Marx does not seem interested in biology or psychology as an argument.

Many philosophers have a problem with Marx's insistence that *all* aspects of human nature will change when the economic basis changes. Why, they ask, should *reason* change? The rules of reason are supposed to be absolute and culturally independent: Logic is always logic, and math is always math, no matter what kind of economy you have. And if we are capable of *dispassionate reason*, which most philosophers assume we are, at least some of the time, then why should our findings be tainted by our economy?

A final objection might be that Marx's vision was meaningful, and perhaps even necessary, for his troubled century, but we are doing much better now, and we don't need a socialist revolution. Many of Marx's goals involved making a better life for the majority (unions, pensions, decent housing, fair wages, better working conditions), and many of these have already been accomplished or at least approached without a revolution. Marx probably would not have imagined that the working class of the Western world would become, by and large, the *middle class*—property owners with conservative interests. If Marx could have looked into the future, would he have changed his mind? That is hard to say, but traditional, hard-line Marxists say no. For one thing, both Marxists and non-Marxists usually can agree that Marx provided one of the main sources of inspiration for the improvement of social conditions in the nineteenth as well as the twentieth century. But Marxists also argue that a content, property-owning working class is not the answer. The philosopher Herbert Marcuse (1892–1979) warned that the seemingly better conditions for workers (and for everybody else, for that matter) are just a result of *repressive tolerance*. The political powers let you think you have a nice life, but they control you with an iron fist nevertheless, by imposing economic restrictions as well as cultural, religious, and moral rules. And when you complain, they pretend to listen to you politely, but your words have no effect on them; your viewpoint is being tolerated yet repressed at the same time. This covert oppression is, Marcuse says, more dangerous than blatant oppression, because you don't realize it—you are duped (*indoctrinated*) into thinking that you are free, whereas you are really a pawn in their game. So what is the duty of the Marxist? To open your eyes to the fact that you are being manipulated. To tell you that you don't know yourself well enough, and once you realize you have been the victim of a *false ideology*, you will realize that Marx was right.

Three Narratives That Explore Political Visions

Chapter 20 includes three stories that examine political visions. The first one, "Harrison Bergeron" by Kurt Vonnegut, is a parody of a futuristic society in which equality is misunderstood as *sameness*. The next is Ayn Rand's critical exposure of communism, *Atlas Shrugged*. The third is a defense for the common man and woman which may or may not have been intended as a socialist rallying cry, but which comes across as an eloquent defense of socialism: John Steinbeck's *The Grapes of Wrath*.

FIGURE 18.2 Sigmund Freud (1856–1939), Austrian doctor and psychoanalyst. Freud originally wanted to become a natural scientist, but such studies were closed to Jews in nineteenth-century Austria, so he chose the medical profession instead. While today Freud is often criticized for his theory of the Unconscious and its implications, there is consensus that he is right in one important respect, that humans do have an Unconscious which affects their conscious self.

Sigmund Freud: We Don't Know Ourselves

Freud shares with Marx not only the honor of being another "master of suspicion," but also shares the dubious honor of having all of his ideas in the "public domain," so to speak. Marx's and Freud's theories have had such an impact on twentieth-century life that we believe we know what they were talking about even if we have never read any of their writings. On occasion, though, we can be mistaken. If we think that all Marx is saying is that everybody should be a communist, we are as wrong as if we think that Freud believes everything has a sexual connection. But just as communism is an important part of Marx's theory, so is the pervasiveness of sexual human nature a vital element in Freudianism.

The Birth of Psychoanalysis

On occasion, philosophers talk about three major events that have occurred in the course of human self-awareness. Three times in Western cultural history, humanity has been shaken loose from its foundation, with irrevocable effects. The first time was when Copernicus determined that we did not live in a geocentric universe. In other words, the heavens did not revolve around our planet. Instead, the earth and its inhabitants were just a minor part of an immense celestial ballet which, it seemed, was not staged for our sake, but happened quite automatically. The second time was when Darwin published *On the Origin of Species*. No longer were humans perceived as the pinnacle and purpose of creation. Darwin showed that humans were directly related to other, previous species, and were presumably part of a process of further evolution.

The third time was when Freud produced irrefutable evidence that we are not in total control of our mind; part of it seems, rather, to be in control of us. These three *blows to human self-assurance* have helped determine our present-day conception of the *human condition*.

Freud (1856–1939) cannot be called the founder of psychology, for in the second half of the nineteenth century there already were schools of thought, primarily in the field of medicine, that probed the idea that the human mind works according to rules. The school of *psychology of association*, for example, was a deterministic theory that held that our thoughts advance along an associative pattern that may be predictable. The French philosopher Henri Bergson (who was intensely opposed to the psychology of association) worked with theories of human memory. He suggested that the memory forms a reservoir in the depths of our mind, shapes our decisions and emotions, and is accessible to conscious thought, but not all at the same time. Even David Hume, in the eighteenth century, had thoughts about the interaction between mind and emotions, and throughout this text we have seen examples of philosophers who discussed the relationship between desire, willpower, and reason. However, Freud is credited with inventing a new discipline, nonetheless—*psychoanalysis*—and with providing evidence for the existence of a part of the mind that is inaccessible, the *Unconscious*. Freud, as a "master of suspicion," "suspects" that we don't know all there is to know about ourselves, and that we can't know it without going into analysis.

Freud's background was in medicine. He worked as a medical doctor in Vienna and became interested in the treatment of hysteria. One common method for treating this problem was surgery—one simply removed the organ that which was supposed to cause hysteria, the *hystera*. The operation is known as hysterectomy, *hystera* being Greek for *womb*. Hysteria thus was considered primarily a "female complaint." Other methods of treatment also were surfacing, such as hypnosis. Freud was interested in a theory developed by a colleague of his, Josef Breuer, who believed that hysteria was caused by some forgotten bad emotional experience. This work led Freud to his first theory, which held that there are two layers in the human mind, the *Conscious* and the *Unconscious*. The Unconscious is not merely what we don't remember right now but will when we are reminded (that is known as *Preconscious*), but an area in the psyche that is completely closed off to conscious probing. How do we know it is there? Because it manifests itself in various forms, some quite ordinary, and others very dramatic.

Dreams Are Wishes

One of the ordinary manifestations of the Unconscious is dreams. Freud's *Interpretation of Dreams* appeared in 1900. Dream interpretation was nothing new at the time—it had been attempted throughout history with occasional political success. Rulers with nasty dreams would have "dream interpreters" standing by to soothe their worries. Books on the meaning of dreams also have enjoyed much popularity. One such dream book, *A Treatise of the Interpretations of Sundry Dreams* (1601), foretells that certain dreams will mean certain changes in your life. In other words, dreams are *omens*, portents of things to come.

Only in the remotest sense could Freud's *Interpretation of Dreams* be said to have any kinship with these other dream theories. There is no precognition hidden in dreams for Freud, although there is a cognition about yourself, of which you are otherwise unaware. What you dream about does not predict what *will* happen, but it does indicate what you *would like to have happen*. Dreams are wish fulfillment.

Instant objections arise: "But I was having a nightmare! How can that be wish fulfillment?" or "I dreamed I was in Paris with my sister—but I don't *want* to go to Paris with my sister." or "I dreamed I was having dinner with my boss. How could I possibly wish for that? I don't even like my boss." Freud has several possible answers. First, *dreams are not what they seem*. In dreams, the images go through a camouflaging process (what Freud calls the *manifest dream-content*) that "hides" their true intention (the *latent dream-content*). This is because your conscious self is so alert that it doesn't allow the true meaning to be expressed clearly, even in dreams. Perhaps you enjoy, subconsciously, the fear of the nightmare (you feel guilty about something, so you torture yourself at night). Perhaps you really weren't dreaming of Paris or your sister, but the dream utilized this image to tell you about some other place you would like to go with someone else. Or your dream was telling you that you really would like not only to have dinner with your boss, but also to make love with him or her. However, you have *repressed* that desire. More likely, your boss is a symbol of *someone else* of authority in your life (most likely your mother or father), and that is the person you really are dreaming about. Then there is the additional process of you remembering the dream and telling about it. This adds an element to the dream which is an important part of it; it is your mind dealing with it and explaining it to yourself.

Why does the dream have to be hidden behind symbolic images? Because our reason will not accept the reality of what the dream expresses—our instincts and drives. We repress them, banish them to the darkest corners of our Unconscious, but the harder we repress them, the more certain they are to reappear in the form of dreams or as slips of the tongue ("Freudian slips"), neurotic behavior, or even psychosis, the most dramatic form of expression of the Unconscious. In particular, *traumatic childhood experiences*, such as emotional rejection, child molestation, or witnessing of unexplained disturbing parental behavior (anything from heated arguments to silence to sex), are likely to be repressed. When the time is ripe, the trauma will resurface in disguise. Presumably the patient will not be able to identify the original experience him or herself, but will need the help of a psychoanalyst to bring it out. This process is likely to cause an emotional bonding—the patient often falls in love with the analyst—but that is supposedly part of the treatment and is known as *transference*. When the treatment has succeeded, the emotion of love and also the trauma will dissipate, or the patient will at least be able to control it.

Today there are other theories of why we dream, such as the theory that dreams don't say anything at all but are merely our computerlike brain's way of clearing the mind for the next day's input. Some dream theories of today build on Freud's theories, but the idea that all dreams are *always* wish fulfillment seems to have lost popularity.

Still, Freud's concept that dreams are hidden messages about ourselves has been immensely influential, not only for psychoanalysis but also for the kind of understanding humans achieve through art. In literature and film in particular, the theory of the Unconscious has flourished in two ways. Freudian theory has served not only as a never-ending source of material, but also as a means for pictorial art, literature, and film to explore the depths of the human mind with the help of symbols, and as a means for theories of art, literature, and film to better understand the works of art created by these media.

Other Manifestations of the Unconscious

That the Unconscious exists can be considered evident; it has been proven empirically, by experiments. Post-hypnotic suggestion reveals that we may think we act freely, but we don't—the Unconscious is capable of taking over in spite of our conscious willpower. (Post-hypnotic suggestion involves a command given by the hypnotist to the hypnotized subject. The subject will forget the command upon waking, but will obey the command nevertheless.) The psychoanalytic technique of "free association" presumably provides another access to the Unconscious. A number of key words are spoken to the patient, and the patient says whatever comes to mind without reflection. Image analysis provides another window to the Unconscious. The Rorshach test is a personality and intelligence test in which a subject interprets inkblot designs in terms that reveal intellectual and emotional factors. The most readily available sign of the unconscious mental life, though, is probably the parapraxis, the "Freudian slip." Freud points out that slips of the tongue, forgetfulness, mistaking one action for another, and other blunders or "beside-doings" (para-praxis) are not a sign of illness. They occur for everybody, and that is why they are such a good tool for understanding the Unconscious. By paying more attention to when they occur, we can use them to understand ourselves, and others, better.

There are several kinds of parapraxes. They include repeatedly forgetting an item (you keep forgetting to call the doctor about test results); mislaying an object (you mislay a gift from your previous boyfriend or girlfriend); forgetting combined with making mistakes (you are so proud that you finally remembered to mail a card to your in-laws—but you mailed it to their old address); forgetting an event or situation (Freud tells of the newlywed woman who saw her husband in the street and forgot she had married him); misreading (as when the radio announcer mistook the title of the old song "There's an Empty Cot in the Bunkhouse Tonight," calling it "There's an Empty *Bunk* in the *Cathouse* Tonight"); mispronouncing something (a frequent mispronunciation among students as well as TV news anchors is to say "orgasm" instead of "organism"); bungling an action (you slam the car door on your girlfriend's leg after she has told you she won't go out with you anymore—and you swear it was an accident); and so on. A Danish professor of psychology tells this classical example of a parapraxis: He was conducting experiments with students at the University of Copenhagen psychology lab in the 1970s. He was presenting them with unusual or culturally unacceptable food items, and registering their reactions. They had eaten horsemeat, ants, maggots, and lizards, and he had detachedly and professionally taken notes and confronted students with their irrational fears of foods. One evening he realized that he had *forgotten* to show up for his class that afternoon—the rat-eating session. He had a particular problem with rats, he admitted, and so he experienced a genuine parapraxis, caused by his own experiment.

What makes these occurrences of forgetfulness parapraxes and not just mistakes is that they reveal a hidden motivation: You forget something you don't want to remember, you mislay something you don't want to see. You forget the name of someone you don't like or someone you couldn't care less about; you forget a meeting you're not interested in, or that you fear. Your forgetfulness also may reveal a hidden interest: You are supposed to call up your mother, but you call up the one you're in love with instead. You forget to answer a question on a test because you want to get out of there in a hurry; you make word contractions (writing "phenoma" instead of "phenomena," for instance) for the same reason.

Are *all* mistakes of forgetting, misreading, mispronouncing, and so on parapraxes? In other words, is there a hidden agenda behind all of our goofs? If so, it's clear we reveal more than we ever intended every time we forget to call someone, forget to videotape a show, misplace a piece of jewelry or an address, forget where we parked our car, or step on someone else's toes by accident—because according to this line of thinking, *there are no accidents*, and, morally speaking, we might be blamed for all such things (if indeed we can be blamed for what our Unconscious does—we shall return to that notion shortly). In his *Introductory Lectures on Psychoanalysis*, Freud explains:

> The governing condition of these cases . . . is that the present psychical situation is unknown to us or inaccessible to our enquiries. Our interpretation is consequently no more than a suspicion to which we ourselves do not attach too much importance. Later, however, something happens which shows us how well-justified our interpretation had been.

So we may not recognize a parapraxis at the time it happens—it just seems like a mistake. But for the professor who forgot his rat-eating experiment it was no mistake—it was a firm, unconscious intention to avoid the situation, and this became clear the second he realized that he had forgotten the class. For the woman who forgot she had married her husband, the hidden intention became clear when the marriage came to an end only a few years later—or so says Freud. He also cites a "happier example"—the time a man forgot his own wedding: "He was wise enough to be satisfied with a single attempt and died at a great age unmarried." Whatever conclusions one might draw about Freud and his ideas of women and marriage is up to the reader.

At any rate, the interpretation of the parapraxis is not straightforward. The boy who slammed the car door on his girlfriend's leg after she broke up with him may be justified in claiming that he didn't do it because he was angry with *her*; perhaps he was reminded of the last time someone broke up with him, and he reacted to *that*. When Pilar forgets to call Carlos and invite him to her party, perhaps he should not feel hurt, because it may be that Pilar has nothing against him, but against his namesake, her uncle Carlos, who pulled her pigtails when she was a little girl. In other words, there is a counterwill at play, and it works against our conscious intentions—but it may not be directed at the "victim" of the parapraxis. It may be indirectly aimed at something or someone in our past.

The point Freud wants to make is that it is *subsequent events* that give meaning to the mistake and make it a parapraxis. If no such revealing event occurs, then perhaps it really was a mistake; perhaps we simply were tired or preoccupied. More often than not, though, it will turn out that mistakes have hidden meanings.

The Oedipus Complex

The French anthropologist Claude Lévi-Strauss (b. 1908) has said that whenever an analysis of some cultural phenomenon becomes influential, then it becomes *part* of that phenomenon. Thus, Freud's analysis of the legend of King Oedipus has become part of the Oedipus phenomenon, as has Lévi-Strauss's own lengthy Oedipus analysis. The *Oedipus complex* has become one of the most famous of Freud's contributions to psychoanalysis, as well as to our popular conception of psychology in general.

The tragedy of King Oedipus was written by Sophocles (c. 495?–406 B.C.E.), but it was a legend before he wrote it down. Oedipus, born to King Laius and Queen Iocaste of Thebes, but raised as the son of the king and queen of Corinth and believing them to be his parents, unknowingly kills his natural father and marries his natural mother, thus fulfilling a prophecy from the Oracle of Delphi. He and his mother rule as king and queen of Thebes until he is exposed. In horror, his mother kills herself, and Oedipus puts his own eyes out. (Chapter 20 includes a detailed outline of the Oedipus story as told by Sophocles). The image of Oedipus marrying his mother has become the symbol of the strong emotional, and even sexual, bonding between a boy and his mother, and of the aggression the boy feels toward his father for taking his mother's attention. (Note that Oedipus did *not* want to marry the woman he *thought of* as his mother; he ended up marrying his *birth mother*. So the Oedipus complex makes a different story out of the legend.) For Freud, any boy in any family will experience the Oedipus complex, but in some cases the bonding is especially strong, and it will cause a neurosis in the boy when he grows up—he will look for a "girl like Mom" or will not look for a girl at all. Furthermore, it will cause the boy to fear Dad, because Dad will be jealous, and Dad might castrate him. So the boy develops a will to kill his father.

What about little girls? Do they have a version of the Oedipus complex? In a sense, no, because the girl's psychological development, for Freud, is not as dramatic as the boy's. Freud seems not to have been as interested in the girl's development as the boy's, but he does postulate two things: that the girl naturally suffers from a *penis-envy*, seeing the little boy as "normal" and herself as "castrated" (this theory is highly disputed today), and that the girl experiences an *Electra Complex* (the girl has a bonding with her father, and feels some animosity toward her mother). The Electra Complex de-

Was Oedipus Real?

The British mythologist Robert Graves (1895–1985) speculates that there may have been a real King Oedipus. He probably did not kill his father and marry his mother, says Graves, but he may have married a *high priestess* of Hera, thus becoming king. This was common practice in many cultures: A man would become king by marrying the queen, who represented the royal or holy bloodline. (This practice is a remnant of a *matrilineal society* in which ancestry is traced through the mother's bloodline, not the father's.) Sometimes the man would live out his normal life span as king, but more often he would be sacrificed after a preset span of time, and the queen would marry a new king, often much younger than herself, and often her own son or someone who became her son *symbolically* for as long as he was allowed to live. Graves speculates that Oedipus may have had the gall to announce that in the future the kingship would be passed from *father to son*, instead of being determined by marriage to a high priestess. Perhaps the citizens of Thebes did not want this, and after the high priestess committed suicide, they banished him. There still is not much evidence for this theory of King Oedipus, but it matches other conditions of kingship and priestess religions that we know of in the ancient world.

rives from the story of Electra, daughter of Agamemnon, who sees her father killed by her mother and the mother's lover, and who, with her brother's help, kills both mother and lover.

To the intellectual Western world that was just emerging from the sexually repressive values of the Victorian era, this was nothing short of blasphemy. To assume that innocent children had sexual interests, and, further, to assume that these were directed toward their parents, was directly offensive to most people and helped cement the fable that Freud thought "everything was sex."

But did Freud believe that sex was everything? No, only that sex drives are very powerful and are present at a very early age. Freud believed childhood experiences are crucial to the further development of the individual, especially the sexual experiences—not necessarily active sexuality, but general feelings of physical well-being that occur as early as infancy. Even in the first weeks of our lives we experience what Freud calls the *pleasure principle*: Everything that happens to us feels good. It feels good to get fed, to be touched, to be washed, and if something doesn't feel good, it generally is taken care of by our parents, so we feel that we are the center of the universe. But one day mother or father is busy and doesn't come when we cry, or tells us "No!" This marks the arrival of the *reality principle*: You can't always get what you want. Humans live under the shadow of the reality principle for the rest of their lives. However, the pleasure principle also remains a demanding factor, and throughout their adult lives humans experience a conflict between these two principles.

Id, Ego, and Superego

In 1923 Freud conceived of a new model for the human psyche, to replace the "Conscious-Unconscious" duality. He now saw not two, but three parts of the psyche: the *Id*, the *Ego*, and the *Superego*. The Id (Latin for "it") is the powerful Unconscious, inaccessible to the conscious mind yet still influential. The Ego is the conscious self with which we are familiar. The Superego is the voice of our parents or teachers, the demands of society and religion, and all the rules and regulations that we internalize as feelings of guilt and conscience; the Superego is that little "inner voice" that tells us what to do.

The Ego thus has three masters: the external world (in other words, the reality principle), the Superego, and the Id. Constantly they battle for control and attention in the psyche. The Id gives us the greatest trouble because it represents the pleasure principle; it challenges both the reality principle and our sense of duty. In the end, we can't hope for reason to control our passions, because the physical drives have their own very powerful voices.

This is not the first time we have encountered a theory of a tripartite psyche (a soul with three parts). For Plato, the psyche consisted of desires (appetites), willpower, and reason. Can we draw any parallels to Freud? The only obvious parallel is the similarity between the *Id* and *desires*. The Ego certainly reflects Plato's *reason*, but it is nowhere near as powerful as what Plato imagined. Can we compare willpower and *Superego*? Possibly, because according to Plato, willpower usually sides with reason against desires, as the Superego would. But in Freud's imagery, the Superego represents guilt and conscience, and for Plato these moral elements reside in our *reason* (because for Plato reason carries moral values). For Freud, morality is a result of acculturation, and thus it is superimposed on the Ego by the Superego. There is no such thing as morality in the Id, and the rationality of the Ego is a fragile one indeed—ethics becomes only a matter of the guilt that is present in the adult mind. One might ask, then, if Freud thinks that the unconscious drives are evil. He might answer that he himself did not impose moral values on the human instincts; he attempted to be descriptive, not normative, in his analysis. It is certain, however, that many of his post-Victorian contemporaries did choose to view the sexual drives as evil, and used Freud's own theories to support their views.

Social Consequences of Freud's Theory of Human Nature

As we have seen, theories of human nature have social and ethical consequences, and Freud's theory is no exception. What would be the social consequence if human nature were not controlled? Human society would become completely unstable, says Freud; therefore, *social repression* is necessary. We must not condemn our drives, because they are not our fault, but we can't let them run loose, either. Freud regrets these necessary repressions but sees no other solution. Eventually, humans can learn to channel their drives into other areas, to *sublimate* the energies by working hard, pursuing hobbies, or participating in sports. In the *theory of sublimation* we see most clearly that Freud, in spite of his supposedly value-free analyses, considered the world of the instincts socially undesirable. But Freud never gives us a complete social theory—the nature of such a society remains speculative.

For some, Freud's theory became an inspiration to design a future society in which the sexual drives are considered a reality rather than something to be controlled and repressed. For Swiss psychologist Carl Jung (1875–1961), Freud's student and successor, the sexual drives and the Unconscious in general were to be seen not as a threat to society and the individual, but as a source of creative energy. They became a way to link up with other humans in a common understanding of human nature, through the *Collective Unconscious*—symbols and images that come to the surface in times of stress or need, and which we share with the rest of humanity.

Others have envisioned a new political system based on Freudian theory. The Austrian psychoanalyst Wilhelm Reich (1897–1957) saw a new future in the combination of the revolutionary theory of Marx and the sexual theory of Freud—a sexual-political revolution that would create a world of social equality without sexual repression. Reich himself became a source of inspiration for revolutionary theories of the sixties and seventies. Thus, a complex of theories thought to be *descriptive* by Freud has come to inspire a *normative* view of human nature.

Humans and Religion

Even if Freud did not consider himself a social thinker, at the end of his life he pondered cultural phenomena such as religion and their effects on society. And it is in Freud's writings that we find what may be the last modern version of a *state of nature* theory: his hypothesis of the *primal horde*.

What is the psychological basis for religion? Freud believed that it it developed out of a historical occurrence. In the days prior to society, when humans lived in small groups (as we now believe they did), the group structure was much like that of monkeys, says Freud. An old male ("Old Man") kept the females to himself, and no other males had breeding privileges. (Anyone who has watched a troop of baboons in the zoo has seen evidence of this). One day, the young males ganged up and killed the Old Man, and took his women, some of whom were their own mothers (we already see shades of the Oedipus complex here). After a while the young men began to *feel guilty*, as if the Old Man was still watching them and plotting revenge. So they got together again and decided to try to placate the Old Man through prayers and sacrifices, and *religion* was born. Soon the old male became the "Old Man in the Sky"—God—who sees all and punishes the wrongdoers, and perhaps forgives, too. So what is religion? Nothing but pure wish fulfillment—the wish that God will be like a father to us, strict but kind.

Did Freud believe that this event actually took place? It seems that he did. There is no evidence that one particular Old Man was killed, but such an event probably happened more than once in prehistoric times. Either way, Freud might say that if it didn't *actually* happen, it happened in the young men's *hearts*, in their *wish* to kill the Old Man and take his women, and this Freud saw as a universal experience for males in the human race.

Objections to Freud's Theories

Does Freud's theory of religion explain all forms of religious faith, then? Hardly. Polytheistic religions don't seem to follow this pattern, nor do religions based on a creator-goddess, or on spirits of nature. But Freud was no scholar of religious studies, and his intent late in life was to explore the psychological background of the religions with which he was familiar, Judaism and Christianity. He never intended a complete theory of the origin of religions. At best, Freud's vision may point to the psychological foundations of monotheistic images, but even so, it explains only why *men* have a guilt complex toward God; it says nothing about females and religion.

When Freud wrote his major works on psychoanalysis, the patients that supplied him with material for his theories came from middle-class families, by and large. Since then, critics have pointed out that given other social patterns we might have seen a totally different theory of psychology develop. In other words, are the complexes and repressions Freud sees as typically human really just typically late-19th-century–early-twentieth-century European middle-class? The ideal Victorian nuclear family, which consisted of the stern father who worked outside the home, the kind and protective mother who worked at home, and a number of siblings in competition with one another might very likely produce an Oedipus complex, or an Electra complex. It also might produce the famed "penis envy" in little girls, it might produce images of a stern but forgiving God, and it might favor a powerful Id in battle against a powerful reality principle and Superego—repressive times make for repressive psyches. But suppose we have a much different family structure. Will we then have the same complexes? There seems to be sufficient evidence today that different family structures (such as any of the following, in which the dad works at home, the mom works away from home, both parents work away from home, the kids are raised by grandparents, the kids have two fathers or mothers because of divorce, or the kids have two lesbian moms or two gay dads) may create other kinds of psychological baggage. Anything a child is exposed to will have some influence on him or her—Freud was right in that—but we still don't know enough about alternative families to agree on a post-Freudian theory of human psychology.

Another objection to Freudian psychoanalysis comes from an ethical viewpoint. If the acts of the human mind as well as those of the body are determined by previous causes, can we then be held morally responsible for what we do? Freud never talks in

ELIZA: The Perfect Listener?

ELIZA is a computer program designed to imitate a psychoanalyst talking to a patient. It was designed by Joseph Weisenbaum, an M.I.T. computer scientist, as a joke. When it registers a key word, such as *mother*, it is programmed to pose the question: "Tell me about your mother." People who have been subjected to the program report that it seemed sympathetic and understanding.

philosophical terms about this, but it is an issue in present-day psychoanalysis: Is there room for *free will* in a system of predictable, mental causality? A compatibilist solution (see Chapter 15) has been suggested which distinguishes between *causes* over which we have no control, and *motivations* that are our moral responsibility. If we accept a psychoanalytic view of human nature which implies that humans have *no* control over their acts (and thus no responsibility), then we allow for a psychological absolution of guilt for anything we do, as well as a social system based on absolute control over citizens in order to prevent them from doing it.

A third objection to Freud's theories involves both the theory and practice of psychoanalysis. When a patient undergoes analysis, the analyst expects *resistance*: The patient will not believe that he or she was attracted to one parent and aggressive towards the other (or whatever). As a matter of fact, the more the patient *denies* this, the more certain the analyst becomes that it is true. *Denial* is taken as a confirmation of the theory. So is psychoanalysis truly scientific, or is it a self-fulfilling hypothesis? A scientific theory, as we saw earlier, must be theoretically *falsifiable* in order to be workable. But can one, as a patient, ever show the analyst that she or he is wrong? If not, then the findings of the analyst can't be viewed as an objective theory, but merely as a viewpoint or, as some critics say, an *article of faith*.

The general assumption of psychoanalysis is that the patient—and in a sense we are all "patients" because we are humans with complex childhoods—can't find the answer by him or herself but must seek the analyst's help to clarify things and bring them out in the open. This, in itself, is a familiar assumption—we have encountered it in Plato, in Saint Augustine, and in Karl Marx. You may think you know yourself, but you don't, and only with help from another will you realize the truth. But when, in psychoanalysis, is the " truth" realized? In other words, when is the treatment *over*? Some therapies come to an end when the patient regains control of his or her life, but other patients see their therapist for years and years, and it is hard to determine if any progress has been made, or indeed what progress is supposed to be made. Some of Woody Allen's films are a poignant take-off on this phenomenon. (Some rather jaundiced critics claim that the only time therapy is over is when your insurance runs out.)

If psychoanalysis offers insight that is available to the patient only through seeing an educated and experienced analyst, then analysis is valuable. If the insight it offers is the kind one experiences after a good conversation with a kind, attentive friend, then it is questionable that it has any *unique* therapeutic value.

Narratives That Explore Destiny and Passion

Chapter 20 includes Sophocles' classic, *Oedipus Rex*, the original drama of the inescapable fate of King Oedipus, and the Alfred Hitchcock film *Marnie,* a story of a young woman with severe psychological repressions.

Chapter 19

The Storytelling Animal

In this chapter we will return to an important theme of this book: the power of storytelling. In discussing theories of human nature, it is important to review all the various ways humans struggle with their identity and destiny. Some scholars think, however, that humans undertake the struggle primarily through one basic format—the narrative format. In other words, humans learn about themselves and each other by telling stories. Because we are *temporal creatures*, we tend to think in terms of before and after, of beginnings, middles, and endings, and so we turn to the story format in order to make sense of our lives. The story is one of the deepest forms of human expression, not just of ethical issues, but also of *metaphysical* ones, those dealing with the nature of reality.

MacIntyre's Call for Stories

In 1981 a book was published which caused quite a stir among ethics scholars in the United States. In his book *After Virtue*, renowned American philosopher Alasdair

MacIntyre claimed that the Western culture is morally confused because we have no founding stories anymore (stories that provide a cultural identity for a people). From the time of the Ancient Greeks until now, the prevailing moral attitude has changed to such a degree that we no longer have a cultural *ethos* to bind us together. What was morally good for the Greek nobleman is no longer what is morally good for us. Does this mean we have nothing in common with those ancient times? No, what we have in common with them is that we are all people whose identity is rooted in a sense of community and history—we all are part of a *tradition*. In spite of what modern individualism would like to think, says MacIntyre, we are part of a greater whole, and we can't understand ourselves if we try to view ourselves outside of that context. We all have relationships with our families, be they good or bad, we affect our friends as they affect us, and we share in the history of our people regardless of whether we took part in it or not. We may not own slaves or be slaves ourselves, but some of our ancestors may have been involved in the slavery issue, on one side or the other. This doesn't mean we should feel guilty about our heritage or bear resentment, but we should understand that we can't divorce ourselves from our past—it is an important part of our culture, and it affects how our culture views the rest of the world.

So how should we properly understand ourselves? Not just as part of a whole, but as part of a *narrative* whole. Here is an example of what this means. You see a man digging in his yard. You can't know what he is doing until you hear his explanation: He is gardening, or exercising, or hunting for treasure, or planning to murder his wife. Each explanation involves a story, and without the story there is no explanation. So our understanding of ourselves and each other is basically narrative: We understand each other through stories and by implying reasons and motivations, causes and effects:

> Man is in his actions and practice, as well as in his fictions, essentially a storytelling animal. He is not essentially, but becomes through his history, a teller of stories that aspire to truth. But the key question for men is not about their own authorship; I can only answer the question "What am I to do?" if I can answer the prior question "Of what story or stories do I find myself a part?"

Unless we have a sense of *narrative continuity* in our lives—unless we think of ourselves as the person (for instance) who knocked over a vase at age seven, fell in love at sixteen, won a scholarship at eighteen, went to Paris at twenty-one—we live our lives merely as a series of disjointed events. By recalling our personal history we give ourselves a *personal identity* similar to that of a character in a story. This is especially true if we use one event in our life to explain another ("I decided to change my major from business to medicine because of my sister's illness"). Furthermore, we are part of the stories of others, just as they are part of our stories, so our narrative is in this way *correlative*. "The narrative of any one life is part of an interlocking set of narratives," says MacIntyre.

What is necessary in order for us to do the right thing, as humans? We must understand that the life we live has a story that it wants to tell: It is on a *narrative quest*. Sometimes it doesn't succeed, and we feel frustrated, but sometimes it succeeds, and we feel that our lives have been well spent. What type of a quest is it? Here MacIntyre goes back to *virtue theory*: It is a quest for virtue in a life. A good life is a life spent searching for the good life—but of course this may mean different things under different circumstances. The *historical traditions* of which we are a part will determine what kind of a narrative quest we are on. In our culture the quest must involve a sense of justice, courage, and truthfulness, says MacIntyre. Others might add that it also should involve a sense of caring and compassion.

Ethics scholars are divided over this approach to ethical behavior. Some believe that personal identity is nothing but a figment of the Western imagination. Some feel uncomfortable with the linking of the individual to his or her culture, and some question the whole idea of conforming to a dominant culture. Others feel uncomfortable discounting *rationality* as the deciding factor, and still others feel it is demeaning to moral human beings to reduce them to characters in a story. But many believe that MacIntyre has given people a tool with which to carve a future, a renewed sense of belonging in a contemporary world, even if we come from faraway places. We find ourselves part of a greater whole that we perhaps didn't realize existed, and it gives us a renewed sense of responsibility.

There still is one problem with MacIntyre's program: the problem of *ethical relativism*. If, for instance, our cultural tradition says to kill the infidel, or practice infanticide, or keep a race or a gender in bondage, is that then part of the virtues that our narrative quest must include? And how can we allow ourselves to refuse to follow such a quest if it is part of our historical narrative?

Narrative Theory: Ricoeur, White, and Nussbaum

Paul Ricoeur: Time and Narrative

Since the time of Plato and Aristotle, philosophy has felt compelled to say something about literature and its effects on human beings. As we saw previously, Plato believed it distracted the mind from its rational course, whereas Aristotle saw it as a *cathartic* (cleansing) experience. Aristotle believed that a story is good if it follows certain rules: It has to have a proper *plot*, with a beginning, a middle, and an ending, and the ending has to make sense morally—a bad person has to come to a bad end, a good person has to be vindicated. A good story has to mimic real life to a certain extent, but it does not have to contain actual details from real-life situations, as long as it represents a general truth.

What Plato and Aristotle were interested in primarily was *tragedy*. Aristotle was also interested in comedy, epic prose, and poetry, but he believed that tragedy was a higher form of art. Prose literature as we know it did not become the subject of philosophical discussions until later, and then it usually was discussed in a general theory of literature. Some philosophical traditions, such as the French tradition, see few boundaries

FIGURE 19.1 Paul Ricoeur (b. 1913), French philosopher. Throughout his professional life and through numerous works, Ricoeur has attempted to create a mutual understanding between British-American and Continental (European) philosophy. Drawing from sources in philosophy from both continents, he proposes that humans are fundamentally temporal beings, understanding themselves as existing in time; but there are many ways to exist in time, and one of them is *narrative time*, reading or listening to the plot of a story.

between literature and philosophy. French philosophers of earlier and present generations are usually more interested in literature as a philosophical phenomenon than are their American and British colleagues. One of the major philosophers of the late twentieth century is Paul Ricoeur, who has divided his time between his native country of France and the United States, and who for most of his life has striven to connect the viewpoints of American and continental philosophers. Through his trilogy *Time and Narrative* (1984, 1985, and 1988), readers have been treated to an overall view of how important the narrative structure is in our lives.

Ricoeur sees three levels to a story. The first is the simple plot structure, which should be based on what we know of real life. In other words, the plot has to be believable in some sense—not that it can't deal with fantastic events, but it must show that the writer understands what Ricoeur calls "the world of action." In other words, it must reflect our belief that our actions have effects and can't be reversed, and that some events may be more than the sum of their parts—in other words, they may contain symbolism. At the second level we read the story and "suspend the question of the relationship between fiction and truth." In other words, we make believe that the story is true while we read it. At this level the story merely entertains us. We read the events chronologically, moving from point to point until we have finished the story. But there is a third level, and without that level we would never *understand* the story. The third level allows us to reach back to remember earlier parts of the story as we read, and to connect the elements. The details of the story come together to form a whole, and we understand *why* things happen in the story. This works even when we read a story we already know. We jump right into the third level, because we know both the beginning and the end. We don't read it for the plot anymore; we understand, in light of the ending, how the early events lead in that direction—our memory repeats the order of events in reverse.

The third level also lets the story involve us personally. We read an exciting book and discover that hours have passed. ("I couldn't put it down!" is the critic's quote we read on the cover of a best-seller.) While we are reading we are immersed in *another time*, the time in which we live the lives of the people in the story. And it is on this level that we become involved in the story, we see the hero as a role model, we are instructed by the terrible fate of bad people, we are seduced by the charm of the rogue—and we close the book and take it with us, in our heart.

Ricoeur finds it sad that the "day of the novel" seems to have come to an end (he perceives that very few people read books these days). He predicts that the narrative time experience will take on new shapes in the future, because if we don't read books, he says, we miss out on that tremendous experience of sharing in another time, of living two lives at once—and understanding the time of the characters in the story allows us to understand how we try to structure our own lives. Ricoeur, though, doesn't seem to know the data: More paperbacks and best-sellers are sold now than ever before. They may not be classics, or avant-garde literature, but they certainly have the classic plot structure: a beginning, a middle, and an ending. The experimental literary forms that tried to dispense with such a structure are no longer as much in vogue as they were before, and today we are seeing novels being published in English whose roots are in non-Western traditions. So it seems that people are reading books. But even if they weren't, they would still be exposed to that special narrative experience of time, because people go to the movies. Ricoeur was once asked about movies and narrative time, and he answered, "I never watch movies." That is Ricoeur's loss, because in the movie theater (and to a lesser extent, with home videos) we experience the same extraordinary thing: We live another life in another time structure for two hours, we follow the plot and the characters through Ricoeur's three levels, and we take them with us and even use them as role models when we find we need to.

It has been pointed out by ethicists that although Ricoeur has helped advance the understanding of the narrative experience, he has not drawn a direct connection between this experience and the concepts of moral values and ethical decision making—partly because he seems to believe that ethics has primarily to do with living up to certain absolute rules of duty and can't be learned merely through reading about people in stories. (You may remember the discussion about duty theory (deontology) from Chapter 6.) The Danish philosopher T. Peter Kemp suggests that it is possible to extract an ethics from Ricoeur's narrative theory, because the stories we are particularly attracted to have a value system built into them. As he says in his piece entitled "Toward a Narrative Ethics: A Bridge Between Ethics and the Narrative Reflection of Ricoeur," a good story "creates a vision of the good life, as distinct from a wasted and frustrated life." And we learn this lesson not so much from absolute rules in a Kantian sense, says Kemp, as from the *ethical attitude* imbedded in the story. This attitude we can make our own. In other words, Kemp is suggesting that we combine Ricoeur's theory of the narrative experience not with an ethical system derived from *ethics of conduct*, but with one derived from from *virtue ethics*: This ensures that we comprehend not only the intellectual value of storytelling, but also the ethical value of stories, which, in the final end, has to do with living in a moral community with others.

An American scholar who explicitly makes the connection between narrative experience and moral values is the scholar we will look at next: Hayden White.

Hayden White: History Is Storytelling

Numerous scholars have made and are making contributions to narrative theory—in philosophy as well as in literature. One of the most important contributions, however, has come from a professor of literature and history. In his book *Metahistory* (1973), Hayden White (b. 1928) explores the relationship between storytelling and history.

The common assumption is that there is a world of difference between literature and history. Stories are made up, but history, as Aristotle said, deals with facts, and if we find out that our written account of history has somehow exaggerated somebody's influence or downplayed the influence of some factor, we do our best to correct it. Consider Christopher Columbus, for instance. Upon the five-hundredth anniversary of his "discovery" of America, there was a tremendous debate over whether his was a heroic deed or the act of a greedy person, and, furthermore, whether the effect of his discovery was a boon for humankind or the beginning of the end for some of the noblest cultures that ever existed. Laypeople usually assume that historians can find out what the proper interpretation should be by studying their sources—*somewhere* there must be sufficient evidence to support one view or another. But most historians know that it is not as easy as that, because what we consider evidence is colored by our viewpoint. There is no such thing as an objective assessment of historical facts. You may remember that Nietzsche was the first modern scholar to claim that there are no facts. By this he (probably) did not mean that we can't determine whether it rained last night, but that everything that passes through our senses and our brains already has been colored by our own preconceived notions. This is what is known as *perspectivism*. It can be said to be a "fact" that Columbus *landed* in the Americas in 1492, but to say that he "discovered" them is not fact, but interpretation. So history does not have privileged access to facts; just as bias is present in eyewitness accounts, so it is present in written history.

What is the relationship between history and historiography (the writing of history)? We take what someone decides, on the basis of research, to write down as an account of what happened during a certain time period to be the *history* of that period. But strictly speaking, it is only *history-writing*, and this is the only access to actual history that we have. We probably can never do more than approximate what actually happened. And today, with the emphasis on rediscovering the histories of groups that have been neglected by most Western male historians (such as women's history, the history of minorities in the United States, and the local histories of suppressed population groups around the world), time periods that we thought we knew are acquiring a new face altogether. Some people even credit Nietzsche for this revolution in history-writing, based on his view of perspectivism, which has found its way into what has become known as *postmodernism*. By now it is dawning on scholars and laypeople alike that there may be no such thing as "historical truth." There are a number of truths, all depending on whose eyes you use to view history.

We may think that the perspectivization of history-writing breaks with an early tradition of regarding history as the ultimate version of what happened and why. But history-writing has not always had that as its goal. Hayden White points out that some early history-writing, such as *annals*, didn't even bother to tell about everything that happened, and they certainly didn't try to explain why. Often, these accounts chronicle important activities, such as coronations, but fail to mention certain important events—for instance, an outbreak of plague—altogether. And there is no attempt to link events causally. Our conception of history as a comprehensive *analysis* of events ("because of famine the kingdom collapsed"), rather than an *enumeration* of them ("In year x there was famine. The next year the kingdom collapsed"), is a fairly modern conception.

But what does that conception entail? According to White it entails that *history works like a story.* (In some languages, like French, the words for history and story are identical.) Something begins, develops, and ends, and it is up to the historian to make sense of it, *because we assume that somehow it must make sense.* We are driven by the need for the world, and our lives, to make sense, and because of this we apply the structure of a story to our historical research. We look for a beginning, a middle, and an end, and, as we saw in a previous section, those choices may be quite arbitrary. If we wish to tell the history of Columbus, where do we begin? With him sailing off into the sunset? Or with his first notion of sailing across the sea to get to Asia, in order to avoid the Muslim trade empire? With Ferdinand and Isabella kicking the Moors out of Spain and then feeling free to indulge themselves in an overseas venture? Or perhaps with the conflict between the scientific notions of the shape of the earth? We also could begin with the Aztec predictions of the fall of their empire upon the return of the bearded white god. One novelist has even chosen to begin the story by assuming that Columbus was of Longobard (Viking) blood, and that was why he had a longing for the sea. We make a choice as to what the beginning of our story will be, and that choice also determines our middle and end.

So modern history-writing is storywriting based on selected evidence, and undertaken with the assumption that history must be made to make sense, just as a novel makes sense. In a more religious age one might have assumed that history made sense because God "wrote the story." But historians make no such assumption; they are concerned only with the idea of *causality*: everything has a cause, and when we have understood the cause, we will have understood the event (see Chapter 15 on determinism). And the storytelling of history goes even deeper than that, says White, because any narrative, even the narrative of history, makes a *moral statement*, approving or disapproving of the story it tells. So when we tell the traditional story of Columbus discovering America, we are applauding his courage and tenacity, and supporting a vision of the future in which the old world comes to the new world and is transformed forever. But when we tell the story of Columbus as the beginning of the genocide of the Native Americans, the beginning of the enslavement of Africans, and the start of a political imbalance in the world, we are disapproving of Columbus and/or his time, and we are disapproving of our culture's behavior since that time. In all fairness a third kind of story can be told, of course—the story of what Columbus *intended* to do (find a trade route), what he didn't accomplish, what he did accomplish, and what the results have been for the world. This we can do without making a judgment as to whether it was "good" or "evil." Our moral judgment would not be absent, though, because our judgment would be that in this case it is morally appropriate not to make a judgment. We mustn't assume, according to White's way of thinking, that we can ever make an objective statement about history, but at least we can try to be open-minded. We can let our moral statement be one of tolerance for the ideals and mistakes of other times and other cultures, and we can include constructive suggestions for how to make the best of our present situation.

White has been accused of being too Eurocentric in his view of history-writing. Indeed, the concept of historiography as a story of cause and effect is very Euro-American. Other cultures see history as something that repeats itself endlessly, or something that is determined by divine powers, or, something that is simply a chronological account of past events. But White doesn't say that all history-writing *should be* storytelling that includes a moral judgment. He just points out that this happens to be the way we have done it in the Western culture for some centuries, and it is about time that we become aware of it.

Martha Nussbaum: Living Other Lives

Ricoeur sees novels as a phenomenon that helps us understand ourselves as temporal beings immersed in crisscrossing plot lines, our own as well as those of others. White sees novels as the realization of a fundamental human cognitive function—to make sense of events by assigning a reason to them. The American philosopher Martha Nussbaum (b. 1947) does not look to the intellectual value of storytelling, as Ricoeur and White do, but to the emotional force of narratives.

Nussbaum believes there was a time when philosophers understood the value of narratives. Aristotle (whom she values greatly) believed that experiencing a drama unfold teaches the viewer basic important lessons about having the proper feelings at the proper time—lessons about life and virtue in general. As modern Western philosophy took shape, however, the idea of emotions seemed increasingly irrelevant. There are signs today that philosophy is making a long-awaited turnaround, that it is allowing itself to take a closer look at emotions as a legitimate subject for research. Nussbaum contributes to this turnaround with her book *Love's Knowledge* (1990). She points out that emotions weren't excluded from philosophy because they did not yield *knowledge*. In other words, it is not because of any lack of *cognitive value* that philosophers have refused to investigate emotions. There is actually much cognitive value in emotions, for emotions are, on the whole, actually quite *reasonable* when we look at them in context. When do we feel anger? When we believe that someone has deliberately injured us or someone we care about—in other words, when we feel *justified* in our anger. Feelings such as disappointment, elation, grief, and even love are all responses to certain situations. They develop according to some inner logic; they don't strike at random. How do we know? Because if we realize that we were wrong about the situation, our anger slowly disappears. Perhaps *love* is not that easy to analyze—people in love don't seem to respond all that logically to situations that ought to change their feelings of love. (The person you love is seeing someone else, and what do you do? Continue to be helplessly in love.) But even love does respond to such changes in a way; we realize that our feeling is, somehow, out of place.

FIGURE 19.2 Martha Nussbaum, American philosopher. The author of *Love's Knowledge*, she suggests that novels are supremely well suited to explore moral problems. Through novels we have the chance to live more than our own lives and to understand human problems from someone else's point of view. Since others can read the same novels, we can share such knowledge and reach a mutual understanding.

Why, then, have so many philosophers refused to deal seriously with emotions? Not because they don't have cognitive value, but because emotions show that we react to situations outside our control: When we are emotional, we are not *self-sufficient*, and most philosophers have, according to Nussbaum, preferred to investigate a more autonomous part of the human character, our reason. (Of course some philosophers and psychoanalysts have pointed out that reason is not immune to outside influence, either, but Nussbaum is addressing the trends in traditional philosophy before the twentieth century, when the idea of reason being affected by the Unconscious was not yet commonly accepted.)

For Nussbaum emotions provide access to values, to human relationships, and to understanding ourselves, so they must be investigated. And where do they manifest themselves most clearly? In narratives. Society teaches values to its children through stories, so stories are actually emotions put into a structure. When we are children and adolescents we learn how to manipulate objects and relate to others; we learn cognitive skills and practical skills, and among the skills we learn are when to feel certain kinds of emotions. The prime teacher of emotions is the story. This means, of course, that different societies may tell different stories teaching different lessons, so we can't avoid adding a social critique to a study of emotions. However, we need not conclude that people in their formative years are just empty vessels into which stories are poured. To Nussbaum there is no rule saying that people accept everything their culture teaches them, so if someone doesn't approve of the stories being told, or thinks the stories haven't been told right, he or she will begin to tell his or her own stories. Nussbaum says that of course cultural relativism will have to be discussed (in terms of how it applies to the values taught by different stories), but we need not conclude that people can never reevaluate what they have been taught. (Remember the discussion of ethical relativism in Chapter 3?)

To understand emotions we must read stories, but that ought to come easily to us, since Nussbaum believes that we already enjoy doing just that. Contrary to Ricoeur she does not seem pessimistic about the fate of the novel. She does stress, however, that we have to read the entire story. We can't just rely on a synopsis, because there is an integral relationship between the form and the content of a story. As she says in her book *Love's Knowledge*, we can't skip "the emotive appeal, the absorbing plottedness, the variety and indeterminacy . . . of good fiction" without losing the heart of the experience. So in a sense Nussbaum does not specifically advocate *using stories to illustrate* moral problems, as we have done in this book. Instead, she supports reading stories as a way of *sharing basic experiences* of values, and using philosophy as a tool for analyzing this experience. For her, the story comes first, in a sense, and then the analysis can follow.

Why use stories, though? Can't we approach moral issues by more traditional avenues, such as examples that are "made to order" by philosophers? You have seen such examples in this book, such as Kant's famous one about the killer asking you to tell him where to find your friend, his intended victim, or the one illustrating the categorical imperative, about the man who wants to borrow money and can't pay it back, so he asks himself if it would be all right to make it a universal moral law that everyone can borrow money on the pretense that he will pay it back. Why not just stick with these fine little examples? Because, says Nussbaum, they lack precisely the rich texture that makes the story an experience we can relate to. Besides, such examples are formulated in such a way that the conclusion is obvious. As you may remember from our introductory chapter, novels tend to be quite open-ended, and this is a feature that Nussbaum believes is valuable. Novels preserve "mystery and indeterminacy," just like real life.

Why not just rely on your own experiences to learn about life? Some of them must certainly contain both mystery and indeterminacy. To some extent we do that already; we draw on our own experience as much as we possibly can when judging concrete and abstract cases. But the trouble is, one human life is just not enough for understanding the myriad ways of being:

> We have never lived enough. Our experience is, without fiction, too confined and too parochial. Literature extends it, making us reflect and feel about what might otherwise be too distant for feeling. . . . All living is interpreting; all action requires seeing the world *as* something. So in this sense no life is "raw" and . . . throughout our living we are, in a sense, makers of fictions. The point is that in the activity of literary imagining we are led to imagine and describe with greater precision, focusing our attention on each word, feeling each event more keenly—whereas much of actual life goes by without that heightened awareness, and is thus, in a certain sense, not fully or thoroughly lived.

Furthermore, it is much harder to talk about events in your own life with others than it is to discuss events in a story. We may not want to share our deepest feelings, or we may not be able to express them. But if we talk with friends about a passage in a favorite book, we can share both an emotional and a moral experience.

Movies, Too?

Does this rehabilitation of novels as a legitimate way to gain access to questions of ethics include a rehabilitation of *movies*? Like Ricoeur, Nussbaum does not seem too interested in films, which she believes lack the textual richness of the written word. If we look at her key points, however, that (1) stories engage our emotions; (2) the story itself is a structured emotion; and (3) we can share the experience of stories, then her narrative theory may be extended to cover films, too.

So it is fruitful as well as enjoyable to investigate emotions through stories, and to enjoy the style and fabric of the story as well as its bare plot line. And after all, why would we want a philosophy so removed from real events that it focuses only on reason as something unaffected by and apart from real life? That kind of attitude resembles a very ancient desire for something permanent, something unchanging, something with a form that never changes regardless of outside forces (remember Plato? and remember Nietzsche's critique of this ancient dream?). It is a dream of immortality and immutability which, to Nussbaum, lies behind much of the disdain for emotions. But do we really want stories in which the hero becomes immortal and immutable? At the beginning of Homer's Trojan War epic *Odyssey*, the hero, Ulysses, has to decide whether to stay with the immortal goddess Calypso (and become immortal himself) or brave endless dangers to try to make it home to his now middle-aged wife, Penelope. Nussbaum says that in spite of our fantasies of immortality, we, as readers, hope that Ulysses will choose to return to his wife, and remain mortal and human, because the other alternative is simply *boring*. So we need stories that tell of emotions and dangers and the unforeseen, because that is part of the way we understand ourselves as human beings.

The Story as Life Experience

Living in Time

Part of the human experience is that we live in *time*. Animals live in time, too, but they are presumably not as aware of it as we are. But what is time? Saint Augustine said "When you don't ask me, I know—but when you ask me I don't know." To refer to the movements of the clock, or of the earth revolving around the sun, is not enough, because those are movements in *space*. Time, on the other hand, is something we experience, and it is the basis for most of our actions and decisions. The key to the human sense of time seems to be our *memory*. We *remember* the past, or at least some of it, or some version of it, and on the basis of that we *anticipate* the future. But the only time we truly experience is the present. And we assume that the passing of time is irreversible (at least that is an assumption of Western culture); we assume the past will not return, and we can't undo what we have said or done.

What kind of life would we lead if we had no clear memory of the past? Some people who suffer brain damage live just such a life, and it seems that it is that sense of being *temporal creatures* which is lost: There is no "resonance" in their personality from past experiences, and there is no anticipation of future events, good or bad. Although the lessons of previous experience are missing, so is the *fear* of what the future might bring. It is doubtful, though, that anyone would think that it is worth giving up the fullness of your temporal personality just to escape the fear of death (in other words, fearing death is the price we pay for remembering our lives). The German philosopher Heidegger calls it *Being-towards-death*—we are constituted so that we always are aware that we are mortal. (This theory doesn't reflect the attitude of most adolescents, who as a rule are convinced that they are immortal.) That doesn't mean we are always afraid, but we carry with us the knowledge that nothing lasts forever, at least not in this world. We are acutely aware of the ending of the story as something that is inevitable for everyone, although we may choose not to think of it. Choosing not to think of it is, by the way, what Sartre would call *bad faith*. But other philosophers have a different opinion. Dutch philosopher Baruch Spinoza (1632−1677) said that "the wise man thinks least of all on death"; by this he may have meant that it is better to live life while you have it, instead of letting the thought of death overshadow your life. Whichever attitude you choose is probably a matter of temperament, but we can't deny that it seems natural to look ahead now and again and ponder, How much time will I have? Have I made the right choices? Will I feel that my life was well spent? Could I have done things differently?

When Bad Things Happen

As we saw in Chapter 11, the psychologist Erik Erikson believes that if we are lucky enough to have become psychologically mature, we will have developed *ego integrity*, and we will stop asking useless questions like "Why did I do/not do such and such when I had the time?" We will learn to accept the events in our lives, those we are responsible for and those that just happened to us, as facts of our life with which we must contend. Knowing individuals who have attained this peace of mind may actually help us along the way.

One challenge to our ego integrity occurs when something happens in our life that we didn't expect and that we find grossly unfair. A man works hard and saves his money so he can enjoy his later years, and then he dies six months after retiring. Parents give up everything they have so that their daughter can go to college, and she ends up on skid row because of drug abuse. A young child who receives a "routine" blood transfusion is infected with AIDS.

Is there a good way to deal with such things? One approach that has provided comfort for many, many people over the ages has been to view such an event as an act of God, or of Fate: It had to happen, we don't know why, but to God it makes sense. Now, we see "through a glass darkly," but later, in heaven, we will see why it happened. Another source of comfort for some is to view it as *karma*: It is the consequence of something you did earlier, or in a previous life. In other words, it is your own fault, and it will do you no good to rage about it or blame someone else. If it is in your karma that things will get better, they will. The best you can do is to realize it, and thus create good karma for next time around.

A more popular, modern Western way of approaching the problem is to assign guilt, or blame. We say the retiree brought on his death himself; he never exercised, and his cholesterol level was too high. The parents of the girl who became a drug addict must have done a terrible job of raising their daughter. And the parents of the child who contracted AIDS should have been more careful about checking up on the hospital. Our accusations are sometimes justified, but they also can be unnecessarily cruel and quite inappropriate. *Sometimes*, common sense will tell us, people really can't be blamed for what happens to them or to those they love. But it is a convenient buffer for disaster to believe that people bring on their own suffering—that they somehow *deserve* what happens to them. Although it may be true in some cases that a person's conduct contributed to what happened to him or her, that is far from being a universal pattern. In any case, we have no right to infer *guilt* from *causality*; in other words, just because someone's conscious or unconscious conduct led to some problem, we can't automatically conclude that he or she is guilty of some *moral wrongdoing*. Such an attitude often reflects a double standard: If it happens to strangers they must have done something "wrong"; if it happens to me or to one of my heroes, we are just unfortunate victims. This double standard is frequently applied to the AIDS crisis; for some people, AIDS is punishment for immoral behavior—unless it strikes someone close to them.

Life as a Story

An alternate way of dealing with life's crises is to see them in the light of *stories*. As we have seen before, humans—at least modern humans in the Western world—seem to have a need for history and their own lives to make sense; they need to understand *why* something happened. Even in traditional cultures where there is little history-writing, people have the same concern about a life well spent. In such cultures the model is usually the myths and legends of that culture: Do as the culture hero did, and you will have lived well. In our pluralistic culture the emphasis is much more on doing something *new*—blazing a trail, inventing something, or writing a paper about something nobody has thought of before. We like our children to be different from their friends, to be individuals (however, we don't want them to be *deviant*). Martha Nussbaum says that stories teach us to deal emotionally with the unexpected, because in so many novels we witness characters having to deal with such situations. Of course the unexpected situation in our own life is not likely to be the same as the one in our favorite story—then it wouldn't be *unexpected*. But we can react to the unexpected in the same way our favorite characters do, and in this way we may be able to rise to the occasion. For persons from a traditional culture, such efforts at being ready for the unexpected, as well as efforts at being different, would be incomprehensible, for what makes persons good is precisely that they do the *same* as their ancestors. The urge to act *well*, however, is the same for members of both modern and traditional cultures. In order to live an accomplished life you must follow a pattern ("do like the ancestors" or "do something new"), and others will deem it a good thing if you succeed. *Havamal*, the ancient Icelandic poem of rules for living, says that your name will live on after you die; in other words, people will tell your story only after they know the ending, be it good or bad. ·

When things go our way, we don't ask about the meaning of life. We find that the whole development makes sense. The mythologist Joseph Campbell compares it to being at a fun party: You don't stop and ask yourself what you are doing there. But at a boring party you might ask yourself that question. Similarly, when things go wrong in someone's life, he or she may question the meaning of life—because somehow, life doesn't make sense anymore. An *unexpected* element interrupts our life's story, and we lose the thread—we experience an *identity crisis* (an expression introduced by Erikson). So how can stories help?

You may remember that Sartre, in his theory of free will, suggested that not only can we change the future, but also we can change the past, by reinterpreting it. In the same way, we can, and we do, reinterpret the story of our life whenever great changes happen that provoke a reevaluation. This idea of Sartre's that we can "reinvent" our past finds a parallel in narrative theory, because what we do when we change our viewpoint and interpretation of the past in the light of the present is *rewrite our own story* and sometimes even the story of our community and our culture. When we decide to major in medicine instead of business because of our sister's illness, we rewrite our story from then on. If our uncle dies just after retiring we rewrite his story and it *does* become a moral lesson; we tell ourselves, I will try not to do what he did, or try to avoid what life did to him, or at least make every day count. (In this way we rewrite our own story as well.) If we lose our money because of bad investments, we may rewrite the story in a number of ways: I was victimized, but now I'm smarter, or, I was too concerned with money, but now I'm smarter. And of course we are not always smarter, but it makes us feel better to think so. At any rate, we rewrite our past so it will make sense to us in the present and give a new, meaningful direction to our future. It is when we feel incapable of finding a new story line in our life—when the change has been so dramatic that there seems to be no new purpose lurking among the rubble—that the identity crisis may be hard to shake. In that case, it takes courage to choose to view the world and human life the way the British philosopher Bertrand Russell described it: as a collection of atoms brought together at random, with no rhyme or reason other than the rules of science and biology. According to this viewpoint there is no meaning to the individual life or to the universe as such. But even this is a story: It is a story of natural forces and how each human fits into the greater whole of biology—rather a romantic notion when it comes down to it. In the face of meaninglessness, we also might choose, with Nietzsche, to say that life is its own meaning. In this case the force and will of life in any shape or form becomes a story we can relate to when no other stories present themselves. We may, of course, choose to say that we just don't know. We would like to think that there is some story, some purpose, but we don't know what it is, or if there is one at all.

Living in the Narrative Zone

Let us tie all of these ideas together. We humans are temporal beings. We live in the present, but we are constantly reaching back to the past and forward to the future—we are in a constant state of tension between memory and anticipation. We live our own story, which has its own beginning and its own end. Furthermore, we live the stories of our culture; we identify with them or criticize them or rewrite them. We seek moral lessons in our own stories and in the stories of our culture. We also just like to hear stories, watch stories, and tell stories, and when we do, the time period we experience multiplies; we are still living our own life, but we also are sharing in the compressed time of a novel or a movie, and we are sharing multiple experiences with fictional characters.

There is a story by Richard Matheson about a man who wanted his life to be like things are in the movies, because he thought his life was extremely dull. His wish was granted, and this is what happened: He fell in love and was married, all in a matter of five minutes. He had kids, made a career, earned money, lost money, and lost his job, all within half an hour. He found that he was living out his life in abbreviated chunks of time, the same as in a movie. After two hours he was old and dying, and the final thing he saw before his eyes was the letters DNE EHT—"The End" to the audience watching him. As the saying goes, when the gods want to punish us, they give us what we wish for.

Obviously this is not what the man truly wished for—he wanted a life with an exciting story line, not a life lived in Narrative Time. But Narrative Time was what he got. We readers and viewers are luckier, because we can have the best of both worlds. We can retain our own real-life time while we share in the accelerated, "telescoped" time of books and movies. When we open a book or enter a movie theater we enter what we might call the *Narrative Zone*. And in the Narrative Zone we can live other lives vicariously, acquire skills and experiences that we might never know of otherwise. We may get an idea of what it feels like to be a member of the other gender or another race, of another time and place, or of another species entirely—and these experiences may help us decide how to live once we leave the Narrative Zone. Nothing else provokes our empathy as effectively as a good story: We weep and rejoice with our friends in the novel or in the movie, even if we know that it is only make-believe. They are not wasted tears or smiles, for they are, ultimately, the building blocks of our character. Would we be more realistic if we didn't involve ourselves with stories? More reliable? Less apt to fantasize? Some people, like Flaubert's Emma Bovary, probably immerse themselves in fiction more than they should, but that only supports Aristotle's idea of the Golden Mean: Everything has to be done in moderation. We may never have to deal with the kind of thirst for revenge that consumes the Count of Monte Cristo, but we can learn what it might feel like, and we can understand the sense of letdown and the self-doubt that occurs when the revenge is complete. We may even decide that the Count was wrong to behave as he did, and that we would not want to react that way. Either way, we are richer for the experience. If we happen to read the story of the Good Samaritan, there is a chance that we will stop to help a mugging victim should we happen to see that crime in progress. There is also a chance that the "victim" will end up mugging us, but that doesn't mean we should not have read the story, or that we should not have come to his aid; it means that life doesn't always conform to the stories we read, and we shouldn't think that it does.

So sometimes we get hurt when we are inspired by stories, and sometimes we are inspired by the wrong stories. Should we play it safe—stay home and stick to reading newspapers? The essayist and science-fiction writer Ursula LeGuin compares our existence as readers and listeners to the hoop snake that bites its own tail: It hurts, but *now you can roll!* The problem comes if you are a poisonous hoop snake—then your own bite will kill you. What is the moral? If the hoop snake doesn't make a hoop, it won't move, and it will be as though it never lived. So we must take chances—we mustn't shy away from taking part in the listening process, in becoming engaged in the story—and we mustn't shy away from becoming engaged in our own story. For LeGuin, telling stories and listening to stories is a kind of life affirmation and an incentive to live life to the fullest. And when we do come to the end of our own story, we may feel that we've accomplished something.

Narratives That Explore The Life Experience

All of the stories discussed in this book are examples of how natural it is for humans to think in terms of stories when we want to discuss a moral problem. At this point, though, I would like to repeat something I mentioned early on in the book. These outlines of stories are by no means a sufficient substitute for reading the stories or watching the films yourself; the outlines merely provide a basis for discussing the specific problems explored in the stories in light of the theories presented in this book. Without actually reading the book or viewing the movie, the essential experience of being in the Narrative Zone—of sharing the narrative time with the work of fiction—is lost, or at least thoroughly diluted, and the emotional impact is at best a weak approximation of the original narrative experience. So do yourself a favor: If you like a certain story, then read the original book or watch the original film. In this way you will add another set of "parallel lives" to your own life experience. As Martha Nussbaum says, we never live long enough to experience for ourselves all the various ways of being human. Stories help us add others' lives to our own life. Besides, it's not a bad idea to let the characters in films and novels make some of our mistakes for us, as long as we don't forget to make ourselves the central character in some stories of our own now and again.

Chapter 20

Narratives of Human Nature

In a sense, most stories are stories about human nature, in some way or other. Often they are reflections of what we believe humans *are* like, and occasionally they are examples of what we think humans *ought to be* like. The selections in this chapter focus on all of the themes discussed in Part 4—personhood, biology as destiny, gender issues, self-knowledge, and political theory.

Personhood

In this section we will look at some fictional stories that ask, What does it mean to be human? Is being human a moral condition or a genetic one? Are all humans persons, and can there be persons who aren't strictly human?

453

ROGER MCBRIDE ALLEN, *Orphan of Creation*
Novel (1988).

Dr. Barbara Marchando, an African-American paleoanthropologist, makes an astounding discovery on the family plantation in Mississippi. The plantation was bought by her ancestors, former slaves, from their former masters, sometime after 1865. One day she discovers a diary kept by one of her ancestors which tells about a disturbing incident in the 1850s, when a new breed of slaves was introduced on the plantation. This new breed was *nonhuman*, so the masters were able to bypass antislave trade regulations. The new slaves looked much like humans, but their heads were misshapen, they had hardly any chins, and they could not talk.

Because her profession is paleoanthropology, Dr. Marchando pursues the discovery, and the slave graveyard yields astounding archaeological evidence. Resting in the earth are the remains of a race of beings who were not quite human and not quite apelike, either: prehominids who supposedly have been extinct for a million years (the remains clearly date back only a little over a hundred years). Marchando's colleagues reluctantly agree: She has found remains of *australopithecus boisei*, which have never before been seen outside of Africa.

Marchando and her colleagues agree that if such creatures could survive in Africa until the mid eighteen-fifties, then perhaps they might still be around somewhere. An expedition is dispatched to the Gabon area in Africa, and contact is made with present-day slave traders who are in charge of the last, pitiful members of a group of prehominids like the ones found by Marchando. The scientists negotiate to examine a female—one who has been scheduled for termination—and they find out that they have actually bought her in the process. Reluctantly they take her home to the United States and begin to establish contact with her, giving her the name Thursday, because "Thursday's child has far to go."

Barbara Marchando's troubles are only just beginning. As the press, the scientific community, and the business world catch hold of the news, Thursday becomes a celebrity as well as an object of speculation. Biologists want to "euthanize" her and perform an autopsy, the world wants to gawk at her, linguists want to teach her to speak, and enterprising businesspeople are already negotiating to acquire the rest of her tribe, whom they would consider "unpaid laborers." Thursday is now relating to Barbara as to a parent, and her spirit is very low, because she senses the unrest around her. Barbara's only chance of protecting her is to prove to the world that Thursday is not an animal but a *person*, with a person's right to life and to privacy. By this time Thursday is able to speak a few words, even though her vocal cords are not developed like humans'. Nevertheless Barbara decides not to argue that Thursday can reason and is thus a person; she chooses instead to focus on Thursday's *genetic* makeup. It turns out that sometime in the past, *humans* interbred with Thursday's ancestors (slave owners raping their slaves seemed to be a common phenomenon). So Barbara artificially impregnates Thursday with human sperm. Thursday conceives, and the news is spread just as scientists are getting ready to terminate her. Because Thursday can conceive by a human, she now is considered genetically a human being. Another slave tragedy has been narrowly averted.

Study Questions

1. If a population of prehuman hominids were discovered today, do you think it is likely that some people might argue they would make good slaves?
2. What do you think is the most important characteristic for determining personhood—having human genes, or displaying traits such as speaking, reasoning, and being able to plan for the future? Which defense would *you* have chosen for Thursday?
3. Can you think of some reasonable arguments why animals should be considered a resource for humans?
4. Is Dr. Marchando acting in an ethically responsible way when she impregnates Thursday? Why or why not?

RIDLEY SCOTT (DIRECTOR), HAMPTON FANCHER AND DAVID PEOPLES (SCREENWRITERS), *Blade Runner*

Film (1982); from the novel Do Androids Dream of Electric Sheep? *by Philip K. Dick.*

At its premiere the critics weren't too impressed with *Blade Runner*; it was too weird for most moviegoers' taste at the time. Over the years, though, the film achieved a near-cult status among film lovers for its "film noir" style and prophetic theme. What looked like cultural mishmash in 1982 is now recognized as an accurate depiction of life in the inner cities—not only in the far-distant future, but even today in the 1990s.

This is the Los Angeles portrayed in the movie: dirty, perpetually rainy because of pollution, and populated with people from all cultures, all of whom are looking out for themselves. The language of the streets is a mix of Japanese, German, and English. Giant blimps cruise the skies advertising "a new life off-planet," away from the hopelessness of earth life. There are almost no nonhuman animals left on earth, so humans are manufacturing mechanical pets—robotic owls and ostriches and snakes and what have you. In addition they are also manufacturing artificial humans, replicants to take on hazardous and difficult work off-world. The latest series of replicants is particularly advanced. Stronger and more intelligent than humans, they already have become a danger to them: They are rebelling and have already killed some humans. Private detective Deckard is assigned the job of hunting them down and destroying them. He meets with their manufacturer, who tells him that these beings have a built-in self-destruct mechanism; five years is as long as they can live. Deckard has no sympathy for these beings; as far as he is concerned, they are mere things to be terminated. A young woman, Rachael, is staying at the house of the manufacturer. Deckard is attracted to her, and his view on replicants begins to change when he realizes that she, too, is a replicant, although she herself is unaware of it. She is an experimental model, and her "brain" contains implants of some-one else's childhood memories, which make her seem more human and make her believe she is human. Given the existence of such extraordinary features, who can say for sure who is a replicant and who isn't? Might Deckard himself also be one?

Eventually, Deckard catches up with the runaway replicants one by one. Their leader, Batty, the strongest and most intelligent of all of them, engages Deckard in a fight to the death. (The replicant's death is approaching anyway, because his five years are almost up.) In the fight, when Deckard is close to losing his own life, he realizes that what the replicant wants is what all humans want—just a little more time to live, to sense, and to breathe.

Study Questions

1. What statement does *Blade Runner* make about humanity and human rights, if any?
2. Are the runaway replicants persons? Is Rachael? Is Deckard? Is the manufacturer? What makes someone a person?
3. The film assumes that humans eventually will kill off all nonhuman animal life on earth, and that they will begin to make artificial animals. Do you think that either assumption might come true?

Jorge Luis Borges, "The Circular Ruins"

From the book The Garden of Forking Paths, *short story (1941).*

A mysterious wizard settles in an old abandoned temple, an ancient circle of ruins. This is the place, he feels, where he can fulfill his purpose: to dream a man, in minute detail. Workmen in the area bring him food so he can concentrate on his dream-work. He dreams that he is lecturing in a circular amphitheater, hoping for a bright student who might question his teachings (those who simply accept what they hear are too docile for him and don't have enough substance to be of use to him). In the end he focuses on one dream-student and imagines the rest gone.

One day he runs into a problem: He can't fall asleep, and without being asleep he can't work on his dream-creation. So he goes through a strenuous purification process and is finally able to dream again. Over the span of a year he constructs a human, piece by piece, in his dreams. Eventually, the god Fire reveals himself to the wizard in a dream. He says he will make the dreamed man come alive, and so it happens: The dreamed man awakens. Now the real teaching begins. The dreamer trains his creature to live in the real world. He thinks of him as his son, and before he sends him out into the world, he destroys all memories the creature might have of being dreamed up. He wants the creature to think of himself as a real man.

Alone, it occurs to the wizard that the god Fire is the only one who knows that his son is not a real man. He is terrified that his son will somehow find out the secret:

> Not to be a man, to be a projection of another man's dreams—what an incomparable humiliation, what madness!

But his worries are cut short. A fire rages in the circular temple, and the wizard realizes that his hour of death has arrived. But when the flames reach him they do not burn him:

> With relief, with humiliation, with terror, he understood that he also was an illusion, that someone else was dreaming him.

Study Questions

1. Why does the wizard feel both relief and terror at realizing that he is being dreamed, too?
2. Compare *Blade Runner* and "The Circular Ruins." What questions do they raise about self-identity?
3. In a symbolic sense, what might Borges intend with this story of a dreamed man dreaming another man? Are we all created by someone else? Is reality not what it seems to be?

WALT DISNEY (PRODUCER), BEN SHARPSTEEN, ET AL. (DIRECTORS), TED SEARS, ET AL. (SCREENWRITERS), *Pinocchio*

Animated film (1940).

An old children's story about a wooden puppet becomes, in the hands of Disney, a moral tale of the virtue of being human. Since I assume that most readers have been exposed to this fabulous cartoon, the outline is kept to a minimum: Old Gepetto, a woodcutter, longs for human company and makes a life-size wooden puppet. Magically, the puppet becomes animated and is told by a fairy that if he is good, he will become a real human boy. This is easier said than done, because Pinocchio has no *conscience*. So the little critter with the top hat, Jiminy Cricket, pronounces himself Pinocchio's conscience. Pinocchio is easily lured astray by evil characters who tell tales of how wonderful it is to skip school and do whatever you please. Together with real boys who also have been seduced, Pinocchio ends up in a nightmarish place that at first seems like heaven. The boys can do whatever they want—they can eat and drink and smoke cigars—but there is a price to pay: one by one, to their horror and dismay, the boys turn into jackasses.

Through a series of events involving fantastic feats of animation (and this was before computer graphics were invented) Pinocchio succeeds in redeeming himself and finally is awarded the ultimate gift, which he wants more than anything else: He becomes a real boy. As the song from the movie says, "When you wish upon a star, makes no difference who you are . . . your dreams come true."

Study Questions

1. What moral lesson is intended by the jackass incident?
2. Is the notion of "a real boy" intended primarily as a descriptive or a normative term in this story?

ROBERT SCHEERER (DIRECTOR), MELINDA M. SNODGRASS (WRITER), *Star Trek: The Next Generation*, episode entitled "The Measure of a Man"

Television series (1989).

First the cast of characters: *Data*, a unique android and high-ranking officer in Starfleet who wants to be human more than anything else; *Captain Picard*, the captain of the Enterprise starship; *Guinan*, the long-lived alien bartender and wise woman; *Maddox*, a visiting scientist; *Captain Levoir*, a visiting, unsentimental courtroom judge; and *Riker*, first officer and a good friend of Data's.

Paying a visit to the Enterprise, Maddox announces that he is going to take Data away to perform experiments on "it." His goal is to create a new breed of androids that could be made available to all starships. When informed that this will involve downloading his memories into a memory bank, shutting him down, and dismantling him, Data refuses, worried that the subtle element that makes up his personality will not survive such a procedure. Maddox insists, and Data's only recourse is to resign from Starfleet in order to avoid being commanded to go with Maddox. As Data packs his things we see what he chooses to take along: a book from Picard, his medals, and a hologram of another crew member, now dead: Tasha Yar.

In the meantime, Maddox has gone to see Picard and the visiting judge, Levoir, to ask them to rule about Data's status. Is Data's refusal to cooperate the same as if the main

FIGURE 20.1 *Star Trek: The Next Generation.* Data (Brent Spiner) is the android who wants to become human, like a child who longs to grow up. He can't experience emotions, although he is more intellectually capable than a human. The question is, is Data a person, and should he be given human rights, or is he a machine belonging to Starfleet, with no rights to self-determination?

computer refused to work? For the main computer to refuse would be unthinkable, says Levoir, because the computer is only property. But in that case, since Data is artificial, perhaps he is just property, too? In that case Data would have no right to life or to privacy. Maddox says Picard is fooled by Data's human likeness—if Data resembled a box on wheels the request would never have been any problem. Levoir does some research and finds that Data is indeed the property of Starfleet and can't resign. Picard challenges the ruling. As a result, a hearing is held, with Levoir presiding. She chooses Picard to defend Data, and, logically, the role of prosecutor falls to First Officer Riker. He refuses at first, because he considers himself a close friend of Data's and doesn't want to risk a possible unfavorable ruling. But when he is told that if he refuses, Levoir will rule summarily that "Data is a toaster," he agrees to do his best.

At the hearing, Riker eloquently demonstrates that Data is a machine: His hand can be removed, and he can be turned off, just like any computer. In Riker's words, "Pinocchio is broken." Picard is shaken and requests a recess. In the lounge he confers with his good friend Guinan (played by Whoopi Goldberg) about the case, and Guinan puts her finger on the real issue: If Data is property, then all other future Datas will be property, too. In that case, what does Starfleet intend to do with them? Put them in dangerous positions, subject them to long hours of hard labor, think of them as disposable? All through history there have been *disposable populations*, she says, and Picard realizes she is talking about slavery.

Back at the hearing, Picard now has a focus for his defense. What is at stake, he says, is whether Data is *sentient* or not. He asks Maddox to define sentience, and Maddox offers the following definition: being self-aware, being intelligent, and being conscious. Of course Data is a machine, Picard says, but that is irrelevant. Of course he is made by humans—but so are other humans. What is relevant is whether he fulfills the three criteria of sentience. Data is certainly *intelligent*, more so than any human on board the Enterprise. And he is *self-aware*; he knows where he is, what is at stake, and what the implications of a ruling against him are. But is he conscious, in the sense that humans are conscious? Picard points to Data's bag containing his few pieces of memorabilia. He asks Data what the items mean to him. Data's response reminds everyone that he and Tasha were "intimate." (Data and Tasha once had a sexual encounter. This relationship, however, does not qualify Data for personhood, for Data is created without emotions in the human sense of the word. However, we do understand from his attachment to his mementos that Data knows the value of friendship and loyalty, and we, as viewers, are not so certain that Data isn't developing emotions after all.)

What exactly does it mean for humans to be "conscious"? Picard admits that he does not know, and neither does anyone else—but if Data is not granted rights as a person, future Datas will be condemned to be members of a race of slaves that can be used as others see fit, without any regard for their personal interests. (As Kant would say, they could be used "merely as a means to an end.") The future of Data's "descendents" depends on this ruling.

Levoir finally speaks, and she asks the fundamental question: *Does Data have a soul?* If we can't say, and if we don't know, then Data should have the freedom to explore that idea without being the property of anyone else. As Picard points out, the Enterprise is always looking for new life forms, and there one sits, looking back at them. So Maddox is denied his request. In the end he even learns to call Data "he" and not just "it."

In the aftermath of the ruling, Data's friends are giving him a party, and Riker hasn't shown up. Data goes to find him and sees that Riker is torn apart by remorse—he realizes he almost cost Data his life. But Data understands that Riker was only doing his duty as first officer, and Data understands well about duty. Riker tells Data that he is a wise man, and Data answers that he is not yet wise, but he is learning.

Study Questions

1. Is Data a "Pinocchio"? What are the similarities and differences between the wooden puppet and the bioengineered android?
2. What does the question of slavery have to do with whether or not we think of someone as a person?
3. The idea of *duty* often is combined with the idea of *rights*. Could Data have duties as a Starfleet officer without having rights?
4. Some scholars say that if you have *interests* then you also have certain rights. Does Data have interests?

Nature or Nurture?

This section contains discussions of questions concerning determinism and its application in sociobiology—of "nature" versus "nurture." All of these stories express the belief that humans somehow are programmed to develop in a certain way, either as individuals or as a species, and because of either their heredity or their environment (or lack of environment).

HANS CHRISTIAN ANDERSEN, "The Ugly Duckling"
Fairy tale (1844),
HENRIK PONTOPPIDAN, "Flight of the Eagle"
Short story (1894).

Children around the world have been exposed to the story of the ugly duckling, but rarely in its original form. Hans Christian Andersen tells a grueling tale of hard times and abuse for the poor ugly duckling who is really a "swan-ling": His mother rejects him because he is ugly and clumsy, his brothers and sisters, the pretty ducklings, peck at him, and even the kitchen maid kicks dirt at him because he is so ugly. All through the winter he struggles to survive, barely escaping dogs and hunters and hunger itself. But his efforts are worth it. In the spring, when the ice breaks, he sees a family of majestic white birds coming toward him. He expects them to kill him because he is so ugly, but they welcome him as one of their own, because now he is a beautiful, full-grown swan. He sails off to glory with them, remembering that when he was an ugly duckling he had no idea life would hold so much happiness for him.

Is this the likely fate of a baby swan whose egg ends up in a duck's nest? And how did it get there in the first place? And why are ducks somehow lesser beings than swans? Such questions are not Andersen's concern. The story is purely symbolic; it is the story of Andersen's own life. He was pushed around and experienced terribly hard times when he was young, but because of what he *really* was, because of his poetic nature, he overcame all hardships and finally even became famous. As long as you have the right qualities, Andersen is saying, your true nature will prevail.

Another Danish author, Henrik Pontoppidan, did not agree with this view. He wrote a "counter-duckling" story, "Flight of the Eagle." An eagle chick is found by some boys and is taken to a parsonage, where kind people raise him. All his life, the eagle knows of nothing but life with the humans who feed him and care for him. He feels comfortable among the chickens in the yard but dreams of the day when he will be free so that he can fulfill his biological destiny. (His wings are clipped, though, so actually he cannot go anywhere.)

One day there is a windstorm, and the eagle finds himself lifted up to the barn roof. He longs to fly more than ever, and the next gust of wind fulfills his dream: It makes him airborne. His wings can barely carry him, but, aided by the wind, he soars over the woods and fields and flies toward the mountains. He is finally a true eagle. A female eagle approaches; she calls him, and he follows, higher and higher. Night arrives, and he lands on a rocky ledge, but the female keeps calling for him to follow. Now he begins to think about how everyone is doing back home. He imagines his friends nice and snug and well fed. He turns away from the call of the she-eagle and makes his way home. The journey takes all night. In the early morning hours he approaches the farm, but a farmhand who doesn't know that he has been missing mistakes him for a wild eagle and shoots him down. Pontoppidan concludes that being born an eagle makes no difference, if you grow up among the ducks.

Study Questions

1. Which story do you think represents the truer picture? Can we overcome our upbringing and realize our true heritage, or not?
2. Can we overcome our heritage by training hard?
3. Both stories are versions of determinism. Could you imagine free will playing a part in the decision of either the duckling or the eagle?
4. Why do you think these authors chose to write about animals rather than people?

FRANCOIS TRUFFAUT (DIRECTOR) AND JEAN GRUAULT (SCREENWRITER), *The Wild Child*

Film, 1969.

This story is based on a real-life event, the life of Victor d'Aveyron. In 1798 a feral child (a "wild" child who did not grow up among humans) was discovered in the woods near Aveyron in France. This discovery excited the intellectual community very much, because they would now be able to test some of the predominant theories of the Enlightenment (such as, humans are endowed at birth with the capacity for reason) and of Rousseau (such as, humans who haven't been corrupted by civilization are morally better than others). However, Victor's case proved inconclusive at best. The film portrays a small segment of Victor's life.

The boy is captured in the woods. He can't speak, and apparently he can't hear, either. He runs on all fours and acts like an animal. Kicking and biting, he is carried off to the Institute of the Deaf and Mute by the authorities. A young scientist, Dr. Itard, takes an interest in the case and obtains permission to take the boy to his home on the outskirts of Paris, to educate him. Once home, he realizes that the boy is neither deaf nor mute, but that his attention is selective toward what directly concerns him, mostly food. Itard's housekeeper becomes the primary care giver to the boy, now named Victor. Up until now the boy has seemed emotionally retarded as well, but little by little he becomes capable of responding to both Itard and the housekeeper. He likes for them to pat his face and his head. Itard puts him on a strict training schedule; he is to learn table manners, proper stance, cleanliness, and the names of objects. Once he catches on to what Itard wants, he is a quick learner, as long as he is rewarded with milk. If he doesn't get his milk, he has a temper tantrum and is locked in the closet. After a while Victor seems to understand the difference between right and wrong, and Itard feels that he has elevated the boy to the level of a human being. By and by, Victor comes to understand the connection between words, things, and written language, but he never speaks except to repeat the word for an object *after* he has obtained the object. Itard despairs at this because he considers it not language acquisition, but parroting. Eventually Victor runs away and is given up for lost, but he returns on his own. Itard feels that this is the beginning of a new phase.

This is as far as the film takes us, and in real life, this was about as far as Itard went. After a while he gave up on Victor as a hopeless case and left the boy in the care of his housekeeper for as long as he lived—another twenty-odd years.

What fascinated researchers so much at the time was that Victor might give the answer to the most burning question of eighteenth-century philosophy: *Is some human knowledge innate, or is it all learned through experience?* The theory that some knowledge is innate (such as logic and mathematics) is known as *rationalism,* and the theory that all knowledge comes from experience (that the mind is a blank slate from birth) is known as *empiricism.*

Study Questions

1. Is Itard's method of training Victor the method a scientist today might use in a similar situation? Would you suggest a different method?
2. What does the story of Victor suggest in terms of a theory of human nature? Would you side with rationalism or empiricism if you were Itard?
3. The "feral child" theme is familiar to most of us. The most famous feral child in Western popular fiction is probably Tarzan, closely followed by Kipling's Mowgli from *The Junglebook*. Feral children do occur in real life, though, and sometimes they actually are reared by animals (such children are sometimes referred to as "wolf children"). On the basis of *The Wild Child*, could we ever realistically imagine a Tarzan or a Mowgli being King of the Jungle? Why or why not?

STANLEY KUBRICK (DIRECTOR AND SCREENWRITER), ARTHUR C. CLARKE (SCREENWRITER), *2001, A Space Odyssey*

Film, 1968.

This film has become a classic. Commercials still borrow from *2001* by using the opening bars of Richard Strauss's "Also Sprach Zarathustra" for music. Some feature evil computers speaking in a soft tone of voice; they too are borrowing from *2001*. And films and novels have explored the theme of "government conspiracy to hide contact with aliens" ever since. The film takes us from the "dawn of man," through the first years of systematic moon exploration, all the way to the era of computers in space, but because we already have considered the question of whether a computer can be a person, we will focus here on the opening sequence of the film, which serves as an illustration of Robert Ardrey's sociobiological theory that humans are aggressive.

It is dawn somewhere in the African desert, at about the time of the "dawn of man." Two groups of knuckle-walking, furry prehominids are fighting over a waterhole. (The movie was made before it became evident that humans have not walked on their knuckles for at least four million years.) One group barely manages to scare the others away with shrieks and gestures. The defeated group retreats, moping and thirsty.

Next dawn: same group of ape-humans, but now there is something new. A giant, black monolith is standing in the sand, calling the creatures to it. It possesses a strange attraction. The creatures touch it and dance around it, and soon something happens to them. Images come into their mind, and mental connections are made. One picks up a thigh bone lying on the ground, smashes it into the dried-up skull of a grass-eater, and imagines doing it to a live one. The connection between *tool* and *food* is made for the first time—a connection between *weapon* and *killing*. What, then, is the monolith's function? It makes the creatures think. It is an intelligence enhancer, and the part of the mind that is enhanced is the part that uses aggression.

Next scene: back at the waterhole. The Other Guys are there, shrieking and threatening as before, but this time there is a difference: Our Guys have weapons—clubs made from bones and rocks—and the other group is quickly defeated. A weapon has caused death within the species for the first time. Elated, the killer throws his weapon, the thighbone, high up in the air. The bone changes into a spaceship that is heading for a space station in the late twentieth century. End of the beginning of *2001*.

Study Questions

1. Evaluate the film's assessment of human intelligence—that we have gotten to where we are now by channeling our aggression into the use of weapons.
2. If the film had been made today, do you think the filmmakers might have had the monolith teach the creatures how to make *baskets* and use them, as well as weapons? Why or why not?

Men and Women: Different Worlds?

In this section we will explore some stories about how men and women need each other, and also how men and women can perceive each other to be different. The stories reflect different times and different views concerning the ways men and women live with each other.

SIA INDIAN MYTH, "Men and Women Try Living Apart"

Reported by Mathilda Cox Stevenson (1889).

The Sia Indians (a New Mexico Pueblo tribe) tell this story, which is similar to many other Native American myths. Many years ago the Sia women began a quarrel with the men. The women worked hard all day, and when the men came home from hunting, the women accused them of being lazy and lascivious. The men answered that although the women might criticize them, the truth was that the women wanted the men more than the men wanted the women. Soon both the men and the women were claiming that they would be happy without sex for a very long time, even years. The women gathered their things and moved to one side of the village, while the men and boys moved to the other side. The next day the men and boys, at the advice of their council leader, moved across the river.

Months passed, and the men were doing fine, because they hunted for meat. But the women grew thin and pale, for they had nothing to eat. As time passed, the women wanted the men more and more, but the men were still doing fine without the women. In the fourth year the women gave up and asked the men to come back. They did. After only a few days, the women were healthy again.

NAVAJO INDIAN MYTH, "The River of Separation"
Reported by Matthews and Washington (1897).

First Man and First Woman quarreled about who could stand to be without the other the longest. First Man moved across the river with the other men of his tribe. For a while everything was well in the men's camp as well as in the women's camp. Once in a while the women would call over and ask if there was anything they were missing out on; there was, but they would never admit it. After a year, though, the women's gardens weren't yielding much, and the women grew thinner. The men were doing fine, because they had both gardens and meat. But First Man was not happy. He missed the way his wife cooked stew, and he didn't sleep well alone. Little by little the men began to feel bad about the situation—about eating while their wives and little girls were going hungry— and they plainly missed their wives. So First Man called across the river, "Have you learned your lesson by now?" First Woman said she had, that the women had realized they couldn't live without the men. So the men went back to the women, and they all had a second honeymoon. Everybody had learned a lesson: Men and women can't live without each other.

Study Questions

1. How do these two versions of the same story differ in their view of the relationship between men and women?
2. The Sia are agricultural, and the Navajo are (or used to be) nomadic. Do you think that makes a difference in the moral of the story?

ALICE WALKER, *The Temple of My Familiar*
Novel (1989).

This narrative weaves threads of destinies together, primarily from the perspective of African-American, African, and South American Indian women. In the face of physical

FIGURE 20.2 Alice Walker, American novelist, author of *The Color Purple*, *The Temple of My Familiar*, and *Possessing the Secret of Joy*. Walker paints a picture of the many cultural strands contributing to the lives of American people of color and relates the African-American experience to that of the African. In particular, the life experiences of African and African-American women are explored by Walker.

abuse and the threat of genocide these women retain their family stories and ancestral memories to build a women's wisdom that the chosen men in their lives are invited to share. Zedé, the South American Indian woman living in California, tells her young lover, the rock musician Arveyda (he is also her daughter's husband) about the Beginning Time, when men and women were struggling to understand the mystery of life. This story, told in the style of a myth, is Walker's way of discarding the Freudian idea that women believe they are naturally "incomplete" compared with men; in other words, this is a "countermyth" to the myth of "penis envy":

In the old, old days the first women created men, and the men got together and observed the world of woman. For the first women, men were only playthings, but men were in great awe of women when they found out that women could give birth. This inspired them to imagine a giant woman, a mother goddess, and they began to worship women as priestesses, although women never thought of themselves as such. For a long time women were revered and spoiled, and yet they didn't take themselves seriously and thought nothing of their powers of creation. But one day the men rebelled, because they had found out that woman gives birth "through a hole at her bottom." So now the men decided that *they* should be the ones creating life, and they began castrating themselves so that they could be like the life-giving women. This was the beginning of the celibacy tradition of priesthood, because men wanted to be like women.

Study Questions

1. Why do you think Alice Walker wrote this pseudomyth?
2. Do you think men are generally envious of female creative powers?
3. Write a pseudomyth in which men and women experience each other as different, but equal.

UMBERTO ECO, *Foucault's Pendulum*

Novel (1989).

This novel, written by the Italian philosopher who made his debut as a fiction writer with the best-seller *The Name of the Rose*, is not directly concerned with gender issues; however, indirectly, the idea of women's values sets the tone for the entire plot. The plot takes the reader in and out of conspiracy theories, secret societies, Freemasonry, the mystique of the medieval order of warrior monks, the Knights Templar (and their purported treasure), and the personal problems of three bored male scholars who make up their own secret society and dig up old letters in code that suggest the existence of a forgotten treasure, an immense power source. The trouble begins when other secret society aficionados become interested in their secret, and the three scholars find that their lives are in danger. Faced with his wife's pregnancy, Pow, one of the scholars, begins to understand that his work is hollow and empty compared to the task of creation that his wife is undertaking:

> I daydreamed. The Thing, with its birth, would give reality and meaning to all the old wives' tales of the Diabolics [alchemists]. Poor Diabolics, who spent their nights enacting chemical weddings with the hope that eighteen-karat gold would result and wondering if the philosopher's stone was really the lapis exillis, a wretched terra-cotta grail—and my grail was in Lia's belly.
>
> "Yes," Lia said, running her hand over her swelling, taut vessel, "here is where your good primal matter is steeping. . . . There are no secrets, Pow. We know exactly how the Thing is formed, its little nerves and muscles, its little eyes and spleens and pancreases."
>
> If I had only stopped there. If I had only written a white book, a good grimoire, for all the adepts of Isis Unveiled, explaining to them that the secretum secretorum no longer needed to be sought, that the book of life contained no hidden meaning; it was all there, in the bellies of all the Lias of the world, in the hospital rooms, on straw pallets, on riverbanks, and that the stones in exile and the Holy Grail were nothing but screaming monkeys with their umbilical cords still dangling and the doctor giving them a slap on the ass. . . . But no. We, the sardonic, insisted on playing games with the Diabolics, on showing them that if there had to be a cosmic plot, we could invent the most cosmic of all.
>
> I should be at peace. I have understood. . . . The Earth turned in her sleep and traded one surface for another. Where ammonoids once fed, diamonds. Where diamonds once grew, vineyards. The logic of the moraine, of the landslip, of the avalanche. Dislodge one pebble, by chance, it becomes restless, rolls down, in its descent leaves space (ah, horror vacui!), another pebble falls on top of it, and there's height. Surfaces. Surfaces upon surfaces. The wisdom of the Earth. And of Lia.

Study Questions

1. What is the understanding Pow has reached?
2. In what sense does Lia have wisdom?
3. Do you think women are primarily concerned with life-giving and life-preserving efforts, and men are primarily concerned with intellectual pursuits? This is Eco's view. Is it fair to men, and to women?

RIDLEY SCOTT (DIRECTOR) AND CALLIE KHOURI (SCREENWRITER), *Thelma and Louise*

Film (1991).

Thelma and Louise are friends living ordinary lives in a small Arkansas town. Louise (Susan Sarandon) is single and works at a family restaurant. Thelma (Geena Davis) is married to a suspicious, jealous husband. They decide to go away for a weekend together; their plans are to go to a cabin that Louise has use of for the weekend. Thelma writes her husband a note and tapes it to the microwave oven.

On the way to the cabin the two women stop at a country-western bar called the Silver Bullet; Thelma hasn't had any fun in ages, and she wants to have a drink and enjoy the music. A local man asks her to dance; Louise finds him pushy and obnoxious, but Thelma thinks he is fun. The fun ends when Thelma goes outside to the parking lot for a bit of fresh air, and the man tries to rape her. His plan doesn't succeed, because Louise comes out of the bar with a pistol aimed straight at him.

As the women back toward their car, the man hurls insults at them. One of his remarks hits too close to home for Louise, and she shoots him. He dies instantly, and the women hit the road.

This is the beginning of the story of Thelma and Louise, and it is the end of their ordinary life. They decide that they can't go home, and they can't go to the police, because there is no evidence of actual rape; Louise can't plead self-defense. As the days go by, they get deeper and deeper into a situation that has no solution. Louise's boyfriend offers his help without asking questions; to Louise his offer is both beautiful and tragic. She realizes he truly loves her, but she can't accept his love because she doesn't want to involve him in her problems. Their money is stolen by a man Thelma spends the night with; she leaves him alone in their motel room, and when she returns the money is gone. To get money, Thelma holds up a convenience store; the robbery is captured on a hidden camera.

A police officer from Thelma and Louise's hometown wants to help them out of their situation; he sees them as victims and knows what happened in the parking lot. But the more crimes they commit, the less they appear as victims to other law officials. Several times Louise and the officer talk on the phone, and it's clear they realize that the other is bound by the circumstances of the situation.

At various times in their journey Thelma and Louise take on men who, as they see it, perpetuate patterns of intimidating women. One sexist trucker finally understands what it is to be harassed when they shoot out the tires on his truck and set it on fire. A police officer whose only offense is that he is about to run a check on them is forced into his trunk and left in the hot desert; Thelma uses her gun to put a few air holes in the lid of the trunk.

On one level Thelma and Louise are leading the life of fugitives; on another they are discovering both freedom and responsibility. They have never felt so much alive as they have during this flight, which, incidentally, takes them from the flat landscape of southern Arkansas, through Oklahoma, and into the tall red rocks of the Southwest, the classic backdrop for outlaw Westerns. They are headed for Mexico, but Louise will not travel through Texas (which is hard to avoid if you're coming from Oklahoma). Louise was once raped in Texas, and that incident is at the core of her decision to run instead of return home and face charges.

In the end Thelma and Louise realize that ultimate freedom is the freedom to make up your mind to act, and to take on the full responsibility of your actions.

Study Questions

1. Are Thelma and Louise heroes or villains?
2. Does it make a difference that this "buddy Western," as it has been called, involves two modern women?
3. What statement, if any, does the film make about modern men and modern women?
4. Is the film fair to modern women? To modern men?

Are We Good or Evil?

The Alter Ego

In Part 1 we encountered the concept of the *alter ego*, the notion of two persons somehow mirroring each other, or one person symbolically represented by two characters, one with a certain set of characteristics (usually good), and the other with the opposite set of traits (usually evil). Traditionally one person represents conscience and reason, and the other temptation and drives, but the theme may vary. Here we will take a closer look at some classic alter ego stories.

ROBERT LOUIS STEVENSON, *The Strange Case of Dr. Jekyll and Mr. Hyde*
Novel (1886).

You may have seen a movie version of this story. The special effects of the movie versions are usually at the cutting edge of whatever decade the movie was produced in, and the transformation of Jekyll into Hyde is generally a grisly process involving lots of contortions. Hyde usually ends up looking like a hairy prehominid. Only one version so far, a British TV movie, portrays an old Dr. Jekyll who is transformed into a dapper, attractive, young Hyde—a mirroring of his innermost dreams. And that is actually not too far from the original story, which we will look at here.

An unpleasant and dangerous person, Edward Hyde is roaming the streets of London. He seems to have a protector in the well-known do-gooder Dr. Jekyll, who has even written out a will leaving everything to Hyde in the case of his own death or disappearance. Hyde gives everyone who sees him the sense that he is deformed, although he is physically normal. Dr. Jekyll's old friend Utterson suspects foul play and imagines that Hyde is somehow blackmailing Dr. Jekyll, but Jekyll reassures him that everything is fine. Incidents surrounding Hyde become more ominous, and an elderly gentleman is bludgeoned to death in the street. Hyde's quarters are searched, but it appears that he has left in a panic, after burning his papers. Utterson, who knows that Jekyll is somehow mixed up with Hyde, goes to Jekyll's house, but the voice that warns him to go away is not Jekyll's, but Hyde's. Utterson imagines that Hyde has murdered Jekyll, and proceeds to break down the door. In the house they find Hyde on the floor, dying from having swallowed poison. There is no sign of Jekyll, but Hyde is dressed in clothes that are much too big for him.

Utterson is now at liberty to read two documents that have been left to him, one from his old friend Dr. Layton, and the other from Jekyll. Layton tells the first part of the astonishing story: He has personally witnessed the transformation, through the help of a chemical potion, of young, small, nasty Mr. Hyde into elderly, portly, kind Dr. Jekyll. The incident disturbed Layton so profoundly that he died shortly after. The next document, from Jekyll himself, tells the whole story, of how he always seemed to be the good and kind person, but has really always had a *dual nature*—one that loved knowledge, science, and a career, and another that sought only pleasure, and cared nothing for the feelings of others. Over the years his "career self" won out, but he has always felt the attraction of his "lower self":

> With every day, and from both sides of my intelligence, the moral and the intellectual, I thus drew steadily nearer to that truth, by whose partial discovery I have been doomed to such a dreadful shipwreck: that man is not one, but truly two. . . . It was on the moral side, and in my own person, that I learned to recognize

FIGURE 20.3 *Dr. Jekyll and Mr. Hyde.* MGM, 1941. Kindly, reliable Dr. Jekyll (Spencer Tracy) has a beast hiding in him, a beast urging him to do what he wants, pursue pleasures, and commit acts of violence. With the help of a drug, the beast emerges and transforms Jekyll into Mr. Hyde, what Freudians would later have called the uncontrolled Id of the doctor. In this promotional still, Mr. Hyde is hovering over Dr. Jekyll like a shadow—in much the same way as in Figure 20.4, an illustration from Hans Christian Andersen's "The Shadow."

the thorough and primitive duality of man; I saw that, of the two natures that contended in the field of my consciousness, even if I could rightly be said to be either, it was only because I was radically both. . . . If each, I told myself, could be housed in separate identities, life would be relieved of all that was unbearable.

So originally Jekyll wanted to suppress his wicked side—but after taking the brew that is to accomplish this, he finds himself instead transformed into a "younger, lighter, happier" person (younger and lighter because his Hyde-side has not had as much time to develop as Jekyll, so he is a smaller image). But in time, Hyde grows and becomes closer in size to Jekyll. In the beginning Jekyll merely enjoys himself, and feels he can get rid of Hyde any time (like all addicts in the beginning stages of addiction). But by and by he realizes that Hyde is not seeking just pleasures, but *monstrous* pleasures, because he is completely evil. He does not have the mediating element of goodness, which Jekyll himself, as a whole person, possesses. This also means that Jekyll is split not into one person of good and one person of evil, but into one of evil and one of the normal mix of good and evil. So the Jekyll persona, which is only partly good, is not forceful enough to restrain Hyde, who is completely evil. And now the drug begins to have erratic effects; one morning he wakes up as Hyde, having gone to bed as Jekyll. The process now happens at random, and he switches from Jekyll to Hyde when he least wants to. During one of these transformations he seeks help from Dr. Lanyon, which is why Lanyon witnesses the disturbing event.

In the end Jekyll hides in his laboratory and writes a letter to Utterson. While he is there he is changed back to Hyde for the last time. As Utterson is trying to break down the door, Hyde swallows the poison that will end his torment, and Utterson finds him dead on the laboratory floor.

Study Questions

1. Is Stevenson right? Do we all have two natures, one good and one evil, fighting for dominance of our souls?
2. Is Jekyll right in classifying the need for "pleasure" as evil? What does this attitude say about Stevenson's own time period?
3. There is a genre of stories that are "Jekyll and Hyde" in reverse, so to speak: An ordinary character has an *alter ego* who is *good* and *strong*. Can you think of some examples?
4. Would a modern version of the story be likely to draw a parallel between being evil and being deformed? Why or why not?
5. How might a Freudian interpret the story of Jekyll and Hyde? (See Chapter 8.)

FIGURE 20.4 Hans Christian Andersen's "The Shadow" (illustration by Vilhelm Pedersen). The shadow side of the scholar is growing and will soon claim its independence. Eventually it will mean the downfall of the scholar. (Courtesy of the Hans Christian Andersen Museum, Odense, Denmark.)

Hans Christian Andersen, "The Shadow"

Short story (1847).

This is one of Andersen's lesser known stories. It is not a fairy tale, although it does contain elements of the supernatural. It is a spooky tale for adults about losing your soul to the dark side of yourself—kind of a Jekyll and Hyde-story, although it was written and published almost forty years before the Stevenson story. Andersen traveled extensively in Italy, and one day he was particularly bothered by the heat and had to stay in his hotel room. Here he thought up the story of the shadow.

A scholar traveling in southern Europe is confined to his hotel room by the heat. He discovers that during the heat of the day his shadow shrinks, but in the cool of the night, by candlelight, his shadow grows long and stretches. He notices that someone in the house opposite his hotel room is playing beautiful music, but he never sees anybody there, except one late evening, when he sees, briefly, a beautiful lady on the balcony, surrounded by a glowing light. Later he notices that his shadow, cast by the light in his room, is now silhouetted on the house across the street, and that the balcony door is open; jokingly he tells his shadow to go in and find out what's going on. The light goes out, and the scholar thinks no more of it until the next day, in the street, when he realizes he no longer has a shadow. "That's too bad," he thinks, "my shadow took me seriously, and now he is gone." But everything grows rapidly in the South, and in another few days a new shadow is growing out from his feet. Soon he leaves for his home in the North and continues his life, but one day there is a knock on his door.

A thin wisp of a man, very elegant, is standing outside. He introduces himself as the scholar's former shadow. Yes, he says, he went inside the house across the street, and there lived Lady Poetry herself. He didn't go all the way in, for the light was too blinding, but he stayed in her antechamber, and that was enough; the exposure to Poetry transformed him, and made a human out of him. But because he had no clothes and still had the appearance of a shadow on a wall, he fled and hid. For a long time he hid in wealthy people's houses and discovered all their secrets; it became easy then to make a fortune. Slowly he has acquired flesh and bones, and now he would like to ask if his old master might like to become *his* shadow, for he can't seem to grow one. The scholar is appalled at the very idea and sends him away, but the damage is done; he now worries so much that friends say he is "just a shadow of himself." The Shadow returns, repeats his offer, and makes the scholar promise that he will never mention that their roles have been reversed. The scholar complies, and off they go.

After a while they arrive in a foreign land, where there lives a princess whose penetrating eyesight allows her to perceive things others can't perceive. She promptly sees that the Shadow can't cast a shadow. But the Shadow tells her she is wrong, for he has a very fancy shadow, a flesh-and-blood one. The princess likes the Shadow and even talks to his "shadow," finding the scholar a shadow of much learning and goodness. If a man's shadow is so wise, the man himself must be a truly remarkable person, she tells herself.

The Shadow calls the scholar to him and informs him that he is about to marry the princess. The scholar will be secure for life, provided that he will promise never to let on that he used to be human and the Shadow used to be a shadow. But the scholar balks, and threatens to reveal everything to the princess. So the Shadow goes to the princess and tells her the sad tale of how his shadow is beginning to think that he is the human and his master is his shadow. The princess suggests a quick removal of this mad shadow, and she and the Shadow have a magnificent wedding. But the scholar has no awareness of it, for he has been quietly put to death.

Study Questions

1. Compare the Shadow to Mr. Hyde: How are they similar, and how do they differ?
2. What is the role of Poetry in this story?
3. Do we all have a Shadow waiting to take over?

(continued)

4. If you read the outline of Borges's "The Circular Ruins" (also in this chapter), you might want to compare "the dreamed man" with the Shadow. Do the stories make the same point, or a different point altogether?

FYODOR DOSTOYEVSKY, *Crime and Punishment*
Novel (1866); film (1935), (1958), (1959).

In a sense *Crime and Punishment* contains *alter ego* elements, but here we witness the struggle the way it ordinarily takes place: inside one person. Dostoyevsky's story is not merely about the struggle between good and evil; it is about evil done in the name of good, by a person who believes himself to be superior to most other people—a person who, by virtue of his personal powers and intellect, can act according to his own set of values. Raskolnikov, a handsome young student who is down on his luck, is thinking about murdering an old, nasty pawnbroker; he knows that it is a terrible thing to do, and yet he feels justified in his plan and mysteriously drawn to seeing it through.

We will look at two scenes that provide clues to Raskolnikov's personality and his struggle with himself. The first illustrates the struggle between good and evil in Raskolnikov himself; the other might serve as a case study of Nietzsche's concept of the Overman, the human who has gone beyond good and evil.

In the first scene Raskolnikov is having a nightmare, the result of psychological pressures relating to his murder plans. In the dream he is a small boy walking with his father past a tavern where a peasant is trying to get a an old, sick horse to pull a heavy load. The cart won't move, even though the little mare does her best, and people come out of the tavern to cheer the peasant on. Soon he is beating the horse, and the others shout suggestions for how best to torture the exhausted animal. The boy is frantic, because he loves the horses and often stops to "talk" with them; his father says that there is nothing they can do and tries to drag him away. The boy breaks loose and runs to the horse to protect her, but he can't help her—the peasant is now beating the horse to death with a crowbar. The crowd gets in on it, and, grabbing whatever they can, they pound on the mare until she dies.

Raskolnikov wakes up in a terror:

Can it be, can it be, that I shall really take an axe, that I shall strike her on the head, split her skull open . . . that I shall tread in the sticky warm blood, break the lock, steal and tremble; hide, all spattered in blood . . . with the axe. . . . Good God, can it be?

FIGURE 20.5 Fyodor Dostoyevsky (1821–1881), Russian novelist. Above all, Dostoyevsky was fascinated by the human psyche and the capacity for evil combined with intellectual rationalization. Such a clever, intellectual person is Raskolnikov, who manages to persuade himself, at least for a while, that he has the right to commit murder.

The second scene takes place much later, after the murder has been committed. Raskolnikov is talking to Razumihin and Porfiry about an article that Raskolnikov wrote some time before the murder. The article suggests that there are some people who are beyond the law because they are extraordinary individuals. Ordinary people have to live by the law, but "extraordinary men have a right to commit any crime and to transgress the law in any way, just because they are extraordinary." Raskolnikov tries to clarify what he meant; he says that these extraordinary people don't *have* to commit crimes against morality, but they have a *right*, within themselves, to break rules in order to carry out their ideas in practice. So if Newton's theories had required him to kill off a certain number of people to prove his point, he would have had the right to do so—for his theories' sake, not just for personal gain. All great men of history, says Raskolnikov, are criminals: They make a new law by transgressing an old one. Everybody else is just ordinary, inferior, conservative, and law-abiding. When a great man embarks on setting an idea in motion, the ordinary people usually won't let him do it—they catch him and hang him. But in the next generation that great man will have become their hero.

How many of these extraordinary persons are there? Very few:

The vast mass of mankind is mere material, and only exists in order by some great effort, by some mysterious process, by means of some crossing of race and stock, to bring into the world perhaps one man out of a thousand with a spark of independence. . . . The man of genius is one of millions, and the great geniuses, the crown of humanity, appear on earth perhaps one in many thousand millions.

Study Questions

1. Is Raskolnikov an evil person? Can anyone have the right to be "beyond good and evil"?

(continued)

2. What might the function of his dream be in the general murder plot?
3. Would Nietzsche have approved of Raskolnikov as an Overman?

Human Nature Is Bad/Human Nature Is Good

WILLIAM GOLDING, *Lord of the Flies*

Novel (1954). Film by Peter Brook (director), 1963, and Harry Hook (director), 1990.

The world is at war. A plane carrying English schoolboys goes down on a small tropical island, and a handful of boys ages six to twelve find themselves stranded, without any adults to take charge. This is the premise of Golding's famous novel, which explores the depths of human nature. I strongly suggest that you read the original story for yourself—it is a classic "what if" story.

At first the boys, like good British subjects, take up a parliamentary existence. They devise rules, hold assemblies, and assign projects; water must be fetched, shelters must be built, and, most important of all, a fire must be maintained at all times to ensure that passing ships will see the smoke. To light the fire they use Piggy's glasses, and during this process he is practically blind. Ralph is the boys' leader, partly because he is a person of confidence, and partly because he has in his possession a great conch shell. Whoever holds the conch has the right to speak, and the conch becomes the symbol of civilization: Where it is, the veneer of orderly life still exists. However, the veneer soon wears thin. Piggy, the overweight boy with glasses and a good mind, becomes Ralph's conscience. He is the person who never lets go of the thought of rescue. But Piggy has a counterpart, Jack, who discovers the lure of island life: There are no adults to set any rules, and life seems to create patterns that are made to be followed. As the weeks go by a change occurs. The boys begin to shed their British clothes and their British identity—all except Piggy and Ralph, who still have hopes of being rescued. They keep insisting that they must keep the fire going; once it went out already, and a passing ship failed to see them.

Jack and a few followers begin seeking out pigs on the island, but their civilized natures make it difficult for them to complete the actual kill. Once they put on masks, which they make themselves, they take on a new identity as hunters. After a quarrel, they split off from Ralph and Piggy and discard the notion of trying to have a civilized society. In an orgy of blood and violence that resembles a ritual rape and murder, they kill their first pig, a sow with suckling babies. They cut off the pig's head and mount it on a sharpened stick as a sacrifice to the beast.

The beast is a shadow that haunts the *littuns*, the smaller boys. There is a rumor of a shape that moves at night, of a thing that comes out of the sea. Piggy tries to convince the others that there is nothing to fear on the island "unless we get frightened of people." But for Jack the beast is a powerful entity that must be placated, an island god. Jack has invented religion.

Simon, a spiritual boy, has two fateful encounters. After the killing of the pig (which he witnessed from a hiding place) he goes to see the mounted pig's head, and has a vision. From the pig's head the Lord of the Flies speaks to him:

> The half-shut eyes were dim with the infinite cynicism of adult life. They assured Simon that everything was a bad business. . . . "There isn't anyone to help you. Only me. And I'm the beast. . . . Fancy thinking the beast was something you could hunt and kill!" said the head. For a moment or two the forest and all the other dimly appreciated places echoed with the parody of laughter, "You knew, didn't you? I'm part of you? Close, close, close! I'm the reason why it's no go? Why things are the way they are?"

When some of the boys encounter a strange thing on the island they are convinced that the beast exists. (The reader knows that the thing is just a dead pilot, all tangled up in his parachute, which moves and bulges with the wind.) Shortly after, Simon finds the beast and realizes what it is—the pilot in his parachute. He frees the dead man from the tangles and runs to tell the others that there is no beast. He bursts in on a pig-killing dance that Jack has initiated. In the hunters' frenzy Simon is not even recognized, but is taken to be the beast himself, and the hunters stab him to death.

This is the end of innocence for everybody. For Ralph and Piggy there is only one solution. They go into denial, refusing to face the fact that they were present at the dance, too. For Jack and the others there is no return to reason: They reject the conch, Ralph, Piggy, and the memories of another life. However, realizing that they need to build a fire of their own, they raid the camp and steal Piggy's glasses. The last glimpse of civilization disappears along with Piggy's own vision. Ralph and Piggy, the only ones left who care about rescue, approach Jack to reason with him to get Piggy's glasses back "not as a favor. I don't ask you to be a sport, I'll say, not because you're strong, but because what's right's right." The others have now all donned war paint, but not Ralph and Piggy, because "we aren't savages." Piggy pleads with them all, one last time, to recognize the value of civilization: "Which is better—to have rules and agree, or to hunt and kill? . . . Which is better, law and rescue, or hunting and breaking things up?" The plea is futile: The boys roll a big rock toward half-blind Piggy, who is thrown off the cliff to his death in the rocky surf below. Now the hunt is on for Ralph, who must run and hide like a pig. In order to smoke him out, the boys set fire to the thicket, but this act leads to Ralph's rescue. The smoke is seen by a British warship, and an officer intercepts the hunt moments before Ralph would have been killed:

"Fun and games," said the officer. [But when he realizes that this was no game, he scolds them]: "I should have thought that a pack of British boys—you're all British, aren't you?—would have been able to put up a better show than that. . . ." And in the middle of them, with filthy body, matted hair, and an unwiped nose, Ralph wept for the end of innocence, the darkness of man's heart, and the fall through the air of the true, wise friend called Piggy. The officer, surrounded by these noises, was moved and a little embarrassed. He turned away to give them time to pull themselves together; and waited, allowing his eyes to rest on the trim cruiser in the distance.

Study Questions

1. The title *The Lord of The Flies* is a translation of the Hebrew *Ba'alzevuv* (Greek: *Beelzebub*). What kind of a "devil" or beast is Golding referring to?
2. Golding reportedly intended this to be more than a story about boys on an island. What is his theory of human nature? Do you agree?
3. What is the symbolic significance of the boys being rescued by a cruiser?

Kevin Costner (director) and Michael Blake (screenwriter), *Dances with Wolves*

Film (1990), from the novel by Michael Blake.

Benjamin Franklin once remarked that white people who had been rescued from long-term captivity with American Indians most often grabbed the first chance to escape back to the woods and their former captors, no matter how well they were being treated by white society. Hollywood has explored this idea in films such as *Duel at Diablo*, *Two Rode Together*, and *A Man Called Horse*. In the film credited with reviving the Western genre in the nineties, *Dances with Wolves*, we get not only a story about a white captive who doesn't want to go back to white society, but also a full-scale Rousseau-style vision of human nature: Civilization (the white soldiers) represents all that is corrupt, crude, and evil, and the Native American represents all the best in human nature—caution toward the unknown, but, eventually, warmth and acceptance.

The film is long, and part of the dialogue is in the Lakota language (subtitles are provided). Critics didn't have much hope for the success of this film, but in spite of everything, *Dances with Wolves* became a tremendous success and was the recipient of several Academy Awards. A brief outline will have to suffice. John Dunbar, hero of the Civil War, is posted to a remote cavalry fort on the plains—a post most other soldiers would have considered sheer punishment. On arrival he realizes that he is the only soldier present—everyone else is gone. He begins to repair the fort and observe his surroundings. His nearest neighbors—a wolf and the local Lakota Sioux tribe—appear dangerous at first, but after a while Dunbar is able to establish friendly relations with both the wolf and the Indians. A captive white woman called Stands With A Fist (now a full member of the Lakota society) becomes his friend and language teacher, and once her mourning period for her dead Lakota husband is over, she becomes Dunbar's wife, for Dunbar has settled in with the Indians. He discovers much about their customs and values, and when he finds himself defending the village against their archenemy, the Pawnee Indians, he realizes that this is the first meaningful battle he has ever participated in: He is fighting for his home and his loved ones, and not for other people's principles.

As the tribe prepares to leave for their winter grounds, Dunbar, now called Dances with Wolves, feels he must go back to the fort to retrieve his diary, which, if found, would give out the location of the Indians. This proves to be a disastrous decision. As Dunbar approaches the fort, he sees that a cavalry troop is stationed there; because he is dressed in Indian gear, they mistake him for a hostile presence, shoot his horse out from under him, and capture him. When they discover his identity, they accuse him of treason, beat him up, and prepare to take him to the headquarters at Fort Hays to be tried and possibly hanged.

But Dunbar never reaches Fort Hays. As the troop prepares to ford a river on the way to the fort, we see that Dunbar's Indian friends have followed him and are preparing to rescue him.

Is Dunbar rescued? What happens to him? What happens to his Indian friends? And Stands With A Fist? I am not going to tell you. I suggest you rent the movie and see for yourself.

Study Questions

1. Dunbar and Stands With A Fist are, by and large, the only sympathetic white people in the film. Why do you think the white race is portrayed that way? Is it a reasonable portrayal?
2. What makes this film a statement in the tradition of Rousseau?
3. Is Dunbar a traitor or not?

The Eternal Return of the Same

The following stories explore exercising one's freedom in the midst of terrible and difficult situations, with the realization that all actions just may be endless repetition of the same situation. If that is the case, do we have any freedom of the will at all?

ALBERT CAMUS, *The Myth of Sisyphus*

Retelling of a traditional Greek myth (1955).

Greek mythology tells the story of Sisyphus, who, in the realm of Hades, is condemned to roll a big rock up a hill. Every time Sisyphus gets to the top, the rock rolls back downhill, and he has to start all over again. Why was Sisyphus condemned to struggle with the rock forever? And who was he? The story tells us that he was a very clever man who, through guile and theft, was able to get away with just about anything, from seducing princesses to cheating Death and putting him in chains. Once, Sisyphus had been sent to Hades (ruler of the Netherworld) by the gods, but he cheated his way out of being dead by claiming that proper death rites had not been performed over him, so he would have to go back to the living to check up on the situation. Once he was back on earth, he evaded Death until he was a very old man. When he finally died of natural causes, Hades put him in charge of the rock rolling, apparently as an occupational device to keep him from disrupting things further in the Netherworld. According to other Greek myths it was customary for offenders in the Netherworld to be condemned to repeat a certain action over and over again—a predicament that people with tendencies toward compulsory actions (such as washing hands incessantly) may be able to sympathize with. By the way, you might think that with Sisyphus's intelligence he could have figured a way to stop the rock from rolling, but that is not the way things work in the Netherworld.

Albert Camus, the existentialist writer of both fiction and nonfiction, uses this original myth to illustrate the absurdity of life. For Camus there comes a day in each person's life when the absurdity of it all becomes apparent—the daily routine, the nonsense that must be put up with—one day the person asks, Why? and from that moment on there are only two possibilities, suicide or recovery. If you recover it is because you have accepted your fate fully, even its absurdity. Indeed, you may even strive to keep the absurdity alive by challenging it at every moment. Suicide is merely giving in to the absurd. So why is Sisyphus condemned to roll the rock? Because he loved life too much and defied the gods in the process. In other words, he was too passionate about life, and the worst thing the gods could do to him was to assign him a meaningless task. So now he has to toil for eternity, and he has all the time in the world to think about how meaningless it all is every time he walks downhill. But, to Camus, if Sisyphus approaches this in the right way he need not be miserable—in fact, he can be happy, because he has the chance to triumph in the face of absurdity. He can choose to love his fate, and if he does, he will feel in control: He will roll that rock because that is what he wants to do.

Study Questions

1. How can Sisyphus possibly display freedom of the will in his eternal, predetermined task?

2. Is there a difference between the original Greek myth and Camus's version?

3. What might Nietzsche say to this terrible vision of an event repeating itself over and over again? (You may want to read the next narrative and then return to this one for further discussion.)

4. Can we use the Camus version of the Sisyphus myth to tell the Marxist that workers should love their boring, alienating, assembly-line work? Why or why not?

FRIEDRICH NIETZSCHE, *Thus Spoke Zarathustra*
Novel (1892).

In his film *Hannah and Her Sisters* Woody Allen ponders Nietzsche's philosophy of the eternal recurrence: "Nietzsche says we'll live this life over and over again in exactly the same way—great. That means I'll have to sit through the Ice Capades again; it's not worth it."

Here we'll see how Nietzsche himself puts it in his philosophical novel *Thus Spoke Zarathustra*, about a prophet who seeks the truth about humans and brings the word of their destiny to them:

"Behold this gateway, dwarf!" I continued. "It has two faces. Two paths meet here; no one has yet followed either to its end. This long lane stretches back for an eternity. And the long lane out there, that is another eternity. They contradict each other, these paths. . . . The name of the gateway is inscribed above: 'Moment'. . . . From this gateway, Moment, a long, eternal lane leads *backward*: behind us lies an eternity. Must not whatever *can* walk have walked on this lane before? Must not whatever *can* happen have happened, have been done, have passed by before? And if everything has been there before—what do you think, dwarf, of this moment? Must not this gateway too have been there before? And are not all things knotted together so firmly that this moment draws after it *all* that is to come? There-fore—itself too? For whatever *can* walk—in this long lane out *there* too, it *must* walk once more.

"And this slow spider, which crawls in the moonlight, and this moonlight itself, and I and you in the gateway, whispering together, whispering of eternal things—must not all of us have been there before? And return and walk in that other lane, out there, before us, in this long dreadful lane—must we not eternally return?"

. . . A young shepherd I saw, writhing, gagging, in spasms, his face distorted, and a heavy black snake hung out of his mouth. Had I ever seen so much nausea and pale dread on one face? He seemed to have been asleep when the snake crawled into his throat, and there bit itself fast. My hand tore at the snake and tore it in vain; it did not tear the snake out of his throat. Then it cried out of me: "Bite! Bite its head off! Bite!" Thus it cried out of me—my dread, my hatred, my nausea, my pity, all that is good and wicked in me cried out with a single cry. . . . Guess me this riddle that I saw then, interpret me the vision of the loneliest. For it was a vision and a foreseeing. *What* did I see then in a parable? And *who* is it who must yet come one day? *Who* is the shepherd into whose throat the snake crawled thus? *Who* is the man into whose throat all that is heaviest and blackest will crawl thus?

The shepherd, however, bit as my cry counseled him: he bit with a good bite. Far away he spewed the head of the snake—and he jumped up. No longer shepherd, no longer human—one changed, radiant, *laughing*! . . .

. . . Courage, however, is the best slayer—courage which attacks: which slays even death itself, for it says, "Was *that* life? Well then! Once more!"

Study Questions

1. Imagine that Nietzsche is right: Everything that has happened will happen again, and again, and again. Could this be true? And how would you feel about it if it were true?
2. One interpretation is that Nietzsche didn't actually think everything recurred eternally, but that he meant we ought to use the theory as a *test* of how much we love life. If we love it so much that we would say, "Well, then! Once more!" then we have conquered absurdity. Could you pass this test?
3. Who is the shepherd into whose throat everything terrible has crawled? And what does it mean that he bites its head off and is no longer human, but radiant? (Here's a hint: Some scholars think that it is Nietzsche himself, and that the evil he bites into is the terror of the eternal recurrence. Do you think this is what Nietzsche intended, or could he have had something else in mind?)

KEN GRIMWOOD, *Replay*

Novel (1987).

Jeff Winston is on the phone with his wife Linda when he has a heart attack. He is in his early forties, and their marriage isn't going too well. They have not been able to have children, and lately communication between them has not been too good. He has let a lot of things slide, always thinking that there would be time to correct them. And now he is dying.

The next thing Jeff knows he is lying in a bed in a familiar room. But it isn't his bedroom at home—it is his bedroom from college. Early sixties music is playing, and his old roommate Martin (who died in 1981) is trying to get him to respond. He is back in time, reliving his life as a college student, but he does not understand why. He discovers that he has the memories and the mind of his adult self, and as he moves through the events he has already lived through—such as going out with girlfriends—he discovers that he is not bound to repeat his previous actions; he has free will. Because he remembers who won the Kentucky Derby in 1963, he bets on the race—and wins big. This time around he will have money! He starts living the wild life, increases his fortune by betting on the World Series, and begins to invest in IBM, Xerox, Boeing, Polaroid. He realizes there may be something else he can do, too: prevent the murder of John F. Kennedy. He sends threatening letters to the White House in Oswald's name, and Oswald is arrested before the fateful date of November 22. But on November 22, President Kennedy is murdered by someone else.

On the day Jeff is due to meet Linda for the first time, he is very excited. He sees her from a distance and can't wait to repeat their romance. But this time around Linda doesn't like him—he is too cocky and self-assured. So he marries someone else, and they have a little girl, who becomes everything to Jeff. He is rich, he has a daughter he loves, and things are working out. He is even in fine health. But on the date that he died the first time around, he has a heart attack—and dies again. And wakes up, back in 1963.

This time around he realizes what he has lost, and is very cautious. He bets on the horses again and wins, and promptly marries a different girl, his college sweetheart. She doesn't understand why he doesn't want to father children, but he is determined never again to bring another child into existence and then see every trace of her existence snuffed out with his own death—for the past to which he keeps returning is his *original* past; the variations he experienced the last time around are wiped out when he comes back.

He and his wife adopt two children, and they lead a rich life. On the date of his previous two deaths he goes to the hospital and gets himself hooked up to a life-support system, just as a precaution—but it doesn't help. He dies just as he did the other two times.

Now life follows upon life. In one life he experiments with drugs and the European jet set; in another he makes Linda like him, and marries her again. He notices that every time he comes back, he is a little further along in his original life, and he anticipates that the next lives are going to be progressively shorter. In one life he meets another time traveller, Pamela, who is undergoing the same experience, and they arrange to meet in all future lives. In one life they decide to go public, and their disclosure leads to a world war. In another they try to contact others with the same kind of experience; they find most of them locked away in asylums. Meanwhile their new lives are getting ever shorter. It is getting harder for them to "link up," because Jeff "wakes up" into his previous life years before Pamela does, and besides, the "wake-up time" keeps approaching the dates of their deaths. In the end Pamela dies for good: Her wake-up date has finally coincided with the date of her death. Soon, the same happens to Jeff: He dies again and again in rapid succession, still without knowing why all this has happened to him.

And then he wakes up—on the phone with Linda. The cycle has been broken, there are no more rebirths. Was it all a dream? No, for on another line is Pamela, who has experienced the same revival. Jeff realizes that his multiple lives had a purpose: to make him understand the importance of making conscientious choices and the importance of time itself, for nothing is predetermined for the rest of his life, and everything he does will have consequences. Jeff approaches the rest of his life as a responsible person. He and Pamela will link up again, but she has responsibilities from her original life, too, and Jeff has a lot of talking to do with Linda.

Study Questions

1. If you knew that you would be living your life over and over again, how would you feel about it? (You might want to discuss Nietzsche here, too).
2. In what sense does Jeff have free will, when he is experiencing the eternal return of his previous life? And in what sense does he have free will after the cycles are over?
3. Is the author right that one would learn the lesson of responsibility from going through Jeff's and Pamela's experience? Why or why not?
4. Is Jeff a Sisyphus who has to learn to love his fate? Why or why not?

Some Visions of the Soul and the State

In this final section of narrative outlines we will look at stories that explore the depths of the soul and the concept of the ideal state. The Greek tragedy of *King Oedipus* provides the original literary background for the Freudian theory of the Oedipus complex, and Alfred Hitchcock's film *Marnie* shows how Freudian theory can be used to unravel a plot centering around a character with deep personal problems. Kurt Vonnegut's short story "Harrison Bergeron" provides a humorous and disturbing image of a future where, politically and otherwise, there are no differences between people; John Steinbeck's novel is the inspiration for the film *The Grapes of Wrath*, which provides a powerful voice for the working class population; and Ayn Rand's novel *Atlas Shrugged* speaks in defense of classical capitalism, aiming a blow at the ideals of communistic economy.

SOPHOCLES, *Oedipus Rex*

Tragedy (fifth century B.C.E.*).*

There is a plague upon the city of Thebes; a murder has occurred which has gone un-avenged. The priest of Zeus implores the King, Oedipus, to instigate a cleansing that will free the land of its curse. The former king, Laius, was killed on a visit to Delphi by persons unknown. Oedipus's brother-in-law, Creon, brings the blind soothsayer Teiresias to tell who the murderers are, so that Laius can be avenged. Teiresias, knowing that he is about to destroy Oedipus's life and peace of mind by revealing the truth, laments that it is "dreadful to have wisdom when it profits not the wise." The terrible truth is spoken: Oedipus has been, for the past many years, living "in unguessed shame with nearest kin." The murderer of Laius is right here; he is both brother and father to his own children, son and husband to the woman who gave birth to him, and killer of his own father.

Oedipus is enraged at the ravings of the blind man and asks Creon, his brother-in-law, why Teiresias hasn't come forward before if he suspected that Oedipus killed Laius. Oedipus blames Creon for causing trouble. Creon says he is willing to lay his life on the line that he is not involved in any conspiracy; he asks Oedipus to consult the Oracle in Delphi himself to hear the truth. Oedipus threatens to kill him, but Queen Jocaste, Creon's sister, (and Laius's former wife) intervenes and suggests that Oedipus investigate the story himself. She remembers that she and Laius once were told by the oracle that their son would kill him one day. The boy, who was only three days old, had his ankles pinned together and was left on a mountainside for the wild animals to dispose of; all this was to ensure that Laius never would be killed by his son. And because Laius's death came when he was murdered by robbers at a crossroads in the land of Phocis, the prophecy was obviously incorrect.

But Oedipus is not relieved, for he realizes that he himself once killed a man at a crossroads in Phocis, a man of Laius's description.

How did Oedipus come to be in Phocis? He was raised as the son of the king and queen of Corinth. At a banquet, though, a drunk claimed that Oedipus was not the true son of his parents. Upset, the young man went to Delphi, without telling his parents, to find out the truth of his parentage. In Delphi he was told something else, something horrible—that he was fated to sleep with his mother, and kill his father. In order to avoid this dreadful fate he decided not to go home to Corinth, and he instead traveled through Phocis. At a certain crossroad a man shoved him rudely aside and hit him on the head, so Oedipus killed him. Now Oedipus realizes that this must have been King Laius. The murderer who should be banished to rid the town of the plague is himself.

But this is only the beginning of Oedipus's undoing, for what about the prophecies? The first one, that Laius would die by the hand of his son, obviously can not be true, says Jocaste, because the boy was left to die. And when they get a message that Oedipus's father, King Polybus, is dead of sickness and old age, it looks as if the prophecy that Oedipus was destined to kill his father was not true, either. Jocaste assures Oedipus that he needn't fear the prophecy of marrying his mother—but Oedipus is still frightened that it may come to pass.

The messenger from Corinth has yet another story to tell: Oedipus need not be afraid of his mother, the queen of Corinth, for she is no relation to him. The messenger himself brought Oedipus to the court when he was a baby and gave him as a gift to the king and queen. Oedipus is a foundling, discovered on a mountainside by a shepherd. He was in poor condition, with his ankles pinned together; this caused his lifelong problems with his feet. (Oedipus means sore feet.) A shepherd gave the baby boy to the messenger, who gave him to the king and queen. Oedipus wants to know who the shepherd was, but Jocaste is getting strangely restless and pleads with him to forget the whole thing; when Oedipus persists, Jocaste runs off in terror.

The herdsman is brought forth, and Oedipus realizes the terrible truth. The boy picked off the mountainside was the son of Laius and Jocaste. Of him it was prophesied that he would marry his mother and kill his father. Jocaste hangs herself, and Oedipus blinds himself with her brooch, not wanting to see the horror he has wrought, or see his children, who also are his own siblings. He cannot bear to look his parents in the eye when he meets them in the land of the dead. Oedipus leaves Thebes forever to live the rest of his life in the mountains with his daughters Antigone and Ismene, and the chorus concludes:

> Therefore, while our eyes wait to see the destined final day, we must call no one happy who is of mortal race, until he hath crossed life's border, free from pain.

Study Questions

1. Does Oedipus have an Oedipus complex?
2. What do you think is the lesson Sophocles intended his audience to learn from this legend?

ALFRED HITCHCOCK (DIRECTOR), JAY PRESSON ALLEN (SCREENWRITER), *Marnie*

Film (1964).

Many contemporary films and novels implicitly make use of Freudian theory in order to help the viewer (or reader) understand the problems of the characters. For example, a woman dreams, and we understand that her dream reveals something significant that she doesn't want to face while awake. Or a man has amnesia but suffers anxiety when he starts to make certain associations, and we understand that there is something he doesn't *want* to remember. Few films, though, actually use the therapy situation as part of the plot. Hitchcock's *Marnie* is one that does. In addition, it presents a view of Freudian theory other than the Oedipal theory, one that is not gender-specific: Both women and men can suffer the effects of a traumatic situation and may need therapy to come to terms with their past.

Marnie is only one of the names (the real one, as it happens) of a young woman (played by Tippi Hedren) who specializes in fraud and theft. Immaculately dressed and giving the impression of a decent and reliable person, she applies for secretarial positions, and after an initial period of establishing her reliability, she cleans out the safe and disappears.

Fairly early in the film we learn where she disappears to in between jobs: a sordid back alley in Baltimore by the harbor where her mother lives. She buys her mother lavish gifts but feels that her mother doesn't truly love her or appreciate her. The elderly woman seems more attached to a neighbor's little daughter, and Marnie suffers classical pangs of sibling rivalry.

A new job for Marnie means another city, another name, and another hair color, but even so, she is recognized by her new boss (Sean Connery), who has had business dealings with a company where she used to work. Without revealing that he suspects she is not who she claims to be, he asks her for dates and introduces her to his family. After a while he has enough information to send her to jail, but because he is now in love with her, he takes another tack: He proposes to her, and makes it clear that if she doesn't accept she will be turned over to the police. Marnie realizes she has no alternative, and accepts, although she actually has no intention of living with him; Marnie suffers from a severe case of sexual anxiety. She believes (as she has heard her mother say) that sex is filthy, and she abhors the touch of a man—any man.

Her new husband realizes that there is a connection between her drive to change identities and commit burglaries, and her psychotic fear of sex, and he sets out to find the solution to the riddle. His interest is heightened by the fact that Marnie is now (thanks to his nosy sister-in-law, who has a crush on him) on the verge of being exposed by a former employer. Through detective work, he follows a trail that leads back to Marnie's mother's place in Baltimore. As he and a reluctant Marnie confront her mother with an old story of death and violence, it becomes clear why Marnie has become a person of such warped character. Through the classical therapeutic technique of reliving the original traumatic situation (which I will not reveal to you), Marnie and her husband finally realize the reason behind all her problems, and Marnie realizes that she has had her mother's love all along.

Study Questions

1. Is Marnie a thief (one who steals deliberately) or a kleptomaniac (one who can't help stealing because of a psychological problem)? Does it make any difference?
2. Do you think it is always the case that people who suffer from a psychological problem like Marnie's can be cured if they are forced to relieve the original situation?
3. Do you think Marnie's husband's primary reason for helping her is that he would like to cure her of her fear of sex? If no, why not? If yes, is that a good or bad reason? Why?

KURT VONNEGUT, JR., "Harrison Bergeron," from the book *Welcome to the Monkey House*

Short story (1970).

It is the year 2081, and everybody is finally equal—not just in the eyes of the law, but in every way. Nobody is stronger or smarter or prettier than anybody else, because to allow some to be stronger or smarter or prettier is to discriminate against those who aren't. If you are strong, or smart, or pretty, you have to assume handicaps designed by the Handicapper General. A strong and athletic person has to carry bags of birdshot and sashweights so that he or she won't make a weaker and less athletic person feel bad. A beautiful person has to wear a mask. A smart person must wear a mental handicap radio that is tuned into a government transmitter, and that emits bursts of noise that disrupt any intelligent thought (because otherwise those who are less intelligent and who can think only for a few minutes at a time will feel left out).

George and Hazel Bergeron are trying to watch television. They are watching a program of ballet, and the ballerinas, being both beautiful and athletic, are all masked and weighted down, so the ballet isn't exactly graceful. (A graceful ballet with beautiful ballerinas would make all the ungraceful and unhandsome people feel inferior.) George is having trouble following the program, for he is very intelligent, and his handicap radio buzzes all the time, so he can't think a clear thought. He can see that some of the ballerinas also have such radios, for they get distracted and fall down periodically. His wife Hazel has an average mind and doesn't need the radio—she is quietly jealous of George, who hears all the interesting government sounds that she doesn't get to hear.

Hazel tells George that she thinks he looks so tired, and he should lie down and take the handicap bag off (for George is big and strong, too, and carries a big bag of birdshot). Hazel says she won't mind being unequal for a while. But George is afraid to follow her advice, because it could cost him two years in jail and a fine for every birdshot he removes. It just isn't worth it. And the minute people start cheating on society, where will we all be? Hazel doesn't quite understand the question, but George has already forgotten he asked it, for he has been buzzed again.

The rest of Vonnegut's story centers on George and Hazel's son, Harrison, who is extremely strong, and also big, smart, and handsome. He has been incarcerated for this reason: He is too dangerous to have running loose. But Harrison escapes, and for a brief moment the nation witnesses the glory of true human talent (for he is shown on live television). But soon things are back to the good old ways of imposed equality, and George and Hazel have forgotten what the whole incident was about.

Study Questions

1. Is being *equal* the same as being *identical*?

2. Is this story about political equality? And how does it compare with the concept that "all men are created equal"?

3. Sometimes it is assumed that in the socialistic state everyone will be equal in the sense of identical. Is that a fair assessment of Marx's ideal state?

4. Is this story insensitive to the physically and mentally disabled?

JOHN FORD (DIRECTOR) AND NUNALLY JOHNSON (SCREENWRITER), *The Grapes of Wrath*

Film (1940), from the novel by John Steinbeck.

When a famous book has been made into a film, scholars of literature usually choose to refer to the story line of the original novel rather than to the film, unless the film has become more famous than the book. In the case of *The Grapes of Wrath* it is probably a toss-up as to which version has become more popular, and in terms of artistic quality most people who enjoy movies as well as books would say that they are different, but equally great, masterpieces. I have chosen to refer to the film rather than to the novel because it is a fascinating example of a director creating one of the most eloquent works about socialism without being himself a socialist, or (probably) even suspecting that he was about to leave a socialistic legacy to moviegoers. Ford, who was a master at depicting human relationships and human emotions on screen, but who never bothered to intellectualize about what he was doing, has succeeded in telling a story of human hardship which has universal appeal.

It is the great depression of the thirties. The Joads have been living on their land as sharecroppers in the Oklahoma "dustbowl" for more than fifty years. But now the bank is kicking them off the land, and everybody else, too. Tom Joad comes home from prison (he has been paroled) just in time to help his family load up the Ford and head for California; they have heard there is work to be had there picking fruit. And so they join the migration of other "Okies" who are fleeing the dustbowl: Tom's pa and ma, his grandma and grandpa, his pregnant sister and her husband, his grown brother, his uncle, and his little brother and sister. Keeping them all company is the ex-preacher Casy; he used to preach up a storm, but he has lost the call and doesn't know what to tell people any more, so he figures that he may as well come along.

As they approach California they have the distinct feeling that they aren't welcome anywhere. People mistake them for beggars, and the Joads' family pride is deeply wounded. At one checkpoint a guard remarks to the other, "Okies ain't human, no human could stand living the way they do." At a truck stop Pa Joad asks if he can buy a

FIGURE 20.6 *The Grapes of Wrath* (1940). Tom Joad (Henry Fonda) learns a lesson about civil injustice and the strength of working people fighting together on the long journey toward recapturing the dignity and self-reliance of the family. Here the Joads are experiencing trouble during a strike on a California farm.

loaf of bread for ten cents for Grandma, for she can't chew, and they can't afford a sandwich. The waitress has no understanding for their plight, but the truck stop owner tells her to give them the bread for ten cents. When Pa Joad asks about the price of candy sticks for the two kids, she looks at the children and suddenly understands what it is all about—she gives him two for a penny. After he leaves, two truck drivers remind her that the candy sticks are five cents apiece, and when she wants to give them their change, they generously refuse to accept it.

En route to California both Grandma and Grandpa die and are buried by the wayside. The rest of the family arrive in California only to learn that the fruit they expected to pick already has been picked, and the cotton is not ready yet. Besides, thousands of fliers were printed, telling how workers were needed, but in fact only a few hundred jobs are available. The employers wanted to create competition for the jobs so that wages could be kept low. All of the employers seem crooked; they pay less than what they initially promised. The contractors are dishonest, and anyone who complains is called a Red and an agitator. Tom doesn't know what a Red is, or an agitator, but he soon finds out. A guard fires at a man who complains about lowered wages; the shot hits a woman instead. Tom and Casy attack the guard. Casy decides to to "take the rap" so that Tom can get away; Tom can't risk violating his parole.

The Joads find work on a farm surprisingly soon. Outside the fence around the property are a lot of what looks like other Okies; police officers seem to be keeping them at bay. But the Joads' pay is good, and they settle into a shack and go to work immediately, picking peaches. When Tom tries to find out about the trouble, he is stopped by a guard. Later he manages to sneak out of the compound and finds, to his surprise, Casy, who is now one of the workers being kept off the farm. Tom learns the whole story: The workers are striking because the owners won't pay them what they promised, but only half the amount. Tom and his family are getting the higher amount, but, says Casy, this is a trick; once the strikers leave, the Joads' wages will be reduced. One of Casy's friends tries to tell Tom that they can win if they would just unite, but Tom sees the situation only from his own perspective: For once, his family has meat for dinner, and why should he give that up for some strangers? Casy, however, has found a new call; he tries to tell Tom that something new is happening—he doesn't quite know what it is yet, but he is learning. Their conversation is cut short when they hear sounds of men approaching. Soon there is a raid on the strikers' camp. Casy gets killed, and Tom strikes out at Casy's killer, killing him.

Now Tom is in trouble, because he got hit in the face, and he can be identified. In the night he and his family sneak out, with Tom hiding in the car.

They finally arrive at a place where they are treated like human beings—a governmental camp for migrant workers. There is no camp police, and the camp elects its own officers. There is a ladies' committee setting up childcare. For a while things are good. But soon the police show up looking for Tom, and he has to leave his family, perhaps for the last time. He and his mother have their last talk at night, before he leaves, and Tom tries to tell her how he feels now. People are living like pigs, he says, while rich men let good land lie fallow, and farmers are starving. But if we all got together. . . . Tom still doesn't quite know what to do, but since he is a fugitive anyway, he will try to find out.

Ma Joad, the strength of the family, is nervous about the family splitting up. She asks Tom how she ever will know what has happened to him. And Tom says that maybe Casy was right: "A fellow ain't got a soul of his own, just a little piece of a big soul, the soul that belongs to everybody"; he tells Ma that she can think of him as being everywhere—"whenever there's a fight so hungry people can eat, I'll be there; whenever a cop is beating up a guy, I'll be there . . . when people are eating the stuff they raised and living in the houses they built I'll be there, too."

Tom leaves, but the story isn't over; in fact, it goes on, and on. Ma and Pa and the remaining children (the sister's husband has run away in the meantime) head for the cotton fields. Pa Joad feels lost and abandoned, but Ma Joad is in much better spirits: "Rich fellers come up, and they die, and their kids are no good and they die out, but we keep a-coming. We're the people that live—they can't wipe us out, they can't lick us, we'll go on forever, Pa, 'cause we're the People. . . ."

Study Questions

1. What is the meaning of the episode in the truck stop?
2. What might it mean that the only decent place they find is a government-run place?
3. Why might this be taken to be a socialistic story? Is it a reasonable assessment?

AYN RAND, *Atlas Shrugged*

Novel (1957).

Embedded in her mammoth novel *Atlas Shrugged* is Ayn Rand's antisocialist narrative about the factory. (We looked at the novel once before in the discussion of ethical egoism.)

The factory used to be a regular automobile company that made a profit, but then the new owners announced to the workers that changes would be made, for the good of everybody. Everybody would now be working according to ability, and would receive payment according to need. The workers weren't really told how it was going to work out, but each thought that the other knew. It sounded like a noble idea, but the next four years turned out to be hell. One of the surviving workers tells the story, which goes like this:

If you are supposed to work according to ability, then you do so, in the beginning, for the ideal is noble, and you are able to work a lot. But then you begin to think about what you are working for—because you don't get anything out of it yourself: you are working for your neighbor's dinner, his wife's operation, his mother's wheelchair, his child's measles, because those are their needs. Of course you get your needs taken care of, too, but if your needs are simple, then you just get the basics: food, shelter, clothing. And if you are an honest man or woman, then you don't create or invent new needs that the others must pay for, but not everybody is like you: soon cousins begin to arrive from the country who must be taken care of, a child needs braces, and some of the families just keep having babies so they have to get more and more of what you make with your ability. So you can't apply for a car until everyone else has one, too. You have to prove you need a new pair of shoes, because you have no right to your own earnings, and so you claim that you need things you don't really need just to get a little extra, because so many are mooching off of you. So what happens? Instead of turning into noble creatures, we all turned into beggars and moochers.

There was one young man who was really bright, and he worked out an improvement for the work system so they would all save money. He was put on extra duty and worked to the bone, because his ability was so great. Next year he made sure he didn't come up with any new ideas. The capitalist system was supposed to show the evil side of human nature, but nothing could be more wicked than all the workers slowing down, trying *not* to work according to their ability, because then they would just be worked all the harder. It destroys your spirit if you have to try to fake unfitness.

And people began to hate those who had extra needs, even if they couldn't help it. If people had more children, they were frozen out. People would pick quarrels with others just to get them thrown out of the community, and spy on each other to see if they could come up with antisocial offenses. An old lady broke her hip on the cellar stairs, and everybody knew how expensive that would be for the community. She was found dead the day she was supposed to leave for the hospital, and the cause of death was never established. So what was supposed to bring out the best in everybody, actually brought out the worst: "to each according to need, and from each according to ability" will, in the end, reduce a human being to a liar, a moocher, a resentful beggar.

Study Questions

1. To your knowledge, is this a fair assessment of a communistic society? Why or why not?
2. What would Marx respond? Remember he thinks that in the world of socialism human nature itself will be different.

A Final Word About Stories and Morals

The Russian author Ilya Ehrenburg tells of a terrible time during World War II:

> During the war I visited Leningrad; it was during the occupation, and people had no water, power, or heat; the thermometer showed 30 Celsius below, the dead lay around in the houses, nobody had the strength to bury them.
>
> As the Germans retreated I returned. This time I was visited by a young woman who used to study music; now she was working in the factories, repairing cannons.
>
> "I've heard you're working on a book about the war," she said; "perhaps this can be of use to you." She handed me her diary from the occupation. I read:

March 15. Mascha dead. Minus 25 degrees Celsius in the room. 125 grams of bread.

March 16. Petrof dead. Minus 29 degrees. 120 grams of bread.

March 18. Minus 25 degrees. Went through *Anna Karenina* at night.

March 20. All night *Madame Bovary*.

March 21. All night *Quietly Flows the River Don*.

When she returned to pick up her diary as arranged, I asked, "How could you read at night with the power out?" She answered, "I didn't read. I just went over the books I could remember in my mind."

They often ask *why* we won the war. Some say it was because our courage is so enormous. Others: It was because we are a people of wild Tartars. Others: It was because the Americans sent us grenades and canned goods. I think it was because we've given our young people good books to read!

Throughout this book we have seen examples of stories being the bearers of moral values. I had three things in mind when I selected the story outlines and excerpts in this book. First, I wanted to find stories that would provide a clear and interesting focus on the types of problems encountered in this book. Second, I wanted to include some stories from non-Western, noncontemporary sources in order to illustrate that the exploration of moral problems through storytelling is a cross-cultural phenomenon. Finally, I selected most of these stories simply because I enjoyed reading and watching them, and I thought you might enjoy them, too. As I have already mentioned, I hope you will choose to experience some of these stories in their original form if you haven't already done so. Of course, we have not even scratched the surface of the treasure of stories available to us, and I hope that our discussion of stories will inspire you to experience and evaluate other narratives in light of these theories of ethics and of human nature. You'll want to explore narratives from your family and cultural tradition as well as narratives that represent the traditions of other cultures. And don't forget the groundbreaking new stories appearing every day, which change our way of looking at the world and ourselves. Enjoy!

GLOSSARY

absolution: Forgiveness; usually God's forgiveness.

absolutism: The ethical theory that there is a universal set of moral rules that can and should be followed by everybody.

absurdity: The existentialist concept that life is meaningless, because there is no God to determine right and wrong (or because we can't know what God's values are, if God happens to exist).

act utilitarianism: The classical version of utilitarianism that focuses on the consequences of a single act.

ad hominem argument: A logical fallacy (a formally faulty argument) that assumes that because a person is who he or she is, his or her viewpoint must be wrong.

agnosticism: The view that God is unknown, or that it cannot be known whether or not there is a God.

alchemy: The speculative science of the Middle Ages, which primarily focused on turning base metals into gold.

alienation: In Marxist philosophy, the worker's loss of contact and control with the product of his or her work. The opposite of self-activity. Also: Feeling estranged from yourself and/or your environment.

alter ego: Another "self," as (1) a hidden and suppressed part of one's personality, or (2) another person who resembles oneself but who has other, usually opposite, characteristics.

altruism: Concern for the interests of others. Extreme altruism: concern for the interests of others while disregarding one's own interests. Moderate altruism (also known as Golden Rule altruism): taking others' interests into account while being concerned for one's own interests as well.

ambiguity: Quality exhibited in an expression or statement that can be interpreted in different ways.

anamnesis: Greek: re-remembering. Plato's theory of remembering the truth about the Forms, forgotten at birth.

497

androgynism: Male and female nature in the same individual, either in terms of sex (biological) or gender (cultural).

android: An artificial intelligence; a robot made to resemble a human being. Literally: manlike. There is no accepted word for a female android, but the equivalent would be *gyneoid*.

angst: Existentialist term for anxiety or anguish, a feeling of dread without any identifiable cause. Most frequently felt when one has to make important decisions. Different from *fear,* where the object of the emotion is known.

antebellum: Before the American Civil War.

anthropocentrism: Viewing everything from an exclusively human perspective.

anthropology: The study of humans. Physical anthropology: the study of human biology and biological prehistory. Cultural anthropology: the study of human cultures.

anxiety: *See* angst.

a posteriori knowledge: Knowledge that is acquired through our senses. Empirical knowledge.

approximation: To approach something with as much accuracy as the conditions allow.

a priori knowledge: Knowledge that we have prior to or independent of our sense experience, such as the capacity for understanding mathematics and logic.

arbitrary: Coincidental, without meaning or consistence.

archetype: A concept coined by the psychiatrist C. G. Jung, meaning a symbol or prototype shared by most of humanity through our collective unconscious.

asceticism: Denying oneself physical pleasures and indulgence.

atheism: The conviction that there is no God.

Australopithecus: A four-million-year-old prehominid species, probably a direct human ancestor.

authenticity: Being true to yourself, having personal integrity. Existentialism: not succumbing to the idea that you have no free choice. *See* bad faith.

autonomy: Independence; a state achieved by those who are self-governing. Autonomous lawgiver: Kant's term for a person using the Categorical Imperative without regard for personal interest, arriving at something he or she would want to become a universal law. Moral autonomy: being capable of and allowed to make moral decisions on your own.

bad faith: Existentialist term for the belief that you have no choice; the belief that you can transform yourself into a thing with no will or emotions.

behaviorism: Philosophy of human nature developed by Watson and Skinner, stating that there is no such thing as mental states; all behavior, human as well as nonhuman, can be explained in terms of material stimulus and response.

Being-there: Heidegger's term for human beings, or at least for beings who are self-aware.

benevolence: Interest in the well-being or comfort of others.

care: (1) Heidegger's concept of human existence, involving a *Care-structure,* being engaged in living; (2) Gilligan's concept of ethics as it is typically viewed by women—an *ethics of care* rather than an *ethics of justice.*

catalyst: A person or agent that causes something to happen.

categorical imperative: Kant's term for an absolute moral rule that is justified because of its logic: If you can wish for your maxim to become a universal law, your maxim qualifies as a categorical imperative.

causality, causal explanation: The chain of cause and effect. Aristotle's theory of causation: Material cause (the material aspect of a thing), efficient cause (the maker of a thing), formal cause (the idea of a thing), and final cause (the purpose of a thing).

chauvinism: Originally: excessive feeling of nationalism, from the Frenchman Chauvin. Today it usually means male chauvinism (sexism from a male point of view). Human chauvinism: *see* speciesism.

cognitive, cognition: The faculty of knowing, examining something rationally.

compatibilism: The theory that determinism (causality) and free will are compatible. Causality determines the external states; free will determines the internal states.

conceptualize: Make a vague notion into a concept with a clear definition that can be used in a description or an argument.

condition of possibility: What makes something possible, or what makes it come into being.

consequentialism: A theory that focuses exclusively on the consequences of actions.

continental philosophy: Philosophical traditions from the European continent (excluding British traditions).

correlative: A term or a concept that is understood in its relation to other concepts. The fallacy of the suppressed correlative: If terms are correlative, like *hot/cold,* and *tall/short,* they help define each other. If one is suppressed, the other ceases to have any meaning.

counter-fable/counter-myth: A story/fable/myth told deliberately to prove another story, type of story, or idea wrong.

criterion: A test, rule, or measure for distinguishing between true and false, relevant and irrelevant. A standard for a correct judgment. Plural: *criteria.*

Crusades, the: Military expeditions undertaken by European Christians from the eleventh through the thirteenth centuries to recover the Holy Land from the Muslims.

cultural diversity: The recognition of a variety of ethnic and racial groups within a given region (all the way from a neighborhood to planet earth).

cultural imperialism: A critical term for the attitude of imposing one's cultural accomplishments and moral convictions on other cultures.

cultural relativism: The theory that different societies or cultures have different moral codes. A descriptive theory.

cynicism: Distrust in evidence of virtue or disinterested motives. Pessimism. Originally a Greek school of thought believing that virtue, not pleasure or intellect, was the ultimate goal of life. Deteriorated into the idea of self-righteousness.

debt-metaphor: English's term for using the terms *owing* and *debt* in situations where it may or may not be appropriate. Appropriate use: a situation where favors are owed. Inappropriate use: a situation of friendship or family relationship.

deduction: The scientific and philosophical method of identifying an item of absolute truth (an axiom) and using this as a premise to deduce specific cases that are also absolutely true.

deontology: Duty-theory. An ethical theory that disregards the importance of consequences and focuses only on the rightness or wrongness of the act itself.

descriptive: A theory that describes a phenomenon without making an evaluative or judgmental statement. Opposite of normative.

determinism: The theory that everything is scientifically predictable. The more you know the better you can predict what will happen. Everything is determined by human heredity and/or environment. There is no free will.

dialectic method: Socrates's method of guiding his students to their own realization of the truth through a conversation, a dialogue. Also called the Socratic method.

didactic: Done or told for the purpose of teaching a lesson.

dilemma: The situation of having to choose between two courses of action that either exclude each other or are equally unpleasant.

dualism: The metaphysical theory that reality consists of matter and mind. Also used as a term for any theory of opposite forces.

egalitarian: A theory that advocates social equality.

Ego: Freud's term for the human experience of the self. *See also* Superego and Id.

ego integrity: Erikson's term for mental equilibrium, accepting one's past, and not playing the "what if" game with oneself.

elitism: The belief that a certain advantage (for instance, knowledge, education, or wealth) should be reserved for a small part of the population, an elite.

empiricism: The philosophical school of thought that claims that humans are born without knowledge, that the mind is an empty slate (*tabula rasa*) at birth, and that all knowledge comes through the senses.

end-in-oneself: Kant's term for a person. Persons (rational beings) should be regarded as dignified beings who have their own goals in life; they should not be used as means to an end only. *See* means to an end, merely.

end justifies the means, the: The statement of a consequentialist: Only the consequences count, not how they are brought about.

enlightenment: Traditional Buddhist term for the realization that life is suffering, and that the endless cycle of reincarnation can be broken.

Enlightenment, the: In the European and American cultural tradition, the eighteenth century saw a new focusing on the rights of the individual, the importance of education, and the objectivity of science. Also called the *Age of Reason,* rationality was considered the ultimate cultural goal by scientists, philosophers, and many politicians.

epistemology: Theory of knowledge. One of the main branches of traditional philosophy.

equilibrium: In this book: A well-balanced mind, capable of fair judgment.

essence: A thing's inner nature. "Essence precedes existence": the traditional philosophical conception of reality, including human nature; the theory that there is a design or purpose that nature must follow.

ethical egoism: The theory that everybody ought to be egoistic/selfish/self-interested.

ethical pluralism: The modern attempt to take the best from each ethical theory and create a realistic and workable ethical system. Also: several moral systems working simultaneously within one culture.

ethical relativism: The theory that there is no universal moral code, and whatever the majority of any given society or culture considers morally right is morally right for that culture. A normative theory. *See also* cultural relativism.

ethicist: A person professionally or vocationally involved with the theory and application of ethics.

ethics: The study, questioning, and justification of moral rules.

ethics of conduct: The study of moral rules pertaining to decisions about what course of action to take or "what to do."

ethics of virtue: The study of moral rules pertaining to the building of character or "how to be."

ethos: The moral rules and attitudes of a culture.

Eudaimonia: Greek: well-spirited, contentment, happiness. Aristotle's term for the ultimate human goal.

Eurocentric: A critical term meaning that American culture is overly focused on its European roots. Possibly a misnomer, since Americans rarely focus on European traditions, politics, and history, but rather on the European *legacy* for mainstream American culture.

euthanasia: Greek for "good death," mercy-killing. Active euthanasia: Helping someone to die at his or her request. Passive euthanasia: withholding treatment that will not help a terminally ill patient.

evidence: A ground or reason for certainty in knowledge. Usually empirical evidence; facts gathered in support of a theory.

exemplar: A model, an example for others to follow.

existence precedes essence: Existentialist belief that humans aren't determined by any essence (human nature) but exist prior to any decision about what and how they ought to be.

existentialism: A Continental school of thought that believes all humans have freedom of the will to determine their own life. Anti-deterministic.

extrinsic value: *See* instrumental value.

fallacy: A flaw in one's reasoning; an argument that does not follow the rules of logic.

falsification, principle of: The concept that a valid theory must allow for the possibility of situations where the theory doesn't apply. In a sense, part of the verification process of a theory is being able to hypothetically falsify it.

fatalism: The theory that life is determined by a higher power, and our will can't change our destiny.

faux-pas: French: a misstep, a social blunder.

Forms, theory of: Plato's metaphysical theory of a higher reality that gives meaning and existence to the world we experience through our senses. This higher reality is accessible through the mind. Example: a perfect circle; it doesn't exist in the world of the senses, but it does exist in the intelligible world of Forms.

fortitude: Strength of mind and courage in the face of adversity.

four noble truths: The content of Buddha's enlightenment: (1) There is suffering; (2) its causes can be identified; (3) suffering can be ended; and (4) the method of ending suffering is the Noble Eightfold Path.

fundamentalism: A religious approach to reality which interprets the dogmas and sacred scriptures of the tradition literally.

gender-neutral: Not gender-specific. Usually used when referring to language. Example: Scientists must do their research well. Nurses should take good care of their patients.

gender-specific: Applying to one sex only. Example of gender-specific language: A scientist must do *his* research well. A nurse should take good care of *her* patients.

general will: Rousseau's conception of democracy. All citizens get together to vote, disregarding their own personal desires and focusing on the common good.

genocide: The murder of all or most of a population.

genre: A literary type of story (or film), such as horror, western, or science fiction.

Ghost in the Machine, the: Ryle's criticism of Descartes' interactive dualism: If the soul is immaterial—a ghost—how does it affect the material world it lives in—the machine?

Golden Mean, the: The Greek idea of moderation. Aristotle's concept of virtue as a relative mean between the extremes of excess and deficiency.

good will: For Kant, having good will means having good intentions in terms of respecting a moral law that is rational and deserves to be a universal law.

Greatest Happiness Principle, the: *See* utility.

hard universalism: *See* absolutism.

Harm principle, the: John Stuart Mill's idea that one should not interfere with other people's lives unless those people are doing harm to others.

hedonism: Pleasure-seeking. The paradox of hedonism: The more you look for pleasure, the more it seems to elude you. Hedonistic calculus: Bentham's pro-and-con system, where pleasures are added and pains subtracted to find the most utilitarian course of action.

heterogeneous: Consisting of dissimilar or diverse elements.

hierarchy: A structure of higher and lower elements, ordered according to their relative importance.

homocentrism: *See* speciesism.

homogeneous: Consisting of similar elements.

human condition, the: What it means to be a human being, usually in terms of inevitable facts: having physical and spiritual needs, being a social creature, and being subject to illness and aging.

hypothetical imperative: A command that is binding only if one is interested in a certain result. An "if-then" situation.

Id: Freud's term for the Unconscious, the part of the mind which the conscious self (the Ego) has no access to, but which influences the Ego.

idealism: The metaphysical theory that reality consists of mind only, not matter.

immutability: Something that remains stable and can't be changed.

inalienable: Incapable of being taken or given away.

incarnation: Literally "being in the flesh." Living, being born; one's present life. *See* reincarnation.

induction: The scientific and philosophical method of collecting empirical evidence and formulating a general theory based on those specific facts. The problem of induction: Because one never knows if one has collected enough evidence, one can never achieve 100 percent certainty through induction.

institutionalized cruelty: Hallie's term for cruelty (psychological or physical) that has become so established that it seems natural to both victimizer and victim.

instrumental value: To have value for the sake of what further value it might bring. Also known as extrinsic value; good as a means to an end. *See* means to an end.

interactionism: The version of metaphysical dualism which believes the soul (mind) and the body (matter) interact with one another.

intrinsic value: To have value in itself without regard to what it might bring of further value. Good in itself, good as an "end in itself." *See* end-in-oneself.

intuition: Usually, an experience of understanding that is independent of one's reasoning. Can also mean the moment of understanding, an "Aha" experience. Moral intuition: a gut-level feeling of right and wrong.

ipso facto: By the fact itself.

irony: Ridicule through exaggeration, praise, or understatement.

karma: A concept used by Hindus and Buddhists to designate the principle of reincarnation. Karma is the accumulation of good and bad deeds in your previous life which led to your position in this life, and the accumulation of deeds in this life which will lead to your position in the next life.

kingdom of ends: Kant's term for a society of autonomous lawgivers who all use the categorical imperative and show each other mutual respect.

leap of faith: Kierkegaard's concept of the necessary step from the ethical to the religious stage. It involves throwing yourself at the mercy of God and discarding all messages from your rational mind or your self-interested emotions.

liberalism: A political theory that supports gradual reforms through parliamentary procedures, and civil liberties. Opposite of conservatism.

libertarianism: (1) A theory of government that holds that the individual has a right to life, liberty, and property; that nobody should interfere with these rights (negative rights); and that the government's role should be restricted to protecting these rights. (2) A theory that humans have free will independent of mechanistic causality.

materialism: The metaphysical theory that reality consists of matter only, not mind.

maxim: Kant's term for the rule or principle of an action.

means to an end: Something used to achieve another goal, an end. *See* instrumental value.

means to an end, merely: Kant's term for using others as a stepping-stone for one's own purpose.

mental state: Any mind activity or mental image.

mentalism: A term used by behaviorists to designate philosophies and theories which assume that humans have a mind and/or a soul. Also: theories of extrasensorial perception, and/or mind-reading.

metaethics: The approach to ethics which refrains from making normative statements but focuses on the meaning of terms and statements, and investigates the sources of normative statements.

metaphor: An image or an illustration that describes something in terms of something different. A figurative image such as "my boyfriend is a tiger."

metaphysics: The philosophical study of the nature of reality, or of being.

millenium: Literally: a thousand years. The term for a great social or religious upheaval or change. In Christianity: the second coming of Christ. Also used to refer to political theories, such as Marxism, which promise a new world after the revolution.

misanthropy: Misgivings about, hatred of, or lack of trust in the goodness of human nature.

misogyny: Misgivings about, hatred of, or lack of trust in female human nature. There is no equivalent term for mistrusting male human nature, but such a term might be *misandry*.

monism: A type of metaphysics which holds that there is one element of reality only, such as materialism, or idealism.

monotheism: A religion that recognizes only one god.

morality, morals: The moral rules and attitudes that we live by, or are expected to live by.

moral agent: A person capable of reflecting on a moral problem and acting on his or her decision.

mores: The moral customs and rules of a given culture.

multiculturalism: The policy of recognizing cultural diversity to the extent where all cultures within a given region are fairly represented in terms of public life and education. Sometimes includes gender as cultural diversity. *See also* cultural diversity, pluralism, and particularism.

mysticism, mystical experience: A religious experience of a direct meeting and coexisting with God or a divine being. A sense of becoming one with God.

myth: A story or a collection of stories that give identity, guidance, and meaning to a culture. Usually these are stories of gods and heroes, but they may involve ordinary people, too. In common language myth has come to mean "falsehood" or "illusion," but this is not the original meaning.

narrative: A story with a plot. Narrative structure: perceiving events as having a logical progression from a beginning through a middle to an ending.

narrative time: The time frame within which a story takes place. The experience of sharing this time frame as one reads or watches the story unfold.

natural law: A view introduced to the Catholic church by St. Thomas Aquinas that what is natural for humans (in other words, what God has intended) is good for humans. What is natural for humans includes: preservation of life, procreation, socialization, and pursuit of knowledge of God.

natural rights: The assumption that humans (and perhaps also nonhumans) are born with certain inalienable rights.

naturalistic fallacy: The assumption that one can conclude from what is natural ("what is") to what should be a rule or a policy ("what ought to be"). Not all philosophers think this is a fallacy.

Neo-classicism: A style of art and architecture in the seventeenth and eighteenth centuries which revived classical Greek and Roman forms. Also, any spiritual and philosophical movement that tries to recover the classical ideals of moderation and order.

nihilism: From the Latin *nihil,* nothing. The attitude of believing in nothing.

Noble Eightfold Path: The Buddhist way to end suffering: right view, right aspiration, right speech, right conduct, right livelihood, right effort, right mindfulness, right contemplation.

normative: A theory that evaluates and/or sets norms or standards. Opposite of descriptive.

objectification: Making an object, a thing, out of someone: disregarding their human dignity. Also reification, making a thing out of someone.

objective: Knowledge that is supported by evidence, and that has independent existence apart from experience or thought.

omniscience: The quality or state of being all-knowing. Usually mentioned as one of God's attributes. Other attributes are: omnipotence (the quality or state of being all-powerful) and omnipresence (the state of being present everywhere simultaneously).

original sin: The Christian belief that the disobedience of Adam and Eve are inherited by all humans from birth, so all humans are born sinful.

Other, the: A philosophical concept meaning either something that is completely different from yourself and all your experiences, or someone who is different from you and is thus hard to understand.

Overman, or Superman: Nietzsche's term for the individual who has recognized his will to power and created his own system of values based on an affirmation of life.

parable: A short narrative told to make a moral or religious point.

parallelism: The theory of metaphysical dualism which views mind and matter as two parallel but unconnected substances. The question of how they seem to interact is answered by claiming that God started both up simultaneously, so they stay synchronous.

parapraxis: Freud's term for a "Freudian slip," a blunder or mispronunciation that reveals an unconscious wish.

parochial: A narrow, provincial viewpoint.

particularism: The branch of multiculturalism which believes that people not belonging to the dominant culture should retrieve their self-esteem by learning about the traditions and accomplishments of their own cultural group rather than those of the dominant group or any other group.

Pater Familias: The male head of the household.

perspectivism: Nietzsche's view that all truth is a matter of the perspective from which you see it.

philanthrophy: Greek: loving humans. Doing good deeds, being charitable.

philology: The study of language, its structure and history.

pleasure principle: Freud's term for the oldest layer of the human mind, which caters selfishly to our own pleasure. For most people it is superseded by the reality principle, at least most of the time.

pluralism: The branch of multiculturalism which believes that racial and ethnic discrimination in a population of cultural diversity can be abolished by a shared orientation in each others' cultural traditions and history. Also: any theory or culture that includes several different viewpoints.

polytheism: A religion that recognizes more than one god.

preconceived notion: An idea that is formed prior to actual knowledge or experience, and which you don't think of questioning.

predestinarianism: A version of predetermination, held mostly by certain Protestant groups, that one's fate after death is predetermined.

predetermination: The view that life is predetermined by God, who knows what we will do in the future by virtue of his omniscience, but that we still retain our free will to choose right or wrong.

prerational: Before the use of reason; instinctive; belonging to human nature prior to the development of reason.

prescriptive: *See* normative.

Principle of Utility: *See* utility.

procreation: Having offspring, giving birth.

protagonist: The hero of the story.

psychological egoism: The theory that everyone is selfish, self-interested.

rational being: Anyone who has intelligence and the capacity to use it. Usually stands for human beings, but may exclude some humans and include some nonhuman beings.

rationalism: The philosophical school of thought which claims that humans are born with some knowledge, or some capacity for knowledge, like logic and mathematics. Opposite of empiricism.

reality principle: Freud's term for the knowledge that we can't always have things our own way.

reductio ad absurdum: A form of argument in which you reduce your opponent's viewpoint to its absurd consequences.

reification: *See* objectification.

reincarnation: Transmigration of souls; action through which the soul after death is incarnated into another body, usually the body of a newborn baby.

relevance: Direct application to a situation; pertinence.

Renaissance: Literally: rebirth. The European cultural revival of the arts and sciences in the fourteenth through sixteenth centuries. This period marked the end of the Middle Ages.

replicant: Term used in the film *Blade Runner* for androids. *See* android.

repression: Freud's term for when a traumatic experience in one's past is suppressed by one's conscious mind, one's Ego. The experience exists as a repressed memory in the Unconscious, the Id, and affects the Ego in various ways.

retribution: The logical dispensing or receiving of punishment in proportion to the crime. Sometimes known as "an eye for an eye," *lex talionis*. To be distinguished from vengeance, which is an emotional response that may exceed the severity of the crime.

revisionism: Advocacy of revision of former values and viewpoints. Today, refers mostly to a cynical revision of heroic values of the past.

rhetoric: The art of verbal persuasion.

Rococo: An artform and architecture prevalent in the seventeenth and eighteenth centuries, emphasizing asymmetrical ornamentation.

Romanticism, the Romantic Movement: A movement among artists, philosophers, and social critics in the late eighteenth and nineteenth centuries, partly based on the idea that emotion is a legitimate form of expression and can give access to higher truths without necessarily involving the intellect.

rule utilitarianism: The branch of utilitarianism that focuses on the consequences of a type of action done repeatedly, and not just a single act. *See* act utilitarianism.

satire: The use of sarcasm in a criticism of conditions one doesn't approve of.

self-activity: Marx's term for meaningful work; the opposite of alienation.

skepticism: The philosophical approach that we cannot obtain absolutely certain knowledge. In practice it is an approach of not believing anything until there is sufficient evidence to prove it.

slippery slope argument: A version of the *reductio ad absurdum* argument; you reduce your opponent's view to unacceptable or ridiculous consequences, which your opponent will presumably have to accept or else abandon his or her theory. Your opponent's argument must "slide down the slope" of logic. A way to defeat the slippery slope argument is to "dig in on the slope" and defend your viewpoint on the basis that there is a difference between the "top of the slope" and the "bottom of the slope."

social contract: A type of social theory, popular in the seventeenth and eighteenth centuries, which assumes that humans in the early stages of society got together and agreed on terms for creating a society.

sociobiology: A theory of humans in society based on findings in human biology and psychology.

soft universalism: The ethical theory that although humans may not agree on all moral rules or all customs, there are a few bottom-line rules we can agree on, despite our different ways of expressing them.

sovereign: A ruler; most often a monarch (king). Can also mean the right each person has to self-determination (Rousseau).

spatial: Associated with space.

speciesism: A critical term for putting the human race ahead of all other species for no other reason than the fact that we are humans. *Compare* racism, sexism. Also: homocentrism, human chauvinism.

state of nature: A type of theory, popular in the seventeenth and eighteenth centuries, usually associated with a social contract theory. Such theories assume that humans prior to the social contract lived as loners in nature without much contact with each other. For Hobbes, the state of nature is dangerous and terrible; for Rousseau, it is healthy and benevolent.

straw man argument: A logical fallacy that consists of attacking and disproving a theory invented for the occasion.

subjective opinion: One that is not supported by evidence, or is dependent on the mind and experience of the person.

subjectivism: Ethical theory that claims that your moral belief is right simply because you believe it; there are no intersubjective (shared) moral standards.

Superego: Freud's concept of the human conscience, the internalized rules of our parents and our society.

teleology: A theory of purpose. A teleological theory such as Aristotle's may assume that everything has a purpose. Also used to designate theories interested in the outcome of an action, that is, consequentialist theories.

temperance: In virtue theory this means moderation. In a modern context it may mean abstinence from alcohol.

temporal: Associated with time. Temporal being: a being living in time and understanding himself or herself in terms of a past, a present, and a future.

territorial imperative: A term used by Ardrey and others to signify a tendency in human nature to defend one's territory with aggression.

theology: The study of God and God's nature and attributes.

totalitarianism: A form of government which views the state as all-important, and the lives of its citizens as disposable.

transvaluation of values: Nietzsche's term for discarding the Christian value system in favor of one that recognizes the will to power and the right of the creative man to set his own values.

universal law: Kant's term for a moral rule that can be imagined as applying to everybody in the same situation, and accepted by other rational beings.

universalizability: A maxim that is acceptable as a universal law.

universalization: The process by which one asks oneself if one's maxim could become a universal law: "What if everybody did this?"

utilitarianism: The theory that one ought to maximize the happiness and minimize the unhappiness of as many people (or sentient beings) as possible.

utility: Fitness for some purpose, especially for creating happiness and/or minimizing pain and suffering. Principle of Utility: To create as much happiness and minimize suffering as much as possible for as many as possible. Also: The Greatest Happiness Principle.

Utopia: Literally, no place. Sir Thomas More's term for a nonexistent world, usually used as a term for a world too good to be true.

vicariously: To experience something through the experiences of others.

Way, the: Chinese: Tao (Dao). The morally and philosophically correct path to follow.

yin and yang: The two cosmic principles of Taoism, opposing forces that keep the universe in balance.

SELECTED BIBLIOGRAPHY

Works of Nonfiction

Ardrey, Robert. *African Genesis*. New York: Delta Books, 1961.

Aristotle. *Nichomachean Ethics*. In *Introduction to Aristotle*. Edited by Richard McKeon. Translated by W. D. Ross. New York: Random House, 1947.

Badinter, Elisabeth. *The Unopposite Sex*. Translated by Barbara Wright. New York: Harper & Row, 1989.

Baigent, Michael, et al. *Holy Blood, Holy Grail*. New York: Delacorte Press, 1982.

Bartlett, Kim. "On Christianity and Animals: A Conversation with Andrew Linzey." *The Animals' Agenda*, April 1989.

Beauvoir, Simone de. *The Second Sex*. Translated by H. M. Parshley. New York: Alfred A. Knopf, Inc., 1952.

————. *The Ethics of Ambiguity*. Translated by Bernard Frechtman. New York: Philosophical Library, 1948.

Belenky, Mary Field, et al. *Women's Ways of Knowing*. New York: Basic Books, Inc., 1986.

Benedict, Ruth. "Anthropology and the Abnormal." *Journal of General Psychology* 10 (1934).

Bentham, Jeremy. *Principles of Morals and Legislation*. In *The Utilitarians*. New York: Anchor Books, 1973.

Berger, Fred. "Gratitude." In *Vice and Virtue in Everyday Life*. Edited by Christina Hoff Sommers. Fort Worth: Harcourt Brace Jovanovich, 1985.

Bergson, Henri. *Time and Free Will*. Translated by F. L. Pogson. New York: Harper, 1960.

Bonevac, Daniel, et al., ed. *Beyond the Western Tradition*. Mountain View, Ca.: Mayfield Publishers, 1992.

Bonevac, Daniel, ed. *Today's Moral Issues*. Mountain View, Ca.: Mayfield Publishers, 1992.

Booth, Wayne C. *The Company We Keep*. Berkeley and Los Angeles: University of California Press, 1988.

————. "Why Ethical Criticism Fell on Hard Times." In *Ethics: Symposium on Morality and Literature,* vol. 98, no. 2, January 1988. Chicago: University of Chicago Press.

Camus, Albert. *The Myth of Sisyphus*. Translated by Justin O'Brien. New York: Alfred A. Knopf, Inc., 1955.

Carmody, Denise Lardner, and Carmody, John Tully. *How to Live Well: Ethics in the World Religions*. Belmont, Ca.: Wadsworth, 1988.

Clark, Kenneth. *Landscape into Art*. New York: Harper & Row, 1979.

Clark, R. T. Rundle. *Myth and Symbol in Ancient Egypt*. London: Thames and Hudson, 1978.

Darrow, Clarence. "Leopold and Loeb: The Crime of Compulsion." In *Vice and Virtue in Everyday Life*. Edited by Christina Hoff Sommers. Fort Worth: Harcourt Brace Jovanovich, 1985.

Diamond, Jared. "The Worst Mistake in the History of the Human Race." *Discover,* May 1987.

Ehrenburg, Ilya. "Bøger." In *Evige Tanker*. Edited by Anker Kierkeby. Copenhagen: Westmans Forlag, 1951.

Eliade, Mircea. *A History of Religious Ideas,* vols. 1–3. Chicago: University of Chicago Press, 1978–1985.

English, Jane. "What Do Grown Children Owe Their Parents?" In *Vice and Virtue in Everyday Life*. Edited by Christina Hoff Sommers and Fred Sommers. Fort Worth: Harcourt Brace Jovanovich, 1985, 1989.

Erikson, Erik. *Childhood and Society*. New York: W. W. Norton and Company, Inc., 1964.

Feinberg, Joel. "Psychological Egoism." In *Ethical Theory*. Edited by Louis P. Pojman. Belmont, Ca.: Wadsworth, 1989.

———. "The Rights of Animals and Unborn Generations." In *Philosophy and Environmental Crisis*. Edited by William T. Blackstone. Athens, Ga.: The University of Georgia Press, 1974.

Foot, Philippa. *Virtues and Vices*. Berkeley and Los Angeles: University of California Press, 1978.

Freud, Sigmund. *Civilization and Its Discontents*. Translated by James Strachey. New York: W. W. Norton & Company, 1961.

———. *The Future of an Illusion*. Translated by James Strachey. New York: W. W. Norton & Company, 1961.

———. *Introductory Lectures on Psychoanalysis*. Translated by James Strachey. New York: W. W. Norton & Company, 1966.

Fromm, Erich. *Marx's Concept of Man*. New York: Frederick Ungar Publishing Co., 1977.

Gilligan, Carol. *In a Different Voice*. Cambridge: Harvard University Press, 1982.

Goodall, Jane. *The Chimpanzees of Gombe*. Cambridge, Mass.: Harvard University Press, 1986.

Graves, Robert. *The Greek Myths*. 2 vols. Penguin Books, 1960.

Grønbeck, Vilhelm. *The Culture of the Teutons*. 2 vols. Translated from *Vor Folkeæt I Oldtiden* (2 vols.) by W. Worster. London: Oxford University Press, 1931.

Gyekye, Kwame. "An Essay on African Philosophical Thought: The Akan Conceptual Scheme." In *Today's Moral Issues*. Edited by Daniel Bonevac. Mountain View, Ca.: Mayfield Publishers, 1992.

Hallie, Philip. "From Cruelty to Goodness." In *Vice and Virtue in Everyday Life*. Edited by Christina Hoff Sommers and Fred Sommers. Fort Worth: Harcourt Brace Jovanovich, 1985, 1989.

Harris, Jr., C. E. *Applying Moral Theories*. Belmont, Ca.: Wadsworth, 1986.

Heidegger, Martin. *Being and Time*. Translated by John Macquarrie and Edward Robinson. New York: Harper & Row, 1962.

Hinman, Lawrence. *Ethics, A Pluralistic Approach*. Austin: Harcourt Brace, 1993.

Hobbes, Thomas. *English Works*. Vol. 3. Edited by Sir W. Molesworth. London: J. Bohn, 1840.

Hohlenberg, Johannes. *Søren Kierkegaard*. Copenhagen: Aschehoug Dansk Forlag, 1963.

Hume, David. *An Enquiry Concerning the Principles of Morals*. In *Enquiries Concerning Human Understanding and Concerning the Principles of Morals,* 3rd ed. Edited by L. A. Selby-Bigge. Revised by P. H. Nidditch. Oxford: Clarendon, 1975.

Kalin, Jesse. "In Defense of Egoism." In *Ethical Theory*. Edited by Louis P. Pojman. Belmont, Ca.: Wadsworth, 1989.

Kant, Immanuel. *Grounding for the Metaphysics of Morals*. Translated by James W. Ellington. Indianapolis: Hackett Publishing Company, 1981.

———. "On the Distinction of the Beautiful and Sublime in the Interrelation of the Two Sexes." In *Philosophy of Woman*. Edited by Mary Briody Mahowald. Indianapolis: Hackett Publishing Company, 1983.

Kemp, T. Peter. "Toward a Narrative Ethics: A Bridge between Ethics and the Narrative Reflection of Ricoeur." In *The Narrative Path*. Edited by T. Peter Kemp and David Rasmussen. Cambridge, Mass.: MIT Press, 1989.

Kierkeby, Anker, ed. *Evige Tanker*. Copenhagen: Westmans Forlag, 1951.

Kierkegaard, Søren. *Stadier Paa Livets Vej*. Copenhagen: Martins Forlag, 1926.

Kittay, Eva Feder, and Meyers, Diana T., eds. *Women and Moral Theory*. Savage, MD: Rowman & Littlefield Publishers, 1987.

Körner, S. *Kant*. Harmondsworth, England: Penguin Books, 1955.

Larsen, Martin, ed. *Den Ældre Edda og Eddica Minora*. 2 vols. Copenhagen: Munksgaards Forlag, 1945.

Leakey, Richard E., and Lewin, Roger. *People of the Lake*. New York: Avon Books, 1978.

LeGuin, Ursula. "It Was a Dark and Stormy Night." In *On Narrative*. Edited by J. I. Mitchell. Chicago: University of Chicago Press, 1981.

Leiber, Justin. *Can Animals and Machines Be Persons? A Dialogue*. Indianapolis: Hackett Publishing Company, 1985. (This entry can also be found in the fiction section.)

Lloyd, Genevieve. *The Man of Reason*. Minneapolis: University of Minnesota Press, 1984.

Lorenz, Konrad. *On Aggression*. Translated by Marjorie Latzke. London: Methuen, University Paperback, 1966.

MacIntyre, Alasdair. *After Virtue*. Notre Dame: University of Notre Dame Press, 1981, 1984.

MacIntyre, Ben. *Forgotten Fatherland*. New York: Farrar, Strauss, Giroux, 1992.

Mackie, J. L. *Ethics: Inventing Right and Wrong*. New York: Penguin Books, 1977.

Mahowald, Mary Briody, ed. *Philosophy of Woman*. Indianapolis: Hackett Publishing Company, 1983.

Malinowski, Bronislaw. "Myth in Primitive Psychology." In *Magic, Science, and Religion,* Garden City, NY: Doubleday Anchor Books, 1954.

Maltin, Leonard. *Leonard Maltin's TV Movies and Video Guide*. New York: Signet, 1993.

Marx, Karl, and Engels, Friedrich. *The Communist Manifesto of Marx and Engels*. New York: Viking Penguin, 1985.

Mayo, Bernard. "Virtue or Duty?" In *Vice and Virtue in Everyday Life*. Edited by Christina Hoff Sommers and Fred Sommers. Fort Worth: Harcourt Brace Jovanovich, 1985, 1989.

Medlin, Brian. "Ultimate Principles and Ethical Thought." In *Ethical Theory*. Edited by Louis P. Pojman. Belmont, Ca.: Wadsworth, 1989.

Mencius. Translated by D. C. Lau. Harmondsworth, England: Penguin Books, 1970.

Midgley, Mary. "Persons and Non-Persons." In *In Defense of Animals*. Edited by Peter Singer. New York: Harper & Row, 1985.

Mill, John Stuart. *On Liberty*. In *The Utilitarians*. New York: Anchor Books, 1973.

———. *The Subjection of Women*. Cambridge, Mass.: MIT Press, 1970.

———. *Utilitarianism*. In *The Utilitarians*. New York: Anchor Books, 1973.

Mitchell, J. I., ed. *On Narrative*. Chicago: University of Chicago Press, 1981.

Muntz, Peter. *The Shapes of Time; A New Look at the Philosophy of History*. Middletown, CT: Wesleyan University Press, 1977.

Nietzsche, Friedrich. *Beyond Good and Evil.* Translated by Helen Zimmern. Riverside, N.J.: Macmillan Publishing Company, 1911.

———. *On the Genealogy of Morals.* Translated by Walter Kaufmann and R. J. Hollingdale. New York: Random House, 1969.

Nussbaum, Martha. *Love's Knowledge.* New York: Oxford University Press, 1990.

Nuyen, A. T. "Sociobiology, morality, and feminism." *Human Studies* 8:97–168. Dordrecht, Holland: Martinus Nijhoff Publishers, 1985.

Oden, Thomas C., ed. *Parables of Kierkegaard.* Princeton, N.J.: Princeton University Press, 1978.

Pagels, Elaine. *Adam, Eve, and the Serpent.* New York: Random House, 1988.

Plato, *The Republic.* Translated by G. R. U. Grube. Indianapolis: Hackett, 1974.

———. *The Republic of Plato.* Translated by Francis MacDonald Cornford. London: Oxford University Press, 1945.

———. *Plato's Phaedrus.* Translated by W. C. Helmbold and W. G. Rabinowitz. New York: The Liberal Arts Press, 1956.

Plotinus. *The Essential Plotinus.* Translated by Elmer O'Brien. Indianapolis: Hackett Publishing Company, 1964.

Pojman, Louis P., ed. *Ethical Theory.* Belmont, Ca.: Wadsworth, 1989.

Rachels, James. *The Elements of Moral Philosophy.* New York: Random House, 1986.

Ricoeur, Paul. *Interpretation Theory.* Fort Worth, Texas: The Texas Christian University Press, 1976.

———. "Narrative Time." In *On Narrative.* Edited by J. I. Mitchell. Chicago: University of Chicago Press, 1981.

———. *Time and Narrative.* 3 vols. Chicago: University of Chicago Press, 1985–1989.

Rosen, Claire Mead. "The Eerie World of Reunited Twins." *Discover,* September 1987.

Rosenstand, Nina. "Arven fra Bergson: En Virkningshistorie." In *Den Skapende Varighet.* Edited by Hans Kolstad. Oslo, Norway: H. Aschehoug & Co., 1993.

———. "Med en anden stemme: Carol Gilligans etik." In *Kvindespind—Kønsfilosofiske Essays.* Aarhus, Denmark: Forlaget Philosophia, 1987. Edited by Mette Boch, et al.

———. *Mytebegrebet.* Copenhagen: Gads Forlag, 1981.

Rousseau, Jean-Jacques. *Emile.* Translated by Allan Bloom. New York: Basic Books, Inc., 1979.

———. *On the Social Contract and Discourses.* Translated by Donald A. Cress. Indianapolis: Hackett Publishing Company, 1983.

Salmon, Wesley C., "Determinism and Indeterminism in Modern Science." In *Reason and Responsibility,* 4th ed. Edited by Joel Feinberg. Encino, Ca.: Dickenson Publishing Company, 1978.

Sartre, Jean-Paul. *Existentialism Is a Humanism.* Translated by P. Mairet. New York: The Philosophical Library, 1949.

Schneewind, J. B. "The Misfortunes of Virtue." *Ethics* 101, October 1990. Chicago: University of Chicago Press, 1990.

Schwartz, Leo W., ed. *Great Ages and Ideas of the Jewish People.* New York: Random House, 1956.

Singer, Peter. *The Expanding Circle.* Farrar, Strauss and Giroux, 1981.

Shapiro, Laura. "Guns and Dolls." *Newsweek:* May 28, 1990.

Shaw, William H. *Morality and Moral Controversies.* Englewood Cliffs, N.J.: Prentice-Hall, 1981.

Skinner, B. F. *About Behaviorism.* New York: Vintage, 1976.

Sommers, Christina Hoff. "Teaching the Virtues." *Imprimis.* Hillsdale College, Michigan: Nov. 1991.

Sommers, Christina Hoff, and Sommers, Fred, eds. *Vice and Virtue in Everyday Life*. Fort Worth: Harcourt Brace Jovanovich, 1985, 1989.

Stace, W. T. "A Defense of Compatibilism." In *Vice and Virtue in Everyday Life*. Edited by Christina Hoff Sommers and Fred Sommers. Fort Worth: Harcourt Brace Jovanovich, 1985.

Stambaugh, Joan. *Nietzsche's Thoughts of the Eternal Return*. Baltimore: Johns Hopkins University Press, 1972.

Stevenson, Leslie. *Seven Theories of Human Nature*. New York: Oxford University Press, 1974.

Stone, Christopher. "Should Trees Have Standing? Towards Legal Rights for Natural Objects." In *People, Penguins, and Plastic Trees*. Edited by Donald VanDeVeer and Christine Pierce. Belmont, Ca.: Wadsworth Publishing Company, 1986.

Tannen, Deborah. *You Just Don't Understand*. New York: William Morrow & Co., Inc., 1990.

————. *That's Not What I Meant!* New York: Ballentine Books, 1986.

Taylor, Mark C. *Journeys to Selfhood: Hegel & Kierkegaard*. Berkeley and Los Angeles: University of California Press, 1980.

Taylor, Paul B., and Auden, W. H. *The Elder Edda*. London: Faber & Faber, 1973.

Taylor, Paul W. *Principles of Ethics: An Introduction*. Belmont, Ca.: Wadsworth Publishing Company, 1975.

Taylor, Richard. "Compassion." In *Vice and Virtue in Everyday Life*. Edited by Christina Hoff Sommers. Fort Worth: Harcourt Brace Jovanovich, 1985.

Trebilcot, Joyce. "Two Forms of Androgynism." *Journal of Social Philosophy*, January 1977.

Trigg, Roger. *Ideas of Human Nature*. Oxford: Blackwell, 1988.

VanDeVeer, Donald, and Pierce, Christine, eds. *People, Penguins, and Plastic Trees*. Belmont, Ca.: Wadsworth Publishing Company, 1986.

Wamberg, Bodil, ed. *Out of Denmark: Isak Dinesen/Karen Blixen 1885−1985 and Danish Women Writers Today*. Copenhagen: The Danish Cultural Institute, 1985.

White, Hayden. *Metahistory*. Baltimore: Johns Hopkins University Press, 1973.

————. "The Value of Narrativity in the Representations of Reality." In *On Narrative*. Edited by J. I. Mitchell. Chicago: University of Chicago Press, 1981.

Williams, Bernard. *Morality: An Introduction*. New York: Harper & Row, 1972.

Wilson, David M., ed. *The Northern World*. New York: Harry N. Abrams, Inc., 1980.

Wollstonecraft, Mary. *Vindication of the Rights of Women*. Excerpt in *Philosophy of Woman*. Edited by Mary Briody Mahowald. Indianapolis: Hackett Publishing Company, 1983.

Yutang, Lin. *The Importance of Living*. London: William Heinemann Ltd., 1931.

Works of Literature

Allen, Roger MacBride. *Orphan of Creation*. New York: Simon & Schuster, 1988.

Andersen, Hans Christian. *Eventyr og Historier*. 16 vols. Odense, Denmark: Skandinavisk Bogforlag, Flensteds Forlag.

Blixen, Karen. *Anecdotes of Destiny*. New York: Random House, 1985.

Borges, Jorge Luis. *Ficciones*. Translated by Emecé Editores, S.A., Buenos Aires. New York: Grove Press, Inc., 1962.

Capek, Karel. *War with the Newts*. New York: Berkeley Medallion Books, 1959.

Conrad, Joseph. *Lord Jim: A Tale.* New York: Bantam Classics, 1981.

Dostoyevsky, Fyodor. *The Brothers Karamazov*. Signet Classic, New American Library, New York, 1957.

————. *Crime and Punishment*. New York: Bantam Books, 1959.

Dumas, Alexandre. *The Count of Monte Cristo*. New York: Bantam Classics, 1985.

Eco, Umberto. *Foucault's Pendulum*. Translated by William Weaver. New York: Random House, 1989.

The Epic of Gilgamesh. Translated by N. K. Sandars. New York: Viking Penguin, 1972.

Erdoes, Richard, and Ortiz, Alfonso, eds. *American Indian Myths and Legends*. New York: Pantheon Books, 1984.

Flaubert, Gustave. *Madame Bovary*. Translated by Lowell Lair. New York: Bantam Books, 1981.

Forster, E. M. *Howard's End*. New York: Random House, 1921.

———. *A Passage to India*. San Diego: Harcourt Brace Jovanovich, 1952.

France, Anatole. *Penguin Island*. New York: Random House, 1984.

Golding, William. *Lord of the Flies*. The Putnam Publishing Group, 1954.

Graves, Robert. *The Greek Myths*. 2 vols. Harmondsworth, England: Penguin Books, 1960.

Grimm's Complete Fairy Tales. Garden City, New York: Nelson Doubleday, Inc.

Grimwood, Ken. *Replay*. New York: Berkley Books, 1988.

Huxley, Aldous. *Brave New World*. New York: Bantam Books, 1958.

Jacobsen, I. P. *Marie Grubbe*. In *Samlede Værker*. 5 vols. Copenhagen: 1924–29.

Jewkes, W. T., ed. *Man the Myth-Maker*. New York: Harcourt Brace Jovanovich, Inc., 1973.

Kafka, Franz. *The Basic Kafka*. New York: Simon & Schuster, 1979.

LeGuin, Ursula. "The Ones Who Walk Away From Omelas." In *The Wind's Twelve Quarters*. New York: Harper & Row, 1981.

Leiber, Justin. *Can Animals and Machines Be Persons? A Dialogue*. Indianapolis: Hackett Publishing Company, 1985.

Malmberg, Bertil. *Åke ock hans värld*. Stockholm: Albert Bonniers Förlag, 1954.

Marlowe, Christopher. *Doctor Faustus*. New York: Signet Classics, 1969.

Marriott, Alice, and Rachlin, Carol K., eds. *American Indian Mythology*. New York: Harper & Row, 1968.

Maugham, Somerset. "Sheppey." London: Wh. Heinemann, 1933.

Melville, Herman. *Billy Budd*. Riverside, N.J.: Macmillan Publishing Company, 1975.

———. *Moby Dick*. New York: Viking Penguin, 1973.

Mitchell, Margaret. *Gone with the Wind*. Riverside, N.J.: Macmillan Publishing Company, 1975.

Mullahy, Patrick. *Oedipus—Myth and Complex*. New York: Hermitage Press, Inc., 1948.

Murdoch, Iris. *The Good Apprentice*. New York: Penguin Books, 1986.

Nietzsche, Friedrich. *Thus Spoke Zarathustra*. Translated by Walter Kaufmann. New York: Penguin Books, 1966.

Njal's Saga. Translated by Magnus Magnusson and Hermann Palsson. Baltimore: Penguin Books, 1960.

Rand, Ayn. *Atlas Shrugged*. New York: Signet Books, 1957.

Pontoppidan, Henrik. "Ørneflugt." In *Håndbog i Dansk Literatur*. Edited by Falkenstjerne and Borup Jensen. Copenhagen: G.E.C. Gad, 1961.

Sartre, Jean-Paul. *No Exit*. New York: Random House, 1989.

Scott, Sir Walter. *Ivanhoe*. New York: Viking Penguin, 1984.

Shakespeare, William. *The Tragedy of Othello*. New York: New American Library, 1963.

Shelley, Mary. *Frankenstein*. New York: Bantam Books, 1981.

Steinbeck, John. *The Grapes of Wrath*. New York: Viking Penguin, 1992.

Stevenson, Robert Louis. *Dr. Jekyll and Mr. Hyde and Other Stories*. London: MacDonald & Co., Ltd., 1950.

Tepper, Sheri S. *Sideshow*. New York: Bantam Books, 1993.

Walker, Alice. *The Temple of My Familiar*. New York: Simon & Schuster, 1990.

Wessel, Johann Herman, "Smeden og Bageren." In *De gamle huskevers*. Edited by Fritz Haack. Copenhagen: Forlaget Sesam, 1980.

PHOTO AND ILLUSTRATION CREDITS

Unless otherwise noted, all movie stills in this book are from the author's collection. Illustrations on pages 24, 164, 176, 189, and 248 are by the author.

Chapter 1 19 © 1980 Warner Bros. All rights reserved. 20 © 1988 Twentieth Century Fox Film Corporation. All rights reserved.

Chapter 2 31 From The Dore Bible Illustrations, Dover Publications, 1974. 37 Copyright © 1993 by Universal City Studios, Inc. Courtesy of MCA Publishing Rights, a Division of MCA Inc. 39 Copyright © 1985 Columbia Pictures Industries Inc. All rights reserved. Courtesy of Columbia Pictures. 45 Copyright © by Paramount Pictures. All rights reserved. Courtesy of Paramount Pictures. 48 From *The Divine Comedy*, Dante Alighieri, Pantheon Books, New York, 1948. 57 © 1956 MGM Inc. All rights reserved. 59 TM & © Lucasfilm Ltd. (LFL) 1989. All rights reserved. Courtesy of Lucasfilm Ltd.

Chapter 3 68 The Bettman Archive. 77 Courtesy of James Rachels. 79 Copyright © Columbia Pictures Industries, Inc. All rights reserved. Courtesy of Columbia Pictures.

Chapter 4 87 AP/Wide World. 96 © 1942 Turner Entertainment Co. All rights reserved. 99 The Bettman Archive.

Chapter 5 102 and 109 The Bettman Archive. 117 Copyright © 1956 Renewed 1984 Columbia Pictures Industries, Inc. All rights reserved. Courtesy of Columbia Pictures.

Chapter 6 120 The Bettman Archive. 125 © 1956 Warner Bros. All rights reserved.

Chapter 7 136 Copyright © 1989 by Universal City Studios, Inc. Courtesy of MCA Publishing Rights, a Division of MCA Inc. 140 Copyright © 1962 Renewed 1990 Columbia Pictures Industries, Inc. All rights reserved. Courtesy of Columbia Pictures. 155 Courtesy of Republic Pictures Corporation. 157 Copyright © 1993 by Paramount Pictures. All rights reserved. Courtesy of Paramount Pictures.

Chapter 8 166 and 170 The Bettman Archive.

Chapter 9 180 and 181 The Bettman Archive.

Chapter 10 198 UPI/Bettman. 202, 205, and 207 The Bettman Archive. 210 Drawing by Ian Mackenzie-Kerr. Courtesy of Harry N. Abrams, Inc. By permission.

Chapter 11 222 Courtesy of Christina Hoff Sommers. 225 and 231 The Bettman Archive. 233 Copyright Munch Museum, Oslo, 1993. By permission. 236 UPI/Bettman.

Chapter 12 252 The Granger Collection, New York.

Chapter 13 267 Copyright © 1965 Columbia Pictures Industries, Inc. All rights reserved. Courtesy of Columbia Pictures. 273 From The Dore Bible Illustrations, Dover Publications, 1974. 282 © 1956 Warner Bros. All rights reserved. 290 TM & © Lucasfilm Ltd. (LFL) 1977, all rights reserved. Courtesy of Lucasfilm Ltd.

Chapter 14 310 The Bettman Archive. 316 AP/Wide World. 317 © 1982 Warner Bros. All rights reserved.

Chapter 15 326 The Bettman Archive. 329 UPI/Bettman. 337 and 343 The Bettman Archive. 348 © 1968 Turner Entertainment Co. All rights reserved. 351 Photo by Dr. Jane Goodall. Courtesy of The Jane Goodall Institute.

Chapter 16 361 The Granger Collection, New York. 364 The Bettman Archive. 369 Photo by Lilian Kemp. Courtesy of Carol Gilligan and Lilian Kemp Photography. 371 © 1990 MGM Inc. All rights reserved.

Chapter 17 377 Centennial Gift of Landon T. Clay. Courtesy, Museum of Fine Arts, Boston. 380, 386, and 397 The Bettman Archive. 398 Goethe- und Schiller-Archiv, Weimar, Germany. By permission.

Chapter 18 420 The Bettman Archive 425 UPI/Bettman Newsphotos.

Chapter 19 440 Photo courtesy of Texas Christian University Press. 445 Photo by T. Scott Niendorf. Courtesy of Martha Nussbaum.

Chapter 20 459 Copyright © 1993 by Paramount Pictures. All rights reserved. Courtesy of Paramount Pictures. 467 AP/Wide World Photos 472 © 1941 Turner Entertainment Co. All rights reserved. 477 The Granger Collection, New York 492 © 1940 Twentieth Century Fox Film Corporation. All rights reserved.

INDEX

Boldface numbers indicate story outlines; numbers in italics refer to illustrations